National Intelligencer Newspaper Abstracts 1854

Joan M. Dixon

HERITAGE BOOKS
2008

HERITAGE BOOKS
AN IMPRINT OF HERITAGE BOOKS, INC.

Books, CDs, and more—Worldwide

For our listing of thousands of titles see our website
at
www.HeritageBooks.com

Published 2008 by
HERITAGE BOOKS, INC.
Publishing Division
100 Railroad Ave. #104
Westminster, Maryland 21157

Copyright © 2008 Joan M. Dixon

All rights reserved. No part of this book may be reproduced or transmitted in any form or by any means, electronic or mechanical, including photocopying, recording or by any information storage and retrieval system without written permission from the author, except for the inclusion of brief quotations in a review.

International Standard Book Numbers
Paperbound: 978-0-7884-4633-7
Clothbound: 978-0-7884-7172-8

NATIONAL INTELLIGENCER NEWSPAPER
WASHINGTON, D C
1854

TABLE OF CONTENTS

Daily National Intelligencer, Washington, D C, 1854: pg 1

Acts passed at 1st session of 33rd Congress: 280-282
American flag: 224
Appointments by the President: see index
Army orders: 283-287
Army pay increase: 74
Assist Surgeons-U S Army: 80; 140
Cadets appointed by the President: 92
Charter Oak tree: 345
Cholera at Martinsburg, Va: 323; 376
Columbia Typographical Society: 429

Commencements: Georgetown College, D C: 234
                St Mary's, Chas Co, Md: 289
                Visitation, Georgetown, D C: 240-241

Court Martial of Assist Surgeon Josephus M Steiner: 99
Court Martial of Maj Wyse: 154
Criminal Court-Wash City-Jurors: 92; 207
Darien exploration: 106

Death of American Citizens: 13-14; 32; 89; 145; 178; 329; 422
Death of Capt John Downes: 289
Death of Capt Robert Burnett: 421
Death of John Bliss: 431
Death of M de Bodisco: 30; 35; 38; 294
Death of Mrs Eliz Benton: 321
Death of Mrs Eliz Hamilton: 160; 389

Dr Geo A Gardiner-guilty: 89
Edward Herndon kin: 326
First ascent of Mount Hood: 406
First Gas Lights: 340
Friday-unlucky day: 369
Georgetown elections: 87

Glenwood Cemetery dedication: 265
Jennings Estate: 2; 134; 153

Justice of the Peace for Washington City: 106
Land Warrants: 66-68
List of ship wrecks: 352
Loss of steamer Arctic: See index
Loss of the Leviathan: 109
Loss of the Waterloo: 109
Massacre of Capt J W Gunnison & party: 35-36; 78
Memoirs of Maj Robt Stobo: 84
Methodist Episcopal Conference: 102
Midshipmen: 348-349
Miss Rooker's School: 293

Ofcrs of the: Erebus: 375
      Cumberland: 433
      Susquehanna: 2
      Terror: 375

Packet Kate Kearny disaster: 75
Pilgrim burial place: 31
Mount Vernon Association: 249
Remains of Pulaski: 57; 309
Revolutionary Claim cases: 131
Railroad disaster near Balt, Md: 228
Reminiscences: 351
Royal Family: 180
Sale of real estate of the late Dr Wm L Powell: 413
Sale of real estate of the late Hanson Clarke: 325
Schnr Ontario disaster: 349
Ship Powhatan disaster: 138
Ship Staffordshire disaster: 4; 8
Ship Townsend disaster: 294
Soldiers of the War of 1812: 76; 396
Steamboat Georgia disaster: 59
Steamer Caroline disaster: 101
Steamer Gazelle disaster: 181
Steamer Kate Kearny: 82
Steamer San Francisco disaster: See index
Steamer Secretary disaster: 163
Steamship Brother Jonathan disaster: 99
Tornado at Louisville: 308
Uncle Sam: 283
U S Grinnell Expedition: 122

Walker's Fillibuster Expedition: 236
War of 1812: 86

Washington City-1853: 1
Washington City-tax sale: 39-48
Washington's letters: 79-80
Washington City teachers: 288
Washington Police Officers: 348
Washington Public School Principals: 337
Washington Seminary students: 11
Wreck of steamer Yankee Blade: 390

Index: pg 446

> Dedicated to the memory of my uncle:
> Edward J Neff,
> b. 1899, Wash, D C d. 1976, Md
> Married 1924 ca
> Alice V Bruchi
> b. 1904, Md d. 1992, Md

PREFACE
Daily National Intelligencer Newspaper Abstracts
1854
Joan M Dixon

The National Intelligencer & Washington Advertiser is hereafter the Daily National Intelligencer. It was the first newspaper printed in Washington, D C; Samuel H Smith, the originator. The same was transferred to Jos Gales, jr on Aug 31, 1810; on Nov 1, 1812, the paper was under the firm of Jos Gales, sr, & Wm W Seaton. The Library of Congress has microfilm of the paper from the first issue of Oct 31, 1800 thru Jan 8, 1870, the final paper. The Evening Star Newspaper of Jan 10, 1870 reports: The Intelligencer is discontinued: the proprietor, Mr Alex Delmar, says that having lost several thousand dollars, & being in poor health, he has resolved to discontinue its publication.

Included in the abstracts are advertisements; appointments by the President; Hse o/Rep petitions; passed Acts; legal notices; marriages; deaths; mscl notices; social events; tax lists; military promotions; court cases; deaths by accident; prisoners; & maritime information-crews. Items or events which might be a clue as to the location, age or relationship of an individual are copied.

No attempt has been made to correct the spelling. Due to the length of some articles, it was necessary to present only the highlights of same. Chancery and Equity records are copied as written.

The index contains <u>all</u> surnames and *tracts of lands/places*. **Maritime vessels** are found under barge, boat, brig, frig, schn'r, ship, sloop, steamboat, tugboat, yacht or vessel.

ABBREVIATIONS:
AA CO	ANNE ARUNDEL COUNTY
CO	COMPANY/COUNTY
CMDER	COMMANDER
CMDOR	COMMODOR
D C	DISTRICT OF COLUMBIA
ELIZ	ELIZABETH
ELIZA	ELIZA
MONTG CO	MONTGOMERY COUNTY
PG CO	PRINCE GEORGES CO
WASH	WASHINGTON
WASH, D C	WASHINGTON, DISTRICT OF COLUMBIA

BOOKS IN THE NATIONAL INTELLIGENCER NEWSPAPER SERIES: 1800-1805/1806-1810/1811-1813/1814-1817/1818-1820/1821-1823/1824-1826/1827-1829/1830-1831/1832-1833/1834-1835/1836-1837/1838-1839/1840/1841/1842/1843/1844/1845/1846/1847/ 1848/1849/ 1850/1851/1852/1853/1854 SPECIAL: CIVIL WAR 2 VOLS, 1861-1865

DAILY NATIONAL INTELLIGENCER
1854

MON JAN 2, 1854
House of Reps: 1-Cmte of Claims: bill for the relief of Henry, of Clinton, Co, Indiana: committed. Same cmte: asked to be discharged from the further consideration of the ptns of John P Shelden & Martha L Patterson: laid on the table. Same cmte: bill for the relief of Capt Geo Sympton, of Galveston: committed. 2-Cmte on Invalid Pensions: bill for the relief of Wm Black: committed. Same cmte: adverse reports on the ptns of Eliza Merrill, of Bangor, Maine, & John Droat, an invalid of the war of 1812. 3-Cmte on Military Affairs: joint resolution of thanks to Gen John E Wool, reported the same without amendment. Sword to be presented to him for his distinguished services in the late war with Mexico, & especially for his skill, enterprise, & courage which distinguished his conduct at the battle of Buena Vista. 4-Memorial of Eliz Hall, of Balt: referred. 5-Ptn of John Nash, praying for the remission of a fine. 6-Ptn of Nathl Riddick, adm of Richd Taylor, a captain in the war of the Revolution, praying for commutation pay. 7-Memorial of Dimock P Huntington, Interpreter to the Indian agency of the Territory of Utah, praying Congress for compensation for performing extra services.

<u>Wash City-1853</u>: total # of dwlgs: 8,265. Completion of the dredging of the Canal between 15th & 17th sts has been neglected, although much needed. Public School in the 7th Ward has had an additional story & other improvements made to it. The Market House in the 5th Ward has been enclosed & fitted up as a primary school for that section. The markets have increased much with the year; an enlargement of the bldg, by erection of the wings on 7th & 9th sts, would double the present; the present fish shed ought to be removed, & a new place erected on the line of B st for the venders of fish. In the city are 48 places of worship, viz: 10 for Methodist & Methodist Protestants, Presbyterians-7, Episcopalian-6; Baptist-5; Roman Catholic-5; Lutheran-2; Friends, Unitarians, Congregational, & Swedenborgian-1 each; & also 9 colored congregations. An extensive bldg has been erected by Mr Coyle on B st, for sawing, planing, & turning & grooving, which is doing a good business. The foundry & machine shops of Messrs Ellis, adjoining, are fully employed, & turn out the best of work of all kinds in that line. There is also the sash & frame factory of McLean & Ager. In the Third Ward there has been an extension of the sewer on 9th st to Mass ave, & on I from 8th to 9th sts. Good improvements made at the City Post Ofc; old bldg pulled down north of the Market & rebuilt in a beautiful style by Mr S Hill. In the 7th Ward a new lime-kiln has been erected near Va ave & the Canal by Mr Seely. The Gas Co have extended their line of lamps to Gtwn, & have commenced laying pipes from the Capitol to 8th st east, on Pa ave. Great progress on the wings of the Capitol & the west wing of the Patent Ofc.

Two convicts escaped from the penitentiary at Richmond on Sunday last: Wm Pogue, a convict from Lynchburg, a white man, 40 years of age; & Chas Jones, alias Geo Morgan, a white man, from Monroe Co, 27 years old. $500 reward offered for their apprehension.

Died: on Jan 1, John Braddock Porter, infant son of John E & Sarah Porter, aged 11 months & 16 days. His funeral will take place this evening at 3 p m, from the residence of his uncle, Mr D S Porter.

The Sandusky [Ohio] Register states that Mr Hector Jennings, of that city, has lately received letters from his atty, just returned from London, assuring him of the entire & complete validity of his claims as one of two heirs to the immense Jennings' estate, in England, value at $60,000,000. Mr Jennings is an old citizen of Sandusky, having resided here most of the time for 17 years. The history of his lineage is a singular one, having much of the air of romance about it.

Geo W Howell, chief operator in the Wash & New Orleans Telegraph ofc at Richmond, Va, was killed there on Thu by being thrown from a wagon.

The Brandywine Springs bldgs, occupied by Capt Partridge as a Military School, were destroyed by fire on Thu. The scholars were mostly obsent for the holydays.

TUE JAN 3, 1853
List of Ofcrs of the Ward-room Mess of the U S frig **Susquehanna** at the time of her passage from Norfolk to Rio Janeiro, in June & Jul, 1851. Lts: S W Gordon, T T Hunter, J B Randolph, F A Parker, Geo H Cooper; Master, John Matthews; Passed Assist Surgeon, Chas Eversfield; Assist Surgeon, Chas F Fahs; Purser, G R Barry; Chaplain, E C Bettinger; Bvt Capt of Marines, W B Slack; Cmdor's Sec, Ferdinand Coxe; Chief Engineer, S Archbold.

U S Patent Ofc, Wash, Jan 2, 1854. Ptn of Jas Rowe, of Tampa Bay, Fla, praying for the extension of a patent granted to him on Apr 24, 1840, for an improvement in machines for crushing hard substances, for 7 years from the expiration of said patent, which takes place on Apr 24, 1854. –Chas Mason, Com'r of Patents.

Household & kitchen furniture at auction: Jan 3, at the residence of A T Burnley, on F st, between 18th & 19th sts. –Green & Scott, aucts

Hon Sam Houston, Senator from the State of Texas, has arrived in Wash City, & is stopping at Willard's.

Mrd: on Dec 28, in the Parish Church of Chestertown, Md, by Rev Clement F Jones, D D, Saml M Shoemaker, of Balt, to Augusta C, eldest daughter of Hon John B Eccleston, of the former place.

WED JAN 4, 1854
Confectionary, preserves, cakes, candies, jellies, fruits, & cigars, at auction: on Jan 6, at the store of Mr John H Arnold, on Pa ave, near 3rd st. –E N Stratton, auct

Trustee's sale of valuable real estate: by deed of trust dated Jun 27, 1853, recorded in Liber J A S, 58, folios 264 thru 268: sale on Jan 27, 1854, in subdivision of square 463, fronting on 7th st, between D & E sts south, with bldgs & improvements, which consist of, on lot 75 of a well & substantially built 2 story frame dwlg house, & a back kitchen, with stable, & other out-house, & on lot 76 a frame bldg for ofcs. The property is situated on the Island, in a rapidly improving part of Wash City. -Chas S Wallach, Trustee -Jas C McGuire, auct

Senate: 1-Message received from the Pres of the U S, transmitting, in compliance with a resolution of the Senate of Dec 12 calling for any correspondence that may have taken place with the British gov't on any subject growing out of the treaty of Wash of Jul 4, 1850, a report of the Sec of State communication certain papers, to wit: Mr Crampton to Mr Marcy, May 19, 1853; Mr Harding to the Earl of Clarendon, Apr 15, 1853; Mr Crampton to Mr Marcy, Dec 15, 1853; Lord Clarendon to Mr Crampton, Apr 29, 1853; same to same, May 29, 1853; Mr Marcy to Mr Ingersoll, Jun 9, 1853; Lord Clarendon to Mr Crampton, Jul 22, 1853. 2-Ptn from the widow of Gen Childs, asking a pension. 3-Ptn from Morris Powers, asking a pension, in consequence of disability incurred in the Mexican war. 4-Ptn from Hammond Howe & others, asking an amendment of the steamboat law. 5-Ptn from Mordecai & Co, of Charleston, S C, asking to be allowed to change the name of the vessel **John Dutton** to **Emma Eager**. 6-Ptn from the administrator of David Richardson, of the Revolutionary army, asking to be allowed the difference between the amount he received & what he represents to be due. 7-Ptn from David Hines, asking remuneration for damages sustained in consequence of the change of grade of Pa ave, in Wash City. 8-Ptn from Edw Hamilton, of Mass, asking that coal may be admitted free of duty. 9-Ptn from Helen Macay, asking that the accounting ofcrs of the Treasury may be directed to receive certain vouchers as evidence in the settlement of her husband's accounts. 10-Ptn from Jas McDaniel & others, asking a tri-weekly mail from Kansas to Platte city, Mo. 11-Cmte on Private Land Claims: bill authorizing Victor Morass to relinquish certain lands & to enter the same quantity elsewhere, accompanied by a written report: passed. 12-Bill for the relief of the legal reps of Joshua Kennedy, deceased: passed. 13-Bill for the relief of Jos Gordon, jr, & John Duff, which was agreed to. 14-Bill for the relief of the heirs of Caleb Swann, was amended as to allow the heirs a commission of one per cent, instead of one-half per cent, as it stood in the original bill, & passed.

Died: on Jan 3, in Wash City, Mrs Jane Kenney, in her 41st year. Her funeral will take place from St Peter's Church, Capitol Hill, on Thu next, at 10 o'clock.

House of Reps: 1-Cmte on Commerce: bills for the relief of Ferdinand Clark, Adolphus Meise & Co, of St Louis, & Wilson & Bros, of St Louis: committed. Same cmte: bill to change the name of the American built brig **John Dutton**, & to grant a register in her new name **Emma Eager**: passed. 2-Bill for the relief of Wm Darby: introduced. 3-Bill for the relief of Eleanor Williams: introduced.

The steamship **Winfield Scott**, which was lost recently, was owned by the Pacific Mail Steam Co of N Y, running between San Francisco & Panama with mails & passengers. The accident happened on Dec 2, during a dense fog, the passengers were immediately dispatched to San Francisco, & the agents of the company forthwith sent off 2 steamers, & on Dec 7 all the passengers were again on the way to Panama, without loss or injury of any kind in persons or property.

Providence, Jan 3. The schnr **Moselle**, from Boston for Virginia, was wrecked on Sunday off Newport, & all on board lost.

Boston, Jan 3. The ship **Staffordshire**, Capt Richardson, from Liverpool for Boston, struck on Blande Rock, south of Sea Island, Dec 31. The 1st & 2nd mates & 17 sailors reached Cape Sable. The 3rd mate & 130 others have been picked up & landed at Albany. 177 persons perished with the wreck.

Burlington, [Vt] Jan 3: the steam saw mill machine shop & iron foundry owned by Henry Simonds, with several adjacent bldgs, were burnt yesterday.

Circuit Court of Wash Co, D C: Ann Tench vs Edmund Burt, Julia A Burt, & Martha Ellen French. The trustee reported that he has sold part of lot 3 in square 928 to John A Golden for $399.84, & parts of lot 1 & 12 in square 975, & part of lot 5 in square 975, to Mrs Ann Tench for $3,373, & the purchasers have complied with the terms of the sale. –John A Smith, clerk

In the Circuit Court of St Mary's Co: in Equity: Dec Term, 1853. Ann B Burch vs Remegius Burch. The object of the suit is to procure a decree for the divorce of Ann B Burch from Remegius Burch; also to return to the custody & possession of the said Ann B Burch all the property, real & personal, which she owned previous to her intermarriage with the said Remegius Burch. The bill states that the plntf was joined to the dfndnt in wedlock somewhere about Jul 26, 1851; that the dfndnt at divers times since said date has treated her unkindly, & that he has deserted her, & no longer lives with her as her husband; that she was possessed of certain real & personal property, named in her bill of cmplnt, before her intermarriage with said cmplnt; that the said Remegius Burch resides out of the state of Md. He is to appear in this Court, in person or by solicitor, on or before the first Monday of June next. –Peter W Crain -Jas T Blakistone, clerk.

THU JAN 5, 1854

Senate: 1-Ptn from Gideon Hotchkiss, asking the extension of a patent for improvements in making water wheels & their appendates. 2-Ptn from John Phagan, asking compensation for exploring a country for the Seminole Indians west of the Arkansas under an order of the Sec of War. 3-Ptn from the heirs of Andrew Buchanan, asking indemnity for French spoliations prior to 1800. 4-Ptn from W W Woodworth, asking the extension of a patent. 5-Ptn from Jos McCracken, asking bounty land for the services of his father in the war of the Revolution. 6-Ptn from L Taliaferro, asking a pension on account of disease contracted in the military service during the last war with Great Britain. 7-Ptn from Maj Jas P Heath, asking to be allowed pay for his services as aid to Gen Winder, cmder-in-chief of the Md militia in the last war with Great Britain. 8-Ptn from Wm Ballard, asking that certain improvements made by him in the construction of vessels designed for the navy may be tried in the construction of one of those about to be built. 9-Ptn from Peter Amey, asking a pension on account of wounds received in the naval service of the U S in 1814, in that memorable battle of the ship **Essex**, with the English ships of war **Phoebe & Cherub**. 10-Cmte on Commerce: adverse report on the memorial of B E Abbott, asking to be remunerated for expenses incurred by his father while vice consul of the U S at Salonica. 11-Cmte of Claims: bill for the relief of the legal reps of Chas Cooper & Co; a bill for the relief of Jas Boyd, of La; & a bill for the relief of Jacob Gideon, accompanied by written reports in each case. Same cmte: bill for the relief of Jas Dunning. Same cmte: bill for the relief of the legal reps of the late Capt Wm Ridgely: ordered to a 2nd reading. 12-Cmte on Pensions: to inquire into the expediency of granting to Maj Jonathan Hensley, an invalid ofcr of the war of 1812, the pension originally allowed him, but subsequently reduced under an opinion of the Atty Gen.

House of Reps: 1-Cmte of Claims: adverse reports on the ptns of Job M Sayton & the heirs of Anthony Gale: laid on the table.

Hon Saml H Walley, a member of Congress from the Fourth Mass District, was prevented by the death of his wife from taking his seat at the opening of the session. He is now detained at home by his own ill health.

Michl McKenna, aged about 17 years, employed in the dye-house of the Woonasquatucket Print Works, at North Providence, was killed on Dec 29, his clothes having been caught by the shaft while he was adjusting a belt.

The hotel at Upper Marlboro, Md, occupied by Mr Leonard H Chew, & owned by John Brookes, was destroyed by fire in the night of Sat last. It was insured in Alexandria for $5,000. Most of the furniture was removed from the burning bldg, but it was so damaged as to be almost worthless.

Mrd: on Jan 4, by Rev Dr Butler, Chas W Beatty, of Balt, to Augusta M, daughter of Dr A J Schwartze, of Wash.

Died: on Jan 3, at her residence, in Gtwn, Mrs Martha J Waggaman, the sister of the Ex-Pres Tyler, in her 70th year. Her funeral will take place from her late residence, on 1st st, near High st, & proceed to St Matthew's Church, this day, at 1 o'clock.

Died: on Jan 3, at the Navy Yard, Mary Ann, wife of Merrit Shecklels, in her 32nd year.

A daughter of Widow Oliver, aged 3 years, residing in this town, was accidentally killed on Sun last by the discharge of a pistol in the hands of a son of Saml Moses, about 4 years old. The pistol belonged to Mr Moses, who was a watchman in the mills, & had that morning been laid by him upon a shelf. The child of Mr Moses, teasing for the weapon, it was handed him by his mother. She was not aware of its being loaded; & in playing with the pistol it was soon after discharged with fatal effect. –Madison [N Y] Observer

On Dec 24, Mr Fred'k A Theudley, paper maker, near Morgantown, Va, met with an accident which eventuated in his death. On closing up the labors of the week he went into the wheel room when the machinery suddenly started, catching him between the wheels.

Copartnership: I have associated with me Ulysses B Ward, for the purpose of carrying on the Lumber business, under the name of J B Ward & Bro.

Circuit Court of Wash Co, D C-in Chancery. Chas H Wiltberger & al, heirs at law of Benj Burche, vs Catherine Caine & Jonathan Cain. The trustees have reported the sale of part of lots 7 & 8, with improvements, in square 728, fronting on East Capitol st, for $2,700, & John C Burche became the purchaser; & that Chas McNamee became the purchaser of part of lot 8 in square 723, fronting on East Capitol st, for the sum of $459.75; & that they have complied with the terms of the sale.
-Jno A Smith, clk

FRI JAN 6, 1854
John A Parker, a distinguished merchant of New Bedford, died in that city on Fri, at an advanced age. He left a fortune worth at least a million dollars, & was grandfather of Gov Clifford's wife.

Mr Abraham Pittsley, of North Fairhaven, Mass, was frozen to death in the woods on Fri last. He had been cutting wood for several days & it is supposed was overcome by the intense cold. His age was about 60 years.

Jas Clough, convicted at Taunton in Dec, 1852, for the murder of Gideon Manchester, the ofcr who underook to arrest him for burglary, the Govn'r of Mass has appointed Apr 28 for his execution.

Senate: 1-Ptn from L P Holladay & Co, asking to be allowed to erect a large & commodious hotel on the public grounds in Wash City. 2-Ptn from R Piemont & others, asking compensation for saving the U S ships **Raritan** & **Vandalia** from destruction by fire on Oct 11, 1847. 3-Ptn from Jas McCormick, asking the payment of an amount due him under a contract with Cmdor Jones while commanding the U S squadron in the Pacific. 4-Ptn from the heirs at law of Capt Thos Buckner, Beverley Hoy/Roy, Lewis Booker, & Ensign Henry Hughes, of the Va line in the continental army, asking the half pay for life to which they were entitled in virtue of a resolution of Oct 21, 1793. 5-Ptn from Isaac Cook & others, asking compensation for the schnr **Tempest**, which was pressed into the service of the U S in 1814. 6-Ptn from Mgt C Hanson, widow of an ofcr who died of disease contracted while in service, asking a pension; & also from Mary Ray, widow of a soldier in the last war with Great Britain, asking to be allowed bounty land. 7-Cmte on Military Affairs: to inquire into purchasing 3 of Thos H Barlow's planetariums for the use of the West Point Military Academy, Annapolis Naval School, & the Nat'l Observatory.

Dr Saml McClellan, an eminent physician of Phil, died in that city on Wed, in his 54th year.

Hartford Courant: Rev Lewis Weld, Principal of the American Asylum for the Deaf & Dumb at Hartford, Conn, died. He had just returned from a European trip, undertaken for his health, which had recently become impaired. The voyage did not alleviate his complaint, a congestion of the lungs. His place was occupied by Rev Wm W Turner, who has been acting Principal for the year. [No death date given- current item.]

The Sandwich [Mass] Advocate says that Capt Bangs Nickerson, of Harwich, drank, through mistake, from a bottle a quantity of bed-bug poison. He died on Dec 26.

House of Reps: 1-Ptn of Jas Robinson for an invalid pension. 2-Memorial from Abner R Hill, A F Zachey, & 14 others, citizens of Chambers Co, Ala, praying a grant of land in aid of a military institution in said State, known as the Southern Military Academy. 3-Memorial of Gen Walbach, Col Taylor, & other ofcrs of the U S army, praying a change in the commutation price of the ration.

A young woman, Adeline Phelps, was recently tried at Greenfield, Mass, charged with the murder of her father by poison. Verdict: not guilty, by reason of insanity. The Court directed her to be sent to the State Asylum for the Insane at Worcester. The fact of the poisoning was pretty conclusively proved.

The packet ship **Staffordshire**, Capt Richardson, from Liverpool, Dec 9, for Boston, struck the Blonde Rock, south of Seal Island, on Dec 30. The 1st & 2nd mates & 17 seamen reached Cape Sable. The 3rd mate, boatswain, & 12 others were picked up & landed at Shelburne, N S. Capt Richardson & about 180 persons, went down in the wreck immediately after striking. The following is the list of passengers by the **Staffordshire**:

Bridget Barrett	Michl Sullivan	John Shell
Bridget Fallon	John Fierney	Jerry Hurley
Homer Lahey	Catherie Mahoney	Michl Hurley
Elijah Brien	Julie Mahoney	Jas Austin
Jos Brien	Jas Tobin	Fanny Austin
Mary Cutter	Chas Moriarty	Edw Granghan
J Carroll	Honora Bruckley	Wm Cayle
J O'Brien	Patt Barry	Mary Copely
- Gillen	Michl Barry	Mary English
Nancy Murray	Patrick Burke	Eliza Boardman
Jeremiah Murray	Thos Burke	Jane Boardman
Mgt Brown	Mary Keeron	Edw Boardman
Julianna Brown	Hugh Keeron	Mgt Dowahy
Wm Brown	Patt Colemar	Julia Dowahy
Patrick O'Conner	Johanna Healey	Danl Delany
Mary Monnaghan	J Scounnell	Mary Garrizan
Michl Smith	Peter Killy	Geo Smith
Edmund Sweeney	John Sullivan	Michl Martin
Danl Sweeney	John Murphy	Thos Barrett
Mary Carroll	C Doherty	Mary Devlin
Catherine Rafferty	M Sweeney	Patt Devlin
Mary Rafferty	Eliza Healy	Sarah Ann McKenna
Catherine Dowling	Mary Nelson	Jas Somers
Ann Dolan	Miles McCarru	Andrew Somers
Wm Alton	Eliza Butler	-Boston Journal
Ann Alton	John Shell	
Thos Sullivan	Mary Shell	
John Sullivan	Julia Martin	

Mrd: on Jan 4, in Wash City, by Rev Geo W Samson, Jos D Green, of Phil, to Mrs Mary A Gold, daughter of Hon A Kendall.

Mrd: on Jan 2, at Grace Church, by Rev Alfred Holmead, Saml C Penington to Anna E Dorsey, daughter of E J Dorsey, all of Wash City.

Died: on Aug 26, 1853, on board the clipper ship **Antelope**, in the Pacific Ocean, Raphael, son of the late Raphael Semmes, of Gtwn, D C, in his 18th year.

SAT JAN 7, 1854

Household & kitchen furniture at auction: on Jan 10, at the residence of a lady declining housekeeping, on East Captiol st, one door west of Maj B B French's, [the flag will designate the house,] at 10 o'clock, a lot of good furniture.
–Green & Scott, aucts

Household & kitchen furniture at auction on Jan 13, at the residence of Mrs McCormick, on the south side of Pa ave, between 4½ & 6th sts.
–Green & Scott, aucts

House of Reps: 1-Bill for the relief of the legal reps of Maj Caleb Swan, deceased. 2-Bill for the relief of the legal reps of Dr Wm Somerville, deceased. 3-Bill for the relief of Jos Gender, jr, & John Duff. 4-Bill for the relief of the legal reps of John Kennedy, deceased. 5-Bills laid aside: for the relief of Lewis B Willis, late a paymaster in the army of the U S; of the legal reps of Isaac B Simonton, deceased; & of Wm Blake. 6-Bills objected to: settling the claims of the legal reps of Richd W Meade, deceased; relief of Saml Colt; relief of Chas Lee Jones; relief of Henry Lewis, of Clinton Co, Indiana; relief of Capt Geo Simpton, of Galveston; relief of Ferdinand Clark; relief of Adolphus Meir & Co, of St Louis; relief of Robt Grignon; relief of Geo G Bishop & the legal reps of John Arnold, deceased; & relief of the widow & heirs of Elijah Beebe.

Murder at Lexington, Ky. A few days ago the wife of Wm H Weigart of said place, entered a confectionary store in that town, when a young man, Luther C Cushing, temporarily employed therein, stepped up to her, & patting her familiarly on the back, observed, "What will you have, pretty?" Mrs Weigart became offended. Cushing apologized. Mrs Weigart informed her husband who soon after entered the store & commenced firing upon Cushing with a revolver, killing him on the spot. Weigart & wife were arrested. She was discharged & he was committed to await his trial on a charge of murder.

John West attempted to ride across the mouth of Pawpaw on the ice, when his horse broke through & was drowned. West was thrown forward on the ice, probably stunned, & was found frozen to death the next morning. It is said he was intoxicated at the time. –Morgantown [Va[Mirror

Mrd: on Jan 5, at Trinity Church, by Rev Mr Hodge, Thos W Brodhead, U S N, to Eliza R, daughter of the late Jas D Barry, of Wash City.

Mrd: on Jan 5, in St Thomas' Church, by Rev S R Gordon, Col Wm D Bowie to Miss Mary Oden, daughter of the late Benj Oden, all of PG Co, Md.

Mrd: on Jan 5, by Rev John C Smith, Mr A B Claxton to Miss E Jennie Fisher, all of Wash City.

Died: on Jan 6, Henry Ashton Bibb, in his 15th year, youngest son of Hon Geo M Bibb. His funeral will take place at St Patrick's Church, this morning, at 10 o'clock.

Died: on Jan 5, in Wash City, Henry R, infant son of Fanny & C R Byrne. His funeral is this afternoon, at 2 o'clock, from the residence of Mrs Middleton, Garrison st, Navy Yard, near Va av

Information has been received at the Dept of State, from the U S Consul at Hamburg, Saml Bromberg, of the death at that place, in Nov last, of Jacob Willet, or, as he was called at Hamburg, Hans Jacob Wehling, late of Wash Co, Ga.

MON JAN 9, 1854
Household & kitchen furniture at auction: on Jan 12, at the residence of O S X Peck, on N Y ave, between 13th & 14th sts, nearly new furniture. –Green & Scott, aucts

Hon Thos Greenleaf died on Thu, at his residence in Quincy, Mass, at age 86 years. He was a graduate of Harvard College in 1784, & for upwards of 6 years has been the only survivor of his class.

Wm D Benson, a young man, residing in New Orleans, on retiring to bed on Dec 26, took a heavy dose of morphine, because he felt slightly indisposed. In the morning he was found dead by the servant.

Wash Corp: 1-Ptn of Dennis O'Neale & wife for the remission of a fine: referred to the Cmte of Claims. 2-Resolved, that Mrs Susan Burche have leave to withdraw her petition from the files of this Board. 3-Ptn of H G Ritter & others in relation to closing shops at 10 o'clock: referred to the Cmte on Police. 4-Cmte on the Compilation of the Laws: act for the relief of Jas W Sheahan: passed. 5-Ptn of Casey Proctor, asking permission to give 2 suppers for the benfit of Bethel Church: read twice. 6-Ptn of J H Hilton & others, engaged in the business of huckstering, praying certain modifications in the laws in relation to hucksters: referred to the Cmte on Police. 7-Ptn of Chas Finnigan, praying for the remission of a fine: referred to the Cmte of Claims. 8-Cmte of Claims: bill for the relief of Sophia Stallings: passed. Same cmte: asked to be discharged from the further consideration of the ptn of W A Snyder. Same cmte: bill for the relief of Wm True: passed. 9-Bill for the relief of Wm Gallant was recommitted to the Cmte of Claims. 10-Bill for the relief of Francis Miller: referred to the Cmte of Ways & Means. Same cmte: bill for the relief of P W Dorsey, reported the same without amendment.

Mrd: on Dec 22, by Rev J F Hoff, Philip Nelson to Emma Page, all of Clark Co, Va.

Sidney S Baxter, late Atty Gen of Va, has removed to Washington to practice Law. Ofc in Morrison's new bldg on 4½ st, east of Pa ave.

Application will be made to the Board of Trustees of the Farmers' & Mechanics' Bank of Gtwn, at the expiration of 30 days from the date hereof, for the renewal of certificate #265, issued by said Bank to the subscriber on Nov 13, 1830, for 80 shares of the capital stock of said Bank of $25 each, said original certificate having been lost or mislaid. –Harriet B Macomb

TUE JAN 10, 1854
Superior stock of groceries at auction: on Jan 14, at the Grocery store of C R Byrne, corner of 10th & Pa ave-his entire stock. -Jas C McGuire, auct

Dayton was the scene on Thu of a tragedy when an uncompleted 3 story brick warehouse on 3rd st, fell. Geo Weathers & A Jennings were killed & others were badly injured. The Methodist Church adjoining was also damaged.

Senate: 1-Cmte on Pensions: bill for the relief of Mary E Hamilton, accompanied by a report. Same cmte: bill for the relief of the children of the late Michl Everly. 2-Cmte on Private Land Claims: bill for the relief of the legal reps of Wm Weeks, accompanied by a report. 3-Cmte on Commerce: adverse report on the memorial of Francis B Ogden. 4-Cmte on Indian Affairs: asked to be discharged from the further consideration of the memorial of Amos Kendall & J E Kendall, & that it be referred to the Cmte on the Judiciary.

Dept of State, Wash, Jan 6, 1854. Information has been received from Wm H Kelly, U S Consul at Tahiti, Society Islands, of the death, on that Island, on May 11, 1853, of John Donnelly, a citizen of the U S, & late seaman on board of the ship **Orosimbo**. His friends, who are said to reside at 44 Orange st, N Y, may obtain further intelligence respecting him by addressing this Dept.

Meeting of the students of the Washington Seminary in memory of the late Henry A Bibb, an accomplished scholar & an honor to society.

Washington Carvalle	Eugene Fitzgerald
Jas Hoban	Chas B Massi
Peter P Fitzpatrick	Willard L Fitzgerald
Jas F Callan	Lawrence O'Toole
Francis Renshaw	Andrie H Kerr
Wm Whelan	Geo Theodore Orme
Chas Carvalle	Walter Hellen
Jos C Caden	Francis Dooley
Francis D Orme	Douglas Cleary
John Callan, jr	Jas K Cleary

Cmte on the part of the Students of the Washington Seminary.

Died: on Jan 5, at his residence in PG Co, Md, Mr Richd Hyatt, in his 70th year, formerly a merchant of Balt.

Young Men's Christian Association meeting this evening at 7 o'clock.
–Robt S Forde, Rec Sec

Mrs Richd Coke has for rent several large Parlors & Chambers, handsomely furnished & lighted with gas. Her residence is the house of her mother, Mrs Cochrane, on F, between 13th & 14th sts.

R Finley Hunt, Dentist, requests all persons against whom he has accounts to come forward & settle them. After Jan 11 all bills on his books will be placed in the hands of a collector, with instructions to close them up immediately.

Orphans Court of Wash Co, D C. Letters testamentary on the personal estate of Ann E Brook, late of Wash Co, deceased. –Robt C Brooke, exec

WED JAN 11, 1854
Senate: 1-Communication from the Dept of Interior, transmitting the report of Willis A Gorman & R M Young, Com'rs appointed by the Pres to investigate the charges alleged against Alex'r Ramsey, late Superintendent of Indian Affairs for Minnesota Territory: referred to the Cmte on Indian Affairs. 2-Ptn from Henry K Brown, asking to be allowed 14 pieces of condemned brass cannon belonging to the U S, & that the Sec of War be authorized to deliver the same to him, for the purpose of casting a large equestrian statue of Washington, to be erected in N Y C. 3-Ptn from John Thomas, asking an appropriation to enable him to test certain improvements made by him in the inclined plane or mill. 4-Memorial of Barnum Whipple, asking the enactment of a law requiring the Sec of the Treasury to report the amount of money collected by each of the collectors of the customs for the support of marine hospitals. He says that he has paid under the act of 1793 a tax of twenty cents per month for over 40 years for the alleged purpose of bldg marine hospitals, & has yet seen any proper account of the disposal of that money. He infers that some millions must have been paid into the treasury since the passage of that act, & it was right & proper that those who pay the tax should know something of the disposition made of it. He has reason to believe that all the money has not reached the object for which it was intended. 5-Cmte of Claims: bill for the relief of Silas Loomis, with a report. 6-Cmte on Pensions: bill for the relief of Rebecca Freeman, with a report. Same cmte: asked to be discharged from the further consideration of the memorial of Mary Ray, & that it be referred to the Cmte on Public Lands. 7-Cmte on Finance: joint resolution for the relief of Geo R C Floyd, late Sec of Wisconsin Territory, reported back with an amendment, & asked the unanimous consent of the Senate to consider the bill: which was granted.

Mr John Leary, of Ky, the late mail agent, who was indicted on a charge of committing depredations on the mail, has received a full pardon from the Pres. The accused is respectably connected, & was & is deranged. This fact having been fully established, the pardon was granted.

House of Reps: 1-Ptn of Capt John A Webster & 24 other ofcrs of the revenue service, praying an increase of compensation & certain modifications of the laws relating to the revenue marine. 2-Memorial of Mrs M F B Leveley, of Phil, asking Congress to grant her the pension formerly prayed for by her husband, commencing from the date of his wounds-from 1812 to 1829-as well as that already now due her under the pension law from 1836, when the payment of his pension ceased. 3-Ptn of Mrs Sarah Vinson for a pension.

The public of N Y C, at least, will learn with deep regret that the Hon Edw Curtis was taken to the insane asylum on Sat. His health has been failing for some time, & during the past year his intellect has been sensibly affected. The malady began with partial loss of memory, an inability to recognize persons & remember names, & more lately exhibited itself in the hallucination that he was possessed of boundless riches, which he was seeking to bestow with a lavish profusion. The case is deemed by the medical faculty to be a softening of the brain, & but faint hopes exist of his recovery. Mr Curtis was formerly Collector of this port, an intimate friend of Webster & Clay, & a prominent man in the ranks of the Whig party. –N Y Mirror

Dept of State, Wash, Jan 9, 1854. Information has been received from Thos Wm Ward, U S Consul at Panama, N G, of the death of the following citizens of the U S:
J B Fitts, late of Lumpkin Co, Ga.
M Roussin, late of St Genevieve, Mo.
Michl Corbit, late of New Orleans, La.
Wm Daggett, residence not given.
Charles, son of J F Winkley.

Dept of State, Wash, Jan 9, 1854. The Spanish Legation in the U S has communicated to this Dept certificates of death of American citizens who have died in the Danish West Indies since Aug 20, 1852, a list of which is subjoined:
At St Thomas
1852, Aug 20, Alfred Gardere, of Balt
Sep 1, J H Myers, of Va, physician
Sep 2, Rev Edm Richards, of Va, pastor of the Episcopal Church.
Sep 11, Thos Tweeny, of Norfolk, Va, sailor
Oct 7, Henry Hunn, of Boston, sailor
Oct 24, Miss Mary Furnass, of Boston
Nov 8, Thos Root, of N Y, sailor
Nov 15, Peter Wilson, of Provincetown, sailor
Nov 22, John Penny, of Eastport, Me, sailor
Nov 23, Wm King, of Maine, sailor
Nov 28, John Snyder, of N Y, sailor
Dec 2, Henry Ballast, of Boston, sailor
Dec 2, Alex'r Letter, of N Y, sailor
Dec 2, Jas Fish, of N Y
Dec 18, Wm Beecher, of New Haven, Conn
Dec 9, Wm H Elliott, of New Haven, Conn

Nov 2, Chas Cooper, sailor
Nov 7, Jas Duncan, sailor
Nov 5, Jas Kirby, Md, sailor
Nov 5, Mrs Mary Gustava Chandler, wife of Capt Judah Chandler
Nov 7, Wm S Brangbridge, of Maine, sailor
Nov 7, Chas Baker, of Bucksport, sailor
Nov 13, Thadeus T Kendrick, of Mass, sailor
Nov 14, Jas Cannon, of Conn, sailor
Nov 15, Hardy M Burton, of Tenn, U S Consul
Nov 16, Wm Hamilton, of Maine, sailor
Nov 19, John Hanson, of Phil, sailor
Nov 23, Wm Hong, of Phil, sailor
1853 Jan 19, C B Adams, professor of astronomy & natural philosophy, Amherst College, Mass
Jan 21, Ezechiel Halfield, of Yarmouth, U S, sailor
Feb 3, Peter Prain, of N Y, sailor
Feb 4, Jas Fellow, of Frankfort, sailor, at St Croix
Feb 22, Stephen Bogardus, of N Y, merchant

Mrd: on Jan 10, by Rev C M Butler, Jas K Smith, of Phil, to Georgie, daughter of Wm G W White, of Wash City.

Mrd: on Jan 10, at Trinity Church, by Rev Dr Butler, Wm Bowie Burford, of Montg Co, Md, to Eliz Ann, eldest daughter of Wm Thompson, of Wash City.

Mrd: on Jan 10, at St Stephen's Church, Balt, by Rev Mr Reed, Norman S Bestor, of New Almaden, Calif, to Willie J Childs, of Balt.

Died: on Jan 10, Kate, youngest child of B F & E E Dyer, aged 2 years & 9 months. Her funeral is this afternoon at 3 o'clock.

N Y, Jan 10. The steamer **Union** has sailed in search of the steamer **San Francisco**. Capt Hudson & 3 ofcrs of the Navy volunteered.

The Marchioness Wellesley, a most excellent & distinguished lady, died at Hampton Court Palace on Dec 16. Lady Stafford & the Duchess of Leeds, her younger sisters, were with her during her final hours, & in the deepest lamentation. The Marchioness will be interred at Cottsey Hall, the late residence of her sister, the Dowager Lady Stafford, & the new residence of the present Lord Stafford. The Marchioness was in her 66th year. [She died in a foreign land; the grand-daughter of that eminent Marylander who periled life & vast domains in opposition to the British rule over these now sovereign & flourishing States. No name given.] -H

Dissolution of the copartnership conducted as Davis & Garrett, this day, by mutual consent. Jos Davis will continue the business at the old stand. Geo W Garrett is authorized to use the name of the firm in settling up the business, & to call upon him at the ofc of the Lumber Yard, 6th & B sts.

THU JAN 12, 1854
Household & kitchen furniture at auction on Jan 18, at the residence of Mrs Langton, on South S st, opposite the east part of Capitol square, an excellent assortment of furniture. –Green & Scott, aucts

Auction of the personal effects of John H Sherburne, deceased, on Jan 14, in front of our Auction Store, by order of the Orphans Court of Wash Co, D C. –Green & Scott, aucts

Public sale of desirable farm in Fairfax Co, Va: on Jan 28, at the auction rooms of Green & Scott, in Wash City, a Farm of upwards of 60 acres. This piece of land is the house lot of the estate of John Hunter Terrett, deceased, located within 8 miles of Wash. –Wm H Ward, trustee -Green & Scott, aucts

Hon Thos W Ligon, formerly a member of Congress, was yesterday inaugurated as Govn'r of Md, & entered upon his duties. He is a native of Va, but has been a resident of Md for many years.

Lt John A Davis, of the U S Navy, was thrown from a buggy while driving through E st, near 6th, on Monday night, & very seriously, if not fatally injured, his skull being severely fractured. He was taken to the Infirmary. He is about 40 years of age, & has no family.

On Fri last Andrew H Trayer, one of the men convicted at Stuanton, Va, of the murder of Wm Coleman, was executed in the presence of about 10,000 persons, including nearly 1,000 females. He addressed the multitude for 15 minutes, assevorating his innocence, as well as the innocence of Wilson, convicted of the same offence.

Senate: 1-Memorial of J Wilson Smith, asking indemnity for the illegal seizure of the steamer **Fanny** by the U S district atty & the ofcrs of the customs at Savannah, Ga; & also 2 other memorials from the heirs of Antoine Pauleut, & the heirs of Lewis Gosline, of the Revolutionary war.

The body of David Jones, of Andover, was found in a clump of woods near the line between Lawrence & that town. On Wed previous to the great snow storm he went to Lawrence to procure some provisions. On his way back it is supposed he became bewildered in the storm, wandered from the road, & died from exhaustion. His dog accompanied him, & stayed with him for 6 days. –Boston Traveller

St Mary's [Md] Beacon: 3 gentlemen of Chas Co, Md, were drowned in attempting to cross Chaptico bay. They were on a ducking excursion, & caught in a gale. They were Messrs E A Lloyd, Francis J Lloyd, & Chas Simms. The first named gentleman leaves a wife & 3 children. The other two were youths from 16 to 20 years old.

On Thu Miss McCann, a young lady, residing in Covington, near the Rolling Mill, went to the cistern to draw a bucket of water, when her foot slipped & she was precipitated into the cistern, whence her body was taken out lifeless after the lapse of some 15 minutes.

Franklin Pierce, Pres of the U S A, recognizes Fitzhenry Homer, who has been appointed Consul of Buenos Ayres, for the port of Boston, in Mass. -Jan 5, 1854

Mrd: on Jan 10, by Rev Jas B Donelan, Wm S Davis to Sarah E, eldest daughter of John T Cassell.

House of Reps: 1-Resolutions of respect for the memory of the deceased, Henry A Muhlenberg, late a Rep from Pa. The brother of his grandfather, Fred'k Augustus Muhlenberg, was the first Speaker chosen to preside over the House of Reps of the U S under the present constitution. Jos Heister, his maternal grandfather, was among the early Govn'rs of Pa. His father, Henry A Muhlenberg, long a distinguished member of this body, during the whole of Gen Jackson's Presidential term was a Rep in Congress: was afterwards chosen by Gen Jackson the representative of his Gov't to the Court of Vienna, Austria; & after discharging those duties, he was shortly after his return to Pa, nominated as the Democratic candidate for Govn'r of Pa, his native State. He was stricken down with the banner in his hands, & died but a short time before the election. The deceased was a man of high character, of inflexible integrity, & of polished education & manners. Mr Brodhead said he was with him much during his protracted & fatal illness. Henry A Muhlenberg was my deceased friend. He breathed his last at my residence last evening . On my way to this place I was a guest for days, with my family, in his hospitable mansion. As a husband & father his happiness was complete. He leaves a devoted wife & an only child, a little boy.

Boston, Jan 11. Death of an Old Merchant. Hon Thos H Perkins, one of our oldest & most respected citizens, died today.

Valuable land at private sale: that tract of land called **Long Green**, adjoining the subscriber's **Westphalia estate**, & also adjoins the lands of Roderick McGregor, Washington J Beall, & Mrs Mary Beall, & contains 357 acres, more or less. There is an excellent Mill Seat upon it, & 2 barns; beautiful situation upon this land for a dwlg house. It was lately owned by Otho B Beall. –Zachariah B Beall

FRI JAN 13, 1854

Hon Wm A Barstow entered upon his duties as Govn'r of Wisconsin on Jan 2.

Letters from Calif bring the painful intelligence of the sudden death [from disease of the heart,] of Lt Jas Blair, formerly of the Navy, & of Wash City. His bereaved wife, [a daughter of Gen Jesup,] is in this city, where she was in critical health, daily expecting cheering letters from her husband, when instead the heart-rending news of his sudden death.

Gen Bankhead has been appointed to the command of the eastern division of the U S army, in place of Gen Wool.

Dr Lutener, an oculist & aurist, was found in his room, in N Y, on Tue, shot through the head, & a pistol lying on the floor. It is not known whether he killed himself or whether he was murdered. Most probably, however, a case of suicide.

Senate: 1-Ptn from Isaac S Bodeman, asking to be allowed the half pay his father was entitled to for services during the Revolutionary war. 2-Ptn from Chas Gordon, asking compensation for services as draughtsman to the Cmte on Public Lands. 3-Ptn from John B Kerr, late charge d'affaires, asking compensation for official services under commissions to other Republics in Central America apart from Nicaragua. 4-Ptn from Francis A Gibbons & F X Kelly, asking compensation for services rendered in the construction of lighthouses on the Pacific coast. 5-Cmte on Naval Affairs: bill for the relief of M K Warrington & C St J Chubb, executors of Capt Lewis Warrington, reported back the same without amendment. Same cmte: bill for the relief of the widows of ofcrs & seamen of the U S schnr **Grampus**, who were lost in that vessel near the coast of the U S. Same cmte: asked to be discharged from the further consideration of the memorials of Harriet Ward & Thos B Parsons, & that they be referred to the Cmte on Pensions: agreed to. Same cmte: bill for the relief of the captors of the frig **Philadelphia**. Same cmte: asked to be discharged from the further consideration of the memorial of Wm Ballard: agreed to. 6-Cmte on Pensions: adverse reports in writing on the ptns of Alex'r Waugh, Wm Bonner, & Catherine M Weaver. Same cmte: bill for the relief of Moses Olmstead. 7-Bill for the relief of Priscilla C Simons: passed.

The steamers **Pearl** & **Natchez** lately came in collision near Baton Rouge, La, by which the **Peal** instantly sunk, & it is supposed that some 8 ot 10 lives were lost. Among the lost are Capt Stanley & Robt Sullivan.

Henry Silverton & 5 colored men were drowned near Newbern, N C, by the upsetting of a boat during the late gale.

A young man, Stephen Hague, lately returned from Calif, was killed in an affray in Allegheny city, Pa, on Monday, by E Hosach.

John B Robertson has been elected District Judge at New Orleans, vice Judge Larue, resigned.

Mrd: on Jan 12, by Rev D X Junkin, Mr E Wood Fogg, of Phil, to Miss Mattie A Wilson, of Wash City.

Died: on Jan 11, Ephraim W Hall, 2nd son of the late Dr Jos Hall, of Anne Arundel Co, Md, & for the last 4 years a resident of Wash City. His funeral is on Fri at 10 o'clock, from the residence of his mother, on 11th st, between G & H sts.

Died: on Jan 12, in Wash City, A Clinton McLean, of N Y C. His funeral is this afternoon at 4 o'clock, from the residence of Col C K Gardner, Capitol Hill.

Died: on Jan 12, after a brief illness, Augustus Lot, aged 3 years, 5 months & 2 days, son of John T & Eliz Costin. His funeral is this afternoon, at 3 o'clock, from the residence of his parents, on the Island.

House of Reps: 1-Ptn of Mr John Wood, a citizen of Chambers Co, Ala, asking indemnity for losses incurred whilst in the service of the Gov't in the Indian war of 1836. 2-Ptn of Chas D Maxwell, asking for a difference between pay of assistant surgeon & that of surgeon in the navy, during the time he performed the duties of surgeon. 3-Memorial of S R Addison, passed assistant surgeon U S Navy, asking the difference between the pay of passed assistant surgeon & surgeon of the navy during the period he performed the duties of the latter grade. 4-Ptn of Elijah L Pomroy for pension money which his father, Jos Pomroy, ought to have received. 5-Memorial of Maj E Harding, praying for an increase of the commutation price of rations to ofcrs of the army. 6-Memorial of Mrs Mary F B Levelly, of Phil, praying arrearages of pension due her late husband may be paid to her. 7-Cmte on Invalid Pensions: bill for the relief of Henry N Halstead; of Benj Hammond, of the State of N Y; of Henry J Snow, of Rome, N Y; & of Chas Staples. Same cmte: adverse reports on the ptns of Bela Sprague, of N Y; of Dudley F Holt; of Anthony Walton Bayard; of Saml C Dickinson, & of Lt Edw Springer. Same cmte: bills committed: relief of Lemuel Hudson; of Harriet Leavenworth, widow of the late Bvt Brig Gen Leavenworth; of Geo S Claflin; & of Jas F Green. Same cmte: adverse reports on the ptns of Mgt C Hanson; of Joshua Lewis; of John Gallagher; of Fielding G Brown; of the daughters of Gen Solomon Van Rensselaer, deceased; of Josiah Martin; of Elijah Armstrong; of the legal reps of Saml J Smith, deceased; & of R R Platt. Same cmte: bills committed: relief of Thos Frazer; of Cornelius H Latham; & of Saml W Brady. Same cmte: adverse reports on the ptns of Cotton Murry; of the widow of Wm Flora; of Jacob Sailor; of Jas Shorey, of Levi M Roberts; of Holly Guile; of Capt Chase, & of Reugen Cahoon. Also, the ptns of Henry Miller; of the heirs of Robt Henry Dyer; of Abraham Pettengill; of Danl Hager, jr; of Parkinson Mitchell; of Robt Stevenson; of Aaron Tucker, of Maine; of Geo Babcock, of Mich; of Thos B Harvey; & of John Baird.

Died: on Nov 30, at **Fort Snelling**, Minn. Eliza, wife of Col Francis Lee, U S Army. The death of this devoted wife & mother on the anniversary of the day that saw her a happy bride has cast an impenetrable gloom over the house which for 28 years she has brightened with her presence, & filled with unutterable sorrow the hearts of her widowed husband & orphan children.

SAT JAN 14, 1854
The fate of the steamer **San Francisco** is at length known, & terrible beyond expression it is. The ship foundered, & 240 of the 700 human beings have perished. They did not go down with the ship, but were swept overboard from her decks some days before she foundered. Lost overboard are Col John M Washington, Maj Geo Taylor & his wife, Capt H B Field, & Lt R H Smith. The ship **Three Bells** arrived in N Y with 160 persons saved from the steamer **San Francisco**, which foundered at sea on Jan 5. Others were taken off by the barque **Kilby**, [about 100,] bound for Boston, & many by the ship **Antarctic**, bound for Liverpool. Maj Wyse & Lt W A Winder are amongst the passengers who have arrived in N Y. Col Gates, Col Burke, Maj Merchant, Capt Judd & wife, Lt Fremont & family, Lt Loeser, Lt Vanvort, & the ladies & children are on board the barque **Kilby**. Capt Watkins, Lt Chandler, & Lt C S Winder are on the ship **Antarctic**.

House of Reps: 1-Cmte of Claims: bill for the relief of Jos Girard: committed. Same cmte: adverse on the ptn of Capt Francis Allyn & the owners of the ship **Cadmus**. 2-Cmte on the Judiciary: bill for the relief of Robt G Ward: committed.

From Texas: Corpus Christi, Dec 23. Gen P F Smith, Maj Chapman, & Capt Gibbs arrived safe at headquarters on Dec 20th from a tour of inspection along the Rio Grande & by the way of San Antonio. They are all in good health & spirits. Maj Chapman leaves today for Indianola to receive from Maj Babbit the documents belonging to the chief quartermaster's depot for his dept, & then returns to this place. Maj Hill, paymaster, leaves also, on leave, to bring his family to this place. Corpus Christi has been spared from the epidemic & is looking up; it is decidedly the most healthy spot in the South.

St Louis, Jan 12. Dr Irley, a member of the Mississippi Legislature, has been killed in a duel with Dr Fant, a member of the same body. [Jan 16th newspaper: fatal duel on Dec 31 near Columbus, Miss, between Dr Irby & Dr Fant, the former a member of the Legislature of that State. Dr Irby was killed at the first fire.]

Stray Buffalo Cow came to my premises in Oct, perfectly dry. Owner is to prove his property, pay charges, & take her away. –C H Wiltberger, near Rock Creek Church, Wash Co.

Mrd: on Jan 5, by Rev Jas H Brown, Mr Jos H Wright to Miss Henrietta Rittenhouse, both of PG Co, Md.

Mrd: on Jan 12, by Rev Mr Marks, Mr Wm W Bradley to Miss Sarah F Simmons.

Mrd: on Jan 12, by Rev Mr Marks, Mr John Pullin to Miss Susanna G Carden.

Mrd: on Dec 27, 1853, by Rev Mr Marks, Mr Jas L Boswell to Miss Mary Ann King.

For sale: an improved & cheap farm in Stafford Co, Va, 2 miles from Falmouth: contains 288½ acres, highly improved: a comfortable dwlg, frame kitchen, carriage-house, ice-house, smoke-house, stables & over-seer's house. Possession immediately. Apply to C H Wiltberger, Wash City; Wm M Mitchell, Fredericksburg, Va; or Jno B Wiltberger, on the premises.

MON JAN 16, 1854
Log of the steamer **San Francisco**: Dec 24: tremendous sea; Dec 25: heavy gale; Dec 26: gales: Dec 27: strong gale; employed in clearing the wreck, pumping, bailing, & lightning ship; Dec 29: continued strong gale; Dec 29: weather moderate & pleasant, sea going down quite fast. Before night we succeeded in getting on board the barque **Kilby** upward of 100 persons, men, women, & children, including Col Gates & family, Maj Merchant & family, Capt Judd & lady, Lt Fremont & family, Lot Loeser & family, Capt Gardner, Lt Murray, of the U S N, Mr Aspinwall, Mr J L Graham, Mr J Farnesworth, & Mr Southwark. Dec 30: cloudy weather & strong gales: continued to throw coal overboard & to free the ship from water. A large number of the troops & hands had become sick of diarrhoea, & many dying daily. Dec 31: moderat gales. Was spoken by the ship **Three Bells**, Capt Robt Creighton, of Glasgow, who told us to be of good cheer, for he would lay by us. Wm Wilson, colored waiter, died. Jan 1: heavy gales. Jan 2: gale continues. Jan 3: moderate gales. **Three Bells** came alongside, & Mr Gretton, 2nd ofcr, was sent on board by Maj Wyse, senior U S ofcr on board, to charter her for the Gov't. The ship **Antarctic** spoke with us. Jan 4: some 70 or 80 passengers were put on the **Three Bells**. Jan 5: weather moderate. We embarked the crew & by sunset we had every soul out of the ship but Capt Watkins, Mr Mellus, the chief ofcr, & Mr Marshall, the chief engineer. These then embarked-Capt Watkins being the last to quit the wreck. Mr Mellus states that the sickness & deaths were confined entirely to the troops, firemen, & waiters. Drowned: Col J M Washington, Maj Geo Taylor, Mrs Taylor, Capt H B Field, Lt R H Smith; 2 ladies, names unknown; ___ Brooks, a waiter, F Duckett, brother to carpenter; the barber, about 150 soldiers, & a sailor named Alexander. Died: ___ Johnson, waiter; Louis Testader; Wm Wilson, Walter Watkins; Arthur Henry, of the engineer corps; Levi Heath, steerage steward; Walter Heath, waiter; & Chas Sandford, steward. The following is a list of the saved, as far as known: On board the ship **Three Bells**, arrived at N Y: Surgeon R S Satterlee; Assist Surgeon H R Wirtz; Lt Col M Burke; Maj Francis O Wyse; Lt J Van Vorst; Edw Mellus, 1st ofcr; J W Marshall, chief engineer; A Auchinlick, 1st engineer; David Dunham, 2nd engineer; Jas Crosby, 2nd engineer; B Donaghan, 3rd engineer; C Hoffman, 3rd engineer; W Buel, M D, Surgeon; W H Wickham, storekeeper; Lt W A

Winter, & the following number of soldiers: of Co G-14; Co A-18; Co D-25; Co L-19; Co B-14; Co J-12; Co H-12; Co K-13; regimental band-8; besides sailors, waiters, & firemen, making the number 230 in all. On board the barque **Kilby**, for Boston: Col Wm Gates, commanding regt, & family, including wife & 3 children; 1st Lt Loeser & wife, Miss Eaton, Capt J W T Gardner, Lt F K Murray, Maj Chas S Merchant, wife & 2 children, Miss Valecia Merchant, Mrs Wyse & child, Capt H B Judd & wife, Lt S L Fremont, wife & 3 children, Mr G W Aspinwall, Mr J L Graham, jr, Mrs Taylor, Mr Southwark, Mr J Farnsworth, 1st engineer, besides 50 soldiers of Co I, & a number of camp women, in all about 120. On board the ship **Antarctic**, for Liverpool: Capt Watkins, Mr Schell, purser; Mr Barton, 3rd ofcr; Mr Mason, 4th ofcr; Washington Duchet, carpenter; Lt Chandler, U S Army; Lt Chas Winder, U S Army; Mr Rankin, U S Army, & 175 non-commissioned ofcrs, musicians, & privates, in all about 183. The sickness & death on board were entirely confined to the troops, firemen, & waiters. Having no means of cooking, these people ate imprudently of preserved meats & fruits, which produced diarrhoea. There was no sickness among the cabin passengers or ofcrs of the ship & crew. The ship **Three Bells** is an iron vessel, owned by 3 brothers named Bell, citizens of Glasgow. The rescued soldiers & crew are loud in praise of her commander.

John Gaskins, a poor old colored man from Gtwn, was found dead on Sat near Mr Douglass' Greenhouse, on 15th & G sts. Verdict of death by intemperance & exposure. He was between 50 & 60 years of age.

Wash Corp; 1-Ptn of Mrs Mary Ann Lewis, for her relief: read twice. 2-Ptn of Catharine Eaton, for the remission of a fine. 3-Ptn of G H Plant & John M Graham, asking permission to use the clay in certain streets in the First Ward: referred to the Cmte on Improvements. 4-Bill to allow Casey Proctor to give 2 suppers for the benefit of Bethel Church: passed. 5-Cmte of Claims: bill for the relief of Mgt McCarty: passed. 6-Ptn of Ellen Mullin for the remission of a fine: referred to the Cmte of Claims. 7-Cmte of Claims: asked to be discharged from the further consideration of the bill for the relief of Chas Vermillion. 8-Bill for the relief of F W Sallhausen: referred to the Cmte on Improvements. 9-Mr Queen moved for leave to withdraw the ptn of P W Dorsey: which motion was agreed to.

N Y, Jan 15. List of those brought up by the steam-tug **Titan**: Lt Murray, U S Navy; Mr Colgate, wife & family; Maj Merchant, disabled, & family; Capt Judd & wife; Lt Col Burke, severely wounded; Dr Satterlee, disabled; Dr Wirtz; Lt Loeser & wife, & Miss Eaton; Lt Fremont & family; Lt Van Vorst, disabled; Capt Gardner; G W Aspinwall; J L Merchant, jr; Rev Mr Cooper, wife & family; Mrs Maj Wyse & child; Mr Southworth, & about 100 soldiers. Additional names of those swept from the decks of the steamer **San Francisco** by the waves: Mr Tenney, Mr D C Stockwell, Miss Belton, Mr Gates, Mrs Chase & child, Mr Lacrade & wife, Miss Lucy Moore, & Mr Farnsworth, an engineer.

Obit-died: on Nov 16 last, at his residence on Wye river, Queen Anne's Co, Md, Wm Carmichael, in his 79th year. He was born on Sep 25, 1775, at Chestertown, Kent Co, & educated at Washington College, near that place. His family were Whigs of the Revolution. His father was a volunteer under Gen Smallwood, & fought at Brandywine & Germantown, remaining in the service more than 2 years, & holding the rank of captain. His uncle was employed in the diplomatic service of his country, being Sec of Legation to Mr Jay while the latter was the Minister of the U S near the Court of Madrid, to which he was afterwards commissioned as Charge d'Affaires by Gen Washington. The subject of this notice was himself a man of marked character & lofty virtues. He studied law at Annapolis, then the seat of the Genr'l Court, the great resort of the Md Bar, & the best school for lawyers in the U S. Among his fellow students were the late Judges Stephen & Magruder, of the Court of Appeals, & the present Chief Justice of the U S, who was, however, several years his junior. They were not students in the same ofc, but were room mates. From 1816 to 1821 he held a seat in the Senate of Md, a small but distinguished body, composed of the first men in the State, & numbering among its members Gen Wm H Winder, Gen Robt Goodloe Harper, his early friend Mr Taney, & others of high talent & influence. He withdrew from practice 15 years before his death & devoted his attention to the cultivation & improvement of a large landed estate on the Wye river.

Lt John A Davis, U S Navy, died on Sat. Although the accident was of so severe a nature as to first to proclude almost any hope of his recovery, he rallied under the kind & skilful treatment at the Infirmary. It proved to be a vain delusion. On Sat he took a change for the worse & died in the afternoon.

Mrd: on Jan 12, by Rev S A H Marks, Mr W Wallace Bradley to Miss Sarah F Simmons, all of Wash City.

Died: Jan 15, Eliz Jane, wife of Jas Miller, & eldest daughter of Alex'r & Mary Borland. Her funeral is today at 3 p m, from the residence of her father, L st, between 15 & 16 sts.

Valuable real estate in market: a bargain. Tract of land in PG Co, Md, 439 acres, 16 miles from Washington. Improvements consist of a large dwlg, containing 10 or 12 rooms, kitchen, smoke-house, stable, [capable of holding 15 or 20 horses,] corn-house, & large barn. The title is perfect. -John A Parker, Potomac House, Wash.

TUE JAN 17, 1854
Franklin Pierce, Pres of the U S A, recognizes Chas Francois Frederic, Marquis de Montholon, appointed Consul Genr'l of his Imperial Majesty the Emperor of the French, to reside at N Y. C Morton Stewart, appointed Consul of Buenos Ayres, for the port of Balt, in Md. –Jan 11, 1854. Carl Friedrich Adae, Consul of Hesse Darmstadt, for the states of Ohio & Indiana, to reside at Cincinnati. – Jan 13, 1854. –Jan 11, 1854

House of Reps: 1-Cmte on Private Land Claims: to inquire into making a grant of land to Jas W Marshall, the discoverer of gold in Calif, & report by bill or otherwise. 2-Bill for the relief of John Gossett. 3-Ptn from the heirs of Jos Pomroy, asking to be allowed arrears of pension. 4-Ptn from Capt Hiram B Sawyer, of the navy, asking to be restored to the pension roll & allowed arrears of pension. 5-Ptn from R M Walsh, asking compensation for his services as charge d'affaires at Mexico. 6-Ptn from the administrator of J Dickerhoff, a soldier in the war with Mexico, asking a pension on account of a disease contracted by that soldier while in service. 7-Cmte on Pensions: bill for the relief of Pamela Brown, widow of Gen Jacob Brown, with a report. 8-Cmte on Patents: adverse report on the ptn of John Thomas.

Dr R G Smith, of Phil, who has been missing since Dec 28, was on Fri, Jan 18, accidentally discovered dead in an upper room on Exchange Pl, Phil. The room was locked on the inside. A quantity of rags had been burnt in the room, & it is supposed suffocated the deceased.

Mrd: on Jan 15, by Rev S A H Marks, Mr John Stamp to Miss Martha White, both of PG Co, Md.

Mrd: on Jan 12, in Wash City, by Rev W McLain, Robt C Farish to Miss Mary F Yates.

Mrd: on Jan 14, by Rev Jas H Brown, Mr Chas W Alcott to Miss Adelaide J Cochran, both of N Y C.

Died: yesterday, Mr Alex'r Wittenauer, in his 30th year, a native of Balt, but for the last 2 years a resident of Wash City.

Copartnership formed this day under the name of Schwartze & Son, for the purpose of conducting the Apothecary & Drug business, on Pa ave, next door to the U S Hotel, where business will be attended to day & night. –A J Schwartze, John Schwartze

Orphans Court of Wash Co, D C. Letters of administration on the personal estate of John W Strong, late of Wash Co, deceased. –Jennings Pigott, adm

WED JAN 18, 1854
Trustee's sale of part of square 546 at auction: on Feb 9, in front of the premises, by deed of trust from Jas Deggle & wife, dated Jan 28, 1852, recorded in the land records of Wash Co, D C: all of lot 19, & part of lots 18 & 20, in square 546, with improvements. –Walter Lenox, Henry Naylor, trustees -Green & Scott, aucts

Died: on Jan 16, Mandeville, 2nd son of Jas Mandeville Carlisle, aged 4 years & 11 days. His funeral will take place at 12 o'clock M, today.

Senate: 1-Ptn from Danl Kelly, asking compensation for losses & sufferings during his imprisonment in the Island of Cuba in 1810. 2-Ptn from Robt Thompson, asking to be allowed the 7 years' half-pay to which his father was entitled for services during the Revolutionary war. 3-Ptn from Mary F B Levely, asking arrears of pension. 4-Ptn from John Reddin, a discharged soldier from the army on account of his disability, asking to be allowed a pension. 5-Ptn from Roger Simonton & Co & Jno Young, asking the enactment of a law giving further remedies to patentees. 6-Cmte on Military Affairs: bill for the relief of Allen G Johnson & a bill for the relief of Adam D Steuart, with a report in each case. Same cmte: asked to be discharged from the further consideration of the memorial of John M McIntosh, & that it be referred to the Cmte of Claims: which was agreed to. Same cmte: adverse reports on the memorials of A H Cole, of Wm C Easton, & of Jas D Cobb. 6-Cmte on Pensions: adverse reports in writing on the ptns of Benj Burton & of Catharine Clark. Same cmte: bill for the relief of Albert Hart & a bill for the relief of Lavinia Taylor, with a report. Same cmte: adverse reports on the ptns of John Brown & of Orson Young. Same cmte: bill for the relief of the heirs of Judith Worthen. 7-Cmte on Indian Affairs: bill for the relief of John Phagan: passed.

Ofcrs lost or missing from the steamer **San Francisco**. Ofcrs lost Brvt Col John M Washington, Brvt Maj Geo Taylor, Brvt Capt Horace B Field, & Lt Richd H Smith. The only names we can gather of persons not military who were lost are those of Mr Tenney, Mr Gates, Miss Belton, Mr J C Stockwell; F Duckett, steerage waiter; Brooks, colored waiter; Alexander, seaman; Chas Sanford, colored; & the barber, colored. The names of the soldiers known to be lost are:

Wm Bennett	Henry Moses	John Downing
Zebediah P Knapp	Carl Mier	Austin Hoban
Johan Miller	John B Philips	Anthony Fleck
Francis Miles	Jos D Sawyer	Patrick Gordon
Geo Parks	Geo H Wallace	Harting R Heller
Kalron Schenck	Richd Welch	Chas Heinricke
Abraham Workman	Wm H Davis	Fred'k Heine
Clark Walters	Richd Hopley	Michl Kennedy
Patrick Graham	Richd Conally	Jas Kelly
Edw Higway	Edw P Balard	John McLane, 1st
John F Salmon	Wm Cameron	John McLane, 2nd
David Sullivan	M Claxon	Peter Murray
Stephen Spilane	Richd Coghlan	John Mitchell
Jos Trumpet	John W Denny	Thos McManus
John F Fisher	Chas Gerk	Thos McNamara
John Donnelly	Dennis Haley	Seth Rowland
Leonard Karg	Jas Henry	Fred'k Smidt
Chas Campbell	Patrick Malahy	Jos Shurman
John Greenway	Thso Moran	Philip Ward
Henry Hilton	John Rowland	Patrick Sheehan

Richd Carland	Michl Rogon	Conrad Steinman
Wm Graham	Wm S Graeff	Const Schweitzer
Jas Hillock	Frank Griffith	Jonas Smith
Thos Kerner	Alex'r Hart	John Smith
Antoine Gross	Chas Heinrich	Geo Walsh
John Button	Peaody Herkimer	Jas Wallace
Wm Ballard	Jas Knowlton	Chas White
Levi H Bentz	Patick Lynn	John Wendt
David Brindle	Abraham Lawrence	John Diehl
Wilhelm Burkhols	Wm Morris	Jos Sutlenberger
Denis Corbett	Abraham Moore	Michl McAlister
F B Clifford	Jas Mathew	Jas Currie
Thos D Cooper	Henry Meyer	Barney Clancy
Geo Calbe	Wm Meyers	Louis Durque
Wm A Dillingham	Carl Meyn	Deschell
John Deacon	Martn Mixel	Mrs C Higney
Wesley S Day	Wm McLaughlin	Corp Smith
Chas Engel	Michl Morgan	John Smith
Henrich Engelbuch	Chas Mayer	Monke
Wm Fauerbach	Hugh McLaughlin	Riley
John Friel	John Scheerer	

The rolls of the regt show that, besides the above, known to be dead, many have not yet been accounted for. Most of these have no doubt perished. Their names [including 15 or 20 who at the moment before the steamer sailed were detached on account of illness] are as follows:

Jas Ludlam	Andrew J Hannah	Wm J Nottingham
Chas Barnes	Robt B Morse	Jas Oliver
John Dulong	Lorenzo H Phelps	Thos Payton
Jas Ennis	David Saxton	Anthony Van Sanford
Abraham Kuept	Wm Steimart	Carl Schmidts
Chas Milvers	Michl Malahy	Dennis Whalen
Michl O'Connor	Jas Conway	Luke White
Wm Power	Robt Balster	Horatio Winship
Wm L Ferne	Elias Clark	Edmund Gardner
Richd Allen	Jas Collins	Andrew Bechtel
Saml Blaurak	Conly Conegham	Martin Dutton
Eugene W Fields	John Dykeman	Jas Fox
Wm Healy	Adolph Ehrhard	Jos Kale
Andrew Shamly	Adolphus Haage	John Mines
John Curry	Peter Hughes	Thos Miller
Robt Great	Michl Ketcher	Wm F Matchler
Jacob Joelinski	Geo Kelson	John Quirk
John Miller	Simon McGill	Jacob Step
John McCleary	John McNeil	Chas H Smith

Saml S Thompson	John Lander	John Lee
Jos McIntyre	Peter McGuire	Laurence MacAnliffe
Timothy Sheehan	Christopher Poman	Francis Burke
Chas Boyle	Andrew J Powell	John Carey
Francis A Baker	Michl Reedy	Jacob Falleegger
Jas Cord	Ferd Rettlebusch	Jas Gilgon
John Dooling	Rufus P Rogers	Henry Schultz
Wm Farrell	Rudolph Smith	Wm Wallace
John Franks	John Sawyer	Alex'r Berkler
Richd Gilmore	John Tully	John J Stone
Michl Healey	John H Sludt	Geo Smith
Chas H Jones	John Haag	

Died: on Jan 16, Peter Little, jr, in his 51st year, of disease of the lungs. His funeral will be on Thu at 2 o'clock, from his late residence on Va ave, between 4½ & 6th sts, Navy Yard.

Wash City Ordinance: 1-Act for the relief of Jas W Sheahan: to be paid $1,000 for his services in preparing & revising the recently published compilation of the laws of this Corp. 2-Act for the relief of G Ruppell: to be paid $60, the amount Ruppel deposited to take out a tavern license, but which was not granted. 3-Act for the relief of Saml W Handy: to credit him the amount of principal & interest which which he was assessed as his share of the expense of constructing a sewer down 14th st west, for the drainage of his cellar, & which, instead of draining said cellar, increased the quantity of water in it. 4-Act for the relief of Wm Gallant: to pay him the sum of $10 for digging a well & the erection of a pump on the front of square 478, on F st.

House of Reps: 1-Ptn of Lee H Thomas, a citizen of Chambers Co, Ala, asking a pension for services rendered the U S as a soldier in the last war with Great Britain & the Indian war of 1836.

THU JAN 19, 1854
Senate: 1-Ptn from John Baptiste Beaubien, of Illinois, asking compensation for the loss of certain lands in the city of Chicago, in said State. 2-Ptn from E J McLane, asking compensation for his services in seizing & detaining horses & mules smuggled late the U S from Mexico. 3-Ptn from Wm C Jones, asking compensation for services as an ofcr in the Florida war, as lt of mounted men on extra duty for a period of 5 months. 4-Ptn from John McCutcheon, asking compensation for the performance of clerical services in the ofc of 2nd Comptroller while a messenger in that ofc. 5-Ptn from Clements Bryan, asking indemnity for losses occasioned by the rescinding of a contract for furnishing supplies. 6-Cmte on the Judiciary: bill for the relief of John G Camp. Same cmte: asked to be discharged from the further consideration of the memorial of Benj B Roberts, & that it be referred to the Cmte on Military Affairs. Same cmte: bill for the relief of Lewis H Hemstead. Same

cmte: asked to be discharged from the further consideration of the memorial & papers of Caleb Green. Same cmte: bill for the relief of the legal reps of Thos Chapman, collector of the port of Gtwn, in the State of S C. 7-Cmte on Naval Affairs: bill for the relief of Purser T B McBlair. Same cmte: bill for the compensation of Jas W Low & others for the capture of the private-armed British schnr **Ann** during the last war with Great Britain. 8-Cmte on Military Affairs: bill from the House for the relief of Lewis B Willis, late a paymaster in the army of the U S, reported the same without amendment, & recommended its passage. 9-Cmte of Claims: bill for the relief of Richd Fitzpatrick, with a report. Same cmte: bill for the relief of Don B Juan Domereq, a Spanish subject. 10-Cmte on Commerce: adverse report on the memorial of Francis Barnes. 11-Cmte on the Judiciary: asked to be discharged from the further consideration of the memorial of Amos & Jas E Kendall: which was agreed to. 12-Bill for the relief of Chas A Kellet, had passed the Senate unanimously on a previous occasion, but was lost in the other House for want of time. Bill was read & passed. 13-Bill for the relief of Chas Cooper & Co, & the bill for the relief of Jas Dunning: both passed. 14-Bill for the relief of Rebecca Freeman: passed.

House of Reps: 1-Cmte on the Judiciary: adverse report on the ptn of Thos Thody. Same cmte: bill for the relief of Lt John E Bispham: committed. 2-Cmte on Military Affairs: bill for the relief of Mrs Helen McKay, widow of the late Col Aeneas McKay, deputy quartermaster in the U S army, & a bill for the relief of D C Cash & Giles U Ellis: each committed. Same cmte: adverse report on the ptn of Capt H B Field; & on the ptn of Jas Sweet. 3-Cmte on Naval Affairs: adverse report on the ptn of Jos Ayres. Same cmte: bill for the relief of John O Mears: committed. 4-Cmte on Invalid Pensions: bill for the relief of Pamela Brown, widow of Maj Gen Jacob Brown, late of the U S Army, deceased: committed. Same cmte: adverse reports on the ptns of Jas Payster, & of citizens of Albany, N Y, relative to the pension act of Apr 14, 1816. Same cmte: bills committed: relief of Lyman N Cook; of Benj Rowe; of Emilie Hooe; & of Wm B Edwards. Same cmte: adverse report on the ptn of Jas Robinson. Same cmte: adverse reports on the ptn of Elias Carpenter. Same cmte: adverse reports on the ptns of Uriah Hanscom; & on the ptn of John Thompson. Same cmte: adverse reports on the ptns of Jonathan Stuart, & of John Cook & others, of Mass. Same cmte: adverse reports on the ptn of Edw Tracy & others, of Wm Tool, of Jas M Halden, of Thos Russell, & of Catherine Jacobs, of Albany, N Y. 5-Cmte of Claims: bill for the relief of John Hamilton & a bill for the relief of Danl Steenrod: committed. Same cmte: adverse reports on the ptns of Thos Copeland, of Eunice Gilbert, of Wm B Cozzens, & of Jas M Duckett.

The venerable Wm Jay departed this life Dec 27, at Bath, in his 85th year. It is on record that he preached in Surry Chapel when only 16. His regular ministry was confined to Bath.

The Jesuit missionaries have finally been expelled from the Grand Duchy of Baden. The Chambers were convened for the 9th of Jan.

Sydney, C B, Dec 30: Archibald Otto Dodge, barrister at law, 27 years of age, was shot dead in the store of Mr Burchill by Nicholas Henry Martin, J P, & late Postmaster at Sydney. Mr Martin immediately surrendered himself up to justice. The reason assigned for the act was an alleged injury done by the deceased to a member of the family of the accused.

The number of soldiers engaged in the War of the Revolution was 231,791. Of this there are less than 1,400 now living, whose ages must average nearly 90 years. 73 have died during the past year. –Albany Transcript

Mrd: on Jan 16, in N Y C, by Rev C C Pyne, D D, Walter Lenox, of Wash City, to Rachel S Ludlow, daughter of Ezra Ludlow, of the former place.

Mrd: on Jan 17, by Rev E Knight, of Wash, at the residence of Mr Edw Fenwick, Richd T Hill, of PG Co, Md, to Miss Eliza A Fenwick, of D C.

Mrd: on Jan 17, by Rev Mr Caldwell, Rector of Christ Church, Gtwn, D C, Zachariah Berry, of Belmont, PG Co, Md, to Eliz Clagett, daughter of Henry Addison, Mayor of Gtwn.

Mrd: on Jan 17, at Gtwn, by Rev Mr Tillinghast, Wm Henry Denny, of Pittsburgh, to Miss Maria Poe, daughter of Geo Poe, jr, of the former place.

Death of Joshua Bates, D D. This distinguished divine died on Jan 14, at his residence in Dudley, after a short & painful illness, at age 77 years. In 1803 he was ordained pastor of the First Congregatioonal Church in Dedham. In 1818 he became Pres of Middlebuy College, which ofc he held for 21 years.

Circuit Court of Wash Co, D C. Edw McGuire vs Richd G Briscoe. The trustee reports that he had sold the particular premises of this cause to C B Cluskey, for $1,953, on Sep 1, 1851; that said Cluskey failed to comply with the terms of sale. Resale was made on Aug 12, 1852, F B Culver being the purchaser, for the sum of $1,975; that said Culver afterwards assigned his said purchase to Benj F Middleton & Benj Beall & they have paid & satisfied unto the trustee the said purchase money with interest. –Jno A Smith, clerk

FRI JAN 20, 1854
The Telegraph announces the sudden death, yesterday, of Capt Alden Partridge, principal of the Military Academy at Norwich, Conn. [Jan 23rd newspaper: for nearly 50 years Capt Partridge had been engaged as an instructor in all the branches of military knowledge, involving the highest mathematical skill. –Phil Ledger]

Senate: 1-Ptn from Jane E Wright, asking an increase of pension. 2-Ptn from Saml C Reid, cmder of the private armed American brig **Gen Armstrong**, in behalf of the claimants of said brig. 3-Ptn from Patrick Shannon, asking to have the amount refunded which was illegally exacted in relation to his ferry. 4-Cmte of Claims: bill for the relief of Zachariah Lawrence, of Ohio: passed. 5-Cmte on Patents: bill for the relief of Geo G Bishop & the legal reps of John Arnold, deceased. 6-Cmte on Private Lands: asked to be discharged from the further consideration of the memorial of John A Ragan: which was agreed to.

Judge Robt M Charlton, lately for a brief period a Senator in Congress from Ga, died at Savannah on Wed.

Obit-died: Maj & Brev Lt Col John *Marshall Washington, of the U S Army, who was swept from the deck of the steamer **San Francisco**, had made himself one of the most distinguished artillery ofcrs belonging to the service. He was a native of Va, & must have attained the age of 58 or 60. He graduated as a cadet at West Point in the class of 1813, was commissioned 3rd lt in the artl in 1817, & rose by rank to his majority in the 3rd artl in 1847, Feb 16. In a week from this promotion he won his brevet as lt col by gallant & meritorious conduct on the field of Buena Vista. In 1824 he was made instructor in the artl school at *Fort Monroe*. [Jan 21st newspaper: correction-his Christian name is John Macrae, not John Marshall; he was born in 1799, & was in the 55th year of his age at the time of his death.
+
Maj Geo Taylor was a cadet of the class of 1833. He won his first brevet, that of captain, in the Fla war, in 1840, & was commissioned captain in Feb, 1847. In 1842 he served as assist professor of mathematics at West Point. In Oct, 1847, he won his brevet of major by gallant & meritorious conduct in the battle of Huamantla, in Mexico; & in Jul 1848, distinguished himself in action at Atlixco. He was a native of Ga.
+
Capt Horace B Field was of N Y; an 1836 graduate of West Point. He was made brevet captain for gallant conduct in the battle of Huamantla, Mexico, in Oct, 1847. He first entered the 3rd artl in Jul, 1840, as a 2nd lt.
+
Lt Richd H Smith was of Tenn, appointed to one of the additional infty regts authorized in 1847 [the 14th] as a 2nd lt, & was transferred to the 3rd artl in Jun, 1848.

Mrd: on Jan 19, by Rev C M Butler, Nathan Reeve, of Newburgh, N Y, to Mary, daughter of Hon Selah R Hobbie, of Wash City.

Died: on Jan 18, Mrs Anna Cunningham, in her 89th year, at the residence of her son, A F Cunningham, Mass ave.

SAT JAN 21, 1854
Household & kitchen furniture at auction on Jan 30, at the residence of Mr Geo W McLane, on E st, between 6th & 7th sts. -J C McGuire, auct

Household & kitchen furniture at auction on Jan 26, at the residence of Dr G W Humphreys, on Pa ave, near 14th st, all his furniture & household effects. -J C McGuire, auct

Mrd: on Jan 19, by Rev S A H Marks, Mr Geo W Durity to Miss Jane Eliz Wise, all of Wash.

Mrd: on Jan 19, by Rev Jas H Brown, Mr Jos T Bell to Miss Harriet F Beckett. Also, by the same, Mr Jas Brown to Mary A Wright; all of PG Co, Md.

Died: on Jan 20, in Wash City, of a pulmonary affection from which he had been a patient sufferer for many years, Mr Jas S Turpin, in his 39th year. He was a devoted husband, an affectionate father, & a friend in whom there was no guile. His funeral is tomorrow at 2½ o'clock, from his residence on D, near 13th st.

Ladies stock of dry goods at auction: on Feb 6, at the store of Mr Wm E Myers, on Bridge st, we will sell his entire stock. –Barnard & Buckey

House of Reps: 1-Senate bills taken up & referred-relief of: Jos Gideon; of M K Warrington & C St John Chub, excs of Capt Lewis Warrington & others; Moses Olmstead; Ezra Williams; John Fagan; heirs of Judith Worthen; of Rebecca Freeman; Chas A Kellett; Jas Dunning; & Chas Cooper & Co.

We are deeply pained to state that M de Bodisco, the highly esteemed Minister of Russia, is laboring under an illness so severe as to have left during the last 2 or 3 days scarcely a hope of his surviving it. [Jan 23rd newspaper: Mr Bodisco was still at 7 o'clock last evening, but we were sorry to learn that there were no hopes of his surviving many hours.]

The Louisville Democrat of Jan 13th has a letter from Leavenworth, Indiana, of an occurrence there. On Jan 9 a man named Ornfield left his house, informing his wife that he would be back in 2 or 3 days. That night Mrs Ornfield heard some one trying to get into the house, took a rifle, & fired through the door, one inch in thickness, & shot her husband through the heart. She brought the body into the house & informed the neighbors of the occurrence. Many think that a cold blooded murder has been committed, & the story was to cover her guilt. She has been committed to jail to answer for the murder of her husband.

I certify that G L Baldwin, of Wash Co, D C, brought before me a trespassing stray Cow. –J W Beck, [Seal] Owner will come forward to prove property, pay charges, & take her away. –G L Baldwin

The Ancient Burying Ground of Marshfield. The **Pilgrim Burial Place** in Marshfield now contains the Tomb of Webster. Here repose the ashes of Peregrine White, the first child of the Plymouth Colony; & the remains of the Mother of Peregrine White, who married for her second husband Edw Winslow, afterwards Govn'r, the proprietor & settler of Winslow. She was not only the first mother, but also the first bride in the Colony. Her son, Gov Josiah Winslow, was the first native-born Govn'r in the country. His remains lie in the family tomb, from which the entire ground derives its name of the **"Old Winslow Burying Ground."** Directly adjoining is the site of the thatched meeting-house, in which these pilgrim fathers & mothers were accustomed to worship God. Next summer a Fair will be held in the Winslow House, still standing on the Webster estate, for the purpose of putting an iron fence around the burying ground, & other improvements. Donations may be forwarded to Mrs Fletcher Webster, Marshfield, during the winter 2 West Cedar st; Mrs Saml K Williams, 68 Boylston st, & John T Dingley, 451 Washington st, Boston, & to either of the cmte, or Mrs Waterman Thomas, Treasurer for the Fair, Marshfield. In behalf of the Ladies of Marshfield:

Alathea Cushman	Abigail P P Hatch
Nancy Waterman	Rebecca Carver
Mary S Hatch	Sibyl White
Charlotte E Leonard	Olive S Bourne
Frances S Clark	Marcia A Thomas,
Louisa Phillips	Cmte-Marshfield,
Wealthy Ford	Oct 20, 1853

Tragedy at Lexington, Va. Thos Blackburn, a son of Dr R S Blackburn, of Charlestown, Va, & a cadet at the Military Institution at Lexington, Va, was killed on Sunday last by a young man named Christian, a member of Judge Brockenbrough's Law School. Christian has been arrested.

On Jan 13 a young man, Henry N Sargent, deliberately killed a young lady, Miss Servilla Jones, aged 17 years, & then shot himself, at New Boston, N H. He said last summer that if she would not marry him he would murder her. Her brother was nearby when he killed her.

Epidemic of a fever recently, by attending a Ball, in Glamorganshire, South Wales. The epidemic broke out a few days afterwards. Still suffering are members of the families of Sir G Tyler, M P; Mr Brocker, M P; & Dr Carne. Rev Geo Traherne, a clergyman in the neighborhood, & Miss Richards, of Reath, a young lady, have fallen victims to the terrible malady. Lt Scroode, a young ofcr of the 1st Royal Regt, a scion of the ancient house of Scroope, of Danby, died on Sunday. –English paper

MON JAN 23, 1854
Subject of inquiry in Congress, to remedy the matter of granting a pension to Mrs Brown. Gen Jas Brown died in 1828, & eminent surgeons testify that his death was hastened by, if not the positive result of, the wounds received by him at Bridgewater, near Niagara Falls, on Jun 25, 1814. One of his wounds was in the shoulder, the other in the thigh, & the former was kept open until a short period before his death. The battle of Chippewa was fought on Jul 5, 1814, & that of Bridgewater on the 25th, both under the command of Gen Brown. He began life with the peaceful tenents of a Quaker; in 1799 he went on to the frontier of N Y & purchased a lot of land, took his axe, & commenced a settlement; & was made agent for M Le Roy de Chaumont, a distinguished Frenchman, who owned a large tract of that county. From the command of a company he soon found himself at the head of a regt, & at the commencement of the war of 1812, was raised to a Maj-gen. He moved on from one degree of fame to another, & at the return of peace he made his headquarters at Wash, & remained there until his death in 1828.

Warren Wood was hung at Catskill, N Y, on Friday last. He made a long address, in which he charged some of the witnesses with perjury. He confessed that he shot Williams, but protested that he did not know what he was doing.

A correspondent of the Norfolk Co [Mass] Journal states that Mr Josiah Hall, of Walpole, was 100 years old on Dec 26. The event was celebrated at the meeting house. After dinner he related a brief history of his several campaigns in the army of the Revolution. Mr Hall is in good health & spirits, & bids fair to live for several years to come.

Official, Dept of State, Wash, Jan 21, 1854. The Danish legation in the U S has communicated to this Dept certificates of death of American citizens who have died in the Danish West Indians since Jan, 1853.
At St Croix: Jan 29, 1853: Horatio Gates Lewis.
At St Thomas, in 1853:
Apr 11: John J Hayes, of Bangor, Maine
Apr 24: John Sylvester, of Boston, Mass
Apr 25: Sousoa Weston, of Gardiner, Maine, sailor
Apr 26: John Milliken, of Maine, sailor
May 16: Edw Dalley, of Walton, sailor
May 16: Isaac Lamberson, of Frankfort, Penn
May 16: Capt Dexter, of American whaler **George**, Westport
Jun 4: Wm Cunningham, of Maine, sailor
Jun 9: Wm Warren, of Bangor, Maine
Jun 13; Robt Craig, of Augusta, Maine, sailor
Jun 19: Brainard Lowring, of Portland, Maine, sailor

In Equity. Jas Adams against Richd Patton. The cmplnt, as exec & devisee of the late Thos Law, contracted with the dfndnt for the sale of lots B & H, subdivisions of lots 1 & 34 in square 695, in Wash City; that the sum of $359.98 remains due of the purchase money, with interest from Nov 17, 1851; that the lots have not been conveyed to the dfndnt, & that he hath neglected & refused to pay the said balance. The object of the bill is a specific performance of said contract & payment of said purchase money & interest or a sale of the said lots. The dfndnt does not reside in this District, but in the state of Md. He is warned to appear at this Court on the first Monday of June next. –Jas S Morsell, Asst Judge -Redin, for cmplnt.

Appointments by the Pres. by & with the advice & consent of the Senate.
Collectors of Customs:
Henry F Hancock, for Washington, N C
Geo Bradford, for Providence, R I
Geo H Reynolds, for Bristol & Warren, R I
John Lynch, for Richmond, Va
Geo Turner, for Newport, R I
Henry Hobart, for New London, Conn
Jas Lytle, for Presque Isle, [Erie] Penn
Eben W Allen, for Nantucket, Mass
Wm Bartoll, for Marblehead, Mass
Wm S Pomeroy, for Fairfield, Conn
Saml T Sawyer, for Norfolk & Portsmouth, Va
Hugh Archer, for St Mark's, Fla
Ezra Chesebro, for Stonington, Conn
John S Parker, for Cherrystone, Va
John A Sherrad, for Burlington, N J
Julius A Barratts, for St Mary's, Ga
Robt N McMillan, for Teche, [Franklin,] Louisiana
Ephraim K Smart, for Belfast, Maine

Among the passengers on board the ill-fated steamer **San Francisco**, was Lt F K Murray, of the U S Navy, of whose conduct throughout the trials of the wreck every narrative of that said event speaks in the highest praises. He encouraged us with hope & bade us not despair. I cannot help repeating the name of Lt Murray, of the navy, who deserves the highest credit for his activity, courage, & intrepidity. Col Gates in his report speaks of the meritorious conduct of Maj Wyse, Capts Judd & Fremont, & Lts Chandler, Loeser, Chas Winder, Wm Winder, & Van Vorst. To Lt Murray, of the navy, for his judicious advice & noble conduct, too much praise cannot be bestowed. The following was signed by ofcrs who came in the barque **Kilby**: Col Gates, Dr Satterlee, Maj Merchant, Capts Judd, Gardiner, & Fremont, Lts Loeser, Van Vorst, & Dr White: to Lt Murray: may you reach your family in safety, & ever enjoy the highest reward a conscientious discharge of duty can give to a good & faithful servant.

New Orleans, Jan 17. Forbes Allison, merchant, & Pres of St Andrew's Society, has absconded. He is a defaulter to the amount of $40,000.

New Orleans, Jan 20. Judah Touro died on Wed night. His fortune is estimated at a million to a million & a half of dollars. It is reported that the bulk of it is bequeathed to the public institutions of New Orleans.

Obit-died: on Jan 10, at his country residence in Brookline, near Boston, Col T H Perkins, aged 89 years. Thos Handysyde Perkins was born in Boston, Dec 15, 1764, & when he died he is supposed to have left a property of some two millions, to be divided among his numerous heirs. He began commercial life in partnership with his elder brother, James, constituting the first American firm engaged in the China trade. During the war of 1812 he was distinguished, in connexion with Otis & Sullivan, as a strenuous opponent of Mr Madison's Administration, & was elevated by the Federalists to several important posts in the State & Nat'l Gov't. –N Y Evening Post

TUE JAN 24, 1854
Senate: 1-Ptn from Eliz C Smith, asking to be allowed bounty land & 3 months' extra pay for her services in the Mexican war. [She states that her maiden name was Eliz C Newton, & that she enlisted in <u>male attire</u> under the name of Bill Newcome, in Co D, of the Missouri infty volunteers; that she was mustered into service, & faithfully performed all the duties of a soldier for 8 months, when her sex was discovered, & she was sent to **Fort Leavenworth**, where she was informally discharged by Lt Col Wharton, being about 10 months from the day of her enlistment; that she has received no pay from Gov't.] 2-Ptn from Jane M Rudolph, widow of a captain in the revenue service, asking a pension. 3-Ptn from Augustin Demera, surviving descendant of Francis Chandonet, asking to be allowed the commutation pay to which said Chandonet was entitled under a resolution of Congress. 4-Cmte on Private Land Claims: bill for the relief of Richd King. 5-Cmte on Pensions: bill granting 5 years' half-pay to the widow of Capt Gunnison. 6-Cmte on Naval Affairs: bill for the relief of David Myerle, accompanied by a report.

The Senate confirmed the following nominations in the Dept of the Navy:
1-John Lenthall, Chief of the Bureau of Construction, Equipment, & Repairs.
2-Danl B Martin, Engineer in Chief of the Navy.
3-Surgeon Wm Whelan, Chief of the Bureau of Medicine & Surgery.

The statement of the Comptroller of Md shows the amount of defalcation of Lambert S Norwood, late Clerk of the Court of Common Pleas for Balt city, to the State of Md, from Jun 1, 1853, to Dec 15, 1853, to be $17,862.

Household & kitchen furniture at auction: on Jan 27, at the residence of Mr T Drury, on I, between 21st & 22nd sts. –Green & Scott, aucts

It is with unfeigned sorrow that we have to announce the death of M Alexander de Bodisco, Envoy Extraordinary & Minister Plenipotentiary of the Emperor of Russia to the Gov't of the U S. He expired at his residence in Gtwn, near this city, at 4 o'clock yesterday morning, the 23rd instant, after an illness of 2 months, but which did not assume a serious aspect until within 10 or 12 days of his death. He has filled the post of Russian Envoy in this country for 17 years, while ever faithful to his own Sovereign. He was familiarly known to all our inhabitants. It may be added that the domestic ties which he formed in our country doubtless strengthened his own claims to the general regard. He leaves an afflicted widow & 5 children, besides a multitude of personal friends, to mourn his loss. Mr Bodisco was a noble by birth, & first entered the public service in Russia about 50 years ago. A few years after his arrival here he married Miss Williams, of Gtwn, a young American lady of remarkable beauty. By her he leaves several children. Mr Bodisco has lived almost 20 years among us. The funeral of Mr Bodisco will take place tomorrow. [Jan 26th newspaper: Mr Bodisco resided here, as the Minister of his Gov't, for some 17 years. The Senate adjourns today to meet on Thu next, to attend the funeral of Mr Bodisco.]

Household & kitchen furniture at auction on Jan 30, at the residence of Mrs Brooks, on G st north, near the corner of 5th st west. –Green & Scott, aucts

Intelligence of the massacre of Capt J W Gunnison, Corps of Topographical Engineers, & of 7 of his party, including his assistant, Mr Richd H Kern, by a body of Utah Indians, on the Sevier river. Capt Gunnison was appointed a cadet at West Point from N H, in 1833; graduated with honor in 1837, being the second in grade of scholarship in his class, & was assigned as a 2nd Lt to the 2nd Regt of Artl; transferred to the Topographical Engineers in 1838, when it was organized. Mr Kern was one of 3 brothers who accompanied Col Fremont as his assistant across the plains in the winter of 1848 & 1849, & were with him at the time of his great disaster in the Rocky Mountains, when more than 100 mules perished in one night on account of the deep snows, & 13 of his men died from cold & starvation. It is said that the eldest of 3 brothers, the physician & botanist, should also shortly after the disaster just referred to have been massacred by this same tribe of Indians. They met a body of Utahs, who informed than that the day before they had an engagement with the dragoons under Lt Whittlsey, had lost some of their men, & that their custom was to take life for life; a portion of their party must died. Dr Kern & Old Bill Williams, trapper, were killed on the spot. Edw Kern, the 3rd in age, was with Fremont; he is now engaged as artist in the Japan expedition. Both he & Richd were good portrait painters & most excellent topographers. The Kerns were natives of Phil, & neither of them married at the time of their decease. They have left a large circle of relatives & friends to mourn their untimely loss. –S -St Paul, Dec 20, 1853 [Aug 3rd newspaper: account from Kanoshe, Chief of the Pauvan Indians. An emigrant party of Americans, under command of Mr Thos Hildreth & 3 brothers, encamped near Fillmore. Some Indians came into camp, as is their usual practice, & solicited food & clothing, & asked permission to remain in camp until moonrise, which was refused & the Indians were ordered out of camp. The Indians did not immediately comply, whereupon the whites unmercifully attacked them, & shot down a chief, two of his sons, & several others. A few days afterwards a brother of the chief who was slain was hunting & heard near him the explosion of firearms. He discovered that it proceeded from two men who were hunting. The Indians attacked while Gunnison's party was eating breakfast. Not a gun was fired by the whites in defence. Kanosha knew nothing of the intended attack. Walker & his band of Utahs were 300 miles off at the time, & were innocent of any participation in the act.]

The Elkton [Md] Whig says that Mr Job Wharton, of Bohemia Manor, has acknowledged the shooting of young Smack, found dead in Nov last. They were out partridge shooting together when the accidental discharge of Wharton's gun proved fatal to young Smack. No one doubts that the shooting was altogether accidental, as they were on the best terms.

Mrd: on Jan 19, in N Y, at the residence of Dr Bern W Budd, by Rev Thos Gallaudet, John C Hunter, Purser of the U S Navy, to Sophia, daughter of the late Rev Thos H Gallaudet, L L D, of Hartford, Conn.

Mrd: on Jan 23, in Trinity Church, Gtwn, by Rev J E Pallhuber, J C Berry, of Howard Co, Md, to Miss Susan Cloud, of Gtwn.

Phil, Jan 23. We announce the death of Dr Bird, one of the editors & proprietors of the North American, who died this morning, after a brief but severe attack of brain fever. In his death our city has lost a most valuable & worthy citizen.

WED JAN 25, 1854
Senate: 1-Memorial from Chas F Fisher, asking Congress to purchase his painting now on exhibition in a cmte room of the Senate, a representation of the battle of New Orleans. [The memorial says this picture has been the result of several years of hard labor; that he resided 15 years in the city of New Orleans, where he had the most reliable means of information, & flatters himself that he had produced a work of art beyond the reach of criticism, & the only current representation of the battle in existence.] 2-Ptn from Michl Nourse, late chief clerk in the ofc of the Register of the Treasury, asking compensation for the several periods during which he performed the duties of register, & also for compensation for acting disbursing agent. 3-Ptn from Abner Bassett & others, owners & master of vessels & pilots, asking that a beacon light may be placed on Black Ledge, at the entrance of the harbor of New London, Conn. 4-Ptn from Wm Rees, asking permission to select 10 or 12 thousand acres of land for the establishment of a Normal school. 5-Additional documents submitted in relation to the claim of Hugh Wallace Wormley. 6-Cmte on Indian Affairs: bill for the relief of Theodore E Elliott. 7-Cmte on Patents: bill for the relief of Hiram Moore & John Hascall. 8-Engrossed bill granting 5 years' half-pay to the widow of Capt John M Gunnison: passed.

House of Reps: 1-Ptn of Luke Hilton for remuneration for losses & injuries sustained while in the employ of the Gov't. 2-Ptn of Betsey A Faulkner, asking for a pension, or such relief as she may be entitled to as the surviving child of the late Ebenezer Floyd, a soldier & ofcr of the Revolutionary war. 3-Ptn of Abner Merrill for increase of pension. 4-Memorial of Chas D Arfwedson, asking compensation for his services as Charge d'Affaires ad interim at Stockholm. 5-Ptn of Jacob Mechlin, jr, Wm C Campbell, & other citizens of Butler Co, Pa, praying that 180 acres of land may be granted to all soldiers of the war of 1812 & all subsequent wars, or their heirs, without regard to rank or duration of service. 6-Memorial of Jane M Rudolph, widow of Thos C Rudolph, late captain in the U S revenue service, asking for a pension.

Mrd: on Sunday last, by Rev Dr Butler, Mr Levi Pumphrey to Mrs Ellen Sweeting, all of Wash City.

Mrd: on Jan 20, by Rev Jas H Brown, Mr Jas B Enroughty to Miss Henrietta C Hardaway, both of Va.

Died: yesterday, Miss Anne Brooke, of Wash City. Her funeral will take place this day, at 10 o'clock, from her late residence on 13th st west, between G & H sts, to which her friends are invited.

Washington Steam Cracker Bakery, C st, between 4½ & 6th st. –Thos H Havenner

Senate: 1-Private bill passed giving half-pay for life to the widow of the late Maj Gen Brown, to whose distinguished gallantry during the war of 1812 Gen Cass, in advocating the bill, paid a well-merited tribute.

Robbery on board the steamer **San Francisco**. On Saturday, 2 negroes, Wm Evans, formerly 2nd steward of the steamer **San Francisco**, & Wm Fields, a waiter on the same steamer, went into a jeweller's shop in Chathan st & offered a large quantity of valuable jewelry at 75% below its actual worth. Suspicion led to their arrest. The double-cased lepine watch was identified by Capt Fremont, of the U S army as the property of his wife. The negroes have confessed their guilt. –N Y Post

American & Foreign Agency, Wash, D C, Jan 24, 1854. Information is solicited of Gerrard von Blonay, of Hanover, who was at Las Vegas, New Mexico, engaged as a surveyor, in Mar, 1850, & then about to return to **Fort Independence**, Missouri. Danl Helm, of Hesse, late a regular or volunteer in the U S Army in the Mexican war, said to have served 14 months, & to have died at New Orleans in 1848 or fall of 1849. –Alfred Shuking, Ofc Clark's Commercial Bldgs.

Valuable Farm for sale: about 70 acres, within 3½ miles of the Capitol. Application may be made to J C G Kennedy, & H N Gilbert, Wash. The owner & occupant, G W Bowie, will be happy to show the premises.

THU JAN 26, 1854
The remains of the lamented M de Bodisco were committed to the tomb yesterday with every mark of public & private respect due to the representative of a great nation. The funeral was attended by the Pres of the U S & by all the members of his Cabinet; by the Pres of the Senate & many members of Congress, both Houses having adjourned over to give them the opportunity of attending; by the Diplomatic Corps, in full official costume; by the Mayors of the cities of Wash & Gtwn, & by a multitude of citizens. The religious services were conducted by Rev Dr Pyne & Rev Mr Caldwell, both of the Protestant Episcopal Church, the latter of whom [pastor of the church at which Mr Bodisco & his family worshipped] delivered an eloquent discourse. The following gentlemen officiated as Pall Bearers: Senators: Messrs Cass, Mason, Everett, & Dawson. Reps: Messrs Benton, Bayly, Preston, & J L Taylor. The Procession was formed at 4 p m, & in lengthened order attended the remains to the Cemetery of Gtwn. The body was conveyed in an open hearse in a coffin of the best material, but plain & unornamented, followed on foot by Mrs Bodisco, her children, & the remaining members of the family & suite of the deceased, all the way from the residence on 2nd st to the cemetery on the heights. This circumstance was peculiarly touching & appropriate, following as it did the affectionate example of Mr Bodisco himself, on a very recent occasion, at the funeral of a near relative of his wife.

Mr Patrick O'Donohoe, one of the Irish exiles who made his escape from Van Dieman's Land, & arrived in this country a few months since, died on Sunday last at his lodgings in Brooklyn.

The total defalcation of Lambert S Norwood, the late Clerk of the Superior Court of Balt, is $36,299, of which the sum of $17,862 is due to the State & $18,437 to the city of Balt. Mr Norwood was the first person elected to the ofc he lately filled under the provisions of the new Constitution.

Mrd: on Jan 24, in Gtwn, by Rev Jos Aschwanden, Mr Francis L Boarman, of Chas Co, Md, to Cecilia, daughter of Capt Wm Peters, of the former place.

Died: on Jan 23, at the residence of her daughter, Mrs Farquhar, Mrs Mary Anna Osterloh, wife of the late Rev John F Osterloh, in her 80th year.

Died: on Dec 28, at San Francisco, Calif, Judge N C Read, formerly of Ohio.

Died: on Saturday last, Robt W S Yeatman, son of Mr J H Yeatman, aged 3 years, 3 months & 27 days.

For rent: 3 story Frame bldg for rent or sale, on 8th st, above the Northern Liberty Market House. Apply to Aza Gladmon, 9th & M sts.

FRI JAN 27, 1854
Wash City property to be sold for taxes, on Apr 12 next. Years for which taxes are due: 1852 & 1853. To whom assessed: [Names that were not legible were omitted.]

Alexander, Chas
Alexander, Columbus
Andrae, Cornel
Addison, Danl D
Atkinson, Francis & Geo
Abbott, Geo L
Atkinson, Geo
Adrian, Geo W
Appleton, Henry
Abert, John J
Abbot, Jos
Adams, Jas
Almy, John
Appleton, John
Aveihle, Louise E
Acker, Nicholas
Adams, Nathl
Arth, Philip
Anderson, Robt P
Alexander, Sandy
Anderson, Saml J
Ackley, Thos
Acton, Wm D
Bateman, Abraham
Baldwin, Al
Byington, Aaron H
Bohrer, B S
Beall, Beverly W
Butler, Benj
Bealle, Benj
Baylor, Collie P
Balt, Chas
Brown, Chas
Bomford & Decatur
Burke, Dorothy
Burr, D V
Barry, David
Booth, Edw
Bett, Eliz
Butler, Franklin
Butler, Geo A
Buckey, Geo
Bomford, Geo
Brown, Geo
Bomford, Geo C
Birch, Geo A
Bergershausen, Geo W
Bray, Geo W
Bergman, Geo
Barry & Holtzman
Bergman, Henry W
Bradford, Henry
Breckenridge, John
Bond, John F
Bridges, Jas A
Barnes, John
Brown, John D
Brereton, John
Brenner, John A
Bergman, John W
Baltimore, Jos
Boyle, John
Bloecher, Johanna
Biglow, Jacob
Bloecher, John
Bradley, Jos H
Bradley, Jos H, exc of Robt E Kerr
Ball, John
Beardsley, Jos
Burche, John C, in trust for Catharine Burche
Barron, Jas
Brent, John Carroll
Burche, John C
Benning, Jas & Lucy
Buttle, John

Barrett, John	Clemens, Augustus D
Bayne, John	Clements, B H
Briethaupt, John G	Cheever, Benj H
Baden, John W & Thos E	Chambers, Benj
Bickley, Lloyd W	Cox, Clement
Brown, Lewis H	Collins, Charlotte & Mary E
Butler, Mary Ann	Coyle, Andrew
Byrne, Maria	Coddington, Camilla
Biss, Noah	Cockerell, Catharine
Bestor, O H	Crump, Danl F
Brown, O B	Conroy, Dom'nic
Boteler, Philip	Carroll, Danl, of Duddington
Bradley, Phineas	Clark, Danl B
Baltzell, Philip C	Cross, Eli
Bates, Robt W	Chew, Eliz
Broom, Robt	Clarke, Edw M
Barry, Richd	Clarke, Frances L
Briscoe, Richd G	Cross, Francis
Brent, Robt Y	Cole, Geo
Barry, Richd	Croggon, Henry B
Brooke/Brocke, Richd	Coburn, Jos L
Bowman, Richd A	Cole, Jas
Battle, Sally	Cruttenden, Joel
Burch, Saml & Offa Wilson	Carr, Julian
Busche, Saml	Callahan, John
Butler, Silas	Conelly, Joh
Brown, Thos	Cope, Jasper
Bowen, Thos H	Caden, Jas
Burch, Thos	Cabot, Jos R
Blagden, Thos	Cock, John T & J R Bowen
Burche, Victor M	Clarke, Jos S & R S Briscoe
Brown, Wm	Connor, Jas
Butler, Wm B	Callan, John F
Brown, Wm	Clarke, Jos S
Beall, Wm D	Crutchet, Jas
Breckenridge, W D	Cannon, John
Belt, Wm M	Cuvillier, Jos
Brown, Wm V H	Cross, Jos
Bayly, Wm F	Cryer, Jas
Bradley, Wm A	Campbell, Marlbro
Bush, Wm	Coombs, Mary E
Birth, Wm W	Caton, Michl, use of E Holland
Berry, Washington O	Calan, Nicholas, in trust for Jane
Bird, Wm	Lynch

Conoley, Owen
Collins, Patrick
Cruit, Richd
Campbell, Robt G
Coombs, Robt M
Cochran, Robt
Clarke, Reuben B
Culienane, Richd
Callin, Sarah
Cole, Seth L
Crown, Saml
Coleman, S S
Crawford, Thos B
Corcoran, Thos & W W
Cramphin, Thos
Corcoran, Thos
Collins, Thos
Connelly, Thos, of John
Conner, Thos
Costello, Timothy
Conway, Wm
Chandler, Walter S
Clarke, Wm
Collins, Wm
Corcoran, Wm W
Coxen, Wm H, jr
Carter, Washington
Clarke, Wm
Carrico, Wm B
Dermott, Ann R
Davis, Chas B
De Selding, Chas
Dougherty, Cornelius A
Day, David G
Dunlan, Eliz
DeKraff, Edw
Deter, Ebender
Doulin, Edw
Douglass, Earl
Darnell, Francis H
Day, Francis
Dunlap, Henry
Dant, H H
Dorsey, Henry C

Dunlap, Jas & R P
Dickenson, John P
Dunlap, Jas
Degges, John O P
Dove, Jos
Downer, Joel
Davis, Jas T
Duvall, John
Duncanson, J A M
David, Jos & Geo W Garret
Donohoe, John A
Devlin, John S
Dulany, John
Diggle, Jas
Dulaney G
Dickerman, Lemuel
Drummond, Lewis D
Dixon, Martha E
Donohoe, Mary
Dale, Mgt T & Mary L Livingston
Duffey, Michl
Dunlap, Robt P
Downing, Robt
Dyer, Robt W
Devaughn, Saml
Digges, Silvia
Drew, Solomon
Day, Sarah
Deckson, Thos
Donn, Thos C
Douglas, Wm
Deitz, Wm H
Durr, Wm
Dowling, Wm
Davidson, Wm
Dixon, Wm
Davis, Wm L
Dulie, Wm
Ellicott, Andrew
Ellis, Chrissy
Ellis, Chas F
Eckloff, Edw C
Edelin, Edw H

Ellicott, Elias
Edmondston, Franklin
Erving, Geo W
Evans, Geo
Ellicott, John
Edwards, Jos
Espey, Jas
Everick, Peter
Ellis, Robt
Estep, Rezin
Elliot, Saml
Easby, Wm
Elliot, Wm P
Evans, Wm
Foster, Adams
Fletcher, Basil
Fales, H
Fenwick, Benj J
Fisk, Chas B
Fisher, Chas
Finch, David
Forrest, Eleanor M
Folsom, Henry
Farrell, Harriet
Franks, Henry N
Frazier, Hannah
Freer, Jas B
Free, J D
Gibson, Geo & others, in trust for heirs of Henry Huntt
Garrett, Geo W & Jos Davis
Greer, Henry T
Goddard, John H, jr
Goheens, John L
Gardner, Jacob B
Gibson, John
Green, John
Gates, Mary
Graff, Michl
Gassaway, Madison
Goodwin, Robt
Gardner, Saml
Griffin, Sarah A
Grey, Thos K
Gadsby, Wm

Foy, John
Fitzgerald, John
Fitzgerald, Jas
Fowler, Jas J
Frye, Jos
Foulkes, John E & wife & others
Fowke, Lucy B
Foy, Mordecai
Fletcher, Mary Ellen
Fitzgerald, Susan
Frazier, Simon
Fenwick, Thoa
Ford, Wm
Fletcher, Wm, sr
Fischer, Wm
Ford, Wm
Griggs, Abel
Green, Ammon
Green, Benj E
Gaston, Catharine J
Gault, Edw
Gillan, E J
Gallant, Edw
Grey, Eliz
Goddard, Emma A C
Godfrey, Francis
Gelacking, Fred'k W
Hoover, Andrew
Heitmiller, A & A
Hagerty, Ann
Higdon, Andrew F
Hines, Ann
Harper, Alex'r H
Hill & Brot
Horton, Cornelius N
Halloran, Cecilia
Hibbs, Chas
Hanson, Chas
Haskett, Danl H, in trust for J J Milligan
Hall, David A
Homans, Danl

Hall, Edw
Houzam, Fred'k
Hall, Fred'k
Hardesty, Henry & wife
Hughes, Hugh
Hoban, Henry
Henning, Henry N
Hazle, Harriet A
Holtzman, Jacob
Harris, Jos G
Harmon, John L
Halliday, Jas F
Harrison, John D
Hall, Jas C
Henderson, Jos W
Halligan, Jas
Higgins, John
Harshman, Jacob
Howard, Jos
Hoye, John
Hepburn, John
Henke, Lewis, trustee
Holan, Marion B, & A Diamond
Hepburn, Peter, jr
Hawke, Robt A
Halliday, Robt
Harkness, Saml
Humphreys, Sophronia G
Hickey, Thornton F
Haines, Washington
Hindman, Wm
Halloran, W E
Hardy, Walter
Hollins, Wm
Ingle, John P
Ingle, Jos
Iddins, Saml
Iseman, Henry
Jones, Andrew Jackson
Jackson, Ap___
Jackson, Alex'r
Jones, Ann
Jackson, Andrew, in trust for J E Fitzgerald
Johnson, A E H
Jarboe, Benedict
Johnson, Henry D
Johnson, Joshua
Jarboe, John
Jones, Jas
Jones, Jas H
Johnson, John
Jones, Joel W
Jones, Morris
Jackson, Philip
Jenifer, Rachel
Jordan, Richd L
Jones, Susan
Jenkins, Thos C
Johnson, Walter C
Johnson, Wm
Jones, Zephaniah
Kerr, Alex'r
Kelley, Betrand
Kummer, Chas
Kierman, Chas
Kellar, Eliz
Knight, Edw A
Kurtz, Eliz
Knott, Geo A
King, Geo of Chas
Kirk, Geo E
Key, Henry S
Keppler, Henry
Key, John Tayloe
King, John A
Kidwell, John L
Knott, Ignatius M
Kehle, John
Keenan, Jas
Kleindeist, Jos
Katzenberger, J
Kern, Mary Ann
Kelly, Moses
Key, Philip
Kinney, Patrick
Kavanaugh, Patrick
Kurtz, Peter

Knowles, Robt O
Key, Saml
Kealey, Sarah A
Kelley, Thos
King, Wm F & others
King, Z M P
Locke, Andrew R
Lindsley, Andrew R
Lindsley, Andrew
Lefevre, Ann M, & others
Lindsay, Adam
Lucas, Bennet
Leadbettar, Danvile
Lancaster, Catharine
Laidler, Eliz
Lewis, Esther M
Lombardi, Francis
Lord, Francis B
Lowry, Geo
Lacey, Harriet
Little, John
Lare, John G
Laurie, John
Lewis, Jos C
Lynch, John & Jas
Liston, John A
Long, Jas
Lewis, John
Lockery, Jane
Little, John E
Lusby, Jas H
Lighted, Joan
Lenox, Peter
Loker, Richd H
Lewis, Saml L
Lunt, Saml
Llewellen, Thos
Lloyd, Thos
Lumpkin, Thos
Law, Thos
Leach, Thos
Lewis, Wm B
Langley, Wm H
McLean, A B

Moore, Ann
Miller, August
Morrison, Alex'r
Middleton, Arthur
Mangate, Antony
Middleton, B F
Milburn, Benedict
Magar, Benj S
McCorkle, Christiana
McCarthy, Chas F
Merrilist, Chas
McNamee, Chas
Myer, Ferdinand F
McKnight, Geo B & M H
Mattingly, Geo
Merkel, Casper
Mudd, Dominic
McCarthy, Eugene
Merida, Eliza
Mile, Eliza
McKenney, Edw
Masi, Francis & Vincent
McCoy, Harriet E
Merryman, Horatio R
Merryman, Horatio R, in trust
Moscrip, Henry
Meddart, Jacob
Myers, John
Mason, Jos
McBride, John
Mountz, John
McConchi, John T
Merman, Jane
Miller, John
McCarthy, Jas
Morss, Jas S
Marks, John
Moulder, John A
Moses, Jas
Major, John
McKuen, Jas P
Mills, John
Maury, John W
McCandless, Juliana

Moore, John & L Ladomus
McCormick, Jas
McCormich, Jas M
McCracken, John
Miller, Jacob
Martini, Jos
Mitchell, Jas
McElfresh, John W
Magar, John
McGee, Jas S
McQudlan, Mary A & Mgt
Miller, Mary
McCarthy, Michl
McPherson, Mary E
McKnight, Martha H
Mackay, Mary
Morris, Maria
McGregor, Nathl M
McCubbin, Nicholas
Maddox, Notley
McMoreland, Peter
Mackay, Philip
Marshall, Priscilla
McDermott, Robt
Murray, Stanislaus
McGuire, Thos
McCoubray, Thos
Madi, Vincent
Maxey, Virgil
Maud, Wm
Markwood, Wm
Myers, Wm
Morrow, Wm
McPherson, Wm S
McDonald, Wm L
Morgan, Wm
Moreland, Wm A
McPeck, Wm
Nailor, Allison
Nourse, Chas H
Nailor, Dickson, in trust for W O Nailor
Neil, Eliz
Nixdorff, Henry

Naylor, Henry & A Rothwell
Neilson, Hall
Nailor, Henry, use E Walls
Narden, Jos & Susan
Nicholson, John N
Nailor, Joshua S
Newton, Isaac
Neale, Jos W
Narden, Mary
Neale, Ramsay
Noyes, Wm
Nicholls, Wm S
Norris, Wm G
O'Couter, Eugene
O'Harra, Jas
O'Ferral, Jas
Owen, John
Owen, Saml W
O'Donoghue, Timothy
O'Neale, Wm
Parker, Albert
Provest, Alex'r
Pollard, Benj
Peter, David
Pancoast, David
Prott, Francis
Parker, Francis E
Page, Geo
Prather, Hugh D
Pierre, Jos B
Parker, Jas
Phillips, Jas B
Peake, John
Parsons, Jas
Parker, Lucinda
Purl, Mary
Prout, Mary
Pettibone, Mgt
Preston, O J & Levi Stowell
Prather, Overton J
Pearson, Peter M, in trust for B R Robey
Phillips, Richd, in trust for A D Davis
Prout, Robt

Peugh, Saml A, improvements assessed to J K Plant
Paine, Saml
Phillips, Saml
Plumsill, Thos
Parker, Wm H
Preston, Wainwright
Philip, Wm H
Pettibone, Wm
Phillips, Wm
Queen, Nicholas L
Quin, Jas
Rothwell, Andrew
Reynoldson, Catharine E
Ridgway, Enoch
Ross, Eliza
Riter, F W
Rider, Geo F
Randall, H K
Rotler, Julius
Richardson, Ira
Rollins, Jas H
Rives, John C
Russell, John T
Raley, Jas
Rowland, Jas W
Ray, Josiah
Ratrie, Jas
Robey, John
Richards, Jos
Roach, Mahlon
Ray, Paul
Rodier, P L
Richardson, Robt R
Riggs, Saml
Reading, Wm
Richardson, Wm
Riley, Wm R
Ratrie, Wm, jr
Ruggles, Wm
Redstreak, Wm J
Russell, Wm H
Sheppard, Alex'r
Sheckett, B O
Simms, Basil

Stubbs, Catharine A
Sengstack, C P
Smith, Clement
Schnebley, DAnl H
Sister, Eliz
Stratton, E N
Shaw, Eliza
Slater, Eliz
Simms, Edw
Scherf, Eterhard
Shorter, Fanny
Seldon, Francis
Schlegel, Ferdinand
Stewart, Geo W
Schaub, Gallus
Semmes, Geo
Stoke, Geo
Smith, Henry
Stewart, Hanson
Shryock, Henrietta
Smith, J B H, trustee
Sutton, Jas
Schultz, John G
Smith, J B H
Smith, Jas T
Sems, Ignatius
Smith, Jas
Shad, John
Scrivener, Jas
Sargeant, John
S-uter, John Q
Steele, Jas R
Smith, Jas H
Smith, John
Stallings, John P
Scott, Jas W
Sinchcomb, John H
Springman, John M
Sturgess, Mary Ann
Speake, Mary Ann
Simpson & Neale
Simmons, Ruthy Ann
Smith, Richd

Stott, Saml
Smith, Saml H
Seibert, Selman
Strong, Saml
Scott, Saml
Shelter, Saml
Sewall, Thos
Sylvester, Thos
Scrivener, Thos
Sibrey, Wm
Smith, Walter
S-uter, Wenderline
Slade, Wm
Spearing, Wm
Stewart, Wm W
Scott, Wm
Sothoron, Wm B
Stickney, Wm
Smith, Wm
Thruston, Bockner
Tayloe, Benj O
Terrett, Colville
Taylor, Emily
Theilick, Fred'k
Tilghman, Tristy
Thomas, Geo
Turner, Henry
Turner, Henry & others
Thomas, John Hanson
Tayloe, John, jr
Tayloe, John
Tabler, John
Throckmorton, John A
Taliaferro, Jas M, in trust
Towson, Nathan
Travers, Sydney
Todd, Wm B
Trock, John N
Todd, Wm B & W H Philip
Van Ness, Chas W
Van Ness, C P
Van Patten, Chas H
Venable, Chas H
Van Ness, Edw

Vernon, Henry T
Vowell, John C
Van Ness, John P
Villard, R H L
Vocable, Thos P
Veitch, Wm
Wilson, Alex'r
Wallingsford, Alfred
Worcester, Benj P
Waters, Benj
Winder, Chas H
Woodward, C, J Maguire, & Chas Miller
Ward, Cassander
Wheelan, Catherine Ann
Wiltberger, C H & others
Wiltberger, Chas H
Wilkerson, Edw
Wilson, Ellen
White, Geo W
Willner, Geo
Willner, Geo F H
Watterston, Geo
Williams, Geo W
Warring, Henry
Welsh, Judy, Mary, Catherine, & Mgt
Ward, John B
Walsh, Jos C & Mary Y
Williams, J & J
Wagner, John
Wood, John
W-se, Jas Alex'r
Wyrick, Jos
Whitney, Jos O
Walker, John
Walker, Jonathan T
Wall, Jesse D
Wimsatt, Jos
Wilson, John A
Werner, John H T
Wormley, Jas
Wilkerson, John
Ward, J C & N S
Wilson, Jesse R

Williams, John
Wilson, John H
Williams, Lemuel
Woodhull, Maxwell
Wall, Mary Ann
Wilson, Marcellus
Walker, Mariah E
Wingate, Mgt G T
Wilson, Patrick
Walker, Patsey R
Wimsatt, Richd
Walter, Robt
Williams, Sarah B
Young, Benj
Young, Henry N
Young, J Rodney
Young, Mgt

Williams, S S
Wilson, Sylvia & Jos Lee
Williams, Thos
Welch, Thos
Ward, Ulysses
Waters, Wm
Winder, Wm H
Wroe, Wm
Wall, Wm
Walker, Wm B
Weaver, Wm A
Ward, Wm H
Whitmore, Wm
Young, Richd
Young, Thos
Yeatman, Thos J

Young, Benj, surviving trustee of E & E M Brooks
Young, Nicholas, Notley, Ignatius, & Benj & Sarah E Clagett

House of Reps: 1-Ptn of Jacob Huglebergor, of Crawford Co, Pa, for remuneration for services in the Indian wars of 1790. 2-Cmte on Military Affairs: bill for the relief of Wm Hankins: committed. 3-Cmte on Naval Affairs: bill for the relief of Jos Gideon: recommended that it do not pass: laid on the table. 4-Cmte on Revolutionary Pensions: adverse reports on the ptns of Chas M Howe, of Benton, N H, & of the heirs of Stephen Hoyt & others, of Bradford, N H. Same cmte: adverse reports on the ptn of Sallyette Bennett, widow of Stephen W Bennett, for a pension. Same cmte: bill for the relief of Geo W Gibson, & a bill for the relief of Parmelia Slavin, widow of John Blue, deceased: committed. Same cmte: adverse reports on the ptns of Wm Murray, of Halifax Co, Va, for a pension; of Wm A Webster, for a pension; of Mgt Bowne, for bounty land; & of John Mitchell, for an increase of pension. Same cmte: bill for the relief of Alton Nelson: committed. Same cmte: adverse reports on the ptns of Horatio Fitch, for arrearages of pension; of Chas H Pointer; & of Abigail Southworth & Rosalind Peters for a pension. Same cmte: bill to provide a pension for Silas Champion, of Genessee Co, N Y. Same cmte: adverse reports on the ptns of Emanuel P Stedman, of Robt Ham, of John W Cameron, & of Ben O'Branham. Same cmte: adverse report on the ptn of John Mills for a pension. 5-Cmte of Claims: bill for the relief of Sarah K Jenks, & the legal reps of Hartshorne R Thomas, in the matter of the brig **Jane**; bill for the relief of Gilbert C Russell: committed. 6-Cmte on Commerce: adverse on the ptn of Jas Irwin, of Pittsburg, Pa. 7-Cmte on Private Land Claims: bill for the relief of Thos C Greene; bill to confirm to Hercules L Dousman his title to farm lot 32 adjoining the town of Prairie de Chien, Wisc; bill authorizing Victor Morass to relinquish certain lands & to enter the same quantity elsewhere: each committed. 8-Cmte on Invalid Pensions:

bill for the relief of Aaron Stafford, of the State of N Y; bill for the relief of Hezekiah Johnson, of Bridgewater, Vt: committed. Same cmte: adverse report on the memorial of Wm Breeding for a pension.

U S Patent Ofc, Wash, Jan 26, 1854. Ptn of Allen & Wm A Crowell, of Salisbury, Conn, praying for the extension of a patent granted to them on Jun 20, 1840, for an improvement in churns, for 7 years from the expiration of said patent, which takes place on Jun 20, 1854. –Chas Mason, Com'r of Patents

Susan R Thompson, aged 7 years, died of hydrophobia at the Massachusetts hospital in Boston on Saturday. She was bitten by a rabid dog some 6 weeks since. Death ended her sufferings.

Senate: 1-Ptn from the heirs of Jos Bindon, of the Revolutionary army asking to be allowed commutation pay. 2-Ptn from H H Maddox, asking compensation for services in taking the 7th census in Ky. 3-Ptn from Dr Wm M Ryer, asking compensation for vaccinating soldiers in Calif, in accordance with a contract made by the U S Indian agent. 4-Ptn from Chas D Arfwedson, asking compensation for his services as charge d'affaires ad interim in Stockholm. 5-Ptn from Sophia G Dillingham, for a pension.

Died: on Jan 26, after a short but painful illness, Wm Keefe, sr, in his 54th year. His funeral is on Saturday, at 9 o'clock, from his late residence, on H st, between 17th & 18th sts.

Died: on Thu, at the residence of Mr S Worthington, 18th st, Mr Roger W Wilcox, in his 21st year. Though he has been long declining, yet his death was sudden. His funeral will be at the E st Baptist Church on Jan 28 at 3 o'clock.

Died: on Dec 16, at Marysville, Calif, John Holmes Magruder, formerly of Montg Co, Md, aged 26 years.

SAT JAN 28, 1854
Wash Corp: 1-Ptn from Mrs Louisa McLean, asking that Mgt Lewis, a colored woman, may have the privilege of holding a supper: referred to the Cmte on Police. 2-Ptn of Geo Page, for the remission of a fine: referred to the Cmte of Claims. 3-Ptn of G Oakley & S Easton, asking leave to give a party to their colored friends, to be continued after the hour of 10 o'clock: referred to the Cmte on Police. 4-Cmte on Improvements: bill for the relief of F W Sellhausen.

The new <u>Presbyterian Church</u> on 6th st, near Md ave, will be dedicated on Jan 29, the Rev Messrs Smith, Sunderland, & Noble officiating.

The house of John Thompson, of Centre Harbor, was burnt on Sat, & Mr Thompson, who was its only occupant, was burnt in it. He had carried out a quantity of books from his library, which were very valuable, & returned to get a chair which belonged to his mother, which he valued very highly, when some part of the bldg fell, & he was seen no more. Mr Thompson was about 50 years of age & had no family.
-Boston Courier

Mrd: on Jan 17, at Trinity Church, Boston, by Rt Rev Bishop Eastburn, John Osborne Sargent, of Wash, to Georgiana, daughter of Benj Welles, of Boston.

Mrd: on Thu last, at the Navy Yard, by Rev Jas H Brown, Mr John M Mitchell to Miss Mary Ann Goodrich, all of Wash City.

Mrd: on Jan 12, in the Church of the Nativity, Huntsville, Ala, Ellen, daughter of Geo P Beirne, to Geo A Gordon, of Savannah, Ga.

Mrd: on Thu, by Rev Jas H Brown, John E Evans, [son of Rev French S Evans,] to Sophia Smiley, daughter of Jas Lawrenson, all of Wash City.

Mrd: on Jan 11, in Tallahassee, Fla, by Rev Jessee W Hume, Col Allan Macfarlan, of Cheraw, S C, to Miss Julia Gamble, youngest daughter of the late Col John G Gamble, of Fla.

Died: on Jan 20, after a long & painful illness, in Salisbury, Md, Mrs Anna C J Briggs, in her 40th year, & for the last 10 years a resident of Wash City.

Senate: 1-Bills passed: relief of-Thos Marston Taylor; Hiram Paulding; Purser F B Stockton; Mrs Mary E D Blaney; sureties of Danl Winslow; & the heirs & reps of the late Capt Wm G Williams. 2-Bills ordered for a third reading: relief of-Jacob Gideon; the children of the late Lt Michl Everly, a Revolutionary ofcr; & of Richd M Bouton; Geo Wright; & the widow of Marvin W Fisher. 3-Bills considered & postponed: relief of-Rinaldo Johnson, & Ann E Johnson; of Wm G Ridgely; & of the legal reps of John G Mackall, deceased. 4-Bill for the relief of Cornelius McCaulay: rejected: yeas 12, nays 21.

House of Reps: 1-Bills referred: relief of-the heirs & legal reps of Wm Weeks; the captors of the frig **Philadelphia**; & the legal reps of Danl Loomis, deceased. 2-Bills laid aside to be reported to the House: relief of-Madison Parton; Henry N Halstead; Benj Hammond, of the State of N Y; Henry J Snow, of Rome, N Y; Lemuel Hudson; Geo S Claflin; Jas F Green; Thos Frazer; Cornelius H Latham; Saml W Brady; Fayette Mauzy & Robt G Ward; John O Mears; Lyman N Cock; Benj Rowe; Emelie Hooe, widow of Capt Hooe; John Hamilton; Geo W Gibson; Parmelia Slavin, widow of John Blue, deceased; Aaron Stafford, & Hezekiah Johnson, of Bridgewater, Vt. Also, a pension for Silas Champion. 3-<u>Bills objected to</u>: settling the claims of the legal reps of Richd W Meade, deceased. Bill for the relief of: Chas Lee Jones; of Henry Lewis, of Clinton Co, Indiana; of Capt Geo Simpton, of Galveston; of Ferdinand Clark; of Adolphus Meier & Co, of St Louis; of Robt Grignon; of Geo G Bishop & the legal reps of John Arnold, deceased; of Chas Staples; of Harriet Leavenworth, widow of the late Brvt Brig Gen Leavenworth; of the heirs of Jos Gerard; of Mrs Helen McKay, widow of the late Col Aeneas McKay, deputy quartermaster general U S army; of D C Cash & Giles W Ellis. Bills objected to: relief of-Pamela Brown, widow of Maj Gen Jacob Brown, late of the U S army, deceased; of Wm B Edwards; of Dan Steenrod; of Anthony G Willis, deceased; of John S Jones & Wm H Russell, surviving partners of Brown, Russell & Co; of Wm Hankins; of Alton Nelson; of Sarah K Jenks, & the legal reps of Hartshorne R Thomas, in the matter of the brig *Jane*; of Gilbert C Russell; of Thos C Green; authorizing Victor Morass to relinquish certain lands & to enter the same quantity elsewhere.

For rent or lease, for one or more years, that large & elegant Mansion House on G st, between 17th & 18th sts, now occupied by Mr Sartiges, the Minister of France. Also, the block of bldgs at E & 13th sts, now occupied by Mrs H D P Wise as a boarding house. Inquire of Dr Benj King or Thos Lawson, Winder's Bldg.

MON JAN 30, 1854
For rent: commodious store, occupied by Jesse B Wilson, on Pa ave, between 6th & 7th sts. Possession on Mar 1. Apply to B H Cheever, opposite Treasury.

Teacher wanted by the Trustees of Primary School #3, Bladensburg district, PG Co, Md. A single man of good moral character. –Horatio Beall, R G Cross, A H Wells

Mr E Mosche, a German apothecary at New Haven, Conn, fell from a 2nd story window of his residence on Wed & broke his neck, killing him instantly.

Jas L Heart was executed on Fri in the court yard of the City Prison, N Y, for the murder of Susan McAnany.

Col Geo McFeely, of Carlisle, Pa, died on Jan 19, in his 74th year. He was appointed by Pres Madison Lt Col of the 16th Regt U S Infty on Mar 14, 1812. He commanded at *Fort Niagara*, which place he defended against a severe attack of the enemy on Nov 21, 1813. He was appointed Col of the 25th Regt of Infty on May 18, 1814.

The wife of Henry R Smith, of Middletown, Conn, while on her way to visit a sick relative on Sun last, complained of indisposition & expired in her husband's arms.

Mr Jas K Hanson, a worthy citizen living near Van Buren, Ark, was lately killed in the woods near his house, when a dead tree fell upon him.

I hereby notify the public not to take certain notes of hand given by me to Francis Langley in June, 1853. The notes were for $50 each, & were given for a consideration that said Langley has failed to execute. –John O'Neil
[After the name O'Neil is an X]

Died: on Dec 27 last, Miss Courtney Waters, of Montg Co, Md, in her 65th year. In the death of this estimable lady her relatives & companions have lost one remarkable for many good qualities.

TUE JAN 31, 1854
Senate: 1-Cmte on Pensions: adverse report on the claim of the children of Geo Felker. 2-Cmte of Claims: bill for the relief of Lt A J Williamson. 3-Cmte on Military Affairs: bill for the relief of Dempsey Pittman. 4-Adverse report on the memorial of H K Brown, asking for 14 pieces of brass cannon to cast an equestrian statue of Washington. 5-Cmte on Public Lands: adverse report on the memorial of Wm Reeves for 10,000 acres of land for a Normal school. 6-Ptn from Thos P Huger, John Quincy Adams, & Payne N Westcott, asking that they may be indemnified for clothing lost on board the U S steamer wrecked on the coast of Mexico. 7-Ptn from the widow & children of John M Baker, late Consul at Rio Janeiro, asking compensation for diplomatic services. 8-Ptn from Horatio G Gibson, of the 3rd Artl of the U S army, asking that extra pay may be extended to the ofcrs, sailors, & marines serving in Calif from May 8, 1846 to Jul 1, 1853. 9-Ptn from Jas Pool, asking the reimbursement of money paid by him for supplies for the Shawnee tribe of Indians. 10-Ptn from Eliz Monroe, asking to have her pension extended & renewed. 11-Ptn from Jas M Goggin, asking to be allowed additional compensation for his services as special mail agent for Calif, & for expenses incurred in the discharge of his duties. 12-Ptn of Calvin K Averill, asking to be allowed commutation pay & a pension. 13-Ptn from John C F Salomon, asking a act of incorporation for the purpose of supplying pure water to the cities of Wash & Gtwn. 14-Cmte on Private Land Claims: bill for the relief of Jos Campan, with a report. 15-Cmte on Patents: bill for the relief of Wm R Nevins. 16-Cmte on Naval Affairs: bill for the relief of Wm S P Sauger. 17-Cmte on Military Affairs: bill for the relief of Mrs Helen Mackay, widow of & excx of Col Aeneas Mackay. 18-Cmte on Indian Affairs: adverse report on the memorial of Henry C Miller, Philip W Thompson, & Jesse B Turley. 19-Cmte on Pensions: adverse reports on the ptns of Eliz R Drane & B M Van Derveer. 20-Cmte on Private Land Claims: to confirm the title of Chas G Gunter: reported back without amendment.

Dr Lewis W Chamberlayne died at his residence near Richmond on Sat last. He was one of the original founders of the Richmond Medical College.

House of Reps: 1-Bills introduced & referred: relief of-John Klock & Decatur Herb; of Hannah Scroggins; of Simon Myers; & of the legal reps of Geo McGirk.

N Y, Jan 29. Yesterday the bldg occupied as a factory for the making of ballcartridges, Lower Ravensworth, Long Island, blew up. List of the killed as far as could be ascertained: Ann Burns, 25; Mary Hague, about 16; Geo Malcomb, about 13; Mary Malcomb, 18; John O'Brien, 13; John Downy, 13; John Gormly, 12; John Riley, 10; Ellen McDonnell, 20; Matthew Hand, 15; Jas Foley, 12; Emma Ryan, 20; & Matthew Ryan, 16.

Mrd: on Jan 30, in Gtwn, by Rev J R Eckard, W H F Gurley, of N Y, to Miss Eliz S, daughter of Benj F Rittenhouse, of the former place.

WED FEB 1, 1854
House of Reps: 1-Cmte on Revolutionary Pensions: adverse report on the ptn of Elmira White, widow of Thos R White, for back pay. Same cmte: adverse reports on the ptns of Ira Whitaker; of the heirs of Jos Wheaton; of Sarah Liscomb; & of Enoch Perkins, heir of Zephar Perkins. Same cmte: to adjust the accounts of Wm Woodbury, agent at Portland Maine: committed. 2-Cmte on Invalid Pensions: bill for the relief of Mary Deany, widow of Jas A Deany, of the U S army; & a bill for the relief of John S King, of Va: committed. Same cmte: adverse reports on the ptns of Chas W Balkeman; of Elijah L Pomroy; & of Washington Porter. 3-Cmte on Patents: adverse report on the ptn of Thos McAnaspie. Same cmte: bill for the relief of Hiram Moore & John Hascall: committed. 4-Cmte of Claims: bill for the relief of Ezra Williams: committed. Same cmte: bill for the relief of Chas Cooper & Co: committed. Same cmte: bill for the relief of John Boyd, of Louisiana: recommended that it do not pass: laid on the table. Same cmte: bill for the relief of Jas Dunning: committed. Same cmte: bill for the relief of Thos S J Johnson, of the Territory of New Mexico: committed. Same cmte: adverse report on the ptn of Wm H Topping. Same cmte: bill for the relief of the administrators of Oliver Lee, deceased: committed. 5-Cmte on Commerce: bill for the relief of Chas A Kellett, to provide for the establishment of a marine hospital at St Mark's, Fla: committed. 6-Cmte on Public Lands: bill for the relief of Jos Mitchell: committed. Same cmte: adverse report on the ptn of Chas Simmons. 7-Memorial of Sarah Benbridge, a daughter of Com Truxton, in relation to French spoliations: presented. 8-Cmte on Indian Affairs: bill for the legal reps of Joshua Kennedy, deceased: committed. Same cmte: bill for the relief of John Phagan: committed. 9-Cmte on the Territories: bill for the relief of Grafton Baker: committed.

Mrd: on Jan 29, by Rev J C Smith, Mr Nicholas O McCubbin to Miss Mary E McDonald, both of Wash City.

The infant Princess of Spain has died suddenly.

Rev Jas C Richmond complains that he is detained a prisoner by the Austrian police at Kochenet, in Hungary, & calls on the U S for redress.

The house of a man named Parker, in the township of Orion, Oakland Co, Mich, was burnt to the ground on Jan 22, while the family were absent at church, & 4 children perished in the flames. A boy of 14, the eldest, appeared to have brought out articles of furniture & returned to the house, probably to save his little brother & 2 sisters.

Wash City Ordinances: 1-Act for the relief of Maurice Roach: fine imposed for an alleged violation by selling chestnuts in the Centre Market without a license: to be repaid to Roach. 2-Act for the relief of Saml J Little: to pay him $10, the amount he overpaid for certain licenses. 3-Act for the relief of Alfred H Parry: the fine imposed for selling butter without a license: is hereby remitted: provided Parry pay the cost of prosecution in this case. 4-Act for the relief of Sophia Stallings: sum of $30 be paid her, she being the legal rep of the heirs of G L Golding, said Golding having overpaid the above sum for running an omnibus.

Senate: 1-Ptn from Chas McCormick, an assist engineer in the U S navy, asking to be allowed per centage on money disbursed by him: referred. 2-Ptn from Geo Alexander, asking pecuniary relief on account of loss of health while in the service of the U S Commission to run the north-eastern boundary line: referred. 3-Ptn from Minerva Cattlett, widow of a surgeon in the army, asking to be allowed a pension: referred. 4-Bill for the relief of John Bronson, with a report. 5-Cmte of Claims: bill for the relief of John P McElderry. 6-Bills passed-relief of: Geo M Bouton, Geo Wright, & the widow of Marvin W Fisher. Relief of Jacob Gideon; & of the legal reps of the late Capt Wm G Williams.

THU FEB 2, 1854
Household & kitchen furniture at auction on Mar 6, at the Irving House, 13th & Pa ave, by deed of trust from Danl D French, recorded in Liber J A S #53, folios 147 thru 148, of the Land Records of Wash Co, D C, all the furniture & effects in the establishment. –B Willett & C E D Wood, trustees -Green & Scott, auct.

Senate: 1-Ptn from Harriet H Saunders, widow of an ofcr of the U S revenue service, who was lost on board the cutter **Hamilton**: referred. 2-Ptn from Abraham Boileau, grandson of Ensign Amable Boileau, of the Revolutionary army, asking to be allowed commutation pay: referred. 3-Ptn from Sarah J Hine, widow of an ofcr in the revenue service lost on board the cutter **Hamilton**, asking to be allowed a pension: referred. 4-Ptn from Jos C Smith, assignee of a certain land warrant, asking to be allowed to locate the quantity of land therein described: referred. 5-Ptn from Ellen Martin, asking that the commutation pay to which Francis Martin was entitled for Revolutionary services may be paid to his legal reps: referred. 6-Cmte on the District of Columbia: asked to be discharged from the further consideration of the memorial of L P Halliday & Co, asking to be allowed to build a hotel on some of the public lots: discharged accordingly. Same cmte: asked to be discharged from the further consideration of the memorial of John C F Saloman, asking an act to supply water to the cities of Wash & Gtwn: discharged accordingly.

Household & kitchen furniture at auction on Feb 7, at the residence of G B Armstrong, on H, between 7th & 8th sts. –Green & Scott, aucts

Died: yesterday, after a long & severe illness, Henry Hoffman, aged 88 years, a native of Germany, but for many years a resident of Wash City. His funeral is on Sunday next, at 2 o'clock.

Died: on Jan 28, at his residence, in the city of Phil, Jas Robertson, having on the day of his death attained his 82nd year. He had formerly, as Cashier of the Branch Bank of the U S, resided many years in Richmond, Va, & in that community has left numerous friends, by whom his memory will be long & warmly cherished.

Died: at her residence in New Albany, Indiana, Mrs Isabella Sengstack, consort of Henry E Sengstack, of Wash, D C, in her 22nd year. [No death date given-current item.]

Orphans Court of Wash Co, D C. Letters of administration on the personal estate of Frederic F Wingenroth, late of Wash Co, deceased. –P Hitz, adm

Unknown heirs. Alfred D Offutt & Eli Offutt, against Esly Offutt's widow, heirs, etc. I Matthew H Fuqua, having been appointed, by a decree of the Logan Co Circuit Court of Ky, Com'r to collect & distribute the money due the estate of Esly Offutt, deceased, do, hereby notify the unknown heirs of Thos L Patterson, Wm H Patterson, Chas Patterson, & Temple Smith, that there is due them from said estate, as heirs of Esly Offutt, deceased, the following sums of money, to wit: to the unknown heirs of Thos L Patterson: $400.42; to the unknown heirs of Wm H Patterson, $400.42; to the unknown heirs of Chas Patterson, $400.42; to the unknown heirs of Temple Smith: $160.16; which they can get by application to me at Russellville, Logan Co, Ky, upon proper proof of indentity of person. –Matthew H Fuqua, Com'r

FRI FEB 3, 1854
Senate: 1-Memorial from Lucy Audubon, asking that Congress will purchase the original drawings of the work of her late husband on the birds of America.
2-Ptn from May F B Levely, widow of the cmder of the privateer **Nonsuch**, asking to be allowed a pension. 3-Cmte on Naval Affairs: memorial of Passed Midshipmen Geo P Welsh & Clarke H Wells, asking compensation for the time they performed the duties of a higher grade: reported a bill for their relief. 4-Cmte on Private Land Claims: asked to be discharged from the further consideration of the ptn of Yates & McIntyre: discharged accordingly.

House of Reps: 1-Memorial of Jos S Kele, asking an extension of his patent for safety beams of railroad cars: presented. 2-Ptn of Sidney P Pool, of Minot, Maine, for a pension on account of injury received in the Fla war. 3-Ptn of Elijah Frye, of West Bath, Maine, for a pension for injuries & loss of health in the war of 1812.

Amelia Wyand, who died in Wash Co, Md, a few weeks ago, has left the following offspring: 14 children, 73 grand-children, 203 great grand-children, & 10 great great grand-children-in all 300 descendants.

Appointments by the Pres, by & with the advice & consent of the Senate.
Consuls of the U S:
Jos W Clark, of N Y, for Arica, Peru
Edw B Buchanan, of Md, for La Rochelle, France
R G Barnwell, of S C, for Amsterdam
Jas H Williams, of Maine, for Sydney, Australia
Noble Towers, of Conn, for Barbadoes
Max Stettheines, of N Y, for Stuttgardt, Wurtemburg
Fayette M Ringgold, D C, for Paita, Peru
John L Nelson, of Md, for Turk's Island
Robt C Murphy, of Ohio, for Shanghai, China
John Higgins, of N Y, for Cork, Ireland
Jas W Green, of Va, for Lima, Peru
G W Fletcher, of Alabama, for Aspinwall, New Granada
John Duffey, of N Y, for Galway, Ireland
C W Denison, of Mass, for Demerara
Stephen Cockran, Pa, for St Jago de Cuba
Chas W Bradley, of Conn, for Ningpa, China
Levi K Bowan, of Md, for Bordeaux

Mrd: on Feb 2, in Wash City, at Trinity Church, by Rev Dr Butler, Lt John J Almy, U S Navy, to Sarah McLean, daughter of Col Chas K Gardner.

Mrd: on Jan 31, by Rev Mr Hodges, Jas Henry Moore to Miss Mgt Ann Farr, both of PG Co, Md.

Died: on Feb 2, in the Wash Infirmary, Mr John A King, in his 52nd year. His funeral will take place this evening at Trinity Church, Gtwn, at 3 o'clock.

Died: on Jan 31, in Wash City, Thos M Boyle, in his 42nd year, only son of the late Capt Thos Boyle, of Balt.

Orphans Court of Wash Co, D C. Letters of administration on the personal estate of Wm G Davidson, late of Wash Co, deceased. –Saml C Davidson, adm

SAT FEB 4, 1854
The Catholic Church at Rockville, Md, under the pastoral charge of Rev Mr Dority, was broken open on Sat & robbed of 3 silver candlesticks, two marked B O, one censer, one gilt double candelabra, & a large quantity of linens.

The remains of Pulaski. A report that the remains of Pulaski had been discovered has caused a great controversy in Georgia. A letter from Col Jas Lynch, of S C, settles the matter. He states, & produces documents to prove, that his grandfather, who was surgeon in the army, extracted the bullet which gave Pulaski his death. Although a desperate wound, my grandfather thought the Count could have recovered from it had he consented to remain under his care & follow the American army on a lifter. Count Pulaski resisted, because he feared a pursuit by the British army & his capture; he believes they would have sent him to Russia, a Power with whom he was in deadly hostility. Rather, he took the chance of a cure in the French fleet, commanded by D'Estaing. He was carried on ship-board, died on the passage round to Charleston, & his body was buried in the seas. [A report that the remains of Pulaski had been discovered has caused a great controversy in Georgia.]

Mrs Landreaux, a widow lady of New Orleans, has recovered for herself & children $20,000 damages from the New Orleans & Carrollton Railroad Co for the death of her husband, Dr Landreaux, caused by a collision between a horse car & a locomotive attached to a passenger car. She laid her damages at $50,000.

The death of Don Manuel Armigo, formerly Mexican Govn'r of the Territory, at Simitar, announced on Dec 17, is contradicted by the Gazette of Dec 24. He was pronounced better & likely to recover.

From New Mexico. Kit Carson, John L Hatcher, & several others arrived in Santa Fe on Christmas Day from Calif, where they left just 2 months previous. They report having met near a 100,000 sheep driven from New Mexico for the Calif market.

Wash Corp: 1-Cmte of Claims: asked to be discharged from the further consideration of the ptn of C H Burgess for the remission of a fine: discharged accordingly. Same for John Kelly. 2-Act for the relief of Albert Hart: passed. 3-Cmte of Claims: act for the relief of John Burns: passed. 4-Ptn of John Grinder, proposing to purchase the surplus clay out of a portion of Ga ave: referred to the Cmte on Police.

Died: on Feb 3, in Wash City, Robert John, son of D R & Ann Lindsay, aged 3 years & 11 months. The friends of D R Lindsay, of Tuscumbia, Ala, are invited to attend the funeral at 10 o'clock tomorrow, from Mrs Taylor's, Pa ave, between 4½ & 6th sts, south side.

Senate: 1-Bills considered in Cmte of the Whole & passed: relief of-Albert Hart; of Lavinia Taylor; of Allen G Johnson; of Adam D Steuart, paymaster of the U S Army; of Wm Senna Factor; of Richd Fitzpatrick; of Don B Juan Domereq, a Spanish subject; of Purser T P McBlair; of John G Camp; of Saml H Hempstead; of Isaac Varn, sr; of Richd King; of Wm Blake; & of the legal reps of the late Thos Chapman, formerly collector of the port of Gtwn, S C.

Died: in Wash City, after a painful & protracted illness, Mrs Sinia Griffin, consort of Jas L Griffin, aged 47 years. Her funeral will take place at her late residence, 9th st, between M & N sts, Sunday at 2 o'clock. [No death date given-current item.]

House of Reps: 1-Recommended that they do pass: relief of-of Harriet Leavenworth, widow of the late Brvt Brig Gen Leavenworth, with an amendment; of Wm B Edwards, with an amendment; of Anthony G Willis, deceased, with an amendment. 2-Bill passed: relief of-Benj Rowe; of Henry N Halstead; of Benj Hammond, of the State of N Y; of Henry J Snow, of Rome, N Y; of Lemuel Hudson; of Geo S Claflin; of Jas F Green; of Thos Frazer; of Cornelius H Latham; of Saml W Brady; of Fayette Maury & Robt G Ward; of the legal reps of the late John E Bispham; of John O Mears; of Lyman N Cook; of Emilie Hooe, widow of Capt Hooe; of John Hamilton; of Geo W Gibson; & of Parmella Slavin, widow of John Blue, deceased. Also, of Aaron Stafford; of Hezekiah Johnson, of Bridgewater, Ct; of Chas Staples; of Alton Nelson; of Grafton Baker; of Mary Deany, widow of the late Lt Jas A Deany, U S Army; & a pension for Silas Champion. Bill to confirm to Hercules L Dousman his title to farm lot 32.

For sale: a new 2 story brick dwlg house, but 1 square from Pa ave, between 11th & 12th sts. The owner is about to leave. –Alfred Shucking, Clark's Commercial Bldg, opposite Centre Market.

MON FEB 6, 1854
Senate: 1-Ptn from Oliver Towles & others, asking to be allowed 7 years half-pay as legal heirs & reps of Capt Towles, who was killed in the war of the Revolution. 2-Ptn from Christopher Spencer, asking remuneration for the sufferings, injuries, imprisonment, & loss of property he sustained during the war of the Revolution. 3-Ptn from John Wilson, asking remuneration for land settled & improved by him under a title from the U S & of which he was dispossessed.

Household & kitchen furniture at auction on Feb 9, at the residence of a family declining housekeeping at the s e corner of 10th & Pa ave, over Byrne's Grocery Store. -J C McGuire, auct

We learn from a letter in the N Y Advertiser that among the Americans in Florence, on Jan 5, was Mr Chas Fenton Mercer, who at the age of 70 had just acquired the Italian language, thus surpassing Cato, who boasted that he learned Greek at 60.

Destructive fire at London, Madison Co, Ohio, on Thu. About 20 bldgs were destroyed with their contents. Names of the sufferers: Jas Smith, V S Chamberlin, J C Kemp, A Shanklin, W Dungan, J Kanncaster, J B Evans, I Warner, H Warner, T Jones, A Winchester; A E Turnbull; H Fellow, Dunkin & Boals, Geo Phifer, Wm Jones, J J Jones, R Acton, G W Sprung, J Lewis, & R Hall.

A fracas occurred at Hagerstown, on Thu, between Peter Reese, a respectable German, & John Beider, during which Beider drew a pistol & shot Reese dead. The murderer was arrested & committed to jail.

Mrd: on Feb 2, by Rev Mr Holmead, Henry D Gunnell to Mary Ann Hinton, daughter of the late Geo Milburn, all of Wash City.

Died: on Sat last, at his residence on Capitol Hill, Geo Watterston, one of the oldest & most esteemed citizen of Wash. A witness in early childhood to the laying of the corner-stone of the Capitol, he manifested throughout his life a constant devotion to the interest of the Nat'l Metropolis. During his mortal illness, protracted for nearly 6 weeks, the universal & deep anxiety of his neighbors was a tribute to his character which cannot be mistaken. His funeral will take place this afternoon, from his late residence on Capitol Hill, at 3 o'clock.

Died: on Jan 25th last, near Bladensburg, Md, Dr Wm Henry Decker, in his 22nd year, son of Rev John Decker.

TUE FEB 7, 1854

New Orleans Delta of Jan 30. The steamboat **Georgia**, Capt Roberts, burned on Sat last at the terminus of the Carrollton & Pontchartrain Railroad. She had 180 passengers on board, & was heavily loaded with cotton. The list of passengers was consumed, &, as no list was taken of those who were saved, the entire loss of life cannot be correctly estimated. Mr Jackson & one child, of Barbour Co, Ala, were lost; his wife & 8 children, were saved; Mrs Jolly & one child, of Randolph Co, Ga, were lost; Mr Jolly was saved. B F Loftin, of Lenoir Co, N C, was saved, but lost two negroes. Rev J McCarter, of Clinton, Ga, lost three negroes; he & his wife were saved, though the latter was badly injured. Dr J M Young, from Hancock Co, Ga, lost his servant boy, his books, surgical instruments & clothing. Mrs Davidson, from Macon Co, Ala, lost several negroes. Mr Graham, from Wmsburg, S C, lost two negroes & $500 in gold. Thos J McLanathan, of Bristol, Conn, is missing. J B Hubbard, of Bristol, Conn, was saved, but lost his baggage.

Auction of fancy goods on Feb 8, at the store of Mr J A Peters, on Pa ave, near 10th st. –E N Stratton, auct

House of Reps: 1-Cmte on Military Affairs: Bill for the relief of the children & heirs of Maj Gen Baron de Kalb: committed. 2-Cmte on Military Affairs: bill for the relief of the legal reps of Maj Caleb Swan, deceased: committed.

J Glancy Jones [Dem] has been elected to Congress from the 8th District of Pa, Berks Co, in place of H A Muhlenburg [Dem] deceased.

Senate: 1-Memorial of Christopher Cory, asking an investigation into his discovery as to the cause & cure of the potato rot, & asking that he may be indemnified for the time spent & expenses incurred in making the discovery. 2-Ptn from John W Kelly, asking to be indemnified for losses sustained in consequence of the abrogation of a contract by the Post Ofc Dept. 2-Ptn from Sarah Somers Corson, neared surviving relative of Richd Somers, who fell at Tripoli in 1804, asking a pension. 3-Ptn from Theresa Dardennus, asking indemnity for losses sustained in consequence of an erroneous sale of land by the land ofcrs at Little Rock to her late husband. 4-Letter from Alex'r Ramsay, enclosing papers in relation to the charges of malfessance in ofc made against him. 5-Documents presented in support of the claim of the children of Leonard Proctor to a pension for services. 6-Additional documents submitted in relation to the claims of the heirs of Uriah Jones. 7-Memorial from <u>citizens of Gtwn</u>, D C, remonstrating against any bridges being built below the harbor of the town. 8-Select Cmte: bill for the relief of Capt Langdon C Easton, assist quartermaster U S army. 9-Cmte of Claims: bill for the relief of the heirs & excs of Saml Priolean, with a report. 10-Cmte on Revolutionary Claims: adverse reports on the memorials of Abraham Hunt; adms of Jos Torry; Wm Johannet; the heirs of Wm Rusewurn; & the heirs of Dr John Morgan. 11-Cmte on Military Affairs: bill for the relief of Sally T B Cochran, widow of the late Lt R E Cochran, U S Army. Same cmte: bill for the relief of the heirs & reps of Col A G Moran, with a report. 12-Cmte on Private Land Claims: bill for the relief of Mrs Eliz C Smith, of Missouri, with a report. [This lady served as a private in the Mexican war until her sex was discovered, when she was discharged. The bill gives her pay up to the time of her discharge & 160 acres of land.] Bill was passed. 13-Bills from the House appropriately referred: relief of-the execs of the late Lt John E Bispham; of Madison Paxton; of Fayette Maury & Robt G Ward; of John O Mears; of Grafton Baker; of Hercules L Dousman; of Benj Rowe; of Chas Staples; of Lemuel Hudson; of Geo S Claflin; of Thos Frazer; of Lyman N Cook; & of Aaron Stafford. 14-Bill to incorporate the <u>Gas Light Co</u> of Gtwn, D C, &, after a brief discussion, it was passed.

Monsignor Edini was a passenger in the steamer which sailed from the port of N Y on Sat for Liverpool.

Valentines! Beautiful assortment of English Valentines for sale. –W C Zantzinger, over Bank of Solden, Withers & Co.

Orphans Court of Wash Co, D C. Letters testamentary on the personal estate of Anne Brooke, late of Wash Co, D C. –Robt C Brooke, exc

WED FEB 8, 1854
Orphans Court of Wash Co, D C. Letters of administration on the personal estate of John Anderson, late of Wash Co, deceased. –Alfred Shucking, adm

Cmder Jas B Cooper, of the U S Navy, died at Haddonfield, N J, on Sunday last, at the advanced age of 93 years. He was a soldier in Lee's Legion in the war of the Revolution, & subsequently was an ofcr in the navy, in which he held the rank of commander at the time of his death. He served in the navy through the war of 1812-1815.

Senate: 1-Memorial from the heirs of Edw Rudd, asking indemnity for slaves carried off by the British during the war of 1812. 2-Ptn from Mary Carlton, widow of a soldier of the Revolution, asking to be allowed a pension under the act of Jul, 1838. 3-Ptn from Barton Ricketson, asking compensation for his services & expenses in removing wrecks at the Delaware breakwater. 4-Ptn from Madalena Van Ness, asking that whatever amount may be found due to her late husband, Cornelius P Van Ness, or whatever other relief Congress may see fit to allow, be paid to her, & not to the administrators on her husband's estate. She represents that at the death of her husband she was left entirely without means, & is now dependent upon her friends for support, & that she has no source from which to expect relief other than her late husband's claim now pending before Congress. 5-Ptn from the heirs of Brig Gen Richd B Mason, asking certain allowances in the settlement of his accounts as civil & military governor of Calif. 6-Cmte on Pensions: bill for the relief of Thos B Parsons. Same cmte: bill for the relief of Amos Knapp. 7-Cmte on Pensions: adverse reports on the ptns of Edw Wheeler; Sophia G Dillingham; & of Claudia Stuart.

Died: on Feb 7, after a brief illness, Maj Thos Fitzpatrick, U S Agent for the Indians on the Upper Platte & Arkansas. His funeral is this morning at 10 o'clock, from Brown's Hotel.

Died: on Feb 2, at his residence in Leesburg, Va, Thos S Dorrell, in his 49th year.

Died: George Horace Ellicott, son of Fanny A & Jas P Ellicott, aged 2 years & 8 months. His funeral is on Wed at 2 o'clock, from his father's residence on D st, between 6th & 7th sts. [No death date given.]

Family Groceries, H H Voss, [successor to C R Byrne,] corner of 10th & Pa ave.

THU FEB 9, 1854
Hon J Wright Gordon, formerly Lt Govn'r of Michigan, came to his death at Pernambuco, in Dec last, in consequence of an accidental fall from a balcony.

Mrd: on Feb 7, at Ryland Chapel, by Rev Mr Hodges, John R Elvans to Georgianna Thompson, all of Wash City.

Mrd: on Feb 7, in Wash City, by Rev G W Samson, Mr Henry West to Miss Catharine Miller, both of Wash City.

Died: on Feb 8, Richard Coxe, son of Alex'r & Mary G Mahon, aged 5 years & 6 months. His funeral will take place today at 2 o'clock, from the residence of his father, near Washington.

Died: on Wed, in Wash City, Mr John Sergeant, in his 53rd year. As a kind husband & father, the deceased was endeared to a large family circle, & as a citizen an upright man, faithful in all the relations of life. His funeral will be on Fri at 2 o'clock, from his late residence on E st, near 10th.

Public sale: by order of the Orphans' Court of PG Co, the subscriber, as administratrix of Wallace Kirkwood, late of said county, deceased, will offer, on Feb 10, at the late residence of said deceased, the personal property of which the said Wallace Kirkwood died seized & possessed: horses, cattle, sheep, hogs, farming utensils, & furniture. –Mary Jane Kirkwood, admx of W Kirkwood

A young man, Geo Edwards, while skating upon the Schuylkill, near Phil, on Wed, broke through the ice & was drowned. His wife was in the vicinity & saw her husband sink without being able to render any assistance.

FRI FEB 10, 1854
Senate: 1-Ptn from the descendants of John Laboutte, of the Revolution, asking to be allowed bounty land & commutation pay. 2-Ptn from Thos B Eastland, late quartermaster in the army in the war with Mexico, asking to be credited an amount of money disallowed by the Gov't in the settlement of his accounts & compensation for the performance of certain services not in the line of his duty. 3-Ptn from Jno H Thompson & others, composing a volunteer company raised under a call from Maj Gen Gaines during the war with Mexico, asking to be allowed the pay due them under said call, & from Jno H Thompson, asking payment for provision & provender furnished to a complement of mounted men raised under the like call from Maj Gen Gaines. 4-Documents presented in support of the claim of Nannie Denman for a pension. 5-Ptn from Eliz Summers, widow of Cornelius Summers, who served in the last war with Great Britain as a substitute for a man named Gray, asking to be allowed bounty land. 6-Ptn from Geo Mattingly, asking the U S to confirm his title to square 495, erroneously sold by the Crop of Wash for taxes & purchased by him. 7-Ptn from the heirs & reps of Col Geo Gibson, a Revolutionary ofcr, asking to be allowed commutation pay. 8-Cmte on Revolutionary Claims: act for the relief of Abigail Stafford. 9-Cmte of Claims: bill for the relief of Benedict J Hurd, accompanied by a report. 10-Ptn of Benj Campt, of Othego Co, N Y, praying Congress to grant him bounty lands for naval services in the Revolutionary war of the U S. 11-Memorial of A Kintring, of Phil, asking compensation for revenue services performed. 12-Memorial of W H Wurick, praying for compensation for services & mileage as Lt in the 1st Regt N Y volunteers.

Circuit Court for Worcester Co: in Chancery. Geo W Landing vs John H Powell & others. The suit is to procure a decree for the sale of the real estate of Arthur M Powell, late of said county, deceased, for the payment of his debts. Arthur died intestate, in 1853, indebted to the cmplnt in the sum of $700 debt, & $5.53 & a third cents costs, with interest from Nov 11, 1848, for which a judgment was rendered in Worcester Co Court Nov 15th, 1848; that the administration of said Arthur's personal estate was committed to John H Powell, & that it is insufficient for the payment of his debts. Previous to his death the said Arthur contracted with Wheatley D Barnes for the sale of all his lands in said county, & that the provisions of said contract were not complied with by said Arthur in his lifetime; nor have they been by his heirs at law since his death, though, the time therein limited for compliance hath long since elapsed, & that the said Wheatley D Barnes, hath abandoned said contract & declines to enforce its provisions. The following persons are heirs at law of said Arthur, to wit: John H Powell, Jackson B Powell, Robt W Powell, & Francis Powell, now residents of Md, & Ann Jones, wife of Mager Jones, of Worcester Co, all of whom are of the full age of 21 years, except Francis Powell, who is an infant. Absent dfndnts are to appear in this Court, in person or by solicitor, on or before the 3rd Tue of August next. –Edw D Martin, Court of Worcester Co. [Sep 30th newspaper: absent dfndnts to appear in this Court, in person or by solicitor, on or before the 3rd Tue of Feb, 1855.]

Orphans Court of Wash Co, D C. Letters testamentary on the personal estate of Henry Hoffman, late of Wash Co, deceased. –Saml Bacon, Peter F Bacon, excs

Toledo, Ohio, Feb 7. The boarding house destroyed by fire here yesterday was occupied by about a dozen persons. Two men, Howard & Busby, & 2 females, one a Miss Stacy, & the other a daughter of Mr Murphy, aged 10 years, perished in the flames. Mr & Mrs Murphy, the keepers of the house, together with a 4 year old child, were badly burnt. Mrs Murphy's injuries, it is feared, will prove fatal.

Phil, Feb 9. The well-known novel writer, Geo Lippard, died in this city this morning.

Mrd: on Feb 9, by Rev A G Marlett, Wm Y Robinson, of Balt, Md, to Matilda F Watson, of Wash City.

Mrd: on Feb 9, by Rev Jesse T Peck, Mr Peter F Kessler, of Pa, to Miss Sylvia Peck, of Wash.

Mrd: on Feb 7, at the F st Presbyterian Church, by Rev Jas R Eckard, Clifford Evans to Miss Mary Jane, daughter of Geo M Dale, all of Wash City.

Died: on Feb 9, Mr Chas F Adams, of the Nat'l Theatre. His funeral is this afternoon, at 3 o'clock, from the Wash Infirmary.

Trustee's sale of part of square 546 at auction: on Mar 14 next, in front of the premises, by deed of trust from Joel W Jones & wife, dated Sep 26, 1848, recorded in Liber J A S #1, folios 53 thru 61, of the land records of Wash Co, D C: all of lot 19 & part of lots 18 & 20 in square 546, with the improvements thereto belonging. -Walter Lenox, Henry Naylor, trustees -Green & Scott, aucts

SAT FEB 11, 1854
Trustee's sale of square of ground at auction: on Feb 21, on the premises, by deed of trust from Geo W McLane & wife, dated May 8, 1853, recorded in Liber J A S 56, folios 161 & 163, of the land records of Wash Co: all that piece of ground & premises numbered square 475. –Nich Callan, trustee -Jas C McGuire, auct

Senate: 1-Memorial of Saml Colt, asking an extension of his patent for certain improvements in fire arms. He shows that he never began to enjoy benefit from his invention until 1850, & an extension of 7 years more will enable him to perfect his fire-arm. 2-Cmte on Private Land Claims: bill for the benefit of the heir-at-law of Lt C A Wickliffe, asking its immediate consideration: passed.

House of Reps: 1-Private bills passed: relief of-Wm B Edwards; of Anthony G Willis, deceased; of Harriet Leavenworth, widow of the late Brvt Brig Gen Leavenworth.

Mrd: on Feb 8, in Gtwn, by Rev J M P Atkinson, Boudinot S Louey, of Balt, Md, to Miss Nannie, daughter of the late Geo French, of D C.

Died: on Feb 8, Elexius Simms, in his 58th year. His remains will be conveyed from his late residence, F & 13th sts, to St Patrick's Church, on Feb 11, at 10 o'clock, when mass of requiem will be sung.

Died: on Thu, after a lingering illness, Mrs Eliza Trego, trusting in her Saviour, aged 62 years. Her funeral will take place today at 2 o'clock, from the residence of Mr Henry Weaver, on the Heights of Gtwn.

Died: on Feb 6, Fanny, 2nd daughter of L B & Augusta L Hardin, aged 1 year, 9 months & 16 days.

Died: on Feb 8, in N Y, Georgeann, aged 14 years, eldest child of Lt D D & Georgeann Porter.

Desirable estate for sale: by decree of the Circuit Court for PG Co, Md, sitting in equity, the subscriber, as trustee, will offer at public sale, at Beltsville, on Mar 3, the real estate of the late Thos Parker. It contains 420 acres, about 12 miles from Wash, with a good dwlg house & other necessary out-houses. –C C Magruder, trustee

Trustee's sale: public auction at the court-house at Brentsville, Prince Wm Co, Va, on Mar 15, by deed of trust from Chas A Vocke, dated Jan 14, 1852, all of the parcels of ground in said county, called **Giliad**, 395 acres, more or less; the other called **Gray's Tract**, containing 184 acres, more or less; for a more particular description, reference may be had to a deed from John Gibson to A Arena, dated Feb 2, 1846, of the records of the clerk of Pr Wm Co, with the bldgs & improvements thereon. –H B Sweeny, Nich Callan, trust

Emma E Berry offers for sale her dwlg house & lot on Capitol Hill, Wash. There are also on the premises a carriage-house, stable, & wood-house, all in good repair. The lot contains an acre of land. Apply to Emma E Berry, at the residence of John Moore, on F st, between 9th & 10th sts.

MON FEB 13, 1854

Michl Jennings, charged with the murder of Mrs Esther Bradley, of North Haven, on Jul 24 last, has been convicted in the Superior Court at New Haven of murder in the first degree. Jennings is only 18 years of age.

Orphans Court of Wash Co, D C. Sale of a large stock of groceries, furniture, & fancy goods, on Feb 14, the personal effects of the late J A King, on 2nd & Fayette sts. –John H King, adm -E S Wright, auct

Henry E Stevens, manager of the Bowery Theatre, N Y, died on Tue from injuries received while wrestling with Wm H Hamilton.

Died: on Feb 10, Jas A Lenman, in his 84th year. His remains will be conveyed from his late residence, on 11th st, between G & H sts, to St Matthew's Church, this morning, at 10 o'clock, when mass of requiem will be sung.

Died: on Feb 11, in Wash City, Mrs Mgt Johnston, aged 77 years. Her funeral will take place this morning at 11 o'clock, from the residence of her son-in-law, Saml Kirby, on 8th st, between D & E sts.

Died: on Feb 11, after a long & painful illness, Richd Ayton, in his 39th year. His funeral will be from his late residence on 8th st, between D & E, [Island] on Tue at half-past 2 o'clock.

Died: on Feb 8, at New Orleans, in his 30th year, Phineas Janney, 3rd son of the late Jonathan Janney, of Alexandria, Va.

Died: on Feb 11, George Henry, infant son of John H & Adelaide Buthmann.

Orphans Court of Wash Co, D C. Letters of administration on the personal estate of Robt H Caffee, late of the State of Ohio, deceased. –Chas H Cragin, adm

Genr'l Land Ofc, Feb 10, 1854. A report has been received at Iowa City, Iowa, that their ofc was entered on Jan 19 last, & military land warrants abstracted therefrom being a part of those located during the month of Dec previous. –John Wilson, Com'r of 160 acre Warrants; Act of 1847.

Name of warrantee	Name of locaters
Robt H Richardson	John Terry
Henry Thompson	John Terry
Alfred Williams	Jas Darcy
Irene Jenkins et al	Frederic Sanxay
Patrick McGuire	Frederic Sanxay
Saml Dunlap	Chas H Berryhill
Moses C Teel	Alfred Lauderback

Act of 1830:

Moses M Matlock	Chas H Berryhill
Robt Mitchell	John Terry
Joel H Angley	John Terry
John Allison	David McCartney
Wm Sharp	Richd J Gatling
Turner G Morehead	Richd Gatling
Timothy P Andrews	Jas L Patterson
Jacob Markle	Jas L Patterson

80 acre Warrants
Act of 1850:

Wm Bledrod	Elisha F Clark
Geo Birdwell	Elisha F Clark
Sarah Straw	Geo W Stoner
Washington Weems	Richd Watson
Chas Edw Minor	Edw Tauburan
Peyton Edwards	Jas H Gower
John Lovell	Danl L Hoover
Abraham Wisner	Danl L Hoover
Henry Holsteen	Wm J Gatling
Susannah Pagnad	Jas H Gower
Alex'r Crockett	John C Culbertson
Catharine Hooper	Jas S Easley
Epaph Y Wimbish	Jas S Easley
Saml Jose	Turner B Switzer
Abraham March	John O Sargent
Hardy F Menhall	Geo Greene

Act of 1852:

Isaac Price	Louis A Macklet
Jesus Martin	Mark Howard

40 acre Warrants
Act of 1850:
Thos Ash
Matt'w C Williamson
So do dune Harjo
Mary Varick
To-wah we ke
Oke-fuike Harjo
Chah-yah-yep-kah
Mary Eliza Rowland
Jacob Hummel
Ann Morris
Julia A Searles et al
Lydia Osman/Orman
Jos Woods
Ann Singles
Eliz Davidson
Stephen D Hutchins
Chandler H Tucker
John F Richardson
Jacob R Fertig
Peola Osler
Reuben Westberry
Eliz Cantrill
John Morganthall
Mary Woods
Simon Canaway
Jas Parker
Rebecca Curry
Eliz Thompson
Eliz Christian
Judith McGinnis
Francis Allen
Rebecca Wilkins
Wm Chenery, jr
Jas Pitler
Randolph B Marcy
Echo Kmarthla
Jas Williams
Act of 1852:
Thos A White
Geo W Wingate
Jas L McLure
Francis A Parks

Louis A Mackleet
John C Culbertson
John M Chandler
Frederic Sanxay
Frederic Sanxay
Chas H Berryhill
Chas H Berryhill
Frederic Sanxay
Hugh D Downey
Wm W Willingham
Julia A Searles et al
Ebenezer Cook
John W Howe
Isaac Gregory
Danl Walrad
John O Sargent
John O Sargent
Jeremiah Plympton
Judson Jaqua
John L Clark
Hugh D Downey
Edw Connelly
Jas R Weagley
Jas Woods
Valentine C Woods
Edw Connelly
Geo L Fifield
Jas H Gower
Jas S Easley
Jas S Easley
Francis Allen
Anderson H McClure
John O Sargent
Jeremiah Plympton
Fred'k Sanxay
Stephen G Levermore
Joshua Williams

Ebenezer Cook
Hugh D Downey
Chas H Berryhill
Jas H Gower

Julius Cent__
Jos Chase
Christopher Meaders
Jos Whalin
David C Craig

Chas H Berryhill
Wm J Gatling
John C Culbertson
Edw Connelly
Geo B Sargent

Appointments by the Pres, by & with the advice & consent of the Senate.
Envoy Extra & Minister Pleni:
Peter D Vroom, of N J, to Prussia
Solon Borland, of Arkansas, to Central America
Wm Trousdale, of Tenn, to Brazil
Minister Resident at Constantinople: Carroll Spence, of Md
Com'r of the Kingdom of Hawaii: David L Gregg, of Ill
Charge d'Affaires to Venezuela: Chas Eames, of D C
Sec of Legation:
John Cripps, of Calif, to Mexico
Danl E Sickler, of N Y, to London
Jas C Marriott, of Md, to Peru
R Augustus Erving, of Conn, to Russia
O Jennings Wise, of Va, to Prussia
Agent for the Indians in Oregon Territory: Josiah L Parish, of Oregon, vice J M Garrison, resigned.
Wm P Davis, of Ill, to be Register of the Land Ofc at Danville, Ill, vice R S Molony, resigned.
John G Reardon, of Fla, to be Receiver of Public Moneys at Newnansville, vice Saml Surrell, deceased.
Wm H Garret, of Ill, to be Agent for the Creeks, vice Wm H Raiford, removed.
Douglas H Cooper, of Miss, to be Agent for the Choctaws, vice Wm Wilson, removed.
Benj B French, to be Com'r of Public Bldgs, vice Wm Easby, resigned.
Charge d'Affaires:
J J Seibels, of Ala, to Belgium
Jas S Green, of Missouri, to New Granada
August Belmont, of N Y, to the Netherlands
Henry R Jackson, of Ga, to Austria
Henry Bedinger, of Va, to Denmark
Philo White, of Wisc, to Ecuador
John M Daniel, of Va, to Sardinia
John W Dana, of Maine, to Bolivia
Robt Dale Owen, of Indiana, to Naples

U S Patent Ofc, Wash, Feb 11 1854. Ptn of Saml Blatchford, adm of Orlando Jones, deceased, of Auburn, N Y, praying for the extension of a patent granted to said Orlando

Jones on Apr 30, 1840, for an improvement in the manufacture of starch, for 7 years from the expiration of said patent which takes place on Apr 30, 1854.
–Chas Mason, Com'r of Patents

Stolen, from the Farm of Capt Wm A T Maddox, [formerly Mr Marshal's,] 1½ miles above Gtwn, on Feb 8, a fine Buffalo Cow, with calf, & giving milk. $5 for delivery of same & $20 for evidence as will convict the thief. –Jas Towles, for Capt Wm A T Maddox, U S M.

TUE FEB 14, 1854
Senate: 1-Bills from the House referred to appropriate cmtes: relief of-Wm B Edwards; of the heirs of Anthony O Willis, deceased; & of Harriet Leavenworth, widow of the late Bvt Brig Gen Leavenworth. 2-Ptn from Jeremiah Simons & Jos Penby, prisoners confined at Dartmoor, England, during the late war with Great Britain, asking to be allowed a pension. 3-Ptn from Rebecca P Stansbury & other children of Thos Peters, deceased, asking to be allowed an amount of money equal to the pensions their father & mother would have been entitled to for the services of the former during the war of the Revolution. 4-Cmte of Claims: bill for the relief of John Develin, with a report. 5-Cmte on the Post Ofc & Post Roads: bill for the relief of Ira Day, with a report. 6-Cmte on Pensions: recommended the bills from the House for the relief of Lyman N Cook, & for the relief of Emelie Hooe, widow of Capt Hooe: recommended their passage. 7-Cmte on Pensions: adverse reports on the ptns of Isaac Bowman; of Michl Hennessy; of Mary Anne Moore; of Jacob T Smith; of Thos Conner; & of Sarah Somers Carson.

House of Reps: 1-Bill for the relief of the reps of Pierre Clermont. 2-Bill for the relief of Nathl Ewing, assignee of the interest of H Richard.

A copartnership formed on Feb 1 for the purpose of conducting the Tailoring business in all its various branches, in Moffitt's bldg, east side of 4½ st, near Pa ave. –J R Thompson, A S Carner, late of N Y

On Thu last, the dwlg house of Mr Geo Lowry, near the corner of K & 24th sts, was ransacked & robbed. The whole value of the property taken is less than $100. Mr Lowry was absent in Balt at the time.

Died: on Feb 11, in Balt, of inflammation of the brain, Joseph Anthony Peck, youngest son of John T & Sarah A Mitchell, aged 3 years & 3 months.

Orphans Court of Wash Co, D C. In the case of Thos Baker & Bernard Giveny, excs of Terence Looby, deceased, the execs & Court have appointed Mar 7 next for the final settlement of the estate of the deceased, of the assets in hand.
–Ed N Roach, Reg/o wills

WED FEB 15, 1854
House of Reps: 1-Ptn of John White, of Polk Co, Tenn, asking a pension for services in the Revolutionary war. 2-Memorial of F W Jett, in behalf of other lighthouse keepers, praying for an increase of compensation. 3-Memorial of Robt Johnson, of Phil, asking relief with regard to land warrants purchased by him. 4-Ptn of Thos D Jervey, deputy collector of the port of Charleston, S C, for an increase of salary.

I certify that Mrs Eliz Wood, of Wash Co, 3 miles north of the Capitol, brought before me, as an estray, a large Bay Horse. –C H Wiltberger [Owner is to prove property, pay charges, & take him away. –Eliz Wood, Mount Harmony]

Trustee's sale of valuable bldg lot: by deed of trust from Wm A Williams, dated Jul 23, 1853, recorded in Liber J A S 60, folios 135 & 136, of the land records of Wash Co, D C: sale of lot 24 in square 515, fronting on L st, near 4th st. –A Green, trustee -Green & Scott, aucts

Two lads, aged about 15 & 12 years, sons of Martin White, residing in N Y, while sliding on the ice on the old canal, on Mon, broke through & were drowned.

Wash City Ordinance: 1-Act for the relief of F C Clark: the sum of $14 to be paid him, for the purpose of purchasing of F C Clark 2 copies of Munk's maps of the U S for the use of the Two Boards of this Corp. 2-Joint resolution in relation to St Patrick's burial ground. The Very Rev Wm Matthews be permitted to retain the fence enclosing St Patrick's burial ground in its present position during the pleasure of this Corp.

Appointments by the Pres. by & with the advice & consent of the Senate.
John W Davis, of Indiana, to be Govn'r of the Territory of Oregon.
David Meriwether, of Ky, to be Govn'r of the Territory of New Mexico.
Francis Huebschmaun, of Wisc, to be Superintendent of Indian Affairs for the northern superintendancy, vice E Murray, removed.
Alfred Cumming, of Missouri, to be Superintendent of Indian Affairs in the central superintendency, vice D D Mitchell, removed.
Edw A Bedell, of Ill, to be agent for the Indians in Utah, vice Jacob H Holeman, removed.
David B Herriman, of Indiana, to be agent for the Chippewas, vice John S Watrous, removed.
Henry C Gilbert, of Mich, to be agent for the Indians in Mich, vice Wm Sprague, removed.
Edmund A Graves, to be agent for the Indians in New Mexico, vice Michl Steck, removed.
Andrew J Dorn, of Missouri, to be agent for the Osages, Senecas, Quapaws, & Senecas & Shawnees, vice Wm J J Morrow, removed.

Saml H Culver, of Oregon, to be agent for the Indians in Oregon, vice A A Skinner, removed.
John W Whitfield, of Tenn, to be agent for the Pottawatomies, ____-ink blurred, vice Francis W Lea, resigned.
Dannl Vanderslice, of Ky, to be agent for the Kickapoos, Iowas, Sacs, & Foxes of Missouri, vice Wm P Richardson, removed.
Alfred J Vaughan, of Missouri, to be agent for the Insians on the Upper Missouri, vice Robt B Lambelin, removed.
Robt R Thompson, of Oregon, to be agent for the Indians in Oregon, vice E A Starling, removed.
Benj F Robinson, of Missouri, to be agent for the Shawnees, Munsees, Stockbridges, & others, vice Thos Mosely, jr, removed.
Eli Moore, of N J, to be agent for the Weas, Plankeshaws, Kaskaskias, & other Indians, vice Asbury W Coffee, removed.
Richd G Murphy, of Ill, to be agent for the Sioux of Minnesota, vice Nathl McLean, removed.

Mrd: on Feb 14, by Rev Jas H Brown, Mr Jas H Shreve to Miss Frances Ann Sewell, both of Wash.

Mrd: on Feb 14, by Rev Jas H Brown, Mr Henry Hammond to Miss Rebecca Stallions, all of Annapolis.

Mrd: on Feb 14, by Rev Rufus Dawes, R B Donaldson to Anna Maria, do G W Hall, of Wash.

Senate: 1-Ptn from Eliza G Townsend, asking a pension on account of the services of her late husband, Maj David S Townsend. 2-Ptn from the reps of Jas Purris, asking to be allowed commutation & bounty land for his services in the war of the Revolution.

Orphans Court of Wash Co, D C. Letters testamentary on the personal estate of John Sergeant, late of Wash Co, deceased. –Adeline Sergeant, excx
+
The Bookbinding Business, conducted by her late husband, on H st, between 9th & 10th sts, will be continued. She has engaged competent assistants for this purpose. -Adeline Sergeant

U S Patent Ofc, Wash, Feb 13, 1854. Ptn of John N Vrooman, of Niskayuna, N Y, praying for the extension of a patent granted to him on Apr 15, 1840, for an improvement in Floating Swing Bridges, for 7 years from the expiration of said patent, which takes place on Apr 15, 1854. –Chas Mason, Com'r of Patents

Died: on Feb 13, Miss Jane Clark, after a short illness. Her funeral will be on Feb 15, at 12 o'clock, from the residence of her father, Mr Robt Clark, PG Co, Md.

THU FEB 16, 1854

House of Reps: 1-Cmte on Invalid Pensions: bill to provide a pension for Jas K Welch, of Fulton Co, N Y, & a bill to provide a pension for David Towle, of Bedford Co, Maine: committed. Same cmte: bill to provide a pension to Capt Thos Porter: read twice. 2-Cmte on Military Affairs: bill for the relief of Allen G Johnson: committed. Same cmte: bill for the relief of Mrs Eliz C Smith, of Missouri, who served as a soldier in the Mexican war, reported the same back without amendment, & it was committed. 3-Cmte on Foreign Affairs: adverse report on the ptn of J R Sands, of the U S Navy. Same cmte: bill for the relief of W D Porter, U S Navy: committed. Same for the bill for the relief of Capt E A F Lavalette: committed. Same cmte: adverse report on the ptn of Mrs Frances A McCauley. 4-Cmte on Invalid Pensions: adverse reports on the ptns of Zachariah Long & Robt Hughes for pensions. Same cmte: bill granting 5 years half pay to the widow of Capt John W Gunnison: committed. Same cmte: bill for the relief of Moses Olmstead: committed. Same cmte: bill for the relief of Mary C Hamilton: committed. Same cmte: adverse reports on the ptn of John Morrison, of N Y; of W F Curry; of Susan Worth; & of O H Whitney & others. Same cmte: adverse report on the ptns of Leaman Gibbs, of Wisc, & of Libeas H Babb, of N H.

Mr C G Baylor, of the Balt Times, has become sole editor & proprietor of that young but already prominent & influential journal. It is now an afternoon paper instead of a morning paper.

Appointments by the Pres, by & with the advice & consent of the Senate.
Consuls of the U S:
Geo M Chase, of Maine, for Lahaina, in the kingdom of Hawaii
Chas L Denman, of Calif, for Acapulco, Mexico
Geo R Dwyer, of Mass, for Mozambique
Geo H Goundie, of Pa, for Zurich, Switzerland
Wm Hart, jr, of Calif, for Port Louis, in the Isle of France
Philip T Heart, of N Y, for Glasgow, Scotland
Thos H Hyatt, of N Y, for Amoy, China
Wm Hildebrand, of Wisc, for Bremen
Duncan K McRae, of N C, for Paris
Jas McDowell, of Ohio, for Leith, Scotland
John T Pickett, of Ky, for Vera Cruz, Mexico
Robt G Scott, of Va, for Rio de Janeiro, Brazil
Jas M Tarleton, of Ala, for Melbourne, Austrailia
Thos M Ward, of Texas, for Panama, in New Granada
Edw Worrell, of Delaware, for Matanzas, in Cuba

Franklin Pierce, Pres of the U S A, recognizes Jas Denoon Reymert, who has been appointed Vice-Consul of Sweden & Norway for the State of Wisconsin.
–Feb 11, 1854

Senate: 1-Cmte on Naval Affairs: bill for the relief of John O Mears: passed. Same cmte: adverse report on the memorial of John C F Salomon. 2-Cmte of Claims: asked to be discharged from the further consideration of the memorial of Elijah H Weed, & that it be referred to the Cmte on Naval Affairs: agreed to. 3-Cmte on Naval Affairs: bill for the relief of Otway H Berryman. Also, a bill for the relief of Capt F Voorhees, of the U S Navy, with a report in each case.

The last intelligence from Texas announced the death of Alex'r Somerville, U S Collector at Salina, who was drowned in attempting to land from a boat at night. Mr Somerville was a native of PG Co, Md, where he had many relatives & friends.

FRI FEB 17, 1854
Senate: 1-Ptn from the heirs of Capt Wm Henry Allen, late of the U S navy, asking renumeration for important services rendered during the late war with Great Britain, & payment of prize money for vessels in the capture of which he was engaged. 2-Ptn from Mary Tasker, widow of a Revolutionary soldier, asking a pension. 3-Ptn from J Doly, a Revolutionary soldier, asking to be allowed a pension. 4-Ptn from Jas Robertson, asking indemnity for his arrest & imprisonment without cause by Robt Beale, late Sgt-at-Arms of the Senate. 5-Cmte on Foreign Relations: bill for settling the claim of the legal reps of Richd W Meade, with a report. 6-Bill for the relief of passed Midshipmen Geo P Welsh & Chas H Wells: passed. 7-Bill to confirm the title of Chas G Guster: passed.

House of Reps: 1-Cmte on Revolutionary Claims-committed: relief of Danl Bedinger's heirs; of Col John H Stone's heirs; of the legal reps of Col Willis Ridick, deceased. Same cmte: asked to be discharged from the further consideration of the ptn of Isaac Bowman, & to refer it to the Sec of the Interior for liquidation: committed. 2-Cmte on Invalid Pensions: adverse reports on the ptns of Danl B Lewis; of Reuben Apperson; of Chas Bemus; of Henry Jackson; of Ephraim Sharp; of Lee H Thomas; of Peter Frost; of Geo Williams; of Judith Taylor, widow of Capt John Taylor; & of John Sleven. Same cmte: bill for the relief of J M Lewis; of Wm Mayo, of Maine; of Jesse R Faulkner, of Missouri; of Albra Tripp; & of Jas Walsh: committed. 3-Cmte of Claims: bill for the relief of Gen John E Wool, & a bill for the relief of legal reps of Col Francis Vigo, deceased: committed. Same cmte: adverse report on the ptn of John T Ball, for extra pay for services rendered in the ofc of the Clerk of the House of Reps.

Mrs Cain & her daughter were drowned a few days since, in the West Fork river, Va, by the upsetting of a canoe.

Mr Foster Bosworth, the Postmaster of Troy, N Y, has been arrested on a charge of having embezzled $8,000 of the public money.

House of Reps: 1-Memorial of Chas J Porcher, acting purser U S navy, for compensation.

<u>Increase of pay to the Army: proposed increased rates of pay in lieu of the present:</u>
Maj Gen-$265 per month
Brig Gen-$165 per month
Colonel-$135 per month
Lt Col-$115 per month
Major-$95 per month
Capt of cavalry-$85 per month
Capt of artl & infty: $75 per month
1st lt of cavalry-$65 per month
1st lt of artl & infty-$57 per month
2nd lt of cavalry-$55 per month
2nd lt of artl & infty-$47 per month
a cadet-$33 per month
a sgt maj, quartermaster sgt, principal musician, chief bugler, principal farrier, & ordnance sgt-$23 per month
to each 1st sgt of a company of dragoons, mounted riflemen, artl, & infty-$21 per month
to all other sgt of those arms-$18 per month
a cpl of dragoons & mounted riflemen-$14 per month
a cpl of artl & infty-$18 per month
A farrier, blacksmith, saddler, & artificer of dragoons, mounted riflemen, & artl-$15 per month
bugler of dragoons & mounted riflemen-$12 per month
A musician of artl & infty-$11 per month
A private of dragoons & mounted riflemen-$11 per month
A private of artl & infty-$10 per month

Died: on Feb 15, at her residence, in Gtwn, Mrs Emily Corcoran, relict of the late Col Thos Corcoran, aged 44 years. Her funeral will take place today at 4 o'clock.

Died; on Feb 16, Charles Gilbert, youngest son of Johanna & Isaac Hill. His funeral will take place this afternoon, at 4 o'clock, from the residence of his father, 9th st.

U S Patent Ofc, Wash, Feb 16, 1854. Ptn of Saml F B Morse, of Poughkeepsie, N Y, praying for an extension of a patent granted to him on Jun 20, 1840, for an improvement in the mode of communicating information by signals by the application of electro magnetism, for 7 years from the expiration of the said patent, which takes place on Jun 20, 1854. –Chas Mason, Com'r of Patents

Mrd: on Feb 14, by Rev Mr Pyne, Henry D Johnson to Mary, youngest daughter of Col J J Abert.

SAT FEB 18, 1854
Senate: 1-First bill on the calendar was for the relief of Hodges & Lansdale & the legal reps of Rinaldo Johnson & Ann E Johnson: Mr Shields argued against the bill on the ground that it would be dangerous to carry the principle of paying for property destroyed by the enemy to the extent contemplated by the bill: postponed. 2-Bill for the relief of Campan: passed. 3-Bill for the relief of John Devlin: passed. 4-Bill for the relief of John P McEldery: passed.

Mrd: on Feb 16, in Phil, by Rev P G Mayer, Wm Clabaugh, of Gtwn, D C, to Mary A, daughter of John Buddy, of the former place.

Mrd: on Feb 16, in the Church of the Epiphany, by Rev J W French, Dr Wm B Magruder to Sarah, eldest daughter of the late Abraham Van Wyck, of Wash City.

Mrd: on Feb 16, in Wash City, by Rev Mr Hodges, John A Thompson to Miss Eliz M Turtin, both of PG Co, Md.

Died: on Feb 17, Mr Robt Cammack, in his 23rd year, son of Mr Wm Cammack. His funeral is tomorrow at 3 o'clock, from his father's residence, above Gtwn.

Mr Armstrong, proprietor of the Wash Union, announced in yesterday's number, he has associated with him the Hon A O P Nicholson in the management of that journal.

Louisville, Feb 16. Dreadful disaster occurred here this morning. The Alton packet **Kate Kearny** exploded her boiler at her wharf this morning whilst about starting, killing & wounding a large number of passengers. Some 20 persons may have been killed, & many are supposed to have been drowned. Maj Beall, of the U S Army was among the wounded. He condition is considered dangerous.

MON FEB 20, 1854
The Pandally case in New Orleans, in which Mr Geo Pandally brought suit for $20,000 damages against Victor Wilts, for an alleged libel in asserting that he was of negro extraction, has been terminated by verdict for the plaintiff, without damages. The suit has exulted great interest in New Orleans, where both the parties are well known.

Gen Wm Paulding, an old & respected citizen, died on Fri at his seat at Tarrytown, N Y, at the advanced aged of 85 years. He succeeded Stephen Allen as Mayor of N Y C in 1823. In 1825 Philip Hone was chosen in his place. In 1826 Mr Paulding was again chosen, & continued in 1828, when he was succeeded by Walter Bowne.

Hon Robt Strange, formerly a Senator in Congress from N C, died yesterday in Fayetteville, N C.

Appointment by the Pres: John L O'Sullivan, of N Y, to be Charge d'Affaires of the U S in Portugal.

An old lady in Washington, N H, undertook last week to explain the operation of a revolver to her 2 little grandsons, children of Otis Metcalf. She succeeded so well that she lodged a ball in the back of one of them.

Old Soldiers of the War of 1812: convention last evening at the Temperance Temple, North Gay st, of the old patriots who participated in the war of 1812-15. Pres: Hon John Smith Hollins, Mayor of Balt. Vice Presidents:

Gen Benj C Howard	Capt Robt D Milholland
Gen Shepherd C Leakin	Capt John J Laty
Gen Geo H Steuart	Capt Jas Frasier
Gen Anthony Miltenberger	Capt Edw Kenly
Gen John Spear Smith	Capt Alex'r Cummings
Col B W Campbell	Capt Jas Blays
Col Elijah Stansburg, jr	Capt Beverly Diggs
Hon Judge Frick	Capt Lemuel G Taylor
Hon Reverdy Johnson	Capt John Dutton
Hon John P Kennedy	Capt Henry Hilbert, sr
Hon Nathl Williams	Capt John Fosset
Capt John A Webster	Dr Saml B Martin
Capt Andrew E Warner	Dr Michl Diffenderffer
Capt Joel Vickers	

Secs:

Col Nicholas Brewer	Col Henry Myers
Mendes I Cohen	Hoshua Atkinson
Capt John F Hoss	Maj Jas J Archer

Resolutions prepared for the occasion were read by Capt Jas C Marriott. -Baltimore "Clipper" of Friday.

Valuable real estate for sale: lot 11 in square 408, which are three 3 story brick houses. Apply to Thos Purcell, opposite Brown's Hotel, or to the subscriber, on Missouri ave, 3rd door from 4½ st. –Rich G Briscoe

Franklin Pierce, of Pres of the U S A, recognizes Carl F Adam, of Cincinnati, who has been appointed Consul of Nassau for the State of Ohio; Consul of Frankfort on the Mayn for the States of Ohio & Indiana; & Consul at Saxony at Cincinnati, in the State of Ohio. Also, John Leffiers, who has been appointed Consul of Bremen for the Port of Phil, in Pa. –Feb 13, 1854

Mrd: on Feb 16, by Rev Chas A Davis, Mr John F Ritter to Miss Alice Welch, all of Wash City.

Co-partnership formed for the purpose of carrying on the Plumbing business, to the citizens of Wash & Gtwn & vicinities. They can be found at F Y Naylor's old stand, south side of Pa ave, near 3rd st. –Francis Y Naylor, Francis McGhan

Circuit Court of PG Co, Court of Equity. Jas Baden vs Araminta Brooke, Geo W Carroll, De Rosey Carroll, Robt Carroll, John M Martin & America his wife, Chas W Carroll, John Ford & Mary his wife. The object of this suit is to procure a decree for the specific performance of an agreement made between Michl B Carroll, now deceased, & the cmplnt, in relation to the sale of certain real estate thereby made to the said cmplnt by the said Michl B Carroll, on or about the time specified in the bill of complaint; & also to procure a decree for the payment to the complainant of whatever sum may be found justly & equitably due to him from the said Carroll in his lifetime on account of said agreement & the general dealing between them. The bill states that, on or about the day named therein, the said Carroll contracted to sell, & did sell to the complainant, the real estate in the said bill mentioned, & upon the terms therein named; that the complainant hath long since during the lifetime of the said Carroll, more than paid & satisfied the whole purchase money for the said land to the said M B Carroll, & that the said Carroll frequently promised to execute the necessary deed or deeds to carry out the said contract of sale, but was prevented from so doing by his sudden death; that the said Carroll died on or about Aug, 1851, leaving a last will & testament whereby he constituted his then wife his sole executrix; that she has since deceased, & that letters d b n on the personal estate of the said M B Carroll have been duly granted to 2 of the dfndnts, Geo W Carroll & De Rosey Carroll; & that the heirs at law of the said M B Carroll & Araminta Brooke, [a sister of said deceased, & a resident of PG Co, Md,] Geo W Carroll & De Rosey Carroll, [brothers of said deceased,] & Robt Carroll, America, now the wife of John M Martin, Chas W Carroll, & Mary, the wife of John Ford, children of Chas I Carroll, a deceased brother of the said M B Carroll, all of whom are non-residents. The bill prays that all the said heirs & reps may be made dfndnts thereto, & that an order of publication may be passed requiring said non-resident dfndnts to appear in this court on or before the 2nd Monday in Jul next. –Owen Norfolk, clerk of the Circuit Court of PG Co, Md.

TUE FEB 21, 1854
Wash Corp: 1-Ptn of John Atchison; of Jos B Moore; & of Michl O'Brien: for the remission of a fine: referred to the Cmte of Claims. 2-Ptn of Vincent Masi & others for the grading & gravelling of 13th st: referred to the Cmte on Improvements. 3-Ptn of Mrs Louisa J Wadsworth, asking to be paid for injuries done by a change of grade in front of her property in square 284: referred to the Cmte on Improvements.

Died: on Feb 20, at the residence of J C Rives, near Wash City, of chronic inflammation of the brain, L Huntington Young, in his 49th year, eldest son of the late Col Guilford D Young, of Troy, N Y.

Senate: 1-Ptn from the executor of Reading Beatty, asking an increase of the pension allowed his father for services as surgeon in the war of the Revolution. 2-Memorial from Citizens of N Y, remonstrating against the renewal of Cyrus H McCormick's patent for improvements in reaping machines. 3-Memorial from Ralph King, late U S consul at Bremen, asking compensation for services rendered the U S during the years 1851, 1852, & 1853, & also for allowance of a balance due to a circular from the Dept. 3-Cmte on Private Land Claims: bill for the relief of Jos Smith; & of John S Wilson: both with a report. 4-Cmte on Pensions: recommended their passage-relief of Hezekiah Johnson, of Bridgewater, Vt; of Mary Deany; of Aaron Stafford; & of a pension for Silas Champion, of Genesee Co, N Y. Same cmte: adverse report on the ptn of Geo Fitzsimmons. 5-Cmte on Pensions: recommended their passage: relief of Harriet Leavenworth, widow of the late Brvt Brig Gen Leavenworth; of Wm B Edwards; & of Mary Carlton. Same cmte: adverse report to the claim of the children of Leonard Proctor: which was agreed to. 6-Cmte on Military Affairs: adverse report on the memorial of Benj S Roberts: which was agreed to. 7-Cmte on Naval Affairs: bill for the relief of Cmder G J Pendergrast, with a report.

Massacre of Capt Gunnison. Great Salt Lake City, Nov 30, 1853. On Oct 23 the late Capt J W Gunnison visited Fillmore city to get a $500 check cashed, which was done by Mr L P Hoyt. At this time he was fully informed of the Meadow creek Indians affair, & the then hostile feelings of the three sons. Capt G expressed strong indignation at the conduct of the emigrant part, & remarked that no difficulty had occurred between his party & the Indians they had met, & manifested much confidence in his ability to preserve peaceful relations with the red men. Oct 28-Brvt Capt R M Morris, with part of his command, rode into Fillmore city & stated that Capt Gunnison & 7 of his party had been killed by the Indians on the Sevier river; that he had just come from the scene of the massacre, but had left the dead unburied, as he had no tools on hand suitable for digging. He wished Mr Anson Call to use the best efforts in his power to recover the instruments, note-books, horses, & other Govn't property taken by the Indians. On Nov 1, Mr Dimock B Huntington, interpreter for Indian Agent E A Bedell, left my ofc for Capt Morris' camp, having 2 guards & a sufficient quantity of Indian presents, with a requisition for men & horses on the route, & to use all possible skill & diligence. On Nov 2, Mr Huntington met Capt Morris & party on their way here to quarter for the winter. Mr Huntington reached Fillmore city on Nov 3, & on the 4th dispatched Mr Call, with 2 friendly Indians & 9 men, to bring in the remains of Capt Gunnison & Mr Potter & bury the rest on the spot. Three graves were then dug, in one of which the remains of Creutzfeldt were deposited, in another those of Kern & those of Bellows, & the 3 soldiers were deposited together. –Brigham Young

Died: on Feb 15, at West River Landing, Md, Andrew Coyle Gibbs.

All persons indebted to the estate of the late W H Peaco are to make settlement before or on Mar 6 next. –Ruth A Peaco, John W Chew, excs [Mr J Wesley Etchison is duly authorized to receipt for us as the excs of Wm H Peaco, late of Wash, deceased. -Ruth A Peaco, J W Chew, excs]

South Branch Land for sale: the subscriber, designing to change his residence to one of the Western States, offers for private sale his Farm, lying upon the South Branch of the Potomac, 4 miles above Moorefield, containing 550 acres. Improvements consist of a spacious Brick Mansion of recent construction & in modern style, with necessary out-bldgs. –Solomon C Vanmeter, Moorefield, Hardy Co, Va.

WED FEB 22, 1854

Washington resigned the Presidency in 1797; returned to Mt Vernon & employed Albin Rawlins, a young man, recommended by Gov Spotswood, to copy into a large book certain letters & papers that would be prepared for such purpose. The letters were delivered to Rawlins by the Chief in person. A portion of the letters of the Rawlins' Book were of a delicate character & are no where to be found. The ancient family vault having fallen into a state of decay, the Chief marked out a spot for a family burial place during the last days at Mount Vernon. [Col Monroe, when President of the U S, order 2 crypts or vaults to be formed in the basement story of the centre of the Capitol for the reception of the remains of the Chief & his consort, which vaults are untenanted to this day.] Mrs Washington had the only right to the disposal of the remains of the Chief. On her death-bed the venerable Lady called the author of the Recollections, her grandson & executor, to her side, & said, Remember, Washington, to have my remains placed in a leaden coffin, that they may be removed with those of the General at the command of the Gov't. Washington ceased to be a sportsman after 1787, when he gave up the hunting establishment. True, he bred the blood horse, & a favorite colt of his named Magnolia, was entered & ran for a purse, but this was more to encourage the breeding of fine horses than from any attachment to the sports of turf. Mount Vernon, in the olden times, was celebrated for luxuries of the table. Father Jack, an African negro, 100 years of age, with his light canoe, was the fisherman to the establishment. His body was greatly enfeebled but his mind possessed uncommon vigor. A hunter, Tom Davis & his great Newfoundland dog, Gunner, were important characters in the dept for furnishing game & wild fowl. Geo Washington Lafayette, & his tutor & friend M Frestel, became members of the family during the last days. These estimbable Frenchmen, driven by persecution from their native country, found refuge in America. While reasons of State prevented Washington as Pres from receiving émigrés, so soon as he became the private citizen he warmly welcomed to his heart & his home the son of his old companion in arms, the young Lafayette. [Arlington House, Feb 21, 1854. The story of the Last Letters of the Rawlins' Book I have put off to the last. It is a painful subject to me, but it was bounden duty upon me, was Washington's Biographer & the last of his domestice family to place this matter in the only light in which it can ever appear to the world. Faithfully yours, G W P Custis to Messrs Gales & Seaton.]

Senate: 1-Ptn from the heirs of Richd Kidder Meade, asking to be allowed commutation pay. 2-Ptn from Gold H Rogers, late Charge d'Affaires of the U S to Sardinia, asking to be allowed arrears of compensation. 3-Ptn from A Kintsing, late special examiner of drugs at Phil, asking extra compensation for performing the duties of one of the assistant appraisers at that port. 4-Ptn from Mary S Maffit, asking an indemnity for the destruction of property by the enemy in the last war with Great Britain. 5-Ptn from E M Gregory & others, asking that a grant of land may be made to aid in the construction of a railroad from Cincinnati to Mackinaw. 6-Cmte of Claims: House bill for the relief of the execs of the late Lt John E Bispham, reported back the same without amendment. 7-Cmte on Indian Affairs: asked to be discharged from the further consideration of the memorial of Richd Fields, & that of Wm M Ryer.

Hon Stephen A Douglas has been appointed by the Pres of the Senate a Regent of the Smithsonian Institute, in place of the late Senator Charlton.

Army Medical Board convened in N Y C on Dec 1 last for the examination of Assist Surgeons for promotion, & of applicants for appointment in the Medical Staff of the Army, adjourned sine die on Dec 4, after a continuous session of more than 2 months. By this Board the following Assist Surgeons, named according to rank, were examined & found qualified for promotion.

Assist Surgeons:

Wm J Sloan	John F Head
Thos C Madison	Israel Moses
Jos K Barnes	John F Hammond
Levy H Holden	Elisha J Bailey
Chas C Kenney	Geo E Cooper
Robt Murray	Glover Perin

The Board examined & approved the following candidates for appointment in the Medical staff of the Army:

Robt Southgate, of Va	John F Randolph, of Louisiana
Robt L Brodie, of S C	Jas C Herndon, of Va
Dewitt C Peters, of N Y	Geo Taylor, of Md
Albert J Myer, of N Y	John J Gaenslen, of Va
Nathl S Crowell, of S C	Geo Hammond, of Md
Jos R Smith, of N Y	Wm J L'Engle, of Florida
Jas T Ghiselin, of Md	Bernard J D Irwin, of N Y
Pascal A Quinan, of Md	

Mrd: on Feb 14, by Rev Edmund H Waring, the Rev J Wesley Boteler, of the Balt Conference, to Miss Susan H Printz, daughter of Mr Cornelius Printz, of Alleghany Co, Va.

THU FEB 23, 1854
Mrd: on Feb 21, by Rev Mr Wisong, Mr R W Barnaclo to Miss Catherine J Turner, both of Wash City.

Died: on Feb 21, Mrs Julia C Fowler, in her 74th year. Her funeral will be today at 11 o'clock, from the residence of her daughter, Mrs Wainwright, on 2nd st, between B & C sts.

Boston, Feb 22. Augustus Wilber, residing in West Randolph, killed his wife today with an axe; then cut the throats of 7 children, & finally his own.

FRI FEB 24, 1854
Senate: 1-Ptn from Ithiel S Richardson, asking an appropriation to test the practicability of an atmospheric telegraph between Wash & Balt for the conveyance of letters & packages: referred to a select cmte of five. 2-Ptn from Thos Bassuett, asking the attention of Congress to his discoveries, of value to the navigation interests, as disclosed in a work written by him. 3-Ptn from Josiah Tatnall, asking to be indemnified for losses sustained while acting as purser on board the U S ship **Dale** on the coast of Africa. 4-Ptn from Jasper Strong & Geo Terrill, asking authority to construct a railroad from Perdido river to the Bay of Pensacola, near the town of Warrington, in that State. 5-Ptn from Manuel Hernandez, asking to be allowed a tract of land equivalent to that subsequently sold by the U S to another person. 6-Cmte on Military Affairs: bill for the relief of Thos S Russell, with a report. 7-Cmte of Claims: bill for the relief of John Metcalf. 8-Cmte on Pensions: adverse reports on the following bills from the House of Reps:, in each case:-relief of Alton Nelson; of Benj Rowe; of John Hamilton; of Pamela Slavin; of Jeremiah; & of Jos Penly. 8-Cmte of Claims: adverse report on the memorial of the heirs of John Burnham. 9-Cmte on the Post Ofc & Post Roads: adverse report on the memorial of John R Jefferson, of Miss.

The negro woman who poisoned the family of the late Coleman Wingfield, at Richmond, Va, & who drank of the coffee in which the ammonia had been dissolved for the purpose of proving her innocence, has since died of its effects. The family are slowly recovering.

John McElwrath, sentenced to 2 years imprisonment for killing R H Peyton, in Sumner Co, Tenn, has been pardoned by the Govn'r of that State. Mr Elwrath is an old man, was a soldier in the war of 1812, & was badly wounded at the memorial battle at New Orleans.

St Louis Democrat: more on the explosion of the steamer **Kate Kearny**: the sad end of Rev S G Gassaway, pastor of St George's Church in St Louis, will cast a gloom over his large circle of friends; he had taken passage for the East; he was identified by the tie in his cravat. Bt Maj Buell, Adj Gen's Dept, was among the passengers & received severe injuries; he was removed to Planter's House. Maj Guthrin, 7th Infty, also a passenger, escaped by the merest chance without injury. His son, 4 or 5 years of age, was severely injured. His condition is deemed somewhat critical.

Elliot Cresson died on Monday, at his residence in Phil, of erysipelas, after a short illness. He was at the period of his death the Pres of the Pa Colonization Society.

Died: last evening, at his residence in Wash City, Gen Robt Armstrong, proprietor of the Wash Union, aged about 64 years. He died of congestion of the brain, & had been confined at home some 10 or 12 days. He leaves a large family of 6 or 7 children & a wide circle of attached friends to mourn his loss.

Died: on Feb 22, after a long illness, Mr Fred'k Goldsborough, in his 60th year. His funeral will take place today, from his late residence, I & 18th sts, at 1 o'clock.

Died: on Feb 21, at Gtwn, Mrs Sarah Cooper, aged 78 years, a native of England, but for the last 40 years a resident of Md & this District.

Died: on Feb 17, Ann Catherine, youngest child of F W & Mgt E Eckloff, aged 13 months & 16 days.

Died: on Feb 16, in Colebrook, N H, Miss Mary Jane Adams, of Wash, aged 23 years.

N Y, Feb 28. A letter dated Canton, Dec 8, states that the U S ship **Plymouth** had just arrived, & that Lt Matthews, with 14 of the crew, had been lost in a typhoon near Bonin Islands.

Phil, Feb 23. Letter from the Delaware Breakwater, received at the Exchange, states that the storm on Monday night was the severest ever experienced there. The beach is completely strewn with wrecks. 13 vessels are ashore within the new breakwater. One of the crew of the vessel **James Maull** was frozen to death, & 2 of the crew of the vessel **Charles Wood** perished in the rigging.

SAT FEB 25, 1854
Household & kitchen furniture at auction: on Feb 27, at the residence of E M Clark, on the south side of Md ave, between 10th & 11th sts, near Mr D B Clark's Drug store. –Green & Scott, aucts

Executor's sale of valuable improved property: on Mar 1, on the premises: sale of subdivision 3, of original lots 20 & 25, in square 252, improved by a 2 story & attic brick house, on 13th st west, between G & H sts north. By order of Robt C Brooke, exc of Ann Brooke.

The soldiers of the war of 1812 in Wash City, whether residents or visiters, are requested to attend the funeral of Gen Robt Armstrong, which will take place on Sunday, Feb 26, at 3 o'clock.

Mrd: on Feb 23, by Rev Jas H Brown, Mr Wm R Jeffers to Miss Bettie M Hunt, both of Va.

Died: on Feb 17, at Farley, Culpeper Co, Va, Rebecca Parke Farley, wife of Dr Wm N Wellford, & daughter of the late Richd Crobin, of Laneville.

In Chancery: Fred'k L Keller vs Henrietta C Keller & Chas Keller. The trustee reports that he sold the premises in the decree passed on Nov 9, 1847, & J T Cassell was the purchaser of lot 20 for $140.44; that H C Keller was the purchaser of lot 21 for $135.10; the D B Clarke was the purchaser of lot 32 for $151.04; that W Bird was the purchaser of lot 23 for $354.76; that J Knight was the purchaser of lot 19 for $194.63½; that G F Dyer was the purchaser of lot 30 for $158.75; that J H Yeatman was the purchaser of lot 31 for $154.97; that J P Headly was the purchaser of lot 32 for $102.14; & that D Roland, by Geo Mattingly, was the purchaser of lot 18 at 10½ cents per foot: all purchasers have complied with the terms of the sale.
–Jno A Smith, clerk

Senate: 1-Memorial from Geo Stealey, asking remuneration for his services & expenses incurred in visiting the Indians of Calif under direction of the Com'r of Indian Affairs. 2-Cmte on Indian Affairs: bill for the relief of Susan Coody & others. 3-Cmte on Private Land Claims: bill for the relief of Conrad Wheat, jr, or his legal reps. 4-Cmte of Claims: adverse report on the memorial of G A Dabney & others.

House of Reps: 1-Referred: bill for the relief of the heir-at-law of Lr C A Wickliffe; relief of Passed Midshipman Geo P Welsh & Clark H Wells; relief of Jos Campan; of John P McEldery, & of John Devlin.

House to let: the very large, commodious, & elegantly finished House at the corner of 11th & Pa ave being now completed, is offered to let, with the exception of the first floor, occupied by R Farnham. –B Bayliss, Missouri ave, between 4 ½ & 6th sts.

Bailiff's sale: by order of a distrain against the Goods & Chattels of D D French, [at the Irving House,] for rent due & in arrears, I have seized Household & kitchen furniture: sale on Mar 2nd, in front of the Centre Market-house. –A E S Keese, blf

MON FEB 27, 1854
N Y: Wm & Clara Hays have againt been arrested for the murder of Dr Lutener, the grand jury having indicted both for the said murder, although they had been honorably acquitted by the coroner's jury.

New Books: Memoirs of Maj Robt Stobo, of the Va Regt: this is the republication of a little work, issued in England in 1760, giving an account of the remarkable adventures of Stobo in escaping from the French at Quebec. Stobo was born at Glasgow, in Scotland, in 17?. He emigrated in 1750 to Va & became a favorite of Govn'r Dinwidde, also a Scotchman. When the French commenced making encroachments Virginia resolved to raise a regt of soldiers to resist them. Mr Fry was made Col of this regt, Gen Washington Lt Col, & Robt Stobo the senior Capt. Stobo acted as engineer in bldg *Fort Necessity*. Finally, when Washington surrendered, 2 hostages were to be given to the French as sureties for the safe return of some French ofcrs previously taken by Washington. These hostages were Jacob Van Braam, a Dutchman, & Robt Stobo. He was conveyed to *Fort Du Quesne* & confined there for 3 months, & then sent to Quebec. The book is sold in Washington by Mr Franck Taylor for the author.

Mrd: on Feb 21, at Trinity Church, Gtwn, D C, by Rev Mr Pallhuben, Francis Harper to Miss Mary A, only daughter of the late Dennis O'Donnoghue, of that place.

Mrd: on Feb 23, at Elmwood, PG Co, Md, by Rev J N Watson, Geo R H Marshall, of Montg Co, Md, to Miss Eleanor F Marshall, of PG Co, Md.

Died: on Sunday, after a short but severe illness, Mrs Jan Freeman Howard, in her 57th year. Her funeral will be from the residence of her son, Wm E Morcoe, on 6th st, between G & H sts, tomorrow at 11 o'clock.

Died: on Feb 27, Mr Jos Thomas, in his 41st year. His funeral will be today, at 3 o'clock, from his residence, corner of 11th & Water sts, Island.

Died: on Feb 25, in Wash City, Anolphus Henry, infant son of J H B Nowland, of Indiana.

TUE FEB 28, 1854
Splendid warehouse for sale: recently erected on the south side of Pa ave, nearly opposite the Nat'l Hotel. Apply to M G Emery, or J C McKelden, F st, between 6th & 7th sts west.

Dr F A Von Moschysker, Oculist & Aurist, will be in Wash on Fri, for those who wish to consult him on diseases of the Eye & Ear. His ofc is at Mrs W Voss', Pa ave, between 12th & 13th sts.

A young man, Jacob Carbaugh, of Adams Co, Pa, was killed on Thu last by the accidental of a gun.

Mrd: on Feb 26, by Rev J B Donelan, Americus Zappone to Miss Mgt A Joyce, both of Wash City.

Died: on Feb 27, William Thomas, son of Jno F & Annie, Havenner, aged 18 months. His funeral will be this afternoon at 4 o'clock, from the residence of his parents, on 11th st, near Md ave.

Valuable real estate for sale: the subscriber offers his estate called **Greenock**, containing upwards of 800 acres, lying in Culpeper Co, on the Rappahannock river, near the Fauquier White Sulphur Springs. The bldgs are substantial & commodious. Letters may be addressed to the subscriber, Warrenton Springs, Va, or to my atty & agent, B H Shackelford, Warrenton, Va. –Jonas Green

Teacher wanted: to be employed in his family. Need not apply without the best testimonials of moral character & capacity to teach. Address Dr J Waring, Chaptico, St Mary's Co, Md.

WED MAR 1, 1854
Extensive sale of 34 bldg lots, at public auction, on Mar 14, being a part of the *Mansion Square*, the well-known residence of the late Gen Van Ness. This square fronts 444 feet 5 inches on the President's grounds. These lots are generally 25 feet front by 100 deep, running back to a 20 foot alley. Two of the lots are 44 feet 5 inches by 100 feet. 17 lots front on 17th st. If good brick or stone dwlgs, at least 3½ stories high, be erected within 18 months from the day of sale, 20% of the whole purchase money will be deducted from the last payment.

Trustee's sale of valuable property: on Apr 3 next, on the premises, by deed of trust from Jos Peck & wife to the subscriber, dated May 5, 1847, recorded in Liber W B 134, folios 99 thru 102, of the land records of Wash Co, D C: these lots: 7, 22, 23, 24, 25, & 27 in square 106, together with the several dwlg houses to the same belonging. –Js Rhodes, trustee -Green & Scott, aucts

Trustee's sale of valuable improved Island property: on Mar 8, on the premises, by 2 deeds of trust, dated Mar 10, 1853, recorded in Liber J A S 35, folios 43 thru 47, of the land records of Wash Co, D C, & the other dated Dec 14, 1853, recorded in Liber J A S 42, folios 409 thru 413, the north part of lot 30, in square 296, being 27 feet 5 inches on 12th st west, improved by a handsome 3 story dwlg, with back bldg. The property is between Va ave & south C st. All conveyances at expense of purchaser. –Richd H Clarke, Danl Ratcliff, trustees -Green & Scott, aucts

Franklin Pierce, Pres of the U S A, recognizes A Rettberg, who has been appointed Consul of Hanover at Cleveland, in Ohio. –Feb 23, 1854

For rent: a 2 story frame house on the corner of 10th st & N Y ave, a first rate stand for any business. Inquire of Mary A Harvey, on the premises.

Orphans Court of Wash Co, D C. Letters of administration on the personal estate of Hannah Bosten, late of Wash Co, deceased. –Smith Harley, adv

In old papers containing accounts of the progress of the war of 1812, we found a notice of a company of boys who took an active part in the defence of Plattsburg. But a few of them were over the age of 16. They are referred to in one of Gen Macomb's despatches, dated at Plattsburg, Sep 13, 1814. He was so pleased with their gallant bearing that he promised them each a rifle, which promise Congress afterwards redeemed for him. The enemy's loss during the siege of Plattsburg amounted to about 2,500 killed, wounded, prisoners, & deserters. Col Wellington was among the killed. Following is the resolution of Congress authorizing the delivery of rifles promised to Capt Aitkin's volunteers [boys] at the siege of Plattsburg. The Pres of the U S to cause to be delivered to Martin J A Aitkin, Azariah C Flagg, Ira A Wood, Gustavus A Bird, Jas Trowbridge, Hazen Mooers, Henry K Averill, St John B L Skinner, Fred'k P Allen, Hiram Walworth, Ethan Everist, Amos Soper, Jas Patton, Baremus Brooks, Smith Batemen, Melancton W Travis, & Flavel Williams, each one rifle, promised them by Gen Macomb, while commanding the Champlain dept, for their gallantry & patriotic services as a volunteer corps during the siege of Plattsburg in Sep, 1814, on each of which said rifles there shall be a plate containing an appropriate inscription.
-Approved, May 20, 1826

Senate: 1-Cmte on Pensions: bill for the relief of Jas Wormsley. Same cmte: adverse reports on the ptn of Mrs Jane A Wright. 2-Cmte on Indian Affairs: the Sec of the Senate be directed to pay to Richd M Young $974.20, the amount of his per diem & compensation allowed him by the Pres as special com'r for investigation charges against Hon Alex'r Ramsey, late Superintentendent of Indian Affairs of Missouri Territory, under resolution of the Senate of Apr 5, 1853.

Smith Rider, age 12 years, was caught in the machinery of a grist mill at West Poultney, Vt, & literally ground to pieces.

Boarding on I, near 7th st. Mrs Tomlin has 2 vacant rooms, neatly furnished. Apply on the premises, between 6th & 7th sts, north side.

Three boys were drowned in the Pennypack, near Holmesburg, Pa, on Sat. Their names are Jas Saul, 13; Francis H Saul, 8, & Jos F Lawton, aged 10. The ice gave way & they were all precipitated into the water & drowned.

House of Reps: 1-Ptn of Fred'k W Miller, of Erie Co, Pa, late surgeon-2nd regt of Pa volunteers in Mexican war, for an invalid pension. 2-Ptn of Wm Pruitt for a pension.

Mrd: on Feb 27, by Rev J C Smith, D D, Robt H, eldest son of Rev A A Marcellus, of N Y, to Miss E Kate Glover, of Wash.

The Gtwn Municipal elections took place on Monday last. To the Board of Alderman for the ensuing year the following gentlemen were elected, viz:

Evan Lyons
Jos Libbey
Robt Dodge

Geo Waters
Esau Pickrell

To the Board of Common Council:
Walter S Cox
A H Pickrell
Wm McK Osborn
Jeremiah Orme
A H Dodge
Saml Cropley

Richd Jones
David English
John A Grimes
Wm H Tenney
Peter Berry

THU MAR 2, 1854

Grey Mare at auction: on Sat next, in front of Centre Market: sold to me by Mr Elias Davis as sound. I sell her on Mr Davis' account, by order of Mr Thos Fahey.
-John Robertson, auct

The Will of Elliott Cresson, who died on Feb 20, was admitted to record at Phil on Monday, & its items are living evidence of his sincerity & ardent philanthropy. Mr Cresson was but in his 58th year of his age; 2nd senior Vice-Pres of the Pa Colonization Society. He bequeathed $50,000 to the American S S Union; & $77,000 to various other causes. His will bears date Sep 3, 1853. Jacob Cresson, Geo Vaux Bacon, & Wm Coppinger are named as executors. -Ledger

Wash Corp: 1-Ptn of Benedict Jarboe for the remission of a fine: referred to the Cmte of Claims. 2-Ptn of Richd G Briscoe, praying the correction of an error in the assessment of his property: referred to the Cmte of Ways & Means.

Mrd: on Feb 28, in Wash City, by Rev Smith Pyne, Capt Lorenzo Sitgreaves, of the U S Army, to Lucy Ann, daughter of Gen Thos S Jesup.

Mrd: on Feb 28, at Trinity Church, in Wash City, by Rev C M Butler, Dr Richd H Coolidge, U S Army, to Harriet B Ringgold, daughter of Com Chas Morris, U S Navy.

Died: on Feb 28, at his residence in Wash City, Michl Keller, in his 58th year. His funeral will be from his late residence on G st, between 2nd & 3rd sts, today at 2 p m.

Died: on Feb 25, at his late residence in Wash Co, D C, Levi Sheriff, aged 76 yers.

Died: on Mar 1, Agnes C, aged 6 months, daughter of Thos F & Mgt Stewart.

House of Reps: Election of the Public Printer: A O P Nicholson received 122 votes; Gales & Seaton received 48 votes; scattering of 33 votes. The Speaker declared A O P Nicholson Printer of the House of Reps for the remainder of the present Congress.

Senate: 1-Ptn from Mrs Mary Baury, of Boston, widow of Louis Baury, an ofcr of the Revolution, asking to be allowed a pension. 2-Ptn from Thos C Nye, asking indemnity for the violation by the Post Ofc Dept of his contract for the transportation of the mails. 3-Cmte on Commerce: bill for the relief of E J McLane. 4-Cmte on Military Affairs: bill for the relief of Wm Harris, of Ga. 5-Cmte of Claims: adverse report on the memorial of Wm C Kyle. 6-Cmte on Pensions: adverse reports on the following ptns: of Phoebe Hascall; of the heirs of Jos Pomeroy; of the administrator of Jos Richardson; & of Jas A Glanding.

FRI MAR 3, 1854
Senate: 1-Cmte on the Post Ofc & Post Roads: bill for the relief of Zadock C Ingram, & asked its immediate consideration: bill was passed. 2-Cmte on Military Affairs: bill for the relief of Wm Claude Jones. 3-Cmte on Private Lands: bill for the relief of the legal reps of Antoine Vasques, Hypolite Vasques, Jos Vasques, & John Colligan to enter certain lands in Missouri. 4-Cmte of Claims: adverse report on the memorial of Franklin Chase. 5-Cmte on Foreign Relations: bill for the relief of Wm A Slacum. Same cmte: adverse report on the memorial of Francis Ann McCauley. 6-Cmte on Commerce: bill for the relief of Alex'r Lea.

Orphans Court of Wash Co, D C. Letters testamentary on the personal estate of Eliza Trego, late of Wash Co, deceased. –J P Kennedy, exc

Mrd: on Feb 28, by Rev Dr Cole, Mr Thos B Turner to Miss Eliz E Lusby, both of Wash City.

The Late Thos Mower, M D: from the N Y Scalpel. On Dec 7 Thos G Mower, senior surgeon of the U S army died in this city, after a protracted illness, surrounded by a devoted family & friends. Thos Gardner Mower was born in Worcester, Mass, Feb 18, 1790; graduated at Harvard Univ, 1810; studied medicine with Thos Babbit, an eminent surgeon of Brockfield, Mass, & formerly a surgeon in the U S Navy. He was appointed surgeon's mate in the 9th regt of the U S Infty, Dec 20, 1812, & joined his winter quarters at Burlington, Vt. In 1818 he received the degree of doctor of medicine at the College of Physicians & Surgeons, N Y, & in 1844 was elected a member of the American Philosophical Society of Phil, an institution over which Franklin & Jefferson in turn presided.

Died: on Jan 17, at Austin, Texas, Miss Eliz Scott, daughter of the late Alex'r Scott, formerly of Md.

SAT MAR 4, 1854
Criminal Court: yesterday, the Jury came into Court with a verdict of Guilty against Dr Geo A Gardiner. The Judge read: You have been convicted by a Jury of your country of the crime of false swearing touching the expenditure of public money, & in support of a claim against the U S. The sentence of the Court is, that you suffer in the penitentiary for the Dist of Columbia imprisonment & labor for the period of 10 years. After receiving his sentence, Dr Gardiner was taken into the custody of the Deputy Marshal, for safe keeping in jail. He had arrived there but a very little time before he was attacked by severe spasms & vomiting inducing the suspicion that he had poisoned himself; but this is not yet positively known. At quarter past 3 o'clock he died. [Two other bills had been found against him for forgery.] [Mar 6th newspaper: The funeral of Dr Gardiner took place yesterday & was attended by his brother, John Chas Gardiner, & a number of friends & acquaintances.] Mar 11th newspaper: verdict rendered yesterday by the Jury of Inquest: we are of the opinion that Dr Geo A Gardiner came to his death from strychnine & brucine, voluntarily taken after conviction & sentence.]

Official: Dept of State, Wash, Mar 3, 1854. Information has been received at this Dept from Alex'r Burton, U S Consul at Cadiz, of the death, at that place, on Jan 9 last, of Henry Hendley, a native of Conn, & late chief mate of the ship **Emblem**, of Portland, Maine.

Mrd: on Mar 2, by Rev J S Pruit, Mr Robt A Payne to Miss Martha Eliz Baldwin, all of Wash City.

Mrd: on Mar 1, by Rev D E Reese, Thos J Miller, of Wash City, to Miss Martha Virginia Reed, of Winchester, Va.

Died: on Mar 2, James Mitchell, only son of Silas H & Mary B Hill, aged 14 years. His funeral is today at 3:30 o'clock, from the residence of his father, E & 6th sts.

Died: on Mar 3, Charles G McKnew, aged 6 months, infant son of the late Chas & Maria McKnew.

Circuit Court of Wash Co, D C-in Chancery. John, Jas, Mary Ann, & Sarah Foy vs Robt A Foy. Order of ratification nisi. The trustees have reported that on Jul 7, 1853, he sold & disposed of parts of lots known as the west parts of of lots 37 thru 40 in square known as reservation 10, in Wash City, to L M Powell, for $5,954.24, & that the purchaser complied with the terms of the sale. –Jno A Smith, clerk

$100 reward for runaway negro man Tom, aged 23 or 28 years of ae. –John G Beale, living near Bealeton, on the Orange & Alexandria Railroad, Fauquier Co, Va.

Some time since Judge D F Vondersmith & Gen Geo Ford, men of wealth & standing, residing at Lancaster, Pa, were arrested on a charge of being concerned in extensive frauds upon the U S Gov't by means of fraudulent pensions. At the time of their arrest they were admitted to bail, & when the time came up for the hearing before the U S District Court it was found that both parties had fled. It is alleged that these frauds have been carried on for a period of 8 years, & that during the time have defrauded the Govn't out of not less than $70,000. On one claim they obtained $10,000 & on another $8,000. The names of some of the most distinguished men in the State have been forged in carrying out these frauds, which are said to be most ingenious & deceptive.

MON MAR 6, 1854
Capt Wm A Spencer, of the U S Navy, died at N Y on Fri last, in his 62nd year. He was a son of Hon Ambrose Spencer, Chief Justice of the State of N Y, & brother of Hon John C Spencer, formerly Sec of the Treasury.

New Haven mail robber: Rowland A Smith, who was arrested there a few days since on a charge of purloining letters from mail bags while under his care, was arraigned at New Haven on Fri, plead guilty to several counts, & was sentenced by Judge Ingersoll to 27 years in the State prison.

Appointments by the Pres, by & with the advice & consent of the Senate:
Consuls of the U S:
John C O'Neill, of Pa, for Belfast, in Ireland.
Wm Lilley, of Ohio, Pernambuco, in Brazil.
Donald G Mitchell, of Conn, for Venice.
Wm B Barry, of Ohio, for Matamoros, Mexico.

Died: on Mar 4, in her 77th year, Mrs Isabella Ellsworth, a native of Chester, Pa, but for more than 50 years a resident of Wash City. Her funeral is this morning, at 10 o'clock, from the dwlg of Ferdinand Jefferson, 11th st, between L & M sts.

Died: on Mar 4, Jas A McLaughlin, [late a clerk in the ofc of the Auditor for the Post Ofc Dept,] in his 33rd year, leaving a disconsolate wife & child to mourn their sad bereavement. He was an affectionate man, fond parent, a firm friend, & an honest man. His funeral is on Monday, at 10:30 o'clock, from his late residence on 11th st, between G & H sts.

Died: on Mar 4, at his residence, near Gtwn, John Lyons, in his 74th year, a highly esteemed citizen. His funeral is this morning at 11 o'clock, from his late residence.

Died: on Mar 4, in Wash City, Elizabeth, youngest child of Richd M & Edmonia Heath, aged 11 months & 11 days.

Mr Michl Anton lost his life at Balt on Thur, in consequence of entering his house, while it was on fire, for the purpose of recovering some valuable effects. He was suffocated & overcome by the smoke & heat.

Second-hand piano for sale: 7 octave piano. –John F Ellis, Pa ave, between 9th & 10th sts.

Wash Corp: 1-Ptn from Wm Jacobs; & of D P Kurtz: for the remission of fines: both referred to the Cmte of Claims.

Dissolution of partnership of Mitchell & Terrett, by mutual consent. Mr Mitchell will continue the business at the old stand. –R P Mitchell, John Terrett
+
We the undersigned have entered into co-partnership, for the conducting of the Dry Good business. –Mitchell & Hazle, successors of Mitchell & Terrett

Orphans Court of Wash Co, D C. Letters of administration on the personal estate of Susan Ballenger, late of Wash Co, deceased. –Francis Ballenger, adm

Orphans Court of Wash Co, D C. Letters of administration on the personal estate of Jos Thoma, late of said county, deceased. –Stanislaus Murray, adm

TUE MAR 7, 1854
Household & kitchen furniture at auction: on Mar 9, at the residence of P A Jay, corner of 32nd & F sts. -J C McGuire, auct

Jacob Albert, one amongst the oldest, wealthiest, & most respected citizens of Balt, died at his residence in that city on Sunday, after several weeks' illness. He is supposed to have left property to the amount of nearly two millions of dollars.

The Delaware Journal announces the death of Maj Philip Reybold, at his residence near Delaware city, on Tue last. He was a thriving & energetic agriculturist, always ready to advance the farming interest of the country.

Criminal Court-Washington: Mar Term: the Grand Jury:

Peter Force, chairman	Leonard Storm	Wm Morgan
Andrew Rothwell	Jeremiah Sullivan	Evan Lyons
Wm F Bailey	Wm Wilson	Esau Pickrell
John P Pepper	Washington Adams	A Hamilton Dodge
Peter F Bacon	Robt Beall	Lewis Carbery
John Purdy	Ephraim Wheeler	Jas Kelley

Jenkin Thomas	Chas R Belt	Saml Pumphrey
Rezin Arnold	Chas H Wiltberger	Geo B Smith
Petit Jurors-1st Panel		
F A Tucker	Wm H Perkins	Thos Stelle
Peter Hepburn	Lem F Clarke	Thos Marshall
Walter Stewart	Jas R Barnacloe	Chas F Wood
Wm B Butt	John M Belt	Wm Boyd
2nd Panel:		
Geo A Bohrer	J B Birch	Giddings
Walter Hooe	W H Thomas	Ferguson
Wm H Tenney	John Ashford	T Arthur Scott
Jas H Tenney	John House	
Jas Lynch	D J Evans	

Mr W H MacFarland has purchased the ***Montpelier***, the former residence of Jas Madison, the 4th Pres of the U S. We are glad that this estate has fallen into the hands of a Virginian, & it is hoped that a suitable monument may now be erected over the remains of Virginia's eminent statesman & patriot. –Alexandria Gaz

WED MAR 8, 1854
House of Reps: 1-Memorial of Abraham Martin, asking to be allowed compensation due to him & paid to others in the custom-house in Phil. 2-Memorial of the heirs of Joshua Fisher & Son, of Phil, asking remuneration for good taken for the Revolutionary army by order of Gen Washington & other general ofcrs of the American army. 3-Ptn of Clarissa Packwood & 4 sisters, daughters of the late Jos Packwood, of Colchester, New London Co, Conn, asking remuneration for services rendered by their father in the war of the Revolution. 4-Ptn of John Owen, of China, Maine, for a pension for injuries received in the war of 1812.

Cadets at large, appointed by the Pres:
1-Martin D Hardin, son of Col Hardin, of Ill volunteers, killed at Buena Vista.
2-Wm E Merrill, son of Capt M E Merrill, U S Army, killed at Molina del Rey.
3-Edw Ross, son of Edw C Ross, late Lt 4th Artl, & Assist Prof of Math at West Point.
4-Wm W Gaines, adopted son of the late Gen Gaines, U S Army.
5-Chas E Jesup, son of Maj Gen Jesup, Quartermaster Gen U S Army.
6-Jas Wilson, son of Col H Wilson, 7th Infty U S Army.
7-Saml M Cooper, son of Col S Cooper, Adj Gen U S Army.
8-John S Saunders, son of Com'r Jno L Saunders, U S Navy.
9-Jonathan P Cilley, great grandson of Gen Cilley, of the Revolution, & son of the late Jonathan Cilley, Member of Congress from Maine.
10-Frank C Goodrich, son of C B Goodrich, of Boston. Ancestors distinguished in the Revolutionary war.

For rent: a new 3 story brick house with basement, on 7th st between D & E sts. For terms apply on the premises to John Jacob Seufferle.

Annual Commencement of the Nat'l Medical College yesterday in the Lecture Hall of the Smithsonian Institution: Rev Dr Bacon, presiding; Deal of the Faculty, Dr R K Stone, pronounced the names of the students whose proficiency entitled them to take rank in the profession. The young gentlemen who have thus become Doctors of Medicine are Messrs Speiden, Moore, Bradley, Dyer, Combs, Johnson, Hellen, & Weaver.

The New Orleans papers have full accounts of the frightful casualty at the French Opera House in that city on Feb 26, when the third gallery gave way. This gallery is occupied by colored people. The second gallery fell as it was attached to the third. The lamplighter of the theatre saw the danger, & turned off the gas on the side threatened in time. Florian Malus, notary, about 27, was killed; Fergus Toledano, about 13, was killed; Mr Salvador Prata, residing in Bourbon st, reported to be dangerously wounded; Dr Chas Delery, badly wounded; Chas Roman, of the firm of Roman & Kernion, severely injured; Henry Boullgay, severe injury; E A Michel, ex-sgt of the ex-general council, severe injury; M'me Lafont, severely hurt; a hair-dresser living in St Chas st, severely injured. Few ladies are ever present at the theatre on Sundays, & but few were there last evening. The theatre was crowded for the benefit of a favorite performer, Mr Carrier.

On Fri Mr Theodore Yahrling, employed in the flouring mill of his father-in-law, 3 miles from Wheeling, was caught on a large vertical shaft, by his clothes getting entangled in the machinery & was horribly mangled. He died on Sat.

Died: on Mar 7, Lilian Longfellow, infant daughter of Saml L & Anna C Harris.

Senate: 1-Ptn from J Burrows Hyde, asking that the patent laws may be so amended as to make the fees chargeable for a patent the same to all foreign inventors applying for a patent in the U S. 2-Ptn from J H Taliafero & other sureties of D F M Thurston, a purser in the navy, asking to be relieved from their liability. 3-Ptn from Sarah D Brigham, asking to be allowed to locate land within the Bastrop grant. 4-Cmte on Patents: bill for the relief of Gideon Hotchkiss. 5-Cmte on Pensions: adverse reports on the ptns of Lucretia W Hubbard for herself & heirs of Elijah Ranson; of John Webb; & of Robt Steele. Same cmte: asked to be discharged from the further consideration of the ptns of David Felker & Jerathmiel Doty: agreed to.

Trustee's sale: by decree of the Circuit Court of Wash Co, D C, in a cause wherein Edmund Hanley's excs are cmplnts, & Susan D Shepherd, Alex'r R Shepherd, & others, heirs & admx of Alex'r Shepherd, are dfndnts: auction on Mar 30, of part of lot 9 in square 450, in Wash City. –W Redin, trustee

Maj Buell, who was severely injured by the explosion of the steamer **Kate Kearney** at St Louis, has so far recovered as to go eastward on his duties. John Gatlin, son of Maj Gatlin, of the army, injured by the same explosion, died on Feb 26.

U S Patent Ofc, Wash, Mar 7, 1854. Ptn of Ralph Bulkley, of N Y, praying for the extension of a patent granted to him on May 8, 1840, for an improvement in life-preservers, for 7 years from the expiration of said patent, which takes place on May 8, 1854. –Chas Mason, Com'r of Patents

THU MAR 9, 1854
Trustee's sale of Household & kitchen furniture at auction: on Mar 11, by deed of trust, duly recorded from Henry R Robertson to Danl Ratcliffe, dated Apr 10, 1853. –Green & Scott, aucts

Orphans Court of Wash Co, D C. Letters of administration on the personal estate of Nathl M Walker, late of Wash Co, deceased. –Levi T Walker, adm [I hereby appoint Mr Francis Wheately, of Gtwn, my agent to settle up the above estate. –Levi T Walker, adm]

Wash Corp: 1-Cmte of Claims: asked to be discharged from the further consideration of the ptn of Stuart Smith: agreed to. Same for the ptn of Geo Seitz: agreed to. Same cmte: bill for the relief of J D Hendley: read twice. 2-Cmte on Improvements: asked to be discharged from the further consideration of the ptn of Mrs Louisa J Wadsworth: agreed to.

Mrd: on Wed, by Rev John C Smith, Mr Henry Boyer to Miss Mary Jane Herbert, both of Va.

Ornamental Iron Warehouse: under Jackson Hall, Pa ave, between 3rd & 4½ sts. -Ralph Haskins

FRI MAR 10, 1854
Senate: 1-Ptn from Harriet A Wilcox, widow of an ofcr in the revenue cutter service, asking a pension. 2-Ptn from Seth Ingram, asking to be allowed arrears of pension. 3-Additional documents submitted in relation to the claim of John Huddy. 4-Cmte on the Post Ofc & Post Roads: bill for the relief of Almansor Huston. Also, a bill for the relief of Robt Jemison & Benj Williamson.

Orphans Court of Wash Co, D C. Letters of administration on the personal estate of Elexius Simms, late of Wash Co, deceased. –Euridice F Simms, admx

First Ward Shoe Store, 7 Bldgs: beautiful assortment of Gentlemen's Congress Gaiters, made by one of the first manufacturere in N Y C. –Henry L Cross

For rent: 3 story brick house, with stabling, on Delaware ave, Capitol Hill, adjoining the residence of Mr David H Burr. Apply to John C Brent, E st, near 7th, & for the key at Mr Burr's residence. Possession given immediately.

Died: on Thursday, Mattie, daughter of Dr Alex'r McD & Martha Davis, aged 8 years. Her funeral is today at 3 o'clock, from the residence of Dr Davis, on E, between 6th & 7th sts.

Wash City Ordinances: 1-Act for the relief of Jas A Wise: the sum of $20 be paid him for work done at the Northern Market. 2-Act for the relief of Geo H Walter: fine for removing sand from the footway is remitted: provided he pay the costs.

SAT MAR 11, 1854
Senate: 1-Bills passed: relief of-Geo G Bishop & the legal reps of John Arnold, deceased; of Asbury Dickins; of Theordore E Elliott; of Lt A J Williamson; of Dempsey Pittman; of W P S Sanger; of Wm N Nevins; & of Mrs Helen Mackay, excx of Lt Col Aeneas Mackay, late a quartermaster in the U S Army. 2-Bill for the purchase of the copyright of a work published by Thos H Sumner, where in he describes his new method of ascertaining a ship's position at sea: passed. 3-Bill for the relief of the exc of the late Lt Col H C W Fanning: passed.

Gen John Cocke, of Tenn, died at his residence in Grainger Co, Tenn, on Feb 16. He was a prominent Rep in Congress from the year 1819 to 1828.

Mr Ruffin, of N C, has been called home on account of the extreme illness of his father.

Mrd: on Thu, by Rev John C Smith, Mr Jas Taylor to Miss Bridget Moore, all of Wash City.

Mr Jacob Albert, who died at Balt last week, has bequeathes liberal sums to several benevolent objects in that city: to the Protestant Orphan Asylum, on Franklin Square, $10,000; to the Female Orphan Asylum of St Paul's Church, $10,000; & to the Male Orphan Asylum of the same, $10,000.

Mr Isaac Duel, aged 50 years, an estimable citizen of Dutchess Co, N Y, accidentally lost his life on Sat, whilst engaged in oiling the gearing of his mill, into which he was drawn & mangled in a horrible manner.

MON MAR 13, 1854
Household & kitchen furniture at auction: on Mar 17, at the residence of Miss Waggaman, on High st, Gtwn. –E S Wright, auct -A Green, crier

Died: on Mar 12, in Wash City, of pneumonia, Mrs Mary Lazenby, aged about 78 years, of short illness. Her funeral will be today at 2:30 o'clock, from her late residence, on 12th st, between M & Mass ave.

Died: on Mar 9, suddenly, William J, infant son of A L & Mary Newton, aged 8 days.

Franklin Pierce, Pres of the U S A, recognizes H de Saint Cyr, who has been appointed Vice Consul ad interim of the Mexican Republic for the port of Galveston, in Texas. Also, Francisco Montaner, who has been appointed Vice Consul ad interim of the Mexican Republic for the port of Charleston, in S C. Also, Francisco Moreno, who has been appointed Vice Consul ad interim of the Mexican Republic for the port of Pensacola, in Fla. –Mar 7, 1854

Dept of State, Wash, Mar 9, 1854. Information has been received from J H Williams, U S Consul at Sydney, of the death at that place of Robt Allen, a seaman belonging to the ship **George**, of New Bedford. Further information respecting the property left by him may be obtained on application to the Treasury Dept.

Orphans Court of Wash Co, D C. Letters of administration de bonis non, with the will annexed, on the personal estate of Ann P Watson, late of Wash Co, deceased. -Geo C Burdett, Adm de bonis non, with the will annexed.

Orphans Court of Wash Co, D C. Letters of administration on the personal estate of Charlotte Garratt, late of Wash Co, deceased. –Simeon Garratt, adm

TUE MAR 14, 1854
Died: on Mar 9, at Poolsville, Md, in his 76th year, Edw Fallon, a native of Ireland, & formerly a resident of Wash City.

Died: on Mar 3, in Tenn, at her residence in Bedford Co, Mrs Gentry, wife of Hon Meredith P Gentry, a lady greatly esteemed for the excellence of her character.

Groceries & liquors at auction: on Mar 10, at the Grocery Store of Mr H G Murray, at the corner of 8th & K sts, near the Marine Barracks. –Green & Scott, aucts

Household & kitchen furniture at auction: on Mar 16, at the residence of the late Mr J A McLaughlin, on east side of 11th st, between G & H sts. -Jas C McGuire, auct

Wash Co, D C: by 2 writs of fieri facias, at the suit of Wm T Dove, & one at the suit of B L Jackson & Wm B Jackson, use of Wm T Dove, against the goods & chattels, lands & tenements of Patrick Goins, to me directed, I have seized lot 8 in square 80, fronting on 22nd st, for public auction, on Mar 30. –Wm Cox, constable

Senate: 1-Ptn from Chas Fletcher, of Kalorama, D C, asking that Congress will adopt measure for the formation of a good harbor for the port of Washington. 2-Ptn from Lewis Ralston, asking remuneration for losses sustained by him contrary to the provisions of the treaty with the Cherokee Indians. 3-Ptn from Denton Offutt, offering to Congress to make public his system of treatment of domestic animals & his mode of improving their breeds, for the general good, for a fair equivalent. 4-Bill for the relief of John Boyd. 5-Cmte on Public Lands: bill for the relief of Mark Bean & Richd H B Bean, of Arkansas. 6-Cmte on Pensions: asked to be discharged from the further consideration of the ptn of Thos Frazer, on the ground that his case was provided for in a general bill: which motion was agreed to.

Mr Fielding Lucas, one of the oldest & one of the most worthy citizens of Balt, died on Sunday last, in his 73rd year.

WED MAR 15, 1854
Senate: 1-Cmte on Pensions: bill for the relief of Andrew J Dickerhoff, & of Anne W Angus, with a report. Same cmte: adverse reports on the ptns of John Boykin; & of Mary Baury. Same Cmte: asked to be discharged from the further consideration of the ptn of Anne Royal: laid on the table. 2-Cmte on Indian Affairs: bill for the relief of Amos Kendall & John E Kendall. 3-Cmte of Claims: bill for the relief of Levi Pierce & Andrew Hodge, jre. Same cmte: bill for the relief of Hezekiah Miller; & for relief of Henry La Reintree. 4-Cmte on Public Lands: bill for the relief of Theresa Dardenne.

From the Dayton [Ohio] Journal of Mar 4. Obit: died: on Sunday last, at the residence of her son, Robt C Schenck, in this city, Mrs Eliz H Schenck, in her 78th year. The eventful life of Mrs Schenck, connected as it is with the early history of the Miami Valley, which she witnessed, would furnish many incidents for a most interesting narrative. Much of history comprised in her single life, covering as it does the whole period of our existence as an independent nation. Eliz Rogers was born at Norwalk, Conn, Dec 27, 1776. The family residence was at Huntingdon, L I; but, the British having taken possession of that town, the mother of Mrs Schenck was compelled to fly for safety to Norwalk. Capt Wm Rogers, the father, holding a commission for the colony of N Y as cmder of a vessel, engaged in active hostilities, his family was particularly abnoxious to the enemy. Capt Rogers had the honor of bringing into port the first prize taken in the Revolutionary war. In 1798 Eliz Rogers married Gen Wm C Schenck, & emigrated with him to Ohio, then almost an unbroken wilderness. In 1801 they removed to Franklin, of which town Gen Schenck was the founder & proprietor. She was the mother of a numerous family. Her husband being dead, the last 18 years of her life were spent in Dayton. Of her 10 children but 3 survive her: Lt Jas F Schenck, U S N; Hon Robt C Schenck, of this city; & Egbert T S Schenck, of Iowa. She was for many years a consistent member of the Presbyterian Church. Her remains were interred yesterday, by the side of her husband, in the old graveyard at Franklin.

Negroes for sale: by order of the Orphans Court of Wash Co, D C. Sale on Mar 18, at the residence of Mrs Ann Bean, near Comb's Wharf, 2 colored boys, or Men, Jas & Charles, belonging to the estate of Geo Bean, deceased. –Ann Bean, admx -Green & Scott, aucts

House of Reps: 1-Bill to confirm the claim of Wm H Henderson, & the heirs of Robt Henderson to 500 acres of land in the Bastrop grant.

Mrd: on Mar 11, by Rev Stephen P Hill, John T Goldsmith to Sarah Van Vassel.

Died: on Monday last, Meeta Dashiell, daughter of Lemuel & Caroline Williams, aged 11 months.

By writ of fieri facias, Wash Co, D C, wherein Geo Parker, Thos Parker & Jos B Bryan, under the firm of Geo & Thos Parker & Co, plntfs, & Chas McGee, dfndnt, I have levied on one new frame house on lot 7 in square 864, & will auction off the right, title, & interest of said Chas Motler in & to the same. –John Davis, constable

Wash City Ordinance: 1-Act for the relief of Eliz Braiden: the fine of $68.75, imposed on Eliz Braiden for the removal of a nuisance on lots H & E, in square 226, is hereby remitted.

THU MAR 16, 1854
From the Tuscaloosa [Ala] Monitor of Mar 2. Gen Thos D King, elder brother of the late Hon Wm R King, Vice Pres of the U S, died on Feb 24, 1854, in his 75th year, in Tuscaloosa. Gen King had for many years withdrawn himself from public life, &, owing to enfeebled health, had ceased to take an earnet interest in business affairs of whatever kind. In his more vigorous days he did honorable service both as a civilian & as a soldier. Gen King was born on Sep 22, 1799, in Duplin Co, N C; educated completed at the Univ of N C; & received the commission of Maj in the 43rd regt, in the war of 1812;

Mrd: on Mar 14, at the Church of the Ascension, by Rev Mr Stanley, Mr Wm Nalley to Miss Virginia A Kersey, both of Wash City. [Mar 17th newspaper: Mrd: on Mar 14, at the Church of the Ascension, by Rev Mr Stanley, Mr Wm H Nalley to Miss Virginia A Kersey, both of Wash City.]

Died: at the residence of her mother, in Gtwn, Annie, daughter of H A & the late Gen T T Wheeler, of Md, in her 18th year. [No death date given-current item.]

Died: on Feb 5, in Camptonville, Calif, after a long & painful illness, Mrs Nancy A, wife of G P Sanders, aged 39 years. The deceased was a daughter of Hon Henry Dodge, of Wisc. -Marysville Herald

Capt Caleb S Sibley, 5th Infty, & Capt Robt Granger, 1st Infty, as supernumeraries. Capt Wm B Blair, Commissary of Subsistence, has been appointed the Judge Advocate. Dr Steiner is supposed to be in the hands of the civil authorities of Texas, & it is not anticipated that he will refuse to deliver himself up to be tried for his military offence. The affray which resulted in the death of Arnold was witnessed but by a single other individual, a sgt, who has since deserted. -Star

The War Dept yesterday ordered a Court Marital upon Assist Surgeon Josephus M Steiner, U S Army, for killing his commander, Maj Arnold, not long since, at a post in Texas. They are to assemble at Austin, Texas, on Apr 17. The detail for this Court is as follows:
Brvt Brig Gen Wm S Harney, Col 2nd Dragoons
Brvt Col Chas A May, Capt 2nd Dragoons
Col Jos Plympton, 1st Infty
Brvt Col Carlos A Waite, Lt Col 5th Infty
Brvt Lt Col Thompson Morris, Major 1st Infty
Brv Lt Col Jas V Bomford, Capt 8th Infty
Brvt Lt Col Danl Ruggles, Capt 5th Infty
Brvt Lt Col Benj S Roberts, Capt mounted rifles
Lt Col Washington Seawell, 8th Infty
Maj J H Lamotte, 5th Infty
Maj Giles Porter, 4th Artl
Brvt Maj H W Merrill, Capt 2nd Dragoons
Brvt Maj N B Russell, Capt 5th Infty

Terrible accident on Lake Nicaragua: steamship **Brother Jonathan** left San Francisco on Feb 16, & after a pleasant passage anchored in the habor of San Juan del Sud on Mar 1. There were nearly 600 passengers on board, about 400 of whom were in the steerage. Later some passengers went on the steamer **Omstepe** & as she slowly proceeded it became apparent to all on shore that she was in extreme peril; wave after wave struck her, the whole column of a heavy sea rolled over her entire length, filling her to the gunwale: a scene of horror. The sea was instantly covered with floating objects, among which were many human forms that had been washed from the boat or had thrown themselves overboard. Names of the lost: Mrs C Sylvester, English, going to Manchester to daughter; had on person $5,000, found; C Sylvester, her husband, not found; Danl McLand, aged about 30, belong to Dover, Maine; David Churchill, Sycamore, De Kalb Co, Ill, aged about 50 years; Chas Lyons, Brooklyn N Y; Geo Seaver, Unity Maine, aged about 35; Francis Harris, Hazel Green, Wisconsin, aged about 30; Edw Thomas, boy, Doleville, Wisc; John Knight, Doleville, not found; Jacob Lewis, N Y; Mearcey Moore, native of Central American, drowned in attempting to save others. Jas Potter, Wm Lins, D W Land; T Smoot, Detroit, Mich. Old man, Battle Creek, Mich, aged about 60 years, crossed the plains to Calif, was a wheelwright by trade. Robt Hutchinson, Nevada, Calif. Isaac Edge, White Oak Springs, Wisc. David Lewis, mulatto man, 27, Phil, Pa.

M W Studley, Branch Co, Mich, aged 41 years; body not found; Wm H Gardiner, C Vise, & Fred'k O'Larey. On Mar 3 the bodies recoverd were buried together by the passengers still on shore.

Farm hand wanted: inquire of Mr E Harte, at Mr Hyatt's, Pa ave; or of Mr Jas B Holmead, 7th st road, adjoining the first Tollgate.

Senate: 1-Ptn from J Balestier, asking remuneration for certain expenses incurred while special agent of the U S to Southeasten India. 2-Cmte of Pensions: bill for relief of Wm Miller; bill for relief of Jas F Green, of Pa; & for relief of Lemuel Hudson. Same cmte: adverse report on House bill for relief of Geo S Claffin.

FRI MAR 17, 1854
Senate: 1-Ptn from Sarah L Russell, one of the creditors of the late republic of Texas, asking to be paid the amount due her. 2-Ptn from A G Bennett, a paymaster in the army, asking to be released from responsibility for certain public money lost by the burning of the steamboat **Velante**. 3-Ptn from Robt Mills, proposing a plan for an improvement of Pa ave. 4-Ptn from Francois Cousin, asking the confirmation of his title to a tract of land. 5-Ptn from Susan Hayne Pinckney, asking remuneration for the services of her father, Richd Shubrick, in the war of the Revolution. 6-Ptn from John O'Leary, asking a pension. 7-Cmte on Foreign Relations: bill making compensation to John Bosman Kerr for diplomatic services in Central America. 8-Cmte on Military Affairs: bill for the relief of the heirs of Bri Gen Richd B Mason. 9-Cmte on Public Lands: asked to be discharged from the further consideration of the ptn of Eliz Summers, & that it be referred to the Cmte on Pensions: agreed to. 10-Bill for the relief of Miles Knowlton & a bill to extend the term for location of certain donation claims in Arkansas.

Appointments by the Pres. by & with the advice & consent of the Senate.
Wm J McCulloh, of La, to be Surveyor Gen of the U S for the district of La, vice J W Boyd, removed.
Paul McCormick, of Fla, to be Register of the Land Ofc at Newnansville, Fla, vice Lemuel Wilson, removed.
Selin W Meyers, of Fla, to be Register of the Land Ofc at Tallahassee, Fla, vice Theodore W Brevard, resigned.
Thos Thornley, of D C, to be Warden of the Penitentiary of the U S for the District of Columbia, vice Jonas B Ellis, removed.

Two white men, Guild & Ingalls, & 13 Chinamen, on a prospecting tour, were slaughtered on McCloud's river, 20 miles east of Pittsburg, Shasta Co, by the Indians. –Sacramento Journal [No date given.]

Died: on Thu, after a short but severe illness, Saml Brereton, in his 80th year. His funeral will be from his late residence, 7th & F sts, this afternoon, at 4 o'clock.

Died: yesterday, Mr Thos Moore, in his 58th year. His funeral is today at 3 o'clock.

Died: on Mar 15, Mrs Julia R Posey, aged 46 years. Her funeral is today, at 2 p m, from her residence, I st, between 12th & 13th sts.

Orphans Court of Wash Co, D C. Letters testamentary on the personal estate of Emily Corcoran, late of Wash Co, deceased. –H C Matthews, exc

Orphans Court of Wash Co, D C. Letters testamentary on the personal estate of Michl Kelly, late of Wash Co, deceased. –Rudolph Eichhorn, exc

House of Reps: 1-Ptn of Bethiah Black, of Oakham, Mass, for pension allowance. 2-Ptn of John Clark, of Belmont Co, Ohio, praying for damages occasioned by the continuation of the nat'l road through his lands.

SAT MAR 18, 1854
Valuable lot & bldgs for sale at public auction: on Mar 25, on the premises, by deed of trust from Aloysius N Clements, dated Sep 26, 1849, recorded in Liber J A S 8, folios 435 & 436, in the Clerk's ofc in Wash Co, D C: a part of lot 9 in square 283/383, fronting on 9th st west, with bldgs thereon. -Jas C McGuire, auct

Household & kitchen furniture at auction: Mar 24, at the late residence of Mrs Mary Lazenby, deceased, on 12th st, between Mass ave & M sts. –Green & Scott, aucts

Household & kitchen furniture at auction: steam engine, lead pipe, benches, bath tubs, & improved property: on Mar 23, at the Wash Assembly Rooms, lately occupied by Moses Copp, on La ave, between 4½ & 6th sts. We shall sell the spacious bldg & the lot on which it stands. –Green & Scott, aucts

The steamer **Caroline**, a regular packet from Memphis, in the White River [Arkansas] trade, on Sunday last, caught fire in the wood pile near the boilers. John R Price, the pilot at the wheel, ran the boat for the shore, when some 15 persons tried to escape, but, over-crowding the yawl, it sunk, & every one perished. Among the lost of the ofcrs & crew are John R Price & Jas Creighton, pilots; Louis Pollock, assist barkeeper; & 8 deck hands & firemen out of ten. Those known to be lost are, wife & child of J Haskins, Marshall Co, Miss; 4 children of S McMullen, Madison Co, Tenn; Mr Smith, wife, & young lady with them; Mrs Haley & 3 children, Tippah Co, Miss; John Horton, wife, & 2 children, Madison Co, Tenn; Mr Parrel, Madison Co, Tenn; M Martin, Tenn; Miss Susan E Pool, Tenn; son of Mr Hinshaw, Tenn; Mr ___, Shelby Co, son-in-law to Mr Wortham; Mrs ___, sister to above, [widow,] & 13 children; Miss ___, sister to above. The cabin passengers forward on the forecastle were saved, except Mr Harslaw, of Clarendon, Ark, & Geo Jones, of Jacksonport. There was about $5,000 of money in the safe belonging to the passengers, not one dollar of which was saved.

Franklin Pierce, Pres of the U S A, recognizes H W Hinrichsen, who has been appointed Consul of Saxony, at San Francisco, for the State of Calif. -Mar 13, 1854

Appointment of Preachers: Balt Annual Conference of the Methodist Episcopal Church, after a 2 week session, adjourned on Wed. Appointed for the Potomac district for the ensuing year: Nerval Wilson, presiding elder
Alexandria: Wm G Eggleston, Jas N Keys, Job Guest, sup.
City of Washington, Foundry & Asbury: Elisha P Phelps, Wm Hank; Wesley Chapel, Jas H Brown, Robt L Dashiell, S S Roszel, sup; McKendree, T T Wysong, Matthew A Tarner, sup; Ebenezer, Alfred G Chenoweth, Ralph Pierce, J W Kelly, sup; Ryland, Alfred Griffith, Wm F Speake, Jas M Hanson, sup; Union Chapel, F Israel, Wm O Lumsden, sup.
Gtwn: B F Brooke, Wm C Steel.
Fairfax: John W Hoover, J H Knotts, John W Bull, sup
Stafford: Jas Bunting, Henry Leber
Fredericksburg: Saml Rogers
St Mary's, Noah Schlosser, P H Smith, Chas L Gibson, one to be supplied
Bladensburg: Alfred A Eskridge, Saml Smith.
Woodville, John Landstreet
Rockville: Thos Sewall, R R S Hough, R Barry, sup.
Henry Slicer, agent of the Metropolitan Church, member of Gtwn quarterly conference. Jasse T Peck, editor of tracts, & corresponding sec of the Tract Society of the M E C, member of the Foundry quarterly conference. Rev Saml Keppler, restored to active duty, has been appointed to Lexington, Va. The Md Conference of the Meth Prot Church, which recently closed its session at Easton, Md, made the following appointments of preachers for this city & neighborhood: Washington. First Meth Prot Church, Navy Yard: W S Hammond; Ninth st: D Evans Reese; Gtwn: S B Sutherland; Alexandria, L W Bates.

We learn that a young gentleman named Scory died suddenly at Gtwn College on Thu, just as he sat down to dinner. He was afflicted by a disease of the heart.

Mrd: on Mar 16, at Doylestown, Pa, by Rev S M Andrews, Col T Bigelow Lawrence, of the U S Legation, London, to Eliz, eldest daughter of Hon Henry Chapman.

Robbery in Wash: on Thu, as Miss McNeill, daughter of the late Gen John McNeill, of Boston, & the niece of Pres Pierce, was walking on 3rd st, near C st, with a portemonnaie in her hand, she received a blow on the breast from a ruffian, who jerked the portemonnaie from her hand & ran off. Stolen was $30 in gold, a ring worth perhaps $100, though being a momento of far greater value to the young lady, & certificates for some $2,000 worth of stock. The police are seeking the scoundrel. -Star of last evening.

Died: at Englfield, N C, Lemuel C Wheat, in his 36th year, son of the late John Wheat. He will be buried from his mother's residence, on Greenleaf's Point, today, at 11 o'clock. [No death date given-current item.]

Marquett [Wis] Mercury, Extra, Feb 29. The land claim difficulties between Messrs Forman & Cartwright which less than 2 years ago terminated in Cartwright shooting & murdering Forman. Cartwright was arrested for the act & lodged in jail to await trial. Last week Cartwright was bailed out. When it was ascertained that he was out, 100 repaired to his residence, intent in lynching him. Cartwright shot from his chambers, killing 2 of the party, Jas Langdon, who leaves a wife & child, & Mr Troop, both of middle age; & then he surrendered. He was taken by the body of men, tied hand & foot, & suspended by the neck until dead. Within one year, four lives have been sacrificed, all for a paltry 40 acre claim.

Mr & Mrs Archer's Academy for Young Ladies, [10or 40] Lexington st, Balt, Md. Mr Archer, Grad of West Point, Principal. Mrs Geo L Van Bibber, Assist. Institution has been in successful operation for more then 10 years. These patrons have their daughters in the institution at this time: Gen Geo Bust, Va; B T Townes, Va; Hon Thos G Pratt, U S Senate, Md; Judge Geo S Gaien, La; Col David Gordon, Miss; Gen Thos F Bowie, Upper Marlboro, Md; Col John H Sothoron, Md; John A Anderson, N C. Mr Archer's farm, **Maiden Bower**, containing 200 acres, in the healthy hills of Deer Creek, has been fitted up for a country retreat.

$300 reward for the recovery of my negro man Hamilton, [age 21 years,] who made his escape from the steamer **Royal Arch**, at Cincinnati, Ohio, on Mar 11. Reward will be paid if lodged in any jail in Ky or Va, so that I may get him again. My address is Sangster's Station, Fairfax Co, Va. –C F Ford, jr

For sale or rent: cottage on Boundary & 7th sts, near the park. Apply at the Franklin Hotel, 8th & D sts. Pump of delightful water at the kitchen door. –R Estep

MON MAR 20, 1854
The Legislature of Ky adopted a resolution authorizing the Govn'r to take steps for the removal of the remains of Wm T Barry, [who died in England on his way as Minister to Spain,] to his native State, & cause them to be interred in the cemetery at Frankfort.

In Phil, on Thu, Eliz Creamer, aged 15, was killed by the accidental discharge of a loaded gun she was carrying. Her younger brother was trying to take it from her.

Mrd: on Mar 16, at Laurel, PG Co, Md, by Rev Mr Waylen, Richd S Eubanks, of Essex Co, Va, to Susan McKenzie, 3rd daughter of Thos J Talbot, of Laurel Farm.

Mrd: on Mar 14, by Rev C M Butler, of the Trinity Episcopal Church, Mr Theodore L Lamb, of N Y C, to Miss Emeline R Watson, of Wash City.

Died: Mar 19, John Sinon, aged 17 years. His funeral is this afternoon at 4 o'clock.

Died: on Sat, in Wash City, Mr Francis N Shaw, a native of Mass, aged about 26 years. He was an intelligent & amiable young gentleman, a reporter by profession, &, previous to his being stricken down by disease, a telegraphic correspondent for the N Y associated press. His funeral is this afternoon from the Fifth Presbyterian [Rev Mr Carothers'] Church. Services will commence at 3 o'clock. The Young Men's Christian Association, the reporters of the press, & his friends generally are invited to attend his funeral.

Died: on Mar 2, after a short but painful illness, Mrs Martha Plater, wife of Dr Nicholas Brewer, & daughter of Elisha W Williams, of Montg Co, Md, aged 23 years & 6 months, leaving a devoted husband & 4 children, together with fond parents, to mourn her early departure. She was a devoted wife, mother, daughter, sister, & friend.

Died: on Mar 17, of scarlet fever, in his 4th year, Henry Bocock Lewis, eldest son of Col Saml L Lewis & Catharine E, his wife. He had an extraordinary intelligence for one of his years, & the most affectionate disposition, especially towards his mother.

The partnership existing between Hubert Schutter & Jas Lamb is dissolved from this day-Mar 20, 1854. We the undersigned have determined on locating themselves permanently in Wash City as Fresco, Decorative, & Ornamental Painters.
-Hubert Schutter, Henry Kahlert, Pa ave, south side, between 13th & 14th sts.

Hon Friend Humphrey, an ex-Senator of N Y, & formerly Mayor of Albany, died in that city on Wed night.

Orphans Court of Wash Co, D C. Letters of administration, with the will annexed, on the personal estate of Ann Garner, late of Wash Co, deceased. –Chas N Garner, adm, with the will annexed.

TUE MAR 21, 1854
Wash City item: the verdict of a Coroner's Jury in the case of Patrick Hurley, who was shot recently on Capitol Hill, was yesterday made up at the Infirmary, where Hurley had been for some time lying previous to his death. It ascribed his death to the wound received on the above occasion.

Died: on Mar 20, in Wash City, Mrs Frances M Greene, in her 53rd year. Her funeral will take place on Wed next, at 11 o'clock, from Mrs Gulager's boarding house, on 4½ st, the residence of her son-in-law, Dr C Boyle.

Died: Mar 19, of typhoid fever, Robt S Reid, late of Fairfax Co, Va, aged 28 years. His funeral will be from his late residence, on 7th st, near F st, tomorrow at 3 o'clock.

Rev W S Loyd, Pastor of two Baptist Churches in Montg Co, Ala, [Elam & Antioch,] died on Sunday week while performing service at the later. His malady was disease of the heart.

By the will of the late Jas F Vanhorn, of N Y C, he has left $15,000 to the N Y Orphan Asylum, $20,000 more to the same institution after the death of his widow, $20,000 to the N Y Protestant Episcopal Bible & Prayer Book Society, $15,000 to the N Y Protestant Episcopal Missions, & the residue of his estate, estimated at $150,000, to the American Bible Society.

Senate: 1-Ptn from John Brown, asking remuneration for losses sustained during the late war with Mexico in Calif. 2-Ptn from Rhoda Loomis, widow of a Revolutionary ofcr, asking to be allowed a pension. 3-Ptn from Wm F Finch, asking a donation of land or money to enable him to establish a manufactory of locomotives, & offering to carry the mails from Cairo to New Orleans. 4-Ptn from John P Brown, asking compensation for the time he acted as Charge d'Affaires at Constantinople. 5-Cmte on Military Affairs: adverse report on the claim of Capt Geo E McClelland's company of Florida volunteers for services during the Seminole war. Same cmte: adverse report on the memorial of Nathl Frye, for compensation for performing the duties of Paymaster Genr'l during the sickness of that ofcr.

Brvt Capt Hampton L Shields, of the 3rd Artl, U S Army, has resigned. His resignation took effect on Mar 17.

WED MAR 22, 1854
The schnr **Hannah Ann** at auction: Mar 24, at Riley's wharf. -Jas C McGuire, auct

Household & kitchen furniture at auction: on Mar 27, at the residence of Rev S S Rozsell, on M st, near 10th. -Jas C McGuire, auct

Senate: 1-Cmte of Claims: bill for the relief of Rulif Van Brunt. Same cmte: recommended the passage of the House bills for the relief of the legal reps of Isaac P Simonton; & for the relief of Madison Parton. Same cmte: asked the immediate consideration of the House bill for the relief of Saml K Rayburn: passed. 2-Cmte on Finance: bill for the relief of Horace Southmead & Son. 3-Cmte of Claims: bill for the relief of the legal reps of Capt Wm Davis, late cmder of the U S transport schnr **Eufaula**. Same cmte: bill for the relief of the legal reps of Robt Sewell. Same cmte: adverse on the memorial of Wm C Parke. 4-Bill introduced for the relief of Margaret A Copley, of the State of Louisiana. 5-Bill for the relief of the heirs of Col Alex'r Morgan: passed.

Dept of State, Wash, Mar 20, 1854. Information is desired at this Dept respecting Mr Louis Rosi, who came to the U S from Modena in 1851, & is supposed to have resided for some time at St Louis.

The Darien exploration: recent intelligence from the Isthmus to the effect that the survey for an late oceanie canal is a failure, & a fear that a gallant party of men, under Lt J G Strain, have lost their lives in the attempt to cross the Cordileras from the Atlantic to the Pacific. A portion of Lt Strains' party returned to N Y by the steamer **George Law**. Nothing has been heard of Lt Strain's party for a long time, about 45 days, & fears are entertained that they have fallen victims to Indians, who are much opposed to the survey. Although they consented to it. Those who separated from Lt Strain's party were Messrs Holcomb, Bird, Hollins, [son of Capt Hollins, of the ship **Cyane**,] Mr Thos Winthrop, of N Y, & one of the crew. The following is a list of Lt Strain's party: Lt J G Strain; Passed Midshipman W T Truston; Midshipman H M Garland; Engineer J M Maury, U S N; Geo W Mayo, Norfolk Va; W S Boggs, Ohio; J S Kettlewell, Balt, draughtsman; A T Avery, N Y, volunteered at Carthagena;
V Gonzales & B Polanes, of Carthagena; Henry Wilson & Thos Johnson, landsmen; Geo B Holmes, Jas McGinnis, W H Parker, Benj Harrison, Peter Vermillion, John Henwood, Thos Miller, Jas Golden, ordinary seamen; Edw Lambart, seaman; John R O'Kelly, corporal of marines; All of U S ship **Cyane**. -Boston Journal.

<u>Justices of the Peace for Wash Co, this District, have been confirmed by the Senate:</u>

Jas A Kennedy	Henry Addison	Jos W Beck
Andrew Rothwell	Geo McNeir	Aquilla K Arnold
Henry S Harvey	John McCutchen	Anthony Hyde
Chas Belt	John D Barclay	Alfred Ray
Albert Greenleaf	Benedict Milburn	Paul Stevens
Saml S Briggs	Rhos Donoho	Robt Clarke

Warning to the public. Whereas Annie Taylor, a young mulatto girl aged 9 years, once my property, but recently manumitted by me, & lately in the service of J L Henshaw, has disappeared from her friends, & it is supposed that she has been carried off or secreted to be sold. All persons are warned against purchasing Annie Taylor, or, if a sale of the girl has been effected, the purchaser is advised to take immediate steps towards the recovery of the purchase money.
–Emma D E N Southworth

Died: on Mar 21, Mrs Lydia Cruit, wife of Richd Cruit, in her 48th year. Her funeral is today from her late residence, on Bridge st, Gtwn. [No time given.]

Died: on Mar 21, William, son of Andrew D & Mary J Melcher, aged 9 years. His funeral will be from his father's residence, on N Y ave, at 2:30 o'clock, this day.

Died: yesterday, at St Vincent de Paul Female Academy, Mary Eliz Corbet, aged 4 years.

Died: on Mar 11, in St Louis, Missouri, in his 45th year, Peter Brooks. He was formerly & for many years a respected citizen of Wash City, where he has left a large number of friends & relatives, who sincerely mourn with his family.

THU MAR 23, 1854
$2 reward for taken or stolen, on Mar 20, out of our ofc, Mass ave & 7th st, a Black Box, containing a Tenor Trombone, John Ham, Nathareth, Pa, engraved on a silver plate on the instrument. Leave at this ofc. –Jacob Hunsberger

My residence is at the Nat'l Hotel, Wash, after Mar 20, where notices of opposition to my petition for extension of my patent must be directed. –Sam F B Morse

Mrd: on Tue, by Rev John C Smith, Geo E House, of Mount Gilead, Ohio, to Miss Ellen W, daughter of Alex'r Elliot, of Wash City.

Mrd: on Mar 21, at the Foundry Church, in Wash City, by Rev Job Guest, of Alexandria, Saml Ridgely, of Howard Co, Md, to Ann Eliza, only daughter of John Ross, of Wash.

Mrd: on Mar 8, near Oxford, Talbot Co, Md, by Rev J H Alday, Alex'r E Beall, of Montg Co, Md, to Nellie M Williss; & at the same time, Rev J H Lightbourn to Lizzie S Williss, daughters of Wm B Williss, of the above place.

Died: on Mar 22nd Christiner Moellor, wife of Chas Schussler, in her 36th year, a native of Eschwege Kurhessen. Her funeral will take place today at 3:30, at his residence, at 7th & N Y ave.

Senate: 1-Ptn from Wm B Kibbey, asking the payment of a sum of money due him by the U S for articles furnished for the Penitentiary in D C. 2-Ptn from Leslie Combs, one of the creditors of the late Republic of Texas, asking the payment of certain bonds held by him. 3-Cmte on Commerce: asked to be discharged from the further consideration of the memorial of Burgess B Long, & that it be referred to the Cmte of Claims: which was agreed to. 4-Cmte on Naval Affairs: bill for the relief of Dr S R Addison, passed assist surgeon in the U S service.

FRI MAR 24, 1854
Died: yesterday, at the Nat'l Hotel, of pneumonia, after an illness of 2 weeks, Miss Eliz Westcott, of Florida, the accomplished daughter of Hon J D Westcott, ex-Senator from Florida, having been on a visit to Wash City for a few weeks past. Her funeral will take place this afternoon at 3 o'clock from the Nat'l Hotel.

Nathl G Taylor [Whig] has been elected in the first Congressional district of Tenn, to succeed Hon Brookins Campbell, who died in the early part of the session.

Mr Wm D Breckenridge, agent for the improvement of the public grounds, has resigned that situation, to take effect on the close of the present month.

Died: yesterday, in Wash City, of a pulmonary complaint which had long affected him, John Selah R Hobbie, the distinguished First Assist Postmaster Genr'l. He was born at Newburgh, N Y, on Mar 10, 1797, & died at the age of 57. At an early day he established himself at Delhi, Delaware Co, in the practice of the law, where he married a daughter of Gen Root, with whom he was connected in business. He was early commissioned Dist Atty & Brig Maj & Inspector; he was elected to Congress in 1826; appointed Assist Postmaster Gen on the accession of Gen Jackson to the Presidency in 1829. His unremitting labors impaired his health, & in 1850 he voluntarily retired from Ofc. On Pres Pierce coming into ofc, he yielded to the request of friends, & consented to resume his duties of First Assist P M Gen. As a husband & a father, he was devoted, kind, & affectionate; as a Christian he was sincere & confiding.

Died: on Mar 19, in Wash City, Gov Wm F Duval, of Texas, aged about 70 years. He was a native of Va, went to Ky in his boyhood, whee he studied law & entered his practice. In 1812 he was elected a member to Congress from Bardstown district, & served as such during the sessions of 1813-1814; in 1822 was appointed Govn'r of Florida by Pres Monroe, & re-appointed by Mr Adams & by Gen Jackson. In 1848 he removed to & settled in the State of Texas, where most of his children now reside. Professional business brought him to Wash some months ago, & it has been the will of Providence that his mortal career should terminate at a distance from his home.

Geo W Mitchell & Jos Reynolds, Real Estate Agents & Dealers: ofc on 7th st, between G & H sts.

SAT MAR 25, 1854
Household & kitchen furniture at auction Mar 27, at residence of Mr Wm E Myers, Bridge st, between Congress & High, his entire furniture. –Barnard & Buckey, aucts

Household & kitchen furniture at auction: on Mar 28, at the house of Mrs Jane G Edwards, on Green st, between West & Stoddard sts, the entire furniture. –Barnard & Buckey, aucts

Sale on Mar 28, at the Stable of A de Bodisco, late Russian Minister, on First st, we will sell: 2 Barouche carriages; 1 family carriage; 1 gig; 1 handsome sleigh; 2 market wagons; carriage, wagon, & other harness; 3 cutting boxes; stone roller, harrow, a number of ploughs, posts & lumber. –Barnard & Buckey, auct

Mr Amos Brown, an esteemed citizen of our village, died in convulsions yesterday by eating cloves, which he had been in the habit of using as a substitute for tobacco. -Greenville Advocate

The fine packet-ship **Waterloo** & the packet-ship **Leviathan**, which both cleared from N Y for Liverpool on Dec 19, are given up as lost, with all on board. The **Waterloo** was commanded by Capt Edmund Harvey, & her ofcrs & crew numbered 26. The **Leviathan** was commanded by Capt Rufus Knapp, & had 29 persons on board. Neither ship had passengers. It is supposed that they foundered in the great gale which destroyed the steamer **San Francisco** on Dec 24 & 25. The ship **Constitution** for Havre, with her cargo valued at $270,000, is also no doubt lost. She sailed on Dec 24. The **Leviathan** & cargo were valued at $300,000; the **Waterloo** & cargo at $125,000. The packet-ship **James Drake**, with a valuable cargo, is also supposed to be lost. –Charleston Mercury

Fire at New Orleans on Mar 16: began in the store of E Wood Perry, 60 Magazine st: destroyed. Fire took the establishments of A Delagrave & Co; stores of A L Addison & Co, Price, Walsh & Co, & J H Heald. Dan S Woodruff, Pres of the Exempt Firemens' Benevolent Association, a most worthy man, perceiving that one of the side walls of a bldg was about to fall, cried out to those in the vicinity to fall back, but his foot slipped, he fell, & he could not escape. When extricated from the ruins he was in the last agonies of dissolution, & died in a few minutes. The same accident took the life of Mr Wm McLeod.

Died: on Mar 23, in Wash City, Maj Selah R Hobbie, First Assist Postmaster Genr'l, aged 57 years. His funeral is this afternoon, at 4 o'clock, at his late residence, on 14[th,] near F st.

Died: on Mar 24, in his 62nd year, Henry Aylmer, a native of Ireland, & for 32 years a resident of Petersburg, Va. His funeral will take place on Sunday, at 4 o'clock, from his late residence, corner of Pa ave & 17th st, & proceed to St Matthew's Church. The friends of the family are requested to attend without further notice.

In reply to the advertisement over the signature of Emma D E N Southworth, regarding a mulatto girl Annie. Her publication is one of a series of acts conceived in bitter malignancy against me, for reasons which for the present I forbear to place before the public. The girl Annie, as well as her mother Caroline, are absolutely of right & in law my property, & no right ever existed to Mrs Southworth to manumit them. Caroline has been in my possession for more than 18 years. Annie was born & raised in my house, & has never left it for a day until she was stolen from it on Fri last. –J L Henshaw

For rent: my 3 story Brick House on Bridge st: possession given on Apr 1 next. I wish to hire a woman as chambermaid & to do house work generally. Apply to W S Nicholls, Gtwn.

Valuable Market Garden & Dairy Farm for sale: by decree of the Circuit Court of Fairfax Co: public auction on May 18, 1854, the Farm owned by the heirs of the late Gen R Jones, U S A. It is in said county, on the Potomac river, 7 miles from Gtwn, D C: contains about 510 acres; farm house, suitable for a small family, with out-houses. Mr Hummer, the manager will show the place. –Catesby Ap R Jones, Wash, D C & W H Dulany, Fairfax Court-House, Va, Com'rs

MON MAR 27, 1854

David Jewell, convicted of murder, was executed at Pittsburgh, Pa, on Fri. He confessed that he struck the fatal blow, but alleged that it was unpremeditated, & was given while he was heated with liquor, & in defence of a friend.

Public auction in Gtwn & Wash, D C: by decree of the High Court of Chancery of the State of Md: auction on Apr 12, on the premises of the property in Gtwn, D C: two 3 story brick warehouses, & adjoining 3 story brick dwlg house on Bridge st, belonging to the estate of the late Thos Cramphin. Also, the following vacant property, namely: lots, in Beale's addition, Nos 1, 5, & 6, & parts of lot, in the orginal survey of Gtwn, Nos 5 & 6, fronting on Gay & Congress sts, likewise known as belonging to Cramphin's heirs: this property has been divided into 12 bldg lots, 4 on Gay st, 30 x 110 feet; & 7 of 30 feet each, & one of 31 feet front on Congress st. Also, Lot 3 in square 84 on N Y ave, Wash. Also lot 3 in square 123, fronting on N Y ave, Wash D C. Title to the above property is deemed unquestionable. For particulars apply to Goodwin G Williams, trustee or to Lloyd W Williams, his solicitor, Law Bldgs, Balt.

Calif & Pacific Territories: 1-Geo W Williams, formerly of Va & Wash City, was killed on Feb 16, on his farm in San Jose valley, by the accidental discharge of his rifle. 2-Mr Nathan Pratt, about 50, formerly of Rhode Island, was murdered by 3 Mexicans, near Quartzburg. Two of them had been captured & were hung by the miners of the vicinity. The deed was to take two & three hundred dollars that Pratt was reported to have buried under his hearth. 3-Horace Bull, a native of Va, a lawyer, committed suicide in Sonora on Mar 23. 4-On Mar 21, Wm Garfield, a blacksmith, cut his throat with a razor in Newcastle, Placer Co. He leaves a wife & 3 children in one of the Atlantic States. 5-On Mar 9 F C Hatch, of Mud Springs, committed suicide by stabbing himself with a pocket knife. 6-Robt Scott, convicted of murder at Auburn, has been sentenced to be hung on Mar 31. 7-J B Gates was convicted of manslaughter in Sacramento on Mar 15. 8-In Calaveras Co, John H Thompson was found guilty of murder, & was sentenced to be hung on Apr 14. Robt Warren at the same term of court, was conviced of manslaughter, & sentenced to 2 years' imprisonment.

We learn from the Western Texas of Mar 2, that Col Stem, late Indian Agent for the State of Texas, was recently killed by a party of Indians, about 4 miles from **Fort Belknap**. Col Stem & another gentleman were riding out in a buggy, & both of them shared the same fate.

TUE MAR 28, 1854
Stock of retail grocery at auction: Mar 31, at the store of Mr J Smith, D st, between 14th & 15th sts, near Birch's Livery Stables: all his stock. -Jas C McGuire, auct

Chancery sale: by a decree of the Circuit Court of Wash Co, D C, in equity, in the cause of Wm J Gray & Susan R Stinger vs Nathan Gray, Benj Gray, & al, No 898, dated Dec 11, 1853. Auction on Apr 11, on the premises: lot 105 in Beatty & Hawkins addition to Gtwn, fronting 70 feet on the north side of First st. Lot 115, in the same addition in Gtwn, fronting 70 feet on the south side of 2nd st, running back 150 feet. –Walter S Cox, trustee -E S Wright, auct

Household & kitchen furniture at auction: on Apr 3, at the residence of G R Herrick, on K st, near 12th st. –Green & Scott, auct

This is to give notice that the original Land Warrant 5,777, issued Apr 6, 1840, for 1,664½ acres of land, to Wm, Jas, Saml W, Martha A T, & Jas Wood, & No 8,949, for 100 acres, issued Jul 19, 1841, to Robt Wood, for which exchange warrant No 499, issued Jul 24, 1841, to Jas M Speed, assignee of Robt Wood, all issued for the services of Jas Wood, a pilot in the State navy of Va, have been lost or mislaid or destroyed; application will be made to the Gen Land Ofc for the issue of scrip upon duplication of said warrants. –John F Webb, for the heirs.

WED MAR 29, 1854
Senate: 1-Ptn from John S Rhea, asking to be credited with a sum of money stolen while in his custody as collector of the customs for the district of Brasos Santiago, Texas. 2-Document in relation to the claim of the widow of Maj Ripley A Arnold, of the U S dragoons, to a pension: submitted. 3-The case of Geo A Gardiner & John H Mears, in the first of which the sum of $428,750 was allowed to Gardiner, & in the second the sum of $153.123 to Mears. Gardiner claimed $500,000 for the destruction of certain mines in the State of San Luis Potosi. A cmte of Hon Henry May, Jas K Partridge, Buckingham Smith, Lt W W Hunter, U S Navy, & Capt Abner Doubleday, U S Army, the last two of whom were designated by the Pres of the U S, went to San Luis Potosi to ascertain the truth of the allegation. At first Gardiner accepted going with them to point out the mines alleged to have been destroyed, & later declined. The com'rs report: 1-Geo A Gardiner is not, never was, a citizen of the U S. 2-Neither Gardiner nor Mears ever owned or were interested in a silver or quicksilver mine, or any kind of mine, in the State of San Luis Potosi, in Mexico. 3-Neither was expelled from that State. 4-Gardiner was not in San Luis Potosi at that time, but engaged as a manager of a small mining concern, as a dentist, & as a

pedlar in small wares. 5-Every paper coming from Gardiner & Mears is false & forged. The money allowed to Gardiner & Mears was obtained upon forged & fabricated papers. The cmte have agreed to ask to be discharged from all the memorials submitted to them, except those of Jonas P Levy & Jose Maria Jarrero. In the case of Alex'r J Atocha the cmte came to no decision.

House of Reps: 1-Ptn of Martha Swain, asking that a pension be allowed her. 2-Ptn from Wm H Wilson, for an increase of his pension as an invalid.

Capt Thos W Wyman, of the U S Navy, died at Florence, Italy, on Feb 25, of an affection of the heart. A letter states that he arrived there, in company with Mrs Wyman, six weeks previous.

Hon K Boyce, who lately died at Charleston, S C, by his will left the College of Charleston, $30,000 & the Orphan House $20,000.

Dabney S Carr, for many years a resident of Balt, died at Charlottesville, Va, on Mar 24, in his 53rd year. He formerly for several years filled the post of Naval Ofcr at Balt, & was subsequently U S Minister to Constantinople for 6 years.

On Tue last, during an experimental trip from Richmond to Staunton over the Central Railroad, the engine was struck & the end of the car was stove in. Mr Geo Clements, after jumping off, fell under the car & had both of his legs crushed. There are no hopes of his recovery.

Valuable real estate at public sale: the private residence of the late Maj Reybold, of Red Line Hundred, near Delaware City, Delaware, consisting of a very superior Brick Mansion 44 by 50 feet, with a wing, also of brick, 34 by 19 feet, & a neat Kitchen attached; with good substantial porches Many necessary out-bldgs, erected within the last 7 years. New Castle, the county town, is within 6 miles. –John Reybold, Wm Reybold, Barney Reybold, Anthony Reybold, excs of the estate of Philip Reybold, deceased. [After the above sale, household & kitchen furniture will be sold at public auction.]

Mrd: on Mar 27, at St Patrick's Church, by Rev Fr Denecker, Mr Louis Marceron to Mrs Rose L O'Bryon, both of Wash City.

Died: on Mar 24, at Sydenham, near Phil, Mrs Catherine Eliza Rush, wife of Hon Richd Rush, in her 71st year.

Died: on Mar 28, Mrs Ann Eliz Lane, consort of Chas H Lane, of Wash City, & daughter of the late Jas B Rooker. Her funeral is on Wed at 3:30 o'clock, from her late residence, on E st, between 6th & 7th sts.

Died: on Mar 28, Doct Danl King, in his 51st year. His funeral is today at 4 o'clock, from the residence of his father, Wm King, on Congress st, Gtwn.

Died: on Mar 27, after a short & severe illness, Sarah A, relict of the late Thos Cross, in her 78th year. Her funeral is this afternoon at 3 o'clock, from the residence of her son, on Ga ave, Navy Yard.

Died: on Feb 26, at Lochbie, East Florida, of consumption, Edw H Oates, 3rd & youngest son of the late Geo Oates, of Charleston, S C, aged 29 years. Affection will cherish his memory. His family & friends mourn his loss.

THU MAR 30, 1854
Mrd: on Mar 29, by Rev Geo Sampson, Dr E M Chapin to Helan M Weaver, all of Wash City.

Mrd: on Mar 19, in Balt, by Rev Dr Jones, Jas L Smith to Mrs Lucinda L Hough, all of Wash.

Senate: 1-Ptn from Henry Chronchey, a British subject, asking compensation for his services as clerk to the U S Legation at London. 2-Ptn from Joshua W Post, asking the aid of Congress to enable him to test a system of telegraphic communications by atmospheric pressure. 3-Ptn from John L Allen & A R Carter, land ofcrs at Augusta, Miss, asking an increase of compensation. 4-Ptn from Robt A Kinsie & John H Whistler, licensed Indian traders, asking payment for supplies furnished the Sac & Fox Indians. 5-Ptn from Wm J Grayson, asking a commission on money disbursed by him on account of the new custom-house at Charleston, S C. 6-Ptn from the Legislature of Alabama, asking the the horses & equipage purchased for Capt French's company of volunteers in the Creek war of 1836 may be paid for. 7-Cmte on Private Land Claims: bill for the relief of Manuel Hernandez; also a bill for the relief of Sylvanus Culver. 8-Cmte on Pensions: adverse report on the ptn of the widow of C L Williamson. 9-Cmte on Revolutionary Claims: adverse report on the ptn of Thos Foster & others.

Jonathan Harrington, the last survivor of the gallant band who were engaged in the first conflict of the American Revolution, died at Lexington, Mass, on Sunday, in his 96th year. He was a fifer for the minute men who assembled at Lexington Green on Apr 19, 1775; at the time but 17 years old, preparing for college, but the events of the day, resulting in the destruction of his books, changed the course of his life. May his reward be commensurate with the wishes of a grateful country.

Philip Greeley, late Collector of the port of Boston, died at Havana on Mar 15, aged about 48 years.

FRI MAR 31, 1854
Senate: 1-Cmte on Private Land Claims: bill for the relief of Jean Baptiste Beaubien. Same cmte: bill for the relief of John Gusman, of Louisana. 2-Cmte on Foreign Relations: bill for the relief of the reps of Thos D Anderson, late Consul of the U S at Tripoli.

Railroad accident on Tue about 9 miles west of Syracuse, killed Mr Coleman, the engineer, & an Indian who was sleeping in one of the freight cars.

House of Reps: 1-Ptn of Jas Adams, of Crawford Co, Pa, for a pension for services rendered the U S in 1794 & 1795, & also for services during the war of 1812. 2-Ptn of Jas Chambers, for the correction of an error in the date of the commencement of his invalid pension.

Ogdensburgh, N Y, Mar 29. The house of Cooper Tyler, at North Lawrence, was burnt last night, while himself & wife were out visiting, & his 7 young children perished in the flames. The oldest was but 9 years of age.

Boston, Mar 29. The dwlg of Wm Flanders, at Londonderry, N H, was burnt yesterday, & 3 children were burnt to death.

Dissolution of co-partnership, under the firm of Statham, Smithson & Co, on Dec 31, 1853. –Chas W Statham, Wm T Smithson, Jas G Hamilton

$50 reward for return of 2 horses, stolen or strayed on Mar 29. –Allen S Dorsey, Livery Stable Keeper, 7th st, between H & I sts, Wash.

SAT APR 1, 1854
Died: on Mar 31, after an illness of a few days, William Clyne, aged 4 years, 4 months & 17 days, only child of the late Geo W & Isabella C Frazier. His funeral will be from the residence of his grandmother, Mrs Isabella Sutherland, East Capitol st, between 1st & 2nd sts, Capitol Hill, Apr 24, at 3 o'clock.

Senate: 1-Cmte on Naval Affairs: bill for the relief of Robt Joyner: the bill is to relieve him from the accountability of certain stores missing at the navy yard at Pensacola, where he was naval storekeeper. 2-Private bill for the relief of Hodges & Landsdale, & the legal reps of Rinaldo Johnson & Ann E Johnson: passed.

House of Reps: 1-Private bills referred: relief of-Theodore E Elliott; of Dempsey Pittman; of Asbury Dickens; of Lt a J Williamson; of Wm P S Sanger; of Mrs Helen Mackay, adm of Lt Col Aeneas Mackay, late deputy quartermaster in the U S army; of W R Nevins; of the excx of the late Bvt Col A C W Fanning, of the U S army; of the heirs & reps of Col Alex G Morgan; & of John Gusman, of La. Also, the purchase of the copyright of a work published by Thos H Sumner.

Improved property at auction: on Apr 12, a large brick bldg, nearly new, fronting on the alley in Reservation 10, it being the bldg lately occupied by Messrs Davis & Garret as a carpenter's shop. —Green & Scott, aucts

A child of Mr Jas S Browning, No 48 South Exeter st, Balt, has been missing since Mar 10. He was last seen by a neighbor on that day with a stranger, in a square covered wagon. Any intelligence concerning him will be gratefully received by his parents.

The remains of the late John Howard Payne, [the author of Home, Sweet Home,] are to be brought to this country & placed in the **Congressional Burial Ground**, & a suitable monument erected to his memory.

Edw Cullen, Thos Vell, & Thos McCoy were drowned on Tue in the Delaware, above Richmond. Their yawl upset.

The copartnership existing under the firm of Corcoran & Riggs, has this day been dissolved by mutual consent. —W W Corcoran, Elisha Riggs
+
The undersigned have formed a copartnership under the name of Riggs & Co, for continuing the Gen Banking Business conducted by their friends, Messrs Corcoran & Riggs. —Geo W Riggs, jr, A T Kieckhoefer

On Mar 16, Justice Talfourd, while charging the Grand Jury at Stafford, was attacked with a fit of apoplexy, of which he died. Thos Noon Talfourd was born at Reading, Jan 26, 1795. His father was a brewer; his mother the daughter of a dissenting minister. He went to London at age 18 & was a student of law under Chitty, the celebrated pleader, in 1813; admitted to the bar in 1821; married in 1822. —N Y Post

The locomotive on the freight train near Providence exploded. John Morris, the engineer, Thos Ratcliffe, the fireman, & John Merrill, a hand on the train, were all killed.

The wife of Joel Willard, residing at Buffalo, N Y, died on Tue of hydrophobia. She was bitten by a cat about 2 months ago. Her sufferings during 2 days were intense.

By writ of venditioni expenas, issued by J H Goddard, J P of Wash Co, D C: I will expose to sale at public auction, in front of the premises, on Apr 10, 1854, all the right, title, claim, & interest, & estate, at law & in equity, of Patrick Goins, in part of lot 8 in square 80, in Wash City, fronting on 22nd st west, running back with that width 62 feet 2 inches, late the property of Patrick Goins. Seized & taken in execution at the suit of Wm T Dove. —Wm Cox, constable

While in pursuit of a deer, a few days ago, John O'Niel, of Whiting, Me, slipped & accidentally discharged his gun, the contents entered the lower part of his body, causing his death after a day or two of excruciating suffering.

MON APR 3, 1854
Died: on Apr 1, Wm A Gunton, in his 28th year. His funeral will be from the residence of his father, Dr Wm Gunton, this afternoon, at 3½ o'clock.

Geo W Kellogg, convicted of altering bank bills & uttering the same, at the present term of the Recorder's Court at Buffalo, N Y, has been taken to Auburn. His sentence is for 20 years & 3 months. Jas Rogers, indicted for passing counterfeit money, was tried, convicted, & sentenced by the same Court to Auburn for 7 years & 1 month.

The funeral of the last of the heroes of Bunker Hill, Jonathan Harrington, the last survivor of Lexington, was celebrated on Mar 30, & was very imposing. The Govn'r, Lt-Govn'r, Exec Council, & members of both branches of the Legislature of Mass were present; 18 miltary companies & several masonic orders were in the procession, & some 6,000 strangers were in the town of Lexington. –Boston Journal

TUE APR 4, 1854
The late Gen John Cocke: died on Feb 16, 1854, closing a life of more than 80 years. He was the oldest son of Col Wm Cocke, & was born in Nottoway Co, Va, in 1772 or 1773. In early childhood his father emigrated into what is now East Tenn, & was a busy & prominent actor in the all the public events during the 20 years which closed the century, being one of the first Senators in Congress from the State. Gen John Cocke was a member of the first Legislature of Tenn in 1796; for 8 years, 1819 to 1827, he was an active member of Congress. His wife, the companion of his youth, his middle life, his old age, united to him for nearly 60 years, had but a few months before died. He has left numerous descendants & a large circle of friends to mourn his loss & to cherish his memory.

Senate: 1-Ptn from Frances Depriest, widow of John Depriest, asking to be allowed the bounty land that her husband was entitled to. 2-Cmte on Military Affairs: adverse report on the memorial of Lt Fremont. Same cmte: asked to be discharged from the further consideration of the bill for the relief of Catharine B Arnot, & that it be referred to the Cmte on Pensions: which was agreed to. Same cmte: bill for the relief of A G Bennett. 3-Cmte on Indian Affairs: bill for the relief of Jas Erwin, of Ark, & others. 4-Cmte on the Post Ofc & Post Roads: bill for the relief of Jas M Goggin: passed. Same cmte: bill for the relief of Thos C Nye. 5-Cmte on Pensions: adverse report on the case of Wyman Badger for an increase of pension. 6-Cmte on Public Lands: adverse report on the memorial of Cadwallader Wallace.

Tragedy in Lexington, Va. Mr Jos W Moore, the keeper of a hotel, was on Thu last deliberately stabbed with a knife or dirk, while standing in front of his hotel, & died in a very short time. —Richmond Enquirer

Mr David Hunt, a wealthy planter of Miss, gave $12,000 to an institution of learning, $5,000 to the Orleans sufferers during the late pestilential scourge, & $5,000 to an orphan asylum in his own State. These sums respectively bestowed when & where they were needed, are worth more than two-fold left in legacies to be consumed in litigation.

House of Reps: 1-Bill for the relief of Jas McCabe: introduced.

I have this day associated with me Mr Fred L Harvey, in the Hardware Business, in the new warehouse next to Messrs G & T Parker & Co. The firm will be under the name of E Wheeler & Co. —E Wheeler, F L Harvey

Mrd: on Mar 23, in Keokuck, Iowa, by Rev Geo Denison, Wm W Belknap, formerly of Gtwn, D C, to Miss Cora Le Roy, daughter of the late Alexis Le Roy, of Vincennes, Indiana.

For rent: two first class Brick Houses in Franklin Place, on I st, between 13th & 14th sts. Inquire of Henry N Lansdale, on 8th st, between M & N sts.

Wash City Ordinances: 1-Act for the relief of Lewis Carusi: the fine imposed on him is remitted: provided he pay the costs of prosecution. 2-Act for the relief of Edw Murphy: the sum of $20 be paid to him, as indemnity for that sum paid by him for a fine. 3-Act for the relief of J T Garner: the sum of $22 be paid to him for paving & repairing the gutter on 10th st, between G & H sts. 4-Act to pay M P Mohun one-half of the expenses of a well & pump: the sum of $55.08 is appropriated.

Barrel timber wanted: copartnership has been formed under the firm of Milburn & Co, for the purpose of conducting the coopering business.
—Benedict Milburn, John Van Riswick

The Supreme Court of the U S re-assembled at the Capitol in Wash City yesterday. There were present Hon Roger B Taney, Chief Justice. Assoc Justices: Jas M Wayne, John Catron, Peter V Daniel, Saml Nelson, B R Curtis, & Jno A Campbell. Jas B Campbell, of S C; C B F O'Neill, of Pa; & Chas Bayard Strode, of Calif, were admitted attys & counselors of this Court.

Fatal accident near Basil, Ohio, on Wed. Mr John S_tphen, of that place, sent out his two sons, aged 11 & 9 years, into the field to attend upon the burning of some logs. The fire communicated to a large beach tree, which falling, killed both the boys instantly.

In Chancery. Jas Adams, Jos Ingle, John Underwood & Christiana his wife, Wm H Campbell & Mary his wife, Eleazer Lindsley & Anna his wife, Jas G Coombe & Mary Coombe, Maria C Fitzhugh, Anne C Carroll, Jane Carroll, Rebecca Carroll, Augustus A Nicholson & Sarah his wife, ___ Fitzhugh & Catherine his wife, Henry M Brent, Henry J Brent, Jas Edelin, Wm B Randolph, Elbert G Emack, Mary P Emack, Thos H Brown & Mary Ann his wife, John D Emack, Rebecca J Emack, Wm Emack, Harriet Emack, & Mgt Emack, & Henry Bradley, cmplnts, & John P Ingle, John A Bailey, Alex'r C Washburne & Ellen M his wife, Frank Moore & Laura M his wife, Chas H Carroll, Danl J Carroll, Wm T Carroll, Henry Fitzhugh & Eliz his wife, Tasker T Gantt & Mary his wife, ___ Littlejohn & Olivia his wife, ___ Peake & Eliz his wife, Ann Tabbs, Hardage Lane, & Julia Thompson, dfndnts.

The bill states that in 1815 an association or joint stock company, called the Capitol Hotel Co, was formed in Wash City, for the purpose of purchasing lots, & erecting bldgs for the accommodation of Congress until the Captiol, then recently destroyed by the enemy, should be repaired; that lots 14 thru 19 in square 728, in Wash City, were purchased for that purpose by the late Danl Carroll, as the agent, & for the use of the company, & the proper bldgs were erected.. That the said Danl Carroll afterwards conveyed the lots & bldgs to the late Griffith Combe, & to John P Ingle, in trust for the shareholders in the company. That the objects of the association have long since been fulfilled by the rebldg of the Capitol, & the abandonment by Congress of the temporary accommodation prepared for them by the company; & in the present condition of the property the rents are wholly inadequate to meet the interest of the capital invested, the taxes, insurance, & cost of repairs of the bldgs, which are now untenanted, & require extensive repairs to fit them for the occupation of tenants. That great changes have taken place in the constituent members of the company, partly by death & partly by transfers of shares, & from the infancy of the reps of some of the deceased members, & the non-residents of others, the burden of the conservation of the premises & of the management of the affairs of the company has devolved chiefly upon the said John P Ingle; & that it will be greatly for the benefit & advantage as well of the minors as adults that the said premises should be sold & the trust closed by the distribution of the proceeds among the shareholders. The object of the said bill is to obtain such sale & effect such distribution. The dfndnts, John A Bailey, Alex'r C Washburn & Ellen M his wife, Frank Moore & Laura M his wife, ___Littlejohn & Olivia his wife, ___ Peake & Eliz his wife, Ann Tabbs, & Hardage Lane, reside out of the jurisdiction of the Court; same are to appear on or before the first Monday of Oct next; or that in default thereof the said bill be taken pro confesso against them. –Jno A Smith, clerk -Redin for cmplnts.

WED APR 5, 1854
For rent, the house lately occupied by Mr J W Thompson, on 11th st, between G & H sts. Apply to Lewis Johnson.

Wash Corp: 1-Wm Douglass confirmed as inspector & measurer of lumber, vice Wm G Deale, resigned. 2-Ptn of P Thyson & others in relation to defective drainage at 7th & H sts: referred to the Cmte on Improvements. 3-Ptns of as T Barnes; Dennis Smallwood; & of Jos Beardsley; for the remission of a fine: each referred to the Cmte of Claims.

Shocking murder in Chapel Hill on Sat last, by J Brockwell, upon the person of Mr Jas Davis. Brockwell went to Davis' & used some very offensive language, & Mrs Davis told him he must go away; he refused. Mr Davis took him by the arm & asked him to leave. Brockwell drew his knife & stabbed Davis several times, killing him almost instantly. The murderer is a worthless drunken loafer; but his victim was a highly respectable mechanic & member of the Methodist Church. Brockwell was arrested & is in prison to await his trial. –Raleigh Star

John Phyfe, Dealer in Ivory & Manufacturer of Ivory Goods, Murray st, N Y.

The foreign papers announce that Signor Rubini, the great Italian tenor singer, the associate of Grial, Lablache, & Tamburtal, in their greatest day, died at Romano, in the province of B_rgamo, on Mar 2. He was 60 years of age, &, having acquired a large fortune as well as lost his fine voice, he had for some years lived in retired but elegant ease.

The Metropolitan M E Church is to be built at the corner of 4½ & C sts. The plan selected was by Mr Saml T G Morsell. The gentlemen elected on the Bldg Cmte are Messrs W G Deale, John C McKelden, Sam Fowler, P W Browning, & Chas H Lane. The general style of the bldg will be Romanesque.

Chas Ahrents, an immigrant from Purssia, met his death at Freeman's Hall, in Cincinnati a few evenings ago. He wagered with Chas Frohlick, a military ofcr in the Austrian war, supposedly with blank cartridges. Ahrents had Frohlick shoot at him first. The cartridge was not empty & it is supposed that Ahrents knew this & wanted to be killed. He had previously attempted suicide.

Mrs L Allen will open, on Apr 8, Spring Millinery: Pa ave, between 9th & 10th sts.

THU APR 6, 1854
Mr Albert Balch, superintendent of car repairs, was killed at St Johnsbury, Vt, on Sat last.

On Sat last, at Lagrange, Miss Lavina Boggs/Beggs, of Wheeling, lost her life from having her clothes caught in the machinery of a paper mill. She was about 17, & an exemplary Christian.

For sale: by deed of trust recorded in Liber J A S 23, folios 31 thru 34, of the land records of Wash Co, D C: private sale, the north 24 feet & 4 inches of lot 8 in square 904, fronting on 7th st, with a 2 story frame dwlg, with necessary outbldgs. For particulars inquire of John W McKim, trustee.

Desirable Farm at public sale on Apr 13, on the premises, a Farm containing 172 acres of land, in Montg Co, Md. It adjoins the lands of Messrs Perry, Duffy, & Radcliff, & is within a quarter of a mile of the turnpike at Bethesda Church. Apply to Mr G E Brent, who resides near the premises, or to the subscribers in Wash, D C. -Green & Scott, aucts

Spring Millinery: Miss E E McDonald, successor to Mrs Ann H Clarke, immediately from N Y. Store is 3 doors east of the Post Ofc, on Bridge st, Gtwn.

Orphans Court of Wash Co, D C. Letters of administration on the personal estate of Catharine Mackall, late of Wash Co, deceased. –Richd Smith, adm

Breakfast at 8 & dinner at 12½ o'clock every day, can be had for 37½ cents each at Casparis', on Capitol Hill. Apply at his Refectory. Lodging 50 cents. Handsome furnished rooms to let, with or without board. –J Casparis

The unfortunate death at Balt of Dr Jos M Tastet, a native of Wash City, & until recently a resident here, will be a subject of painful interest to a large circle of friends. He was located at Woodberry, in Balt Co, Md, & on a visit to Balt City on Apr 3, & whilst riding his horse leisurely on Cathedral st, between the Bolton depot & Biddle st, the animal stumbled over the iron rail of one of the numerous switches in that vicinity, throwing the doctor, & afterwards falling on him, causing concussion of the brain & other fatal internal injuries, from the effects of which he did not rally, & death ensued the same night. He was attended to by Drs Ridely, Johns, & Smith, & attentively waited on at home by Dr Cherbonnier, of Washingtonville, until he expired. Dr Tastet was a regular Sunday school teacher.
+
Died: at Woodbury, Md, on Apr 4, Dr Jos M Tastet, eldest son of Nicholas Tastet, of Wash City, aged 31 years. The subject of the above obituary lost his life by injuries incurred from being thrown from his horse, & the horse falling upon him, on Monday last, in the city of Balt. His funeral will take place this afternoon, at 3:30 o'clock, from the residence of his father-in-law, Mr Thos Mustin, on G st, between 13th & 14th sts.

Senate: Cmte on Patents: bill for the relief of the heirs of the late Uri Emmons. 2-Cmte of Claims: bill for the relief of Michl Nourse. 3-Bill for the relief of Wm Claude Jones: passed.

House of Reps: 1-Cmte on Invalid Pensions: adverse reports on the ptns of Morris G Holmes; of Danl Ladd; of Elijah Frye; of Benj F Wesley; of Constance A Palmer; of Oliver Main; of John Owen; of Hiram Cook & others, heirs of Archibald Cook; of Levi Colmus; of E P Hastings; of Jas M French, of N Y; & of Robt H Stephens, of N Y. Also, from the same cmte: bills committed: relief of Saml McKnight, of Ky; of Wm Wallace, of Illinois; & of Geo M Bentley, of Indiana. Same cmte: bill increasing the pension of Albert Hart: recommended that it do not pass: laid on the table. 2-Cmte on the Post Ofc & Post Roads: bill for the relief of Zadoc C Inghram: committed. Same cmte: bill for the benefit of J C Buckles; & a bill for the benefit of McAtee & Eastham: committed. Same cmte: bill for the relief of Jas S Graham & Walter H Finnall: committed.

F N Roche has removed to the store corner of F & 13th sts, for many years occupied by the late Elexius Simms, & has on hand a selected stock of Groceries, Wines, & Liquores.

Notice: the original Land Warrant, 1,579, issued Aug 18, 1783, for 2,666 2/3 acres of land, to Given Summerson for his services as a Midshipman in the State Navy of Va; Land Warrant 576, issued May 14, 1783, for 200 acres of land, to Burnell Bacon for his services as a Cpl in the Va State Artl or Continental Establishment; Land Warrant 2,563, issued Feb 21, 17__, for 2,666 2/3 acres of land, to John Vaughan for his services as a Lt in the Va State Line; Land warrant 84, issued Dec 31, 1782, for 4,000 acres of land to Jas Quaries for his services as a Capt in the State Line of Va, have been lost, mislaid, or destroyed. Application will be made to the Gen Land Ofc for duplicate warrants. –John F Webb, for the heirs.

FRI APR 7, 1854
A Baldwin, at his Factory, corner of 3rd st & Indiana ave, is prepared to fill all orders for doors, sash, blinds, & mouldings.

Senate: 1-Ptn from Geo B Clarke, asking that a certain amount of Continental money owned by him may be redeemed by the U S. 2-Additional documents submitted in support of the claim of John W Kelley, for indemnity for losses sustained by the abrogation of a contract with the Post Ofc Dept. 3-Bill for the relief of Harriet Leavenworth, widow of the late Brev Brig Gen Leavenworth: passed. 4-Bill for the relief of Jos Smith: passed.

Jos Mayo, was on Wed last, re-elected Mayor of the city of Richmond, without opposition.

Mrs M A Scrivener has removed to 11th st, over Wm P Shedd's millinery & fancy stores, where she would be pleased to receive orders for ornamental needlework.

Election of municipal ofcrs in Annapolis on Mon: Dr Abram Claude [Whig] was elected Mayor by a majority of 4 votes over Col Walton, [Democrat.]

House of Reps: 1-The Pres transmits a large mass of documents, covering correspondence from 1835 to the present time, with reference to all matters not yet settled between the U S & Spain. The papers have relation to the following named cases: Crescent City; steamer **Ohio** & schnr **Manchester**; John S Thracher; steamer **Falcon**; schnr **Lamartine**; Ray, alias Garcia; Peire Rocices; Chas Peter; B V Esnard; John Salivero; Capt Larrabee; the annulling of the Cuban decree; Michl D Haran; seamen belonging to the brig **Jasper**; Black Warrior; opening of the mails of the U S by the authorities of Cuba; & the Centoy prisoners. Referred to the Cmte on Foreign Affairs & ordered to be printed.

Gtwn Municipal election yesterday, to fill the vacancy in the Common Council of Gtwn, was caused by the resignation of Mr Tenney. It resulted in Mr Tenney's re-election by 21 votes over Mr Robt White, his competitor. The vote was Tenney 224, White 203. Mr Tenney represented the one dollar party, & Mr White the one dollar & a half.

I have just received from the northern markets a very large supply of Spring Goods, of every kind. –Ruth A Praco, Pa ave, between 8th & 9th sts.

Household & kitchen furniture at auction: Apr 12, at the residence of Nicholas Halter, on north M, between 5th & 6th sts, opposite Col Seaton's gardens: excellent assortment of furniture. –Green & Scott, aucts

For rent: a 2 story & basement brick house, on I st, between 6th & 7th sts. Apply at the House-furnishing Warerooms of N M McGregor, 7th st.

SAT APR 8, 1854
New Book: The U S Grinnell Expedition in Search of Sir John Franklin. A Personal Narrative by Elisha Kent Kane, M D, U S Navy. N Y: Harper & Brethrem, 1854. The expedition consisted of the brig **Advance** & the brig **Rescue**, commanded respectively by Lt Edwin J De Haven, commanding the expedition, & by Acting-Master Saml P Griffin, both of whom, together with the other ofcrs of the personnel engaged in this undertaking, were detailed from the U S navy for this purpose by Wm Ballard Preston, the Sec of this Dept during Gen Taylor's administration. The expedition took its departure from N Y on May 22, 1850. [Dec 6th newspaper: The Journal of Commerce says: "Dr Kane was when last heard from at Smith's Sound, & it is improbable that any of his party should have since then found their way down to the Back river, where Sir John Franklin is supposed to have perished. We fear that the story will prove to be a distorted version of the account of Dr Rae, originating in the substitution for his name of that of Dr Kane."]

Chancery sale: by decree of the Circuit Court of Wash Co, D C, made in the case of Wm Bird et al, vs Horatio R Maryman, exc of Zachariah Hazel et al, public auction on Apr 19, on the premises, of lots 14 & 15 in square 867, at the corner of 6th & H sts. –Walter S Cox, trustee -Green & Scott, aucts

Franklin Pierce, Pres of the U S A, recognizes Geronimo Roca, who has been appointed Consul of Spain for the port of Phil, in Pa. –Apr 1, 1854

Mrd: on Apr 3, at Pembroke, N H, Rev Wm Hawes, M G Every, of Wash, to Mary K, youngest daughter of Wm Haseltine, of the former place.

Mrd: on Thu, by Rev John C Smith, Mr Robt H Graham to Miss Ann S Hiller, all of Wash City.

Died: on Apr 6, after a lingering illess, Rebecca, consort of A Dixon, in her 31st year. Her funeral will be from her late residence on 8th st, between D & E sts, tomorrow at 3 o'clock.

Died: on Apr 7, in Wash City, Charles W Cox, aged 2 years, 9 months & 15 days, son of C A & Eliz Cox. His funeral is this afternoon, at 2 o'clock, from 4th & Pa ave.

Died: on Apr 5, at Annapolis, after an illness of 12 hours, Maria, youngest daughter of Prof J E & Sarah W Nourse.

Senate: 1-Bills passed: relief of-Thos Butler; of Mrs Sally T B Cochrane, widow of the late Lt R E Cochrane, U S Army; of Thos B Parsons; of Amos Knapp; of Lyman N Cook; of Emilie Hooe, widow of Capt Hooe; of Hezekiah Johnson, of Bridgewater, Vt; of Aaron Stafford; of Wm B Edwards; of Mary Carlton; of Cmder G H Pendergrast; of the execs of the late Lt John E Bispham; of Thos S Russell; of Alton Nelson; of Jas Wormsley; of E J McLane; of Alex'r Lea; of Gideon Hotchkiss; of Robt Jemison & Benj Williamson; of Almanzon Huston; of Mark Bean & Richd H Bean, of Ark; of Levi Pierce & And Hodge, jr; of Andrew J Dickerhoff; of Theresa Dardenne, widow of Abraham Dardenne, & their children; of Henry La Reintree; of Hezekiah Miller; of Wm Miller; of Lemuel Hudson; of J F Green; of Llewellyn Washington; of the heirs of Brig Gen B Mason; of Madison Parton; of the heirs & reps of the late Robt Sewall; of Dr S R Addison, passed assist surgeon in the U S navy; of Manuel Hernandez; of Sylvanus Culver; of Jean Baptiste Beaubien; of Thos Rhodes; of Robt Joyner; of Jas Erwin, of Ark, & others; of A G Bennett; & of Michl Nourse. Also, a pension for Silas Champion, of Genesse Co, N Y. 2-Bill introduced for the relief of L E & L A Lawson, sole surviving heirs of Gen Eleazer W Ripley, deceased. 3-Bill introduced to change the name of the barque **Abeona** to barque **Mount Vernon**.

Appointments by the Pres, by & with the advice & consent of the Senate. 1-Chas S Frailey, of Ohio, to be principal clerk of public lands in the Gen Land Ofc, vice E A Cabell, resigned. 2-John W Whitfield, of Tenn, to be Indian agent at the Upper Platte Agency, vice Thos Fitzpatrick, deceased. 3-Richd C J Brown, of Ark, to be Agent for the Pottawatomies Indians & Kansas Indians, vice John W Wringfield.

A young man named Hilles accidentally shot his sister last week, near Gtwn Cross Roads, Md, whilst trifling with his gun. Her physician thinks she cannot recover.

At Portland, on Tue, J B Cahoon, [Whig] was re-elected Mayor, in opposition to Neal Dow, the author of the Maine law.

A fight occurred at the Monticello House, Charlottesville, Va, on Monday last, between W Edw Garth, of Albemarle, & David W Flournoy, of Charlotte Counties. The fought with pistols & bowie-knives. Both parties were wounded; Mr Garth dangerously, & Mr Flournoy slightly.

Jas Marshall, residing in Phil Co, drank a pint of liquor on Thu last, on a wager of $500, & in 3 hours became insensible, & died the same evening.

Mrs Judith Town, of Marshall, Oneida Co, N Y, died a few days since, aged 107 years. Her eldest daughter is living, aged 85 years.

For sale: at the Citizens' Line Stables, near the Capitol, one fine large dark gray Mare; & one roan Horse, both perfectly gentle. –Wm Weeden

MON APR 10, 1854
Names of the Board of Visitors appointed to attend the examination of the Military Academy at West Point, Jun 1, 1854:

Hon John J Morrison, of Indiana
Winslow Turner, of Missouri
J B Luckie, of Ark
Chas W Whipple, of Mich
Dr H M Kinsey, of Texas
Saml Y Bayard, of N Y
*Geo Holtzbecker, of Delaware
Hon J Clemens, of Wheeling, Va
[*Added per Apr 11th newspaper.]

Wm W Lea, of Tenn
L V Dickerson, of Ky
Richd De Treville, of S C
Jacob Kent, of Vt
Hon Wm C Clarke, of N H
John B Harmon, of Calif
Rev Robt Allyn, of R I
John A Campbell, of Illinois

At N Y, on Thu, while 4 young men were standing on a temporary platform, which had been raised over the hatchway in the Sugar Refinery of Peter Maller & Co, gave way & precipitated them to the floor beneath, a distance of 40 feet. Fred'k Noyman was instantly killed, & John Pauls, John Stansbury, & Augustine Pourman were dangerously wounded.

Franklin Pierce, Pres of the U S A, recognizes Ricardo W Heath, appointed Consul of the Republic of Salvador for the port of San Francisco, in Calif. -Apr 4, 1854

Jas Ticer, 18 years of age, son of Mr Lewis Ticer, of Alexandria, on Sat fell into the hold amongst the machinery of the steamboat **Thomas Collier**, whilst it was in motion, & was almost instantly crushed to death.

At Albany, N Y, on Friday last, John Hendrickson, jr, was re-sentenced to be hung for the murder of his wife. He was convicted & sentenced, after a long & tedious trial, some months ago, but application was made to the Court of Appeals to allow him a new trial on the ground that his own evidence before the Coroner, given before he was arrested, if not before he was even suspected of the murder, was wrongfully used against him on his trial. The Court of Appeals decided that where testimony has been given by a party who has not been formally accused of crime, it may subsequently be used against him. Five of the Judges concurred in this opinion, & three were in favor of a new trial. The case then went back to the inferior Court, which again sentenced him to death.

Criminal Court-Wash-tired during the week. 1-Mrs Barnard, of Gtwn, charged on 4 counts with ill-treating a negro child, was found guilty of assault & battery on one count only, the rest being discharged. Motion for arrest of judgment with a view to a new trial. 2-*Ignatius Grimes, colored servant to the Mexican Minister, guilty of having willfully injured a child while driving a carriage on the street. 3-John Monroe, formerly a marine in the service of the U S, was acquitted of a charge of assault & battery with intent to kill John A Golden, of the Navy Yard, by shooting him with a pistol. Satisfactory proof was brought of the man's mental alienation. He will be taken proper care of. 4-Alfred Hunter was convicted of an assault on Mr Geo Savage, on the avenue, the Court fined the party one cent. 5-**Patrick Goings, tried for setting fire to his own house on 23rd st, in the 1st Ward, was found guilty. [**Apr 11th newspaper: Correction-Patrick Goings is not guilty.] [*Apr 21st newspaper: Ignatius Grimes sentenced to 4 months' imprisonment in the county jail & to pay a fine of one dollar.]

Mrd: on Apr 6, at *Locust Hill*, the residence of the bride's father, by Rev Mr Pinkney, Wm F Holtzman to Mary M, daughter of Richd Patten, all of PG Co, Md.

Died: on Apr 8, at his residence in Wash City, John Stevens, of the Treasury Dept, 2nd son of the late Wm Stevens, No 3 Bedford row, John st, London. Mr Stevens came to the U S in 1817, & for the last 4 years he has resided in Wash City. His funeral will be at the Church of the Ascension, on H st, at 3½ o'clock, this afternoon.

TUE APR 11, 1854
By a vote of the villages of **Hamilton & Rossville**, on Monday last, the two are hereafter to be united under one gov't, with the name of the city of Hamilton. It will embrace a population of about 8,000. –Cincinnati Gaz

Senate: 1-Ptn from S T Van Derge, an ofcr in the Quartermaster's Dept in the war of 1812, asking an amendment of the bounty land & pension laws. 2-Ptn from E H Wingfield, late Indian agent in New Mexico, asking remuneration for expenses incurred in the settlement of his accounts. 3-Additional evidence in support of the claim of J S Smith to be released from a forfeiture incurred under a contract for carrying the mail.

For rent: the house now occupied by Hon C J Faulkner, on 6th st, between E & F sts, will be rented from May 20, furnished. All modern improvements. Address P Hevner, through the City Post Ofc.

Farm at private sale, the well-known farm, in Montg Co, Md, about 7 miles from Wash, containing 200 acres. The dwlg contains 8 rooms, pump of good water in the year, & the necessary out-houses. Inquire of David Hines' Grocery Store, on Pa ave, corner of 20th st.

Panama Star of Mar 26. Lt J G Strain reports that the Indians inhabiting the route over which he traveled always fled on his approach, first setting fire to the ranches or huts, destroying their canoes, & carrying off all stock & provisions. At one of their settlements he found the remains of not less than 5 canoes. Two of the 4 men who accompanied Lt Strain died, & the other two were on board the British steamer **Virago**, which arrived on Mar 16, at the mouth of the Savana. [Apr 8th newspaper: from Calif: Lt Strain & party, engaged in exploring a route for a canal across the Isthmus, & who were reported to have been killed by wild beasts, have been heard from, & are safe.]

Orphans Court of Wash Co, D C. In the case of Alex'r McIntire, acting executor of Alex'r McDonald, deceased, the executor & Court have appointed May 3rd next for the settlement of the estate with the assets in hand. –Ed N Roach, Reg o/wills

WED APR 12, 1854
Senate: 1-Ptn from Chas Vinson, asking for compensation for extra services as a clerk in the Ofc of the 3rd Auditor. 2-Cmte on Pensions: adverse reports on the ptns of Rebecca Bright; & of Morris Powers. 3-Bill for the relief of the legal reps of Isaac P Simonton: passed.

Groceries & liquors at auction: on Apr 18, at the Grocery Store of R E Simms, on 7th st, between I st & Mass ave. –Green & Scott, aucts

House of Reps: 1-Cmte on Land Claims: bill for the relief of John Gurman, of La, reported without an amendment, & recommended it pass. 2-Ptn of Wm Taylor & others, of Hallowell, Maine, tobacconists, that a specific duty of forty cents a pound may be levied on all imported cigars.

Orphans Court of Wash Co, D C. Letters testamentary on the personal estate of Saml Brereton, late of Wash Co, deceased. –John F Sharretts, exc I appoint Louis I Davis my agent in the settlement of the above estate. –John F Sharretts, exc

Orphans Court of Wash Co, D C. Letters of administration, with the will annexed, on the personal estate of Sarah Cooper, late of Wash Co, deceased. -Wm Cooper, adm with the will annexed.

Died: on Mar 23, in Dummerston, Vt, Mr Sumner Bust, aged 43 years. He was employed not long since as a Clerk in the Census Bureau, where, by his diligence & efficiency, added to his blandness of deportment, he endeared himself to all with whom he was associated. -C

Wash City Ordinance: 1-Act for the relief of Luke Richardson: the sum of $6 is paid to him for removing a nuisance in square 226 on Jun 8, 1852.

Orphans Court of Wash Co, D C. In the case of Richd H Laskey, admof Barbara Hoover, deceased: the administrator & Court have appointed May 2 next for the settlement of the estate, with the assets in hand. –Ed N Roach, Reg/o wills

THU APR 13, 1854
Household & kitchen furniture at auction: on Apr 18, at the residence of Chas Eames, north side of G st, near 15th. -Jas C McGuire, auct

Hon Edwin Polk, late Pres of the Senate of Tenn, died at his residence in that State on Apr 4.

Fatal duel on Mar 9 last, near Sacramento, Calif, between P W Thomas, D A of Placer Co, & Dr Dickson, physician of the State Marine Hospital in Sacramento. Duelling pistols at 13 paces: Dickson fell at the first fire. He died at midnight. Thomas had made some severe remarks regarding the character of J F Rutland, a clerk in the State Treasurer's ofc, for which Rutland demanded satisfaction. Thomas refused to fight with Rutland, & he was then challenged by Dickson.

Died: at St Michael's, Talbot Co, Md, where he had gone in the fruitless effort to regain his lost health, Christopher R Byrne, of Wash City. He died on Sunday last, in his 24th year. He leaves a large number of attached friends to console with his wife & immediate relatives in his demise in the prime of early manhood.

Died: on Apr 12, Mrs Harriet McHanney, wife of Mr Jacob McHanney, in her 44th year. The deceased was a native of Balt Co, Md, but for the last 16 years a resident of Wash City. Her funeral will take place this afternoon at 4 o'clock, from the residence of her husband, corner of F & 5th sts.

Died: on Apr 10, at Harrisburg, Rebecca, wife of Judge E Herrick, of Athens, Pa, daughter of the late Andrew Ross, of Gtwn, D C.

Appointments by the Pres: by & with the advice & consent of the Senate. Consuls of the U S: 1-Danl S Lee, of Iowa, for Basle, in Switzerland. 2-Wm L Winans, for St Petersburgh, in Russia. 3-Arnold Graef, of N Y, for Dresden, in Saxony. 4-G C Hesse, of D C, for Aix La Chapelle, in the Prussian province of the Rhine.

Senate: 1-Ptn from Jno B Chapman & Clarinda P Chapman, asking that steps may be taken to colonize & civilize the Indians at Puget's Sound, in Washington Territory. 2-Ptn from the legal reps of Henry Payson, assignee of John Randall, asking indemnity for the confiscation of a vessel & cargo at the island of Margaretta. 3-Ptn from John J Hildreth, in favor of a pension for the widow of John Hildreth. 4-Cmte on Commerce: bill for the relief of Saml Bray, keeper of the Dog Island lighthouse on the coast of Florida. 5-Cmte on Military Affairs: bill for the relief of Seneca G Simmons. 6-Cmte of Claims: bill for the relief of Thos Crown; same cmte: bill for the relief of the heirs of Anthony G Willis, deceased, & recommended its passage. 7-Cmte on Pensions: bill for the relief of Thos Snodgrass: with a report. Same cmte: adverse report on the memorial of Lawrence Taliaferro.

Trial in the first district court of New Orleans, on Mar 20, of Jas Patton for the murder of Col Wm Turnbull. The occurrence took place on Dec 3 last, when Patton shot Turnbull as he was getting on an omnibus. Patton stepped into the omnibus & shot Turnbull again, & in a few minutes Turnbull was a corpse. Before he died he recognized a man named Kelly, who asked him who shot him, & he replied Mr Patton. The jury returned a verdict of guilty, without capital punishment.

FRI APR 14, 1854
Wm Strickland, Architect of the State Capitol of Tenn, died on Apr 6 at Nashville, where he has resided for the last 8 years. He was formerly a resident of Phil, where various public bldgs attest his skill as an architect.

Wash Corp: 1-Act for the relief of Mary James & Sarah Harris: passed. 2-Ptn of Lewis A Tarleton for the remission of a fine: referred to the Cmte of Claims. Same for Thos Lewis for the same. 3-Cmte of Claims: asked to be discharged from the further consideration of the ptn of Danl Graham, asking to be refunded certain money paid for a license. 4-Ptn from Francis B Lord & others for grading & paving the alley in square 516: referred to the Cmte on Police. 5-Cmte of Claims: ptn of Alex'r Matthews: passed.

Information wanted of David Patterson, a young man about 25 years of age, who left his home in Brooklyn, Long Island, N Y, by railroad for Kingston, N C, on Mar 20. He is supposed to be the person seriously injured on the Mountain Virginia Central Railroad on Mar 21, as reported in the papers of that date. Any information respecting him will be thankfully received by telegraph to his afflicted parents, 143 Prospect st, Brooklyn, Long Island, N Y.

The firm of Michl Nourse & Co is this day dissolved by mutual consent, the said Michl Nourse retiring on account of impaired health. The business will hereafter be conducted by Jas Morss & Chas F Stansbury. Mr Morss will attend to the business in the U S & Mr Stansbury in London.

Wash Criminal Court: on Sat last a free colored man, Geo Gaines, was convicted of bigamy; but the Judge discharged Gaines on the ground that the prior marriage was void, one of the parties having been a slave & married without the consent of the owner.

The Old Mansion House on the banks of the river, a little east of the steamboat landing, known also as the "*Young Mansion*," from the name of its original proprietors, is being pulled down to open the street it obstructs. This house was erected with bricks, stone, & timber imported from England, & is probably the oldest bldg in this county. The rooms are lofty & spacious & suggest of wealth & style as belonging to its first occupants.

Died: on Apr 13, Mr Hanson Barnes, of Wash City. His funeral will be this afternoon at 4 o'clock, from his residence, 6th & D sts, on the Island.

Died: on Mar 22, of smallpox, in Charleston, S C, Capt Saml J Duncan, a native of Bath, Me, aged 45 years.

Trustee's sale: by deed of trust executed by N B Tapscott & wife. Public sale on May 15, 1854, the following parcel of land lying & being in Montg Co, Md, being a part of A Nailor's tracts of land in said County & States; near the old road leading to Rockville, & near the Stone Tavern, & adjoining the land of Mr John Councilman. -J B H Smith, Silas H Hill, trustees

SAT APR 15, 1854
Old Govn'r Glass, of the island of Tristan d'Acunaha, east coast of Africa, died in Dec of a cancer in the throat. His people, 8 men & about 100 women & children, are anxious to leave the island on account of the winds, which prevent their raising crops. Our whalers will miss the departure of the colony very much.

Mrd: on Apr 8, by Rev Chas A Davis, Stephen Y McNail, of Norristown, Pa, to Miss Martha E Knowles, of Wash City.

Mrd: on Apr 13, by Rev J E Eckard, Andrew Martine, of White Plains, N Y, to Mrs Eliz A Coolidge, of Wash City.

Fatal Casualties. 1-On Monday a can of alcohol exploded in the house of Chas A Morris, Boston, shattering the house, burning Mrs Morris seriously, & her child, 2 years old, fatally. 2-Calvin Palmer was killed at the Manchester N H depot on Monday by falling from a car-load of wood. 3-In Bureau Co, Ill, the shanty of Dennis Daly was lately destroyed by fire communicated from a burning prairie. The approach was so sudden that Mr Daly, his wife, & 3 children, together with a man who was boarding with the family, were unable to escape, & perished in the flames.

In Sussex Co, Va, Mr J Seward ploughed up an antiquated piece of pottery in the form of a jug, containing about $500 in gold & silver coin. One piece bore date of 1507, & another had on it Josephus L, the only words legible. Nearly every piece had been clipped.

Died: on Apr 3, in Washington, Pa, Charles Mason, son of Rev Dr E C & Emma S Wines, in his 15th year. The deceased at the time of his death was a member of the preparatory dept of Washington College. The disease of which he died was inflammation of the brain, brought on as it it believed by a too close & severe application to his studies. He died in Christian hope.

Appointments by the Pres, by & with the advice & consent of the Senate. 1-Donn Piatt, of Ohio, to be Sec of the Legation of the U S in France. 2-Rowland H Bridgman, Collector of the Customs, district of Penobscot, Castine, Maine.

Fair Hill Boarding School for Girls, Sandy Spring, Montg Co, Md: will commence on May 1. Apply to R S Kirk, or Wm H Farquhar, Olney Post Ofc, Montg Co, Md. Reference may be had from Lambert Tree, John T Towers, D C; & Benj Hallowell, Alexandria, Va.

Farm for sale: located in Montg Co, Md: 5 miles from Poolsville: about 300 acres; the dwlg is of brick, large & convenient, with all necessary out-houses. Apply to me on the farm, or by letter to Poolsville, Montg Co, Md. –F S Key

I have for sale one large brick store & dwlg house on 7th & K sts, opposite the Northern Market. –Jas A Wise, 7th st

MON APR 17, 1854
U S Patent Ofc, Wash, Apr 15, 1854. Ptn of Fones McCarthy, of Putnam Co, Fla, praying fro the extension of a patent granted to him on Jul 3, 1840, for an improvement in the cotton gin, for 7 years from the expiration of said patent, which takes place on Jul 3, 1854. –S F Shugert, Acting Com'r of Patents.

Richd C Derby, who died in Phil lately, in his 78th year, left by his will the following: to the Boston Farm School, $5,000; to the Boston Female Orphan Asylum, $2,599; to the Rev John T Sargent, of Boston, for distribution among the poor, $5,000. Mr Derby was a native of Salem, Mass. For the last few years of his life he has resided at Newport, Rhode Island.

Mrd: on Apr 11, at Portsmouth, N H, by Rev Dr Burroughs, Capt W H Treadwell to Ellen, daughter of Com G F Pearson, U S Navy.

Died: on Apr 11, at New Brunswick, N J, Mrs Charlotte M Frelinghuysen, wife of Hon Theodore Frelinghuysen.

Died: on Apr 14, after a short illness, in his 10th year, Clarence P, youngest son of Walter H & Eliza Fennal. His funeral is this afternoon at 8 o'clock, from his father's residence, on Pa ave, opposite Willard's Hotel.

Wash City Ordinances: 1-Act for the relief of Sarah Kearney: the sum of $5 be paid to her, that amount having been paid into this Corp by Lawrence Kearney for a fine imposed on him for keeping a dog without license. 2-Act for the relief of John Sweeny: the sum of $15 to be paid him for a huckster's license, by the son of said Sweeny, & which license has not been used.

TUE APR 18, 1854
Congressional: cmte on Revolutionary Claims-cases which are embraced in the report made Jul 6, 1853: First Class: those who have received the commutation & are to receive the half pay for life, deducting the comutation on proof:

Benj Mooers	Garrat Tiniece	Andrew Finck
Simon Summers	Thos Reed	Peter J Vosburgh
Wells Clift	Saml Gibbs	Lewis Booker
Wm Beaumont	Derrick Schuyler	Thos Buckner
Joshua Danforth	Saml Lewis	Saml Cliff
Wm Riley	Nicholas Schuyler	Jedediah Huntington
Philip G Vanwick	Thos Mounts	Henry Hughes
Jas Sawyer	Jas Clinton	Beverly Roy
Clement Gosline	Peter Gansvort	Pierre Ayot

Second Class: those who claim half-pay or commutation, & are tobe allowed half-pay for life:

J De Treville	Gerard Wood	Jos Bendon
Antoine Paulent	Uriah Forrest	Feliz Vinter
Francis Chaudonet	Francis Marten	Maria Stephenson
Geo Gibson	Amable Borliace	
Louis Gosline	Lewis Marnay	

Third Class: the children of ofcrs who died in the service:
Nathan Weeks; Mary Perry; Jacob Cooper

Household & kitchen furniture at auction: Apr 21, at the residence of Wm Linton, on 9th st, between H & I sts, all his furniture & effects. -Jas C McGuire, auct

U S Patent Of, Wash, Apr 17, 1854. Ptn of Simon Fairman, of Stafford, Conn, praying for the extension of a patent granted to him on Jul 18, 1840, for an improvement in the expanding & contracting or universal chuck for lathes, for 7 years, from the expiration of said patent, which takes place on Jul 18, 1854.
–S T Shugert, Com'r of Patents

Hon Thos D Eliot, recently elected to Congress from New Bedford, is a Boston boy, born in Boston, where his ancestors have lived for several generations. His great grandfather was Rev Dr Andrew Eliot. For many years the pastor of the New North Church. The Eliot School is named in honor of his memory. His grandfather on his mother's side was Hon Thos Dawes, of Boston, from whom he is named. He is the 6th generation in a direct line from the first settlers in the colony of Mass Bay. Rev Wm G Eliot, of St Louis, the well-know Unitarian clergyman & author, is his brother. Mr Eliot has resided in New Bedford some 25 years past. The new member is a son of the late highly esteemed Wm G Eliot, who resided in Wash upwards of 30 years in the able & faithful discharge of a responsible ofc under the Govn't. Mr T D Eliot, the member, was educated here at Columbian College.

Senate: 1-Ptn from D McManus, a chaplain in the army, asking to be allowed bounty land. 2-Cmte on Indian Affairs: asked to be discharged from the further consideration of the memorial Jas Pool, & that it be referred to the Cmte of Claims: which was agreed to. Same cmte: adverse report on the memorial of Henry Conner. 3-Cmte on Private Land Claims: adverse report on the memorial of Robt C Steptoe & others. Same cmte: asked to be discharged from the further consideration of the memorial of Gray Barrell & others, asking confirmation of their title to land said to have been purchased of certain Indian chiefs on the Pacific by Capt Robt Gray. To be referred to the Cmte of Claims. Same cmte: bill for the relief of Juan M & Jose E Luco. Same cmte: bill for the relief of Thos D Jennings.

WED APR 19, 1854
Capt Augustus Canfield, a valuable & esteemed ofcr of the Corps of Topographical Engineers, son-in-law of Hon Lewis Cass, died at Detroit yesterday.

Jos L Savage, Wholesale & Retail Dealer in Hardware, Pa ave, & 10th st.

Hon Nehemiah R Knight, formerly a Senator in Congress from Rhode Island, died yesterday at Providence. Mr Knight first entered the Senate in 1821, to fill a vacancy, & was subsequently re-elected for 3 successive terms, making the entire term of his service in that body 20 years.

Senate: 1-Ptn from Mgt Chandler, mother of Walter S Chandler, of the U S Army, who was drowned while in the discharge of his duty, asking a pension. 2-Ptn from Adelle Sands, widow of Richd M Sands, of the army, asking an increase of pension. 3-Cmte on Private Land Claims: bill for the relief of Francois Cousin. 4-Cmte on Pensions: adverse report on the bill for the relief of Sophia Kirby; same for the ptn of Anne Royall, widow of the late Capt Wm Royall. 5-Cmte on Revolutionary Claaims: bill for the relief of Eliza M Evans. Same cmte: bill for the relief of Robt C Thompson, only surviving child & legal rep of Wm Thompson, deceased, formerly a brig gen in the army of the Revolution. 6-Cmte on Pensions: bill for the relief of Sarah Crandall. Same cmte: adverse report on the ptn of Rhoda Lewis.

U S Patent Ofc, Wash, D C, Apr 18, 1854. Ptn of Chas Spafford, adm of Geo Spafford, late of Windham, Conn, praying for the extension of a patent granted to him on Sep 2, 1840, for an improvement in a machine for boiling & washing rags for the manufacture of paper, for seven years from the expiration of said patent, which takes place on Sep 2, 1854. –S T Shugert, Acting Com'r of Patents

Died: on Apr 17, at the residence of her son, Hon W S Ashe, in Wash City, Mrs Eliz H Ashe, of N C, in her 72nd year. Mrs Ashe had survived for many years her husband, Col Saml Ashe, who when quite a youth performed distinghuished services in the war of the Revolution, & contributed much to embalm the Ashe family of Cape Fear river in the grateful memory of N C. Mrs Ashe was the mother of a large & interesting family.

Died: on Apr 14, at Du Pont's Mills, near Wilmington, in her 76th year, Mary Alletta Belin, relict of the late Augustus Belin.

Died: on Apr 7, at his residence, **Oakleigh**, near Greensborough, Ala, Dr Robt C Randolph, aged 61 years. Of the distinguished Randolph family of Va, Dr Randolph served creditably in the navy during the last war with Great Britain, became afterwards eminent as a physician at New Orleans, &, on establishing his valuable plantation in Ala, endeared as he was to the large circle of his numerous friends, being held in the highest esteem, his residence became extensively known for its liberal hospitality, refinement, & elegance. -T

THU APR 20, 1854
Mrd: on Apr 13, by Rt Rev Bishop Potter, Mr Campbell Morfit to Miss Marie C Chancellor, daughter of Mr Henry Chancellor, of Germantown, Pa.

Died: on Apr 15, in the valley of the Kishacoquillas, Mifflin Co, Pa, of typhoid pneumonia, Rev Joshua Moore, in his 54th year. He was formerly of Wash City, & son of the late Joshua J Moore, who was Chief Clerk of the Land Ofc during the administration of Mr Jefferson. He was of the Presbyterian denomination, [old school,] & has been in the pastoral ofc in the above locality for about 20 years.

Senate: 1-Ptn from Geo W Lippitt, U S Consul at Vienna, asking compensation for diplomatic services. 2-Ptn from Jos S Kite, asking an extension of his patent for the improvement in the construction of railroad cars. 3-Cmte on Pensions: adverse reports on the ptns of the prisoners confined at Dartmoor prison during the last war with Great Britain; also, on those of Harriet A Wilcox & Eliz A W Gibson. 4-Cmte of Claims: bill for the relief of Wm Darby.

Mr Wm O Hoffman, who was shot at St Louis on Apr 4 by Mrs Mary C W Baker, died from his wounds on Apr 13.

House of Reps: 1-Cmte on the Post Ofc & Post Roads: bill for the relief of Almanzon Huston: recommended that it do not pass. Same cmte: bills for the relief of Llewellyn Washington; & relief of Jas M Goggin: recommended that they do pass: they were committed.

The Jennings estate. It is rumored that an immense property in England is about to be divided among the Corbins of Va, descendants from a Miss Jennings, who intermarried with a Corbin. From the Herald's ofc, London, it has been ascertained that the Corbins of Va are descended from Robt Corbion, alias Corbin, [first to 7th year of Henry II,] the father to Wm; & from him, lineally, by Hamon, Wm, Thos, Wm, of Birmingham, Wm, of Kings Swinford, in the county of Stafford, [Edward III, 1332,] Henry, [Richd II, 1884,] John, Thos, Nicholas, of Hall Ead, in Warwick Co, [Henry VIII,] Richd Thos, Geo, to Thos Corbin, [14th in descent from the first Robt Corbin,] born 1594, died 1637. This Thos Corbin was married, 1620, to a daughter of Gawen Grosvenor, [lineal ancestor to the present Marquis of Westminster,] of Sutton Colfield, Warwick Co. Their 3rd son, Henry Corbin, emigrated to Va, settled in the county of Middlesex, & died there, as supposed, 1675. Henry Corbin's daughter Ann was married to Wm Taylor, [or Taylor, of Va,] of London, & died in Va 1694. Henry Corbin's son Gawin married Jane, daughter of & co-heir of John Lane, of York river, Va. Their eldest son, Richd Corbin, of Laneville, in King & Queen Co, Va, [Pres of the King's Council & Receiver-General of the Quit Rents, 1775,] married Eliz, daughter of John Tayloe, of Mount Airy, in Richmond Co, Va. She died in 1784, leaving the following children: John Tayloe Corbin, grand-father of the present Jas Park Corbin, of Moses; Richd Corbin, ___ Neck, near Fredericksburg, Va; Thos Corbin, of Laneville; & Francis Corbin, of The Reeds, in Caroline Co, Va. The arms or crest of the Corbin family of Va, as above, is a crow-corvus, in Latin, hence the name. -T

Prof John Wilson, celebrated as the Christopher North of Blackwood's Magazine, died on Apr 3. He was born at Paisley, Scotland, & was educated at Glasgow University & at Oxford.

Jenny Lind [Madame Goldschmidt] is giving concerts at Vienna with great éclat.

$50 reward for runaway negro woman Sarah, age 20 years, who ran away from the residence of Mrs Mary Ghiselin, in Nottingham, PG Co, Md, about 2 weeks ago. She belonged to the estate of the late Mgt Ann Ghiselin.-C C Magruder, adm d b n c t a of M A Ghiselin.

FRI APR 21, 1854
In Balt City Orphans' Court: in the matter of the estate of Manuel J *Desouga, deceased, it is ordered that Lounes Draper, adm of Manuel J *Desouza, deceased, give notice to all persons interested as distributees of the estate, warning them to appear in this Court on or before Aug 1 next. –Jas A Reed, J J Gross
[*Note: 2 spellings.]

Circuit Court of Wash Co, D C-in Chancery. Susan Barber & Catharine Wright vs Mary A W Harrington, admx of Richd Harrington, Gordon Forbes & Mgt his wife, & others. Wm B Webb, trustee, reports that he sold at public auction, on Dec 29, 1853, a parcel of ground in Wash City, & that Jas Rhodes, of said city, became the purchaser for the sum of $415.15. –Jno A Smith, clerk

Senate: 1-Ptn from M Tarver, asking a grant of public land in the State of Missouri for the establishment & support of a juvenile reform school. 2-Cmte on Indian Affairs: bill for the relief of Calvin B Seymore & Wm H Boynton. 3-Cmte on the Judiciary: adverse report on the memorial of Chas Stearns. 4-Cmte on the Post Ofc & Post Roads: bill for the relief of Jas Jeffries & Jeremiah M Smith: passed. 5-Cmte on Pensions: bill for the relief of the heirs of Wm Van Wart, deceased. Same cmte: adverse report on the ptn of Seth Ingram. Same cmte: bill for the relief of Ann Eliza Childs, widow of Gen Childs: act to continue half-pay to certain widows & orphans. 6-Bill to confirm the claim of Wm H Henderson & the heirs of Robt Henderson to 500 acres of land in the Bastrop grant: introduced.

House for rent & furniture for sale. Contains gas fixtures. Apply to Pollard Webb, Pa ave, near the Nat'l Hotel.

$10 reward for stolen or strayed fine sorrel Mare: missing from my dwlg, corner of 5th & P sts. –Thos Hollidge

Wash Corp: 1-Act for the relief of Cornelius Regan. 2-Act for the relief of Lewis A Tarlton: passed. 3-Act for the relief of Zener Haight: passed.

Mrd: on Apr 18, by Rev Wm Hodges, John T Burch to Mary G Hatton, all of Wash City.

Died: on Apr 19, Agnes M Edes, daughter of the late Col Benj Edes, of Balt. Her funeral will be from the residence of her brother-in-law, Chas W Pairo, on Prospect st, Gtwn, this afternoon, at 4 o'clock.

Appointments by the Pres, by & with the advice & consent of the Senate. 1-John R Jones, of Indiana, to be Register of the Land Ofc at Vincennes, vice John C Clark, removed. 2-John C Claiborne, of Ark, to be Receiver of Public Moneys at Batesville, vice J T Safford, resigned.

On Friday at the quarry of John McCormich, N Y, a sand blast exploded, striking Wm Pettigrew, a wheelwright, working near by, killing him instantly.

SAT APR 22, 1854
Wash City Ordinance: 1-Act for the relief of Rachel Stone: the fine imposed on her for selling liquor without a license is remitted: provided she pays the costs.

The Duke of Parma was attacked in the street on Mar 27, at half past five o'clock, the assassin having plunged a knife into his abdomen, fled & escaped, & yet remains undetected. The Duke died the next day. Ferdinand, Charles III, Jos Maria Villma Balthasar de Bourbon, Duke of Parma, Placentia, Infant of Spain, was the long name & title of the defunct prince. He was born on Jan 14, 1823, & was age 31 at his death. He succeeded his father upon his abdication in 1849 in the Duchy of Parma. He was connected by marriage with the French Bourbons. His wife was the daughter of the Duke de Berry, who was assassinated at the opera in Paris, & accordingly sister to the Duke de Chambrod, called by the French legitimists Henry V, of France. The Duke leaves 4 children, the second of whom, his son Robt Chas, who is only 6 years old, succeeds him. During his minority his mother will be regent.

Mr Wm Carmines, aged 60, eloped on Wed last with Miss Lucy Smith, aged 16, the daughter of a respectable farmer in York Co, Va. They were married in Portsmouth by Rev Wm Knott. The bride said she was of the lawful age of 21. The father of the bride got out a warrant for the arrest of Carmines. He was held to bail for his appearance before the next grand jury.

Oliver M Whipple, the millionaire or wealthiest man in Lowell, presided at the Vermont Festival in that city the other evening, & remarked that in his early life in Vt, he left home on foot for the city of Boston in 1815, with a cash capital in pocket of $15, & of his arrival at Southwick, & engaging in service for $8 per month.

Mrd: on Apr 20, by Rev Mr Henry, Benj F Gettener, of Balt, to Miss Mary C Ford, of Wash.

Mrd: on Apr 18, at Saten_, N J, by Rev J J Helm, of Phil, Mr J Hackett, of Wash City, to Emeline, youngest daughter of Calvin Belden, of the former place.

Mrd: on Apr 19, by Rev Mr Vincinanza, Thos F Darnold, of PG Co, to Miss Harriet A Sheirburn.

Died: on Apr 21, Grayson Page, eldest child of M W & Mary Jane Galt, aged 8 years. His funeral will take place from the residence of his parents, 8th st, between E & F sts, this afternoon, at half-past 3 o'clock.

House of Reps: 1-Cmte of the Whole: discharged from the further consideration of the ptn of Isaac S Bowman, son & executor of Isaac Bowman, deceased, to the Sec of the Interior for liquidation under the act of Jul 5, 1832, & it was recommitted to the Cmte on Revolutionary Claims.

MON APR 24, 1854

For lease: the large Brick Yard called Red Banks, on the Eastern Branch, 4 & 5 miles from Wash. –Walter D Davidge, La ave, opposite 5th st.

Appointment by the Pres, by & with the advice & consent of the Senate: Thos B English, of Missouri, to be Register of the Land Ofc at Jackson, Mo, vice Saml A Hill, deceased.

Only 6 of Lt J G Strain's party died, namely, the two New Grenadian Com'rs & the following seamen belonging to the ship **Cyane**: Geo B Holmer, P Vermilie, Wm H Parker, & Edw Lombard.

Mrd: on Apr 20, in Wash City, by Rev D Pyne, of St John's Church, Rev O K Nelson, of Annapolis, Md, to Mary M, youngest daughter of the late Peter Hagner, of Wash City.

Mrd: on Apr 18, in Columbia, S C, by Rev Mr Shand, Hon Chas J Jenkins, of Augusta, Ga, to Emily Gertrude, daughter of the late Judge Barnes, of Phil.

Mrd: on Apr 17, in the First Presbyterian Church, Lancaster, Pa, by Rev Abeel Baldwin, Mr Z D Gilman, of Wash, to Miss Emma H, daughter of the late Robt M Barr, of Pa.

Mrd: on Apr 18, at Christ Church, Detroit, Mich, by Rev Chas Aldis, Lt Henry Rodgers, U S Navy, to Kate S, daughter of Chas C Trowbridge, of Detroit.

Died: on Apr 23, Mr Thos Hall, in his 29th year. His funeral will take place from his late residence on B st south, between 6th & 7th sts, tomorrow, at 2 o'clock.

Died: on Apr 22, in Wash City, of consumption, James Emmett, only son of Wm & Laurantine Ryan, aged 2 years & 6 months. His funeral will be this evening at 4½ o'clock, from the residence of his parents, 11 st west, between F & G sts.

Died: on Apr 23, Mary Catherine Barrett, the eldest daughter of Thos J & Susan Barrett, aged 8 years. Her funeral will be this evening, at 3 o'clock, from the residence of her father on D st north, between 5th & 6th sts east, Capitol Hill.

Meeting of the vestry of St John's Parish, held at St Barnabas Church, PG Co, Md, consisting of Rev John Martin, Rector, Henry A Callis & Dr John H Bayne, to prepare resolutions expressive of the deep sense of the vestry & congregation at the lamented death of Mr Wm A Gunton. We mourn the loss of one whose youth gave promise of much usefulness among us. For several years he was a member of this congregation & vestry. We cordially sympathize with his family.

Chickering & Sons' [not Jacob Chickering] Pianos. From the factory of Chickering & Sons, late Jonas Chickering, established for more than 30 years. [A person named Jacob Chickering has a Piano Factory in Boston, who has nothing to do with this old & celebrated establishment.] –Rich Davis, Wash City

Wanted, a place as a housekeeper, well qualified. Apply at Mr J O Sargent's ofc, 14th st, opposite Willard's Hotel.

The ship **Powhatan**, Capt Meyers, with 311 passengers on board, bournd from Havre to N Y, was cast ashore on Sat night on the outside bar, about midway halfway to Egg Harbor inlet. She was first discovered by Capt Jennings. Many persons were swept off by the heavy surf. An immense wave washed a full 100 persons overboard, who were carried away down the beach by the undertow. Capt Meyers called out to Mr Jennings to try & save some of those who might be washed ashore. The sea presented a black mass of human heads & floating pieces of the wreck, but in a few moments all had sunk to rise alive no more. The beach was strewn with the dead bodies of women & children, pieces of the wreck, the baggage of the passengers, & empty casks. One man was found about 50 yards from the beach, with a child in his arms, &, from his condition, it is supposed that he alone of all on board reached the shore alive. They were found frozen to death & it appeared they died from exposure. Bodies were strewn on the beach & upon the sand hills. On Wed a wagon arrived with the bodies of some of the dead. Too much praise cannot be awarded to the inhabitants of Manahawkin for their zeal & industry in giving a decent burial to the dead.

TUE APR 25, 1854
At Wheeling, Va, on Apr 16, Henry Craig, who killed Alex'r Garden, was convicted of murder in the 2nd degree, & sentenced to imprisonment in the penitentiary for life at hard labor.

Mrd: on Sep 12, 1853, by Jas Crandell, Justice of the Peace, A Zappone to Miss Mgt A Joyce, both of Wash City.

Senate: 1-Ptn from John Makin, a pilot, in relation to a claim to salvage for relieving the U S frig **Saranac** while in distress off the harbor of Savannah. 2-Ptn from Sherman Pierce, asking a pension. 3-Ptn from the heirs & legal reps of John Neilson, asking compensation for the services of his ancestor, in remuneration for losses sustained during the Revolutionary war. 4-Ptn from C M Clarke, asking remuneration for losses sustained by her father under a contract to furnish muskets. 5-Cmte on the Post Ofc & Post Roads: bill for the relief of Jos Knock. 6-Cmte of Claims: asked to be discharged from the further consideration of the memorial of Chas Gordon, & that it be referred to the Cmte on Public Lands: agreed to. Same cmte: bill for the relief of Grafton Baker: passed. 7-Cmte on Pensions: asked to be discharged from the further consideration of the ptns of of the heirs at law of Geo Hoyle; of Frances Depriest; & of D McManus: that they be referred to the Cmte on Public Lands: agreed to. 8-Cmte on Pensions: asked to be discharged from the further consideration of the ptns of Eliza G Townsend; of Arabella Riley; of Minerva Cattlett; & of Nannie Deaman.

Dissolution of copartnership, by mutual consent, existing under the firm of Maxwell & Sears, Jas W Sears withdrawing from the firm. –John S Maxwell, Jas W Sears
+
John S Maxwell has associated his brother, David Maxwell, in the Riband, Trimming, & Embroidery business: Maxwell & Bro. –John S Maxwell, David Maxwell

Serious disaster in the destruction of the 2 spans of the new iron bridge at the Little Falls of the Potomac yesterday, whilst the hands were at work. Danl MacNamara was thrown from the abutment on the bank of the river, & fell into the warter, His body has not yet been recovered. Another laborer, John Frizzle, is very seriously injured in the head & face, & can hardly survive. MacNamara leaves a wife & a numerous family of small children. In raising one end of the Va or completed span uniting the two shores, in order to set the bed plates on which the span was finally to rest, the bar of iron connecting the jack screws gave way, & let the frame of the bridge into the river. The other span, on the Md side of the river, being tied to the Va span, was dragged from its position, oversetting the trussels on which it rested, & bringing all down into one mass of ruins. Frizzle was entangled under this.

For sale: a square of ground on the Island containing about 60,000 feet. Also, a small 2 story frame house & several fine bldgs in the Northern Liberties. Apply to Gideon W Larner, Gen Agent, D st, between 6th & 7th sts.

WED APR 26, 1854
Household & kitchen furniture at auction: on Apr 28, at the residence of J B Tree, 11th st, Between G & H sts: all his furniture & effects. -J C McGuire, auct

The Naval Medical Board of Examiners, recently convened in Phil for the examination of Assist Surgeons for promotion & of candidates for admission into the Navy, the following is a list of the candidates who have passed satisfactorily, arranged in the order of merit, viz:

1-Michl O'Hara, of Pa
2-B P Daniel, of Fla
3-Sam Richd Swann, of Va
4-Frank A Walen, of Va
5-Wm G Hay, of Ala
6-Danl B Conrad, of Va
7-J E Sample, of Pa
8-W F Hord, of Ky
9-Wyatt M Brown, of N C

Good business stand at auction: on May 1, in front of the premises: lot 14 in square 117, fronting on 20th st, between L & M sts, with a good frame house, with feed house attached. It is the place formerly occupied by Mr Jas Daly as a grocery store. Terms at sale. –Green & Scott, aucts

Died: on Apr 25, Mrs Ann Espey, in her 60th year. Her funeral will take place this afternoon, at 4 o'clock, from the residence of her son-in-law, Jno H Thorn, on 5th st, between G & H sts.

Died: on Apr 25, of cramp colic, in his 20th year, John McLean Addison, late of the U S Army. His funeral is this afternoon, at 4 o'clock, from the residence of his father, Thos B Addison, on the Heights of Gtwn.

Died: on Apr 24, in Wash City, Dr Edw H Carmichael, late of Fredericksburg, Va, in his 58th year. He has been extensively known as an eminent practitioner of medicine & surgery. He leaves a disconsolate family & numerous friends to deplore his loss.

Four companies of the unfortunate U S 3rd Artl, which was delayed by the wreck of the steamer **San Francisco**, again embarked from N Y on Tue last, on board the steamer **Falcon**, bound for Panama. Soldiers on board number 255, under the command of Lt Loeser, Lt Winder, Lt Van Vorst, & ADj Winder. The families of some of the ofcrs are also passengers, viz: Mrs Loeser, Miss Eaton, Mrs Simpson, Mrs Capt Jones & child.

Hon Luther Severance, of Maine, late U S Com'r at the Sandwich Island, has returned to his home in Augusta. We regret to learn from the Banner that Mr Severance is afflicted with an incurable cancer & is fully aware of his situation. He is thankful that Providence has permitted him to return home to die in the bosom of his family, & to have his body buried amongst his kindred.

Orphans Court of Wash Co, D C. Letters of administration, with will annexed, on personal estate of Hanson Barnes, late of Wash Co, deceased.
–Alex'r Lee, adm, W A

Suicide. Mr S A Krugar took passage on the cars at Richmond for N Y, on Sat last. When he arrived at Taylorsville he left the cars, & was later found suspended from the limb of a pine tree a short distance from the place where he left the cars. He had on a good suilt of black clothing, a gold watch in his pocket, & $300 in money, $100 of it in gold. He also had a receipt from the agent of the steamer **Hermann** for $60 for a second cabin passage for Bremen.

Senate: 1-Memorial from Robt C Forbes, asking the establishment of Floating schools in the principal sea ports of the U S & on one of the lakes for the partial education of seamen. 2-Ptn from the heirs at law of the firm of Joshua Fisher & Sons, asking payment for goods taken by the Cmte of Safety of Phil in 1774 for the use of the army. 3-Ptn from Henry Vethake & others, asking that a portion of the public domain be set apart for the gratuitous education of female teachers. 4-Cmte on Pensions: bill for the relief of Nancy Bowen; & of Sarah Larrabee. Same cmte: adverse reports on the ptns of C C Beatty; of Catharine White; & of Hiram Upson, of N Y. 5-Cmte on Revolutionary Claims: adverse report on the memorial of Mgt Barnitz, heir of David Greer. 6-Cmte on Revolutionary Claims: bill for the relief of Robt C Thompson, only surviving child & legal rep of Wm Thompson, deceased, formerly a Brig Gen in the army of the Revolutioanry war, reported it back without amendment. Same cmte: adverse report on the memorial of Wm L Meredith. 7-Cmte on Foreign Relations: asked to be discharged from the further consideration of the ptn of the memorials of Wm G Morehead; of Jean Duplaigne; & of Jno S De Wolf: which was agreed to.

Extensive sale of lands in Bath Co, Va: the administrators of John W Frazier, deceased, & Guardians of his infant son & heir at law, setting as Com'rs under a decree of the Circuit Court of Bath Co, will sell at public auction: on Jun 15, all that valuable body of lands known as *Cloverdale* [2,917 acres;] & *Wilderness Farms* [1,985 acres;] formerly owned by Gen Blackbun, with all the additions thereto made by the deceased. **Cloverdale** includes the *Dove Spring Tract*, recently acquired by purchase; & the *Beaver Dam Meadows*; with an overseer's house on the meadows. The *Matthews Farm* contains 1,364 acres-no bldgs. The *Wilderness*, or *Home Place*, was the residence in his lifetime of the late Gen Saml Blackburn, & the bldgs are extensive; contains the *Grist Mill* on Stuart's creek. The *Fowler Tract* contains 2,206 acres; is less improved than the others. Mr Fawcett, residing at Cloverdale Hotel, will show the lands, & letters of inquiry to Wm Frazier, P M, Rockbridge Alum Springs, will receive prompt attention. –Wm Frazier, Wm M Tate, Comr's. On the same day, after the above are sold, I will sell at public auction the Farm & Tavern Stand known as *Green Valley*: contains 711 acres, with excellent house & out-houses. Day of sale Jun 15. –Wm Frazier

THU APR 27, 1854
Senate: 1-Additional documents submitted in support of the claim of Paul J Kelly to remuneration for certain discoveries made by him in the Territory of Oregon. 2-Ptn from the widow of Capt Geo C Westcott, of the U S Army, asking to be placed on the pension list. 3-Ptn from John F Moses, of N H, asking such action on the indigent insane bill as will secure its passage, irrespective of the vote. 4-Cmte on Commerce: bill for the relief of Geo Dennett, of N H. 5-Cmte on Naval Affairs: asked to be discharged from the further consideration of the memorial of E A F Lavalette, of the U S Navy, & that it be referred to the Cmte on Foreign Relations: which was agreed to. Same cmte: asked to be discharged from the further consideration of the ptn of Michl Hanson, & that it be referred to the Cmte on Foreign Relations: which was agreed to. 6-Cmte on Pensions: bill for the relief of Urban Scott.

Havanna Cigars: many of the favorite brands, & at prices which cannot fail to give satisfaction. –Sam Hamilton & Co, Pa ave, opposite Jackson's Hall.

New Cash Store: Our motto, We study to please. Large assortment of Dry Goods direct from Phil & N Y. –Latimer & Fogg, Pa ave, between 8th & 9th sts.

FRI APR 28, 1854
Senate: 1-Ptn from Nathl Hayward, asking an extension of his patent for an improvement in the manufacture of India rubber goods. 2-Cmte on Foreign Relations: bill for the relief of Henry Crouchey: passed. 3-Cmte of Claims: asked to be discharged from the further consideration of the memorial of Jas L Collins asking indemnity for property lost in the Mexican war, & that he have leave to withdraw his memorial & papers: which was agreed to.

Geo Larkin, son of Mr John Larkin, of this place, aged about 17 years, with others, were shooting at pigeons on Tue last, near town, when the breech of the gun he was using was blown out, striking him in the forehead. He survived 36 hours, & died on Wed. -Meadeville paper, Apr 11th

Robt Greenhow, associate law agent of the U S before the U S Land Commission, died at San Francisco on Mar 27. The cause of his death was a fall, on Feb 17, off the pavement of Pacific st to the street as graded, a distance of about 6 feet. Mr Greenhow was 54 years of age, & leaves a wife & 4 children in Wash, D C. He was a native of Richmond, Va, came to Calif in 1850, we believe, & was commissioned as associate law agent on Aug 30, 1852, which position he occupied when he died. He was educated as a physician, & took his degree at the College of Physicians & Surgeons in N Y, & completed his medical education at Paris.

Boston, Apr 27. Mr Hugh Jamieson, Naval Storekeeper at Charleston, died this morning, after a brief illness. He was a relative of Pres Pierce.

Real estate for sale: under authority of the will of John Roberts, late of this city, deceased: public auction on May 4, of a large 3 story slated Warehouse, on the north side of King st, between Wash & Columbus sts. –P E Hoffman, W C Page, excs of J Roberts, deceased. –S J McCormick, at Alexandria

Obit-died: on Mar 20, at the residence of Lloyd W Bickley, at Taconey, Miss Eliz Bickley, in her 93rd year. In 1692 Abram Bickley, a member of the Society of Friends, & a worthy associated of Wm Penn, arrived in America, & very soon afterwards, with a few others, constituted the then Legislature of Pa. His son Saml followed in his footsteps & became a leading shipping merchant of his day; & was succeeded by Abram, the father of the deceased, who, avoiding all business, lived & died a Rentier, who thus probably imbued his children with that taste for ease & retirement which afterwards, in a domestic point of view, rendered them so remarkable. It was he at his own expense who imported the first fire engine into the city, which is still in existence, known as the Bickley engine. He also stept forth during our Revolutionary struggle to procure provisions for the army. The sister of Mrs Bickley [mother of the deceased.] was married to Benj West in England, leaving America for that purpose. Miss Hanna Bickley died in Mar last. From the fact of the deceased, & all her brothers & sisters, having been born subjects of George III, & from their having, soon afer the termination of the Revolutionary contest, withdrawn themselves from the world, they were thoroughly imbued with English ideas & prejudices. More than a half century ago 6 brothers & sisters, opulent, attractive, & in the highest social position, retired to their estate in the country, & lived & died single & unmarried. Of the six who thus retired from the world the shortest lived reached the age of 71, the longest 93. Now they are all gone. The family vault has the simple inscription: Vault of the Bickley family, originally from Sussex, England. Eliz Blickely attained the verge of human existence. She & all her family were Episcopalians, having returned to the faith of their forefathers in England.
–Phil Evening Bulletin

J S Landon was killed in a duel at Volcano Bar, El Dorado Co, by David E Hackner. They fought at 11 o'clock at night, on Mar 20, with pistols, at 15 feet. The difficulty grew out of the Senatorial election question.

Died: on Apr 14, at the residence of Prof J C Fr Salomon, in Bladensburg, Md, of inflammation of the lungs, G L Sala De Taroni, of Berlin, Prussia, in his 29th year. He was the personal friend of Baron Humboldt, the great Naturalist, & traveled with him 3 years in Asia & Africa, when they parted, Humboldt going to Europe, & G L Sale de Taroni coming on a visit to the U S, 2 years since.

Mrd: on Apr 25, at St Rose's Chapel, Montg Co, Md, by Rev John Dougherty, Dr Geo Alex'r Dyer, of Wash, D C, to Mary Roberta, 3rd daughter of the late Geo Ashton, of King Geo Co, Va.

Mrd: on Apr 25, at Trinity Church, by Rt Rev Bishop Wainwright, Wm Sewell, late Chief Engineer U S N, to Miss Caroline M, daughter of the late Col D E Dunscomb, of Wash City.

Mrd: on Apr 25, at **Locust Hill**, near Washington, by Rev Dr O'Toole, Jas E Harvy, of Phil, to Miss Selina M Moore, of Wash City.

Rev Jos Sawyer died on Monday, at his residence in Westcheser Co, N Y, in his 84th yea. It is supposed he was the eldest Methodist clergyman in the State, & the first missionary sent by the Methodist Church late Canada.

Norfolk, Apr 27. Peter Brown, the tunner of the Farmers' Bank, committed suicide here today by taking laudanum. Some family difficulty is said to have been the cause of the rash act.

From the Detroit Inquirer. The funeral of Capt A Canfield took place yesterday from his residence on Fort st, attended by a large concourse of our citizens, all of whom share in the great grief which has so heavily fallen upon his afflicted family. The pall bearers were Maj Gaines, Capt Macomb, Maj Woodbridge, & Lt Reynolds, of the U S service, & Messrs C C Trowbridge, John Winder, A S Williams, & F W Backus. The funeral services were conducted at the house of the deceased by Rev Dr Duffield. Gen Cass being absent at Wash with his daughter, the immediate members of the family who followed the dead to its final resting place were the much afflicted widow, & the only remaining son-in-law of Gen Cass, our fellow citizen, Henry Ledyard, & his family. The procession wound its way to the family burial place in Elmwood.

Boarding House on 11th st, between H & I sts. Mrs J P Tubbs has several vacant rooms, with or without board.

SAT APR 29, 1854
John C McKinsie, who was implicated with some 7 others in the alleged killing of Eben Floyd in Clinton Co, Ohio, over 4 years ago, & who left the State at that time, returned on Apr 15 & gave himself up to the Sheriff, declaring he would rather suffer the penalty the law might inflict on him than to remain any longer a wandering outcast, away from his friends & his home. He will stand his trial at the next term of the Court. –Zanesville Courier

Gtwn Municipal election took place on Thu. The following are the candidates: Aldermen: Evan Lyons, Robt P Dodge, Jos Libbey, Geo Waters, & Esau Pickrell. Common Council: A H Dodge, John A Grimes, Peter Berry, A H Pickrell, Jeremiah Orme, Walter S Cox, David English, & Richd Jones.

Dept of State, Wash, Apr 27, 1854. Information has been received at this Dept from the Legation of the U S in Central American that of the persons drowned at Virgin Bay on Mar 2 last the bodies of the following had been recovered & identified. The effects found upon their persons have been transmitted to this Dept, & will be deposited in the Treasury Dept for the benefit of the legal claimants:

List:
Wm Lane
D Churchill
Edw Thomas
*___ Learin, [or Leaven,]
*Copied as written.

Isaac Edge
Jacob Lewis, colored
W H Gardner
Francis Harris

We learn from the Washington [Ark] Telegraph that Capt Richd H Finn was assassinated at his residence in that vicinity on Apr 3. He was shot through the window, while in the presence of his family. He died instantly. The infamous deed was committed in the darkness of the night.

An inquest was held in N Y on Sat on the body of Mary Bogard, aged 80, who was found dead at 5 East Clinton Pl. She & her 50 year old son, a half lunatic, had subsisted for some years by begging & collecting rags. Her son had concealed her body under a large pile of rags for 2 days, so that their funds might not be discovered. They had an account of $206.31 at the Bowery Savings Bank, & $10.05 in cash, but nevertheless the old woman perished from destitution.

Mrd: on Apr 27, in Wash City, by Rev Smith Pyne, Geo P Frick, of Balt, to Miss Kate Turnbull, eldest daughter of Col Wm Turnbull, U S Army.

Mrd: on Apr 25, at Luray, Page Co, Va, by Rev A C Booton, Gen Thos L Price to Miss Caroline V Long, of the former place.

Died: on Apr 15, at Buena Vista, Delaware, in her 24th year, Ellen Sinclair, wife of Jas C Douglass. A gentle spirit called away from the ties clinging round her of wife, mother, & home. There is but left for those to mourn her loss.

Valuable farm for sale: by deed of trust, executed by Temple M Washington, on Jan 15, 1853, of record in the County Court of Prince Wm Co, Va: sale on May 29 of **Buckland Farm**, containing 600 acres, in the counties of Prince Wm & Fauquier, Va: the farm is in a good state of improvement, & has an excellent commodious dwlg house, & all necessary out-houses. –John P Phillips, Eppa Hunton, trustees

MON MAY 1, 1854
Rev Wm Matthews died last night, in his 84th year. He was for the last 50 years Pastor of St Patrick's Church, in Wash City. No one ever died in this community more universally beloved, or whose death will be more generally deplored.

Surgeon A G Gambrill, of the sloop-of-war **Plymoth**, died yesterday at Hong Kong. The death of Lt S F Blunt, of the Navy, is also announced.

The trial of Matthew F Ward, at Elizabethtown, Hardin Co, Ky, for the murder some weeks ago of Prof Butler, of Louisville, was closed on Thu by a verdict of acquittal from the jury.

Dept of State, Wash, Apr 27, 1854. Information has been received at this Dept from Edw Worrell, U S Consul at Matanzas, of the death, in that city, of Henry Cavalier. Further information respecting the disposition of his property may be obtained at this Dept.

Jas Clough was hung at Taunton, Mass, on Fri, for the murder, in 1852, of the deputy sheriff of Manchester while arresting him for burglary.

Trustee's sale: by deed of trust from Henry Sauer to E C Morgan & H B Sweeny, recorded in Liber J A S 43, of the land records for Wash Co, D C: sale on Jun 2, of lots 10 & 11 in square 583, in said city. –E D Morgan, H B Sweeny, trustees

Mrd: on Apr 29, by Rev Jas B Donelan, Lt R A Morsell, U S Revenue Service, to Rosa, only daughter of S Calvert Ford, all of Wash City.

Mrd: on Apr 29, by Rev Jas H Brown, Mr Michl Henry Carlisle to Miss Louisa Oden.

Mrd: on Apr 27, at Cambridge, Md, by Rev Mr Barber, in the Episcopal Church of that place, Dr N S Jarvis, Surgeon U S Army, to Mrs J B Mumford, niece of Col T Staniford, U S Army.

Mrd: on Apr 20, in N Y, by Rev J W Alexander, John Wilkes, jr, U S Navy, to Jane R Smedberg, of that city.

Died: on Apr 29, Mrs Sarah Ann Williams, in her 45th year, after an illness of 3 weeks. Her funeral is this afternoon at 2 o'clock, from her late residence on F st, between 2nd & 3rd sts.

Died: on Apr 30, Anna M Fenwick, only daughter of R M A & Lavinia L Fenwick, aged 3 years & 9 months. Her funeral is this afternoon at 4 o'clock.

Died: on Thu last, Eliot Dickinson Condict, aged 9 years & 2 months. His funeral is today at 12 o'clock, from the residence of his father, Dr H F Condict, on 11th st, between G & H sts.

Died: on Apr 28, in Fairfax Co, Va, Harriet W Sheldon, wife of Israel Sheldon, of Gaston, Ala, in her 40th year.

Died: on Apr 27, in Balt, after a short illness, Lt Simon Fraser Blunt, U S Navy, in his 35th year. He entered the navy in 1831, at a very early age, an appointment as midshipman having been tendered him by Pres Jackson, in consequence of the great gallantry he had displayed & the highly important services he had rendered in the suppression of the negro insurrection of that year in the southern counties of Va. To his bereaved family we offer deep felt sorrow. –U S N

The Vestry of Washington Parish have appointed Mr Saml Arnold to be Sexton of the *Washington Cemetery*, in place of Robt Clarke, resigned. –John P Ingle, Treas, V W P.

In Chancery: Arthur P West & others, cmplnts, against Mary Bowie, Wm D Bowie, & others, heirs of Stephen West. I am directed to ascertain whether the property described in the bill is susceptible of division in specie between the parties. Above parties to appear on May 8th, at my ofc, City Hall, Wash. –W Redin, auditor

In Equity: Wm Noyes, cmplnt, against Peter M Pearson, adm, & Eliz Parsons & others, heirs of Jas Parsons, dfndnts. I am to state an account of the personal estate of Jas Parsons, & of the debts due from him at the time of his death. Meeting on May 10th at my ofc, City Hall, Wash. –W Redin, auditor

For rent: large frame house at 10th & N Y ave. Inquire of Mary Ann Harvey, on the premises.

In Equity: Wm S Laurie, Jos N Laurie, Cranstown Laurie, Jas Colegate & Eliz M his wife, Blair Laurie, Wm H F Gurley & Eliz his wife, Sarah R Rittenhouse, & Jos H Nourse & Isabel his wife, cmplnts, & Lizzie D Mc Laurie & Jas C Hall, dfndnts. I am directed to report whether the lot in square 226, fronting on Pa ave, with the dwlg house thereon, be susceptible of division in specie. Notice is hereby given to the said parties, & to Corinne J Laurie, guardian of Lizzie D Laurie, at my ofc on May 8, for the purpose above stated. –W Redin, auditor

Circuit Court of Wash Co, D C. Wm J Gray & Susan R Stinger vs Nathan Gray et al. The trustee reported that he has sold the east half of lot 105, in Beatty & Hawkins' addition to Gtwn, to Chas Slemmer for $525, & the west half of said lot & all of lot 115, in said addition, to Richd Pettit for $1,342.50, & Gray's lot, in Threlkeld's square, to E M Linthicum for $101, & that the purchasers have complied with the terms of the sale. –Jno A Smith, clerk

TUE MAY 2, 1854
Three boys, members of Mr Marshall Wilkins' family, Hamptonburgh, Orange Co, N Y, were drowned in the Wallkill creek on Sat. They were aged 14, 16, & 19.

Mrd: on Apr 27, by Rev Jas B Donelan, Mr Wm Nash to Miss Jane Virginia Chism, all of Wash City.

Died: on Apr 30, Mrs Ann Salony, wife of Mr Henry Thomas, a native of PG Co, Md, but for the last 29 years a resident of Wash, aged 53 years. Her funeral will be from her late residence, on L, between 6th & 7th sts, this morning at 9 o'clock.

The Windham Co [Conn] Telegraph records the death of Deacon Danl Clark, of Brooklin, at the advanced age of 101 years, 6 months & 1 day. He was born in Chatham, removed to Brooklin in 1785, resided there till 1840, then removed to Plymouth, Vt, & thence back to Brooklin about 10 days previous to his death, having made the railroad journey of 160 miles from his Vt home in a single day. Though long delayed, death came suddenly at last. He complained of a pain in his side, & died peacefully within 5 minutes. Deacon Clark belonged to a family of which longevity has been regularly characteristic. Both his grandfather & father lived to the age of 94, while his grandmother lived to 99. Two of his uncles died at the age of 99, one aged 94, & one aged 86, one aged 84. Of his own generation, two attained to the ages of 88 & 81, while younger brothers & sisters still living have already passed their 3 score years & ten.

Chas B Christian, recently on trial at Lexington, Va, for the murder of Mr Blackburn, the Jury was unable to agree, & the case has been removed to Bedford Co, to be tried in Sept next.

Shepphard H Houston was convicted last week in the Sussex Co [Del] Court of selling for exportation from that State a negro girl who was a slave for a term of years, & was entitled to her freedon in 1861. The Court fined him $500 & costs, & committed him until paid.

Bridgett Little was scalded to death in Boston by the upsetting of a pot of boiling water on Monday.

Sally Ann Connis, 8 years old, was burnt to death at York, Md, on Friday last, while playing near some bushes which her companions had set on fire.

Orphans Court of Wash Co, D C. Letters of administration on the personal estate of Benj Riston, late of Wash Co, deceased. –Wm D Wise, adm

WED MAY 3, 1854
Household & kitchen furniture at auction: on May 3, at the residence of Mr Henry Smith, on 4th st, between M & N sts. –Green & Scott, aucts

Household & kitchen furniture at auction: on May 10, at the residence of Mrs Wise, corner of 13th & E sts. –Green & Scott, aucts

Senate: 1-Ptn from the heirs of John Underwood, asking to be confirmed in the title to certain lands. 2-Ptn from Franklin Chase, late Consul at Tampico, asking that his claim in relation to the confiscation & sale of the schnr **Oregon**, adversely reported on by the Cmte of Claims, may be again recommitted to that cmte with the papers on file in the archives of the Senate. 3-Cmte on Agriculture: memorial from Denton Offutt, offering to make public, for an equivalent, his system of taming wild horses & the improvement of the different breeds of domestic animals for the public good. 4-Cmte on Pensions: bill granting bounty land to Eliz Summers, widow of Cornelius Summers, a soldier in the late war with Great Britain; & a bill for the relief of John McVey, accompanied by reports in each case. Same cmte: bills for the relief of Benj Rowe, & for the relief of Geo W Gibson: recommending their passage. Same cmte: adverse reports on the ptns of Jas Steward, of Stamford Co, N Y; & on the additional documents in the case of Benj Burton. 5-Cmte on Revolutionary Claims: bill for the relief of Fred'k Vincent, adm of Jas Le Caze & Mallet. 6-Cmte on Indian Affairs: asked to be discharged from the further consideration of the memorials of John B & Clarinda P Chapman: which was agreed to. 7-Cmte on Pensions: asked to be discharged from the further consideration of the ptn of S T Van Derze: which was agreed to. 8-Cmte on Naval Affairs: asked to be discharged from the further consideration of the ptn of Mrs Mgt Chandler, & that it be referred to the Cmte on Pensions: which was agreed to.

Mrd: on May 2, at the Fourth Presbyterian Church, 9th st, by Rev Dr John C Smith, J M Stanley to Alice, daughter of the late John C English, all of Wash City.

Mrd: on May 2, by Rev Chas A Davis, Mr Danl L Webster, of N Y, to Miss Lydia B Cross, of Wash City.

In Chancery. Ann R Dermott, cmplnt, against Edwin C Morgan, Hooe, Brother & Co, C S Fowler, Yerby & Co, Sampson Camp, N M McGregor, J W Thompson, Stewart & Jones, Jas Dempsey, J C Smith, G A T Parker, Howard & Hill, J B Kibbey, Hall, Brother & Co, J P Wilson, ___ Harrover, Middleton & Beall, W Parkerson, Israel & Green, Maria B French, & Geo French, dfndnts. I am directed by a decree of the Circuit Court in the above cause to state the account of the trustee & to apportion the proceeds of sale among the creditors, according to the decree & the several deeds made by Maria B & Geo French, filed in the cause. Meeting at my ofc in City Hall on May 12. –W Redin, auditor

Died: on Apr 29, in Balt, Anna M, wife of Robt Leslie, in her 58th year.

Died: on May 2, Janet B Philips, in her 74th year. Her funeral will take place from her late residence, on East Capitol st, between 1st & 2nd sts, on May 4, at 3 o'clock.

Died: Feb 12, at Hong Kong, China, Surgeon Amo G Gambrill, U S Navy, aged 48.

THU MAY 4, 1854
On the Equity side of the Circuit Court of Queen Ann's Co, Md, Apr 28, 1854. Richd T Larrimore, adm of Mary Ann Quin; vs the heirs at law of the said Mary Ann Quin. This suit is to procure a decree for the sale of the real estate of which the said Mary Ann Quin died seized to reimburse the cmplnt for certain expenses incurred by him as her administrator, & the amount of her debts paid by him in his aforesaid capacity, & also for the benefit of any other creditors of said deceased. The bill states that a certain Frances Quin, late of Queen Ann's Co, Md, died in 1845 seized of a house & lot in Centreville, in said county & State; that said Frances had at one time two children, to wit, the said Mary Ann & a certain Arthur F Quin; that the said Arthur left the State of Md in or about 1835, & was last heard from in or about the year 1838, when he was residing in New Orleans, La, & that at that time he was & had always been unmarried; that the said Mary Ann died in 1853 intestate, unmarried & without issue, & leaving no personal estate; that the said Richd T Larrimore was appointed administrator of the said Mary Ann by the Orphans' Court of Queen Ann's Co, Md, shortly after her death, & could find no assets to administer; that he incurred liabilities for the costs of administration & other expenses, & particularly by payment of an account for medical services, which he prays to be reimbursed by the sale of the real estate of the said Mary Ann Quin, for which purpose, & for the payment of all other debts of the said Mary Ann Quin, the said real estate is liable to be sold; that said last named account amounts to $37.00 principal; that if the said Arthur F Quin, or any lineal descendant from him, was living at the time of the death of the said Mary Ann, such person would be her heir at law, but if not, then the said Richd T Larrimore, Thos F Larrimore, Anna M Bryan, formerly Larrimore & wife of Wm Bryan; Eliz Ford, formerly Larrimore & wife of Wm J Ford, & Sarah Harris, formerly Larrimore & wife of Robt Harris, all of Queen Ann's Co, Md, & John N Larrimore, a non-resident of Md & supposed to be a resident of Illinois, are her heirs at law, they being children of Robt Larrimore, grandfather of said Mary Ann Quin on the part of her mother Frances Quin, who were living at the time of the death of the said Mary Ann. Notice is given to Arthur J Quin, or any lineal descendant of said Arthur, & to the said John N Larrimore, & to all others who are or may claim to be heirs at law of said Mary Ann Quin, to appear in this Court in person, or by solicitor, on or before the first Monday of Nov next. -John Palmer, Clerk of the Circuit Court of Queen Ann's Co.

$100 reward for runaway negro boy Oliver, about 19 years of age.
–Wm J Berry, living near Upper Marlborough, PG Co, Md.

Household & kitchen furniture at auction: by order of the Orphans Court of Wash Co, D C. Sale on May 8, in front of our Store, the personal effects of Thos Moore, deceased. –Green & Scott, aucts

For rent: large 3 story brick House, with attic & basement & 3 story back bldg, with pump & stable, presently occupied by Mrs Matthews, on C st, between 3rd & 4½ sts. Possession given on Jun 1. Inquire of J P Pepper, or J W Hicks, for the heirs.

Letters from Cantonment Burgwin, near Taos, to Mar 31, received at St Louis, from which the Republican gathers the following authentic particulars of the late desperate battle between the command of Lt Davidson & the Apache Indians, a few miles from Taos. On Mar 26 Lt Davidson left Burgwin in command of 57 men in pursuit of the Apaches, who were supposed to be 100 strong. Next morning he came upon the Indians posted upon a mountain, & far exceeding in numbers, at least 200. The Indians raised the warhoop on the approach of the command, & attacked upon them at once. After a fight of 3 hours, during which Lt Davidson lost 22 men killed & 21 wounded, he was forced to retire, fighting his way over 2 miles, & with the disadvantage of having the wounded to carry with him. Lt Davidson received an arrow wound, not very severe, in a hand to hand conflict Surgeon Magruder was also wounded slightly. The Indians had about 50 killed, & nothing but their vast superiority in numbers gave them the triumph. Maj Blake & Thompson with a few troops & a large number of Mexicans started to bring in the dead bodies, & to attack the Indians, if they could be found.

The San Antonio Ledger of Apr 17 states that Mr Gallagher's rancho, about 23 miles from the city, had been attacked by a party of Indians, supposed to be Camanches, who killed & drove off a number of sheep & carried off or killed a man & a woman, the shepherd & his wife. They also killed an American named Forrester, knocked his wife down with a club, & probably killed their 4 children.

Loudoun, Va land: Jonathan Hirst sold on Apr 24, in said county, a tract of land, near Goose Creek meeting-house, containing 56 acres, for $7,000, being $125 per acre.

Died: on May 2, in PG Co, Md, Mary Ann Wall, wife of J H D Wall, in her 55th year. Her funeral will take place from Wesley Chapel this afternoon at 3 o'clock.

Died: on May 3, at Brooklyn, N Y, Catharine H, wife of Rosewell Woodward.

Senate: 1-Ptn from Alex'r Mitchell, asking an extension of his patent for screw-pile lighthouses. 2-Ptn from the Brotherton Indians, asking a final settlement of their claims. 3-Cmte on Pensions: adverse report on the ptn of Lewis Humbert. Same cmte: asked to be discharged from the further consideration of the ptn of Patience Hurd: which was agreed to. 4-Cmte of Claims: bill for the relief of Asa Andrews. 5-Bill for the relief of Jonas C Levy & Jose Maria Jarrero: introduced.

Appointments by the Pres, by & with the advice & consent of the Senate:
Chas K Gardiner, Surveyor Gen for Oregon, vice John B Preston, removed.
John Westcott, to be Surveyor Gen for Fla, vice B A Putnam, removed.
Eugene Wartelle, to be Receiver at Opelousas, La, vice H L Garland, resigned.
Patrick Quigley, to be Receiver at Dubuque, Iowa, vice M Mobley, removed.
Geo McHenry, to be Register at Dubuque, Iowa, vice Thos McKnight, removed.
John N Culbertson, to be Receiver at Fairfield, Iowa, vice W H Wallace, removed.
Jas Thompson, to be Register at Fairfield, Iowa, vice F Springer, removed.
Thos A Walker, to be Register at **Fort Des Moines**, Iowa, vice R I Tidrick, resigned.
Phineas M Cassaday, to be Receiver at **Fort Des Moines**, Iowa, vice T A Walker.
Burton A James, to be Agent for the Osage River Sacs & Foxes, Ottowas, & Swan Creek & Black River Chippewas, vice John R Chanault, removed.

Thirty-one slaves, manumitted by the late Wm Jennings, of Hanover Co, Va, left Richmond Monday for Norfolk, where they will speedily embark for Liberia.

On Monday the jury in a case in the N Y Supreme Court, in behalf of Irene Winchell, a girl of 12 years, who was run over, on 4th ave in that city, by a horse & light wagon driven by Benj Snow, a young man from Boston, brought in a sealed verdict of $4,000 damages. It is said that Snow, at the time of the accident, was driving at the rate of 7 miles an hour, & the injuries of the girl were very severe.

In Furman st, under Brooklyn heights, below the foot of Cranberry st, the heavy rains caused a large mass of earth to slide against a frame house, demolishing it & killing Mgt McColligan, aged 17, the daughter of the woman who kept the house as a boarding house, & Wm Curran, a laborer, unmarried, aged 30 years. [No date given- current item.]

Orphans Court of Wash Co, D C. Letters testamentary on the personal estate of Andrew Stepper, late of Wash Co, deceased. –Mary M Stepper, excx

FRI MAY 5, 1854
On Friday last a girl named Clancey, 11 years of age, residing in Ellicottville, N Y, while standing in a chair, was called by her sister. Turning suddenly, her clothes became entangled in the chair, & she was thrown upon an axe which laid with its edge upwards between 2 sticks of wood. Her head was split open, & instant death ensued.

Wash Corp: 1-Ptn from Jas W Scott, praying to be refunded certain money erroneously paid for taxes: referred to the Cmte of Claims. 2-Ptn for the relief of Jacob Smull: referred to the Cmte of Claims. 3-Ptn from P W Dorsey, praying to be refunded certain money erroneously paid for taxes: referred to the Cmte of Claims.

The Jennings Estate: several errors in the account of the Corbins of Va in the article of Apr 20, per writer signed "B." Henry Corbin settled in the parish of Stratton-Major, King & Queen Co, about 1650, or earlier. Col Richd Lee, of Strafford Langton, in Essex Co, England, was a burgess of York, Va, in 1647; & in 1650 settled at Stratford, Westmoreland Co. His 2nd son, Richd Lee, married the eldest daughter of Henry Corbin, & was the father of Col Thos Lee, who was the father of Richd Henry Lee, etc. Thos Corbin, one of the sons of Henry Corbin, died without children. Gawin Corbin, the other son of Henry Corbin, married a daughter of Wm Bassett, & left 3 sons & 4 daughters, viz: Richd Corbin, of Laneville; John Corbin, Gawin Corbin, Mrs Jenny Bushrod, Mrs Joanna Tucker, Mrs Alice Needles, & Mrs Allerton. Richd Corbin, of Laneville, married Miss Betty Tayloe, a daughter of Col John Tayloe, & Carter Braxton married his oldest daughter. Gawin Corbin, the 3rd son, married Hannah Lee, daughter of Col Thos Lee, & sister of Richd Henry Lee. He left an only child Martha Corbin, who married Mr Geo Turberville. Geo Turberville left 2 sons, Gawin Corbin Turberville & Richd Lee Turberville, the father of the present Mrs C C Stuart, of Chantilly, Fairfax Co. Gawin Corbin Turberville left an only daughter, Mary, who married Wm F Taliaferro, of Peckstone, Westmoreland. The writer has in his possession several pieces of plate, on which are the blended arms of the Corbins, Lees, & Turbervilles, on one escutcheon: the Corbin arms, 3 crows passant, [corvus;] the Lee arms, a lion rampant, [leo;] & the Turberville arms, a tower, from the French, Tour-de-ville. But he can trace no connexion with the Jennings family, except that Gawin Corbin owned lands in Prince Wm, which came to him by conveyance & descent from Edmund Jennings. Edmund Jennings was once Pres of the Council, & was succeeded by Robt Carter, who was the last Pres of the King's Council in Va. –B

+

The Jennings Estate, again. From A Jennings, Rockingham Co, Va, Apr 28, 1854, who possesses some knowledge of the genealogy of the Jennings family. No decision has ever been had in the case. One notice purports that a family of Corbins will obtain the estate, as the intestate will his estate to his wife, who was a Corbin, & she left no children; & another purports that a Mr Corbin married a Miss Jennings. Now, in relation to the first of these statements, the intestate, Wm Jennings, never had a wife; & in relation to the second, it is not probable that the descendants of this one Miss Jennings would inherit the estate to the exclusion of all others, when it is well known that said Wm Jennings, who died leaving this immense estate, made no will. The facts in these anonymous notices being at fault, so are their conclusions; & I would advise all who are concerened in the premises that the ostensibly friendly warnings of most of these anonymous writers should be but little regarded, especially when they tend to advance the interest of those who are known to have paid $100,000 to a solicitor to procure the dismissal of a suit brought for the recovery of this property; & when it is further known that the money thus paid went into the pocket of the lawyer & not the client who instituted the suit. –A Jennings

The trial by court-martial of Maj Wyse, of the 3rd Regt of U S Artl, commenced at Govnr's Island, N Y, on Tue. Maj Wyse was arrested on Apr 18, by order of Maj Gen Scott, for refusing to go on board the steamer **Falcon** with his detachment, consisting of companies D, J, I, & K. Maj Wyse had been on the unfortunate steamer **San Francisco**, & deemed the **Falcon** unfit for the transportation of troops. [This steamer was compelled to run into Norfolk with her passengers, & afterwards return to N Y for repairs.] The Major is to be tried on two charges: first, disobedience of order in refusing to lead his troops on board the **Falcon**; &, secondly, conduct unbecoming an ofcr & a gentleman. The result of the trial of Col Gates for alleged misconduct in command of the 3rd Reg of U S Artl, on board the wrecked steamer **San Francisco**, has not yet been officially announced. [Jun 9th newspaper: It is reported in the newspapers that the court martial in the case of Maj Wyse have found him guilty of disobedience of orders in refusing to embark on board the steamer **Falcon**, & that he has been sentenced to dismissal from the army; but that the court recommend him to reinstatement in the service. [Jun 12th newspaper: The court finds the accused Brvt Maj Francis O Wyse, Capt 3rd Artl, as follows: Charge I: guilty of the charge. Charge II: not guilty of the charge. Sentence: to be dismissed the service. This was laid before the Pres of the U S & by him examined & considered, the following order of his in this case: Jun 2, 1854: The Pres is pleased to mitigate the sentence to suspension from rank & command & pay for the period of 6 calendar months. The War Dept regrets that due care & judgment have not in all cases been exercised in the selection of transports for troops, this particular case it does not appear that the board of ofcrs appointed by the Genr'l commanding the army to examine the steamer made the thorough examination & inquiry which the circumstances & importance of the case suggested & demanded. These observations are not intended to justify or extenuate the conduct of Maj Wyse in assuming to oppose his judgment to that of his cmder, & to disobey a positive & reiterated order by refusing to embark with troops to the command of whom he had been assigned, & whose fate it was his duty to share. -Sec of War: Jefferson Davis. III: The sentence awarded will be duly executed, & at the termination of the period for which he is suspended he will proceed to join his company wherever it may then be serving. IV: the Gen Court Martial of which Brvt Brig Gen Henry Stanton is Pres is dissolved.]

Senate: 1-Ptn from Wm Moran, asking remuneration for a horse accidentally killed on the work of the extension of the Capitol. 2-Documents relating to the claim of J C Edwards for the payment of a draft drawn by G W Barbour, Indian Agent in Calif: presented. 3-Cmte on Commerce: adverse report on the memorial of Saml J Peters. 4-Cmte on the Judiciary: adverse report on the memorial of Wm Field. 5-Cmte on Pensions: bill for the relief of Cornelius H Latham, reported back without amendment. 6-Cmte on Military Affairs: asked to be discharged from the further consideration of the memorial of Hardy H Holstead & others, & that it be referred to the Cmte on Public Lands, which was agreed to.

John Baja, the son of a widow lady of Allegheny City, some 6 months ago injured his right leg in a fall & the whole shaft of the bone became decayed. To save the limb Dr Walter removed last week, while the boy was under chloroform, the main bone from the knee to the ankle by extirpation. Experience has taught that new bone will be rapidly regenerated in childhood, & the limb may be preserved. The boy is doing well & is free from pain. –Pittsburg Journal

Indian Affairs: 1-A letter from C H Beaulieu, of Crow Wing, to his brother in this city, says that a little son of Hole-in-the-Dau, head chief of the Chippewas, was burnt to death a few days since by a fire on the prairie. 2-Little Six's brother, a Sioux Indian, was killed & scalped by a party of Chippewas near Little Rapids, on the Minnesota river, on Thu last.

Mr Stephen Holbrook, of Amherst, N H, was accidentally killed on Monday last while engaged in ploughing. The horse became frightened & started upon the run. Mr Holbrook fell in front of the plough, & was carried about 100 feet before he could be extricated by his son, who was at work with him. He survived his injuries but half an hour.

Mrd: on May 2, by Rev Fr Birns, at St Matthew's Church, Danl W Slye, of St Mary's Co, Md, to Miss Genevieve Agnes, elder daughter of Jas D King, of Wash City.

Mrd: on May 4, in Union Chapel, by Rev J H Dashiell, the Rev Robt L Dashiell, of the Balt Annual Conference, to Mary Jane, only daughter of the late Edmund Hanly, of Wash City.

Died: on May 3, in her 64th year, Mrs Mgt Lucey, formerly of Phil.

Wash City Ordinances. 1-Act for the relief of Geo W & John S Hopkin: that the fines imposed on them is remitted, provided they pay to this Corp $34.53, being part of the fines & all the costs imposed on them by Justice Drury, for removing sand from Rhode Island ave: & provided they pay for the number of loads of sand acknowledged by them to have been taken from said avenue. 2-Act for the relief of Jas Grace: that the fine imposed on him for a violation by making a bonfire on Pa ave in June last is remitted.

Private sale of **Overton**, beautifully located in Balt Co, adjoining the Relay House, on the Balt & Ohio Railroad. Seventy-seven acres of this tract were sold to gentlemen of Balt for Villa & Cottage sites, & are now preparing to erect their bldgs, I will sell the remainder 100 acres, with all the improvements. The dwlg upon the propery is very commodious, having been occupied several summers as a first-class Boarding house. –J H Luckett, Balt.

Valuable James River estate in Isle of Wight Co, Va, for sale at public auction. As the atty for Hon John Y Mason, I shall offer at auction, on the premise, on Jun 27, 1854, the estate called **Day's Neck**, containing, by recent survey, 2,121 acres, & bounded by the lands of Gen Francis M Boykin & others. The estate has been subdivided into 4 tracts: **House Tract**, 403 acres; **Shiver's Tract**, 635 acres; **Halstend Tract**, 260 acres, & **Landing Tract**, 723 acres. It will be sold separately or together, as may suit purchasers. The bldgs, though not extensive, are sufficient for the accommodation of a moderate-sized family. Refer to John A Selden, of Chas City Co, Va, or to Gen F M Boykin, Isle Wight. –W Goddin, atty in fact for John Y Mason. -Goddin & Apperson, aucts

Orphans Court of Wash Co, D C. Letters testamentary on the personal estate of Henry Aylmer, late of Wash Co, deceased. –Phoebe Aylmer, Robt R Alymer, excs

Barkeeper & Cook wante: at the Waverley House, Capitol Hill. Inquire at P D Desaules'.

SAT MAY 6, 1854
On Thu a human body was entangled in his net by a fisherman engaged in his occupation near the Potomac Aqueduct at Gtwn. The body was identified as Danl Macnamara, [who was struck down by the falling of the new iron bridge,] by the widow & friends of the poor man, but chiefly by the remnant of clothes on his person. A severe contusion, that must have instantly killed him, appears on his forehead. Macnamara's widow is left with a large family of quite small children

At Gloucester, England, in Apr, the trial of Sir Richd Hugh Smyth, alias Thos Provis, came on. He was charged with forging a codicil to the will of Sir Hugh Smyth, Bart, with the intent to defraud the rightful heir of his property. The trial resulted in the conviction of the prisoner, who was sentenced to 20 years transportation.

Criminal Court-Wash: the case of John Connor, charged with the murder of Patrick Hurley, was concluded yesterday. The jury found Connor guilty of manslaughter.

Mrd: on May 4, by Rev Jas H Brown, Mr Jas F Marr to Miss Eleanor A Hubbard, both of Wash.

Mrd: on May 4, in Gtwn, by Rev J G Butler, Esli D Reed, of Wash City, to Mary E, daughter of John Moore, of Gtwn.

Mrd: on May 4, by Rev Jas H Brown, Mr Wm A Franklin to Miss Sallie W Scrivener, daughter of Mr Thos Scrivener.

Died: on May 4, at his residence in Wash City, Alex'r S Wotherspoon, M D, Assist Surgeon U S army. His funeral is this afternoon at 3 o'clock, at St John's Church.

Died: on May 3, in Brooklyn, N Y, suddenly, of congestion of the brain, Catharine H, wife of Rosewell Woodward, in her 55th year. For a few years the family resided in Gtwn, D C. Her efforts were untiring to fulfill the duties of wife, mother, & friend.

Senate: 1-Senate bills passed-relief of: the legal reps of John G Mackall, deceased; of John Bronson; of Capt Langdon C Easton, assist quartermaster U S army; of John S Wilson; of Isaac Cook & others; of John Metcalf; of Sylvester Pettibone; of Jas Edwards & others; of Wm Harris, of Ga; of the personal reps of Wm A Slacum, deceased; of Rulif Van Brunt; of Horace Southmayd & Son; of the reps of Thos D Anderson, deceased, late U S Consul at Tripoli; of Saml Bray; of Seneca G Simmons; of Thos D Jennings; of Juan M & Jose L Luco; of Eliza M Evans; of Sarah Crandall.
2-House bills passed: relief of the heirs of Anthony G Willis, deceased; of Fayette Manzy & Robt G Ward; & of the legal reps of Capt Wm Davis, late cmder of the U S transport schnr **Eufalia**. 3-House bills adversely reported on: relief of John Hamilton; of Parmelia Slavin, late the wife of John Blue, deceased; & of Wm Darby.

In Chancery. Wm P Pumphrey vs Wm Bird, adm of Simon Fraser, deceased, & others. Wm T Swann & Chas S Wallach, the trustees, reported they have sold part of lot 3 in square 730, with the brick house thereon, to Danl Gen__, for $1,225, who made an assignment of his interest to Morris McConnell; that they have sold lot 1 in square 334 to John Walker & John A Fraser, for the sum of $717; & also they they have sold to Saml Byington lot 1 in square 630, at the price of two cents & three miles per square foot; & the purchasers have complied with the terms of the sale. -Jno A Smith, clerk

Fred'k W Seward, son of W H Seward, John Ten Eyck, & Philip Ten Eyck have beome associated with Messrs Weed, Dawson, & Visscher Ten Eyck as joint & equal owners of the Albany Evening Journal establishment. –Buffalo Comm Advertiser

The U S sloop-of-war **Jamestown** has just arrived at Phil, after a 3 years' cruise on the coast of Brazil. On board are a large number of invalids sent home from the various ships belonging to the Brazil squadron. Her ofcrs & crew will be detached in a few days. The following is a list of her ofcrs: Sam W Downing, Cmder; Chas F McIntosh, 1st Lt; Roger N Stembel, 2nd Lt; Chas Deas, 3rd Lt; John P Hall, 4th Acting Lt; John M Foltz, Surgeon; John S Gulick, Purser; Fred'k Horner, jr, Assist Surgeon; Jos DeHaven, Acting Master; Geo Holmes, Lt of Marines; Wm Cheerer, Midshipman; Henry A Adams, Midshipman; Albert J DeZeyk, Capt's Clerk

The U S steam frig **Massachusetts**, R W Meade, Lt Commanding, went into commission at Norfolk on Monday.

John Hendrickson was executed at Albany yesterday for the murder of his wife. [May 9th newspaper: John Hendrickson was only 21 years of age, & of highly respectable parents. In Jan, 1851, he married Maria Van Dusen, daughter of Lawrence Van Dusen, formerly clerk of Albany Co. Maria was 17 at the time of her marriage, & at the time of her decease she was 19. She was the youngest child of her parents, well educated, accomplished, affectionate, & devotedly attached to her father & mother. In 1852 he became dissatisfied with his wife, gave her poison, the effects of which she died, & for which he was executed.]

Mrs Cecilia Young will give her first Grand Vocal & Insturmental Concet on May 11, at Carusi's Saloon.

Montg Co land for sale: on May 23, at the Court-house door in Rockville, Montg Co, Md: two lots of land in said county. One contains 72 acres, & the other contains 112½ acres. Both are well wooded, but unimproved, & as portions of the real estate of the late Jas B Higgins. –W Veirs Bouic, John M Kilgour, trustees

MON MAY 8, 1854
Household & kitchen furniture at auction: May 8, at the residence of Mr A Lehmann, on East Capitol st, between 1st & 2nd sts. –Green & Scott, aucts

Household & kitchen furniture at auction: on May 9, at the residence of J H Moulton, on 11th st, between G & H sts. –Green & Scott, aucts

Franklin Pierce, Pres of the U S A, recognizes Rudolph K Topp, who has been appointed Consul of Brunswick & Luneburg, for the States of Ohio, Indiana, Ill, & Ky. –Apr 19, 1854

The Chesapeake & Ohio Canal did a fair average business during the week past. Between 60 & 70 boats arrived at Gtwn variously freighted.

Mrd: on Apr 27, at Collington Meadows, by Rev Mr Berne, Richd S Hill to Eliz S, daughter of the late Francis M Hall, of PG Co, Md.

Mrd: on Fri, by Rev John C Smith, Mr Wm C Keyes to Miss Selma V Simms, of Va.

Died: on May 7, Mary Malvina, youngest child of John T C & Jane E Clark, aged 15 months. Her funeral is this afternoon at 3:1/2 o'clock, from the residence of her parents, corner of H & 10th sts.

Summer Millinery: Miss E A McDonald, successor to Mrs Ann H Clark: open on May 10th. Store, 3 doors east of the Post Ofc, Bridge st, Gtwn.

The Jennings' Estate: Article printed from Connecticut for "the heirs of the estate of Wm Jennings who died in England in 1798." The Buckingham letter may refer to the same Wm Jennings, who died intestate & never had a wife. Within a few days, too, "T" has learnt for the first time, that John Tayloe, of Mount Airy, by a codicil to his will, dated in Jan, 1744, & admitted to probate 1747, says: I give & devise to my friend & relative, Edmund Jennings, of the Province of Md, etc. He also leaves a legacy to his friend & relative, Thos Lee, of Stratford, Westmoreland Co, in Va. This Thos Lee, according to the statement of B, was father of the distinguished Richd Henry Lee. The relationship of the present Tayloe family to Edmund Jennings of Md, & to the Lee family of Stratford, is not to be traced in any other channel than the English blood of Wm Taylor or Tayloe, or from his wife, Anne Corbin, the daughter of Henry Corbin, the first of the name who emigrated from England & settled in King & Queen County, Va, about 1650, or a little earlier, according to the genealogy of the Corbin & Lee families, as furnished by your correspondent B. He also states that an Edmund Jenning was Pres of the Council in Va. The late Col John Tayloe, of Wash, owned the Corbin Patent in Prince Wm Co, part of which is now owned by the writer, T, that he concluded were the lands owned by Gawin Corbin, which came to him by conveyance & descent from Edmund Jennings. According to B's statement, & the corroborating circumstances here furnished, it would appear that the connexion, if any, between the Corbins of Va & the Jennings, whence comes the claim to the great inheritance, was formed anterior to the emigration of Henry Corbin to Va, as along ago as 1650. This may be still a subject of nteresting inquiry to all the descendants, who may be legion, of that Henry Corbin. It would seem that the several errors, chiefly of omission, late which I had fallen, in his account of the Corbins of Va, were of no material consequence. It may be worthy of ___, to prevent mistakes as to the present Corbin, of the Reeds, that the gentleman referred to is Robt B Corbin, son of the late Francis Corbin, whose father was Richd Corbin, of Laneville, who married a daughter of John Tayloe, as correctly stated by B. [We must beg to close the discussion, as all our space is demanded by matters of more general interest. –Editors]

Orphans Court of Wash Co, D C. Letters of administration on the personal estate of Christopher R Byrne, late of Wash Co, deceased. –Jas F Haliday, adm

Orphans Court of Wash Co, D C. Letters testamentary on the personal estate of Rev Wm Matthews, late of Wash Co, deceased. –Thos Carbery, W H Ward, excs

TUE MAY 9, 1854
Senate: 1-Report from the Sec of State, in relation to the arrest of Conrad Schmidt, at Bremen, & the arrest at Heidelberg of E P Dana. 2-Ptn from the widow of Andrew A Jones, asking compensation for the services of her late husband.

The first & only duel ever fought in Illinois was in 1820, with rifles, between Alphonso Stewart & Wm Bennett; the former was killed & the latter arrested, tried, convicted, & hung. There has been no duel in Illinois since this example. –Phil Sun

From the New Orleans Crescent. Mrs Eliz Hamilton, the widow of Alex'r Hamilton has reached the great age of 95, & retains in an astonishing degree her faculties, & converses with much of that ease & brilliancy which lent so peculiar a charm to her younger days. She insists her visiters take a merry glass from Gen Washington's punch bowl, which, with other portions of his table-set, remains in her possession. Mrs Hamilton completes her 96th year on Aug 16 next. Her life in its prime was overcast by the bloody death of her eldest son Philip, a young gentleman of great promise, & soon after the fall of her beloved lord, by what was nothing less than a deliberately executed assassination; for Aaron Burr knew when, upon the mere pretence of a quarrel, he summoned Gen Hamilton to the field, that he woulnd not decline to meet him, but would never take the life of a fellow-being in private combat. Mrs Hamilton was seen less than a year since visitng unattended, on foot, friends who lived a half a mile from her. Two years before we saw her arrive at her own house on H st, Wash, [the Menou bldgs,] from a morning's walk to visit her old friend, Judge Cranch, on Capitol Hill: about 3 miles. The Gov't acquired Hamilton's papers from her in 1849, edited by Mr John Hamilton, who had previously given to the world a more limited selection, with a biography of his father.

Laban Mercer, indicted for the murder in Wetzel Co, Va, on the authority of a ghost, has been acquitted. The ghost failed to appear when his testimony might have amounted to something.

Mrd: on May 8, at Trinity Church, by Rev C M Butler, Jacob Carter Gibson to Miss Mary Arkansas McCutchen, both of Wash City.

Died: on May 7, Mrs Ann White, in her 62nd year.

Died: on May 4, at Lexington, Mass, Lt Henry T Wingate, U S Navy. He was a native of Maine, & entered the naval service in 1831.

In Chancery. Wm P Pumphrey, cmplnt, against Wm Bird, adm of Simon Frasier, & John Walker & Martha his wife, John Frasier, Ellen S Frasier, Georgiana Frasier, Chas B Calvert, & Nathl Soper & Maria Ellen Soper his wife, heirs of said Simon Frazier, deceased. Creditors of Saml Frasier, if there by any, to file their claims with me on or before May 15 next. –W Redin, auditor

WED MAY 10, 1854
Trustee's sale: by deed of trust, executed to me by John A King, deceased, & of record in Liber J A S 39, of the land records of Wash Co, D C: sale on May 18, of lot 4 in square 72, containing 7,000 feet. –F W Risque, trustee -Jas C McGuire, auct

The **Independent**, a tri-weekly newspaper published in Gtwn since August last, announced its own exit yesterday.

Church of the Ascension At a meeting of the Vestry of this Church held yesterday, the Rev Henry Stanley was unanimously elected Rector. [May 11th newspaper: Rev Mr Gilliss, who had been for 10 years the Rector, resigned on May 2.]

Mrd: on May 9, by Rev Jas H Brown, Mr Thos J Hardisty to Miss Eliz Jones, both of Montg Co, Md.

Senate: 1-Ptn from Geo W Greene, of Rhode Island, grandson of Gen Green, of Revolutionary memory, setting forth that he has a mass of valuable manuscripts which he desires to have published partly at the expense of the Gov't. 2-Ptn from Robt C Schenck, of Ohio, asking an appropriation for the compensation of his services as Envoy Extra & Minister Pleni on special mission to the Argentine Confederation & to the Orietnal Republic of Uruguay in 1852 & 1853. 3-Ptn from H S Sanford, late Charge d'Affaires at Paris, asking the difference between his pay as Sec of Legation & Charge d'Affaires during the time he acted as such, & reimbursement of sums paid for clerk hire. 4-Cmte on Pensions: adverse report on the ptn of John T Hildreth. 5-Bill for the relief of David Myerle, objected to last Fri, it was again taken up & considered: passed.

A fine old Irish Gentleman. The Dublin Freeman says: Owen Duffy, of Monaghan Co, is 122 years old. When 116 he lost his second wife, & married a third, by whom he had a son & daughter. His youngest son is 2 years old, his eldest 90. He still retains in much vigor his mental & corporal faculties, & frequently walks to the county town, a distance of 8 miles.

Meeting of the Superintendents of Insane Hospitals yesterday at the Smithsonian Institution: Dr Luther V Bell, of Boston, took the chair. Besides the ofcrs, the following superintendents, old members, viz:
Dr Francis Stribling, of the Western Asylum, Va
Dr Tyler, N H Asylum, Concord
Dr John Curwen, of Pa State Lunatic Asylum, Harrisburg.
Dr C H Nichols, U S Hospital for the Insane, Wash, D C
Dr J H Worthington, Friends' Asylum, Frankfort, Ky
Dr Clement A Walker, South Boston Asylum
The following are the new members:
Dr Fisher, N C Hospital
Dr Ingraham, of King's Co Hospital, N Y
Dr Cheetham, of Tenn Hospital
Dr Smith, of Missouri
Dr Bell, of Mass
Dr Ray, of Providence, R I

Died: yesterday, in Wash City, Patrick H Brooks, of Wash City, in his 37th year.

Died: on May 4, in Cincinnati, in her 86th year, Mrs Katherine Browne, a native of Mass, but for the last 6 years a resident of Ohio. Mrs Browne resided in D C 35 years. She was for a long time a member of the family of the late Dr Sewal, & enjoyed the confidence & friendship of John Quincy Adams, Danl Webster, Rufus Choate, Senator Peace, & Judge McLean. Her life was blameless & her end peaceful.

THU MAY 11, 1854
House & lot in Cabot's subdivision of square 677 at auction: May 17, in front of lot 109; it being the property belonging to Mr John C Frantman. -Green & Scott, aucts

Senate: 1-Ptn from Nathl M Wolverton, asking the confirmation of his title to land in the Ouachita district, in Louisiana. 2-Ptn from Jas T V Thompson, asked to be indemnified for loss of flour purchased by him at a Gov't sale as in good condition; & also remuneration for cattle lost while on their way for delivery at *Bent's Fort*, under a contract with the Gov't. 3-Ptn from Alex R McKee, asking to be allowed to locate certain lands in the State of Texas on copies of certificates alleged to have been lost while in possession of an ofcr of the Gov't. 4-Ptn from Jas Herron & others, of Fla, asking the right of way through the lands reserved by the U S for military & naval purposes for the construction of a plank road on the Perdido river & the Bay of Pensacola, & a grant of land for a depot & landing wharves in the harbor of Pensacola. 5-Cmte on Naval Affairs: adverse report on the memorial of John Makin. 6-Cmte on Military Affairs: bill for the relief of Capt Chas G Merchant. Same cmte: adverse report on the memorial of Thos B Eastland. 7-Cmte on Patents & the Patent Ofc: bill to extend a patent granted to John Schley, of Georgia.

Mrd: on May 9, by Rev Mr Hodges, Lewis Williams to Mrs Eliz Pruderoski, all of Wash.

Mrd: on May 9, by Rev S A K Marks, Mr Wm W Duley to Miss Susan Sansbury, both of PG Co, Md.

The court-martial for the trial of Dr Steiner, charged with killing his superior ofcr, convened in Austin, Texas, on Apr 17, & adjourned until the 21st, in consequence of the absence of the accused. A military dispatch was sent for Steiner. We are not advised what course the Court will pursue because of his absence. Slidell McKenzie, who hung young Spencer, was tried before the civil court, & then before a court-martial.

The *Weverton* Manufacturing Co will offer for sale on May 31 their unrivalled water-power & all their lands. Address to Weverton, Md, to John H T Hayes, Gen Agent. By order of the Board of Directors.

Explosion of the steamer **Secretary** on Apr 15, while crossing San Pablo bay. The steamer **Nevada** happened to be close by & rendered assistance. List of the killed & missing as far as ascertained:

D Johnson	W H Tripp
D H Van Byrne	Thos Cameron
Lewis Johnson	C W Rogers, capt
Jas McGuire	Mr Lundy
Edw Bruce Bracket	Mrs Hillman
Mrs Harlon	J D Cookingham
Richd A Lewis	Chas Smith
L Lamberton, clerk	G Walker
Geo Clark	G P Henry
J Foster	Emma Holmes
Mrs Hillmans & child	Geo Robertson
Jas Wright	E A James
Mr Miller, deck hand	R Parker
Judge Ferrill	Wm Lunky, wife & child
John Ebbetts	The cook & deck hand

Died: on May 10, Jane Heyer, in her 85th year, a native of N Y C, but for the last 43 years a resident of Wash City. The deceased leaves to her family & friends a memory honored & endeared by the exercise of meek piety, active kindness, & warm affection. For some years her health has been gradually declining. Her funeral will be from her late residence, corner of N Y ave & 8th st, this afternoon, at 4 o'clock. The friends of the deceased, as well as those of her sister, Mrs Louisa F Zantzinger, are invited to attend.

Died: on Apr 30, at his residence in Charlotte Co, Va, John Jas M Bouldin, who was for several years a member of the Va Legislature, & after the decease of his brother, Judge Bouldin, was elected from the Charlotte district a member of Congress, in which capacity he served for many years.

Died: on Mar 27, at Gibsonville, Calif, Edw DeKrafft, aged 36 years, son of the late F C DeKrafft, of Wash City.

Orphans Court of Wash Co, D C. In the case of Edw Swann, adm of Barry Dixon & Michl Dixon, deceased, the administrator & Court have appointed Jun 10 next for the settlement & distribution of the estates of said deceased, of the assets in hand.
-Ed N Roach, Reg/o wills

For sale: *Seneca Mills*, in Montg Co, Md, adjacent to the C & O Canal: contains 93½ acres, more or less; with a merchant mill, commodious 2 story dwlg, with ice house, corn house, blacksmith shop, & stabling. Apply to F & A H Dodge, or Robt F Dodge, Gtwn, D C.

FRI MAY 12, 1854
Henry Haw, Henry Naylor, Joshua Pierce, Chas R Belt, Robt White, Lewis Carbery, John N Fearson, Benj K Morsell, Saml Drury, Franklin S Myer, & Jas A Kennedy, were re-appointed members of the Levy Court of Wash Co, D C, on May 1.

An elderly gentleman from the West, Mr Richd Deering has devised a plan for providing against the perils of fire. A tin or sheet copper reservoir in the roof of each bldg to be protected, to be fed by rain collected on the surface, from which lead pipes of small capacity connected with each room are to pass. At the departure of each of these pipes from the reservoir is a valve, to be under the control of a combustible cord passing into each other, so that the burning of the cord causes the valve to open & the water to flow. He proposes to to patent his plan.

A fire in Gtwn yesterday, on Prospect st, whereby 2 unfinished frame bldgs were wholly consumed, together with 2 inhabited frame dwlgs adjacent. The first two were the property of Mr O M May, the latter of Mr David Oyster, & were occupied by Mr Isaac Birch & Mr Oats. The fire is referred to an incendiary origin.

Died: on May 11, at his residence in Wash City, Capt Thos L Ringgold, Ordnance Corps, U S Army. His funeral will be at the Church of the Epiphany [Rev Mr French's, on G st,] this afternoon at 5 o'clock.

Died: on May 11, in Wash City, of pneumonia, Mrs Jane Stafford Ely, wife of Albert Welles Ely, M D, formerly of New Orleans. Her funeral will take place this afternoon at 3 o'clock.

Died: on May 8, at his residence in Michigan, in his 50th year, Hon Isaac E Crary, formerly a Rep in Congress from Michigan for several years immediately succeeding the admission of that State into the Union.

Senate: 1-Memorial from Edw Riddle, of Boston, asking that he may be reimbursed for the expenses incurred by him while acting as agent of the American contributors to the Industrial Exhibition at London in 1851. 2-Cmte of Claims: bill for the relief of the legal reps of the late Col John Anderson.

In Boston, on Sat, the venerable John Hancock, nephew of Govn'r John Hancock of Revolutionary memory, now nearly 85 years of age, was standing in front of a mansion, looking at the new church nearly opposite, he lost his balance & fell over backwards down the area between a very low iron fence & the house, a distance of about 6 feet from the sidewalk. He was taken into the basement window of the house, & subsequently conveyed in a state of insensibility to his residence, where he now lies in a critical state.

Mrd: on Apr 11, by Rev Mr Dubois, in Putnam, Ohio, Mr H Safford, of that place, to Mrs Frances L Bowers, formerly Miss Wilson, of Petersburg, Va.

Upholstery & Paper Hanging Store: 3 door north of Pa ave. –David A Baird

SAT MAY 13, 1854
Binghampton [N Y] Republican of Monday: Deacon Joab Hathaway & wife, Chas Hathaway & wife, G Hathaway & his 2 sisters, & 2 granchildren of Saml Hathaway, of Windsor, Broome Co, on Sunday last entered a skiff & proceeded as usual on their way to church, across the Susquehanna river. Having reached the opposite side, the boat upset throwing the whole party into the water. Chas Hathaway & his wife & the 2 children mentioned, as well as a sister of G Hathaway, were all drowned.

Senate: 1-Ptn of Geo W Torrence, a soldier in the late war with Mexico, praying compensation for injuries received in the discharge of his duty, & for extra services rendered at the Nat'l Bridge, in Mexico: referred to the Cmte on Military Affairs.

Mrd: on May 11, by Rev A G Carothers, Mr Arthur G Pumphrey to Miss Lavinia F Childress, both of Wash City.

Mrd: on May 10, at Castle Hill, Va, Henry Sigourney, of Boston, to Miss Amelie Louise, daughter of Hon Wm C Rives.

MON MAY 15, 1854
Household & kitchen furniture at auction on May 17, at the residence of Mr S Brintnall, on E st, between 9th & 10th st. -Green & Scott, aucts

Leonard Houslet shot himself dead at Hamelton, near Cincinnati, in his rage because the moulds in which he was running candles leaked. His wife was present, but was petrified by the man's horrible curses.

Mr Laidlaw, an artist & scene painter at the People's Theatre, St Louis, was murdered on the road known as the King's Highway, which runs across the country from the St Chas road to the Central plank road, near St Louis, on May 7. A man named Jackson is suspected of the crime & the ofcrs are in pursuit of him.

John O'Sullivan, who beat his wife to death at **Fort Hamilton**, N Y, last autumn, has been sentenced to the penitentiary for 21 years.

Mrd: on Apr 20, near Selma, Ala, F Henry Quitman, son of Gen Quitman, of Miss, to Mary, only daughter of Col Virgil H Gardner, of Dallas Co, Ala.

Died: on May 14, Antonio Catalano, a native of Palermo, Sicily, a residenct of Wash City for the last 37 years. His funeral will be from his late residence, near the Navy Yard, this day, at 2 o'clock.

Died: yesterday, Miss Mary Eliz Remington, youngest daughter of the late Mr Jas Remington, in her 18th year. Her funeral will take place from the residence of her uncle, Mr Richd W Clarke, on 10th st, between N Y ave & K st, today at 4 o'clock.

Died: on Sunday, after a long & severe illness, Mr Jabez Young, in his 24th year. His funeral will be from the residence of his sister, Mrs Peddicord, on E, between 6th & 7th sts, at 4 o'clock this day.

Died: on May 12, at Richmond, Va, in her 83rd year, Mrs Susanna Pleasants, relict of the late Gov Jas Pleasants.

Died: on May 18, George William, youngest child of Andrew J & Frances M Joyce, aged 17 months & 16 days.

Orphans Court of Wash Co, D C. Letters testamentary on the personal estate of Sarah A Williams, late of Wash Co, deceased. –Saml W Magruder, exc

TUE MAY 16, 1854
Orphans Court of Wash Co, D C. Letters of administration on the personal estate of Geo Watterston, late of Wash Co, deceased. –M Watterston, admx

U S Patent Ofc: Wash, D C, May 16, 1854. Ptn of Richd Montgomery & Lewis W Harris, of Sangerfield, N Y, praying for the extension of a patent granted to them for an improvement in the mill for breaking & grinding bark, for 7 years from the expiration of said patent, which takes place on Aug 12, 1854.
–Chas Mason, Com'r of Patents

At the recent session of the Berkeley [Va] Circuit Court Jos H Morgan obtained a verdict of $5,000 damages against Z Silvers for shooting & wounding him in 1852.

Improved property & bldg lots at auction: on May 23, being the real property of the late John Myers: eastern part of lot 7, fronting on Dunbarton st, improved with a good 2 story brick dwlg; eastern part of the same lot, improved by a good brick dwlg with back bldgs. This was the residence of Mr Myers. Lot adjoining the above on same street. Part of lot 171, on Fred'k st, between 3rd & 4th sts. Part of lot 23, in Beatty's & Hawkins' addition to Gtwn, on High st, improved by 2 small brick houses. Part of same lot on High st. Title indisputable. –Chas Myers, adm for heirs
-Barnard & Buckey, aucts

From Europe: Montgomery, the poet, died on Apr 30, aged 82 years. [May 18th newspaper: Jas Montgomery, the distinguished poet, presided at the weekly board of the Infirmary as late as the day before his death, & walked home, more than a mile. He was born Nov 4, 1771, in Irvine, in Ayrshire, Scotland. His father was a Moravian minister, who, leaving his son in Yorkshire to be educated, went to the West Indies, where he & the poet's mother both died. When only 12 years old the boy's mind was shown by the production of several small poems.]

Foreign Obit: the death of Wm Henry Paget, first Marquis of Anglesey, is announced. He was the eldest son of the third Earl of Uxbridge, born in May, 1768, & was 80 years of age. Lord Paget began his military career as cmder of a regt of volunteers; served under the Duke of York in Flanders; in 1818 attained the rank of Maj Gen; distinguished himself in the Parthian retreat of Sir John Moore, ending in the battle of Corunna; in 1812 succeeded to the title of Earl of Uxbridge; commanded the heavy brigade, under Lord Wellington during the Peninsular war; was in command of the British cavalry at Waterloo, where he lost a leg.

Mrd: on May 11, at Gtwn, D C, by Rev J M P Atkinson, Geo Arnold, of Balt, to Miss E M Tilley, of Gtwn, D C.

Died: on May 15, in Wash City, John W Simonton, aged about 65 years, formerly a citizen of Key West, Fla, & recently a resident here. His funeral is this afternoon at half past 4 o'clock, from Mrs Wallingsford's Boarding-house, on 4½ st.

Senate: 1-Ptn from Ester Coulter, asking compensation for the services of her father, late quartermaster in the Revolutionary war. 2-Additional documents in support of the claim of Harriet Dela Parm Baker: submitted. 3-Memorial from Castner Hanway, stating that he was arrested at Christiana, Lancaster Co, Pa upon a charge of high treason, in Sep, 1851, of which he was acquitted, & discharged from the custody of the U S. The memorialist complains that in obtaining witnesses for his defence he was subjected to an expense of $3,000, which had entirely absorbed his property, & that many of the witnesses were still unpaid; that his health has been impaired by his imprisonment, which is not yet restored. He asks that Congress may pass an act providing for the payment of the cost of his witnesses, etc. [Mr Cooper alluded to the fact that in the case of Aaron Burr, his witnesses were paid by order of the Court, Judge Marshall having made the order, but in the present case the judges thought they had no power to make such an order. He would commend it to the Cmte on the Judiciary.] 4-Ptn from John C Hand, asking to be allowed a pension on account of disease contracted in the military service. 5-Cmte on Foreign Relations: bill for the relief of Chas Arwedson, charge d'affaires ad interim at Stockholm. 6-Bill to authorize T H McManus to enter by pre-emption certain lands in the Greensbury land district, Louisiana: introduced.

Lord Cockburn is dead. He was one of the Scotch judges, & is known to the literary world as the biographer of Lord Jeffrey. He was an able lawyer.

Fine fresh gentle cow for sale: she has twin calves 4 weeks old & fit for the butcher. Price $50. At W T Geffers', near the Bladensburg Toll-gate.

WED MAY 17, 1854
The Govn'r of Va has appointed Richd G Morris, of the city of Richmond, the Com'r on the part of that Commonwealth to & in conjunction with the Com'rs appointed by the Govn'r of Md to run & mark the boundary line between the States of Md & Va, as prescribed by the act of the Gen Assembly of Va passed on Mar 3 last.

Choloroform counteracted. This valuable discovery had been just announced by Dr Robt de Lambelle, a distinguished physician of Paris. He states that a shock of electricy given to a patient dying from the effects of chloroform will immediately counteract its influence, & return the sufferer to life.

Senate: 1-Ptn from Simon Smith, asking to be allowed arrears of pension. 2-Ptn from Abigail Sanders, asking to be allowed bounty as the widow of Jos Davis, a soldier in the war of 1812. 3-Ptn from Ithamer W Beard, assist treasurer of the U S in Boston, asking that Congress authorize the permanent employment of 2 clerks in his ofc. 4-Ptn from Stephen Michaels, asking to be placed on the pension roll in consequence of disease contracted while in the service of the U S. 5-Ptn from Asa Arnold, formerly of North Providence, R I, now of Washington, asking the renewal of his patent for the machine called "The Double Speeder." 6-Cmte on Revolutionary Claims: bill in relation to the accounts of Gen Stephen Moylan. 7-Bill for the relief of Sylvester T Jerault, assignee of the interest of Henry Richard.Oneonta [Otsego Co] Herald: a son of O D Barnes, of that town, came to his death in a horrible manner. He was living home, near Canajoharie, Montg Co, & while grinding an axe on a grindstone which was driven by water, the band slipped off, & as he tried to put it on, his head was caught between the band & the wheel, which drew him in, crushing out his brains, breaking ribs, & both legs.

Died: on May 16, in Wash City, after a short illness of pneumonia, Susan Borrows, aged 67 year. The deceased came with her father, the late Jos Borrows, on the removal of the offices of the Nat'l Gov't from Phil, to Wash City, & has resided ever since among us. She lived to see what was then a mere wilderness converted into a large city. She was at the time of her death a member of the Shiloh Baptist Church. She died in the midst of her family. Her funeral is on Thu, at 4 o'clock, from her late residence on E st north, between 9th & 10th sts.

Mrd: on May 11, by Rev Mr Fisher, Chas Werner to Sophia Mary Bogusch, all of Wash City.

Mrd: on Tue, by Rev John C Smith, Zechariah L Winston, of Montg Co, to Miss Mary Jane Stone, of Gtwn, D C.

THU MAY 18, 1854

Report to the Senate's cmte: the Cmte on Agriculture, to whom was referred the memorial of the Md State Agricultural Society, submit the following report: That they have under consideration the said memorial proposing the establishment of an agricultural school & experimental farm at **Mount Vernon**, under the auspices of the Genr'l Gov't, & ask for in the favorable consideration of the Senate. The Smithsonian Institution at Washington has been spoken of as a secondary around which might spring up that nat'l board or school of agriculture, with an experimental farm annexed, contemplated by Washington. During his Presidency he favored such a plan. The principal professor of the Smithsonian Institution [Mr Henry] does not consider the funds at his disposal more than sufficient to accomplish what he considers the main object in which it is now engaged, & it would need the aid of Congress. –Jas T Earle, Oden Bowie, Clement Hill, F P Blair, & Geo W Hughes

Senate: 1-Memorial of Alex'r S Taylor, representing that he is in possession of manuscript papers & documents of great value regarding the early history & settlement of Calif: asking an appropriation as will issure their early publication as part of the archives of the Gov't. These papers will fill 2,000 pages of an ordinary sized Congressional document, & extend from 1770 to 1846. 2-Ptn from Isaac Hulse, asking indemnity for injuries sustained in the erection of the barracks of the U S at San Carlos. 3-Cmte on Pensions: adverse report on the ptn & documents of Leonard Proctor.

Rev John C Webber, a Millerite divine of Manchester, N H, unfortunately became forgetful of the fact that he had a wife & 7 children at home, & passed himself off upon Miss Nancy Mead, a warm-hearted sister in the Methodist church, as a marriageable man. Alas! he was false & she undone. Both are now in prison, he for a State prison offence, & she for one that a censorious world seldom forgives, that of having been deceived. –Springfield Republican

Franklin Pierce, Pres of the U S A, recognizes Fred'k Borcherdt, who has been appointed Consul of Saxony for the State of Wisconsin. –May 15, 1854

Local: Severe thunder-storm yesterday: lightning hit the dwlg house of Mr Saml C Roemmle, at K & 18th sts, striking his wife, aged about 50 years. Mrs Roemmle survived only a few moments. [May 19th newspaper: Roemmle is spelled Roemmelle.]

Mrd: on May 17, by Rev Mr Sunderland, Lt John E Wilson, of the U S R service, to Miss Susaan H Osbourn, of Wash City.

FRI MAY 19, 1854
Wash Corp: 1-Ptn of G Fridley for the remission of a fine; same for Peter Rechter; same for John Soper; & same for Christian Schultze: each referred to the Cmte of Claims. 2-Ptn of Wm Begnan & others for curbstone & footway on squares 163 & 164: referred to the Cmte on Improvements. 3-Ptn of John K McClokey, praying to be refunded certain taxes erroneously paid: referred to the Cmte of Ways & Means. 4-Ptn of Richd A Boarman & Ann Biscoe, remonstrating against a proposed change in the grade of L st south: referred to the Cmte on Improvements. 5-Ptn of Wm Cooper & others, in taking up & relaying certain pavements in the 7th Ward: referred to the Cmte on Improvements. 6-Cmte of Claims: asked to be discharged from the further consideration of the ptns of John Considine & Alex'r Cole: which was agreed to. Same cmte: bill for the relief of Lewis A Tarleton: passed. Same cmte: bill for the relief of Danl D French: passed. Same cmte: bill for the relief of Cornelius Regan: passed. Same cmte: bill for the relief of Thos McGrath: passed. Same cmte: bills for the relief of J Callaghan; of John A Minnehein; of Thos Lewis; & of Geo Adrien: passed. 7-Appropriation to pay for walling **Tiber Creek** through a portion of square 630: adopted. 8-Ptn of Wm Hagerty & others for a pavement on the west front of square 75: referred to the Cmte on Improvements. 9-Ptn of Saml Drury &others for a pavement on I st: referred to the Cmte on Improvements. 10-Ptn of Robt Wise, asking to be relieved from the payment of a penalty incurred as surety for Mgt McCarthy: referred to the Cmte of Claims. 11-Julius L Rider nominated as Com'r of the Western Market: considered & confirmed.

The Fred'k Examiner says that Mr John P Gallion, a dairy farmer of that neighborhood, believes himself to have discovered an effectual remedy for heven, or bleat in cattle, an affection very common at this season of the year. His plan is to open the mouth of the animal & pull its tongue forward quickly 3 or 4 time to its furthest tension. This produces instant relief. So simple a remedy is well worth attention.

Wash City Ordinance: 1-Act for the relief of F W Sellhausen: the sum of $38 be paid to him for the damage sustained by him in condemning an alley in square 429, the said damage not being considered by the jury. 2-Act to refund money paid for a license not issued: refunded to Mary Ann Cuthbert, the sum of $50.

Bailiff's sale: by order of distrain from Matthew H Stevens, for rent due & arrears against the goods & chattels, lands, & tenements of Benj Riston, deceased; I have seized one white mare, property of the deceased; sale on May 20 in front of the Centre Market-house. –Chas Kemble, Bailiff

Senate: 1-Ptn from Alex J Atocha, complaining of the action of the late Board of Com'rs to settle the claims of American citizens against the Republic of Mexico.

From Mexico: Gen Nicholas Bravo died at Chilpanciugo on Apr 22.

On Sunday last a fire occurred on Light st wharf, by which the lumber yard of Messrs Lloyd & McEldery was destroyed, with several large warehouses adjoining. The gable wall of the warehouse of Mr Michl Dorsey bound the alley next to their ofc. Yesterday the wind, with heavy rain, blew the wall down with the second floor, & the whole was precipitated upon the ofc where Mr Wilson L Lloyd & Saml C Atkinson, who had been clerk in the establishment for many years were engaged in business. When the bodies were removed Mr Atkinson was dead & Mr Lloyd expired soon after. The remains were removed to their late residence, & received by their horror-striken families, from whom they had separated but a short time before. –Balt American of Thu..

Mrd: on May 18, in Foundry Church, by Rev E P Phelps, Mr Nathan Walker to Miss Anna R Scott, of Gtwn.

Mrd: on May 17, in Wash City, at the residence of Mr A G Southall, by Rev Mr Wingfield, Mrs Anna Cocke to Col Simeon Wheeler, all of Portsmouth, Va.

Mrd: on May 16, at Balt, by Rev Mr Ridout, Mr Belt S Norwood to Miss Isabella McElray, both of that place.

Died: on May 17, by sudden visitation of Divine Providence, by lightning, Mrs Ellen, wife of Mr John C Roemmelle. Mrs Roemmelle was a very worthy member of St Paul's Lutheran Church, in all things adorning her profession. Her family is in painful bereavement. Her funeral will take place this evening at 3:30 o'clock, from St Paul's Church, corner of H & 11th sts.

Vienna: on Apr 24, 1854, the Archbishop of Vienna concluded the marriage ceremony & Austria had a third & reigning Empress. The Princess was conducted by the Archduchess Sophia & the Duchess Louisa in Bavaria [the mother of the bride] to her seat, & his Majesty took his place on her right hand. The marriage service was read & Elizabeth, Duchess in Bavaria, had become Empress of Austria. The Emperor passed round to the left of his consort, gave her his right hand, & led her from the church to a flourish of trumpets & kettle-drums. The Empress of 16 got through the severe ordeal of the Court & the marriage ceremonies wonderfully well.

Human life vs Freight. Chas H Haswell, surveyor of sea steamers for the Boards of Underwriters of N Y, Phil, Boston, & Lloyds, London, in his testimony before the Wyse court martial, in reply to a question, that vessels were often used for carrying passengers which would not be used for freight, as the former were not insured. Mrs Lyon & her child were drowned in crossing the Niagara river on Sat. A flaw of wind struck the boat & it capsized. Her last words were "Leave me & save my child," but the little one perished with her.

Saml Walker, Portrait Painter: studio & gallery in Mr Morfitt's bldg, 4½ st, next to Shillington's, third story.

SAT MAY 20, 1854
Senate: 1-Memorial of John D Gibson, asking to be allowed commission on disbursements made as acting purser of the U S schnr **Enterprise**. 2-Cmte on Private Land Claims: adverse reports on the memorials of Sarah D Bringham; of F A Underwood & H A Crane; & heirs of John Underwood. Same cmte: adverse report on the bill to confirm the claim of John Ervin to a tract of land in the Bastrop grant. 4-Bill for the relief of Hiram More & John Hascal: considered. 5-Bill for the relief of Wm G Ridgely: passed.

Valuable brick dwlg on 10th st at auction: by deed of trust: public auction on May 30, 1854, of part of original lot 15 in square 347, on 10th st, between E & F sts, improved by a nearly new 4 story brick dwlg: gas was introduced during the process of building, & the parlor & hall are heated by a portable furnace. –G W Cutter, trustee

In Chancery. Susan Barber & Catherine Wright against Mary A W Harrington, Forbes, & Mgt Forbes, & Caroline & Anna Maria Harrington. Such of the creditors of Richd Harrington [if there be any] to file their claims with me on or before May 30, at the City Hall, Wash. –W Redin, auditor

Died: on May 19, in Gtwn, Mrs Mary A O Gannon, aged about 65 years. Her funeral will take place on May 21, at 2 o'clock, from the *Wash-house of Gtwn College, when & where her friends are requested to attend without further notice. [*Wash-house as copied.]

Toronto Colonists: on Sat at Yorkville, the 8 year old daughter of Mr Peter Hutty was strangled when she put her head between the boards of a fence & her foot slipped. She was suspened by the neck.

MON MAY 22, 1854
Cows, horses, milk wagons, cutting box, & milk cans: at auction, on May 23, at the dairy of Mr Henry Newman, on north D st, near Md ave, about 5 squares northeast of the Capitol. -Green & Scott, aucts

Household & kitchen furniture at auction: May 26, at the residence of Mrs Matthews, on C, between 3rd & 4½ sts: also paintings & a cow. -Green & Scott, aucts

Household & kitchen furniture at auction: on Jun 1, at the residence of Lewis Warrington, on H st, between 19th & 20th sts. -Jas C McGuire, auct

Extensive sale of cigars, tobacco, & snuff: on May 24, at the Tobacco Store of Mr C J Cook, on 7th st, opposite Odd Fellows Hall. -Green & Scott, aucts

Announced in the Boston papers that Hon Edw Everett has resigned his seat in the U S Senate, to take effect from Jun 1st next.

Miss Caroline Plumer died at Salem on May 15, at the age of 74 years. By a course of rigid economy & self-denial she accumulated a fortune of $100,000. By her will she bequeathed more to public uses than has ever been left by any resident in Salem, viz: $15,000 to Harvard College; $30,000 to the Salem Anthenaeum, & the residue of her estate to found a Farm School at Salem. –Boston Trans

Crafts J Wright, for many years the able editor of the Cincinnati Gaz, is compelled by ill health to abandon his post. Col Schouler & L J Bauer now take charge of the paper.

Boiler explosion of the steam saw-mill of Messrs Gray & Co, about 2 miles of Painsville, Amelia Co, Va, exploded Wed, & killed Mr Mateson, bruised Mr Gray, & a child of Mr Mateson, about 2 years of age, & there is no hope of recovery.

On Sat the lowest bridge on Rock Creek, between Washington & Gtwn, fell in at the moment 2 omnibuses were passing. The worst sufferer is Gen Roger C Weightman, of Wash City, whose left arm was broken just above the elbow. The driver, McGinniss, suffered a fracture of a leg, endangering the loss of the limb. The horses were got out without material hurt. The bridge was constructed by Mr Rider, of this city. [May 24th newspaper: young McGinniss is doing well & the limb will not require amputation.]

Orphans Court of Wash Co, D C. Letters testamentary on the personal estate of Solomon Drew, late of Wash Co, deceased. –Chas Calvert, exc

TUE MAY 23, 1854

In Chancery, Circuit Court of Wash Co, D C. Frasy_er's adm & heirs vs Peck, Walker & others. Wm R Woodward, trustee, reported that he sold lot 4 in square 161, in Wash City, to Geo W Emerson, for $855. & he hath complied with the terms of the sale. –Jno A Smith, clerk

Chancery sale of valuable unimproved real estate: by decree of the Circuit Court of Wash Co, D C, made in the cause wherein Jas F Haliday & others are cmplnts & Thos J Haliday & others, heirs at law of Thos Haliday, Anna Haliday, Wm W Haliday, & Lydia J Hanlon, deceased, are dfndnts: public auction on Jun 13 at the Auction Store of J C McGuire, Pa ave & 10th sts, the following parcels lying in Wash City: lot 16 in square 104; lot 10 in square 703; lots 4 thru 7 in square 770; lots 1, 2, 14 in square 1136; part of lot 3 in square 835; part of lot 3 on 4th st. –Chas S Wallach, trustee -Jas C McGuire, auct

Household & kitchen furniture at auction on May 29, at the residence of Mr Wm Nicholson, H, between 17th & 18th sts. -Green & Scott, aucts

$200 reward for runaway negro man Gustavus Shaw, about 24 years of age. He has relations living in Wash City; his grandmother goes by the name of Ann Shaw; he has relations in this county belonging to Mr Allen P Bowie, Miss Sarah Talbert, & Gov Saml Sprigg. –Z B Beall, near Upper Marlborough, PG Co, Md.

Senate: 1-Additional documents in favor of the claim of the heirs of Joshua Chamberlain, of the Revolution: presented. 2-Ptn from Mary Reeside, excx of Jas Reeside, asking the payment of a judgment rendered in favor of the said Jas Reeside on a suit instituted against him by the U S in the Circuit Court of the U S for the eastern district of Pa. 3-Ptn from the heirs of Jos Boynton, asking to be allowed the commutation due him as a lt in the Revolutionary war. 4-Ptn from the widow of Robt McMillan, asking to be allowed a pension. 5-Ptn from Wm Fields & other members of Capt Gee's company of Alabama mounted volunteers, asking the reimbursement of losses sustained in consequence of the sale by the Gov't at reduced prices of their horses & furniture for which transportation to the U S was refused. 6-Cmte on Private Land Claims: adverse reports on the following bills: relief of Mgt A Copley, of Louisiana; of John Boyd; bill to authorize T H McManus to enter by pre-emption certain lands in the Greensborough land district, La. 7-Cmte on Indian Affairs: asked to be discharged from the further consideration of the ptn of letter of O M Wosencraft, late Indian agent & of the documents relating to the claim of J C Edwards: which was agreed to.

Patrick Doyle was hung at Naperville, Ill, on May 12, for the murder of a fellow-laborer on the railroad. On ascending the platform he avowed that "if they would untie his hands he would lick any three men in the crowd."

Mrd: on May 16, in Union Methodist Episcopal Church, by Rev F Israel, Chas Carroll to Susanna P Millson, all of Wash City.

Mrd: on May 20, at St Patrick's Church, by Rev Dr O'Toole, Thos P Watson, of Detroit, to Miss Mary Ann Burgevin, of New Bern, N C.

Mrd: on May 21, by Rev Mr Hodges, Gabriel Cross to Miss Mgt E Langley, of D C.

Died: on Sunday last, aged 78 years, Mrs Martha Sessford, wife of Mr John Sessford, sr, a resident of Wash City for the last 54 years. Her funeral is this afternoon at 3 o'clock.

Died: on May 21, John T Frost, in his 89th year. His funeral will take place at Mrs Sprigg's boarding house, on C, between 3rd & 4½ st, at 10 o'clock, this morning.

Died: on May 22, at Richmond, Va, in his 36th year, Thos Ritchie, jr, one of the Editors of the Enquirer, & 3rd son of Thos Ritchie, of this place.

The Standards taken at the Surrender of Yorktown & presented by the Congress of the Revolution to Gen Washington, Cmder-in-Chief of the combines armies of America & France. These trophied memorials of the Heroic Age & the Father of his Country were on Thu last brought over from *Arlington House* by the venerable Mr Custis, the sole surviving executor of Washington & last surviving member of his domestic family, & presented to the Pres, & through him to the Gov't & People of the U S. The Pres accompanied by the Sec of War, escorted them to the War Ofc, where they will for the present remain under the care of the Secretary. Among these old standards are a British & Hessian one. Both flags are of silk, & nearly 80 years old, dilapidated by time, the British flag having suffered somewhat from relic-seekers, who have appropriated to themselves scraps of the renowned banner.

Explosion of powder took place at the Hopewell Copper Mine, in Mecklenburg Co, N C, on May 10, by which Marshall McKoy, the superintendent. & Capt Varker, late of Greensboro, N C, lost their lives. Mr McKoy leaves a wife & 9 children. Capt Varker leaves a wife & 6 children. They were highly esteemed citizens.

Rev Robt Newton died at his residence at Easingwold, Yorkshire, England, on Apr 30, having the previous Tue been seized with paralysis. He had been 55 years a minister in the Wesleyan connexion.

WED MAY 24, 1854
Senate: 1-Ptn from Emma C P Thompson, widow of Chas C B Thompson, late of the U S Navy, asking to be allowed a pension to which her husband was entitled for wounds received at the battle of New Orleans in 1814. 2-Additional documents presented relating to the claim of Isaac Swain. 3-Cmte on Pensions: bill for the relief of Wm Brown. Same cmte: adverse report on the ptn of Gideon Prior. Same cmte: asked to be discharged from the further consideration of the ptns of Adele Sands; & of Charlotte S Westcott, on the gound that a general bill had been reported: which was agreed to. Same cmte: adverse report on the ptn of John T Hand. 4-Cmte on Indian Affairs: asked to be discharged from the further consideration of the memorial of E H Wingfield: which was agreed to.

Indian massacre in Texas on May 2: the Gov't train of Maj Chapman, in charge of a number of men, was attacked 5 miles from *Fort Ewell* by 20 mounted & well-armed Indians, who killed & scalped Mr McIntosh, the wagon master, & 5 others. Several others are missing, & were probably taken prisoners. All the mules & horses, about 100, connected with the train, were taken & the wagons destroyed.

Died: yesterday, at his residence on N, between 12th & 13th sts, in his 68th year, Alex'r Morison. His funeral is this evening at 5 o'clock.

THU MAY 25, 1854
Senate: 1-Cmte on Indian Affairs: documents in relation to the claim of David Carter & Nancy Thornton, submitted: ordered to be printed.

Appointments by the Pres, by & with the advice & consent of the Senate.
Jas A Peden, of Fla, to be Charge d'Affaires of the U S in the Republic of Buenos Ayres, vice Wm R Bissell, declined.
Wm W B David, of the Territory of New Mexico, to be Sec of said Territory, from & after Aug 1 next, vice Wm S Messervy, resigned.
Geo Hepner, of Iowa, to be Agent for the Ottoes, Missourias, Pawnees, & Omahas, vice Jas M Gatewood.
Marcus L Olds, of Minnesota Territory, to be Register for the Minneapolis Land District, in Minnesota Territory.
Roswell P Russell, of Minnesota Territory, to be Receiver for the Minneapolis Land District, in Minnesota Territory.
John R Bennet, of Missouri, to be Register for the Root River Land District, in Minnesota Territory.
John H McKenny, of Iowa, to be Receiver, for the Root River Land District, in Minnesota Territory.
Geo H Taylor, of Michigan, to be Register for the Sheboygan Land District, in Michigan.
Hiram A Rood, of Michigan, to be Receiver for the Sheboygan Land District, in Michigan.
Saml S Houston, of Alabama, to be Receiver at St Stephens, Alabama, vice Jackson W Faith, removed.

Orphans Court of Wash Co, D C. Ordered, on application, that the administrator of Benj Riston, deceased, sell at public sale the personal estate of said deceased for cash, first giving notice of day of sale by advertisement 3 times previous to day of sale. -Ed N Roach, Reg/o wills

Mrd: on May 23, by Rev Jas B Donelan, Thos G Clinton to L Rebecca, 2nd daughter of the late Thos Jones.

Mrd: on May 17, at Boston, by Rev J C Stockbridge, Mr Edw Tuckerman to Miss Sarah E S Cushing, daughter of Thos P Cushing.

Mrd: on May 23, at St Peter's Church, in Wash City, by Rev John F Hickey, Edw M Hamilton to Henrietta R, eldest daughter of John C Fitzpatrick.

Died: on May 24, suddenly, Ann Douglass, infant daughter of Saml E & Eliz A Douglass, aged 2 years, 2 months & 7 days. Her funeral will take place from the residence of her parents, on 20th st west, near E st, this afternoon, at 4 o'clock.

Notice: Application will be made for a duplicate Land Warrant, issued Apr, 1831, being No 3,175, for 160 acres of land, in favor of Erastus T Collins for services rendered in Tenn militia, war of 1812, the original warrant being lost. –D W Collins

In Chancery: Estate of Michl McCarty. Edw McGuire against Richd G Briscoe. By order of the Circuit Court of Wash Co, D C I am directed to state the account of the trustee: same to be done on May 21, at my ofc in the City Hall, Wash. –W Redin, auditor

Orphans Court of Wash Co, D C. Letters of administration on the personal estate of Capt Jos L C Hardy, late of the U S Marine Corps, deceased. –T F Semmes, adm

FRI MAY 26, 1854
New Book: The Life of Archibald Alexander, D D, First Professor in the Theological Seminary at Princeton, N J, by Jas W Alexander, N Y. –Chas Scribner, 1854. He was born in a house built of square logs in what is now Rockbridge Co, Va. His early education was prosecuted by what in Va is called, "an old field school," kept by a redemptioner, or a convict servant who had been transported to America for crime, & of whom his father purchased several in Balt. At 11 he was under Rev Wm Graham, a graduate of the college of N J; at 17 he left his father's house to commence that scholastic novitiate which in a higher sphere was to fill the measure of his days & usefulness. He became for a time a private tutor in the family of Gen John Posey, in Spottsylvania Co. He married the daughter of Dr Waddel, the blind preacher; he removed to Phil; & he settled at Princeton.

Senate: 1-Documents presented in support of the claim of S L Collins to indemnity for the seizure & confiscation of his property by the Mexican Gov't. 2-Ptn from Andrew Rankin, asking an extension of his patent for an improvement in the manufacture of hats. 3-Cmte on Foreign Relations: joint resolution manifesting the sense of Congress towards Cmder Ed Marshall, of her Britannic Majesty's ship **Virago**, & the ofcrs & crew who were detached by his orders for the relief of the surveying party under the command of Lt J G Strain. 4-Cmte on the Judiciary: bill for the relief of L E L A Lawson, surviving heiress of Gen Eleazer Ripley, deceased: adverse report on the same. 5-Cmte on Pensions: adverse report on the ptn of Mrs Mgt S Chandler. 6-Cmte on Private Land Claims: bill to confirm the claim of Wm H Henderson & the heirs of Robt Henderson to 500 acres of land in the Bastrop grant, reported the same without amendment. 7-Mr Benjamin asked to have the bills for the relief of T H McManus; & for the relief of John Boyd recommitted to the Cmte on Private Land Claims, as an adverse report had been made on each through an error of his own which he was desirous to correct: which motion was agreed to.

On Fri last, the farm-house of Mr Jos Fisher, 8 miles east of Peekskill, Westchester Co, N Y, was destroyed by fire & 3 children perished in the flames. Mr & Mrs Fisher, parents of the little ones, were absent at the time, having left their children at home.

Official: Dept of State, May 22, 1854. The following description of the effects found on persons drowned at Virgin bay, in Feb last, identified as American citizens, is published for the information of their legal reps, who may make application, with the necessary proofs, at the Dept, for the portions to which they may be respectively entitiled:
Wm Lane: gold & silver coin, $355.03; one large gold ring, elliptical, cornellan set.
D Churchill: gold & silver coin, $45; three specimens of gold ore.
H Leavil, Lezron, or Leavin: gold coin, $170; second of exchange on Messrs Adams & Co, of Boston, to order of Charlotte Leavil, $100; steerage passage ticket.
Isaac Edge: gold dust, stated to be 100 ounces; specimens of gold ore, 1 ounce; gold & silver coin, $122.05; three pins, heads, gold specimens; gold ring marked I E; large ring, shield pattern.
Jos Lewis, [colored]: first of a set of exchange, of Page, Bacon & Co, on the American Exchange Bank, N Y, $110; second, same on same, $107; second, same on same, $60; gold & silver coin, $31.52; second-cabin ticket, San Francisco to N Y; brass trunk key; carpet bag key.
Wm H Gardner: canvass bag with letters M A marked with thread; silver watch, [Olivier Quartier;] gold & silver coin, $942.85; a receipt, signed T O Spring, for various sums received from D Churchill; second of a set of exchange on Adams & Co, N Y, $1,450; pocket comb & small key.

Suicides committed in N Y on Sat. A German woman, Charlotte Lancaster, inconsolable for the loss of her husband, poisoned herself, leaving 2 children. A German, Seglamund Klein, shot himself at Hoboken, owing, it is said, to his having caused the death of his infant child by administering an overdoes of some narcotic drug to quiet it. Three bodies were recovered from the rivers on Saturday. Their names are unknown.

Circuit Court of Wash Co, D C, Mar Term, 1854. Ptn of Wm A Bradley to keep a Ferry between Analostan Island & some point to be designated by the public authorities of Gtwn, in said town, & at some point in Wash opposite said Island: same to be considered. All persons interested are to appear in this Court on Monday next, & show cause, if any they have, against the establishment of said proposed Ferry. –Jno A Smith, clerk

Mrd: on Thu, by Rev John C Smith, Wm H B Butler, of Fauquier Co, Va, to Miss Mary A Thomas, of Wash City.

Mrd: on May 25, at *Ellerslie*, near the city, by Rev T B Sargent, Wm T Landstreet, of Balt, to M Virginia, daughter of Enoch Tucker.

SAT MAY 27, 1854
Household & kitchen furniture at auction: on May 31, at the residence of Mrs Greenhow, on H st, between 15th & 16th sts. All her furniture & effects, including a superior rosewood piano forte. -Jas C McGuire, auct

For sale: several pleasantly situated dwlg houses, prices ranging from $2,500 to $4,000: on G st, near 6th st. Inquire of W G Deale, D & 7th st, 2nd story.

For rent, the large dwlg house & garden recently occupied by Brooke B Williams, on the corner of Montg & Dunbarton sts, Gtwn. Apply to A Hyde, near the Female Seminary.

For rent: 2 parlors, with bed-rooms, at present occupied by Hon Senator Johnson, can be obtained by applying to Mrs M A Stettinius, on La ave. Possession on Jun 1.

Obit-died: on May 8, at *Horn's Point*, Dorchester Co, Md, the residence of her son-in-law, Wm Goldsborough, in her 79th year, Mrs Sally Scott Lloyd, relict of Hon Edw Lloyd, formerly Govn'r of Md & a Senator of the U S from Md. It was but a few weeks ago that the Editors recorded the death, also at an advanced age, of Mrs Catherine Eliza Rush, wife of Hon Richd Rush, which occurred at *Sydenham*, near Phil, the residence of her distinguished husband. These venerable Ladies were sisters, & the death of each, occurring within a few weeks of that of the other, has been received with sorrowful interest by a wide circle of acquaintances & friends. Each were companions of the Carrolls, the Catons, & the Wellesleys, & others of that period in Annapolis, where they were born & grew up, then the center of high fashion & refinement in Md, & as now the seat of its gov't, Mrs Lloyd & Mrs Rush, at that time two of the three beautiful Miss Murrays, are remembered as among the most attractive young ladies of the day. The third still lives, relict of the late Gen John Mason & mother of the present distinguished Senator of Va. Who that has ever shared the delightful hospitalities of Analostan Island can forget the distinguished & high-bred woman who added to the house & home she graced.

Circuit Court of Wash Co, D C-in Chancery, Mar Term, 1854. Edmund Hanley's excs vs Alex'r Shepherd's heirs. The trustee reported that on Apr 6 last, Peter Lammond & Nicholas Vodder became the purchasers of part of lot 9 in square 480, in Wash City, for $224.10, & they have complied with the terms of the sale.
-Jno A Smith, clerk

Mr Henry Quinn, of Nashua, N H, on Sunday, intending, as is supposed, to take a nipper, by mistake swallowed a dose of bed-bug poison, & was soon a corpse.
-Manchester Mirror

The Royal Family of Great Britian: Her Britannic Majesty, Alexandrina Victoria 1, Queen of Great Britain & Ireland, whose birthday was celebrated on May 24, was born in 1819, so that she is just 35 years old. We are quite sure there is no Sovereign in Europe who has a firmer hold upon the affections of her people, or none more deserving of it. Queen Victoria was married at age 21, Feb 10, 1840, & the issue has been: Victoria Adelaide Mary Louisa, born Nov 21, 1840
Albert Edw, born Nov 9, 1841
Alice Maud Mary, born Apr 25, 1843
Alfred Ernst Albert, born Aug 6, 1844
Helen Augusta Victoria, born May 25, 1846
Louisa Caroline Alberta, born Mar 18, 1848
Arthur Wm Patrick Albert, born May 1, 1850
A son not yet named, born Apr 7, 1853. Eight children, 4 sons & 4 daughters, in 13 years, & all well & alive. -Express

Information from Oregon confirming the death by drowning on Mar 27, in Puget Sound, by the upsetting of the Gov't boat of **Fort Steilacoom**, of Maj C H Larned, Capt Isaiah G Barlow, & privates Jas Fitzsimmons & Lawrence Fitzpatrick, & musician John McIntire, of Co A, & Musician Henry Hall, & privates John Clarke & Henry Lees, of Co C, all of the 4th Infty; also, John Hamilton, a citizen boatman. This tragical accident accurred in the Sound, near **Fort Madison**. Maj L, with ten men, was on his return to **Fort Steilacoom**, which post he commanded. He had been in Whidley Island, where he had been engaged for a week in quelling Indian disturbances. The Major was a gentleman of remarkable fine abilities. -Star

MON MAY 29, 1854
Gen Nathl Greene, the illustrious patriot, who figured during our Revolutionary struggle, is dear to every American heart. A daughter of Gen Greene, Mrs C L Littlefield, is on a visit to Wash City, & she can be seen by her friends at Brown's Hotel. This lady, as the heir of her father, has a claim before Congress; & the object of her visit to the seat of gov't is to facilitate her interest. -Union

Queen Isabella, of Spain, has presented to Capt Wm Burrows, of the American barque **Zenobia**, a splendid massive antique chased silver speaking trumpet, in attestation of his humane conduct in saving the crew of the Spanish vessel **Perservancia**, wrecked off Cape Horn.

Mrd: on May 24, at St Patrick's Cathedral, in N Y, by his Grace Archbishop Hughes, Hon John Mckeon to Jeannette E Whittemore, daughter of Cmdor John D Sloat, U S Navy.

Mrd: on May 25, in Foundry Church, by Rev E P Phelps, Mr John Henry Stinchcomb to Miss Emma Eliz Wright, all of Wash City.

On Thu evening, in N Y C, Deputy Marshal De Angules arrested 3 negroes, father & 2 sons, who ran away last Sunday week from the farms of their owners in Wash Co, D C. They are Stephen H Pembroke, 44; the boys are Bob Pembroke, about 18, & Jake Pembroke, aged about 19 or 20. The boys were claimed by Mr David Smith as his slaves, & their father was claimed by Jacob H Graves as his slave. They were quite willing to return home with their masters.

Balt Evening Times: we were informed yesterday by Dr Snowden, of PG Co, of the death of a female servant on Sat last who was upwards of 130 years of age. She was raised by his great-grandfather, & has been blind since 1812, & had given birth to 20 children, the youngest of whom is 80 years of age.

Oregon Spectator Extra. Fatal explosion of the steamer **Gazelle**, at Canemah, on Apr 8 last. Names of the killed:

David Woodhull, of Mich	Jas White, of Salem
Rev Mr Miller, of Albany, O T	John K Miller
John Bloomer	J M Fudge
Jos Hunt, of Mich	Mr Morgan, of Laersole, O T
Mr Hatch	Mr Hill, of Albany, O T
John Daly	Danl Lowe
John Clemens	Mr Blanchet
David Fuller, of Portland	J Henald
Mr Wadsworth	Michl McGee
Judge Birch, of Lockm_uke	

Missing: Mr Knauss, David McLean, & others not known.

Died: on May 4, at his residence, near Port Tobacco, Gen John Matthews, in his 71st year. The large concourse of persons who attended his interment testified the regard & esteem in which he was held. In early life he entered the ofc of Clerk of Chas Co, which he discharged with fidelity. During the war of 1812-15 he promptly became a soldier & entered the field, ready to defend his country. He was later called to represent the Legislature of the State. In the two branches he continued for a period of 15 years. He continued a member of the State Senate until the close of the session of 1853, when his advanced age & feeble health warned him that he could no longer serve as a public servant. He was possessed of very large wealth, which he had accumulated by his own exertions, he had never oppressed any one. To his large number of servants he was the kindest of masters. The approach of his death came with a slow & easy tread.

Died: on May 26, suddenly, Sgt Lewis Meinzesheimer, of the U S Marine Corps, aged 38 years.

Died: on May 20, at **Fort McHenry**, Francis Harwood Taylor, in his 24th year, son of Lt Col Francis Taylor, U S Army.

Died: on May 16, at his late residence, near Warrenton, N C, Jas Somerell, in his 71st year. A kind father, his children entertained for him the affection which generosity such as his never failed. Afflicted by disease in the last years of his life, he obtained that peace of mind which the sincere Christian alone can fine.

Died: at Meadville, Pa, of apoplexy, in his 75th year, Harm Jahn Huidekoper. Descended from an ancient family in Holland, the subject came to this country when a young man, & early entered into the service of the Holland Co, which was possessed of large landed estates in this country, & took charge of the company's ofc at Meadville, which he superintended until he became the purchaser of the company's interests in that portion of the State. The flourishing theological institute & Unitarian church of Meadville are the results of his efforts. In his domestic relations he was a model of excellence. [No death date given-current item.]

TUE MAY 30, 1854
Letter from Corpus Christi, dated May 10, received by a gentleman in this city: Since I commenced writing Lt Cosby, of the Rifles, has come in wounded. He attacked, with 10 men, a party of about 40 Indians, near Lake Trinidad, 45 miles from this place; lost his sgt, 2 men, & escaped himself almost miraculously. He is wounded by an arrow above the elbow, but was shot by 4 arrows in his clothes, & the head of an arrow he found today broken off in his pocket-book, it having penetrated between the clasps. He carried the portmonnale in his pantaloon's pocket. Lt Roger Jones is in pursuit of the same party, with 16 men, & has not yet been heard of since he started. It is not known what Indians they were. -Union

A B Chambers, for many years past the Editor of the Missouri Republican, died at St Louis on May 22, in his 46th year. He was a kind husband & an honorable citizen.

Boston: on May 20 Jas Batchelder was assaulted with firearms, wounding him as that he died. Luther A Ham, deputy chief of police arrested the following for the crime:

A J Brown
John J Roberts, colored
Walter Phoenix, colored
John Westerly, colored
Walter Bishop, colored
Thos Jackson, colored
Henry Howe
Martin Stowell
John Thompson

[Jun 7th newspaper: Coroner's verdict: Jas Batchelder received a wound in the left groin, severing the femoral artery & causing death, which was inflicted by a long, narrow & sharp instrument.]

John Tape, celebrated submarine diver, whilst searching in his submarine apparatus for a wreck on Lake Erie, last Sat, died suddenly, while under the water, from the effect of a rush of blood to the head. In all cases going under water to a great depth tends to this result. He had followed the business successfully for many years.

While a gang of men were removing a twelve pound boat howitzer Fri from the navy yard gate to the new ordinance shop, the piece ran on those dragging it, & Chas De Bevoice fell, the wheel striking him in the breast, it is feared seriously injuring him. –Wash Sentinel of Sat.

Mrd: on May 28, by Rev Mr Hodges, Benj F McCathran to Miss Sarah Ellen Mitchell, all of Wash.

Died: on May 6, at Glasgow, Scotland, of which he was a native, Andrew Smith, aged 85 years, formerly for many years a resident of Wash City.

Alex Randall & Alex B Hagner have this day entered into a Law Partnerhsip, under the name of Randall & Hagner. They will continue to practice in the Court of Appeals & the Circuit Courts of Anne Arnudel, Calvert, PG, Howard, & Montgomery Counties, Md.

WED MAY 31, 1854
Senate: 1-Ptn from A S Robinson, cashier of the Bank of the State of Missouri, at St Louis, asking the payment of a balance due that bank for advances for the use of certain companies of Missouri volunteers, called into service during the late war with Mexico. 2-Ptn from the heirs of Wm Turvin, asking permission to enter any public lands subject to private entry, a quantity equal in value to certain land claimed by them under a Spanish grant & sold by the Gov't. 3-Ptn from Jane Moore, widow of S H Moore, wounded in the battle of Little York, in the war of 1812, asking a pension.
4-Cmte on Indian Affairs: bill for the relief of Overton Love & John Guest, of the Chickasaw nation. 5-Cmte on Pensions: to inquire into providing by law a suitable pension for the support of the widow & children, if any, of the late Jas Bachelder, of Mass, who was killed while assisting the marshal of the U S for that State in executing an act of Congress.

Metropolitan School of Design, Pa ave, over Parker's Store, will open on May 29, when particulars may be obtained. –W J Whitaker, Principal. [In consequence of the illness of Prof Whitaker the re-opening will be postponed until Jun 5.]

The real estate of the late Maj Reybold, of Delaware, was sold on May 8. The *Miles farm*, containing 267 acres, was sold to Jas Shuster for $83.50 per acre, making $22,294.50. The *Spring Garden farm*, containing 304 acres, was sold to Thos Clark for $57 per acre, making $17,828. The *Shuster farm*, containing 202 acres, was sold to John Reybold for $90 per acre, making $18,180. The mansion property was bid off by John C Clark for $10,700.

Mrs Henrietta Robinson has been convicted of murder at Troy, N Y. She is charged with having poisoned Timothy Lanagan. During the trial she insisted in keeping herself veiled.

Jas Dixon & Son's superior quality Tea Ware, plated extra heavy, on fine white metal. Just received by the last steamer from England. –T Bastianelli & Co, Importers of French & English Fancy Goods, under Brown's Hotel.

J L Brown was recently nominated for the Legislature in Pacific Co, Washington Territory, but died very suddenly the day before the election. Mr Scudder was then elected, & he died suddenly a few days after. A special election was then ordered, & H Fiester chosen to fill the vacancy. The late steamer brings news that Mr Fiester proceeded to the seat of gov't, & on the next day fell dead in the House.

The Aberdeen [Scotland] Journal claims that the widow of Alex McBeath, a seaman belonging to Aberdeen, on board the ship **Three Bells**, of Glasgow, whose exertions cost him his life, has had transmitted to her, the sum of L76 16s 6d, the greater part of which was contributed at N Y, Balt, & Phil, & the remainder by Capt Creighton & the crew of the **Three Bells**, on behalf of the survivors of McBeath & another lost comrade, the latter receiving an equal sum.

Harford Co Court, Md. Thos W & Sam Levering have been fined $200, including costs, on some 15 presentments for selling guano without licenses. Jas Nelson, on one presentment for the same offence, was fined $12.25, the amount of the license.

THU JUN 1, 1854
Household & kitchen furniture at auction on Jun 6, at the residence of Saml Reeve, on 12th st, between H & N Y ave. -Jas C McGuire, auct

Clarendon, N Y, on 4th ave & 18th sts, in the upper & most fashionable part of the city, has been enlarged during the past year; accommodations are of the latest & most approved character. –O C Putnam, Proprietor, N Y

Mrd: on May 30, by Rev Alfred Holmead, Anthony Buchly to Miss Eliz J Martin, all of Wash City.

Wash Star of yesterday: Lt E F Deale, Superintendent of Indian affairs in Calif, has been removed from ofc, & the trust confided to the charge of Hon T J Hendley, Postmaster at San Francisco.

Mr Chas Borders & his eldest daughter were drowned in the south branch of Hogan's Creek, Ohio, on Sunday last. Six of the family had started to church & in attempting to ford the stream, which had swollen by a heavy rain during the previous night, the father & daughter lost their lives.

On May 22, 3 daughters of Rev Mr Perry, Methodist preacher, living at El Dorado, 6 or 7 miles from Harrodsburg, Ky, lost their lives by the explosion of a camphene lamp. Mr Perry, his wife & infant child, were absent from home in Jessamine Co, to fill an appointment. There 3 daughters & a servant woman were at home. The girls were 19, 17, & 9 years of age. The 9 & 17 year old died the next day, the eldest died on Tuesday. –Frankfort Commonwealth

Mr Francis H Appleton, son of Hon Wm Appleton, of Massachusetts, died at his residence in Boston on Tue.

On Sat last Henry Augustus Lake, age 8 years, went with his father, Ansley Lake, to the blacksmith's shop of John Graham, in N Y C, to get a horse shod. The father left the son there with instructions to bring the horse home as soon as he had been shod. Francis Graham offered the boy some brandy, which he drank. The child died at home that evening at 8 o'clock. Graham was held to bail for trial. He said he gave the boy but a tablespoon full of brandy.

Senate: 1-Cmte on Pensions: bill granting an increase of pension to Mrs Frances Smith, of S C.

Wilmington, Delaware May 31. Three powder wagons from Dupont's mills blew up here this morning killing 6 or 7 men, & 15 horses. The explosion happened at 14th & Orange sts, opposite Bishop Lee's residence. John Keys, John Walters, & Thos Chambers, the drivers, were instantly killed. A colored woman in Mr Lee's house & a colored waiter of Jas E Price were also killed. Mr Jas McLaughlin's child is missing, supposed killed. Thos Hughes was killed & some of his family hurt. The residences of Bishop Lee & Jas E Price, & of 5 other persons, together with 6 stables, were destroyed. 75 houses in the neighborhood were more or less damaged. [Jun 2nd newspaper: The residence of Mr Thos Hughes was leveled with the ground; & the residences of Jas E Price, Jas Canby, John H Price, Jos T Price, & J Fleming Smith, were injured. Injured, but not seriously, were Mr Hughes, his wife, & child; Mrs Reynold & a little girl; a girl living with Bishop Lee & 2 of his children; & a colored woman living with Mr Conly.]

FRI JUN 2, 1854
Hon Angus Patterson, long the Pres of the State Senate of S C, died at his residence in Barnwell on Friday last.

Six houses burnt a couple nights since on Mass ave, between 1st & 2nd sts, the property of Mr Chas Stott, apothecary. His loss will exceed $2,000, the insurance having been comparatively small.

Mrd: on Jun 1, in the Fourth Presbyterian Church, by Rev J C Smith, D D, Thos P McGill to Miss Mary Osborn, only daughter of Wm Douglas, all of Wash.

Senate: 1-Ptn from Cynthia M Clark, asking indemnity for losses sustained by her father, Ethan Stillman, in the execution of his contract for supplying muskets for the U S, in consequence of the embargo laws & the war of 1812. 2-Ptn from Jos Grafton & other settlers on the Bastrop Grant, asking such relief as was granted to claimants under the Maison Rouge grant by the act of Jan, 1851.

Information wanted of Mary Farren & John Tighe, natives of Ireland, who resided at Providence, R I, about 14 months ago, & recently in Wash City. Any one knowing of the whereabouts of the above persons will confer a favor on their relatives by addressing Ann Tighe, at this ofc.

SAT JUN 3, 1854
Laws of the U S passed at the 1st session of the 33rd Congress of the U S A.
1-To pay the expenses incurred by Edw Cunningham, acting consul at Shanghai, for a police force for the preservation of the peace by American citizens: $575.80.
2-Payment of the claim of Thos N Johnson for his services as marshal at the port of Shanghai, from Dec 9, 1851, to Sep 15, 1853: $1,781.74.
3-Payment to John Bozman Kerr, in addition to his salary & allowances as charge d'affaires to Nicaragua, the amount of his expenses on a journey to San Salvador & Guatemala, & of his expenses at those capitals under his commissions to the Gov'ts of those Republics, together with a full outfit as charge d'affaires to the nat'l representation of Central America.

Three young ladies, Miss Pickett, Miss Maddin, & Miss Adams, were drowned a few days since at Port Royal, Tenn, by the upsetting of a canoe.

Mr Thos Thornley, the Warden of the Penitentiary of D C, offers a reward of $100 each for two convicts who escaped from there yesterday. They are Frank Camper, who was convicted in 1850 for the willful murder of Ragan & sentenced to 8 years; & Jos Allemander, an individual from Balt, who figured in the robbery of plate from several citizens & was arrested on his return to Balt. [Jun 9th newspaper: Camper & Allemander have been arrested & are now secured in the jail of Hagerstown, Md.] [Jun 10th newspaper: the young men arrested at Hagerstown, who carried off the buggy & horse on Fri last from the livery stable of Mr Sotheron, [late Birch's,] on 14th st, in Wash City, are not the convicts Camper & Allemander, but two young men of Washington. They said they were out on a spree. At the best they have laid themselves open to a very serious charge.]

Jos Varady & Franz Bartalis, agents of Kossuth, were hanged at St George, in Transylvania, Apr 29. Two of their associates were sentenced to 18 years' imprisonment.

Mrd: on Jun 1, at Sydenham, Phil, by Rev Dr Hare, Rector of St Matthew's Church, John Calvert, of Mount Airy, PG Co, Md, to Julia, daughter of Hon Richd Rush.

Public sale of valuable Ky land: by authority of the last will & testament of Julia A Wilson, [who was one of the devisees of Maj Wm B Harrison, of Loudoun Co, Va,] & the decree of the Circuit Court for that county: public auction before the Courthouse in Morganfield, Union Co, Ky, on Jul 14. Six-tenths of an island, lying in the Ohio river, at the mouth of the Wabash, in Union Co, Ky. This island was conveyed to Wm Harrison by patent dated Jun 13, 1790, & the taxes have been regularly paid at the Auditor's ofc in Frankfort to this date. The whole island contains between 1,200 & 1,300 acres. –Burr W Harrison, Wm H Gray, excs & Com'rs, Leesburg, Va

Buffalo, Jun 2. Fanny Forrester, late Mrs Judson, [Emily Chubbuck,] widow of the distinguished Baptist Minister, died on Jun 1 in Canada, after a lingering illness, which she contracted when with her husband on a mission to Burmah.

Farm at private sale: formerly owned & occupied by F Darnall, & more recently by Mrs H S Newbold, lying on the road from Rockville to Poolesville, Montg Co, Md, containing 252¼ acres. It has on it a comfortable dwlg house & all necessary outbldgs. To view the premises please call on the subscriber, near the premises, or B S Pleasants, near Poolesville. Address the subscriber, at Dawsonville, Montg Co, Md. –Geo W Dawson

MON JUN 5, 1854
Mr Anthony St John Baker, many years British Consul Genr'l at Washington, died at Tunbridge Wells, where he had resided for some years, on Tue last.

In 1852 Jonathan Lemmon, a citizen of the State of Va, brought 8 slaves to N Y in transit to Texas, whither he was emigrating with his family & property. These slaves were taken before the late Judge Paine, of the Superior Court, by virtue of a writ of habeas corpus issued on the application of a colored man named Louis Napoleon, & Judge Paine ordered them to be discharged from the custody of their master, on the ground that slaves brought voluntarily into N Y by their owners are ipso facto made free. A subscription of $5,000, to which the Judge himself contributed $100, was afterward raised among residents of N Y, & Mr Lemmon was compensated for his loss. The Legislature of Va adopted a resolution to prosecute an appeal from Judge Paine's decision to the Supreme Court of the State of N Y. Mr Lemmon, being a non-resident, shall be required to file security for costs. It was argued on Friday before Mr Justice Clerke, by Mr Lapaugh against & Mr Culver for the motion. Mr Justice Clerke reserved his decision. –N Y Commercial Adv

Wash Corp: 1-Ptn of Timothy Bresneham, for the remission of a fine: referred to the Cmte of Claims. 2-Cmte on Finance: act for the relief of Jas W Scott; & for W C Johnson: passed.

The 4 Irishmen who were indicted for murder at the Kane Co [Ill] Circuit Court for killing Albert Story at La Salle last winter had their second trial at Geneva last week before Judge Isaac G Wilson. All were convicted of murder & sentenced to be hung.

Orphans Court of Wash Co, D C. Letters testamentary on the personal estate of John W Simonton, late of Wash Co, deceased. –Wm Jones, exc

Circuit Court for Somerset Co, Md, in Equity. Experience Lore, Jacob H Hill & wife, Alfred Lore, John Voshell & wife, & Geo W P Smith, vs Eliz Lore. This bill is to procure a decree for the sale of certain real estate in said county, of which Auley Lore died seized. The bill states that some time since 1840, Auley Lore departed this life intestate, leaving Experience Lore, his widow, & Jane Hill, wife of Jacob H Hill, Alfred Lore, Anne Voshell, wife of Jno Voshell, & a certain Rachel C Records, & a grand-daughter, Eliz Lore, daughter of a certain Geo W Lore, who was a son of Auley Lore, his only heirs at law; that the said Rachel hath sold & conveyed her interest in the said real estate to Geo W P Smith, as appears by an authenticated copy of her deed to said Smith, filed as part of the bill & marked Exhibit A; that all the said complaints are of full age, & none of them desires to take the said real estate at the valuation thereof by the com'rs, according to the act of Assembly in such case made & provided; & that the said Eliz Lore is an infant, under the age of 21 years, & resides in the State of Alabama; that the said real estate is not susceptible of division amongst the said parties; & that they are then entitled to have the same sold & the proceeds distributed amongst the parties entitled thereto in proportion of their respective interests. The absent dfndnt is to appear in this Court in person or by solicitor, on or before Oct 10 next. –Ara Spence –Levin Woolford, clerk

Oak Hill Cemetery. The proprietors of lots in the *Oak Hill Cemetery*, Georgetown, [D C] who are members of the Corporation, that is, owners of lots containing 300 square feet, are notified & requested to meet at the chapel within the enclosure of the Cemetery ground on Tuesday, the 13th instant, at 5 o'clock P M, to elect four persons from among their own number to be managers of the said Corporation for the ensuing year. –Jno Marbury, Pres *Oak Hill Cemetery*

TUE JUN 6, 1854
Last week in Luray, Va, Mr Henry Houser, living near Front Royal, while going through the town of Luray in a carriage, the back strap attached to his horse gave way, & the horse, becoming frightened, ran away, precipitating down a steep hill near the bridge, injuring Mrs Houser very seriously, if not fatally. Mrs Jennings, standing in a yard, seeing the accident, was seized with a palpitation of the heart, & fell dead in the yard.

Died: on Jun 3, after 24 hours' illness, Mary, in her 23rd year, wife of Wm H *H___, & daughter of John & Eliza Humphreys. The deceased was from Devonshire, England. [*After the H the next 3 letters are not legible.]

Died: on Jun 4, in Wash City, at the Washington Infirmary, John Roche, in his 26th year. His funeral will be from the above place at 10 o'clock this morning.

Petersburg Express: the body of a drowned man found at Aquia Creek appears, by the papers found in the pockets of the deceased, to be that of Capt Rich'd McRae, who commanded the Petersburg Canada Volunteers in the war of 1812. Capt McRae left Petersburg for Washington a few days since. It is supposed he fell from the steamboat.

U S Patent Ofc, Wash, Jun 5, 1854. Ptn of Fred'k J Austin, of N Y, praying for the extension of a patent granted to him on Jun 10, 1841, ante-dated Dec 16, 1848, for an improvement in machines for cutting paper & trimming books, for 7 years from the expiration of said patent, which takes place on Dec 16, 1854.

Alexandria, Jun 5. Fire broke out here this morning which destroyed the warehouses of Messrs Masters & Co & of Messrs Perry & Sons. Loss supposed to be $10,000. Edw S Hough, the Collector of the Port, was seriously hurt, but not dangerously injured, by the falling of a wall.

Fire yesterday broke out in a shop in the rear of the bldg, on 7th st, opposite this ofc, occupied by Mr Jas W Williams, Cabinetmaker. Mr Williams has had the misfortune to be burnt out several times during a series of years. The fire is presumed to have resulted from an accident.

The first & last duel in Illinois: the year was 1820, the place was Belleville, St Clair Co, between Alphonso Stewart & Wm Bennett, two obscure men. They were to fight with rifles. The guns were loaded with blank cartridges, & Bennett rolled a ball into his gun without the knowledge of the seconds or of the other party. The word to fire was given, & Stewart fell mortally wounded. Bennett made his escape, but 2 years afterwards he was arrested in Arkansas, brought back to the State, indicted, tried, & convicted of murder. Bennett suffered the penalty of the law by hanging.

On Tue last, after the very heavy rain, 3 children, Martha Hyde, 13, Rebecca Davis, 9, & Geo Schlobecker, aged about 5, returning from school at Davis' school-house, taught by Mr Whittemore, in Hartford Co, Md, went to see the water rushing from one of the stream's late Winter's run, which was very high & full, & falling from a plank which they used as a footway all 3 were drowned.

Wash Co, D C. I certify that Jos Fry, of said county, brought before me, as an astray, one Buffalo Heifer. –John L Smith [Owner is to prove property, pay charges, & take her away. –Jos Fry, on 11th, near Boundary st.]

WED JUN 7, 1854
Trustee's sale: by decree of the Circuit Court of Wash Co, D C, made in the case of Abram Barnes et al vs John Mason & others: public auction, on the premises, on Jul 11 next, the following lots of ground in Wash City & District: lots 24 in square 5; lots 13 & 14 in square 17; lots 5 & 6 in square 28; lots 2, 10, 14, & 15 in square 31; lot 8 in square 44; & lots 1, 2, & 13 in square 55. The first mentioned lots front on 26th st, between I & K sts west. –Jno Marbury, trustee -Mitchell & Reynolds, aucts

Trustee's sale of books, periodicals & fancy goods: by deed of trust, recorded among the land records of Wash Co: sale on Jun 14, at the store lately kept by Hugh Cameron, on 7th st, between La ave & D st: all the stock in trade.
-G W Cutter, trustee -Jas C McGuire, auct

Jas D Nourse, associate editor of the St Louis Intelligencer, died of cholera on Thu last, after an illness of about 24 hours, aged 37 years. *Mr A B Chambers, the editor of the St Louis Republican, had been lost to the press of that city the week preceding, & a meeting of the citizens had just resolved to erect a monument to his memory. By the will of Mr Chambers his widow succeeds to all his interest in the establishment. The editorial dept is committed to the charge of Mr Paschall, who has been the assistant editor for many years. [*See Chambers-May 30th newspaper.]

From Salt Lake City: Maj E A Bedell, Indian Agent for Utah died at Green river on May 3.

Mr Jas Wickham & his wife, & a colored boy, were brutally murdered on Fri last, at his farm at Cutchogue, Long Island. Mr W was formerly of the firm of Wickham & Corwin, grocers, in N Y, but had retired from business with a considerable fortune. Nicholas Dane, formerly in his employ, is supposed to have been the murderer, as 2 servant girls, who slept upstairs heard Mrs Wickham exclaim, Nicholas, don't kill him, don't kill him. The girls got out of an attic window & fled to the nearest house & gave the alarm. Mr Wickham & Mrs Frances Wickham, his wife, were found dead. The negro boy about 15, who was living in the family, was also beat to such an extent that he cannot survive. The deed was committed with a post axe. It is supposed the murderer sought revenge upon Mr W for discharging him. Nothing in the house was carried away.

A sailor named Thos Averill was instantly killed at New Orleans last week by falling from the 2nd story window of a boarding house while attempting to descend to the pavement by the gutter-pipe. For a wager, he forfeited his life.

Mr Leftwich's tavern, in Liberty, Bedford Co, Va, was destroyed by fire on Jun 1. The bldg was erected only a few years since at a cost of $14,000, & was insured for $9,000.

New Wash City Council:
Aldermen:
Wm T Dove
Wm F Bayly
French S Evans
Common Council:
W G H Newman
Jas Kelly
Oris S Paine
J R Barr
Geo H Plant
J M Donn
Jonathan T Walker
-John W Maury, Mayor

John P Pepper
John H Houston
Saml A H Marks

Jos W Davis
J A M Duncanson
John Ball
Alex'r McD Davis
Joshua L Henshaw
Saml C Busey
John T Kilmon

Peter M Pearson

John McCauley
Jeremiah Cross
Geo R Ruff
Henry Stewart
John L Smith
Wm C Bamberger
John F Gill

Mrd: on Jun 1, by Rev Jas A Brown, Mr Thos Douglass Walker to Miss Ellen Virginia Warwick, both of Wash.

Mrd: on Jun 4, by Rev Jas H Brown, Mr Chas Keller to Miss Ann Rebecca Walker, both of Wash.

Mrd: on Jun 1, at Leeds, Fauquier Co, Va, by Rev Wm H Pendleton, the Rev Geo Norton to Miss Nannie Burwell, daughter of Jas K Marshall.

Mrd: Jun 1, at Christ Church, Balt, by Rev Dr Johns, Danl P Bedinger, of Nicholas Co, Ky, to Ann Eliz, daughter of the late Matthew Ranson, of Jefferson Co, Va.

John T Cookson, a young married man in Cincinnati, was bit on the leg about 9 weeks since by a dog & on Thu last he felt unwell & retired to bed. He suffered convulsions & died on Wed at 1 p m. An action for damages is to be instituted.

Occidental Messenger: Jas Stallcup, a worthy citizen died on May 19th of hydrophobia. He was bitten by a dog some 10 weeks since. For 36 hours he suffered all the horrors of madness, when death closed his miseries.

THU JUN 8, 1854
Jun 5th was the day fixed for the opening of railroad communication between Cincinnati & Louisville. The tie between the cities will be reduced to 6 hours. 87 miles of the distance will be performed on the Ohio & Mississippi railroad, which great work rapidly approaches completion.

Mrs Sargent, a widow lady residing in Portland, came to a sad death on Sunday by taking oxalic acid in mistake for a dose of salts. It was taken in the morning & resulted in death about 1 o'clock in the afternoon.

The Santa Fe Gaz of Apr 29 notices a report that a party of Indians had attached, some 3 or 4 days previous, the ranche of Mr Maxwell, on the Rayado, about 40 miles from Taos, & killed every body living in it, in all 8 women & 10 men & 2 or 3 children, not leaving a soul to bear witness to the terrible details.

Nicholas Bain, the murderer of Mr & Mrs Wickham, was captured on Monday in Hermitage swamp, about 8 miles from Cutchogue, Suffolk Co, Long Island, where the murders were committed. He had cut his throat with the intention of committing suicide, & was weak from the loss of blood. He was placed in custody of the sheriff of Suffolk Co, & taken to River Head, the county town, where he was locked up for trial. Mr & Mrs Wickham were buried on Monday afternoon.

The Journal de Quebec says the coroner was called on Tue to make an inquest on the body of a farmer, J B Cantin, who lost his life in a combat with a bear on Monday last. Cantin leaves 5 children.

Mrd: on Jun 6, by Rev Jas B Donelan, J De Barth Littele to Columbia, youngest daughter of the late Jos Thaw, all of Wash.

Potomac Pavilion, Piney Point, Md: will be open on Jun 15. –W W Dix, proprietor

Hot-air furnaces & cooking ranges: Loud's improved double oven range for cooking. Cooking stoves for burning wood or coal, also superior articles. Furnace registers & Arnott's Ventilators. –Ralph Haskins, Ornamental Iron Warehouse, Pa ave & 3rd st.

Administrator's sale: by order of the Orphans Court of Wash Co, D C: on Jun 10, the personal effects of Benj Riston, deceased, consisting of household & kitchen furniture. -Green & Scott, aucts

FRI JUN 9, 1854
Senate: 1-Memorial from Royal Phelps, atty in fact of James, Earl of Selkirk, asking that a patent may be issued for certain lands granted to his father by the Hudson's Bay Co: referred. 2-Ptn from John S Waterous, late agent for the Chippewa Indians, praying indemnity for losses sustained by him in consequence of the burning of the Chippewa agency bldg. 3-Ptn from Wm Duer, asking compensation for expenses & services rendered as Consul in Valapraiso in the case of Wm N Stewart. 4-Ptn from Dimitry Carma & others, asking the correction of an error in the location of certain lands in the State of Mississippi. 5-Ptn from Abraham Cutler, asking payment of a balance due for services as a Lt in the late war with Great Britain, & that he may be allowed a pension. 6-Ptn from C H B Fessenden, collector & superintendent of lights for the district of New Bedford, Mass, asking an increase of compensation. 7-Ptn from Ephraim Hunt, asking compensation for his services as a soldier in the last war with Great Britain.

Trustee's sale in square 536: by a decree of the Circuit Court of Wash Co, D C, sitting in equity, in a cause wherein W W Corcoran is plntf & Chas Kiernan is dfndnt, the subscriber, as trustee, will offer at public auction, on Jun 22, the eastern part of lot 6 in square 536, fronting on Va av & south D st. –Anthy Hyde, trustee -Green & Scott, aucts

Mrd: on Jun 6, by Rev Jas H Brown, Mr John H Alison to Miss Anna May, both of Alexandria, Va.

Mrd: on Jun 7, in the Foundry Church, by Rev E P Phelps, Mr Chas W Sherwood to Miss Mgt M Digges, all of Wash City.

Mrd: on Jun 1, at Christ's Church, Winchester, Va, by Rev C Walker, Arthur M Allen, of Clarke Co, to Jane Scott, eldest daughter of the late Alex'r S Tidball.
+
Mrd: on Jun 1, by Rev C Walker, Beverley R Jones, of Fred'k Co, to Rebecca J, 2nd daughter of the late Alex'r S Tidball.

Died: yesterday, after a painful & protracted illness, Mrs Ann Taliaferro Miller, wife of Jas J Miller, of Wash City, & daughter of the late Dr Taliaferro Stribling, of Clarke Co, Va. Her funeral will take place this evening at 5 o'clock.

The case of Lewis Montague, charged with the murder of Gardiner G Thompson on Jun 17, 1852, has been brought to a close. For 2 years he has been incarcerated in the jail of Petersburg, Va, during which time he has been once tried, condemned, & sentenced to be hanged; but a judicial error in the proceedings set aside the verdict. On Monday the jury brought in a verdict of not guilty. Thompson, it appears, on the day of his death had presented a pistol at Montague & told him to defend himself, but no violence was then committed. Thompson told him to meet him that night, when one or the other should be killed. Montague armed himself, met Thompson, & shot him. Thompson it seems was not armed. For this offence the former was arraigned.

SAT JUN 10, 1853
House of Reps: Mr Faulkner announced the death of Hon John F Snodgrass, a Rep from the Parkersburg District of Va.

Proposals will be received at the Mayor's Ofc until Jun 20th for grading & gravelling a roadway 25 feet wide on M st north, between North Capitol st & Delaware ave. Separate proposals for constructing a wood bridge across the creek & mill race, according to the plan to be seen in the Surveyor's ofc. –Fras B Lord, Com'r 3rd & 4th Wards -S H Peugh, Alfred Heitmiller, Assist Com'rs

The U S steamship **Massachusetts**, Lt Commanding R W Meade, is now ready for sea at Norfolk, & awaiting orders from the Dept. The U S sloop-of-war **Cyane**, Cmder Hollins, having lately undergone repairs in Brooklyn dry-dock, will shortly leave N Y for Norfolk, to resume her place in the home squadron.

Mrd: on Jun 8, by Rev F Israel, Wm H Calvert to Frances Anna James, all of Wash City. [Jun 12th newspaper: Mrd: on Jun 8, by Rev Mr Israel, Mr Wm Calvert to Miss Frances R James, all of Wash City.]

Died: on Thu last, Mrs Ann Taliaferro Miller, wife of Jas J Miller, of Wash City, & daughter of the late Dr Taliaferro Stribling, of Clarke Co, Va. In the death of this estimable lady a husband has sustained the loss of a companion whose virtues shone conspicuous in the domestic circle; children a mother affectionate, watchful, & judicious; the Presbyterian Church a member whose worth & conversation illustrated the graces which adorned her Christian character; the poor a friend. –S T

Dissolution of copartnership by mutual consent: under the firm of Wm T Hook & Co. Wm T Hook is authorized to settle the business & will continue in the Coach-making business at the old stand. –Wm T Hook, Anthony W Thomas, Edw Locksey

MON JUN 12, 1854
House of Reps: 1-Cmte on Private Land Claims: bill for the relief of John Rice Jones, deceased: committed. Same cmte: bill authorizing a patent to be issued to Peter Poncin for certain lands therein described: committed; relief of Conrad Wheat, jr, or his legal reps; relief of the heirs & reps of Uriah Prewitt, deceased; relief of Richd King; bill to confirm the claim of Duncan de la Croix to a lot of land therein described: bill for the relief of Robt F McGuire & Louisa his wife, late Louisa Larny: all committed. 2-Cmte on Indian Affairs: adverse on the ptn of Jas M Coleman & his wife, Cherokees, asking that the provisions of the law of Jul 29, 1848, for the benefit of Cherokee Indians of N C, might be extended to the Cherokees of Tenn. Same cmte: bill for the relief of the legal reps of Jas Erwin, of Ark, & others: committed, with a favorable recommendation. Same cmte: bill for indemnifying Moses D Hogan for cattle destroyed by the Indians in 1842: committed. Same cmte: adverse report on the ptn of John Johnston. Same cmte: bill for the relief of Wm Senna Factor: committed. 3-Cmte on Military Affairs: bill for the relief of Richd M Bouton, Geo Wright, & the widow of Marvin W Fisher, with the recommendation that it pass: committed. Same cmte: bill for the relief of the heirs & reps of Col Alex'r G Morgan, with the recommendation that it do not pass: laid on the table. Same cmte: adverse report on the ptn of Lt Edw Cantwell. Same cmte: bill for the relief of Lt Geo H Paige, U S Army, a & joint resolution for the relief of Brevet Capt J H Lendrum, U S Army: both committed. 4-Cmte on Naval Affairs: bill for the relief of Thos Pember; & for relief of Saml Mickum, with the recommendation that they do not pass: committed. Same cmte: bill for the relief of Passed Midshipmen Geo P Welsh & Clark H Wells, with the recommendation that it pass: committed.

Same cmte: bills committed: relief of Thos Marston Taylor; of Purser Francis B Stockton; of the widows & orphans of the ofcrs & seamen of the U S surveying schnr **Grampus**, who were lost in that vessel in Mar, 1843, near the coast of the U S. 5-Cmte on Revolutionary Pensions: adverse reports on the ptns of Mary Chesly, Eliz Martin, & Mary Blakeney. 6-Cmte on Invalid Pensions: adverse reports on the ptns of John Russell, & Mary R Adrain. Same cmte: bill for the relief of Andrew J Dickerhoff, with a favorable recommendation: committed. Same cmte: to provide a pension for Oliver Brown, of Chemung Co, N Y; pension for Edmund Mitchell, of Carroll Co, Ky; & pension to G W Torrants. Same cmte reported bills for the following & same were committed: relief of Jas Butler; of Jno H Hicks, of Indiana; of John Brown, second, of N Y; bill for the relief of Mrs Anne W Angus, widow of the late Capt Angus, U S Navy; relief of B Nash. Same cmte: adverse reports on the ptns of Lydia Prather; of Louisa J Brown & Jas H Casey; of Harvey Thompson; of members of the Pa Legislature in behalf of Lenox Rea; of Phoebe Marvin, of N Y; of Fred'k W Miller, of Erie Co, Pa; & of Jno Campbell. Same cmte: adverse reports on the ptns of Ezekiel Hook; of citizens of Michigan for an extension of the pension laws; & of Peter H Willett. Same cmte: bill for the relief of Lavinia Taylor: committed. Same cmte: bill for the relief of Amos Knapp, with the recommendation that it do not pass: laid on the table. Same cmte: adverse reports on the ptns of Chester Parish; of Eunice Morrison; of Orange Mansfield; of Henry Welch; & of Horatio Seymour. Same cmte: bill for the relief of Thos Bronaugh; of Anna E Cook; & of Abraham Ansman: committed. 7-Cmte on Patents: bill for the relief of Francis Pettit Smith: committed. 8-Cmte of Claims: adverse reports on the ptns of Stephen Warren; of Woodbury & Foster; of Saml Holgate; of John Wilson; of Jos D Ward; & of Jas B Estes, of Wisc. Same cmte: bill for the relief of Sylvester Humphrey & the heirs of Alex'r Humphrey, deceased. 9-Cmte on Commerce: bill for the compensation of Jas W Low & others for the capture of the British private armed schnr **Ann**, during the late war with Great Britain: committed. 10-Cmte on Private Land Claims: bill for the relief of A B Brown, of Louisiana: committed. 11-Cmte on Commerce: bills committed: relief of Jacob McClellan; & of Nathl Goddard & others. Resolution for the relief of the owners of the brig **Kate Boyd**; & of the owners of the steamer **Fanny**. 12-Cmte on Public Lands: adverse report on the ptns of Geo Messersmith. 13-Cmte on Revolutionary Claims: bill for the relief of the heirs of Capt J Davis: committed. 14-Cmte on the Post Ofc & Post Roads: joint resolution for the adjustment of the accounts of John D Colmesuil: committed. 15-Cmte on the Dist of Columbia: adverse report on the memorial of J C F Salomon, asking a charter for a company to suppy the cities of Wash & Gtwn with pure & wholesome water. Same cmte: bill for the relief of Wm G Howison. Same cmte: bill authorizing the Wash Gas Light Co to increase their capital stock to $150,000: committed. 16-Cmte on the Judiciary: adverse report on the ptn of Joshua Shaw & others for a change in the present system of surveying the public lands. Same cmte: adverse report on the ptn of David Hitchcock & others, asking Congress to prohibit the sale of slaves for debts due the U S; & on the ptn of Isaac Burr & others, of N Y, against paying for the Amistad negroes. 17-Cmte on Revolutionary Claims:

committed-relief of the heirs of Capt Nehemiah Stockely, deceased; of the heirs of Capt Matthew Jack, deceased; of the widow & children of Ezra Chapman, deceased; & of the heirs & legal reps of Jos Savage, deceased. Same cmte: adverse reports on the ptn of the legal reps of Tarpley White, deceased; & on the ptn of Wm V Heard, of Wash Co, Md. Same cmte: bill for the relief of the heirs of Thos Park, deceased; of Wm A Duer, John Duer, & Benj Robinson, trustees of the estate of Sarah Alexander, widow of Maj Gen Wm Alexander, commonly known as Lord Stirling: committed. Same cmte: bill for the relief of the heirs of Lott Hall, deceased; & of the legal reps of Henry Hoffman: committed.

On May 14 Mr Geo W Bowman, on his farm in Bullitt Co, Ky, killed a rattlesnake 6 feet 4 inches long & about 18 around the body, with 21 rattles. This was the largest & oldest rattlesnake ever seen in the Western country.

Household & kitchen furniture at auction: on Jun 14, at the residence of Mr J C Greer, on 12th, between G & H sts. -Green & Scott, aucts

The undersigned, representing respectively the Gov't of the U S & the [so-called] Republic of Sonora, have agreed as follows: Col Wm Walker, [Pres of the Republic of Sonora,] & party, agree to surrender to the U S as prisoners, to abide an investigation of their alleged violation of the act of 1812, in reference to the neutrality of the U S, on the following conditions, to wit: Maj J McKinstry & Capt H S Burton, of the U S Army, agree to provision & quarter Col Walker & command at San Diego until the arrival of a steamer, when they shall be furnished with transportation to San Francisco, upon condition of reporting themselves [under the direction of Capt Burton] to Maj Gen J E Wool, U S Army, at San Francisco, as prisoners on their parole of honor. At anchor off Lunto, Calif, May 8, 1854. J McKinstry, Brvt Maj U S Army; H R Burton, Capt U S Army; Wm Walker, Pres't Republic of Sonora. [Whilst in Lower Calif 13 of the party were killed, [2 of them having been shot by order of Walker,] 3 died, & 1 was lost in the desert.

Wm E Roberts, a young man of genteel appearance, from Pa, has been convicted of arson at New Orleans, in setting fire to his store, the contents of which were appraised at $206, & on which he had insurance of $4,000. The punishment is imprisonment in the penitentiary for life.

For rent: the upper or dwlg portion of that large bldg at the corner of 7th st west & fronting south on Market Space & Pa ave: it is 4 stories high above the stores, & contains 60 rooms. It has all the modern improvements of gas, tanks, bath-rooms, hot & cold water conveyed through it, & a dumb waiter from the kitchen to each story in the house. Possession given immediately. –Anne R Dermott, 12th st west, between G & H sts north.

Court of Inquiry instituted by Special Orders, No 17, of Jan 28, 1854, from the War Dept, whereof Maj Gen Winfield Scott is President, which convened in N Y C on Feb 6, 1854, to examine into all the circumstances attending the embarkation, in Dec last, of the troops under the command of Col Wm Gates, 3rd Artl, on board the steamer **San Francisco**, destined for Calif; the cause of the failure of the expedition, & of the disorganization of the command at sea; & all other facts which may concern the conduct of the cmder & of the ofcrs & men of the command, has submitted the following: the wreck of the transport was caused by a storm; the command was further disorganized by the transfers from the wreck to the 3 relieving vessels & the partial mixing of companies; the court is obliged to add blameable of disorganization at the head of the command; & the result of panic or physical incapacity, for Col Gates, the loss of an interesting son washed overboard, seems to have been cool & active on foot; but disorganization resulting from fatuity or crookedness of mine, which, leaving him alive to his own immediate wants & those of his family & to be the first accidental chance of escape, caused him to neglect nearly every high duty imposed by his rank & the circumstances, such as the duty of going often among his men to cheer & animate then; of organization directing their labors; of organizing all the company ofcrs fit for duty, etc. On the wreck, 2nd Lts Chas S Winder, Van Voast, & Chandler particularly distinguished themselves. Capt Gardiner, of the 1st Dragoons, crippled with the rheumatism, who embarked with the 3rd Artl as a passenger for Calif, & 2nd Lt Van Voast, seem entitled to special notice. Col Gates made the declaration on board the **Kilby**, in respect to extra water, that he cared nothing for his men, [with an oath,] I would rather 20 of them should die than his child should suffer, [or die,] when there was no immediate danger that any one board would perish from thirst. The Court regards the conduct of Col Gates in these instances as highly selfish & censurable. An accusation was submitted by Col Gates against Capt Gardiner relative to the purloining of food on board the barque **Kilby**; the Court directed Col Gates, as prosecutor, to adduce the evidence on which he had made grave allegations. The Court is constrained to say that the said allegations against Capt Gardiner were entirely groundless, & seem to have originated in a spirit of gross malignity. –Winfield Scott, Maj Gen & Pres of the Court. J F Lee, Judge Advocate. VI: The Court of Inquiry is dissolved. Sec of War: S Cooper, Adj Gen

The N Y papers announce the death of Mr Chas C Wright, the well known medalist, who executed the gold medals ordered by Congress for Generals Taylor & Scott & the celebrated medal for Mr Clay. He was a most amiable & excellent man.

Mrd: on Jun 8, by Rev S D Finkel, Mr Hubert Schutter to Miss M Esther McConnell.

Mrd: on Jun 6, by Rev S D Finkel, Mr Chas A Schott to Miss Therese Gildermeister, all of Wash City.

Mrd: on Jun 8, by Rev Mr Israel, Mr Wm Calvert to Miss Frances R James, all of Wash City.

Mrd: on Aug 25 last, in Wash City, by Rev Mr Williams, of N Y, & on Jun 7, by Rev Mr Boyle, of Wash City, Mr Thos Grosvenor King, of N Y, to Miss Catharine McNerhany, of Wash.

Died: on Sat, at his father's residence, of consumption, Dr Saml J Anderson, in his 29th year. His funeral is on Monday at 5 o'clock.

Died: on Jun 5, near Rockville, Montg Co, Md, Mr Thos Read, aged 60 years.

Nahant House will be open for the reception of guests on Jun 12. The new & swift steamer **Nelly Baker** will make 4 trips each way daily, between Boston & Nahant. -P Stevens & Co, Nahant House, Nahant, Mass.

TUE JUN 13, 1854
Senate: 1-Message received from the House of Reps announcing the death of Hon John Fryatt Snodgrass, a member of that body from the State of Va.

Chancery sale of valuable property: by decree of the Circuit Court of Wash Co, D C, in chancery, passed in a cause wherein Iardella & others are cmplnts & Bulger & others are dfndnts: sale on Jul 6, on lot 13 in square 317, with a 2 story frame house, on north H st, between 4th & 5th sts. –John F Ennis, trustee -Green & Scott, aucts

For sale: a likely young negro woman, 23 or 24, a first rate cook, washer, & ironer. The owner, having no further use for her, wishes to sell her & her child. Apply to the owner, Mrs Ann Scott, on K st, near the *Congressional Burial Ground*.

Inauguration of John T Towers as Mayor of Washington City, for the ensuing 2 years, was held yesterday. He succeeds Mayor Maury.

WED JUN 14, 1854
Hon Jas P Heath, an old resident of Balt City & Co, & formerly a Rep in Congress, died on Monday at the residence of his son-in-law, Robt P Dodge, in Gtwn, where he had been spending the season. Mr Heath had attanined the age of 78 years.

Cmdor Rousseau relieved Cmdor Tattnall of the command of the Navy Yard at Pensacola on Jun 1.

Died: on Jun 9, in Wash City, at the residence of A B Walles, Mrs Helen M Noyes, wife of Hon Jos C Noyes, of Portland, Maine. She faithfully discharged her duties as wife, mother, daughter, & friend, & met death with Christian hope.

Died: on Jun 7, at *Summerfield*, the residence of Jas Carroll, jr, near Balt, Miss Sarah J Wethered, daughter of the late John Wethered, of Kent Co, Md.

Senate: 1-Ptn from Oakely H Wright, asking a pension for services in the Tripolitan war, & bounty land for services in the last war with England. 2-Ptn from Jane A Bowen, asking a pension. 3-Ptn from A S Bender, for his services as Superintendent of the Lead Mines of the Upper Mississippi: referred. 4-Ptn from Adolphus Allen, asking an extension of his patent. 5-Ptn from Mrs Anne Royal, widow of Capt Wm Royal, of the Revolutionary army, asking to be allowed interest on the amount due her husband at the close of the war. Mr Shields commended it to the consideration of the Senate as a case of merit. 6-Memorial from Adam D Stewart & others of the army, asking compensation for extra services rendered during the late war with Mexico. 7-Ptn from Jesse D Carr, asking indemnity for property destroyed during the late war with Mexico. 8-Ptn from Chas Parsons, of New Orleans, asking the issue of an American register for the Russian brig **Amella**. 9-Ptn from Horace H Smith & Chas Steevens, asking indemnity for the loss of the schnr **Drumscale** & cargo, wrecked in consequence of obstructions placed at the mouth of the Patapsco river by order of the Gov't. 10-Ptn from Saml A Belden Co, claimants against the Gov'nt of Mexico under the treaty of Guadalupe Hidalgo, asking indemnity for property seized & confiscated, & asking that measures may be taken to enforce the payment of their claims. 11-Ptn from Rachel Herbert, asking compensation for extra services rendered by her late husband, Nat Herbert, while messenger in the Post Ofc. 12-Cmte on Pensions: bill for the relief of Betsey Whipple. Same cmte: adverse report on the ptn of Abigail Saunders. Same cmte: bill for the relief of Peter Amey, [colored man.] Same cmte: adverse reports on the ptns of Wm B May & others; of John K Presher; & of Jane M Rudolph, widow of a captain in the revenue service. 13-Cmte on Indian Affairs: bill for the relief of the widow & heirs of Elijah Beebe: asked its immediate consideration: passed. 14-Bill for the relief of the assignees & legal reps of Jacques Moulon: introduced. 15-Cmte on Invalid Pensions: bill for the relief of Mrs Mary A M Jones: committed. 16-Question of Privilege: A O P Nicholson, printer to this body, editor & proprietor of the Wash Union, in his paper of this morning has published an article most evidently designed to excite unlawful violence upon members of this body: therefore-Resolved, that said A O P Nicholson & all other persons connected with the Wash Union be expelled from the hall. Modified to simply refer to the editor of the Union. Yeas 101, nays 32. 17-Cmte on Military Affairs: bills committed: relief of Thos S Russell; of A G Bennett; to provide 3 months' extra pay to the 3rd Regt of Missouri volunteers; & a bill for the relief of Chas H Wilgus. 18-Cmte on Naval Affairs: bills committed: relief of: Purser T P McBlair; & of M K Warrington & C St J Chubb, executors of Capt Lewis Warrington, & others. 19-Cmte on Indian Affairs: adverse reports on the ptns of Chas A Grignon & of Jos Vandruff. Same cmte: bill for the relief of Jos Watson, deceased: recommendation that it pass: committed.

Mrd: at Durhamville, Tenn, at the residence of Mrs Mary J Lee, by Rt Rev Bishop Opey, Jas B Thornton, of Memphis, to Miss Susan Stuart, daughter of Col John S Thornton, formerly of Va, & lately of Gtwn, D C, & grand-daughter of Mrs Lee. [No date given-current item.]

Chicago Democratic Free Press of Jun 7. At Lasalle, while the canal boat **Flying Cloud** was coming through the locks, one or two of the scrow's crew came on board & wantonly threw a favorite dog of Capt Brown's wife into the lock. The Capt put them off the boat in no gentle means. They went to their boat & rallied 20 or more to lay in wait for the boat & to take vengeance. Capt Brown was informed of this danger. He loaded 2 Colt revolvers & a shot gun, & with one of his men, they started for the Collector's ofc to settle his business there. The party fell on him with axes & clubs. His man fired one shot, which dropped one of the assailants, & he then fled, leaving the Captain alone. He shot dropping a man & the party vanished. The Capt was not seriously wounded. He went to the town, surrendered himself to the authorities, was held to bail, gave security, & was discharged.

Circuit Court of Wash Co, D C, sitting in Chancery. Geo C Cramphin, Thos A Cramphin, Alpheus Morse & Mariella his wife, W W Mason & Hannah his wife, Alex'r Cramphin, Jas T Beaumont & Henrietta his wife, cmplnts, versus Geo H Calvert, Chas B Calvert, Thos W Morris, husband, & Anna M Morris, Geo C Morris, & Julia M Morris, heirs at law of Rosalie E Morris, deceased, Chas H Carter, husband, & Rosalie E Carter, Alice Carter, Bernard Carter, Ella Carter, Mildred Carter, Annetta Carter, & Mary R Carter, heirs at law of Caroline Carter, deceased, Richd H Stewart & Julia his wife, Caroline Calvert, Thos Cramphin & Francis Cramphin, Caroline A Smith, Alice E Smith, Richd T Smith, & Sherbourne Smith, heirs at law of Jos & Caroline Smith, deceased, & Allen Brown Davis, executor of Eliz Davis, deceased. The bill states that Thos Cramphin, deceased, was in his lifetime seized & possessed of valuable real & personal estate in Montg Co, Md, & in the Dist of Columbia, & made certain instruments of writing purporting to be his last will & testament & codicil thereto, & thereby, after sundry legacies, demised & bequeathed the residue of his estate to Geo Calvert, late deceased, for the support, benefit, & advantage of the children of said Caroline Calvert-that is to say, Geo, Thos, Marretta, & Henrietta, cmplnts; Caroline, Henry, & Richd since deceased-with certain powers & rights of control in the management, disposal of, & distribution of said estates set forth in said instruments, & named the said Geo Calvert his sole executor; that the said instruments of writing were afterwards, by the finding of a jury & the judgments of the proper judicial tribunal, adjudged not to be the last will & testament of the said Thos Cramphin; that Eliz Davis, the heirs at law & next of kin of the said Thos Cramphin, afterwards by her 2 deeds, one dated Dec 1, 1835, & duly recorded in Wash Co, D C, the other dated Jan 11, 1836, conveyed all the real & personal estate of the said Thos Cramphin at the date of the last said instruments to Geo Calvert, of PG Co, Md, in trust, first, to raise out of the said estate & pay to her, the said Eliz, the sum of $30,000, to reimburse himself all expenses incurred or to be incurred in connexion with the said estate; &, lastly, to hold & apply the same or the proceeds of the sales thereof for the same uses & objects expressed in the said instruments of writing purporting to be the last will & codicile thereto of the said Thos Cramphin; that the said Caroline Calvert had then other children born after the execution of the last of the said instrument of writing, to wit, Hannah & Alex'r, two of the said named cmplnts & Robt, since dead, intestate & without issue, & that the said children, named as residuary legatees in the said instruments of writing, agreed to admit & did admit the said Hannah, Alex'r, & Robt to an equal participation with themselves in the benefits of the said estate. The bill states that the said Geo Calvert took on himself the ofc of trustee under the deed aforesaid of the said Eliz Davis, & disposed of all the real & personal estate of which the said Thos Cramphin died seized & possessed in Montg Co aforesaid, & with the proceeds thereafter paid to the said Eliz Davis the said sum of $30,000; that all other preliminary legacies, pecuniary & specific, in the said instruments mentioned & bequeathed, were paid or delivered to the legatees; that John Henry, one of the residuary legatees named in the said instruments of writing, is dead, intestate, leaving 2 children, Thos Cramphin & Jas Cramphin, two of the dfndnts to the said bill, his heir at law; that Richd & Robt, two other of the children of the said Caroline Calvert, died intestate & without issue; that Caroline, one other of the said children & residuary legatees, married one Jos S Smith, & that she & her husband sold & assigned all her interest in the said estate, & the same is now the property of the cmplnt, Alpheus Morse; that after such sale & assignment the said Jos & Caroline died, leaving 4 children their heirs at law, to wit, the dfndnts Caroline, Alice, Richd, & Sherburne Smith. The cmplnts claim that they & the said Thos Cramphin & Francis Cramphin, heirs at law of John Henry Cramphin, deceased, are entitled to the whole residuence of the said estate; they state that Geo Calvert leaving the trusts so assumed by him unexecuted; that the real estate in the Dist of Col remains to be sold; that the dfndnts, Geo & Chas Calvert, Thos, Anna, Geo, & Julia Morris, Chas, Rosalie, Alice, Bernard, Ella, Mildred, Annetta, & Mary R Carter, Richd Stewart & Julia his wife, & the heirs at law of the said Geo Calvert, & are incapable from their number, dispersed residences, & non-age to execute the trusts devolved on them under said deed by the death of the said Geo Calvert. The object of the said bill is to have some proper person appointed trustee in the stead & place of the said Geo Calvert to execute the trusts of the said deeds; that the real estate in Gtwn aforesaid may be sold, & the proceeds thereof distributed by the trustee, as by the said deeds & instruments purporting to be the last will & codicils thereto of said Thos Cramphin is directed, & for such other relief as to the Court shall seem right. The bill further states that the parties named dfndnts in the preceeding caption & titling are not inhabitants of the Dist of Col, & that they reside in the States of Md, Va, & N Y, beyond the reach of the process of this Court; it is therefore ordered that they appear in this Court on or before the 3rd Monday in Oct next, & answer the said bill, & show cause, of any they have, why a decree as prayed for by the cmplnts should not be passed by the Court. By order of the Court, John A Smith, clerk

Mrd: on Jun 13, at **Green Hill**, by Rev Mr Knight, Prof J E Morgan, of Wash, to Norah, daughter of the late Wm Dudley Digges, of PG Co, Md.

Mrd: on Jun 13, by Rev Wm Hanes, Wm Campbell to Miss Rachael Graham, all of Wash.

Mrd: on Monday, by Rev John C Smith, Mr Geo Small to Miss Eliza Groves, all of Wash City.

Due to the indisposition of Mr Manypenny, Com'r of Indian Affairs, the duties are now performed by Mr C E Mix, Chief Clerk, as acting Com'r.

THU JUN 15, 1854
Mr Isham Williams, of Madison Co, died on May 29 from being stung on the arm by a wasp. He died in less than 10 minutes after being stung. –Athens [Ga] Banner

Mrd: on Jun 13, by Rev G W Sampson, Mr Jas A King to Miss M D Virginia, daughter of Jos Peck, all of Wash.

Mrd: on Jun 13, in Wesley Chapel, by Rev Jas H Brown, Mr John R McGregor to Miss Mary McGregor, both of Wash.

Mrd: on Jun 13, at St Patrick's Church, by Rev T O'Toole, Mr Thos F Maguire to Miss Martha M Reeves, all of Wash City.

Senate: 1-Ptn from the heirs at law of Benj Grover, a Revolutionary soldier, asking to be allowed a pension. 2-Documents submitted in support of the claim of Serepta Cleveland. 3-Cmte on Naval Affairs: joint resolution giving the consent of Congress to the acceptance by Lt M F Maury, of the Navy, of a gold medal from his Majesty the King of Sweden. This was given as an acknowledgment of the kind disposition shown by Lt Maury to make the merchant navy of Sweden, in common with that of other nations, a recipient of the benefit of the discoveries made in the sciene of navigation. Same was passed. 4-Cmte on Revolutionary Claims: bill for the heirs of Capt Joshua Chamberlain, deceased. Same cmte: bill for the legal reps of Jas Bell, deceased. 5-Cmte on Pensions: bill for the relief of Jas Walsh: recommended its passage. Same cmte: to inquire into the propriety of allowing a sum to the heirs of Benj Grover, deceased, of Maine, equal to what was justly due the widow of said Grover as a pension at the time of her decease. 6-Joint resolution introduced authorizing the Sec of the Territory of New Mexico to adjust & pay to Juan C Armijo, Jose L Peres, & Jas L Collins the amount by them loaned to the Legislative Assembly of said Territory under authority of the joint resolution of that body approved Jun 17, 1851.

Wash City Ordinances: 1-Act for the relief of Robt T Mills: fine imposed for violating an ordinance prohibiting shooting within the limits of the city, is remitted; provided Mills pays the cost of prosecution. 2-Act refunding certain moneys to P A Sellhausen: the sum of $4.50, amount of taxes erroneously paid by him on south part of lot 3 in square 527.

Died: on Jun 13, Samuel Emory, only child of Hon Jefferson Davis, aged 22 months & 14 days. His funeral will be at the residence of his parents, on Jun 15, at 4 p m.

Rev Thos W Higginson was arrested at Worcester on Sat on the charge of participating in riotous proceedings in Boston on May 26. He was taken to Boston before the Police Court, where he waived an examinaition, & gave sureties, Dr Walter Channing & Wm I Bowditch, in the sum of $3,000 for his appearance at the Municipal Court for trial.

FRI JUN 16, 1854
Mrd: on Jun 14, by Rev Mr Hodges, Hon Wm R Smith, of Alabama, to Miss Wilhelmina, daughter of Capt Wm Easby, of Wash, D C.

Mrd: on Jun 15, by Rev Mr Donelan, John A Middleton, of N Y, to Annie Maria Berry, daughter of Washington Berry.

Died: on Jun 15, R H Crozier, in his 29th year. His funeral will be this morning at 10 o'clock, from the residence of his mother-in-law, Mrs R Sears, on 12th st, between I & K sts.

Trustee's sale: by decree of the Circuit Court of Wash Co, D C, made in the case of Jeremiah Williams, his wife, & others, cmplnts, against Mary Rhodes & others, dfndnts: public auction on Jul 7, of ground in Wash City, D C, late the property of Mrs Ann Steuart, to wit; lots 14 & 15 in square 324, at G & 14th sts west. Conveyance made at the expense of the purchasers. –Jno Marbury, trustee

Two young men, Jas H Longman, of N Y, & John Downes, of Scotland, residents of Charleston, S C, were drowned in that harbor on Sat last, whilst on a pleasure excursion, in consequence of their boat having collided with a schnr.

Senate: 1-Ptn from the heirs of Col John B Thompson, of the Revolutionary army, asking to be allowed the commutation pay & bounty land to which their ancestor was entitled. 2-Ptn from P C Miles, asking an increase of pension. 3-Cmte on the Post Ofc & Post Roads: resolution for the relief of Rebecca J Birdsall, & asked its consideration. 4-Cmte on Foreign Relations: bill for the relief of Wm Duer, & asked its consideration: Passed. 5-Cmte on Pensions: adverse reports on the ptns of Saml Crapin; & of the citizens of Massachusetts in favor of Josiah Mann.

SAT JUN 17, 1854
Trustee's sale: by deed of trust dated Nov 30, 1852, from John E Baker & Catherine B Baker his wife, recorded in Liber J A S, v 49, pp 470 thru 473, of the land records of Wash City: public sale on Jul 17 of lot 31 in square 387, fronting on south D st. –Jno M McCalla, trustee -Green & Scott, aucts

Senate: 1-Joint resolution for the relief of Abigail Stafford was taken up, &, after argument, was defeated by a vote of yeas 25, nays 13. 2-Bill for the relief of the heirs of Capt Joshua Chamberlain, deceased: passed. 2-Bill for the relief of the claimants of the private armed brig **Gen Armstrong**: agreed to.

House of Reps: 1-Cmte on the Post Ofc & Post Roads: bill for the relief of Thos Rhodes: committed. 2-Bill for the relief of Saml Colt was taken up: laid over, as was also the bill for the relief of Chas Lee Jones. 3-Bill for the relief of Henry Lewis, of Clinton Co, Indiana, was considered: laid aside. 4-Bill for the relief of Capt Geo Simpton, of Galveston, was laid aside with the recommendation that it pass.

Pleasant farm for sale in Montg Co, about 10 miles from Wash, D C, & about 5 miles east of Mr Blair's Farm, & near the *Burnt Mills*. It consists of 154 acres; good frame bldg, a stable, corn-house, & a fine Spring of excellent water. Also for sale, a small brick dwlg & a larger frame dwlg near the Eastern Free School, Capitol Hill. Apply to the Editor of the Wash News.

Wash City Ordinances: 1-Act for the relief of Geo W Fridley: fine imposed in relation to stove pipes is remitted; provided he pays the costs of prosecution. 2-Act for the relief of Alex'r Cole: fine imposed is remitted; provided he pays the costs of prosecution. 3-Act to pay John Purdy for lumber furnished for the 5th Ward: the sum of $50.96. 4-Act for the relief of Jas W Scott: to pay him $13.27, that amount having been erroneously paid by Scott on lot 18 in square1,027. 5-Act for the relief of Jas T Barnes: to pay him $88 for work done by him on L st. 6-Act for the relief of W C Johnson: the sum of $9 be refunded, the amount erroneously placed in his taxes. 7-Act for the relief of J Callaghan: to pay him $15, to reimburse him for a fine recently imposed on him. 8-Act for the relief of Danl File: fine imposed on him for selling tin ware on stall 112 in Centre Market is remitted; provided he pay the costs of prosecution. 9-Act for the relief of Catharine Eaton: fine imposed for a violation of firing guns is remitted; provided she pay the costs of prosecution.

Mrd: on Jun 7, by Rev Mr Todd, Henry Starr Wattles, of Alexandria, Va, to Caroline, daughter of Richd H Clagett, of Swan Point, Md.

Mrd: on Thu, by Rev John C Smith, Bartholomew Oertly to Miss Eliz Ann, daughter of Saml Cunningham, of Gtwn.

Died: on Jun 16, at the Wash Infirmary, Daniel Ettienne, aged 4 years, 10 months & 12 days, son of Jane E & the late Danl Dunscomb. His funeral is this morning at 10 o'clock from the Wash Infirmary.

$100 reward for runaway negro boy Bob Fletcher, age 15 years. He has relatives living in Wash, & Upper Marlborough. I purchased him of Thos W Clagett, formerly of this county. –John H Berry, jr, near Bladensburg, PG Co, Md.

Circuit Court of Wash Co, D C-in Chancery. Bill of Revivor. Wm Lowder, against Caroline R Lowder, admx, de bonis non, of Saml Lowder, deceased. The bill states that the said cmplnt, on May 13, 1851, filed his bill in the Court of D C, making claim to one quarter of the amount of a certain award by the Com'rs under the treaty of the U S with Mexico, which was issued to John Wilkins, then the executor of Saml Lowder, deceased. That the said bill was against the said Wilkins, who made answer thereto, & took depositions in reply to the same. That the said Wilkins afterwards died, & Mrs Caroline R Lowder was duly appointed admx, de bonis non, of the said Saml Lowder; & this cmplnt prays that she may be fully made a dfndnt in this bill of revivor; & she not being a resident of the Dist of Columbia, or within the jurisdiction of this Court, that she may by due process of publication be summoned to be & appear in this Court on or before the first Monday in Nov next. –Jas S Morsell, Assoc Judge Circuit Court D C. –Jno A Smith, clerk

Charleston, Jun 16. A duel was fought a few days since in Mississippi between Gen J C Saunders, of Ala, & Judge Evans, of Miss. Five shots were exchanged, & both were wounded; Evans dangerously.

MON JUN 19, 1854
Mrs Etheridge, wife of Hon Emmerson Etheridge, died at the residence of her husband in Dresden, Tenn, on May 25 last. Her husband is absent attending to his duties as a member of Congress. She was young; she had not reached the meridian of womanhood, except in amability of character & the graces of her sex. Mrs Etheridge was the only daughter of Dr Pulaski B Bell, of Weakly Co. –Trenton [Tenn] Banner

The fire at Worcester, Mass, on Wed has occasioned great suffering in that city, principally among the mechanics & working classes. Below is a list of the more prominent suffers: Williams, Rich & Co, machinists; Saml Flagg & Co, manufacturers of machinists' tools; Danl Tainter, woolen machinery; C Hovey & Co, straw cutters; C Whitcomb & Co, machinists' tools; Howard & Davis, sewing machines; Thayer, Houghton & Co, machinists' tools; Worcester Machine Tool Co; Wm T Merrifield, owner & leasee of bldg & motive power; Dwight Foster, owner of a portion of Merrifield's bldg; Allen & Thurber, pistol makers; Austin W Bixby, Taber & Chellar, manufacturers of furniture; Jno Gates, lumber & grocery dealer; & Howard & Davis, manufacturers of sewing machines.

Illinois Register of Jun 8: John Lewis, postmaster at Waynesville, Dewitt Co, Ill, was arrested on a charge of secreting & embezzling a letter containing $60. He was examined & committed for trial.

Mrd: on Jun 16, by Rev J W Shackelford, Rector of St Mary's, Brooklyn, Rev E A Washburn, Rector of St John's, Hartford, to Fanny H, daughter of Dr Harvey Lindsley, of Wash.

Mrd: on May 21, at Rome, Hon Lewis Cass, jr, American Charge d'Affaires, to Miss Mary Ludlam, daughter of Nicholas Ludlam, of N Y.

Death in *Mount Vesuvius*: a letter from Paris, in the Boston Atlas, says: Young Mr J Delius, of Bremen, fell into the crater of *Mount Vesuvius* on May 11 & perished; his body was found. He was the assist professor of English literature at Berlin, who is so kindly remembered by all American students who have resided in Berlin, from his marked hospitality to them. His father & several of his family are the partners of the well known Bremen house that has a branch establishment in Balt, Md.

New Orleans: B Schlessinger, during a scuffle with a man named S G Ladd, at New Orleans, on Jun 9, was shot with a pistol & expired in a few minutes. Ladd surrendered & was locked up to await trial. A duel he was in was a scham & he became indignant at the trick played on him.

Died: on Jun 8, at Indian Springs, Ga, Lt Geo H Talcott, U S Army, in his 43rd year.

Died: on Jun 16, in N Y, of bilious remittent fever, Saml Humes Houston, U S Navy, in his 24th year. His funeral is this morning at 9 o'clock, from the residence of his parents, on Missouri ave, between 4½ & 6th sts.

Died: on Jun 17, Henry McGill, in his 22nd year. His funeral is this afternoon, at 5 o'clock, from his late residence, between G & H, on 5th st.

The Farm offered for sale by Geo W Dawson, under a delegated authority, formerly owned by Fielder Darnall, & more recently occupied by Mrs Hope S Newbold, was deeded by Fielder Darnall in trust to me, & a cash payment of $3,000 made on it, & the deferred payments secured by a mortgage on the property. To any person desirous of purchasing, a clear & undisputed title will be given on the payment of the whole purchase money. –B B Pleasants

TUE JUN 20, 1854
Jos Radcliff & Son: Commission Merchants & Manufacturers' Agents, Wholesale & Retail Dealers in Agricultural & Horticultural Implements & Machinery, Fertilizers, Seeds, etc, Odd Fellows' Hall, 7th st, Wash.

Senate: 1-Ptn from John Freeman & other citizens of Portsmouth, Va, asking to be reimbursed for their sufferings & imprisonment in Dartmoor during the last war with England. 2-Ptn from Jas Selkirk, asking the settlement of his claim against the Mexican Gov't for the seizure & destruction of his vessel by the authorities of that Republic. 3-Cmte on Foreign Relations: bill for relief of Capt E A F Lavalette, U S Navy: passed. 4-Cmte on Pensions: bill for relief of Jesse R Faulkner, of Missouri: recommended its passage. Same cmte: adverse report on ptn of John Reddin.

Chancery sale of valuable & improved real estate on Pa ave: by decree of the Circuit Court of Wash Co, D C, passed in a cause wherein Wm S Laurie & others are cmplnts, & Jas C Hall & Lizzie Delle Laurie are dfndnts: public auction on Jul 10th next, of that piece of ground contained in square 230, fronting on the south side of Pa ave, with a 3 story brick dwlg-house & back bldg attached. The said property is directly opposite Willard's Hotel. –A Austin Smith, trustee -Jas C McGuire, auct [Oct 18th newspaper: Chancery sale, passed in the same cause: auction on Nov 13, that piece of ground contained in square 226, fronting on Pa ave. -A Austin Smith, trustee -Jas C McGuire, auct]

From Texas: 1-On the 26th a violent storm or tornado swept over San Antonio: two esteemed citizens, Simeon C Rogers, of the firm of G F Rogers & Bro, & M S Ragland, a son of Judge Ragland, were struck by lightning during the storm. The riders & their animals were found lying together, struck down by a bolt so terrible that death ensued without a struggle. 2-Murders in different parts of the State: Jas Holt, Postmaster at Pine Grove Post Of, was recently shot down in cold blood by a man named Forrest, who made his escape. A stranger in feeble health, whose name is not known, was killed near Victoria by Owen D Eagan. A few days since a man named Odam deliberately shot down an unarmed German named Smith, residing on Buffalo Bayou. 3-The celebrated Vigil A Stewart, the capturer & historian of the land pirate John A Murrell, died recently at his residence in Wharton Co.

<u>The Criminal Court-Wash, met yesterday. The Grand Jurors are:</u>

Jacob Gideon	Dearborn B Johnson	Robt S Patterson
B F Middleton	John C McKelden	Thos Berry
G C Grammar	Chas H Lane	Valentine Harbaugh
Wm Easby	John M Donn	Wm T Dove
Robt Clarke	Esau Pickrell	Selby Scaggs
Almon Baldwin	John L Kidwell	Wm B Magruder
Augustus E Perry	Wm H Edes	Henry Haw
Reuben B Clarke	Joshua N Fearson	Saml McKenney

<u>The Petit Jury:</u>

Albert P Waugh	Saml McKnight	John M Thornton
Alex'r Borland	Thos J Stelle	Wm A Kennedy
Jas Miller	Henry H McPherson	John T Bradley
J L Miller	Saml Iddins	Thos Tanner
Joh Scribner	Benedict Milbern	Geo W Godey
Lewis C Hootee	John Howse	Jas B Holmead
Jos Lyons	Edw H Edelin	John R W Mankin
David W Oyster	Aaron Divins	Wm B Dyer
Joshua Hilton	John D Evans	Chas McCarty
Geo Harvey	Saml Wroe	Geo W Stewart

Mrd: on Jun 15, at the Univ of Va, by Rev Wm H McGuffey, Wm Walker Stewart, M D, of Colerain Forges, Pa, to Miss Mary H McGuffey, eldest daughter of the officiating clergyman.

Died: on Jun 18, in Wash City, Jos J Merrick, formerly of Md, in his 64th year. His funeral is Jun 21, from his late residence on F st, between 6th & 7th sts, at 11½ A M.

Died: on Jun 18, of dysentery, Lina, the infant daughter of Wm H & Selina Haslam, of Wash, aged 7 months & 16 days.

Died: yesterday, in Wash City, Jos Elgar, formerly Comr's of Public Bldgs, in his 81st year. Mr Elgar died at a ripe & golden age, venerated & beloved for his integrity & intelligence. In the full possession of his mind & all its affections, he fell gently asleep. His funeral will take place today, at 4½ o'clock, from the residence of his son-on-law, Chas E Sherman, on 3rd st.

U S Patent Ofc, Wash, Jun 19, 1854. Ptn of Geo Draper, of Milford, Mass, praying for the extension of a patent granted to him on Oct 28, 1840, for an improvement in Rotary Temples for Looms, for 7 years from the expiration of said patent, which takes place on Oct 28, 1854. –Chas Mason, Com'r of Patents

Providence, Jun 19. On Sat night, at Millville, Mass, Alex'r Herett, in a fit of jealousy shot his own wife & a man named Owen Brown, to whose house she had fled for protection. He then commited suicide by taking strychnine. Mrs Hewett lingers, but cannot live.

At Sandusky, Ohio, on Tue, Alex'r Derr, a carpenter employed in shingling the cupola of the new Presbyterian meeting-house in that city, stepped on a loose plank at the height of 60 feet, fell, & was killed. The plank in its fall struck a stone Mason, Michl Western, who was also killed.

Jos Radcliff & Son: Commission Merchants & Manufacturers' Agents, Wholesale & Retail Dealers in Agricultural & Horticultural Implements & Machinery, Fertilizers, Seeds, etc, Odd Fellows' Hall, 7th st, Wash.

WED JUN 21, 1854
Mrs Richardson, wife of Amasa W Richardson, of North Adams, Mass, died on Thu in consequence of inhaling chloroform administered by Dr C E Streeter for the purpose of extracting a tooth. –Springfield Republican

Nurse wanted, a steady & competent person, well recommended. Apply to Mrs W C Zantzinger, corner of E & 9th sts.

Farm for sale: 226 acres in PG Co, Md, near Beltsville, Md: adjoins the farm belonging to Mr H Kiernan. –Morss, Stansbury & Co, corner of 8th & E sts.

Heavy robbery: the jewelry store of Mr Claudius Redin, at New Orleans, was robbed of jewelry to the amount of fifteen or eighteen thousand dollars on Jun 10th & 11th.

One Cent reward, & no thanks, will be given for the return of my indentured apprentice Fred'k Langlots, who ran away from me on Jun 15, which is the 3rd or 4th time he has run away from me. –Geo Bower, Confectioner, on the Island.

Mrd: on Jun 20, by Rev Mr Hodges, Wm L Nelson to Miss Ann R Duncan, of Prince Edw Co, Va.

Died: on Jun 18, in Gtwn, D C, in his 71st year, Mr Jos Chick, a native of Cecil Co, Md, & for 52 years a resident of Gtwn.

Died: on Jun 18, in Balt, Edw Ferry, aged 44 years.

Senate: 1-Ptn from John S Pendleton, asking compensation for services on a special mission to negotiate a treaty with the Oriental Republic of Uruguay in the years 1852 & 1853, under instructions from the Pres of the U S. 2-Ptn from Thos W Mather, of N Y, & Wm R Glover, of Ky, merchants trading with Mexico, asking indemnity for property forcibly seized by ofcrs of that Republic. 3-Cmte on Revolutionary Claims: asked to be discharged from the further consideration of the ptns of Rebecca P Stansbury & others, heirs of Thos Peters & of Moven Moore, & that they be referred to the Cmte on Pensions: which was agreed to. Same cmte: bill to pay the heirs of Stephen Morrell, deceased, the amount due their father for a pension. Same cmte: adverse report on the ptn of Jas H Bradford. 4-Cmte of Claims: asked to be discharged from the further consideration of the House bill for the relief of Henry Lewis, of Clinton Co, Indiana, & that it be referred to the Cmte on Pensions: which was agreed to.

THU JUN 22, 1854
Household & kitchen furniture at auction Jun 28, at the residence of J P Tubbs, on 11th st, between H & I sts. -Green & Scott, aucts

Theodore Parker, Saml G Howe, Wendall Phillips, C M Ellis, & other leading Abolitionists are sending printed circulars to different towns in New England, requesting that the usual Fourth of July celebration be omitted & that the bells be tolled instead. The Selectmen of Marblehead, Mass, have deemed it unworthy of notice & returned it from whence it came.

Senate: 1-Ptn from Mary Kinner & Mary C McCoy, asking to be indemnified for losses sustained in depreciation of their property in consequence of delays interposed by the land ofcs in proving their title. 2-Ptn from Robt Mills, architect, in relation to a central railroad to the Pacific. This is an elaborate document of some 40 or 50 pages. 3-Cmte on the Dist of Columbia: bill for the relief of Jas Dixon: passed. Same cmte: asked to be discharged from the further consideration of the memorial of Wm Gunton & others, asking a further allowance for the bridge across the Eastern Branch of the Potomac: which was agreed to. 4-Cmte on Patents: bill for the relief of Cyrus H McCormick. 5-Cmte on Indian Affairs: adverse report on the memorial of Geo Stealey. 6-Cmte on Pensions: adverse reports on the ptns of Fred'k Drurio; of P C Miles; of Uriah Jones ; & of Sarah Harman.

R F Phelps, a young man, was drowned on Monday whilst bathing in the Potomac. He was from Fauquier Co, Va, & was in the employ of Mr Baker, of the Exchange Hotel. His age was about 20 years. The body was yesterday committed to the keeping of the tomb at St Patrick's Church.

Special meeting of St John's Lodge, No 11, of Free & Accepted Masons, was held at the Masonic Hall, in Wash City, on Jun 17, on the occasion of the death of our Brother Saml H Houston, to adopt measures for testifying our grief & pay tribute to his many virtues. A cmte, Brothers Lynde Eliot, Marcus Bull, & Hopkins Lightner were appointed to draft the resolutions.

Died: on Jun 21, in Wash City, in her 60th year, Joanna, wife of Maj Parke G Howes, of the Marine Corps. Her funeral will take place at St Patrick's Church on Jun 23 at 9:30 o'clock. The friends & relatives of the deceased are to meet at the residence of the family at 9 o'clock.

Died: on Jun 21, Nathan H Topping, infant son of Mary E & Nathan H Topping, aged 8 months. His funeral is this evening at 5 o'clock, without further notice.

Died: on Jun 18, in Wash, Geo Duncan, aged 36 years, a native of Scotland, but for the last 16 years a citizen of the U S.

House of Reps: 1-Cmte on the Post Ofc & Post Roads: bills for the relief of Jas Jeffries & Jeremiah M Smith; of John W Kelly; & of Rebecca J Burdsall. 2-Cmte on Military Affairs: jont resolution for the settlement of the claim of Don Juan Jesus Vigil: committed.

Springfield [Tenn] Intelligencer: at Port Royal Mills on Sat week, Miss Adams, Miss Maddon, & Miss Picket, with Mr S Weatherford, were attempting to cross Red river in a canoe, when it upset. The young ladies all drowned.

FRI JUN 23, 1854
Senate: 1-Ptn from John C Fremont, asking that the Sec of the Interior may be authorized to examine & settle upon principles of equity his claim for beef furnished by him under a contract with the Com'rs of the U S for treating with the California Indians in 1851 for the use of said Indians. 2-Cmte on Pensions: bill for the relief of Catharine Dickerson. Same cmte: adverse report on the ptn of Sarah Morey. 3-Cmte on Revolutionary Claims: bill for the relief of Phineas M Nightingale, adm of the estate of Gen Nathl Greene, deceased.

The 12 year old son of Richd Avery, was drowned a few days ago in the Chenango river, N Y, from diving into the river & getting his head fast in the roots of a large tree, so that he was unable to extricate himself.

Died: on Jun 22, John W Gibbons, of Mississippi, [late a clerk in the Treasury Dept,] in his 40th year. His funeral will take place from his residence on Indiana ave, between 2nd & 3rd sts, Jan 23, at 10 o'clock.

Died: on Jun 18, at the residence of her brother, Dr W S Keech, Chas Co, Md, Miss Catharine A Keech, leaving a large circle of devoted friends to mourn her sudden death. Being the eldest of her family, her loss will be severely felt by her 2 brothers & several surviving sisters. She was not only by her own family beloved, but a favorite with all who knew her.

Died: on May 20, at his residence, in PG Co, Md, Thos Wood, in his 60th year. Protracted disease had long since shattered his health & forbidden his engaging in the duties or pleasures of life, yet he was ever a bright example to those around him of Christian contentment & resignation. As a husband, parent, master & neighbor, he was beloved by a large acquaintance & esteemed by those who knew him.

Lynchburg Virginian: yesterday the lifeless body of Josiah Holbrook, of Wash, D C, was found in Black Water creek, near the mouth of the Tunnel. He had been staying in this city for several months, occupied in scientific pursuits, especially geological, to which he was enthusiastically devoted. It is supposed that he met his death by falling down a cliff into the creek. He had been absent from his boarding house since Sat morning.

Richmond Enquirer: some 40 free negroes, liberated by the will of Mr Gunnell, late of Jefferson Co, Va, were taken to Pa 2 or 3 days ago, but, after remaining there a few days, a number of them returned to Va, intending to go to Liberia.

Orphans Court of Wash Co, D C. Letters of administration on the personal estate of Jas Payne, late of Wash Co, deceased. –John Payne, adm

Orphans Court of Wash Co, D C. Letters of administration on the personal estate of Francis N Shaw, late of Wash Co, deceased. –Thos C Connolly, adm

$200 reward for runaway, light color, Joshua Holmes, about 17 years of age. –Philip Mackey, corner of 4th & I sts.

SAT JUN 24, 1854
House of Reps: 1-Cmte on the Judiciary: adverse report on the ptn of Pierre Menard & Jos Bogy. Same cmte: bill for the relief of Henry Gardner & others; & a bill for the relief of Geo Mattingly: committed. Same cmte: bill for the relief of Thos Ap Catesby Jones, surety for a former postmaster at Norfolk, Va: committed. 2-Cmte on Revolutionary Claims: bill for the relief of Thos Underhill, exc of Thos Underhill, deceased: committed. Same cmte reported the following bills-each committed: relief of the legal reps of Everard Meade; of the heirs of Larkin Smith; of the heirs of Lt Willis Wilson; & of Nathl Reddick, adm of Richd Taylor, deceased. Same cmte: adverse reports on the ptns of the heirs of Dr Benj Ellis, of Maurice Langhorne, jrs, adm of Capt Wm H Avery's heirs; of the heirs of Lt Robt Eliott; & of the heirs of Rev Jas Craig. 3-Cmte on Private Land Claims: bill for the relief of John McVea & John F McKneely, of La; & a bill for the relief of Wm Curran: committed. Same cmte: following bills committed: relief of John Frazier & the adm of the estate of John G Clendenin, deceased; of Enoch S More; of Patrick Gass; of Rosalie Cazillo; of Wm J McElhenny, E P Matthews, & Lawrence Kribben; of A S Lougheny; & of Conrad Wheat & his legal reps. Same cmte: bill for the relief of Sylvanus Culver, with the recommendation that it do not pass: laid on the table. Same cmte: bill to confirm the claim of Wm H Henderson & the heirs of Robt Henderson to 500 acres of land in the Bastrop grant: committed. Same cmte: bills recommended that they pass & were committed: relief of Sylvester T Jerauld, assignee of the interest of Henry Richard; of Ira Baldwin; of Thos D Jennings; & of Juan M Luco & Jose L Luco. Same cmte: bills committed with the recommendation that they do pass: relief of Jos Campau; & of Manuel Hernandez. 4-Cmte on Military Affairs: bills with the recommendation that they do pass: committed: relief of Mrs Helen Mackay, admx of Lt Col Aeneas Mackay, late a deputy quartermaster in the U S Army; relief of Mrs Sally T B Cochrane, widow of the late Lt R E Cochrane, U S Army; relief of the excx of the late Brevet Col A C W Fanning, of the U S Army; relief of the heirs of Brig Gen Richd B Mason; & relief of Wm Claude Jones. 5-Cmte on Naval Affairs: bill for the relief of Jos Gonder, jr, & John Duff, with the recommendation that it pass: committed. 6-Cmte on Revolutionary Pensions: bill for the relief of Rebecca Baggerly, widow of David Baggerly, deceased: committed. Same cmte: bill for the relief of Rebecca Freeman, with the recommendation that it pass: committed. Same cmte: bills recommended that they pass: committed: relief of Jas Wormsley; of Mary Carlton; & of Sarah Crandall. Same cmte: bill committed: relief of Lt Francis Ware. Same cmte: adverse report on the ptn of Mary Boyd for a pension. Same cmte: bill for the relief of Jas Capen: committed. Same cmte: adverse reports on the ptns of Martha Scott; of Saml Ross, of Ohio; & of the children of Robt McNeil & Sarah his

wife. Same cmte: adverse report on the ptn of Julia Sherburne; & on the ptn of the heirs of Epaphras Ripley, of Vt. 7-Cmte on Invalid Pensions: bill for the relief of Jas Wright, of Tenn; & a bill for the relief of Wm Miller: committed. Same cmte: adverse reports on the ptns of Jas Chambers, of Pa; of Isaac Plummer; of Wm Guinard; of Benj Cressey; of Eli Darling; of Stephen Connor; of Mathew Wreford; of Wm Young, of F W Raborg; of Maj Wm Keller; of Washington Porter, of Edw Taylor, & of Wm Wilson. 8-Cmte on Naval Affairs: bill for the relief of Lewis E Simonds: committed. 9-Cmte on Invalid Pensions: bills committed: relief of Danl Morse, of Essex, Chittenden Co, Vt; of Ira Call; & of Isaac M Sigler, of Putnam Co, Ind. Same cmte: adverse reports on the ptns of Saml Cleveland; & of Geo Blake. 10-The bill of the Senate for the relief of Jas Jeffries & Jeremiah M Smith was referred to the Cmte of the Whole: passed. 11-Bills to which no objection was made: relief of: Moses Olmstead; pension for David Towle; pension for Capt Thos Porter; relief of Priscilla C Simonds; relief of Saml McKnight, of Ky; relief of Wm Wallace, of Ill; relief of Geo M Bentley, of Indiana; relief of Zadoc C Inghram; relief of Llewellen Worthington; relief of Ira Day, of Vt; relief of Wm G Howison; relief of the heirs of Capt Mathew Jack, deceased; relief of the heirs of Lot Hall, deceased; & relief of the legal reps of Henry Hoffman.

News comes to us clothed in mourning for the death of Elder Willard Richards, one of the Mormon saints, who leaves some 20 desolate wives to mourn his loss. At his funeral Elder G A Smith made a prayer, blessing the widows of thy servant Willard.

Household & kitchen furniture at auction: Jun 29, at the residence of the late Jos J Merrick, No 6 Union Row, on F st, near 7th st. -J C McGuire, auct

Richd M Eskridge, of Sumter Co, has been sentenced to 11 years' imprisonment in the penitentiary; crime, mayhem on a slave. It appears that Eskridge was intoxicated, & about to whip the slave; she retreated with an axe in her hand; he seized his gun & shot her in the leg, just below the knee, rendering amputation necessary.

Mrd: on Thu, by Rev John C Smith, Mr Danl McRae to Miss Mgt Cunningham, all of Wash City.

Died: on Jun 22, at the residence of her father, in Wash City, Mrs Eulalia Crawford Edwards, wife of Dr Lewis A Edwards, U S Army, & daughter of Hon T Hartley Crawford. Her funeral will take place this afternoon, at 4 o'clock.

Died: on Jun 21, in Wash City, Mrs Joanna Howle, wife of Maj P G Howle. As wife, mother, sister, mistress, & friend, she was pre-eminently a pattern. From early childhood she had been a firm & devoted member of the Catholic Church.

Died: on Jun 22, Edwin Cecil, only child of Edwin C & Evelyn P Morgan, aged 1 month & 8 days.

Prospect Hill for sale: contains 65 acres, overlooking Wash City, Gtwn, Navy Yard, & Alexandria. Come & see for yourself, John A Bartruff.

MON JUN 26, 1854
Appointments by the Pres: 1-A Herbemont, of S C, to be Consul for the port of Genoa, in Sardinia. 2-S Ricker, of Louisiana, to be Consul for Hesse Cassel, Hesse Darmstadt, & Nassau.

The legacies which have been bequeathed under the will of the late Mr Jas Montgomery, the poet, to local charities are as follow: Fulneck Moravian schools, 500L; Moravian missions, 300L; Sheffield boys' charity school, 50L; girls' charity school, 50:; national schools, 50:; the Aged Female Society, 50:; the boys Lancasterian school, 25:; the girls Lancasterian school, 25:. All to be paid exempt from duty & to be paid 12 months after the decease of the testator. The will was made 27 years ago, in the year 1827. –Sheffield Times

House of Reps: 1-Ptn of Levi Eldridge, in behalf of himself & others, for allowance of bounty to schnr **Harriet**, of Chatham, was withdrawn from the files & referred to the Cmte of Commerce. 2-Bills passed: relief of: Moses Olmstead; of Priscilla C Simonds; of Saml McKnight, of Ky; of Wm Wallace, of Ill; of Geo M Bentley, of Ind; of Zadoc C Inghram; of Llewellen Washington; of Ira Day, of Vt; of Wm G Howison; of the heirs of Capt Mathew Jack, deceased; of the heirs of Lot Hall, deceased; & of the legal reps of Henry Hoffman. Also, a pension for David Towle; & a pension for Capt Thos Porter.

The brig **Union**, from Turks Island Jun 6, has arrived at Boston: Mr Nelson, the American Consul, has been sent to prison for the non-payment of a fine imposed by a court for an assault upon an official of the island. He was still in prison when the **Union** left the island. Mr Nelson was determined not to pay the fine, saying that he would leave his Gov't to take him out. Some of his friends on the island advised him to pay the fine, but he declined. Mr Nelson alleges the sentence was the result of a personal feeling against him & calls upon the American Gov't to redress his wrongs. -Boston Traveller

Hon Danl Wells, Chief Justice of the Court of Common Pleas of Mass, died suddenly on Fri at his residence in Cambridge, his malady appearing to be a disease of the heart. He was about 63 years of age.

Mrd: on Jun 22, at Princeton, by Rev Mr Peterkin, Lt John C Howell, U S Navy, to Mary, daughter of Hon Robt F Stockton.

Mrd: in Wash City, on Sat, by Rev Mr Sunderland, F Cosby to Anna Smith, daughter of Robt Mills, Architect.

Died: on Sunday, in Wash City, at the residence of Dr Green, of consumption, Wm B North, late of Newark, N J, & son of the late Stephen North, of Phil.

New Boston, Clermont Co: on Sunday, Anderson Patterson, aged 20 years, out of wanton mischief, pointed a loaded shot gun at his widowed mother, not believing it to be loaded, pulled the trigger, & shot his mother in the face, completely tearing away the whole of her lower jaw & a greater portion of the tongue. At last report she was still alive. –Albany Register

Army Genr'l Order: War Dept, Adj Genrl's Ofc, Wash: Jun 21, 1854. The Sec of War has received from the Dept of Texas & New Mexico the official accounts of the engagements which have recently taken place between the detachments of the army & hostile bands of the warlike tribes of Indians inhabiting those regions of country. In these various encounters the conduct of Lt Col P St Geo Cooke, 2nd Dragoons; 2nd Lt John W Davidson, 1st Dragoons; 2nd Lt David Bell, 2nd Dragoons; 2nd Lt Geo B Cosby, Mounted Riflemen; & Sgts C B McNally, John Green, & John Williams, of the same regt, severally in command on the different occasions, merit special praise for gallantry, fortitude, & devotion exhibited by the troops in every instance of combat; & receive the marked approbation of the Pres & of this Dept. The measures adopted by Brv Maj Gen Smith & Brvt Brig Gen Garland, respectively in command of the Military Depts of Texas & New Mexico, are approved. By order of the Sec of War: W G Freeman, Assist Adj Gen.

Liberal reward for runaway negro boy Wm Javis, formerly the property of Hon Senator Walker, & known by the name of Bill Walker. –Alfred Jones, First Ward

TUE JUN 27, 1854
Brvt Maj Benj Alvord, capt 4th Infty, has been appointed a Paymaster in the army, vice Van Buren, resigned on Jun 1. Jos Bryan, Purser U S Navy, has resigned, & Henry Myers, of Georgia, appointed in his stead, has been confirmed. -Star

Missing soldier from **Fort Myers** found on Jun 7, by Capt Snell, having subsisted entirely upon wild fruit for about 37 days. Surely Florida is a great country, starvation being next to an impossibility. The little daughter of Mr Tillis, about 10 years of age, who was lost 19 days in Dec last, subsisted upon raw palmetto.

Wm A Jenkins was tried in Jefferson Co, N Y, last week for seduction, under the promise of marriage, under the law of 1848. It was the first tried of the kind ever had in that county. The jury rendered a verdict of guilty. The prisoner was sent to the State prison at Auburn for the term of 3 years.

A healthy wet nurse wanted, without child. Apply to G M Singleton, at the U S Hotel.

Senate: 1-Ptn from Lewis Dent, asking compension for the supplies of cattle & flour furnished to the U S Com'rs for treating with the Calif Indians in 1851. 2-Ptn from Myles T Wooley, a soldier of the Revolution, asking a pension. 3-Ptn from citizens of N Y, asking that a contract may be entered into with Christian Hanson for carrying the mails in steamers from Brooklyn & N Y C to Bremen. 4-Ptn from Capt Thos Ap C Jones, asking the restitution of his pay suspended by order of court martial. 5-Ptn from Wm B Scott, late navy agent in Wash City, asking to be allowed a commission on disbursements made by him as pension agent. 6-Ptn from Moses Pettit, of Crawfordsville, Ind, asking to be indemnified for certain moneys deposited by him with the register of the land ofc at Crawfordsville, Ind, for the purchase of land, & by that ofcr converted to his own use. 7-Cmte on Pensions: recommended their passage: relief of Benj Hammond, of the State of N Y; of Henry N Halsted; of Albro Tripp; of Jas M Lewis; & of Jas K Welch. 8-Cmte on Private Land Claims: bill for the relief of the assignees or legal reps of Jacques Moulon, recommending its passage. Same cmte: asked to be discharged from the further consideration of the memorial of Mary Kinnier & Mary C McCoy, & that it be referred to the Cmte of Claims: which was agreed to. 9-Cmte on Indian Affairs: asked to be discharged from the further consideration of the memorial of Jas Pool, & that it be referred to the Cmte of Claims: which was agreed to.

Gifted young townsman, Wm D Washington, is now an art-student with Leutze, the head of the Dusseldorff school. At the house of his gratified parents, I was invited to look at his filial offering from a foreign land. Beyond doubt he will make a painter.

Mrd: Jun 26, by Rev Mr Hodges, Judson Butler to Miss Mary Garner, of PG Co, Md.

Mrd: Jun 26, by Rev Mr Hodges, Wm Vension to Julia Ann Curtin, of PG Co, Md.

Mrd: Jun 24, by Rev Mr Finckel, Mr Jos Reese to Isabella C Brown.

Wash Co, D C: two estray cows came to my premises on Jun 5; both give milk. Owner is to come forward, prove property, pay charges, & take them away. -Sarah Ann Nally, Pa ave, near the **Congressional Burying Ground**.

I certify that John Fitzgerald, of Wash Co, D C, brought before me, as an estray, a large Red Cow & her calf. –John L Smith, J P [Owner is to come forward, prove property, pay charges, & take them away. –John Fitsgerald, **English Hill**, between 2nd & G sts.]

WED JUN 28, 1854
Died: on Mar 30, at sea, Oliver Henry Melville, a native of Edinburgh, in his 39th year. Four years ago Mr Melville left this place for the gold regions of Calif, where he worked assiduously for nearly 2 years without success. Thence he went to Australia & engaged in the mines; disappointment again met him, & he lost his health. Finally, he resolved to rejoin his family in the U S, & took shipping for America. But he was destined never to revisit his adopted country & his waiting friends. Before the voyage was half completed his broken constitution gave way, & he breathed his last among strangers.

Died: on Jun 14, at his residence, in PG Co, Md, John H Marbury, in his 51st year.

Madame Sontag, the opera singer, died at Vera Cruz of cholera on Jun 16.

Proposals will be received by the undersigned until Jul 6, for walling & flooring *Tiber Creek* through that portion of square 630 occupied by John Foy. –Francis B Lord, Com'r 2nd & 4th Wards. -T H Parsons, Jas Crutchett, Assist Com'rs

Senate: 1-Ptn from John Shaw, asking compensation for services as interpreter at the trial in the Circuit Court of the U S in the Territory of Michigan in 1828 of certain Winnebago Indians who were indicted for murder. 2-Ptn from Andrew Allison & others, asking that provision may be made in our treaties with foreign nations for the settlement by arbitration of all international difficulties. 3-Cmte on Pensions: bill for the relief of Sherman Pierce. Same cmte: adverse report on the petition of Mgt Johnstone. Same cmte: bill for the relief of Henry J Snow: recommended its passage. Same cmte: asked to be discharged from the further consideration of the ptn of Eliz Monroe. 4-Cmte on the Judiciary: bill for the relief of Chas Sterun. 5-Cmte of Claims: adverse report on the ptn of Chas Horner. 6-Bills from the House referred: to create & provide a pension for David Towle; for relief of Saml McKnight, of Ky; of relief of Wm Wallace, of Ill; of Geo M Bentley, of Ind; of Wm G Howison; of the heirs of Capt Matthew Jack, deceased; of the heirs of Lot Hall, deceased; & of the legal reps of Henry Hoffman. Also, to create & provide a pension for Capt Thos Porter.

Two men, Clark & Elkins, were killed by lightning on Jun 7, while sheltering themselves under a tree near Defiance, Ohio.

Simon S Stubbs was elected Mayor of Norfolk, Va, on Sat. His competitor was Humphrey Woodis.

Orphans Court of Wash Co, D C. Letters of administration, with the will annexed, on the personal estate of Francis N Shaw, late of Wash Co, deceased. –Edw Shaw, adm, with the will annexed.

THU JUN 29, 1854
Senate: 1-Ptn from Mrs Jane Gaston, of S C, widow of Jos Gaston, asking that the invalid pension granted to her husband in his life may be granted to her. 2-Ptn from Gaston T Raoul, asking permission to enter a section of land under a certificate duly issued by the register & receiver of the Greensburg land district. 3-Ptn from Wm Brown, asking compensation for services rendered & losses sustained in the war of 1812. 4-Ptn from Anne S P Chew, of Pa, asking that a claim for outfit of Wm S Chew as Charged d'Affaires to Russia, preferred by him in his lifetime, may be allowed to his estate. 5-Cmte on the Judiciary: asked to be discharged from the further consideration of the memorial of Clements Bryan & Co, & that it be referred to the Cmte of Claims: which was agreed to. 6-Cmte on Pensions: bill for the relief of Abraham Cutter. Same cmte: adverse report on the ptn of Gabriel Denton.

A man named Alex'r A Thompson, convicted last week of kidnapping a free negro boy, Chas Barnes, & attempting to sell him in Richmond, Va, has been sentenced to 4 years' imprisonment in the penitentiary & to pay a $50 fine.

Mrd: on Jun 15, at Lancaster, Pa, by Rev H A Schultz, Dr J M Foltz, Surgeon U S N, to Miss Rebecca Steinman, daughter of John F Steinman.

Columbian College, D C: annual commencement yesterday in E st Baptist Church, Rev Dr Bacon, Pres of the College, opened with prayer: Mr Geo French Bowie, of PG Co, Md, one of the candidates for the degree of Bachelor of Philosphy, pronounced a judicious oration on the abuses of the press. Oration on American Youth by Willis J Palmer, Milton, N C; & Women's Rights, by Wm T Robins, Gloucester Co, Va. The Times We Live In was pronounced by Edw Hartley, of Wash City, one of the candidates for the First Degree in the Arts. Degree of Bachelor of Philosophy was conferred on: G F Bowie, Md; S J Cook, D C; W J Palmer, N C; W T Robins, Va; & J D Stanford, N C. First Degree in the Arts & Sciences conferred on: L D Gowen, Mr; E Hartley, D C; & R H Rawlings, Va. Second Degree was conferred on: Geo S Bacon, N Y; A F T Biewend, Missouri; J W Garlick, Va; Robt Hall, Va; B Johnson Hellen, D C; C C Speiden, D C; & J I Wallace, Ga.

The clothing & woolcarding works of Mr Wm Pierce, of Albany, N Y, worth $1,600, & insured for $1,000, were destroyed by fire on May 3. He forwarded the proof to the insurance company; but, before it was obtained, he committed suicide by hanging himself, & left a letter to his family: I wish to make a confession that I fired my clothing works without any of my family having any knowledge of the same, & I see the great injustice I have done myself & family by injuring us all. My desire is that the Almighty would be merciful to you all. Oh, my children, take warning of this; let nothing tempt you. –Wm Pierce

Died: on Jun 27, at her residence in Montg Co, Md, Maria A Waterman, wife of Edwin Waterman. Her funeral will be at the residence of her brother, Adam L Rose, 7th st east, at 3 o'clock this afternoon.

Died: on Jun 27, at the residence of her brother, after a long & painful illness, which she bore with Christian fortitude, Miss Mary Colclazer, in her 74th year.

FRI JUN 30, 1854
Household & kitchen furniture at auction: Jul 3, at the residence of Dr S C Smoot, on the south side of Pa ve, between 19th & 20th sts. -J C McGuire, auct

Trustee's sale of house & lot at auction: on Jul 21, by deed of trust from Mary Barnes, dated Jul 9, 1852: recorded in Liber J A S No 45, folios 110 thru 113, of the land records for Wash Co, D C: all that part of lot 4 in square 783, Wash City, fronting on Md ave, near 3rd st. –Jas Rhodes, trustee -Green & Scott, aucts

Wash Corp: 1-Ptn of Philip T Ellicott & others, asking remission of taxes erroneously paid the Corp: referred to the Cmte on Finance. 2-Act to refund G W Fridley the amount of a fine: referred to the Cmte of Claims. 3-Election of police magistrates for the remaining districts: Franklin S Myer, Saml Grubb, Benj K Morsell, Jos W Beck, Jas Crandell, & Craven Ashford. Jas W Barker elected assessor for the 2nd Ward in place of Geo H Plant, who resigned. 4-Mr Clarke moved that Saml Armstead have leave to withdraw his petition & papers from the files of this Board: carried in the affirmative. 5-Ptn of Leonard Baum & others respecting the drainage of squares 483, 515, & north of 514: referred to the Cmte on Improvements.

Orphans Court of Wash Co, D C. Letters of administration on the personal estate of Harriet E Jardine, late of Wash Co, deceased. –B L Jackson, adm

Mrd: on Jun 27, in Phil, by Rev Henry J Morton, D D, Ferdinand Coxe to Fanny Travis Cochran, daughter of Wm G Cochran, of Phil

Mrd: on Jun 28, by Rev Jas H Brown, Mr Jas R Harrover to Miss Virginia Larker, both of Wash.

Mrd: on Jun 29, by Rev A G Carothers, Mr Wm W McCathran to Miss Maria V Bradley, all of Wash City.

Died: on Jun 29, Dr Alex'r Speer, of the 5th Auditor's ofc. His funeral services will be at the 1st Presbyterian Church, 4½ st, on Sat, at 8:30 o'clock.

St Louis, Jun 28. Death of an Indian Agent. Despatches from Independence report the death of Judge Brown, agent for the Pottawatomie Indians.

Lt Payne, U S Army, died at Jefferson Barracks on Jun 23. Some cases of cholera have happened, it is said, at that post.

SAT JUL 1, 1854
House of Reps: 1-Bill for relief of A B Roman, of La, passed. 2-Cmte on Invalid Pensions: bill to provide a pension for Sgt G W Torrents: passed. 3-Act for relief of the reps of John Donaldson, Stephen Heard, & others: referred to the Cmte on Revolutionary Claims. 4-Cmte on Public Lands: adverse reports on ptns of John Ketchum; of Eliz Evans & Henry Lake, of Ohio; of the heirs of Jas Thompson; & of Mgt Bowne. Same cmte: bill for relief of Mary H Cushing. 5-Cmte on Judiciary: bill for relief of John G Camp: committed. 6-Cmte on Revolutionary Claims: discharged from the further consideration of the ptn of Isaac S Bowman: laid on the table. Same cmte: bills for relief of the legal reps of Saml Prioleau, deceased; & for relief of Eliza M Evans, with the recommendation they pass: committed. Same cmte: adverse report on ptn of the heirs of Lt Silas Goodal, of the continental line. 7-Cmte on Private Land Claims: bill for relief of the legal heirs of Benj Metoyer, deceased: committed. 8-Cmte on Military Affairs: bills recommended that they pass: committed-relief of Wm Harris, of Ga; of Jas Edwards & others;& of Thos Snodgrass. Same cmte: ptn of Capt Langdon C Easton, Assist Quartermaster of the U S Army, with the recommendation that it do not pass: laid on the table. Same cmte: bill committed: relief of Wm H Weirick; of the heirs of Jas Greer, deceased; of John H King; & of Eleanor Hoople, of the Province of Canada. Same cmte: granting boundy land to Cornelius Coffey; & granting 160 acres of land to Francis M Gwyn, of Indiana. Same cmte: adverse reports on the ptns of Russell Rice; of N G Evans, lt 2nd dragoons, U S Army; of Saml M Latimer; of Chas J Burgess; of John H King, of Harpers' Ferry; of Henry K Brown; of Edw B Shelton; of Chas F Fisher, & of Capt H B Field. 9-The bill for the relief of the heirs & reps of Col Alex G Morgan, heretofore reported from the Cmte on Military Affairs with the recommendation that it do not pass, was recommitted to said cmte for further examination. 10-Cmte on Military Affairs: bill for relief of Chas W Carroll: committed. Same cmte: bill for the relief of Jean Baptiste, with the recommendation that it pass: committed. 11-Cmte on Revolutionary Pensions: adverse reports on the ptns of Robt Babcock; of Betsey A Faulkner; & of Bethiah Black. Same cmte: bill for increasing the pension of John Cole: committed. 12-Cmte on Invalid Pensions: adverse reports on ptns of Eliz Wilson; of Saml McCleland; of Sherman McLean; of Saml Moore; of A Chamberlain; of Martia Townsend; of John Belding; & of Lewis Washburn. Same cmte: adverse reports on ptns of Mrs Clarrissa Poole; of Jos Pullen; of Gardner Herring; & of Bela Young. Same cmte: bill for relief of Evalina Porter, widow of the late Cmdor David Porter, U S Navy: committed. Same cmte: bill for relief of Geo Lynch: committed. Same cmte: adverse reports on ptns of Wm Trumbull; of Silas Chatfield; of Pressley M Kellup; of Jos H Bailey; of John Henry; of Richd Oothoudt; of Geo Babcock; of A Coulter; of Chas Stuart;of Wm Pace; of Sophia Davis; & of Danl Lookingbill. Same cmte: bills committed: relief of-Jos Webb; of John Steen; of Geo Willcott; of Mary Rutherford; & of Warren Raymond.

13-Cmte on Indian Affairs: adverse report on the memorial of Dr J R Wooster, praying the establishment of schools among the Calif Indians.

Senate: 1-Cmte of Claims: bill for the relief of Isaac Swain. 2-Bill for the relief of Phineas M Nightingale, adm of the estate of Gen Nathl Greene, deceased. Mr Bell moved to amend the bill by allowing interest on the claim from 1794: it was passed & amended. 3-Bill for the relief of Francis Lope Urriza: postponed. 4-Bill for the relief of Fred'k Vincent, adm of Jas Le Case, the survivor of Le Case & Mallet: passed. 5-Claim of Wm H Henderson & Robt Henderson to 500 acres of land in the Bastrop grant: passed. 6-Bill for the relief of Cornelius H Latham: pending-the Senate adjourned.

Mrd: on Thu, by Rev John C Smith, Mr John P Hurley to Miss Amanda Johnson, all of Wash City.

Mrd: on Jun 27, by Rev W C Steel, Mr Abner Parrot, of Gtwn, to Miss Eliza A Collins, of Wash, D C.

Died: on Jun 30, in Gtwn, D C, Mrs Sarah Cruikshank, in her 83rd year. Her funeral will be from her late residence on Potomac st, at 5:30 o'clock.

MON JUL 3, 1854
Senate: 1-Ptn from Frances Ann McCauley, widow of D S McCauley, late U S Consul Gen for Egypt, & Consul at Tripoli, asking indemnity for losses & expenses incurred by her husband while Consul at that place. 2-Ptn from Geo Gibson, asking the payment of certain bills of credit issued by the Continental Congress, which were deposited in the Treasury for redemption, & destroyed by the conflagration of the Treasury bldg in 1832. 3-Ptn from Richd S Coxe, Wm A Bradley, & Gilbert L Thompson, proposing to furnish for the use of the navy, composite coal, an article of fuel recently invented by them. 4-Ptn from Frederic Chatard, a Lt in the navy, asking certain allowance in the settlement of his accounts as acting purser of the U S storeship **Fredonia** in 1852. 5-Cmte on Naval Affairs: bill for the relief of Foxall A Parker, of the U S Navy. Same cmte: bill granting to Jasper Strong & his associates the right of way for a railroad through the reserved lands near the navy yard, Pensacola, in Florida. Same cmte: adverse report on the memorial of Jonathan D Ferris. 6-Cmte on the Judiciary: bill for the relief of Geo W Harris. [This bill vests in Mr Harris the copyright to the 13th, 14th, & 15th volumes of the Pa State reports.] 7-Cmte on Foreign Relations: bill for the relief of H S Sanford, late charge d'affaires at Paris. Same cmte: adverse report on the memorial of Robt M Hamilton, U S Consul at Montevideo. 8-Cmte of Claims: adverse report on the memorial of Henry Payson.

Orphans Court of Wash Co, D C. Letters testamentary on the personal estate of Jeremiah Cissell, late of Wash Co, deceased. –Sidney Evans, exc

Cincinnati [Ohio] Gaz: A stranger called upon Dr A H Baker making inquiries about Mr Isaac Allison, a student in the Cincinnati College & Medicine & Surgery & steward of the Marine Hospital. On Monday a box was delivered addressed to Mr Allison, Marine Hospital, corner of Western row & Longworth st, Cincinnati. The box was given to several people, warning them not to open it, & it was finally given to the matron of the house, Mrs Allison, who took the box to her room. She gave the box to her husband who opened the box & an explosion took place. Mrs Allison's clothes caught fire & her husband was mortally wounded. Mr Allison died in great agony. Mrs Allison had one arm badly torn, which was amputated. Her other hand, face, shoulders, & breast were dreadfully burnt. She died the next day. The perpetrator of the crime was Dr Wm H Arrison, who left on Tue by the way of the Ohio & Mississippi railway. He & Mr Allison had a disagreement, each being of the opinion that the other wanted to be arbitrary. Hard words had passed between them. Marshal Rufflin will leave this morning with the proper documents for the apprehension of Dr Arrison. [Jul 20th newspaper: Wm H Arrison has been arrested in Iowa.] [Jul 28th newspaper: it appears that Arrison was not arrested in Iowa, but stopped at his father's house but a short time, & then went further westward.] [Nov 14 newspaper: Wm Arrison was arrested in Muscatine, Iowa, a town on the Mississippi, by the Mayor & his party, in the drug store of Mr I B Dougherty, were Arrison was employed. He had been passing under the name of Willetts. He was brought back to Cincinnati, arriving here last night & is in the watch-house for safe-keeping.] [Dec 21st newspaper: The trial of Wm Arrison, at Cincinnati, for the murder of Mr Allison & his wife, was brought to a close yesterday by the Jury rendering a verdict of guilty of murder in the 1st degree.] [Dec 29th newspaper: Judge Flinn sentenced Arrison to be hung on May 11 next. The prisoner heard his terrible doom without the least apparent emotion.]

Louisville Journal: Henry Herriman, age 13 years, committed suicide. He had lost a little sister who belonged to the church. She had given him a prayer book on her death bed. He appeared desirous to be with her. He cut his throat from ear to ear, severing both jugular veins. He has left heart-broken parents & distressed relatives.

Died: on Jun 2, near Woodville, Sandusky Co, Ohio, Capt John D Hart, a citizen of Hancock, Md. He left his home on Apr 25 last to visit the scenes in which he took so conspicuous a part in the war of 1812 & 1814. He was at that time a captain of cavalry under Gen Thomas, of Pa, & from his efficient services received the highest encomiums from his superiors in command. He, with others, represented Wash Co in the Legislature of Md in 1844, when his State was dishonored by a refusal to discharge liabilities, etc, but he nobly sustained the Executive in all his measures proposed to redeem the fallen & degraded character of the State. He has left a large number of relations & friends to mourn his loss. Capt Hart died from cholera, supposed to have been contracted on the railroad. He was in his 68th year, & was for 30 years a punctual subscriber to the Nat'l Intelligencer.

Appointments by the Pres, by & with the advice & consent of the Senate.
David A Starkweather, of Ohio, to be Envoy Extra Ordinary & Minister Pleni to Chili, in place of Saml Medary, resigned.
Robt Dale Owen, Lewis Cass, jr, John M Daniel, Henry R Jackson, Francis Schroeder, Henry Bedinger, August Belmont, J J Seibels, John L O'Sullivan, John W Dana, Jas A Peden, Philo White, Chas Eames, Jas S Green, to be Ministers Resident of the U S in the countries in which they are now Charge d'Affaires of the U S.

For the Territory of Nebraska:
Wm O Butler, of Ky, to be Govn'r.
Thos B Cumming, of Iowa, to be Sec.
Fenner Ferguson, of Mich, to be Chief Justice of the Supreme Court.
Edwin R Hardin, of Ga, to be Assoc Justice of the Supreme Court.
Jas Bradley, of Ind, to be an Assoc Justice of the Supreme Court.
Experience Estabrook, of Wisc, to be Atty.
Mark W Izard, of Ark, to be Marshal.

For the Territory of Kansas:
Andrew H Reeder, of Pa, to be Govn'r.
Danl Woodson, of Va, to be Sec.
Madison Brown, of Md, to be Chief Justice of the Supreme Court.
Sanders W Johnson, of Ohio, to be Assoc Justice of the Supreme Court.
Rush Ellmore, of Ala, to be an Assoc Justice of the Supreme Court.
Andrew J Isaacs, of Louisiana, to be Atty.
J B Donaldson, of Louisiana, to be Marshal.

Mrd: on Jun 20, at the residence of his father, by Rev L Campbell, of Vicksburg, B G Wyche, M D, to Miss Sallie E Gordon, all of Hinds Co, Miss.

Died: on Jul 2, in Wash City, Louther Taylor, of Md, in his 79th year. His funeral will be from the residence of his son-in-law, Col Chas Thomas, on N Y ave, at 4:30 this afternoon. His friends & those of his son-in-law are invited to attend.

Died: on Jun 30, after a few hours' illness, Julia May Wise, aged 5 years & 5 months, youngest daughter of Geo D Wise, of the U S Coast Survey.

I have this day sold my entire stock of Hardware to Messrs Elvans & Thompson, under which firm & at the same place the business will be conducted as heretofore. -H Lindsley -John R Elvans, Wm Thompson

Wed afternoon, during the thunder storm, two young fisherman of Kensington, F G Prescott & S Kennard, were out fishing near Petty's Island when they were both killed instantly when struck by lightning. Their bodies were found the next day in their boat. –Phil Ledger

Terrible affray: Mr C D Kelley, 2nd engineer on board the boat **G W Sparhawk**, told the boy washing upstairs to stop until he had finished working on the engine. The boy continued & Kelley struck him in the face. Kelley was met by Edw Augustus Dedieman & John Hyland, 1st & 2nd stewards of the boat, who said they would have revenge for the injury done the boy. Dediemen has a heavy piece of iron & Hyland has a loaded pistol. Kelly was unarmed, & snatched a carving knife, stabbing Dedieman just as he was about to hit him with the iron pipe, killing him instantly. Hyland discharged his pistol at Kelley, missing him, when Kelley rushed on him with his knife, & could have killed him if he had been disposed to do so. Hyland was taken to the hospital & bled to death before the wound was dressed. Kelley went to the police ofc & gave himself up for trial. He is a young man, & the ofcrs of the boat represent him to be a peaceable & well disposed person. –St Louis Republican of Jun 28.

Orphans Court of Wash Co, D C. In the case of Ann G V McKenstry & Wm B Webb, adms, with the will annexed of Wm McKenstry, deceased: the administrators & Court have appointed Jul 25th next for the distribution of the assets in hand.
-Ed N Roach, Reg/o wills

Western Presbyterian Church: Rev John C Smith has purchased from Messrs Silas H Hill & Jos B Varnum, jr, their valuable lot on H, near 19th st, & acknowledge the donation of $600 from those liberal gentlemen. Steps will be taken for the erection of a chaste & commodious house of worship on the lot purchased. Rev Thos N Haskell, Pastor, & congregation, worship in the house at the corner of E & 22nd sts.

TUE JUL 4, 1854
The **American Flag**. The first national flag of the present design, adopted in 1818, was made under the direction of the gallant Capt Reid, who commanded the privateer **General Armstrong**. It was made at his house in N Y, by his wife & a number of young ladies, & was first hoisted over the Hall of the House of Reps: on Apr 13, 1818, at 2 o'clock P M. On the admission of Indiana into the Union in 1816, Mr Peter H Wendover, of N Y, offered a resolution that a cmte be appointed to inquire into the expediency of altering the flag of the U S. A cmte was appointed but it was not acted upon. Mt Wendover called on Capt Reid, who was in Washington at the time, & requested him to form a design of our flag so as to represent the increase of the States without destroying its distinctive character. Capt Reid recommended that the stripes be reduced to the original number of 13 States, & to form the number of stars representing the whole number of States into one great star in the Union, adding one star for every new State, thus giving the significant meaning to the flag, symbolically expressed, of E pluribus unum." This design was adopted but did not pass till the next Congress in 1818.

Mrd: on Jul 3, by Rev Stephen P Hill, Henry Hagan to Louisa Jane Patterson.

Fatalities. 1-The 4 year old daughter of Mr Hoag, was drowned in the Blackstone river at Valley Falls, R I, on Mon. 2-In Boston on Tue night a child 6 months old, named John Crues, was suffocated while in bed with its parents. 3-Thos Kennedy, 12 years of age, while at play around a car-house in N Y on Wed, was run over & killed. 4-John Smith was shot dead by the accidental discharge of his own musket at Yorkville, Oneida Co, N Y, on Monday. 5-Andrew McGuire was instantly killed at Richmond, Va, on Tuesday by falling from the roof of a 5 story bldg, on which he was at work, to the ground. 6-At Rock Hill, S C, on Jun 20, Wm Wheeney was killed by the bursting of a cannon which he was engaged in firing, in consequence of neglecting to swab it properly. 7-Abram Williams, an Indian of the Oneida tribe, was run over by a locomotive & killed while walking upon the railroad track at Rome, N Y, on Tue. 8-Mrs Louisa Andrews, wife of Mr Jacob Andrews, of York, Pa, on returning from a visit to Lancaster on Wed, fell under the cars & had both legs so badly crushed as to require amputation. She died soon after, leaving a husband & 6 children. 9-A private letter states that Mr Gray, who was wounded in the battle with the Imperialists at Shanghai, has had his leg amputated. The Chinese loss in killed & wounded is estimated at from 200 to 500.

Anchorage off Yokohama, Bay of Jeddo, Mar 8, 1854. The reception of Cmdor Perry, today at Yokohama: the object was to lay before the Imperial Com'rs from the Court of Jeddo certain stipulations growing out of the letter of the Pres of the U S to the Emperor of Japan which was presented last summer. The boats, extending more than a mile in front of the shipping in line abreast, were under the command of Capt Buchanan, aided by Capt Pope on the right & Capt Lee on the left. Before returning to the shipping we were profusely supplied with bunches of the japonica tree, now in full bloom & towering to the height of 20 or more feet, & said to be abundant in the country.

Boston, Jul 3. In the U S Circuit Court this morning Capt Chas Kehrman, master of the brig **Glamorgan**, taken on the coast of Africa by the brig **Perry** & sent to this port, was convicted on the charge of being engaged in the slave trade. The **Glamorgan** sailed from N Y on Sep 3 last under command of Capt John Sterling. When a few days out she was so disabled that she had to return for repairs. A day later Capt Kehrman came on board when the mate & seamen were on shore.

Died: on Jun 30, Julia-May Gaither, 3rd daughter of the late Greenbury Gaither, of Wash City.

Died: on Jun 17, at St Paul's, Minnesota Territory, Albert N Sergeant, M D, of Meadville, Pa, in his 45th year. Dr Sergeant had gone to St Louis on account of the illness of his daughter, who was visiting there, &, thinking to improve the time taken in her convalescence by a trip to the Upper Mississippi, he was seized with cholera, & after a short illness died.

Died: on Jun 29, suddenly in Port Tobacco, Chas Co, Md, Mr Jas McCormick, formerly of Wash City, aged 54 years.

Report of Mr Marsh, U S Minister at Constantinople. The Greek Gov't sequestered certain lands belonging to Rev Dr King for national purposes, & refused to allow compensation therefore. Mr Marsh has examined the title connected with the affair, & decided the claim of Dr King is fully made out, & his only hope is to be found in the action of his own Gov't. With interest that has accrued, the lands in question are worth nearly $100,000.

Gunpowder explosion & loss of life: the opening of the new railroad from Cincinnati to Louisville was celebrated by an excursion on Thu. The train from Aurora, when nearing the Seymour depot, was firing salutes from a cannon, attached to the last platform car in the train. A small furnace, used for heating the rod with which the cannon was set off, lay close by the breech of the gun, & the wind, it is supposed, blew a spark of this fire into the chest where about a keg of two of powder had been emptied. An instant explosion occurred & 6 men who were on the car at the time were blown into the air & horribly mangled. Mr Robt P Squibb, age 45, died in a few hours; Mr John L Bailey, age 46, died that night; Mr Henry Doolan, a young Irishman, age 21, died the next day; Mr John R Watkins had his arm amputated-there are hopes of his recovery; Mr John Bailey, a young printer, had his face & ears badly burnt, & received other bodily injury; Mr Jas L Redding was severely burnt in the face & hands.

Died: on Jul 3, in Wash City, Thos Ritchie, in his 76th year. His funeral will take place at his residence tomorrow at 5 o'clock. His remains will afterwards be conveyed to Richmond. [Jul 7th newspaper: Large attendance at the funeral, on Wed, of the late venerable Thos Ritchie, at his residence. Among those present were the Pres of the U S, several heads of Depts, Sidney Webster, the Private Sec of the Pres, several Senators & many reps of the U S, as well as ofcrs of the army & navy. The funeral discourse was pronounced by Rev Dr Pyne, of St John's Church. Several of the children & relatives of the deceased were present. After the service, a funeral cortege proceeded to the steamboat wharf, whence the remains were conveyed in the mailboat en route for Richmond, their final resting-place. The pall-bearers were Senators Hunter & Mason, Messrs Bocock, Caskie, & Powell, of the House of Reps, & Sec Dobbin & W W Corcoran. The scene was most imposing. –Union]
:
Simpsonville for sale: the subscriber, intending to engage in another occupation, is desirous of selling the above property, situated immediately on the Plank Road, 5½ miles from Wash, & directly opposite the farm of Francis P Blair. This place contains 221 acres; a handome brick dwlg house, stables, & numberous out-houses. -Thos P Simpson

THU JUL 6, 1854

The *West Market*, 20th st & Pa ave, was completely destroyed. The cause was incendiary of course.

Criminal Court-Wash: 1-Geo King, from Balt, who robbed the room of Dr Morton & wife at the Nat'l Hotel, of jewelry, was convicted. 2-Chas Ross charged with stealing money, gold, & silver, value about $100, from Mr Ruppel, hotel keeper on 9th st: acquitted.

Mrd: on Jul 4, in Union Methodist Episcopal Church, by Rev F Israel, John E DeVaughan to Mary S Millson, all of Wash.

Mrd: on Jul 3, at Foundry Parsonage, by Rev E P Phelps, Mr Richd A Hyde to Miss Eliz A Tucker, of Wash City.

Mrd: on Jul 5, at the Woodyard, PG Co, Md, J W T Gardiner, 1st U S Dragoons, to Annie E West, daughter of the late John Hays, of Carlisle, Pa.

Died: on Jul 4, Hanson Gassaway, formerly & for many years a merchant in Wash City.

Died: on Jun 10, 1854, Emily Rebecca, aged 5 years, the youngest child of Hamilton & Louisa Loughborough.
+
Died: on Jul 3, David Augustine, youngest son of Hamilton & Louisa Loughborough.

Died: on Jul 2, at the *Vineyard Farm*, Chas Co, Md, George W, aged 17 months, only son of Thos & Pamela Milburn, of Wash City.

Household & kitchen furniture at auction: on Jul 10, at the residence of Mr Dement, on Pa ave, between 3rd & 4½ sts. -Green & Scott, aucts

Senate: 1-Cmte on Pensions: House bill for the relief of Chas Staples, reported it back without amendment, & recommended its passage.

C O Wall, Undertaker in all its branches. Funerals attended to at the shortest notice, in the best manner, & on the most reasonable terms. 7th st, between D & E. Residence on 6th st, between E & F sts, south side.

For rent, my 3 story brick house on Bridge st, my former residence, one of the best houses on that street, now in complete order, being newly painted, papered, & other improvements lately made. Apply to W S Nichols.

To Teachers: S L Slack offers for sale his School Property, located in one of the most thriving towns of South Arkansas, on the line of the Fulton Railroad. Address at Minden, Claiborne Parish, Louisiana. –S L Slack

Horrible railroad disaster on Tue to an Excursion train of Cars on the Susquehannah Railroad, not far from Balt, Md. The train was largely occupied by citizens who had been celebrating the day at **Rider's Grove**. The train hit the York train. Among the dead was Mrs Robinson, a young & beautiful woman, & Henry Clay Jeffers, the son of Madison Jeffers, a bright & beautiful boy. Benj Merryman, the baggage-master, met death standing manfully at his post on the front platform of the York train. Names of those killed: [Some persons have not been identified.]

Henry Reynolds	Julius Counsellor
Dr Thos Dorsey	Michl McCormick
Mrs Robinson	Lewis Cochran
David Murray	Benj Merryman
Henry Rose	Jas Boyd
Fred'k Decomb	Chas Boyd
Geo Pringol	Wm J Breaker
Patrick Tearney	John Wise, [colored]
Henry Clay Jeffers	B H Eareckson
Philip Magraw	Mr Munnymon
Robt Preston	Madison Jefferson
Jas Rea	

[Jul 7th newspaper: The accident was the result of carelessness, or rather of criminal impatience, on the part of Mr Wm Scott, the conductor of the York train. He did not strictly observe the time in the schedule.]

Washington C Page, the esteemed cashier of the Alexandria branch of the Farmers' Bank of Va, died suddenly on Tue. He spent the fourth in a happy rural excursion with his family, & in the succeeding night died of a stroke of apoplexy. Mr Page's father died many years ago with almost as much suddenness, & a brother, while delivering a 4th of July address to the Masonic Lodge of Alexandria, suddenly fell & expired.

A conspiracy to assassinate the Emperor Napoleon has been discovered in the South of France. One hundred & fifty arrests have been made.

FRI JUL 7, 1854
Trustee's sale of real estate: by deed of trust from Jas Thos Trundell, duly recorded in liber J A S No 69, folios 113 thru 117, of the land records for Wash Co: sale of lot 10 in square 675, fronting 58 feet on North I st, with a 2 story frame dwlg house. -C E Walker, Jno Y Donn, trustees -Jas C McGuire, auct

Household & kitchen furniture at auction: on Jul 17, at the residence of E A Keene, on North A st, near 1st st. -Jas C McGuire, auct

Senate: 1-Ptn from the execs of Danl Randall, late deputy paymaster general of the army, asking compensation for the services of the testator in receiving & disbursing the assessments levied in the city of Mexico for the support of the army during the late war with that Republic. 2-Cmte on Pensions: adverse reports on the ptn of Rebecca Stansbury & other heirs of Thos Peters: & on the ptn of Morin Moore. 3-Cmte on Territories: resolution to adjust & pay to Juan C Armijo, Jose L Perea, & Jas C Collins, the amount by them loaned to the Legislative Assembly of the Territory of New Mexico: passed. 4-Bill for the relief of Robt C Thompson, only surviving child & legal rep of Wm Thompson, deceased, formerly a brig gen in the army of the Revolutionary war: after protracted discussion the Senate adjourned without taking any questions.

Geo Hourine, in the employ of Messrs Shoenberger, of Pittsburgh, while uncoupling a pair of driving wheels in the machinery, slipped backwards between the roller, when his head was completely severed from his body.

Died: on Jul 6, in Wash City, after a lingering illness, Mary Ann, wife of John B Floyd. Her funeral will be from the residence of her father, Isaac Beers, on 3rd st, near Pa ave, on Jul 8, at 4 o'clock.

Died: on Jul 5, at his residence in Wash City, in his 47th year, Dr A J Schwartze, son of the late Dr A J Schwartze, of Balt Co, Md.

Died: on Jul 6, in Wash City, Elizabeth Jane, youngest child of Wm E & Teresa Ann Morcoe, aged 6 months. Her funeral is this morning at 9 o'clock.

Members of the Board of Health-Washington:
Dr S C Smoot: residence, Pa ave, between 19th & 20th sts.
Mr Chas Calvert: residence, 19th st, between I & K sts.
Dr Thos Miller: residence, Pa ave, near 14th st.
Dr John Riley: residence, 12th st, near Pa ave.
Dr Jas C Hall: residence, Pa ave, between 9th & 10th sts.
Mr W P Young: _____ [blank-Third Ward]
Dr Alex J Semmes: residence, 4½ st, near the City Hall.
Mr G C Grammer: residence, A st south, opposite the Capitol.
Mr John P Ingle: residence, N J ave, between C & D sts.
Dr F S Walsh: residence, 8th st east, between I & K sts north.
Dr Jas E Morgan: residence, Md ave, near 11th st.
Mr W B Randolph: residence, Md ave, beween 12th & 13th sts.
-Thos Miller, M D, Pres

R W Robertson & John G McBlair have purchased this day of J H McBlair his entire stock of Groceries, Wines, & Liqores & will continue the business at the Store, on Pa ave, between 17th & 18th sts, under the firm of R W Robertson & Co. J H McBlair can be seen by persons having business with him on the 2nd floor of the Store-house.

Josiah Emory, late postmaster at New Vineyard, has been sentenced by the U S District Court of Maine, in session at Bangor, to the State prison for 10 years, for purloining letters containing $150.

On Jun 12th, Purnell Jackson, of Worcester Co, Md, was bitten on the end of his fingers by a copper-head snake, from the effects of which he died the next day. When he died the whole of his arm & a portion of his body, the Shield says, were perfectly green.

Mr John Roper, of Dundalk, Ireland, was lately married at that place to Mrs Martha Porter. The groom is 91 years old, & has before had 2 wives, the last of whom was buried on Easter Monday. He is a pensioner from the 88th regt, & for more than 50 years has been receiving 1s per day from the Gov't. The bride is 72 years old, & has been a pensioner for 39 years, at 6d per day, on account of having lost her husband at the battle of Waterloo.

SAT JUL 8, 1854
The Galena & St Louis papers notice the death of Wm Hempstead, which took place at Galena, Ill, on Jun 20. He was an early settler of St Louis & a brother of Hon Edw Hempstead, the first Delegate in Congress from the Territory of Missouri. He removed from St Louis to Galena many years ago, & was a pioneer of the Upper Mississippi lead mines, & the contemporary of Gov Dodge, of Wisconsin, & Gen Jones, of Iowa, both of the U S Senate, in developing the vast mineral wealth of that country. He was the proprietor of the celebrated Shullsburgh mines, supposed to be the richest land mines in the U S.

The dwlg house of Mr Danl Wells, in the upper part of Alexandria Co, was destroyed by fire on Thu. Mr Wells is a worthy farmer, & the loss to him is very considerable.

Mr Shepard, the actor who lost his life by the burning of the Theatre at Phil, had time to escape with the other performers, but became a sacrifice by having stopped to change his clothes. He was about 28 years of age.

At the firing of a salute on the Fourth at Trenton, N J, Washington Reginald & Jacob Storms were badly injured by the accidental discharge of one of the guns. Mr Reginald's arm was amputated above the wrist at once, & it is said Mr Storm's arm will be amputated.

The Mason will case, involving $20,000 worthy of property, which has occupied Worcester Co [Md] Circuit Court for 3 weeks, has been disposed of by a verdict against its validity, on the ground of fraud & undue influence of the wife.

Mr Wm King, who for a half century or upwards has followed the business of Undertaker in Gtwn, conducted to the tomb more persons than now constitute its whole population. He died yesterday at age 82 years, & leaves behind him a large family, variously distributed throughout our Union, & all useful, moral, & intelligent members of society. As father, husband, citizen, & consistent Christian, Mr King has left an honored named. His funeral will take place at 3:30 P M, on Jul 8, from his late residence on Congress st, Gtwn, of which place he was a resident for nearly 60 years.

Died: on Jul 6, in Gtwn, in his 12th year, Nelson W, son of the late Thos J Davis.

Died: on Jul 5, Joseph, infant son of J E & Emma Todhunter.

Died: on Jul 6, in Wash City, Jane Seabrook, only daughter of John D & Rosannah Brandt, aged 7 months & 8 days.

Criminal Court-Wash. 1-Geo King, convicted of stealing jewelry from Dr Morton at the Nat'l Hotel, was sentenced to 2 years in the Penitentiary, to take effect on Jul 13. 2-Geo Montgomery, convicted of passing 2 counterfeit notes of $100 value each on Messrs Galt & Lewis of Wash City, was sentenced to 2 years in the Penitentiary in each case.

Wash City Ordinance: 1-Act to refund to G W Fridley the amount of a fine: the sum of $10. Approved Jul 6, 1854.

Senate: 1-Bills passed: relief of-the heirs of Lt John White & others; of Otway H Berryman; of Mrs Ann W Angus; of Thos C Nye; of the heirs of the late Uri Emmons; of Thos Crown; of Obed Hussey; of the estate of Isaac L Battle; of Wm Darby; of Calvin B Seymore & Willard Boynton, surviving partner of the firm of W & H Boynton; of the heirs-at-law of Wm Van Wart, deceased; of the reps of Henry King, deceased; of Nancy Bowen & Sarah Larrabee; of Geo Dennett, of Portsmouth, N H; of John McVey; of Asa Andrews; of Jonas P Levy & Jose Maria Jarrerro; of Capt Chas G Merchant; of Mrs Frances Smith, of S C. Also, a bill relative to the accounts of Gen Stephen Moylan. 2-House bills passed-relief of: Saml W Brady; of Geo W Gibson; of Cornelius H Latham; & of G W Torrence.

Proposals will be received at the Mayor's Ofc, City Hall, until Jul 17, for numbering the houses in Wash City, according to the provisions of the act entitiled "An act to provide for number the houses in the city of Washington," approved May 18, 1854. -Jno T Towers, Mayor

Mr Matthew Jeffers, who was dangerously wounded by the late accident on the Susquehanna railroad, is not dead, as reported, but is improving.

MON JUL 10, 1854
Household & kitchen furniture at auction on Jul 18, at the residence of Wm Wall, on E st, between 10th & 11th sts. -Jas C McGuire, auct

House of Reps: 1-Private bill to confirm the claim of Wm H Henderson & the heirs of Robt Henderson to 500 acres of land in the Bastrop grant was read twice: passed. 2-Bills referred: relief of David Myerle; of Tredwick Vincent, adm; of the legal reps of the late Col John Anderson; of Phineas M Nightingale, adm of the estate of Gen Nathl Greene, deceased; & of Wm Brown. 3-Cmte on Military Affairs: bill for the relief of the heirs & reps of Col Alex'r C Morgan, deceased: committed. 4-Cmte on Commerce: bill to change the name of the American built brig **Hallowell** to that of the brig **James Rose**: passed.

Prof McFail, of Carlisle Seminary, Schoharie Co, N Y, with a number of students, were exploring a cave near the Seminary on Jul 1. All hands ascended from a pit some 100 feet deep, safely, but when the Professor nearly reached the platform, he slipped from the rope seat & fell to the bottom of the cave, expiring in a few minutes.

Died: on Jul 8, in his 74th year, Saml Smoot. His funeral will be from the residence of his son, L R Smoot, on K st, between 26th & 27th sts, this morning at 10 o'clock.

Died: on Jun 29, near Logan, Hocking Co, Ohio, of a lingering illness of 5 months, Sophia Aurand, wife of Jacob Aurand, aged 56 years, 3 months & 17 days.

Died: on Jul 9, in Wash City, Jas McCarthy, in his 57th year. His funeral will be from his late residence, on E, near 6th st, tomorrow, at 8:30 A M.

Died: on Jul 7, at the residence of her son-in-law, Mr John R Magruder, in Balt, after a short illness, Mrs Eliz Waring, in her 75th year. She was the only surviving child of the late Gov Bowie, of Md, & was especially dear to her relations & friends from her affectionate disposition & winning character of manner.

Trustee's sale: by decree of the Circuit Court of Anne Arundel Co, in equity: public sale, at the Exchange, in Balt city, on Jul 27, the following Farms, being part of the real estate of Jas Kent, late of said county, deceased: The Farm, **Over the Creek**, adjoining Lower Marlborough, in Calvert Co: supposed to contain about 500 acres: with a small frame dwlg & good out houses. It adjoins the lands of Messrs John H Ward, Richd Gantt, & M C Fowler. Also, the Farm, **Grahame's Farm**, at the town of Lower Marlborough, Calvert Co, containing about 402 acres: with a fine large brick dwlg & good out-houses. It adjoins the lands of Messrs John Parren & S L Brook. –Thos G Pratt, Wm H G Dorsey, trustees -Gibson & Co, auctioneers, Balt.

On Jul 2, at the residence of Mr J W Swan, Newton Co, Ga, Dr J W Hitch, Wm Wilson, & Isaac Christian, jr, were instantly killed by a stroke of lightning.

TUE JUL 11, 1854
Senate: 1-Ptn from A B Fairfax, a Lt in the navy, asking compensation for services as acting purser on board the brig **Heda**, & the storeship **Relief**, & also as acting Govn'r of Alvarado, in Mexico, in 1847. 2-Ptn from Jas L Collins asking payment for services as secret & confidential agent of the U S Gov't during the war with Mexico. 3-Ptn from Col Wm Gates, asking to be indemnified for losses sustained in the wreck of the steamer **San Francisco**. 4-Additional documents in relation to the claim of Henry C Miller, Philip W Thompson, & Jesse B Turley: submitted. 5-Ptn from Jas H Gale, asking to be allowed the bounty land to which his brother was entitiled as an ofcr of the U S army. 6-Ptn from Davidge Ridgely, asking a pension for injuries received while in the naval service. 7-Cmte on Foreign Relations: bill for the relief of Lt W D Porter, U S navy. 8-Cmte on Private Land Claims: bill for the relief of John Boyd & to authorize T K McManus to enter by pre-emption certain lands in the Greensburg land district, La, submitted an adverse report on each bill. Same cmte: bill for the relief of Wm Turvin, deceased.

Mrd: on Jul 5, at Christ Church, by Rev Mr Hodges, Geo G Butler to Adeline, daughter of the late Edw Ingle, of Wash City.

Died: on Jul 10, Mrs Anne Smoot, in her 60th year. Her funeral will take place this afternoon, at 4 o'clock, from her late residence, Pa ave, between 3rd & 4th sts east.

Died: on Jul 10, of dysentery, George W, aged 9 years, only son of Julius A & Mary A Peters. His funeral is today at 5 P M, from his father's residence, D & 22nd sts.

Reward for return of a strayed or stolen Cow. Information leading to her recovery left at Patrick O'Donoghue's Soap & Candle Factory will be rewarded.

In Bangor, on Fri, Miss Eliz Rand was burnt to death by the explosion of camphene while filling a lamp.

WED JUL 12, 1854
In the list of births published in the Liverpool Courier of Jun 28: Lately, the wife of Jarvise Wilkinson, laborer, Wallaton, Notts, birth of her 25th child.

Meeting of the soldiers of the war of 1812, was held at Phil on Jul 4. Reading of the Declaration of Independence by Col Judson; address by Col Sutherland; & address by Col Judson. Thanks to Hon Mr Middleswarth, himself a soldier of the war of 1812, for his efficient support in cmte of the bill now ready for action of the houses of our Nat'l Legislature.

Annual Commencement of Gtwn College took place yesterday. The order of exercises, duly interspersed with music, consisted as follows:
The American boy, by H Pinkney, Northrop.
Influence of Philosophy, by Fred L Smith.
Alaric, by Chas B Kenny.
The Constitution, by Robt Ray.
Ode on the Potomac, by Henry E Wotton.
Social Progress, by Eugene Longuemare.
Marshal Ney, by Jas B Randall.
The Operative Clases, by Ludim A Bargy.
The Triumph of Woman, by Sam Robinson
Peter the Hermit, by B Rochford Rierdan
Modern Revolutions, Harvey Bawtree.
Progress of Empire, by Frank Waters.
The address of the Philodemic Society was delivered by Robt J Brent, & the valedictory by one of the accomplished students, Mr Robt Ray. The degree of D D was conferred on Very Rev John Teeling, or Richmond, Va. The degree of LL D on Robt J Brent, of Balt, Md. The degree of M D on T C McIntire, D C; J Hall Moore, D C; & John G Goulston, England. The degree of A B on the following students: Fred'k L Smith, Pa; Jos H Blandford, Md; Jules D D De La Croix, La; Wilson J Walthall, Ala; Ludim A Bargy, D C; Jeremiah Cleveland, S C; Harvey Bawtree, England; Eugene Longuemare, Mo; Robt Ray, La; & John J Beall, D C.

Died: on Jul 11, after a long & painful illness, Mr Henry Hines, aged about 76 years, & for the last 54 years a resident of Wash City. His funeral is today at 4 P M, from his late residence on H, between 18th & 19th sts, First Ward.

Died: on Jul 10, in Wash City, Mr Edw Addison, in his 32nd year, leaving a wife & one child, a native of Accomac Co, Va, & a resident of Wash City for the last 2 years. His funeral will be on Jul 12, at 4 o'clock, from his late residence on K st east, near the Navy Yard.

Senate: 1-Ptn from J Hosford Smith, U S Consul at Beirout, in Syria, setting forth the utter inadequacy of his compensation, & asking that it may be increased. 2-Ptn from Jos Goddart, of N Y, & men & women of Cambridge, Mass, in favor of the repeal of the fugitive slave law. 3-Cmte on Patents & the Patent Ofc: adverse report on the memorial of Adolphus Allen, asking an extension of his patent for a water wheel. 4-Cmte of Claims: asked to be discharged from the further consideration of the memorial of Mary W Perrine, & that it be referred to the Cmte on Roads & Canals: which was agreed to. Same cmte: bill to provide a pension for David Towle: recommended its passage. 5-Bill for the relief of A G Penn: referred to the Cmte on Private Land Claims. 6-Bill from the House of Reps to change the name of the American built brig **Hallowell** to that of the brig **James Rose** was referred to the Cmte on Commerce.

$20 reward for stray or stolen from the subscriber on Fri last a grey mare Pony, with a small scar on her right hind leg. $5 if the Pony is returned, & $20 for the Pony & thief. –Thos Denany, Va ave, between 3rd & 4½ sts.

Mrd: on May 31, at Sacramento, Calif, by Rev B T Crouch, jr, Mr Elliott Aubury to Miss Emily J, daughter of C A Tweed, both of Sacramento.

Mrd: on Jul 9, by Rev F S Evans, Geo W Strother to Ann Thomas.

Mr Chas A Peverelly & his brother Theodore, a boy of 15 years, were arrested at N Y on Wed night in the act of setting fire to a warehouse occupied by the elder Peverelly, in Front st.

Appointment by the Pres, by & with the advice & consent of the Senate. 1-John McKeon, of N Y, to be atty for the southern district of N Y, vice Chas O'Conor, resigned. 2-Chas L Weller, of Calif, to be postmaster at San Francisco, vice Thos J Henley, resigned.

New Haven, Conn, Jul 11. Michl Jennings, the murderer of Mrs Bradbury, at North Haven, was hung today in presence of an immense concourse of spectators.

Boston, Jul 11. J Wetherbee, jr, broker, is reported to have failed today. Stocks have materially declined, & the money panic is increasing.

Boston, Jul 11. Mr Marsh, of Penbroke, & Miss Sampson, of Stoughton, lashed themselves together & jumped into the mill-pond at Abbington yesterday & were drowned.

Albany, N Y, Jul 11. Five deaths have occurred within the last 12 hours in the family of J K Wylie. Much alarm exists, & rumors are afloat of the prevalence of the cholera.

THU JUL 13, 1854
Capt J M Scarritt, U S Engineer in charge of the construction of *Fort Taylor*, died at Key West on Jun 22nd of yellow fever. Between Jun 22 & Jul 8 seven deaths had occurred at Key West of yellow fever.

Susquehanna Railroad late calamity at Balt: Wm D Scott, the conductor & A P Winchester, the superintendent of the road, have both been arrested & held to bail for trial. The time of starting the excursion trains from *Rider's Grove* was changed by the superintendent without Mr Scott's knowledge.

Three days from Europe. Prince Chas Lucien Bonaparte fractured his leg by a fall from his horse.

Senate: 1-Ptn from Chas Hubbs, asking such modification of the letter & newspaper postage as will do away with fractional parts of a cent. 2-Additional documents on the claim of Myles T Wooley, for services in the late war with Great Britain. 3-Ptn from the owners of the fishing schnr **Brothers**, of New London, asking to be allowed fishing bounty. 4-Cmte on the Judiciary: memorial of Mrs Madalena Van Ness, asking that whatever amount may be allowed on the claim of her late husband may be paid to her & to his administrators, submitted a report accompanied by a bill for the relief of Madalena P Van Ness, widow of Cornelius P Van Ness, deceased. [This bill provides $9,000 to be paid to her in consideration of the services of her late husband in the seizure of goods imported into the district of Vt, in violation of the laws of the U S, in the years 1813 & 1814.] 5-Cmte of Claims: bill for the relief of Nancy D Holker, of Va. 6-Cmte on Indian Affairs: adverse report on the ptn of Chas Christy, praying indemnity for losses sustained by Indian depredation in Calif. 7-Bill for the relief of Robt C Thompson, legal rep of Wm Thompson: referred to the Cmte on Revolutionary Claims.

Letters from the U S ship **Portsmouth**, under date of May 28, announce that 30 Americans, taken prisoners & carried to Mazatlan by the Mexicans, suspected of being concerned in Walker's Fillibuster Expedition, had all been released, & at last dates were on board the U S revenue cutter **Marcy**, en route for San Francisco. The story these rescued persons tell is this: they had supposed from the numerous reports that our Gov't had purchased the country, & they were on their way to Lower Calif & Sonora to settle on the lands. Twelve of these passengers had pass-ports, the remainder had none. Eight of them were native-born Americans, 22 were English, Irish, French, & Swedes. We append a list of the names of the whole party:

Wm Snelling, Boston
W Warren, N Y
John Lewis, N Y
A R Clemens, N H
Deal Eaton, La
J M Lempark, Ohio
S Johanneson, Calif
Ferdinand Shang, Ohio
Lewis Batts, Pa
Michl Kemp, Ohio
Henry Gammander, Ohio
Geo Groff, N Y
Miles Courtright, Pa
John V Morrison, Ohio
E Simpson
Geo Henshone, N Y
H Longey, N H
J A Ealott, Mo
John Victor, Ohio
Chas Herr, Ohio
August Stabs, Texas
Geo Shiel, Ind
D'l Byrnes, South Boston
Peter H Hayes, R I
Peter Blokin, N Y
Henry Hofman, N Y
J Kendall, Buffalo, N Y
John Humpster, Ohio
Geo Lower, Pa
Philip Dehl, Mo

Wash Corp: 1-Ptn from H G Lorch for the remission of a fine: referred to the Cmte of Claims. 2-Cmte on Improvements: ptn of A G Swansman for relaying gutter: passed.

Died: on Jul 6, at the residence of her husband, near Wash City, Eliz Godfrey Agg, wife of John Agg, & daughter of the late Edw Blackford.

Died: on Jul 9, at his residence, Mr Wilfred Van Reswick, in his 73rd year, a native of St Mary's Co, Md, but for the last 39 years a resident of Washington.

Rev J H Cargill, a Methodist clergyman, who had just been stationed at Montrose, Pa, was killed on Jul 4, at Susquehanna, Pa, by the discharge of a cannon. Mr Cargill, after a fair warning, passed in front of a cannon just at the instant of its discharge, & he survived but a few hours. He was a young man highly esteemed.

FRI JUL 14, 1854
Senate: 1-Ptn from John A Suter, of Calif, asking the confirmation of his titles to lands in that State under Mexican grants, & indemnity for losses sustained in consequence of forcible seizure of his property by settlers. 2-Ptn from Francis Dalnese, asking compensation for services as acting Consul at Constantinople; from Chas D Arfwedson, for services ad interim at the Court of Stockholm; from Henry Savage, for services rendered the U S in Central America; from J B Holman, asking extra compensation for services as Sec of Legation at Chili; from Jos Graham, late Consul at Buenos Ayres, asking compensation for services as charge ad interim at the place; & documents relating to the claim of John D Diemateri, late U S Consul at Athens. 3-Ptn from John Thompson, asking compensation for his services as a seaman in the late war with Great Britain. 4-Ptn from John Ackerman, asking a balance due him under contracts for supplying stone for bldg barracks at Sacket's Harbor. 5-Cmte on Foreign Relations: bill for the relief of Robt C Schenck & John S Pendleton. Same cmte: bill for the relief of Wm Rich, late Sec of Legation at Mexico. 6-Cmte on Military Affairs: bill for the relief of Brvt Brig Gen B Walbach. 7-Cmte on Pensions: bill for the relief of Patrick C Miles. Same cmte: bill for the relief of Wm Wallace, of Ill; & relief of Saml McKnight, of Ky. Same cmte: resolution providing a pension to the widow of Jas Batchelder, who was killed by a mob in Boston, while in the discharge of his duty, assisting the U S marshal for the district of Mass in the execution of a law of Congress. This bill gives to the widow $3,000, to be held in trust by her for the benefit of said widow & her child, or children. 8-Bill for the relief of Thos K Glenn: referred to the Cmte on the Post Ofc & Post Roads.

Fatal termination to a case of cholera morbus occurred yesterday, in Gtwn, the deceased was named Lightfoot, & he lived near the market-house.

Criminal Court-Wash: on Wed the case against Remigius Birch, charged with assault & battery on Geo Savage at a secret meeting in Temperance Hall, continued till last evening, when the jury was discharged without coming to a verdict.

A coroner's inquest was held yesterday on the dead body of a man named Peter Lakeman, an Englishman, found yesterday in the water close to the western most pier of the recently fallen iron-bridge over Rock Creek, between K & Water sts, Gtwn. Lakeman was a workman in Mr Davison's brewery on K st west, & went to Gtwn with Mr McGarvey, an Irishman, also living near the brewery. The character of the deceased was excellent, quiet, & every way a deserving man.

Prof Benj T Ewell has been elected Pres of Wm & Mary College, vice Bishop Johns, resigned.

Thos Atwood, aged 19, was drowned while bathing at Nashua, N H, on Fri; & Anna, aged 11, daughter of John W North, was drowned at the Portsmouth, N H, navy yard on Thu.

On Jul 4, Mrs Geo W Brownell, of Keesville, N Y, left her infant daughter asleep upon the bed while she went to witness the fire-works, & on her return she found the child hung by the neck between the bedstead & the wall, quite dead.

Wm Percival, aged 20, & Eli Hoyle, 24, were drowned in Holliston on Sunday. The latter had but just arrived from England, & had lost a brother-in-law by drowning on the voyage out.

C C Hall & Jas Hennessy died from the effects of sun stroke in Boston on Saturday.

Mr Isaac P Nash, of Pembroke, & Miss Adriana Sampson, of the same town, but lately of Stoughton, Mass, drowned themselves on Monday at Reed's pond, in Abington. The deceased had formed an attachment for each other, but were prevented by some reason from being married. The female was in Boston on a visit to her aunt, & when there was in her usual spirits.

Orphans Court of Wash Co, D C. Letters of administration on the personal estate of Mary Kelley, late of Wash Co, deceased. –Gottlob C Schneider, adm

Mrd: on Jul 12, at St John's Church, Gtwn, D C, by Rev Mr Tillinghast, Mr W D Stuart to Miss Frances A, daughter of the late S B Harris, of Hagerstown, Md.

Died: on Jul 2, at the residence of her son, Dr A H Buchanan, in the city of Nashville, after a brief illness, Mrs Sarah Buchanan, widow of the late Alex Pitt Buchanan, & youngest daughter of the late John Hite, of Berkeley Co, Va.

Died: on Jul 1, at Lacton, Cedar Co, Iowa, after a short illness, Nancy H, wife of Franklin Butterfield, aged 25 years & 4 months, daughter of Isaac H Wailes, of Wash City.

Died: on Jul 13, in Wash City, William A, son of Wm P S & Martha N Sanger, in his 20th year. His funeral will take place at the residence of his father, on I, between 17th & 18th sts, at 5 P M, this day.

Died: on Jul 13, John E Van Riswick, aged one year, only son of John & Mary Van Riswick. His funeral is this evening at 3 o'clock.

SAT JUL 15, 1854

House of Reps: 1-Bills appropriately referred: relief of-Mrs Ann W Angus; of Susan Coody, & others; of Otway H Berryman; of Thos C Nye; of Obed Hussey; of the heirs of the late Uri Emmons; of Calvin B Seymore & of Wm Boynton, surviving partner of the firm of W & H Boynton; of Wm Darby; of the heirs at law of Wm Van Wart, deceased; of the legal reps of Henry King, deceased; of Nancy Bowen & Sarah Lawrence; of Geo Dennett, of Portsmouth, N H; of John McVey; of Asa Andrews; of Jonas P Levy & Jose Mario Jarrero; & of Capt Chas G Merchant. Also, granting an increase of pension to Mr Frances Smith, of S C. Also, granting bounty land to Eliz Summers, widow of Cornelius Summers, a soldier of the late war with Great Britain. Act to authorize the payment of invalid pensions to the heirs of Lt Robt White & others. 2-Act relative to the accounts of Gen Stephen Moylan: referred. 3-Cmte on Commerce: bill for the relief of Alex'r Lee, with the recommendation that it do not pass: laid on the table. 4-Cmte on Revolutionary Claims: bill for the relief of the legal reps of Gustavus B Horner, deceased: committed. Same cmte: adverse report on the ptn of Dr B R Wellford, one of the reps of Col Wm Nelson, deceased. Same cmte: bill for the relief of Phineas M Nightingale, adm of the estate of Gen Nathl Greene, deceased: committed. Same cmte: bill for the relief of the heirs of Lt Andrew Finley, & a bill for the relief of the adm of Thos Wishart: committed. Same cmte: adverse report on the ptn of the heirs of Capt Wm Van Lear. 5-Cmte of Claims: bill for the relief of Lincoln Bates: committed. 6-Cmte of the Whole: discharged from the further consideration of the resolution for the relief of the owners of the brig **Kate Boyd**: referred to the Cmte on Commerce. 7-Cmte on Private Land Claims: bill for the relief of the legal reps of Chas Pavle: referred. 8-Cmte on Indian Affairs: bill authorizing the Sec of the Treasury to pay John Chas Fremont for beef furnished the Calif Indians: committed. 9-Cmte on Military Affairs: bill authorizing the Sec of the Treasury to settle the accounts of Thos Jordan, assist quartermaster U S army. Bill for the settlement of the claims of W P Buckner & Pierce Crosby, passed midshipmen in the U S Navy. 10-Cmte on Naval Affairs: bill for the relief of Dr S R Addison, passed assist surgeon in the U S Navy, with the recommendation that it pass: committed. 11-Cmte on Revolutionary Pensions: adverse reports on the ptns of Mary Young & of citizens of Phil relative to the half pay of Revolutionary ofcrs. Same cmte: adverse report on the ptn of Joel Kelsey.

12-Cmte on Invalid Pensions: relief of-Homan Chittenden; of Wm Gove, of Maine; of Jonathan Pearce; & of Wm Parker. Same cmte: adverse reports on the ptns of Thos G Brown, of Tenn; of Wm J Sears; of Solomon Honey; of Chas Bussell; of Thos Byron; of Wyman Badger; of Eliz Van Ranst, widow of John Van Ranst; of Zerah Whitney; of Elias Bullock; of Edw Cotter; of Augustus Cooper; & of Jas McCowley. Same cmte: bill for the relief of Zabina Rawson: committed. Same cmte: adverse report on the ptn of Wm Starry & of Voucher Benzinska. 13-Cmte on Patents: bill for the relief of Gideon Hotchkiss, with the recommendation that it pass: committed. Same cmte: adverse report on the ptn of Zebulon & Austin Parker. 14-Cmte on Naval Affairs: bill for the relief of David Myerle, with the recommendation that it pass: committed. 15-Bills considered with the recommendation that they pass: relief of-Chas Lee Jones; of Capt Geo Simpton, of Galveston; of Robt Grignon; of the heirs of Jos Gerard; of Mrs Helen McKay, widow of the late Col Aeneas McKay, deputy quartermaster genr'l U S Army; of D C Cash & Giles U Ellis; & of Pamela Brown, the widow of Maj Gen Jacob Brown, late of the U S Army, deceased. 15-The bill for the relief of Geo G Bishop & the legal reps of John Arnold, deceased, with the recommendation that it be laid on the table: a bill for their relief having already been passed.

Annual distribution of premiums took place on Jul 12 of the Academy of the Visitation, Gtwn, D C. Premiums distributed by his Excellency the Pres of the U S, assisted by Rev Bernard A Maguire, S J, Pres of Gtwn College, to:

Eliz Poe, Gtwn, D C
Mary Spalding, Wash, D C
S Franklin, Wash, D C
Frances Renshaw, Caraccas, Venezuela
Mary Peabody, Wash, D C
N Penn, Richmond, Va
Susan Perkins, Concord, N H
Kate Shackelford, Culpeper, Va
Agnes Montague, Fayettsville, N C
Frances Beckham, Warrenton, Va
Victoria Philips, Warrenton, Va
Eliz Durfee, Marion, Ohio
Louisa Benson, Montg, Ala
Jane Crommelin, Montg, Ala
Mary Crommelin, Montg, Ala
Alice Murray, Gtwn, D C
Anna Goldthwaite, Montg, Ala
Sallie Ames, Montg, Ala
Beverly Rudd, Fredericksburg, Va
C Sauve, New Orleans
Rosa Cole, Balt, Md
Martha Rice, St Paul, Minn
Eliza Finley, Havana, Cuba
Alexandrine Godfrey, Detroit, Mich
Adelaide Granger, Manchester, N Y
Victoria Rosenbaum, Malaga, N J
Malvina Favier, Wash, D C
P Neale, Chas Co, Md
Rosalie Lloyd, Gtwn, D C
Regina Lloyd, Gtwn, D C
Laura Lancaster, Chas Co, Md
Caroline Philips, Warrenton
Florence Poe, Gtwn, D C
Amanda Payne, Gtwn, D C
Emma Granger, Manchester, N Y
Jane Poe, Gtwn, D C
Florence Lavender, Balt, Md
Elisa Whyte, Petersburg, Va
Mary Ann Welch, Boston, Mass
V Hempstone, N Y
Kate Potter, Binghamton, N Y
Caroline Lancaster, Chas Co, Md
Maria Briscoe, Wash, D C

Susan Plowden, St Mary's, Md
Martha Easton, Greenville, N C
Belle Crommelin, Montg, Ala
Kate O'Connor, Gtwn, D C
Mary Lavinia Philips, Warrenton, Va
Eugenia Moore, Columbus, Ga
Mary Ellen Smith, Gtwn, D C
Ellen Posey, Chas Co, Md
Eliza L White, N Y
Mary Eliz Philips, Warrenton, Va
Caroline Cheever, Wash, D C
Carlota Morcira, Rio Janeiro
Rose Cullings, Gtwn, D C
Maria Devereux, Gtwn, D C
Dolores Madan, Havana, Cuba
C McWilliams, Cobb Neck, Md
Eliza Woolard, Gtwn, D C
Agatha O'Neile, Gtwn
Lucinda Clements, Chas Co, Md
Victoris Hicks, Gtwn, D C
Helen Brooks, Gtwn, D C
Eliza Newman
Fanny Pettit
Josephine Clarke
Clara Kidwell, Gtwn
M J Cannon, Wash
Ainee Stubbs, Gtwn, D C
Diana Jones, Gtwn, D C
Mary Belle Mathews, Wytheville, Va
Celestia Semmes, PG Co, Md
Virginia Laub, Wash, D C
Mary Smith, Middleburg, Va
Charlotte Turner, King Geo Co, Va

Frances Robinson, Montg, Ala
Helen Kirby, Wash, D C
Mary O'Connor, Gtwn, D C
Augusta McClelland, Gtwn
Eliz Pizzini, Richmond, Va
Sarah E Bohrer, Gtwn, D C
Sarah E Barbarin, Gtwn, D C
Harriet Stanton, Memphis, Tenn
Jane Tyler, Gtwn, D C
W Emmart, Gtwn, D C
Francili Alexander, Wash, D C
Mary Olds, Circleville, Ohio
Ellen Denman, Lancaster, Ohio
Kate Smith, Louisville, Ky
Bettie Whitworth, Petersburg, Va
Elisa Finlay, Havana, Cuba
Mary Ann Gallagher, Wash, D C
Louisa Sohler, Boston, Mass
Rose Cullings, Gtwn, D C
Mary Josephine Herron, Gtwn, D C
Octavia Prudhomme, Opelousas, La
Agnes Hayes, Opelousas, La
Charlotte Labadie, Galveston, Texas
Mary Clusky
Mgt Clusky
Kate Potter
Ada Barelli
A Penrice
Malvina Favier, Wash, D C
Sydney Palfrey
Eliza Baasen, Milwaukie
Mgt Gormley, Gtwn, D C

Appointments by the Pres, with the advice & consent of the Senate: 1-Henry E Wood, of N H, to be Consul of the U S for the port of Beirut, in Syria. 2-Jas T Miller, Collector of Customs, Wilmington, N C, vice Wm C Bettencourt, resigned.

Mrd: on Tue last, in Emanuel Church, Warrenton, N C, by Rev Dr Smith, Lt Thos M Crossan, U S Navy, to Rebecca, only child of the late Dr Jas G Brehon, of N C.

Sale of blood horses in N Y day before yesterday: Mr Mann of Wash City, purchased Mac for $4,100; & Frank Forrester for the sum of $2,350. Tacony brought $3,700, purchased by J G Bevens, of N Y.

Mrd: on Jul 5, at Columbus, Ga, at the residence of her brother-in-law, Jos B Hill, by Rev F Bowman, D D, Miss Emma C Dawson, daughter of Hon Wm C Dawson, to Edw W Seabrook, of Edisto Island, S C.

Mrd: on Jul 18, in Union Methodist Episcopal Church, by Rev F Israel, Wm W Hough to Sarah Jane Robertson, all of Wash.

Died: on Jul 13, at **Tudor Place**, Gtwn Heights, D C, after a short illness, Martha Custis Peter, relict of the late Thos Peter, in her 77th year. Mrs Peter was the last survivor but one of the family of the wife of Washington. We learn that her remains will be conveyed early this morning to the family grave yard near **Seneca Mills**, Montg Co, Md.

Valuable land for sale: I will offer for sale my undivided interest [one-third] in all of the outlands belonging to the estate of Geo C Harness, deceased, lying in the counties of Randolph, Pocahontas, & Hardy. Apply to Jno F Williams, Moorefield, Hardy Co, Va. The above lands consist in part of one tract known as **Canaan Lands**, & contains 14,350 acres; a second tract of 7,150, & a third tract of 2,520 acres, all lying in Randolph Co, Va, & valuable for timber & minerals.

Valuable real estate in Dinwiddie Co, Va, for sale: sale of the commodious Hotel & appurtenances at Dinwiddie Courthouse, including the land which surround the Courthouse, about 400 acres, the ofcs & residences, together with all the numerous privileges connected with the property. The property will be shown by Maj Anderson or me, both residing on the premises. –E H Smith

Senate: 1-Ptn from Albert C Ramsay & Ed H Carmick, asking an appropriation by Congress to enable them to fulfill their contract for carrying the mails between New Orleans & San Francisco. 2-Ptn from Wm G Donahoe, late private of the 6th Regt of Infty, asking to be allowed arrears of pension & traveling expenses to the military asylum at Wash. 3-Bill for the relief of Gaston T Raoul: passed. 4-Bill for the relief of A G Penn: passed. 5-Bill for the relief of Chas Staples: passed.

Gtwn Female Seminary, Gtwn, D C: Rev Wm J Clark & Miss A H Clark, principals. This Seminary will be resumed on Sep 1. Reference is made to Dr Grafton Tyler, Capt Geo F de la Roche, W G Ridgely, W Hunter, W S H Taylor, Francis Dodge, Robt P Dodge, Dr O M Linthicum, Gtwn, D C; & to Jos H Bradley, Aaron C Dayton, & Mr Fitzhugh Coyle, Wash, D C.

On Fri morning the house of Mr Wm W Moore, corner of F & 6th sts, was burglariously entered & rifled, by persons obviously adept at the business. The burglars succeeded in carrying off about $300; & his clothes were taken from his bedside & the pockets rifled.

Died: on Jul 13, Agnes, wife of Jas Harmon, in her 20th year. Her funeral will take place today at 10 A M, from her late residence, on H st, between 6th & 7th sts.

Mr Chappell, of Fairfax Co, returning from Gtwn to his residence, was thrown from a vehicle in which he was riding into the canal on Tue & killed. His daughter were also thrown in the canal, but saved.

MON JUL 17, 1854
Auction of Wholesale & Retail, stock of Groceries: on Jul 19, at the store of Mr Geo B Lipscomb, on the Canal, near the Market-house. –Barnard & Buckey, aucts

Brief memoir of the late John Diddier Readel, M D, of Balt. The father of Dr Readel was a native of Bavaria: he emigrated to the U S when quite a young man, & was a resident of Phil at the time of the adoption of our Federal Constitution. The subject of this memoir was born in that city in 1790. Five years afterwards his father removed with his family to the city of Balt, where, by industry & good conduct, he amassed a considerable portion of the goods of this world. At age 15 young Readel was an accomplished scholar, his acquaintance with the Greek & Latin languages more than familiar. He graduated from the Phil School of Medicine in 1811; went on a tour of Europe for 3 years. In 1822 Dr Readel married Martha, sister of John T H Worthington, of Balt Co. Four sons & a daughter were born to him. The oldest son, who was educated for his father's profession, died in 1845, in his 21st year, just before his expected graduation. His 3rd son, who was also educated for the same profession, graduated in 1849, before he was of age, was associated with his father in the practice, & died in 1851. Dr Readel received from the Govn'r of Md the appointment of Judge of the Orphans' Court of Balt city & county. Dr Readel died in his 65th year, leaving a widow & 3 children, & we are sorry to learn left them in circumstances far from independent. He was buried with Masonic honors. -P P

Judge Haile, of the Supreme Court of R I, died of cholera at Warren, R I, on Sat.

Senate: 1-Ptn from the heirs & legal reps of Capt Thos Dinsmore, of the war of 1812, asking arrears of pension. 2-Memorial of the widow of Gen Roger Jones, late adj genr'l of the U S Army. 3-Cmte on the Post Ofc & Post Roads: Bill for the relief of Thos K Glen: passed. 4-Bill for the relief of Chas W Carroll: referred to the Cmte on Military Affairs.

Died: on Jul 13, at Saratoga Springs, Mr Timothy O'Neale. His funeral will be this morning at 10 o'clock, from his late residence in Gtwn, D C.

A woman named Ann Hall, of about 34 years of age, was carried over the Falls at Niagara last Monday. She was seen floating in the river above the falls, & while preparations were making to rescue her, she was carried over the cataract.

M M Howes, of New Milford, who was sent to the State prison for 10 years on a charge of attempting to kill a school mistress in his neighborhood, died in the prison at Wethersfield on Sunday last. He had been confined about 2 years. He was a mild inoffensive young man about 21 years of age at the time of his sentence. He had always lived on his father's farm on the side of the mountain. The school mistress boarded in his father's family, & received the attentions of Howes for a time, but finally, on removing to an adjacent district, she wrote him a letter cutting off further intimate relations. This troubled Howes & one day he went to the school-room & demanded $100 in cash or a promise of marriage. She ordered him to leave, when he seized her by the hair, &, with a jack-knife, inflicted several wounds upon her neck & face. The cuts were not deep. He was a mere skeleton when he died. His parents are very worthy people & are highly respected. On Monday the chaplain, as he had promised Howes, delivered his body to the care of his parents.

House of Reps: 1-Cmte of Claims: joint resolution for the relief of John A Bryan, & bills for the relief of Andrew H Patterson & of Polly Carver: committed. Same cmte: bill for the relief of Asbury Dickins, with the recommendation that it pass: committed. Same cmte: bill for the relief of Zachariah Lawrence, of Ohio: committed. Same cmte: resolution for the relief of Geo R C Floyd, late Sec of Wisconsin Territory, & securities: laid on the table. Same cmte: bills of the Senate: with the recommendationt that they do not pass: & they were committed: relief of Michl Nourse; of the sureties of Danl Winslow; of John Boyd, of La; of the legal reps of the late Capt Wm G Williams; of Jacob Gideon; of John McAvoy; & of John Devlin. Same cmte: adverse reports on the ptns of Coale & Barr, of the heirs of Capt John Burnham; of stone-cutters on the Capitol extension; of Dr S A Thompson; of Jas Mackall; of Jno S Gatewood; of the widow & heirs of John Hogan; & of Chas Winters, et al. 2-Cmte on Invalid Pensions: bill granting a pension to Sidney P Pool: committed. 3-Cmte on Foreign Affairs: bill for the relief of Jonas P Levy & Jose Maria Jarero, with the recommendation that it pass: committed. 4-Cmte on Private Land Claims: bill for the relief of Lloyd Dorsey & others: committed. 5-Mr Davis, of R I, said he would ask consent to present the preamble & act of the Legislature of that State reversing & annulling the sentence rendered by the Supreme Court of R I against Thos W Dorr for treason in 1844. 6-The bill for the relief of Chas Lee Jones: passed. 7-Bills laid aside with the recommendation that they pass: relief of: Danl Steenrod; of John S Jones & Wm H Russell, surviving partners of Brown, Russell & Co; of Wm Hankins; of Gilbert C Russell; of Thos C Greene; of John Phagan; of John S King, of Va; of Ezra Williams; of Chas Cooper; of Jas Dunning; of Jos Mitchell; of the adms of Oliver Lee, deceased; & of the legal reps of Joshua Kennedy, deceased. Also a bill authorizing Victor Morass to relinquish certain lands & to enter the same quantity elsewhere. Joint resolution directing the adjustment of the accounts of Wm Woodbury, late pension agent at Portland, Maine. 7-Bill for the relief of Sarah K Jenks & the legal reps of Hartshorne R Thomas, in the matter of the brig **Jane**, was laid aside, with the recommendation that it do not pass. 8-Cmte on Invalid Pension: ptn of Elijah Frye: adverse report: laid on the table.

TUE JUL 18, 1854
Trustee's sale of strip of ground fronting on Pa ave at auction on Jul 20. The property having been sold but the purchaser did not comply with the terms of sale. Public auction by deed of trust from Michl McCarty to the subscriber dated May 5, 1852, recorded in Liber J A S No 39, folios 341 thru 343, one of the land records for Wash Co, D C: a strip of ground fronting 7 feet 5 inches on Pa ave, & adjoining the east side of lot Nov 25, in square A, & containing 945 square feet.
–Jeremiah Murphey, trustee. -Green & Scott, aucts

David Moreland & Mr Deavor, residing on the Levels, were cradling wheat on the Little Capon Mountain, Va, on Jul 8, when they both were instantly killed by a flash of lightning. It is supposed that their scythes attracted the fiery element.

Senate: 1-Cmte on Naval Affairs: bill for the relief of Wm Clark. 2-Cmte on Pensions: asked to be discharged from the further consideration of the ptn of the widow of John Balster: which was agreed to.

For sale, a beautiful & valuable estate. Desirous to close my business in Fred'k Co & remove to a central part of Va more convenient to a large Landed Estate I own in that quarter, I offer for sale *Springdale*, upwards of 800 acres; & *Bartonsville*, with various Mills, forming certainly one of the finest estates in the whole country. On *Springdale* is a well constructed dwlg house of 2 stories, covered with tin roof, with 6 chambers, besides 4 cellar & 3 attic rooms. The bldg is 90 feet in length, including the wings. The improvements of this estate are those which taste & a free expenditure of money for 50 years could make. This property is 5½ miles from Winchester. –R W Barton, near Winchester, Va References:
Hon Jas M Mason, Senator
Hon A A H Stuart, Staunton, Va
Chas Barnard, Boston
Moncure Robinson, Benj Etting, Phil
A P Kennedy, S K Burkholder, Balt
Capt L M Powell, Capt Wm McBlair, U S Navy, Wash
Robt B Bolling, Petersburg, Va
Wm H Macfarland, R B Haxall, Saml Marx, Richmond, Va
Myer Myers, Norfolk, Va
Jas K Marshall, Alexandria, Va
Jno G Meem, Lynchburg, Va
Dr Rice, New Market, Va
Dr R T Baldwin, T A Tidball, H M Brent, Jas Marshall, Jos H Sherrard, D W Barton, Winchester, Va
Jno S Magill, Wm S Jones, Jos Long, Jas Chipley, F B Jones, Jas Gilkeson, Fred'k Co, Va.

4,168 acres of valuable Meherrin River land, in Brunswick Co, Va, for sale. By decree of the Circuit Court for Brunswick Co, pronounced in the case of Stark vs Cunningham: public auction on Aug 29, 1854, if not sold privately before. The plantation is known as **Fort Hill**, & formerly belonging to the late Col Wm Allen, of Surry. Mr Thos Kirkland, on the premises, or the undersigned, in Lawrenceville, will take pleasure in showing the land. –Robt D Turnbull, Com'r

Jas Murray, the Mayor of the town of Alexandria, in Louisiana, was killed on Jul 4 whilst endeavoring to suppress a disturbance at a barbecue. John C Culbertson was the murderer, & such was the indignation of the populace that it was with difficulty he was saved from summary execution under the Lynch code.

Died: on Jul 17, Col Geo C Washington, in his 65th year. His funeral will be this day at 5 o'clock P M, from his late residence on the Heights of Gtwn.

Died: on Jul 16, Harriot, daughter of Wm C & H A Zantzinger, aged 4 years, 5 months & 18 days. Her funeral is this afternoon at 4½ o'clock.

Boston, Jul 15. Edw Crane, Pres of the Vermont Central Railroad, resigned his ofc today. Previous to his resignation it was discovered that he had over-issued 8,000 shares of the Vermont Central Railroad.

N Y, Jul 17. 1-N B Blunt, District Atty, died yesterday at Lebanon Springs. 2-Ex-Judge Merritt, of this city, died yesterday of cholera.

Boston, Jul 17. Mathew Matthews, John Gull, Wm L Mentzer, & C Saxton, from Phil, who recently obtained $3,700 from the Rutland Bank, Vt, on forged checks, have been arrested. Matthews & Gill were taken at Montreal, & Mentzer at Rouse's Point. There was recovered from then $3,300.

WED JUL 19, 1854
Household & kitchen furniture at auction on Aug 1, at the residence of Mrs J B French, on south side of E st north, between 6th & 7th sts. -Green & Scott, aucts

Trustee's sale of 2 story frame house & lot at auction: on Aug 8, by deed of trust, dated May 11, 1854, from Henry B Robertson & Mahaley Jane Robertson his wife: sale of lots 51 & 52 in square 465, with the house & back bldg. –Craven Ashford, trustee -Green & Scott, aucts

Groceries & liquors at auction on Jul 22, at the store of J M L Carusi, corner of 7th & G sts. -Green & Scott, aucts

John C C Hamilton, Atty-at-Law, Washington: ofc on La ave, between 4½ & 6th sts.

The late Hon Geo C Washington, of Md, died at his town residence in Gtwn, D C, on Jul 17, after several months' gradual decline. He was a native of Va, & was at the time of his decease the oldest & nearest surviving relative of his grand uncle, Gen Washington. He was the first President of the Washington Club. He was for several years a member of the House of Reps from his district in Md; & filled the post of Pres of the Chesapeake & Ohio Canal, & also Com'r for the settlement of Indian claims. His remains were followed to the grave yesterday by many sincere friends.

The Petersburgh Express has received a telegraphic dispatch announcing the death of Hon Geo W Townes, formerly Govn'r of Ga. For some years he represented his district in Congress. [No death date given-current item.]

Died: on Jun 29, at Mobile, Ala, Lemuel R Townsend, formerly of Wash City, in his 40th year.

Criminal Court-Wash. The youth John Rollins, alias Whit Cissell, was yesterday convicted of arson.

House of Reps: 1-Memorial of Gen Nathan Towson, for himself & others, asking to be paid for the capture of the British brig **Caledonia**, captured by Capt Towson's artillery company in 1812. 2-Ptn of David Much & 84 other citizens of Amherst, Mass, praying for the immediate repeal of the fugitive slave law. 3-Bill for the relief of Thos K Glenn: passed.

THU JUL 20, 1854
Wash Corp: 1-Ptn of Jos Harbaugh for the repair of the gutter on 7th st: referred to the Cmte on Improvements. 2-Act to authorize Wm H Faulkner to lay a foot pavement along the line of his property on Pa ave: passed. 3-Cmte on Unfinished Business: ptn of Wm Dixon & others for paving the footway on First st east, in front of squares 820 & 825: referred to the Cmte on Improvements. 4-Uriah B Mitchell to be a Police Ofcr, in place of David Westerfield, declined. 5-Geo W Cochran to be a Com'r of the Centre Market, in place of S P Franklin, declined. 6-Jeremiah McNew & Alex'r Forrest to be Comr's of the Northern Market, in place of C F Queen, declined, & B F Bogan, who resigned some time since. 7-Jas W Dileway to be Com'r of the West Market, in place of B Random. 8-Michl H Grimes to be Com'r of the Eastern Market, in place of W S Venable, declined. 9-Wm Baum to be a Measurer of Wood & Coal. 10-Dr Jos D Stewart to be a Physician for the poor of the 7th Ward, in place of Dr John McCalla, declined. 11-Jos H Bradley to be Corp Atty, in place of Walter Lenox, declined. 12-Ptn of Geo Junemann, praying the remission of a fine: referred to the Cmte of Claims.

The dwlg of Mr P W Browning was entered by burglars, on Monday night. They took $80 from his pantaloons & stole a gold watch valued at about $150.

An inquest was found on the body of Mrs Reid, found in the Wash Canal. She kept a boarding-house on the Island, but her pecuniary affairs looking desperate & her family relations being unhappy, she took the premeditated but false step of committing self-destruction. It is supposed she left her house yesterday on the desperate errand.

Criminal Court-Wash: on Mon the jury in the case of Brown & others rendered a verdict finding John Brown, King Atkins, Bill Lomax, Geo Hicks, Geo Simms, & Fred'k Newton guilty on the second count, charging the prisoners with an affray. The above were sentenced to be imprisoned in jail 6 months, & fined $10 each, except Simms, who, having been in jail 7 months, was fined $10. On Tue John Rollins, alias Whit Cissil, charged with arson in setting on fire the dwlg of John Malone on Jun 4, 1854, was found guilty. Regimus Burch, [the former jury discharged] was again tried for an assault on Geo Savage, & acquitted. –News.

Senate: 1-Ptn from the heirs of Henry C Walker, asking to be allowed to locate certain lands stipulated to be granted to the Wyandotte Indians, or a grant in money equal to the value of the same. 2-Ptn from Horatio J Perry, Sec of Legation of the U S at Madrid, asking compensation for services as Charge d'Affaires ad interim at that Court. 3-Ptn from Peter Parker, Sec of Legation & Chinese interpreter at Canton, asking compensation for services as Charge d'Affaires ad interim at that Gov't. 4-Ptn from Elliot Smith, Wm C Green, & Nathan Farnsworth, asking to be allowed salvage on the ship **Charles Wharton**, employed as a Gov't transport, & rescued by them when in distress off Tampa Bay, & compensation for their time & the cargoes of their vessels, which they were compelled to throw overboard to effect the rescue of said ship. 5-Ptn from Wm L Blanchard, asking remuneration for losses sustained on account of a contract having been abrogated for carrying the mail from Salt Lake City to Sacramento. 6-Cmte of Claims: bill for the relief of Ephraim Hunt. 7-Cmte on Naval Affairs: asked to be discharged from the further consideration of the memorial of Cyrus Palmer & Lafayette Bach: that it be referred to the Cmte on Commerce: which was agreed to. Same cmte: asked to be discharged from the further consideration of the memorial of Jas P Espy: which was agreed to. Same cmte: asked to be discharged from the further consideration of the memorial of Richd S Coxe, Wm A Bradley, & G L Thompson, offering to furnish the navy with compressed coal: which was agreed to. 8-Cmte of Claims: bill for the relief of Israel Kitcham. 9-Bill for the relief of Lt Col Edw R S Canby: referred to the Cmte of Claims.

Died: on Jul 18, John Thomas, son of Jas & Rachel Henry, aged 11 months. His funeral is this morning at 9 o'clock, from the residence of his parents, I st between 4th & 5th.

Died: on Jul 11, in N Y C, suddenly, of congestion of the brain, Mrs Sarah Aborn, wife of Hon Henry B Anthony, of Providence, R I, & daughter of Christopher Rhodes, of Pawtuxet.

House of Reps: 1-Cmte on Invalid Pensions: bills committed: relief of Geo J Rallston; of Jos McMinn; & of Asa Leach.

The Fred'k Female Seminary is a fully organized Female College; chartered & endowed with $50,000 by the State of Md. It is located in Fred'k City, Md, as healthy & pleasant a town as any in the Southern States. The school is not sectarian. For particulars see Rev Septimus Tustin, D D, Wash, D C.

U S Patent Ofc, Wash, Jul 19, 1854. Ptn of Ross Winans, of Balt, Md, praying for the extension of a patent granted to him on Nov 26, 1840, for an improvement in the mode of regulating the waste steam in locomotive steam engines, for 7 years from the expiration of said patent, which takes place on Nov 26, 1854.
--Chas Mason, Com'r of Patents

The Ladies of Richmond & Manchester, Va, have held a meeting & formed a society to be known as the Va Central **Mount Vernon Association of Ladies**. The object of the association is to raise a sufficient sum of money to secure the purchase of **Mount Vernon**, to be held in trust by the Govn'r of Va & his successors. John H Gilmer was appointed to correspond with the proprietor of **Mount Vernon**, to ascertain at what price he will agree to sell **Mount Vernon**. All ladies present registered their names, & the following permanent ofcrs were elected:

Pres: Mrs Julia M Cabell
First Vice Pres: Mrs Eliza Semmes
Second Vice Pres: Mrs Pellet
Third Vice Pres: Mrs Dunlop
Fourth Vice Pres: Mrs Wirt Robinson
Fifth Vice Pres: Mrs Gen Pegram
Sec: Mrs W F Ritchie
Corr Sec: John H Gilmer
Treasurer: Wm H McFarland

The two daughters of Fred'k Howes, who were crushed in a carriage on Monday last near North Danvers, Mass, by coming in contact with a railroad train, were not killed as reported by telegraph. One is recovering from her injuries, & the other remains in a precarious condition.

Yesterday, as the lightning train was passing the flag station at Allen's creek, a stick of wood fell from the tender upon one of the wheels, by which it was projected with the velocity of a rifle ball in the direction of the house of the flag-man, Mr Farrenberg, who was standing in his door. The stick struck him square in the head, passing nearly through it, killing him instantly. He leaves a wife & 3 or 4 children.
-Rochester Advertiser of Jul 13

Dr Linton, formerly surgeon in the U S Navy, shot two men at Laredo, Texas, recently. He was seized by a mob & hung on a gallows erected on the public plaza.

Escambia Co, Florida: bill filed in the Circuit Court for this county by Robt Mitchell vs S V S Wilder, Wm L Booth, & others, praying for the partition of a tract of land lying in the city of Pensacola, containing 800 arpens, known as *Cassa Blanca* tract: it appearing to the Court that some of the dfndnts do not reside in Florida. Case to be continued on the 1st Monday of Oct next & dfndnts of this bill are to appear, or the same will be taken as confessed. --J J Finley, Judge

FRI JUL 21, 1854
Senate: 1-Additional documents submitted to the claim of Capt Thos Dinsmore.

Maj Gen Nathan Towson, Paymaster Gen of the Army, died yesterday, from paralysis. His name is associated with almost every brilliant action upon the Niagara frontier from 1812-1815. He was especially distinguished in the battles of Chippewa & Bridgewater, & in the sortie from *Fort Erie*. Gen Towson was a native of Md, & at the time of his death had attained the age of 71 years.

Alex'r Kyle, the Sec of the Harlem Railroad Co, has been arrested & held in custody for having over-issued the stock of the company.

The last of the Choctaws. Mr Wm Fisher & Mr Russel Lewis left yesterday for the Indian territory west of the Mississippi with the last remnant of the once powerful tribe of Choctaw Indians, amounting to about 80 persons. No more will go to Mobile, for the few still remaining, not exceeding 10 persons, are married here & connected in marriage, & therefore will be permitted to linger around the graves of their kindred. --Mobile Tribune, Jun 30

House of Reps: 1-Memorial & ptn of Cyrus Buckland, master machinist at the U S armory at Springfield, Mass, praying compensation for inventions & improvements in machinery for the benefit of the Gov't.

St Paul, Minnesota, Jul 10, 1854. It is my sad duty to announce to you the sudden decease of D H Dustin. I was with him in his ofc at 9 o'clock this morning, at which time he went into court to try a case, being at the time affected with a slight diarrhoea. At 2 o'clock he was brought home in a carriage, his disease defying the skill of his physicians; & now, at 10 P M, I am sitting by his corpse. He has left a bereaved wife & 2 young orphaned children. Mr Dustin was the District Atty of Minnesota, & but 11 months ago had a child & its nurse killed by the side of himself & wife on the Amboy railroad, the rest of the family miraculously escaping the same fate.

Frank Smith was hung at New Orleans on Jul 8 for the murder of his wife. He met his fate with much trepidation.

Abraham Hews died at Weston on Sat last, at the age of 88 years. He was at the time of his death, perhaps the oldest postmaster in the U S, having retained ofc through all the changes of Administrations, from the time of his appointment under Pres Madison in 1812. –Boston Courier

Mrd: on Jul 18, in Gtwn, by Rev Mr Cooper, Geo C Coleman, of Pilot Grove, Md, to Miss Mary A Rush, of Wash Co, Md.

Died: yesterday, Maj Gen Nathan Towson, Paymaster Gen U S Army. His funeral will be on Sat afternoon, on Jul 22, from his late residence, F & 17th sts. [Jul 22nd newspaper: he had attained the age of 73 years.] [Jul 24th newspaper: the funeral of Gen Towson: Rev Mr Gurley, of the Presbyterian Church, portrayed the patriotic career of the veteran; the Pres of the U S & Members of his Cabinet & other ofcrs of the Gov't were present; a company of U S Flying Artl was in attendance from Balt, & Col Hickey's regt of District Volunteers attended in tolerable force, accompanied by the venerable cmder of the division, Maj Gen Walter Jones. The calvacade moved to the *Gtwn Cemetery*.]

Died: yesterday, at the residence of Hon John H Eaton, in Wash City, Lt John Brockenbrough Randolph, of the U S Navy. He had just returned to his family from Japan, after an absence of more than 3 years. But his return was only to die, for in 10 days after reaching home he sank a victim to chronic dysentery, under which he had been laboring for a considerable time. His funeral is this afternoon, at half past 5 o'clock, from the residence of Mr Eaton.

Died: yesterday, in Wash City, Mrs Agnes Wilson, relict of the late David Wilcox, aged about 89 years. Her funeral will take place from the Infirmary at 6 o'clock this evening.

Died: on Jul 19, Mrs Sarah Chapin, relict of the late Rev Stephen Chapin, D D, aged 70 years. Her funeral is this morning at 9½ o'clock, from the residence of Rev G W Samson, on 6th st, between D & E sts.

Died: on Thu, Mrs Mgt D Little, wife of Saml L Little. Her funeral is on Sat at 2 o'clock, from the residence of her husband, near the Navy Yard.

Died: on Jul 15, in Wash City, at the residence of Wm Aiken, of S C, Mrs Amanda Siebels, wife of Edwin W Siebels, of Edgefield district, S C, aged 28 years.

Died: on Jul 5, at Salem, Iowa, Rev Jas Nourse, of Wash City, in his 50th year. He was returning to his family after a short absence.

N Y, Jul 20. It is positively asserted here that Com'r Gregg has nearly concluded a treaty annexing the Sandwich Islands to the U S, with the approbation of the Pres. The only unsettled question, it is said, is whether they shall come in as a State.

Fatal accident near Trenton N J, on Thu. Mr Aaron Bennett, aged 65 years, tender of the canal bridge, was endeavoring to keep some cows off the track, but standing himself too near, & being a little deaf, was instantly killed by the fast train of cars which then came along at a rapid rate.

A young woman, Mary Kelly, lost her life at Jersey City a day or two ago, by using camphene carelessly. She poured some upon the fire to make it burn & the flames caught, setting her on fire. She died during the night.

SAT JUL 22, 1854
House of Reps: 1-Bill for the relief of Mrs Pamela Brown, widow of Maj Gen Jacob Brown, late of the U S Army, to be allowed a pension, at the rate of $50 per month from Feb, 1838. [Jul 25th will be the 48th anniversary of the hard-fought battle of Bridgewater, in which Gen Brown received 3 wounds, the closing up of one of which caused his death in 1828.] 2-Cmte of the Whole: bill to confirm the claim of Dusuan de la Croix to a certain lot of land: passed. 3-Cmte on Revolutionary Pensions: adverse reports on the ptns of Achsa Ayers, of N Y; & of the children of Wm Peters, deceased. 4-Cmte on Invalid Pensions: bill to authorize payment of invalid pensions to the heirs of L Robt White & others, with the recommendation that it pass: committed. Same cmte: bill for the relief of John McVey, with the recommendation that it do not pass: laid on the table. 5-Cmte of the Whole: bills passed: relief of the legal reps of Joshua Kennedy, deceased; of John P Hagan; of Ezra Williams; of Chas Cooper; of Jas Dunning; of Jos Mitchell; & a bill authorizing Victor Morass to relinquish certain lands, & to enter the same quantity elsewhere. 6-Cmte of the Whole: bills passed: relief of Capt Geo Simpton, of Galveston; of the heirs of Jos Gerard; of Mrs Helen McKay, widow of the late Col Aeneas McKay, deputy quartermaster general U S Army; of D C Cash & Giles U Ellis; & of Robt Grignon.

Mrd: on Jul 20, by Rev Mr Gross, Mr Sylvester Mudd to Miss Joannah Peake, both of Wash City.

Senate: 1-Cmte on Private Land Claims: asked to be discharged from the further consideration of the memorials of the heirs of Wolcott Lawrence, & that it be referred to the Cmte of Claims: which was agreed to. 2-Cmte on Naval Affairs: asked to be discharged from the further consideration of the memorial of L F Frazee. 3-Cmte of Claims: bill for the relief of Elbert Smith, Wm C Green, & Nathan Farnsberth. 4-Bill for the relief of Mrs Madelena Van Ness, widow of Cornelius P P Van Ness: passed.

Trustee's sale: by deed of trust from Chas Mondy to Chas C Klunk: public auction on Aug 12, on the corner of E st & 12th st, Wash City, a brick-nogged Carpenter's Shop, a Horse, & one Spring Wagon & set of Harness. Terms cash. –Henry E Clarke, trustee -J C McGuire, auct

Died: on Jul 21, aged 64 years, John M Farrar. His funeral will take place from his late residence, on Missouri ave, on Sunday, at 3 o'clock.

Died: on Jul 19, in Wash City, William Dent, infant son of Maj Jas Longstreet, U S Army.

Died: on Jul 13, at Cincinnati, Ohio, Andrew Jackson Porter, late of Lancaster, Pa, youngest son of Geo B Porter, deceased, Govn'r of Michigan Territory. Born at Detroit on Jun 23, 1832.

U S Patent Ofc, Wash, Jul 21, 1854. Ptn of Reuben Daniels, of Woodstock, Vt, praying for the extension of a patent granted to him on Oct 10, 1849, for an improvement in machine for reducing worn-out cloths & silks of various kinds to the fibrous state, so as to be capable of being manufactured into cloth, for 7 years from the expiration of said patent, which takes place on Oct 10, 1854.
–Chas Mason, Com'r of Patents

MON JUL 24, 1854
Household & kitchen furniture at auction: on Jul 25, at the residence of J J Smith, on First st, opposite the old Catholic Church, excellent nearly new furniture & one very fine Piano Forte. –Edw S Wright, auct -A Green, crier

Household & kitchen furniture at auction on Jul 27, at the residence of the late Dr Alex'r Speir, D & 3rd sts west: excellent assortment. -Green & Scott, aucts

The wife of one of our subscribers, Mr Elias Metcalf, living near Jacksonville, presented her husband a few days since with a son, who, like Richard III, was born with teeth. We are told the little fellow has a mouthful of them. Mother & son are doing well. -Jacksonville [Fla] Constitutionalist

Senate: 1-Ptn from Jas Thompson, of Louisville, Ky, asking indemnity for losses sustained by reason of violation of a contract for carrying the mail. 2-Documents in relation to the case of J G Schonair, late consul of the U S at Vienna, asking compensation for diplomatic services: presented. 3-Additional documents in the case of H S Sanford: recommended to the Cmte on Foreign Relations. 4-Cmte on Military Affairs: bill for the relief of Chas Lee Jones: passed. 5-Bill for the relief of Capt Geo Simpton: passed.

Household & kitchen furniture at auction on Jul 28, at Mrs Belle Gulager's boarding house, on 4½ st, between Pa ave & C st. -Green & Scott, aucts

House of Reps: 1-Cmte of Claims: bills with the recommendation that they do not pass, & were committed: relief of-Mary E D Blaney, widow of the late Maj Geo Blaney; of Hezekiah Miller; of John P McElderry; of Lt A J Williamson; of Rulef Van Brunt; of the legal reps of the late Col John Anderson; & of the legal reps of Danl Loomis, deceased. 2-Same cmte: bills with the recommendation that they do pass, were committed: relief of-Jas Dixon; of Wm Darby; of Fred'k Vincent, adm of Jas Le Caze, survivor of Le Caze & Mallet; of Levi Pierce & And Hodge, jr; of Henry La Reintree; & of A C Andrews. Same cmte: to provide compensation for services of Geo Morell in adjusting titles to land in Michigan. Same cmte: bill for the relief of Wm G Smith & a joint resolution for the relief of Jonas W Nye: committed. Same cmte: adverse reports on the ptns of Christopher Gill; of John Robinson; of Edw H Herbert; of Wm Brown; of Capt Henry Eagle; of Jas Van Horn; & of Robt Latham.

3-Cmte on the Judiciary: bill for the relief of Sylvester Pettibone, with the recommendation that it pass: committed. 4-Cmte of Claims: bill for the relief of L R Lyon & Dean S Howard, of the State of N Y. 5-Cmte of the Whole: bills passed: relief of Danl Steenrod; of John S Jones & Wm H Russell, surviving partners of Brown, Russell & Co; of Wm Hankins; of Gilbert C Russell; of Thos C Greene; of John S King, of Va; & of the administers Oliver Lee, deceased. Adjustment of the accounts of Wm Woodbury, late pension agent of Portland, Maine. 6-Cmte of the Whole: bills with the recommendation that they do not pass: laid on the table: relief of Geo G Bishop & the legal reps of John Arnold, deceased; & of Sarah K Jenks & the legal reps of Hartshorne R Thomas, in the matter of the brig **Jane**. 7-No objection to the bill for the relief of the widows & orphans of the ofcrs & seamen of the U S schnr **Grampus**, who were lost in that vessel, in Mar, 1843, near the coast of the U S. 8-Bills with no objection: relief of-

Andrew J Deckerhoff
W D Porter, of the U S Navy
Danl Bedinger's heirs
Brig Gen John E Wool
J C Buckles, of Louisville, Ky
Jas Butler
John H Hicks, of Ind
John Brown, second, of N H
Betsey Nash
Thos Ellis
Charlotte S Westcott
Lavinia Taylor
Thos Bronaugh
Anna E Cook
Abraham Ausman

Titian R Peale.
Jacob McLellan
John S Wilson
Thos S Russell
A G Bennett
Chas H Wilgus
Purser T P McBlair
Saml H Hempstead
John W Kelly
Geo Mattingly
Wm Curran
Enoch S More
Patrick Gass
Rosalie Caxillo
A S Laughery

Ira Baldwin
Thos D Jennings
Jos Campau
Manuel Hernandez
Wm Claude Jones
Rebecca Freeman
Jas Wormsley
Mary Carlton
Sarah Crandall
Jas Capen
Wm Miller
Wm Harris, of Ga
Jas Edwards & others
Thos Snodgrass
Wm H Weirick
Richd King
Wm Senna Factor

Mary H Cushing
Capt Lewis E Simonds
Jas Wright, jr, of Tenn
Heirs of Larkin Smith
Jos Gonder, jr, & John Duff
Legal reps of Lt Francis Ware
Ira Call, of Huron Co, Ohio
Isaac M Sigler, of Putnam Co, Ind
Legal reps of Saml Prioleau, deceased
Legal heirs of Benj Metoyer
Legal reps of John Rice Jones
Lt Geo H Paige, of the U S Army.
Reps of Jos Watson, deceased
Conrad Wheat, jr, or his legal reps
Lt Geo H Paige, of the U S Army.
Danl Morse, Essex, Chittenden Co, Vt

Robt F McGuire & Louisa, his wife, late Louisa Lamy
Richd M Bonton, Geo Wright, & the widow of Marvin W Fisher
Jas S Graham & Walker H Finnall; of Jas M Goggin
Joint resolution for the relief of Capt J H Lendrum, of the U S Army.
Legal reps of the late Thos Chapman, formerly Collector of the port of Gtwn, S C.
Wm A Duer, John Duer, & Beverly Robinson, trustees of the estate of Sarah
Alexander, widow of Maj Gen Wm Alexander, commonly know as Lord Sterling.
Jas S Graham & Walker H Finnall; of Jas M Goggin
Legal reps of the late Thos Chapman, formerly Collector of the port of Gtwn, S C
Wm A Duer, John Duer, & Beverly Robinson, trustees of the estate of Sarah
Alexander, widow of Maj Gen Wm Alexander, commonly know as Lord Sterling.
John Frazer & the adm of the estate of John G Clendenin, deceased
Rebecca Baggerly, widow of David Baggerly, deceased
Mrs Sally T B Cochrane, widow of the late Lt R E Cochrane, U S Army
Execx of the late Brevt Col A C W Fanning, U S Army
Thos Ap Catesby Jones, surety for a former postmaster at Norfolk, Va
Chas J Davis, adm of Capt John Davis, an ofcr in the war of the Revolution
Mrs Anne W Angus, widow of the late Capt Angus, U S Navy
John McVea & John F McNeely, of La
Nathl Reddick, adm of Richd Taylor, deceased
Wm J McElhiny, E P Mathews, & Lawrence Cribben
Sylvester T Jerauld, assignee of the interest of Henry Richard
Also, pension for Oliver Brown, of Chemung Co, N Y; & a pension for Edmund
Mitchell, of Carroll Co, Ky.
Compensation of Jas W Low & others, for the capture of the British private armed
schnr **Ann**, during the late war with Great Britain.

9-Settle claim of Don Juan Jesus Vigil, of New Mexico 10-Bill authorizing a patent to be issued to Peter Poucin for certain lands therein described.

Geo W Phillips, deputy U S Marshal, returned to Wash City on Sat from Buffalo, where, on Wed last, he arrested Wm W Mann, on a requisition from the U S District Atty for D C, on an indictment of obtaining the sum of $2,300 under false pretences of a banker in this city. The dfndnt was released upon giving bail to the amount of $3,000 for his appearance here at the next term of the Criminal Court. -Union

List of members of the British Cabinet: Earl of Aberdeen, First Lord of the Treasury; Marquis of Lansdowne, without ofc; Lord Kranworth, Lord Chancellor; Lord John Russell, Pres of the Council; Viscount Palmerston, Home Sec; Duke of Newcastle, War Sec of State; Sir Geo Grey, Sec of State for the Colonies; Mr Gladstone, Chancellor of the Exchequer; Sir Jas Graham, First Lord of the Admiralty; Sir Chas Wood, India Board; Duke of Argyle, Privy Seal; Earl of Granville, Duchy of Lancaster; Sir W Molesworth, Ofc of Works; Hon Sidney Herbert, Sec of War.

Criminal Court-Wash: Wed: 1-Wm H Mortimer, charged with stealing money over the value of $9, the property of Thos J Butler: sentenced to 1 year imprisonment in the pentitentiary. 2-Wm Dant sentenced to 4 years' imprisonment in the penitentiary. 3-Robt Holloway, Patrick Butler, & Matthew Butler, free negroes, convicted of grand larceny, & each sentenced to 1 year in the penitentiary. 4-Christian Krouse to be imprisoned in the penitentiary for 2 years. 5-Martin, convicted of grand larceny, to be imprisoned in the penitentiary 2 years. 6-Franklin Bell, free negro, convicted of petit larceny, to be imprisoned in jail 9 months. 7-Henry Byrle, free negro, convicted of grand larceny, sentenced to 18 months imprisonment in the penitentiary. 8-John Rollins, alias Whit Cissel, convicted of arson, was sentenced to 4 years imprisonment in the penitentiary. Same person, convicted of grand larceny, sentenced to 2 years in the penitentiary.

Mrd: on Jun 22, in Phil, by Rev Jno Dowling, D D, Mr Israel E James to Mrs Mary S Walter, eldest daughter of the late John Struthers, all of that city.

Mrd: on Jul 11, near Warrenton, by Rev Josiah Solomon, Mr Wm P Rose to Miss Ann Winifred Collins, eldest daughter of the late David Collins, all of Warren Co, N C.

Died: on Jul 21, in Wash City, Wm Benter, after a short illness, in his 51st year. He was a native of Alexandria, Va, but for the last 20 years a resident of Wash City.

Died: on Sunday, Michl McGinnall, in his 22nd year. His funeral is this evening, at 4 o'clock, from his residence, corner of 15th & M sts.

Obit-died: on Jun 22, at Key West, Capt J Mason Scarritt, U S Engineers, of yellow fever. He graduated at West Point Academy in 1838; served in Florida under Gen Taylor; was afterwards assist Prof of Mathematics at West Point; in 1841 was ordered to Pensacola as assist to Maj W H Chase, where he remained until ordered to join the army of observation at Corpus Christi. He was in the battles of Palo Alto & Resaca de la Palma, where his gallant conduct received the commendation of Gen Taylor, & rendered important services in the siege & capture of Monterey, for which the brevet of captain was conferred on him by the Pres, & the Legislature of his native State [Illinois] presented him with a sword

For sale or rent: large 2 story frame house, with basement, containing in all 14 rooms, on 11th st, between G & H sts. –J H Wheat, Post Ofc Dept

TUE JUL 25, 1854
House of Reps: 1-Cmte on the District of Columbia: bill to incorporate the proprietors of **Glenwood Cemetery**, with an amendment, which provided that each of the stockholders should be held liable, in his or her individual capacity, for all the debts & liabilities of said company, however contracted. The bill was passed.

Obit-died: on Jul 5, in Salem, Henry Co, Iowa, Rev Jas Nourse, of Wash City, in his 50th year. He received the rudiment of his classical & mathematical education under Rev Jas Carnahan, D D, in Gtwn, D C. He attended during one year at Dickinson College, when Dr John M Mason was Pres there. He was licensed to preach the gospel by the Presbytery of D C; preached in Germantown, Pa, about 18 months; & he remained 19 years in service at the Presbyterian church of Perryville, Pa. In 1849 he was compelled from ill health to relinquish his position as a pastor, & in 1850 he became the Principal of the Central Academy in Wash. His sudden departure is a severe blow to all his relatives, but especially to his infirm & aged parents; & as to his bereaved widow & her 9 fatherless children, no pen can describe their agony.

Wm B Foster, of Boston, aged 19, & son of a widowed mother, was drowned at Abington, Mass, on Wed. He was with a picnic party & going in the water to bathe was seized with cramp.

Miss Lucy Howes, of Boston, one of the young ladies injured by a locomotive at Danvers early in the week, died of her injuries on Wed.

Livingston Union: on Sunday, Adam Straley, of Cuylerville, & his son, were on a fishing excursion. The boy was carrying a small sack, which contained a large butcher knife, when he accidentally fell. When he did not arise, his father attempted to help him, when he found the knife had pierced his son's heart, & he was a corpse.

Died: on Jul 22, at **Oak Hill**, Montg Co, Md, Elizabeth Graham, daughter of Edmund H & Emily Brooke, aged 13 months.

The Albany papers of Thu announce the death of Col Robt E Temple, Adj Gen of the State of N Y. He has been for some time suffering from pulmonary consumption. Educated at West Point, he served for some time in the army resigning his commission at the close of the Florida war. At the breaking out of the Mexican war he accepted the command of a regt of volunteers which went to Mexico.

Mrd: on Jul 18, at the chapel of the Theological Seminary, Va, by Rev Dr Sparrow, Rev T Grason Dashiell, of the diocese of Va, to Wilhelmina, daughter of the officiating clergyman.

Senate: 1-Ptn from Wm Hunter, asking compensation for his services as Acting Sec of State during a part of the time when the late Danl Webster was Sec of State. 2-Additional documents submitted in relation to the claim of Robt Johnson to locate certain land warrants of which he is the holder, but which were improperly assigned. 3-Ptn from Geo Frasier, asking remuneration for losses sustained in consequence of the seizure of his property & imprisonment of his person by the Mexican authorities in 1848.

Beautiful & elegant residence for sale: the undersigned offers for sale his residence in Gtwn, corner of Green & Gay sts: a superior dwlg; contains 14 rooms & is finished with all the modern improvements-a bath-house, which furnishes all the rooms with water & cistern of water in the yard. Apply to John E Carter.
P S: I will also dispose of my horse & carriage.

Orphans Court of Wash Co, D C. Letters of administration on the personal estate of Alex'r Socor, late of Wash Co, deceased. –Leonidas Coyle, adm

Guion's Hotel for sale: located in the city of Raleigh; offered for private sale until Sep 20th. If not sold by that time it will be sold at public sale. –E P Guion, Raleigh

WED JUL 26, 1854
House of Reps: 1-Bill for the relief of John Carpenter, jr, & others: referred. 2-Bill for the relief of the heirs of Jacob Moyer: referred. 3-Cmte on Revolutionary Pensions: bill for the relief of Urban Stoll, with the recommendation that it pass: committed. 4-Cmte on Commerce: adverse reports on the ptn of John Connell; on behalf of sundry claimants for a return of duties under the tariff of 1828; on the papers in relation to the wreck of the ship **Aberdeen**, in San Francisco bay; on the ptns of Huntington & Brooks; of Knox & Strain; of A Delmas, of Mississippi; of Edw H Swift, of N Y, for return of duties; & of Anne Dudley. 5-Cmte on Military Affairs: bill for the relief of Capt Chas G Merchant, with the recommendation that it pass: commited. 6-Cmte on the Post Ofc & Post Roads: bill for the relief of John Frink: committed. 7-Cmte on Invalid Pensions: bill for the relief of Jacob Baker, of Sandusky City, Ohio: committed. Same cmte: bill for the relief of Wm Brown; & of Tunstall Quarles, of Ky: committed. Same cmte: bill for the relief of Thos B

Parsons, with the recommendation that it do not pass: laid on the table. 8-Cmte on Revolutionary Claims: bill for the relief of the heirs of Rignald, alias Nick Hillery: committed. 9-Cmte on Private Land Claims: adverse report on the ptn of Jacob Kerr, of Seneca Falls, N Y. Same cmte: bill for the relief of Jos Smith, with the recommendation that it do not pass: laid on the table. Same cmte: bills with the recommendation that they pass, & they were committed: relief of-Gaston T Raoul; A G Penn; & of Francois Cousin. 10-Cmte on Naval Affairs: bill for the relief of Wm P S Sanger, with the recommendation that it pass: committed. 11-Cmte on Indian Affairs: bill for the relief of Theodore E Elliott, with the recommendation that it do not pass: laid on the table. 12-Cmte on Private Land Claims: bill for the relief of the legal reps of Geo McGirk: committed.

Senate: 1-Cmte of Claims: House bill for the relief of Oliver Lee, deceased, reported it back without amendment & recommended its passage. 2-Bill for the relief of the executrix of the late Brevet Col A C W Fanning, U S Army: passed. 3-Act for the relief of the reps of Jos Watson, deceased: passed.

Mrd: on Jul 25, by Rev Danl Motzer, John S Gulich, Purser U S N, to Miss Eliz Milligan, of Waverley, Va.

Furnished cottage on the Heights of Gtwn for rent: occupied until recently by E Corbett, Attache of the British Legation. Apply to Jas C McGuire, auct.

THU JUL 27, 1854
Senate: 1-Bill for the relief of Geo Mattingly: passed. 2-Bill for the relief of John Frasier, & the admx of the estate of John G Clendennin, deceased, might be put on its passage. 3-Memorial of Chas E Shirman, atty in fact of Robt Harrison, & other claimants under the 9th article of the treaty of 1819 with Spain, asking the payment of the decrees in his favor as atty aforesaid, made under the acts to carry said treaty into effect: referred to the Cmte on the Judiciary. 4-Cmte of Claims: bill for the relief of Danl F Douglass, late marshal of the northern district of Calif: passed. 5-Cmte on the Post Ofc & Post Roads: bill for the relief of the legal reps of Seth M Leavenworth: passed. 6-Cmte on Foreign Relations: adverse report on the memorial of Anne S P Chew, admx of Wm Chew, asking to be allowed the outfit of Charge d'Affaires. 7-Cmte on the Judiciary: bill for the relief of J H F Thornton, Lawrence Taliaferro, & Hay T Taliaferro, sureties of D F M Thornton, late a purser in the U S Navy.

Phil papers bring to us the intelligence, not unexpectedly, of the death of Jonathan Roberts, who, in the prime of life, bore a distinguished part in the Legislative Councils of the country. He was born in 1771: was elected to the U S House of Reps: supporter of the war of 1812: at one time a Canal Com'r of Pa: called from retirement in 1841 & appointed by Pres Harrison Collector of the port of Phil. [No death date given-current item.]

Dover [N H] Observer: Chas L Chase, aged 9 years, became so intoxicated on Jul 4 that he died about 12 o'clock at night. The scoundrel who furnished the child with liquor was not known.

Public auction, by deed of trust from John N Trook & wife to Jas *I Fowler, dated Jun 27, 1851, recorded in Liber J A S No 30, folios 227 thru 230, of the land records of Wash Co, D C: sale on Aug 26 of lots 6, 7, & 8 in square 464; all those parts of lots 9, 10, & 11, running on south D st, about to the rear of the back bldg of John N Trook's house; near the house of Mrs Mgt Milburn & John N Trook.
-Jas *J Fowler, trustee -Jas C McGuire, auct [*Copied as written.]

Wash Corp: 1-Ptn from Jackson Pumphrey & others, praying that the curb be not set in front of square 820: referred to the Cmte on Improvements. 2-Cmte of Claims: bill for the relief of Corbin Baker, & a bill to pay for work done at the West Market: which lie over. Same cmte: discharged from the further consideration of the ptn of Geo W Burgess & others. 3-Cmte on Unfinished Business: ptn of John McK Klokey, asking to be refunded taxes erroneously paid: referred to the Cmte of Claims.

Calif: 1-Jos Mansfield, one of the publishers of the San Joaquin Republican, was shot in the street on Jun 22 by John Tabor, editor of the Stockton Journal. Mr Mansfield met Tabor, a few words passed, when Tabor drew a pistol & shot Mansfield. The wound was mortal. Tabor was arrested & lodged in prison. 2-Jas P Kelly, formerly of Balt, was murdered by A K Ward, who struck the fatal death-blow while intoxicated. Ward stabbed Kelly with a bowie-knife in the region of the heart. 3-J Gorham Bond, of Boston, was drowned on Jun 26 off the island of Molate, in the Bay of San Francisco, while attempting to recover a small boat that had got adrift. 4-Wm B Shephard, convicted of the murder of Henry C Day, has been sentenced to be hung on Jul 26. 5-Jas MacFarlane Foley, who killed J H Dunn, editor of the Police Gaz, pleaded guilty of manslaughter, & was sentenced to 3 years imprisonment. 6-Christina Spohn was murdered in Sacramento on Jun 26, by her husband, Adam Spohn, a butcher. He made his escape, but subsequently committed suicide by drowning. 7-Capt Wm Paine was killed at Angel Island on Jun 28 in an affray with a man named First. The coroner's jury returned a verdict of justifiable homicide. 8-Jas Caldwell, aged 45, committed suicide at the Trement House, Sacramento, by taking an overdose of opium while laboring under a temporary fit of insanity. 9-Mary Brady committed suicide at San Francisco by drowning herself in a cistern in a fit of temporary insanity, caused by the loss of $1,000 which she had invested with a person who had failed in business. 10-Stanton Brown was killed at Rocky Barr, near Downieville, on Jun 15, by the caving in of a bank.

Land for sale: 370 acres, more or less, in Prince Wm Co, Va, being part of the well-known **Piedmont estate**, bounded by the land of Chas H Hunton; & of Judge John Tyler. –Jas W F Macrae, Buckland, Prince Wm Co, Va.

The Long Island Vindicator of last week says: Mr Saml Nolan, late of the city of Dublin, now resident of N Y, with the assistance of his brother-in-law, Dr Antisel, has invented & patented at Washington a paper-making machine & pulp that meets all the difficulty.

On Sunday last, a fire broke out on Princess st, between Royal & Fairfax sts, Alexandria, & the whole block of 6 dwlg houses, occupied by several families, was in a short time destroyed. The houses belonged to Mr David Appich & Mr John T Gordon.

Confession of a murderer. A prisoner in the St Josephs' county jail [Michigan] disclosed that he knew the men who robbed & killed Easterbrook, who had gone to St Josephs' Co, Mich, from Reading, Vt, to be married to a young lady living near White Pigeon. Easterbrook & the young lady to whom he was to be married formerly lived in Alden, Erie Co. Two of the men charged with the murder have been arrested & put in prison. The body was buried under a tree. This story was confirmed by the discovery of the body in the place described.

Buffalo, Jul 26. Miss Fillmore, daughter of Ex-Pres Fillmore, left here last night for Aurora, where she was attacked with cholera & died this morning, aged 22 years. An express reached here this morning informing Mr Fillmore of her sickness, & he, with his son & a Doctor, immediately started for Aurora, but they arrived only a half hour before her death, & she as then insensible. It is a sad bereavement.

The Battle of Bridgewater: Tue was the 40th anniversary of the battle: fought on Jul 25, 1814, against a very superior British force, led by Gens Drummond & Riall. Both Gen Brown & Gen Scott received severe wounds, compelling them to retire from the field, leaving Gen Ripley in command. Gen Brown received his wounds at the same instant, late in the action, one in his shoulder, & other in the upper part of the thigh. Gen Scott has 2 wounds, one in the shoulder & the other in the leg. Capt Spencer, one of the aids of Gen Brown, Maj McFarland, Capts Ritchie, Hull, Kinney, & Goodrich, Lts Bigelow, Turner, & Brighardt, & Ensign Hunter, of the regulars, were killed; also, Capt Hooper, of the N Y volunteers, & Adj Poe, of the Pa volunteers, were killed. Capt Towson's artl was the first & last engaged. Distinguished gallantry displayed by Gens Scott & Porter, Col Miller, Maj Jesup, & Maj Hindman. Pres Madison conferred brevets upon the following ofcrs, giving each an addition rank: Brig Gen Scott, Maj H Leavenworth, Maj T S Jesup, Maj J McNeal, Capt T Crooker, Capt Nathan Towson, Capt T Harrison, Capt L Austin, Lt W J Worth, & Lt G Watts.

Orphans Court of Wash Co, D C. Letters testamentary on the personal estate of Martha Peter, late of Wash Co, deceased. –Mrs B W Kennon, excx

FRI JUL 28, 1854
Chancery sale: by decree of the Circuit Court of Wash Co, D C, in equity. Made in the cause of N P West et al vs Bowie et al: public auction on Aug 19, on the premises, the following valuable bldg lots in Gtwn: 1-Part of lots 74 & 75 of Old Gtwn, 2 fronting on High st, north of Dodge's property. Five lots: parts of lots 74 & 75 of Old Gtwn, adjoining Dodge's property at the corner of High & Water sts, fronting each 25 feet on Water st. In front of the last lots, lot 33 in Beatty & Hawkins' addition to Gtwn, fronting 80 feet on High, nearly opposite 7th st. –Walter S Cox, trustee -Edw S Wright, auct

At Peterham, on Sat, the barn of Ellis Cook was destroyed by lightning; at Boylston the barn of Eli B Bannister was struck & destroyed; & at North Oxford, the barn of Mrs Larned, was also burnt. In Leicester the house of Jos Cheney was struck & injured, & one each of two yokes of oxen were killed. –Boston Courier

Miss Mgt Webb was dangerously if not fatally injured at Norfolk on Tue by the discharge of a pistol in the hands of a person who shot at a dog.

Died: Jul 14, at Opelousas, La, after a lingering illness, Judge John McLean, of N Y.

Died: on Jul 26, at Warrenton Springs, Neal, infant son of Dr C & Fannie R Boyle, aged 10 months & 18 days.

Obit-died: on Jun 21, at the residence of his son-in-law, Gen Waddy Thompson, in Greenville, Col John D Jones, of Wilmington, N C. The deceased was the son of Maj David Jones, who served with distinction in the war of the Revolution. Shortly after he returned from college he was elected by his native county to the House of Commons of N C, & elevated to the Speaker's chair. He never afterwards sought or would accept political employment, preferring the calm vale of private life. He was for many years Pres of the Bank of Cape Fear.

Senate: 1-Cmte on Pensions: to inquire into allowing to Capt Leslie Combs all the arrearages of pension justly due him. 2-Bill for the relief of the widow of Jas Batchelder, killed by a mob in Boston while aiding the U S Marshal in the execution of his duties: bill taken up.

Nashville, Jul 26. Eccentric case of suicide. Dr Jayne blew himself & house up last night by putting a keg of powder under it. Four adjoining bldgs were burnt with it. Loss considerable; supposed to be insured.

New Orleans, Jul 26. Advices from Corpus Christi report that Capt Van Buren, with 12 men, pursued a party of 25 Camanches 300 miles, & then attacked & defeated them. Capt Van Buren was shot through the body, but would probably recover.

A New Paper in Washington: the State Rights Register & Nat'l Economist made its first appearance yesterday. Mr C G Baylor is the editor & proprietor, & he is known as the founder of the Balt Times & the Cotton Plant. The Register will contain a large number of State papers & historical documents. –Sentinel

SAT JUL 29, 1854
Senate: 1-Cmte on Foreign Relations: submitted reports in each case with the following bills: relief of-Horatio J Perry; of Robt M Walsh; of Geo W Lippitt; of Henry Savage; of J B Holman; of Peter Parker; of Jos Graham; & of Ferdinand Coxe. 2-Cmte on Naval Affairs: bill for relief of Capt Lewis E Simonds: passed. 3-Cmte on Post Ofc & Post Roads: bills for relief of J C Buckles, of Louisville, Ky, & for relief of Jas S Graham & Walker H Finnall: recommended their passage. Same cmte: bill for relief of Capt Thos Ap Catesby Jones. Same cmte: asked to be discharged from the further consideration of memorial of Jas L Howison. 4-Cmte on Private Land Claims:recommended their passage: relief of Wm J McElhiney, E P Mathews, & Lawrence Cribben; of A S Laughery; of Rosalie Caxillo; of Patrick Cass; of Enoch Moore; of Wm Curran; of John McVea & John F McKneely, of La; of Robt F McGuire & Louisa his wife, late Louisa Larny; of the legal reps of John Rice Jones, deceased; & of Thos C Green. 5-Cmte of Claims: bill for relief of Sylvester Humphrey & heirs of Alex Humphrey, deceased: recommended its passage. Same cmte: bill for relief of Gad Humphreys. Same cmte: bill for relief of Danl Steenrod: asked its immediate consideration; but objection was made. 6-Resolved: that the Pres of the U S be requested to communicate to the Senate all the information in his possession respecting the bombardment of Greytown or San Juan de Nicaragua by Capt Hollins, in command of the U S sloop-of-war **Cyane**; with copies of all orders or instructions, if any, given by the Executive to said Hollin in relation thereto.

We learn from the Abingdon Virginian that a little daughter of Mr Barker, living in the lower part of Wash Co, was killed a few days ago by a panther. Mrs Barker had sent the little girl to a spring for water. The child staying longer than was necessary, the mother went in search of her. Near the spring she found traces of blood & a short distance beyond a portion of her child's body. The mother raised a small company to search for the animal. Near the remains, the panther was discovered in a tree. The unerring rifle of one of the company brought him to the ground.

War Dept, Wash, Jul 27, 1854. Information of the Cmte on Military Affairs: copy of a communication from Govn'r I J Stevens, of Washington Territory, to the effect that the ***Fort Simpson*** Indians have recently made an attack on the border settlements of that Territory & killed several persons, & among them, it is feared, the Chief Justice of the Territory, Hon Edw Lander. –Jeff'n Davis, Sec of War to Hon C J Faulkner, Chairman Com Military Affairs, House of Reps.

At St Johnsbury, Vt, on Jul 17, Mr Levi Brigham was attacked by a ferocious stallion & so severely injured that he died shortly after.

House of Reps: 1-Bills to which no objection was made: relief of:
Jean Baptiste Beaubien
John Cole
Geo Lynch
Jos Webb
John Steene
Geo Elliott
Warren Raymond
Julia Aiken
adm of Thos Wishart
Lincoln Bates
legal reps of Chas Pavie
Heman Chittenden
Wm Gove, of Maine
Jonathan Pearce
Wm Parker
Zebina Rawson
John A Bryan
Polly Carver
Geo J Rallston
Jos McMinn
Asa Leach
Wm Brown
Gaston T Raoul
A G Penn
Asa Andrews
Wm Darby
Wm G Smith
Urban Stoll
Capt Chas G Merchant
John Frink
Levi Pierce & Andrew Hodge, jre
Henry La Reintree
Legal reps of Geo McGirk
Lloyd Dorsey & others
Eleanor Hoople, of Province of Canada
Jacob Baker, of Sandusky City, Ohio
Sidney P Pool, of the State of Maine
Jonas P Levy, & Jose Maria Jarrero
Legal reps of Maj Caleb Swann, deceased
heirs & reps of Col Alex'r G Morgan
L R Lyon & Dean S Howard, of the State of N Y
Mary Rutherford, widow of Saml Rutherford
Phineas M Nightingale, adm of the estate of Gen Nathl Greene, deceased
Dr S R Addison, passed assist surgeon in the U S navy
Pay John Chas Fremont for beef furnished the Calif Indians
Settle accounts of Thos Jordan, assist Quartermaster in the U S army
2-Bill granting bounty land to Cornelius Coffey. 3-Bill for the purchase of the copyright of a work published by Thos H Sumner, wherein he describes his new method of ascertaining a ship's position at sea. 4-Payment of invalid pension to the heirs of Lt Robt White & others. 5-Compensation for the services of Geo Morell in adjusting titles to lands in Michigan. 6-To pay Jonas W Nye $525, in full satisfaction of his claim for compensation for the use of horses & carryalls furnished the post ofc of the House under a contract with the postmaster, dated Jun 15, 1844.

Ephraim Bee killed a rattlesnake in Doddridge Co, Va, last week, which measured 5' 10" in length, 7" in circumference, & weighed 9¾ pounds.

Dedication of **Glenwood Cemetery** will be on Aug 1, at 5 o'clock. Prayer by Rev R L Dashiell; address by Rev Dr Butler; & poem by Rev Mr Sunderland.

Chas B Calvert	Wm A Bradley	Jos B Close
Geo Parker	Chas S Wallach	Wm Phelps
Wm B Todd	Abner Mellen	Wm S Humphreys
Jas C McGuire	Wm Banks	Randolph S Evans

N B: **Glenwood Cemetery** lies north of the Capitol; distance one mile & a half; formerly the estate of Junius J Boyle.

Died: on Jul 28, in Wash City, of bronchitis, Rev Edw L Dulin, of the Balt Annual Conference of the Methodist Episcopal Church. His funeral will be from his late residence on 6th st, between D & E sts, this morning at 11 o'clock.

Died: on Jul 23, at Columbus, Ohio, of cholera, Jonathan Phillips, formerly a resident of Wash City.

Died: on Jul 21, Elizabeth, daughter of Jeremiah & Mary Deasy, aged 14 months & 4 days.

Orphans Court of Wash Co, D C. In the case of Lisette J Voss, admx of Wm Voss, deceased, the admx & Court have appointed Aug 19 for the settlement & distribution of the estate of said deceased, of the assets in hand. –Ed N Roach, Reg/o wills

Circuit Court of Wash Co, D C-in equity. The Balt & Ohio Railroad Co, vs, John H Gassaway, Jane A Gassaway, Mary A Darne, A C H Darne, Geo Peter, Lavinia Peter, Nicholas Gassaway, Wm A Gassaway, & Laura Gassaway. The original bill & bill of reviver in substance states the the cmplnts purchased lot 2 in Reservation 12, in Wash of John Sinon, subject to a deed of trust to Hanson Gassaway, to secure a debt to him for $683.33; that Gassaway transferred said debt to John Withers, & cmplnts paid it; that Gassaway becoming insane, they never could procure a release from him of said deed of trust; that Gassaway has recently died, & the dfndnts are his heirs at law, & reside out of D C; & it is prayed that a trustee may be appointed in the place of Hanson Gassaway, deceased, to execute a release of said deed of trust. Absent dfndnts are to appear in Court, in person or by solicitor, on or before the first Mon in Dec next. –Jas Dunlap -Jno A Smith, clerk

Phil, Jul 28. Riot this morning, between the Fairmount Engine & the Moyamensing Hose. John Paine, aged 20, received a ball in his back, which lodged in his right breast, & John Raftrice was shot in his right arm. Several arrests were made.

Hon John R Thurman, a Rep in the 31st Congress from the State of N Y, died at his residence in that State on Jul 24. Though a young man, he had filled several stations of distinction in his district.

Balt, Jul 28. Sad accident this morning, or during the night, at the corner of Howard & Barre sts. Mr John R Perkins, of the well known commercial firm of Perkins & Traverse, Light st, by some unaccountable accident, fell from the window of his bed chamber during the night & was so badly injured that he died soon after. The bed of the deceased was near the window.

Western Military Institute, Tyree Springs, Sumner Co, Tenn. Address B R Johnson, Superintendent, or Richd Owen, Commandant, Tyree Springs, Tenn.

Library House of Reps: Wash, Jul 21, 1854. Books should be returned before the close of the session. –Mathias Martin, Librarian House of Reps.

MON JUL 31, 1854
Household & kitchen furniture at auction: Aug 7, at the residence of W D Tuely, Pa ave, near 6th st, over J Wilson's grocery store. –T L Potter, trustee
-Green & Scott, aucts

Senate: 1-Bills passed: relief of Wm G Smith. Joint resolution giving 160 acres of land to Francis M Gwin, of Indiana. Bill for the settlement of the claims of W P Buckner & Pierce Crosby, passed midshipmen in the U S navy. Joint resolution for the relief of John A Bryan.

Wm Easby, late Com'r of the Public Bldgs, & for many years past an active & useful citizen, died on Sat last, after a few days' illness.

Obit-died: on Jul 11, suddenly, of cholera, at La Pointe, on Lake Superior, Hon Wm Griffith Ewing, of **Fort Wayne**, Ind. He was on a business tour to Fond du Lac, at the head of Lake Superior, where he had a trading post. He was the son of Col Alex Ewing, a tried soldier of the Revolution, & who belonged also to Capt Wm Griffith's company of spies that piloted the American army to the battle of the Thames in Oct, 1813. Wm Griffith Ewing was born at the town of Monroe, on the River Basin, in the Territory of Michigan, in Oct, 1800, & was in his 54th year. Originally educated at Cincinnati for the bar, & at age 21 he settled at Natchez, where he soon reached a high point of standing in his profession. The extreme heat of that Southern climate determined him, however, to return North. He founded a trading-house May 1, 1822, which became known from London to N Y & to the Pacific Ocean; his junior brother, G W Ewing, the partner. He happily presided as husband, gentleman, neighbor, & friend.

Died: on Sat last, in his 64th year, Capt Wm Easby. His funeral will be this afternoon, at 4½ o'clock, from his late residence on Pa ave & 8th st east.

Died: on Jul 28, Mary Teresa, infant daughter of Michl R & Catharine Shyne, aged 8 months & 15 days.

The obsequies of Miss Mary Abby Fillmore, daughter of Ex-Pres Fillmore, took place at Buffalo on Thu. She was a dutiful daughter, devoted sister, & an affectionate friend.
[Aug 8th newspaper: Miss Fillmore was a skilful performer both upon the piano & the harp. In Wash, the etiquette of the place & her mother's feeble health combined to devolve upon her, almost unaided, the entire performance of the social duties incident to her father's station. She was but a young girl fresh from school.]

Died: on Jul 28, near Balt, Ellen C, wife of Thos J Carson, of N Y, & daughter of the late Col Benj Edes, of Balt.

Died: on Sat, Richard Grafton Hyatt, infant son of Richard G & Mgt Ann Hyatt, aged 1 year & 11 days.

Died: on Jul 14, at The Cave, Jefferson Co, Va, Mrs Anne R Selden, wife of John Selden, & daughter of Andrew Kennedy, in her 29th year.

On Tue, as five men were being drawn up from the tunnel on the Portage [Pa] railroad, 180 feet deep, two of them, P Strain & John Shields, were precipitated to the bottom & instantly killed. Two others, John Mageham & H Sweeny, had their arms & legs broken.

Buffalo, Jul 29. A private dispatch from a reliable source announces the death of Pres Fillmore's brother yesterday at St Paul's, Minnesota, of cholera. [Aug 2nd newspaper: Mr Chas Fillmore, brother of Ex-Pres Fillmore, died suddenly on Thu at St Paul, Minnesota.]

Death of Four <u>Sisters of Mercy</u>. It is with feeling of the deepest sorrow that we have to record the sudden demise of Mother Agatha, [Mgt O'Brien,] & her two sisters in religion, Sisters Mary Bernard Hughes & Louisa Connors, of whom the 2 former died at the Mercy Convent, in this city, on Sat, Jul 8, & the latter on Jul 9. A fourth has since been added to the melancholy list by the decease of Sister Mary Veronica Hicky, at the Mercy Hospital, on Jul 11. The death of Mother Agatha leaves now but one, Mother Vincent, of the original band of 6 Sisters who founded the order in this diocese, five of them having been already gathered to the bosom of their Father who is in Heaven. -Chicago Western Tablet

Hon Henderson Young, Judge of the Sixth Judicial Cicruit of Ky, died at his residence near Lexington on Jul 23.

A telegraphic dispatch from Quebec announces the death there on Monday, by cholera, of Col Hogarth, commanding the 26th Regt of British Infty. He was in command of the regt during the Gavazzi riot.

The tobacco factory of Messrs Geo W Gilliam & Brother, at Richmond, Va, with the whole of its contents, was destroyed by fire on Thu: entire loss about $40,000.

Dr Avery Downer, the last survivor of the battle of **Fort Griswold**, died at Preston, Conn, on Sat, aged 91 years & 8 months. He was at **Fort Griswold** with his father, who was also a physician, at the time of the massacre, & assisted to dress the wounds of the soldiers.

TUE AUG 1, 1854
Senate: 1-Ptn from Elijah D Brigham, asking permission to change the name of a vessel, & that a register be issued under the name of **Wizard**. 2-Ptn from J C McFenan & Saml D Sturgiss, ofcrs of the army, asking compensation for services rendered by them respectively in grades higher than that to which they belonged. 3-Cmte on Public Lands: memorial of Chas Gordon: to be paid the sum of $1,500, it being for his services as draughtsman for the Senate from Mar 3, 1838 to Jan 1, 1840. 4-Cmte on the Post Ofc & Post Roads: joint resolution for settlement of the claims of the late firm of C M Strader & Co, mail contractors. 5-Cmte on Military Affairs: recommended the passage of-relief of: David C Cash & Giles U Ellis; of Wm Hankins; of Lt Geo H Paige, U S N; & of Brvt Capt J H Landrum, U S N. Settle the accounts of Thos Jordan, U S Army; settle the claim of Don Juan Jesus Virgil, of New Mexico. 6-Cmte on Pensions: resolution to adjust the account of Wm Woodbury, late pension agent at Portland, Maine: passed. Same cmte: bill for the relief of John S King, of Va, & recommended its passage. Same cmte: bill for the relief of Betsy Nash, a widow of an ofcr of the war of 1812: the amendment struck out 10 years & inserted 5, so as to limit the provision to that period.

Explosion of Garresche's powder mills, about 1½ miles from Wilmington, on Sat, killed the watchman, Jas Lynch, & severely injured Dennis Cannon, the engineer.

Mrd: on Jun 30, in Foundry Church, by Rev E P Phelps, Mr Wm H Goodger to Miss Sarah E Wood, all of Wash City.

Obit-died: on Jun 29, at his residence in Wash City, after an afflicting illness of 9 days, Capt Wm Easby, in his 64th year. From 1812, the date of his settlement here, he has been actively identified with the growth & interest of the city & its inhabitants. The deceased was an Englishman by birth; but, having been brought to this country by his parents in his infancy, he was thoroughly Americanized. He revisited England in 1849 as bearer of despatches to the American Minister & as Com'r to the World's Fair. In 1812 Capt Easby was one of the most energetic & dauntless of the young volunteers who acted against the British army in its approach to Wash. He was later appointed Com'r of Public Bldgs in Wash, by Pres Fillmore. At the time of his death, & for many years previously, he was the Treasurer of the Nat'l Institute. He met death with the utmost fortitude surrounded by most of the members of his immediate family.

Coroner's inquest was held on the body of Jas Gunner, which was found on the line of the wharf, at the foot of 11 st. He was last seen on Jul 29 in a debilitated condition. He was an old man, about 60 years of age. His death came from exposure & debility.

Died: on Jul 28, Wm Irving, in his 41st year, formerly a citizen of N Y, but for the last 3 or 4 years a resident of Wash City. He filled the post of Chief Clerk in the Census Bureau, & at the time of his death held a responsible clerkship in the ofc of the 4th Auditor of the Treasury. He traveled extensively in his own country & in Europe.

Died: on Jul 29, aged one year, Ellen Augusta, infant daughter of Dr Wm P Johnston, of Wash City.

Wash Corp Ordinance: 1-The sum of $10.75 be paid to W B Wilson for cleaning the snow from the Northern Market-house.

Teacher wanted to act as Principal in a Female Seminary in Charlestown, Jefferson Co, Va. He must come highly recommended. Apply in person to R S Blackburn, sec

The Cincinnati Gaz gives an account of the arrest of Jas Roundtree, on Sunday, at Paris, Ky, on a charge of swindling some Kentuckians out of $900.

Two women were drowned on Jun 27, in the Monongahela river, 6 miles from Pittsburgh. It appeared that two men named Nelson & Woods, both residents of Peebles township, had crossed the river on a shooting excursion, & when returning they did not reach the bank of the river opposite their dwlgs until 9 o'clock at night. They shouted to those residing on the opposite side of the river to send them a skiff. Nelson's wife hearing her husband's voice ran to get them help & on her way met Ellen Woods, daughter of of her husband's companion. They pulled a skiff into the water & commenced to whirl around in the water & the women fell overboard & drowned. Mrs Nelson was the mother of 3 children & very much respected. Miss Woods was about 16 years of age, a sprightly intelligent girl.

Co-partnership existing between the undersigned is dissolved by mutual consent. –Geo Burns, Harmon Burns. Geo Burns has disposed of his interest in the Boot & Shoe Store, on Pa ave, between 4½ & 6th sts, to his brother, Harmon Burns.

All persons are cautioned against trusting any one on my account either by order or otherwise, as I shall positively pay no debts contracted by any one except myself. -Mrs Robt S Wood, Eliz Wood

WED AUG 2, 1854
Jacob Richardson, formerly Collector of Customs at Oswego, NY, died at Kingston, in Canada, on Jul 25.

Senate: 1-Cmte on the Dist of Col: bill for the relief of Wm B Kibbey. 2-House bill for the relief of Chas Steenrod: passed. 3-Cmte on Private Land Claims: bills from the House of Reps without amendment: relief of the legal reps of Geo McGirk; of the heirs of Benj Metoyer; of the legal reps of Chas Pavie; & of the legal reps of Lloyd Dorsey & others. 4-Cmte on Pensions: bills from the House of Reps: recommended their passage: relief of

Julia Acken
Herman Chittenden
Wm Gove
Wm Parker
Geo M Butler, of Ind
Jas Butler
Jas Cassen
Jas Wright, of Tenn
Thos Ellis
Abraham Ansman
Thos Bronaugh
John Cole
Geo Lynch

Jos Webb
John Steene
Geo Elliott
Warren Raymond
Geo J Rollston
Jas McMinn
Asa Leach
John H Hicks, of Ind
John Brown, 2nd, of N H
Irs Call, of Huran Co, Ohio
Isaac M Sigler, of Putnam Co, Ind
Jacob Baker, of Sandusky Co, Ohio

Danl Morse, of Essex, Chittenden Co, Vt
Rebecca Baggerby, widow of Jas Baggerby, deceased
5-Pension for Oliver Brown, of Chemung Co, N Y. 6-Pension for Edmund Mitchell, of Carroll Co, Ky.

Died: on Aug 1, Mr John W Ferguson, in his 42nd year. His funeral will take place tomorrow, at 3 o'clock, from the Methodist Protestant Church, on Va ave, near the Navy Yard.

Died: on Aug 1, in his 4th year, Franck Pinckney, son of R W Latham, of Wash City. His funeral is at 5 o'clock this evening.

Died: on Jul 20, at Gtwn, Ga, Robt Lowry Moore, a native of Wash, & eldest daughter of the late Jas Moore, of Wash City, aged 42 years.

Died: on the 20th ult, at Petersburg, Va, Mrs Sarah Melleville Bolling, aged 41 years, consort of Robt B Bolling. Her bereaved husband & family have sustained an irreparable loss. As wife, mother, or friend, she had no superior.

Died: on the 22nd ult, at Buchanan, Botetourt Co, Va, Saml R G Ould, son of Robt & Sarah A Ould, aged 18 months.

For sale, the property of Mr Corbett, of the British Legation, who is returning to England: a chestnut horse; a lady's saddle; a set of single buggy harness; double reined bridle, & a quantity of horse clothing. Apply at Mr Earle's Livery stables, on H st, between 20th & 21st sts.

THU AUG 3, 1854
The N Y papers mention that Gen Jose Barrundia, Minister from Honduras, is in that city very ill.

Senate: 1-Cmte on Private Land Claims: adverse reports in the cases of Wm Gitt & of Martin Fenwick. 2-Cmte on Naval Affairs: asked to be discharged from the further consideration of the memorial of Wm Black. 3-Cmte on Military Affairs: bill for the relief of Wm H Weirick: passed. 4-Cmte on Commerce: bill for the relief of Jacob McLellan: passed.

House of Reps: 1-Cmte on Private Land Claims: confirm the title of Chas G Gunter: passed. 2-Cmte on Revolutionary Claims: bill for the relief of the heirs of Capt Joshua Chamberlain, deceased: laid on the table. Same cmte: recommended that they pass, Senate bill for the relief of Robt C Thompson, legal rep of Wm H Thompson, deceased. Also, for the relief of the legal reps of Henry King, deceased: both committed. Same cmte: bill relative to the accounts of Stephen Moyer: committed.

Lt Maes, of the Rio Arriba battalion, started from Valecito with 6 Indians to bring to Santa Fe. On the way down they made an attempt to escape, when they were fired upon by the guard & 3 killed. Their scalps were then taken off & brought in; which we saw dangling at the saddle of one of the men in front of the place.

On Jul 18, Mr Jose Antonio Casados was coming to town to attend court, when he was shot in the Apache canon between here & Pecos, & has since died. The murder is supposed to have been committed by a party of Gov't teamsters who were encamped at that place.

In the recent Jersey City conflagration, an Irish widow, Mgt McClennan, was burnt to death in one of the houses while intoxicated. She was rescued but went back into the house to search for her little girl who was supposed to be there.

The Salem Register discredits the late rumor from Oregon that Chief Justice Edw Lander [son of Capt Edw Lander, of Salem] had been massacred by Indians at one of the settlements on Puget Sound.

At Kansas, on Jul 20, whilst Judge Walderan, who was in pursuit of runaway negroes, was attempting to dismount from his horse, he accidentally discharged his gun & killed himself.

Died: on Aug 2, in Wash City, in her 75th year, Mrs Mgt Stewart, consort of the late Saml Stewart. Her funeral will take place of Fri, at 10 o'clock, from her late residence, on 11th st, & proceed from thence to St Patrick's Church, on F st, where mass will be said & other funeral services performed.

Died: on Jul 4, 1854, at sea, on his passage from the Sandwich Islands to N Y, Phineas Bradley Sanders, in his 23rd year, son of B C Sanders, late Collector of the port of San Francisco, Calif. For several months in declining health, he had been advised by his physician to try the more genial air of Honolulu, whither he went early in March. Finding his disease, consumption, increasing so rapidly, he desired to return to the bosom of his family to die, but when within a week's sail of N Y his spirit returned to God, who gave it.

Died: on Aug 2, Dora, aged 3 months & 15 days, daughter of Metta & Adolphus Eirhstedt.

N Y, Aug 2. An affray with bowie knives took place on Aug 1 at the St Nicholas Hotel between a Southerner, Dr Graham, & a Californian, Mr Lowrie. Lowrie lingered but an hour. Both gentlemen had families who are boarding at the hotel. [Oct 11th newspaper-N Y, Oct 10: the jury in the case of Dr Graham came in with a verdict of manslaughter in the 2nd degree. The punishment is to be not less than 4 nor more than 7 years' confinement in the penitentiary. The counsel for Dr Graham have obtained a stay of proceedings for 20 days, to enable them to file exceptions.]

A large new bldg of the Manhattan Gas Co, on 14th st, N Y, fell down on Sat. The killed are Cornelius Wykoff, master mason, Patrick Sheer, & Jas Gilhooley.

On May 20, 1736, the body of Saml Baldwin was in compliance with an injunction in his will, immersed sans ceremonie in the sea at Lymington, Hants. He wanted to prevent his wife from dancing over his grave, which she had threatened to do in the case she should survive him. –English paper

Penn Female College, Perkiomen Bridge Post Ofc, Montg Co, Pa: established by authority of the Commonwealth for the liberal education of young women. -J Warrenne Sunderland, Pres

FRI AUG 4, 1854
Household & kitchen furniture at auction: on Aug 7, at the residence of Jas Walters, 7th st, below L st, near the Navy Yard. -Green & Scott, aucts

Mrd: on Thu, by Rev John C Smith, Mr Wm H Goodman to Miss Sarah Ann Ingram, all of Wash City.

Mrd: on Aug 3, by Rev J W French, Saml W Owen, of Va, to Kate E Evans, of Wash City.

Murder at the St Nicholas Hotel, in N Y, of Mr Chas Loring, of Calif, by Mr R M Graham, of New Orleans. Mr Loring was a resident of Calif & receiver of public moneys at Benicia. The parties had no acquaintance with each other. Mr Graham disturbed Mr & Mr Loring, by ringing the hall bell a number of times for a servant, after the Lorings had gone to bed. Mr Loring opened his door a few times to ask Mr Graham to dress himself & go down stairs for a servant. On his return, Graham met Loring, angry words were exchanged, & Graham stabbed Loring with a sword cane which he had in his hand, killing him almost instantly. He had been committed to prison to await his trial.

Appointments by the Pres. by & with the advice & consent of the Senate.
Jas Tilton, of Ind, to be surveyor-gen for the Territory of Wash.
John Calhoun, of Ill, to be surveyor-gen for Kansas & Nebraska.
Wm Pelham, of Texas, to be surveyor-gen for New Mexico.
Geo P Steles, to be assoc justice of the supreme court of the Territory of Utah, vice John U H Underwood, declined.
Reuben H Gibson, of Ohio, to be receiver at Defiance, Ohio, vice Wm Sheffield, removed.
Ralph Wilcox, of Oregon, to be register for Oregon.
Jas Guthrie, jr, of Oregon, to be receiver for Oregon.
Diedrich Upman, of Wisc, to be register for the Minona land district, in Minn.
Lorenzo D Smith, of Minn, to be receiver for the Minona land district, in Minn.
Wm W Phelps, of Mich, to be register for the Redwing land district, in Minn.
Christopher Graham, of Ind, to be receiver for the Redwing land district, in Minn.
H C Moseley, of Wash Territory, to be register for said Territory.
Elias Yulee, of Ohio, to be receiver for the land ofc for Wash Territory.

Died: on Aug 3, in Wash City, Miss Eliz Catharine Crawford, daughter of Hon T Hartley Crawford. Her funeral will take place from the house of her father, corner of F & 7th sts, this afternoon, at 5 o'clock.

Died: on Thu, of whooping cough, Catharine Harriet, youngest daughter of Mary W & Moses Kelly, aged 20 months. Her funeral will take place from the residence of her grandmother, Mrs *Walker, Missouri ave, this afternoon, at 5 o'clock.
[*Walker was Wblker in the paper].

Died: on Jul 27, at his residence in PG Co, Md, Henry H Waring, in his 58th year.

Died: on Jul 31, at Dunham, Conn, Wm M W Smith, only child of E Goodrich & Mrs Susan W Smith, of Wash City, aged 14 years.

Michl Malone, a contractor on the Pa railroad, was robbed on Monday night of a carpet bag containing $4,000 at the American Hotel, Phil. When arriving at the hotel he deposited his carpet bag in a room downstairs & left the house on business of importance. While absent a stranger directed a servant to bring the bag to his room, which was done, & later the stranger handed the key to the servant & walked out.

Orphans Court of Wash Co, D C. Letters of administration, with the will annexed, on the personal estate of Edw L Dulin, late of Wash Co, deceased.
–Burr P Dulin, Adm W A

Senate: 1-Cmte on Foreign Relations: bill for the relief of Saml A Belden & Co. Same cmte: bill for the relief of Betsy W Eve. Same cmte: adverse reports on the memorials of H Gold Rogers; of Chas D Arfwedson; of J G Schwarr; of Geo Frasier; & of J Balestier. 2-Bills considered & passed: relief of-Wm D Porter, U S N; of John McVey & John McNeelly, of La; of Jas Walsh; of Jesse R Faulkner, of Missouri; of Henry N Halsted; of Benj Hammond, of the State of N Y; of Jas M Lewis; of Albro Trip; of Henry Lewis, of Clinton Co, Ind; & of Henry J Snow, of Rome, N Y. Also, a pension for Jas K Welch. 3-Ptn of John Bronaugh was taken up, to which Mr Pearce moved to add a section repealing the Minnesota land bill.

SAT AUG 5, 1854
For sale: a handsome site for a country residence, 4 miles from the Centre Market, Wash, on the plank road: front of over 500 feet on said road. Aply to me on the premises, or to Capt Thos Carbery, Wash, D C. –Thos Fitnam

U S Patent Ofc, Wash, Aug 4, 1854. Ptn of David Matthew, of Phil, Pa, praying for the extension of a patent granted to him on Dec 31, 1840, for an improvement in spark arresters, for 7 years from the expiration of said patent, which takes place on Dec 31, 1854. –Chas Mason, Com'r of Patents

By order of distrain for house rent due to Wm H Langley by Michl Frelinburger, I will expose at public sale, for cash, on Aug 12, in front of the Centre Market-house, Wash City, D C: 23 glass jars, 3 chairs, 1 glass case, 2 buckets, & 1 keg.
-H R Maryman, constable

Mrd: on Aug 3, by Rev Byron Sunderland, John C Pedrick, of N Y, to Mrs America Fatio, only daughter of the late Col Saml Burche, of Wash City.

Mrd: on Aug 3, by Rev Andrew G Carothers, Mr John Roberts to Miss Mary Eliz Peters, both of Wash City.

Orphans Court of Wash Co, D C. Letters testamentary on the personal estate of Timothy O'Neale, late of Wash Co, deceased. –Ann R O'Neale, H B Sweeney, excs

Obit-died: yesterday, at his residence in Wash City, after a brief illness, Dr Bailey Washington, honored as an ofcr & beloved as a man wherever he was known. Dr Washington was born in Westmoreland Co, Va, on May 12, 1787, & connected by blood & birthright with the illustrious man whose name he bore. At the time of his death he was one of the senior surgeons in the U S Navy, having entered it in 1810. He was the surgeon of the brig **Enterprize** when she captured the ship **Boxer** during the last war, & afterwards served with efficiency on Lake Ontario under Com Chauncey, & selected by that high ofcr as his fleet surgeon, though a junior. He was successively fleet-surgeon under Cmdors Rodgers, Elliott, & Patterson, in the Mediterranean, & closed his active sea-service during the Mexican war. At the time of his death he was consulting & visiting sugeon of the navy yard & marine barracks in Wash City. As a physician few surpassed him in the soundness of his judgment & the calm reflections which a long medical practice had afforded. As husband, father, & brother, his memory will always be remembered. The death of his gallant brother on board the ill-fated steamer **San Francisco** clouded his spirit the past few months affecting his health. His closing hours of life were soothed by the intense love of his now bereaved widow & children, & he breathed his last under the cheering influence of Christian faith & hope.

+

The funeral of the late Dr Washington will be this evening at 5 o'clock, from his late residence. [Aug 7th newspaper: the funeral of Dr Bailey Washington, of the navy, took place Sat. The long array of carriages was preceded by a company of U S marines & the band from the barracks, in full uniform, making a fine appearance, while 12 sailors walked on each side of the hearse.]

Senate: 1-Bills passed-relief of: David C Cash & Giles U Ellis; of Ira Call, of Huron Co, Ohio; of the legal reps of John Rice Jones, deceased; of Jacob Baker, of Sandusky City, Ohio; & of Thos C Green. Also, settle the accounts of Thos Jordan, assist quartermaster in the U S Army. 2-Cmte on Private Land Claims: bill for the relief of F A Whitney: passed. 3-Cmte on Pensions: bill for the relief of Jonathan Pearce, of Muskingum Co, Ohio: passed. Same cmte: bill for the relief of the heirs of Capt Thos Porter: passed. 4-Bills passed: relief of: Rosalie Caxillo; of Patrick Gass; & of A S Longberry. 5-Bills passed: relief of-the legal heirs of Benj Metoyer; of the legal reps of Chas Pavie; of John S King, of Va; of Gad Humphreys; of Horatio J Perry; of Robt F McGuire & Louisa his wife, late Louisa Lanny; & of ___ Gore.

<u>Appointments by the Pres, by & with the advice & consent of the Senate.</u>
Robt B Campbell, of Texas, to be Consul of the U S for the port of London, vice Geo N Sanders.
Roger Barton, of Miss, to be Consul of the U S for the port of Havana, in the island of Cuba, vice Alex'r M Clayton, resigned.
Saml H Montgomery, of Ark, to be Agent for the Indians in New Mexico.

MON AUG 7, 1854

Gen Jose Barrundia, Minister to the U S from Honduras, died at N Y on Fri. His age is stated at 70 years. He left Honduras in Apr in rather infirm health, & has been declining gradually until the time of his death.

Jos F Robinson, aged 20, was killed at Nantucket on Mon by the accidental discharge of his gun.

Harvey Chase, of the firm of Boughton & Chase, of Rochester, N Y, was fatally injured by being caught in a belt & carried around a revolving drum at the rate of 80 times a minute.

Two Irish girls, Ellen Winn & Bridget Dugan, both 13 years of age, & John Murray, a man of intemperate habits, were drowned at Providence on Wed afternoon.

The graduating class of the Patapsco Institue at Ellicott's Mills, Md, at the late commencement numbered 28. Hon Judge Dorsey & Edw Gray, having resigned their ofcs as members of the Board of Trustees, Dr Wm Denny & Hon John P Kennedy have been elected to fill their places.

Died: on Aug 5, Edward Francis, second & only son of I Andria & M A Iardella, aged 3 months. His funeral is this evening, at 5 o'clock, from the residence of his father, N J ave & B st.

Died: on Aug 6, Thomas, aged 16 months, only child of Thos & Mary Duffy. His funeral is this evening at 5 o'clock.

Died: on Aug 2, at *Edge Hill*, Caroline Co, Va, Wm C Nelson, in his 48th year.
+
Died: on Aug 3, at *Edge Hill*, Caroline Co, Va, Wm D Schooler, in his 24th year. They rest from their labors, & their work follows them.

Died: on Aug 6, Margaret Anne, youngest daughter of Chas F & Catharine McCarthy, aged 22 months. Her funeral is this afternoon, at 4 o'clock, from their residence.

Russia: Prince Paskiewitch is not dead as reported, but it is stated has so far recovered from his injuries that he will soon assume the command of the Danubian army.

Mrd: on Aug 3, in St Anne's Church, at Annapolis, by Rev C K Nelson, Jas K Howison to Sally, daughter of Jas Murray.

Appointments by the Pres, by & with the advice & consent of the Senate.
Francis A Chenoweth, of the Territory of Wash, to be an Assoc Justice of the Supreme Court in that Territory, vice Victor Munroe, removed from the Territory.
Wm Claude Jones, of Missouri, to be Atty for New Mexico, vice Wm W H Davis, resigned.
John E Warren, of Minn, to be Atty for Minn, vice Danl H Dustin, deceased.

Consuls of the U S:
Jos C Hart, of N Y, for Teneriffe.
Townsend Harris, for Ningpo, in China.
John Higgins, of Pa, for Belfast, Ireland.
Hugh Keenan, of Pa, for Cork, in Ireland.
Darius A Ogden, of N Y, for Honolulu.
Robt S Cassat, of Pa, for the kingdom of Hanover
Wm Hubotter, for Lagund, Mexico

Collector of the Customs:
Jas E Gibble, Beaufort, N C, reappointed.
T L Shaw, Gtwn, S C, reappointed.
Horace Moody, Ogdensburgh, N Y, vice Thos Bacon, rejected.

Surveyors of the Customs:
David S Ruddock, of New London, Conn
Henry N Dowd, of Albany, vice Robt S Cushman

Indian Agents:
Garland Hunt, of Ky, agent in Utah
R H Lansdale, of Washington Territory, agent in said Territory
Aquila Jones, of Indiana, to be agent in Wash Territory
Edw Hunter to be marshal for southern Calif, vice Pablo Noriega, resigned
John S Hacker, to be surveyor of Cairo, in Ill
Wm Stotts, to be surveyor of Keokuk, Iowa
Wm H Merritt, to be surveyor of Dubuque, Iowa
Wm A Buffum, of N Y, to be consul for the port of Trieste, vice Wyndham Robertson
Wm H Emory, of the U S Army, to be Com'r on the part of the U S to run the boundary line between the U S & the Mexican Republic, according to the treaty of Dec 30, 1853.
Jas W Rhea to be surveyor & inspector of the revenue for Tuscumbia, Ala
Pashal Bequette, of Calif, to be Receiver at Benicia, Calif, vice Chas Loring, deceased.
John A Wheeler, of N C, to be Minister resident of the U S to Nicaragua.
John L Marling, of Tenn, to be Minister resident of the U S to Guatemala.
Wm Grayson Mann, of D C, to be sec of the legation of the U S to Brazil
Fred'k A Beelen, of Pa, to be sec of the legation of the U S to Chili
Francis Burt, of S C, to be Govn'r of the Territory of Nebraska
Chas H Mason, of R I, to be Sec of the Territory of Wash.

Orphans Court of Wash Co, D C. Letters of administration on the personal estate of Thos Hudal, late of Wash Co, deceased. –Mary Hudal, admx

TUE AUG 8, 1854
7th st property for sale, now occupied by M Ruppell as a tavern. The property is lot 5 in the subdivision of square 461. -Jas C McGuire, auct

Trustee's sale of real estate: by deed of trust dated Dec 30, 1847, from Geo H Plant & Eliza Ann his wife, recorded in Liber W B No 137, folios 452 thru 456, of the Land Records of Wash Co, D C: public auction in Wash City, on Sep 13, of lots E thru K, of subdivision of original lot 4 in square 378, made by Selby Parker on May 12, 1845, recorded in the Surveyor's ofc, in Wash City. Improvements are six 2 story brick tenements. –John E Norris, trustee -Jas C McGuire, auct

Trustee's sale of valuable improved real estate on 15th st, near H. By deed of trust, executed to Wm B Webb, from Chas Wierman & wife, recorded on Oct 15, 1852, among the land records of Wash Co; of another deed of trust from said Wierman & wife to Saml Fowler, recorded Nov 2, 1852, & also another deed of trust to Robt Farnham, recorded Jun 14, 1853, with the concurrence & by the direction of the parties for whose use the said trust deed were given: public auction on Aug 28, of lot 11 in Davidson's subdivision of square 222, fronting on 15th st, 25 feet more or less, with a three story brick dwlg house. –S S Williams, Atty for trustees
-Green & Scott, aucts

For rent: the Valley House, new hotel, in Chillicothe, Ross Co, Ohio. Chillicothe is situated in the midst of the far-famed Scioto Valley. Apply to D A Schutte, Sec of the Valley House Assoc.

Brookeville Academy, Montg Co, Md. The Fall session will commence on Sep 4.
-E B Prettyman, A M, Principal. References in Wash:
Prof S F Baird, Smith Institute   Rev R L Dashiell, A M
John C Rives   Thos P Morgan
Chas H Lane   Messrs Gray & Ballantyne

Hagerstown Female Seminary: next session will commence on Sep 21. Address Rev C C Baughman, Principal, Hagerstown, Wash Co, Md. –F R Anspach, Pres of the Board

Thos Bushrod Washington, aged about 40 years, of Jefferson Co, Va, died at Albany, N Y, on Friday. The deceased was a son of Bushrod Washington, & grandson of John A Washington, consequently a grand nephew of Gen Geo Washington.

Mrd: on Aug 5, by Rev C M Butler, D D, J D B De Bow, of Louisiana, to Caroline, daughter of Geo Poe, of Gtwn, D C.

Mr Hubbard W Varnon, of Bourbon Ci, Ky, narrowly escaped a violent death on Monday. An imported bull broke his halter, threw his owner upon the floor, & attempted to gore him, which was prevented by the timely arrival of some of the field hands. Mr Varnon was badly hurt, having his collar-bone & some of his rib bones broken, besides other injuries.

Deaths by lightning: 1-Miss Cordelia Gathright was killed by lightning a few days ago in Goochland Co, Va. 2-On Monday last Mr Wm Richards, overseer of Mr J W George, about 5 miles east of Culpeper Courthouse, Va, was struck by lightning & instantly killed. 3-Two negroes belonging to Mr Wm Palmer, of Mecklenberg Co, Va, were killed by lightning on Wed. 4-Last week the 17 & 18 year old sons of Mr Wyatt Brown, of Bedford Co, Va, were found in the Staunton river, the supposition of the jury was that the boys were struck by lightning while wading in the river.

On the Eastern [Mass] Railroad, very lately, a man named John Donaval attempted to get off the train at West Lynn while it was passing through there, & was killed almost instantly. He had been told there was no stop of West Lynn.

WED AUG 9, 1854
Chancery sale of valuable real estate: by decree of the Circuit Court of Wash Co, D C, made in the cause wherein Jas F Haliday & others are cmplnts, & Thos J Haliday & others, heirs-at-law of Thos Haliday, Anna Haliday, Wm W Haliday, & Lydia J Hanlon, deceased, are dfndnts, the subscriber, Trustee appointed by said decree, will sell at public auction those parcels of ground in Wash Co as being: lot 16 in square 104; lot 16 in square 703; lots 4 thru 7 in square 779; lots 1, 2, & 14 in square 1,136; part of lot 3, in square south of square 825, said part of said lot 3 on 4th st, part of square 905; lot 1 in square 996, with a 2 story frame house. –Chas S Wallach, trustee -J C McGuire, auct

Mrd: on Aug 8, by Rev J G Butler, Upton H Ridenour to Lizzie Miller, both of Wash City.

Died: on Jun 20 last, at *Auvergne plantation*, Talahatchie Co, Miss, Col Geo W Martin, aged 65 years. He was in the late war, & accompanied Gen Jackson throughout his campaigns in 1813, 1814, & 1815, & in the Creek war. In the last campaign of Gen Jackson, Col Martin served as an aid of Gen Coffee. In this capacity he rendered efficient service in the defence of New Orleans.

For sale: a two horse-power [railway] Thrasher, in good order. –Hy L Carlton, Bladensburg, Md.

THU AUG 10, 1854
Household & kitchen furniture at auction on Aug 16, at the residence of Prof Coffin, 19th & I sts. -Jas C McGuire, auct

Acts passed by the First Session of the 33rd Congress: Private Acts-relief of:

- Madison Parton
- Benj S Roberts
- Wm Blake
- Chas Staples
- Lemuel Hudson
- Jas F Green
- Thos Frazer
- Cornelius H Latham
- Saml W Brady
- John O Mears
- Lyman N Cook
- Benj Row
- Wm B Edwards
- Geo W Gibson
- Allen Nelson
- Silas Champion
- Grafton Baker
- Saml K Reyburn
- G W Torrence
- A B Roman
- Chas Lee Jones
- Robt Grignon
- Charlotte Westcott
- Jas Capen
- Asa Leach
- Julia Aiken
- A S Laughery
- Rosalie Caxillo
- Patrick Gass
- Thos C Green
- Catharine Pierce
- Jos McMinn
- Jas M Lewis
- Mary H Cushing
- Henry N Halsted
- Jas Walsh
- John Frink
- Albro Tripp
- Wm H Weizick
- Danl Steenrod
- Wm Curran
- John S Jones
- Betsey Nash
- Geo Mattingly
- Priscilla C Simonds
- Jos Mitchell
- Mary C Hamilton
- Moses Olmsted
- Allen G Johnson
- Zadock C Ingraham
- Lewellyn Washington
- Thos K Glenn
- Richd King
- Jas M Goggin
- Andrew J Deckerhoff
- Wm Senna Factor
- John S Wilson
- Thos S Russell
- A G Bennett
- Purser T P McBlair
- Saml H Hempstead
- John W Kelly
- Ira Baldwin
- Thos T Jennings
- Jos Campau
- Manuel Hernandez
- Wm Claude Jones
- Rebecca Freeman
- Jas Wormsley
- Mary Carlton
- Sarah Crandall
- Wm Miller
- Thos Snodgrass
- John Baptiste Beaubien
- Wm Brown
- Gaston T Raoul
- A G Penn
- Henry La Reintree
- Asa Andrews
- Wm Darby
- Wm G Smith
- Urban Stoll
- Sylvanus Culver
- Capt Chas G Merchant
- Jas Dunning
- Ezra Williams

John Fagan
Lavinia Taylor
Sylvester Pettibone
Ira Day, of Vt
John Gusman, of La
Aaron Stafford, of the State of N Y
Wm Mayo, of Maine
Fayette Mauzy & Robt G Ward
Emelie Hooe, widow of Capt Hooe
Heirs of Anthony G Willis, deceased
Capt Geo Simpton, of Galveston
Geo M Bently, of Ill
Lloyd Dorsey & others
Legal reps of Geo McGirk
Heirs of Capt Matthew Jack, deceased
Widow & heirs of Elijah Beebee
E A F Lavalette, U S Navy
J C Buckles, of Louisville, Ky
Jacob Baker, of Sandusky, Ohio
Ira Call, of Huron Co, Ohio
Hezekiah Johnson, of Bridgewater, Vt
John McVea & John F McKneely, of La
Legal reps of John Rice Jones
Legal reps Maj Caleb Swann, deceased
Levi Pierce & Andrew Hodge, jr
Henry J Snow, of N Y
Mrs Eliz C Smith, of Missouri
Juan M Luco & Jose L Luco
Jesse R Faulkner, of Missouri
Geo P Welsh & Clark H Wells
Rebecca Baggerly, widow of D Baggerly
Benj Hammond, of N Y
W D Porter, of the U S Navy
Reps of Jos Watson, deceased
Heirs & reps of Col Alex'r G Morgan
Legal reps of Joshua Kennedy, deceased
David C Cash & Giles U Ellis

Authorize Victor Morass to relinquish certain lands, & to enter the same quantity elsewhere
Claim of Dusuan de la Croix to a lot of land therein described
Mary Deany, widow of the late Lt Jas A Deany, U S Army
Robt F McGuire & his wife, late Louisa Laney
Lewis B Welles, late Paymaster U S Army
Legal reps of Isaac P Simonton, deceased
Sylvester T Jerauld, assignee of the interest of Henry Richaud
Harriet Leavenworth, widow of the late Brvt Brig Gen Leavenworth
Compensation for the services of Geo Morell in adjusting titles to lands in Michigan
Pamela Brown, widow of Maj Gen Jacob Brown, late of the U S Army, deceased
Thos Ap C Jones, surety for former postmaster at Norfolk, Va
John Frazer, & the adm of John G Clendenen, deceased
Geo G Bishop & the legal reps of John Arnold, deceased
Change the name of the American built brig Glamorgan to that of the brig **Wizard**
Confirm to Hercules L Dousman his title to farm lot 32, adjoining the town of Prairie du Chien, Wisc
Change the name of the American built brig **Hallowell** to that of the brig **James Rose**, & to grant her a new register
Change the name of the barque **Oleona** to the barque **Mount Vernon**.
Change the name of the American-built steamer **Falcon** to that of the steamer **Queen City**.

Authorize the issue of a register to the brig **Amelia** by the name of the brig **Abby Frances**.
Thos Bronaugh, for the repeal of the act to aid the Territory of Minn in the construction of a railroad therein, approved Jun 29, 1854
Mrs Sally T B Cochrane, widow of the late Lt R E Cochrane, U S Army
Excx of the late Brvt Col A C W Fanning, of the U S Army
Jos Gonder, jr, & John Dugg
Legal reps of Capt Wm Davis, late cmder of the U S transport schnr **Eufaula**
Settle the accounts of Thos Jorgan, assist quartermaster of the U S Army
Conrad Wheat, jr, or his legal reps
Capt Lewis E Simmonds, W P Buckner, & Pierce Crosby, passed midshipmen U S Navy
Richd M Bouton, Geo Wright, & the widow of Marvin W Fisher
Compensation of Jas W Low & others, for the capture of the British private armed schnr **Ann**, during the late war with Great Britain
Wm G Smith, Conrad Wheat, jr, or his legal reps
Pamela Brown, widow of Maj Gen J Brown, U S Army
Legal reps of the late Thos Chapman, formerly Collector of the port of Gtwn, S C
John S Jones & Wm H Russell, surviving partners of Brown, Russell & Co
Confirm the claim of Wm H Henderson & the heirs of Robt Henderson to 500 acres of land in the Bastrop grant
Mrs Helen Mackay, widow of the late Col Aeneas Mackay, deputy quartermaster genr'l U S Army
Patent to Peter Poucin for certain lands therein described
Wm J McElheney, E P Matthews, & Lawrence Cribben
Five years' half-pay to the widow of Capt John W Gunnison
Incorporate the <u>Gtwn Gas Light Co</u>
Joint resolution for the relief of Alex'r P Field, late Sec of Wisc Territory, & sureties
Joint resolution of thanks to Gen John E Wool
Pension for Silas Champion; to David Towle; pension for Capt Thos Porter

A young man, Benj Adkinson, of Kent Co, Md, in attempting to pull his gun out of a shallop boat, on Jul 31, the trigger caught & the charge passed into his abdomen & wrist, producing death in one hour.

Extensive sale of Fine Cigars & tobacco, at auction: on Aug 16, at the store of Mr Saml Simmons, Pa ave, two door west of Adams & Co's Express Ofc.
-Green & Scott, aucts

Died: on Aug 8, in Wash City, Mr Fred'k Speiscer, in his 56th year, a native of Germany, but for the last 34 years a resident of Wash, leaving a wife & 7 children to mourn their irreparable loss. His funeral will be on Thu at 4 o'clock, from his residence, 11th st, between K & L sts.

Uncle Sam: the death of Saml Wilson, an aged, worthy, & formerly enterprising citizen of Troy, will remind those who were familiar with incidents of the war of 1812 of the origin of the popular sobriquet for the United States. Mr Wilson, who was an extensive packer, had the contract for supplying the northern army with beef & pork. He was every where known & spoken of as Uncle Sam, & the U S branded on the heads of barrels for the army were at first taken to be the initials for Uncle Sam Wilson, but finally lost their local significance & became throughtout the army the familiar term for United States. The Wilsons were amongst the earliest & most active citizens of Troy. Uncle Sam, who died yesterday, was 84 years old.
–Albany Argus

FRI AUG 11, 1854
Official: Army Order
Gen Order No 11: War Dept, Adj Gen Ofc, Wash, Aug 7, 1854
Promotions & appointment in the U S Army, made by the Pres, by & with the advice & consent of the Senate.
I-Promotions
Pay Dept
Deputy Paymaster Gen Benj F Larned, to be Paymaster Gen, with the rank of Col, Jul 20, 1854, vice Towson, deceased.
Paymaster Adam D Steuart, to be Deputy Paymaster Gen, Jul 20, 1854, vice Larned, promoted, & Leslie, who declines promotion.
Corps of Engineers:
Brvt 2nd Lt Thos L Casey, to be 2nd Lt, Jun 22, 1854, the date of Capt Scarritt's death
Brvt 2nd Lt Newton F Alexander, to be 2nd Lt, Aug 1, 1854, the date of Capt Halleck's resignation
Corps of Topographical Engineers
Brvt 2nd Lt Nathl Michler, to be 2nd Lt, Apr 7, 1854, the date of Capt Webster's resignation
Brvt 2nd Lt John G Parke, to be 2nd Lt, Apr 18, 1854, the date of Capt Canfield's death
Ordnance Dept:
1st Lt Chas P Kingsbury, to be Capt, Jul 1, 1854, having served 14 years continuous service as Lt
1st Lt John McNutt, to be Capt, Jul 1, 1854, having served 14 years continuous service as Lt
2nd Lt Silas Crispin, to be 1st Lt, Jul 1, 1854, vice Kingsbury, promoted
2nd Lt Geo T Balch, to be 1st Lt, Jul 1, 1854, vice McNutt, promoted
Brvt 2nd Lt Joshua W Sill, to be 2nd Lt, May 11, 1854, date of Capt Ringgold's death
Brvt 2nd Lt Francis J Shunk, to be 2nd Lt, Jun 8, 1843, date of Capt Talcott's death
First Regt of Dragoons:
1st Lt Henry W Stanton, to be Capt, Jul 25, 1854, vice Chilton, appointed Paymaster. Co B
2nd Lt Geo Stoneman, jr, to be 1st Lt, Jul 25, 1854, vice Stanton, promoted. Co C

Brvt 2nd Lt Nelson B Sweitzer, of the 2nd Dragoons, to be 2nd Lt, Jul 25, 1854, vice Stoneman, promoted. Co C

Second Regt of Dragoons:
Brvt 2nd Lt Thos Hight, of the First Dragoons, to be 2nd Lt, May 24, 1854, vice De Lano, deceased. Co K

Regt of Mounted Riflemen:
1st Lt Washington L Elliot, to be Capt, Jul 20, 1854, vice Van Buren, deceased-of wounds received in action. Co A
Brvt 2nd Lt John S Bowen, to be 2nd Lt, Jul 20, 1854, the date of Capt Van Buren's death, Co B

1st Regt of Artl:
2nd Lt Adam J Slemmer, to be 1st Lt, Apr 30, 1854, vice Dement, resigned. Co G

2nd Regt of Artl:
2nd Lt Armistead L Long, to be 1st Lt, Apr 5, 1854, vice Rush, resigned. Co F

3rd Regt of Artl:
2nd Lt Chas S Winder, to be 1st Lt, Apr 5, 1854, vice Fremont, resigned. Co L

4th Regt of Artl:
2nd Lt Delavan D Perkins, to be 1st Lt, May 27, 1854, vice Holmes, deceased. Co I

2nd Regt of Infty:
Brvt 2nd Lt John P Hawkins, of the 6th Infty, to be 2nd Lt, Jun 23, 1854, vice Paine, deceased. Co E

3rd Regt of Infty:
Brvt 2nd Lt Alex'r McD McCook, to be 2nd Lt, Jun 30, 1854, vice Maxwell, killed in action. Co D

4th Regt of Infty:
1st Lt Thos J Montgomery, to be Capt, Mar 27, 1854, vice Larnard, deceased. Co A
1st Lt David A Russell, to be Capt, Jun 22, 1854, vice Alvord, appointed Paymaster. Co K
1st Lt De Lancey Floyd-Jones, to be Capt, Jul 31, 1854, vice Grant, resigned. Co F
2nd Lt Benj D Forsythe, to be 1st Lt, Mar 27, 1854, vice Montgomery, promoted. Co K
2nd Lt Wm A Slaughter, to be 1st Lt, Jun 22, 1854, vice Russell, promoted. Co A
2nd Lt John Withers, to be 1st Lt, Jul 31, 1854, vice Floyd-Jones, promoted. Co C
Brvt 2nd Lt Wm Myers, of the 5th Infty, to be 2nd Lt, Mar 27, 1854, vice Forsythe, promoted. Co I
Brvt 2nd Lt Lawrence A Williams, of the 7th Infty, to be 2nd Lt, Jun 22, 1854, vice Slaughter, promoted. Co C
Brvt 2nd Lt Hezekiah H Garber, of the 5th Infty, to be 2nd Lt, Jul 31, 1854, vice Withers, promoted. Co F

II-Appointments:
Medical Dept:
Robt L Brodie, of S C, to be from May 15, 1854. Assist Surgeon, vice Wotherspoon, deceased, to date

Pay Dept:
Brvt Maj Benj Alvord, Capt in the 4th Regt of Infty, to be Paymaster, vice Van Buren, resigned, to date from Jun 22, 1854.
Steuart, promoted, to date from Jul 25, 1854. Brvt Maj Robt H Chilton, Capt in the 1st Regt of Dragoons, to be Paymaster, vice
1st Regt of Artl:
Rank
8. Cadet Henry W Closson, to be 2nd Lt, vice Slemmer, promoted, to date from Jul 1, 1854. Co I
2nd Regt of Artl:
9. Cadet Judson D Bingham, to be 2nd Lt, vice Long, promoted, to date from Jul 1, 1854. Co F
15. Cadet John R Smead, to be 2nd Lt, vice W S Smith, resigned, to date from Jul 1, 1854. Co D
3rd Regt of Artl:
7. Cadet Jas Deshler, to be 2nd Lt, vice C B Winder, promoted, to date from Jul 1, 1854. Co H
16. Cadet Michl R Morgan, to be 2nd Lt, vice Arnold, promoted, to date from Jul 1, 1854. Co M
4th Regt of Artl:
17. Cadet Stephen D Lee, to be 2nd Lt, vice Perkins, promoted, to date from Jul 1, 1854. Co D
III-The following named Cadets constitute the first class of 1854:
Corps of Engineers: to be Brvt 2nd Lt, Jul 1, 1854
Rank
1. Cadet Geo W Custis Lee
3. Cadet Thos H Ruger
Corps of Topographical Engineers: to be Brvt 2nd Lt, Jul 1, 1854
2. Cadet Henry L Abbot
6. Cadet Chas N Turnbull
Ordnance Dept: to be Brvt 2nd Lt, Jul 1, 1854
4. Cadet Oliver O Howard
5. Cadet Thos J Treadwell
Dragoon Arm: to be Brvt 2nd Lt, Jul 1, 1854
10. Cadet John Pegram: Co A, 1st Regt.
11. Cadet Chas G Rogers: Co E, 2nd Regt
12. Cadet Thos J Wright: Co G, 2nd Regt
18. Cadet Milton T Carr: Co D, 1st Regt
22. Cadet John R Villepigue: Co H, 2nd Regt
Regt of Mounted Riflemen: to be Brvt 2nd Lt, Jul 1, 1854:
13. Cadet Jas E B Stuart: Co B
33. Cadet Jas Wright: Co G
37. Cadet Wm M Davant: Co K

Artl Arm: to be Brvt 2nd Lt, Jul 1, 1854:
19. Cadet Wm D Pender: Co A, 1st Regt
20. Cadet Loomis L Langdon: Co D, 4th Regt
21. Cadet John T Greble: Co C, 2nd Regt
23. Cadet Henry A Smalley: Co D, 1st Regt
24. Cadet Saml Kinsvy: Co H, 1st Regt
25. Cadet Abner Smead: Co K, 4th Regt
26. Cadet Oliver D Greene: Co D, 3rd Regt
27. Cadet Stephen H Weed: Co I, 2nd Regt
28. Cadet E F Townsend: Co G, 3rd Regt
29. Cadet Alfred B Chapman: Co K, 2nd Regt
30. Cadet Geo A Gordon: Co M, 3rd Regt
Infty Arm: to be Brvt 2nd Lt, Jul 1, 1854:
14. Cadet Archibald Gracie, jr: Co G, 4th Regt
31. Cadet John O Long: Co C, 2nd Regt
32. Cadet Benj F Davis: Co C, 5th Regt
34. Cadet Waterman Palmer, jr: Co A, 8th Regt
35. Cadet David P Hancock: Co C, 7th Regt
36. Cadet Saml T Shepperd: Co G, 2nd Regt
38. Cadet Chas G Sawtelle: Co K, 2nd Regt
40. Cadet John T Mercer: Co I, 6th Regt
41. Cadet Zenas R Bliss: Co F, 1st Regt
42. Cadet Edgar O'Connor: Co F, 7th Regt
43. Cadet John Mullins: Co I, 7th Regt
44. Cadet David H Brotherton: Co G, 5th Regt
45. Cadet Horace Randal: Co C, 8th Regt
46. Cadet John McCleary: Co C, 3rd Regt
IV-Transfer:
Brvt 2nd Lt Wm R Boggs, Jun 28, from the Corps of Topographical Engineers to the Ordnance Dept, to stand on Army Register next below Brvt 2nd Lt Francis J Shunk.
V-Casualties:
Resignations:
Brvt Lt Col Abram Van Buren, Paymaster, Jun 1, 1854
Brvt Maj Robt H Chiltonk Capt 1st Dragoons, his regimental commission, [only] Jul 25, 1854, the date of his appointment as Paymaster
Brvt Maj Benj Alvord, Capt 4th Infty, his regimental commission, [only,] Jun 22, 1854, the date of his appointment as Paymaster
Capt Henry W Halleck, Corps of Engineers, Aug 1, 1854
Capt Ulysses S Grant, 4th Infty, Jul 31, 1854
Capt Jos D Webster, Corps of Topographical Engineers, Apr 7, 1854
1st Lt Sewall L Fremont, 3rd Artl, Apr 5, 1854
1st Lt Richd H Rush, 2nd Artl, Jul 1, 1854
1st Lt John Dement, 1st Artl, Apr 30, 1854
2nd Lt Wm S Smith, 2nd Artl, Jun 19, 1854

Deaths:
Brvt Maj Gen Nathan Towson, Col & Paymaster Gen, in Wash City, D C, Jul 20, 1854.
Brvt Maj Chas H Larnard, Capt 4th Infty, drowned in Puget's Sound, near **Fort Madison**, W T, Mar 27, 1854
Brvt Maj Geo H Talcott, Capt of Ordnance, at Indian Springs, Ga, Jun 8, 1854
Capt Augustus Canfield, Corps of Topographical Engineers, at Detroit, Mich, Apr 18, 1854
Capt Michl E Van Buren, Regt of Mounted Riflemen, at Corpus Christi, Texas, Jul 20, 1854, of wounds received Jul 11th in an affair with Camanche Indians
Capt Jeremiah M Scarritt, Corps of Engineers, at Key West, Fla, Jun 22, 1854
Capt Thos L Ringgold, Ordnance Dept, in Wash City, D C, May 11, 1854
1st Lt Jas Holmes, 4th Artl, at **Fort Independence**, Mass, May 27, 1854
2nd Lt Ferdinand Paine, 2nd Infty, at Jefferson Barracks, Mo, Jun 23, 1854
2nd Lt Jos E Maxwell, 3rd Infty, killed in a skirmish with the Apache Indians, near Moro river, New Mexico, Jun 30, 1854
Assist Surgeon Alex S Wotherspoon, in Wash City, D C, May 4, 1854
-S Cooper, Adj Gen

Mr Jos Brelsford, an actor, of Phil, met with a fatal accident at Coney Island on Tue. He was, with others, playing an out-door game, leap-frog, or something of the kind, when one of the party jumped upon Brelsford instead of upon the ground, & accidentally fractured his spine. Mr B died soon afterwards.

Died: on Aug 9, in Wash City, after a lingering illness, Mrs Eliz E Page, relict of the late Danl Page, formerly of PG Co, Md, in the 77th year of her age. Her funeral will be from the residence of her son-in-law, Jno L Chubb, on I st, between 6th & 7th sts, this afternoon at 3 o'clock.

Died: on Jul 31, at the **Grove**, the residence of Mrs Saml Latimer Barron, Prince Wm Co, Va, Mrs Rebecca A Barron, wife of Henry A Barron, late of said county.

Died: on Aug 10, after a few days' illness, Kate M, youngest daughter of Wm T & Eliz T Duvall, in her 4th year. Her funeral is this morning at 9 o'clock, from the residence of her parents, on Pa ave, opposite Brown's Hotel.

SAT AUG 12, 1854
Wash-Local matter: teachers elected:

Saml Kelly	Miss M P Middleton, Princ
Miss M A S David	Miss Harriet Baker
Mrs M E Rodier, Princ	Miss Charlotte Campbell
Mrs E M Kelly	Thos M Wilson, Princ
Miss A K Lowe, Princ	Hector Grant
Mrs S E Coale	Mrs S P Randolph

Mrs R M Ogden	Miss Isabella Acton
Miss E Parsons	Mrs M Freeman, Princ
Miss Lucy H Randolph, Princ	Miss H N Henshaw
Miss Kate McCarthy	Mrs E Clarke
Miss Frances Henshaw	Miss Jane Moss
Miss E V Billing, Princ	John E Thompson
Mrs E Myer	Miss M A Milburn
John Fill, Princ	S J Thompson
J T Goldsmith	Mrs M A Skidmore
Mrs C D Martin	Miss M A Lee
W M McCathran	Miss Annie Adams
Miss France Elvans, Princ	

Mrd: on Aug 10, by Rev S A H Marks, Mr Chas Lusky to Miss Matilda A Nalley, all of Wash City.

Died: on Aug 11, at Miss Nancy Carroll's, Montg Co, Md, Mrs Caroline M Hall, in her 65th year. Her funeral is this morning at 10 o'clock.

Died: a few days ago, at Niagara Falls, Mrs Mary C Porter, wife of Peter A Porter. She was the eldest daughter of the late Rev John Breckenridge, of New Orleans, one of the sons of Mr John Breckenridge, of Ky, Atty Gen of the U S under the Administration of Pres Jefferson. Her mother was a daughter of the late Rev Dr Miller, of Princeton, one of the most eminent of the American clergy, so that upon both sides Mrs Porter was connected with 2 distinguished American families. Blessed with wealth, she used it in the exercise of a generous & refined hospitality. –Buffalo Commercial Advertiser

Died: on Aug 11, in Gtwn, after a protracted illness, Miranda M Guy, in her 54th year. Her funeral is this afternoon at 3 o'clock, from the residence of her son-in-law, Levi Davis, Market st, above 3rd st, Gtwn.

Died: yesterday, Frank, aged 14 months, infant son of Wm E & Hannah Howard. Hid funeral is this afternoon at 5 o'clock.

Died: on Thu, of dysentery, William Stanhope, 3rd son of Benj A & Mgt B Janvier, of Wash City, formerly of Delaware, aged 4 years, 5 months & 15 days. His funeral is this afternoon at 4 o'clock, from his fathers' residence, Phil Place, H st.

Died: on Aug 11, Andrew, aged 1 year & 11 days, youngest son of Jas B & Eugenie Orem. His funeral is this morning at 10 o'clock, on 6th st, between F & G sts.

Passed by the First Session of the 33rd Congress:
1-Purchase of Barlow's planetarium for the use of the Military Academy at West Point: $2,000. 2-For sword ordered to be presented to Brvt Maj Gen Wool: $1,500.

Capt John Downes died at Charlestown, Mass, yesterday. This gallant ofcr entered the Navy in 1802, & was in active service during the war of 1812. He was a Lt with Cmdor Porter on board the ship **Essex** in his sanguinary conflict at Valparaiso, in 1814, with 2 British vessels, the frig **Phoebe** & the sloop-of-war **Cherub**. The gallantry of Lt Downes was conspicuous in this affair. The loss of the British was very severe. Capt Downes was in command of the Charlestown Navy Yard at the time of his death, & was the 3rd upon the list of post captains, Cmdors Stewart & Morris being his seniors. [Aug 16th newspaper: on the authority of a Boston paper, that he was cmder of the naval station at Charlestown, is a mistake. He had been formerly in command of the station, but when he died he was awaiting orders at his private residence in Charlestown. Cmdor Gregory is the naval cmder at Charlestown.]

Distribution of Premiums at St Mary's Female Institution, near Bryantown, Chas Co, Md, Jul 27, 1854. Students who received premiums:

Anna M Fitzpatrick, Wash, D C
Eliz Bowling, Chas Co, Md
Celestia Mattingly, St Mary's Co, Md
Marian J Burch, Chas Co, Md
Mary B Hamilton, Chas Co, Md
Amelia R Lancaster, Wash, D C
Hortense Digges, Chas Co, Md
Kate S Hamilton, Chas Co, Md
Jane C Gwynn, PG Co, Md
Maria Conlan, Wash, D C
Thora Siebert, Wash, D C
Mary Keating, Wash, D C
Kate Lloyd, Chas Co, Md
Eliza Matthews, Chas Co, Md
Minna Seibert, Wash, D C
Louisa Keating, Wash, D C
Alice A Morgan, Balt
Mgt E Keleher, Wash, D C
Mary McWilliams, St Mary's Co, Md
Louisa Hamersley, Chas Co, Md
Helen Hamersley, Chas Co, Md
Savina Matthews, Chas Co, Md
Bettie Digges, Chas Co, Md
Rosetta Scott, St Mary's Co, Md
Josephine Mudd, Chas Co, Md
Mary Ellen Talty, Wash, D C
Maria Conlan, Wash, D C
Mary A Caffee, Ohio
Mary Agnes Bowling, Chas Co, Md
Ellen Burke, Faifax Co, Va
Kate Montgomery, Chas Co, Md
Honora Fitzpatrick, Wash, D C
Christiana Durr, Wash, D C
Kate Lloyd, Chas Co, Md
Alice Hamersley, Chas Co, Md
Marian Lancaster, Chas Co, Md
Mary Clare Sanders, Chas Co, Md.
Sarah Savage, PG Co, Md
Mgt Marshall, Chas Co, Md
Clodine Miles
Mary Rose Montgomery
Honorably mentioned:
Mary M Berry
Anna C King
Edmonia Maddox
Helen Blake
Mgt Marshall
Malvina Seibert
Mary C Keating, Wash, D C
Marian Fenwick, Wash, D C

MON AUG 14, 1854
Mrd: on Aug 10, by Rev W C Steel, Wm Vanscriver to Miss Ann Matilda Lightford, both of Gtwn, D C.

Died: on Aug 13, in Wash City, of bilious dysentery, Mrs Mary E Gates, wife of the late Jas Gates, in her 66th year. Her funeral will be this evening at 3 o'clock, from her late residence, near the Navy Yard.

Died: yesterday, in her 7th year, Kate M, daughter of Geo H Holtzman. Her funeral will be from their residence on 11th, between H & I sts, this morning at 10 o'clock.

Died: on Aug 13, Herbert Reginald, infant son of Edw & Isabella J Myers, aged 14 months. His funeral is this morning at 10 o'clock, from Mrs Farquhar's, on 12th st, 3 doors above G st.

Died: on Aug 10, George Washington, son of David E & Sarah A Irving, aged 1 years, 1 month & 15 days.

Orphans Court of Wash Co, D C. Letters of administration on the personal estate of Orris S Paine, late of Wash Co, deceased. –Mary A Paine, admx

The Wash [Pa] Reporter announces the death, on Aug 5, of Jas Spriggs, aged about 53 years. On the preceding Wed, as Mr Spriggs was going to his farm on a cart, the horse took fright & ran away, causing Mr Spriggs to jump off. He fell upon his head, causing a concussion of the brain, with which he suffered till the time of his death. The last ofcs he filled were those of Sheriff & Register.

TUE AUG 15, 1854
Drug store for sale: having determined to enter into the practice of medicine, I will sell the stock of Drugs, Medicines, & Store Fixtures, in my store, corner of I & 7th sts. –T C McIntire

Household & kitchen furniture at auction: on Aug 17, at the residence of Mr Bennett, on the west side of 13th st, between E & F sts. -Jas C McGuire, auct

The sloop-of-war **Cyane** arrived at the Charlestown Navy Yard on Sat. Mr Farens, the U S Commercial Agent from Greytown, came passenger. The **Cyane** brought from San Juan the remains of Purser Ashman, who died & was buried there some time ago, & also the body of Felix Hewlett, boatswain, who died on the passage of the **Cyane**.

W C Highams, Civil Engineer, belonging to N Y, was shot at New Orleans a few days since by John Chandler, formerly of Boston. The wound proved fatal. Chandler has been arrested. There had been a previous quarrel.

The Chinese Mail brings an account of the murder in China of Mr Geo Perkins, a Bostonian, formerly of the house of Thwing & Perkins. He left the barque **Concordia**, from San Francisco, at the entrance of Hong Kong harbor, on May 15 in a Chinese boat for Macao. Not appearing at the place, search was made by the U S Consul, Mr Spooner, when it appeared that the crew of the Chinese boat had murdered him in his sleep in order to obtain his effects. Several of the murderers have been arrested & have confessed the crime. Mr Perkins, though a young man, had amassed a large fortune, with which he was about to return home.

Trustee's sale of valuable bldg lots near the railroad depot: on Sep 14, by deed of trust from Elias Yulee & wife to the subscriber, recorded in Liber J A S No 56, folios 262 thru 264, of the land records for Wash Co, D C: sale of square 630, near a lot occupied by Ryne. –Henry Naylor, trustee -Green & Scott, aucts

A few days since Dr Bomino, supposed to be reduced to extreme penury & who had for a long time lived very meanly, died at St Louis, & the public administrator proceeded to take possession of his effects to sell them to pay his funeral expenses. He found a box containing $1,700 in gold, an old pocket in which he found $4,000 in Missouri bank bills, & other deposites, all amounting to $6,300.

The N Y Evangelist states that Rev John Sawyer, of Garland, Me, is in all probability the oldest officiating clergyman in the U S. Father Sawyer will be 99 years old next Oct. He was born in Hebron, Conn, Oct 9, 1755. He was ordained in 1787, & has ever since been active in the duties of the Christian ministry. He recently preached 3 times on one Sabbath.

A clerk in a dry goods store in Cincinnati, named Jessup, shot & dangerously wounded last Sat Stephen R Smith, for sending him, during 3 months, a series of letters purporting to come from a young lady, & then having the matter published in a Sunday paper.

Galena Advertiser: a lad, Geo Jackson, aged 12 years, was committed to jail in that city, a day or two since, for the murder of a playmate, Elias Horn, aged 16. Both were residents of Millville, in this county. Jackson said he shot him by snapping the gun at him, without knowing it to be loaded. –Galena [Ill] Jefferson, Aug 6.

Under the head of deaths will be found those of Thos Bacon, at the age of 90 years, in Jun last, & Jerusha Bacon, his wife, at age 84 years, who resided in Ware. They were united in the bonds of matrimony 66 years ago, & were parted scarcely for a day until death. They had 12 children, & their children have had 59 children. Their great grandchildren are numerous & widely spread over the land. We know that one of them, aged 15, is married, & has a child. Thos Bacon was a patriot of the Revolution, & has always been a reliable Whig. He went to the polls in Ware & voted the Whig ticket last fall. –Worcester Transcript

Arrest of incendiaries: Claiborn Wilson was accused of the late incendiarisms, when, in alarm, he owned to being a participant in the crimes, naming Claiborn Mocabee, John Merriman, Jas Bulger, & Geo Todshinder as accomplices.

Mrd: on Aug 10, at Foundry Parsonage, by Rev E P Phelps, Mr Wm Judge to Miss Margaret Fasnaught.

Died: on Aug 1, in Wilkesbarre, Pa, Mrs Sarah Hollenback Butler, wife of the late Hon Chester Butler. Mrs Butler spent much of her time in Wash when her husband was in Congress, & greatly endeared herself to a large circle of friends.

Boston, Aug 14. The funeral of Cmdor Downes took place in Trinity Church, & his remains were interred at **Mount Auburn**. The religious exercises were conducted by Bishop Eastburn.

Boston, Aug 12. A son of Chas Francis Adams & his Lady were thrown from a carriage this morning, & both much injured; the son, it is supposed, badly.

The partnership between G W Utermehle & J Hunsberger was dissolved on Aug 1, by mutual consent. –G W Utermehle, J Hunsberger J Hunsberger will continue the business: Wood & Anthracite Coal: 7th & Mass ave. –J Hunsberger

The copartnership existing under the name of Ellicott, Jay & Co, is this day dissolved by mutual consent. –Elias Ellicott, Peter Augustus Jay, Jas F Ellicott, John Ellicott, jr, Phil T Ellicot. Peter A Jay, having disposed of his interest, the business will hereafter by conducted by Elias, Jas F, John Ellicott, jr, & Phil T Ellicott, under the name of Ellicott & Co.

Teacher wanted: trustees of Primary School No 5, Bladensburg District, wish to employ a teacher for said school. –Dionysius Sheriff, Lewis Magruder, Philip Hill

The valuable estate in Albemarle known as **Farmington** is for sale: the property of the late Gen Bernard Peyton, lying in Albemarle Co, on the waters of Ivy Creek, adjoining the lands of Messrs Wm Garth, John T Randolph, & others, containing by recent survey 881 acres. The dwlg, built of brick, is not only remarkably spacious, but is in the most perfect repair, with bldgs used for a farm. The negro quarters are new & built of good materials. Apply to Thos J Peyton, or to Goddin & Apperson, aucts, Richmond, Va.

Orphans Court of Wash Co, D C. Letters testamentary on the personal estate of Bailey Washington, late of the U S Navy, deceased. –Ann M Washington, excx

WED AUG 16, 1854
$5 for delivery of estray cow, with leather collar marked with the initials M B R. -M B Renner, residing on G st, near 11th.

Died: on Aug 11, at the residence of his son-in-law, Col Francis H Smith, at the Va Military Institute, Dr Thos Henderson, U S Army, aged 65 years. Dr Henderson was widely known as a practitioner of medicine in Wash & Gtwn prior to his entrance into the army in 1833. He was a tender husband, father, brother, & friend.

Died: on Aug 10, at Leesburg, Va, in her 70th year, Mrs Jane Byrd Robertson, widow of Thos Robertson, & daughter of the late Robt Beverly, of Blandfield.

It is stated in a letter quoted by the Parlamento of Turin, of June 2, that the tomb of Odoacer, King of the Heruli, has been discovered at Ravenna by some workmen, who it appears found the body encased in a suit of armor of gold, which they broke into pieces & secretly sold. Odoacer was king of the Barbarians who overthrew the Western Roman Empire in 476. He was murdered by his conqueror, Theodoric the Great, A D 498, & was buried at Ravenna, where, after the lapse of 1,360 years, it appears his remains have been found.

Hon Solomon U Downs, late a Senator in Congress from the State of Louisiana, died at Orchard Springs, Ky, on Monday last. He had been in bad health for some time.

The venerable Wm Gwynn, of Balt, formerly for many years editor of the Federal Gax, died in Harford Co, on Monday, in his 80th year. He was the oldest lawyer in Md, most kind-hearted & esteemed.

Misses Rooker's Family Boarding & Day School for Young Ladies, E st, between 6th & 7th sts, Wash, D C: in successful operation for some years, the next quarter will commence on Sep 11. References:
Washington:
Rev C M Butler, D D
Rev J W French
Maj P G Howle
Dr J F May
P R Fendall
R C Brooke
Thos U Walter
Maj B B French
Col M Nourse
Rt Rev A Potter, D D, Phil
Prof N R Smith, Balt
Hon A G Brown, U S S, Mississippi
Capt H Stansbury, U S Army, Cleveland, Ohio

John A Lillington, Whig Senator elect from the counties of Roman & Davie, N C, died at his residence in Davis Co, on Sunday, immediately succeeding his election.

Mr Bodisco did not sail from N Y for Europe on Sat last, as was stated in our papers of yesterday.

Mrd: on Aug 15, by Rev Mr Griffith, Mr Robt Jones, of Boston, Mass, to Miss Ellen C Noble, of Loudoun Co, Va.

Wash Corp: 1-Cmte of Claims: bill for the relief of J D Hendley, Richd Briscoe, & Henry Pardon. 2-Cmte of Ways & Means: bill for the relief of Mrs Mary Nevitt.

THU AUG 17, 1854

Lt Jerome Napoleon Bonaparte, of the rifle regt, has forwarded to the Sec of War from Paris the resignation of his commission in the army of the U S. Lt Bonaparte is an American by birth, & a grandson of Prince Jerome, youngest brother of the great Napoleon. He was educated at West Point Military Academy, where he graduated with credit in Jul, 1853. After serving with his regt a year, he went, with his father, Jerome Bonaparte, of Balt, on a visit to France, where, report said, he was received with distinction by his kinsman the Emperor, & the consequence, as appears, has been the resignation of his commission in our army.

Another Revolutionary Soldier gone. One of our oldest citizens, & the only living representative among us of the heroes of '76, departed this life at his residence in Albany, on Sunday, in his 90th year. We allude to the venerable Durell Williams. Though not free from the infirmities of age, he retained in a remarkable degree the elasticity of mind which ever characterized him, & until within the last few years had enjoyed comfortable health. Mr Williams was a native of Pa; entered the service of his country at the opening of the Revolutionary war, & continued in it until its glorious close. He was with Washington at Newburgh & Valley Forge, was present at the evacuation of N Y by the British, & participated in many of the stirring scenes which preceded. –Albany Argus

Mrs Catharine Flinn on Tue accidentally fell from a 3rd story window of her dwlg in N Y, & was so badly injured as to leave no hope of her recovery.

Capt Wooderson, the master of the ill-fated ship **Townsend**, which was destroyed by fire on May 15 last, while on her voyage from Boston to San Francisco, arrived in Boston on Sat. On May 13 one of the open boats swamped: lost were Chas Bastow, Chas Green, Geo Small, Alex Rowe, G E Allen, & A A Hall, passenger. On May 23 a second boat capsized & all of the crew drowned: lost were Mr Jackson, 2nd mate; Chas Stidder, carpenter; Chas Tewksbury & Antonio Silova, seamen; Phil Spalding, boy. On May 24, the Capt's boat was capsized & Chas Naton, steward, drowned. On May 26, after 10 days & 6 hours in the boat, they landed on the east side of the island of Massafuera, & getting a fire & a few crabs & some dock leaves, were the only eatable things to be found. They saw a whale boat with 2 skeletons alongside of it. They had apparently starved to death some time ago. On May 29 they launched the boat & on May 31, they landed on the island of Juan Fernandez, & were received kindly by the cmder of the garrison, who supplied them with food.

FRI AUG 18, 1854
Thos Bertram, a native of England, was accidentally shot & killed a few days ago, in N Y. Mr Cornelius J Quackenbosh fired a pistol at a rat & the ball from the pistol struck a paving stone & glanced off, entering the back of Mr Bertram. Quackenbosh was acquitted of any criminal intent.

In North Lewisburg, Ohio, on Thu of last week, Mr & Mrs Good were riding in a buggy during a rain storm, when they were struck by a falling tree, which instantly killed Mrs Good & badly bruised Mr Good who was unconscious for some time.

The Grand Jury at N Y have returned true bill of indictment for murder in the first degree against Dr Robt Graham, of New Orleans, for killing Col Loring, a few days since, at the St Nicholas Hotel.

Mr J F Smith, a merchant from Wrightville, Pa, fell suddenly dead at Baltimore yesterday whilst in a counting-room on Smith's wharf.

Austin, Texas: the Govn'r of the State has awarded to Hon Robt J Walker & Thos Butler King, as reps of the Atlantic & Pacific Railroad Co, the contract for bldg the railroad from the eastern boundary of Texas to the town of El Paso, on the Rio Grande, through the whole state, a distance of 800 miles.

Twenty-one years ago the newspapers of the day were praising the workmanship & sailing qualities of the ship **Russia**, built at Wash by the late Capt Wm Easby.

Mrd: on Aug 15, at the **Hermitage**, near Balt, by Rev Dr Wyatt, Benj Jomans, jr, of Cincinnati, to Fanny Ellen, daughter of Nathl F Williams, jr, of the former place.

A little boy named Edward, aged 5 years, was lost yesterday somewhere on the Island. He started to follow his father from 8th st to Page's wharf, & has not been seen since. Any information concerning him will be gratefully received by Mr Stephen Moore, living on 8th st south.

SAT AUG 19, 1854
The old *Swan Tavern*, well known in Richmond, Va, near the Fredericksburg Railroad Depot, has lately been sold at auction for $20,640. It was the resort 50 years ago of the Judges of the Court of Appeals, in the days of Spencer Roane & Geo Wythe, & of other eminent men of the State.

Three men, Lewis Hazlitt, Francis Neville, & Wm Neville, lost their lives on Aug 7 by the falling on them of a tree which a man named Ensign, of Camden, [C W] was engaged in grubbing up.

The wife of Wm H Brown, of Coldwater, Mich, & her child 9 weeks old, were fatally burnt a few days since by the explosion of a camphene lamp.

Orphans Court of Wash Co, D C. Letters testamentary on the personal estate of Wm Easby, late of Wash Co, deceased. –H N Easby, J W Easby, Agnes M Easby, excs

U S Patent Ofc, Wash, Aug 18, 1854. Ptn of Jordon L Mott, of Mott Haven, N Y, praying for the extension of a patent granted to him on Dec 1, 1840, for an improvement in the mode of constructing a combined caldron & furnace for the use of agriculturists & others, for 7 years from the expiration of said patent, which takes place on Dec 1, 1854.

U S Patent Ofc, Wash, Aug 18, 1854. Ptn of Solomon Andrews, of Perth Amboy, N J, praying for the extension of a patent granted to him on Dec 5, 1840, for an improvement in the manner of constructing padlocks for mail bags & other uses, called the clam-shell padlock, for 7 years from the expiration of said patent, which takes place on Dec 5, 1854.

The execution of Weigart took place on Sat last. He had been found guilty of the murder of Cushing, in the city of Lexington, Ky, during the last winter. The murder was committed in a fit of passion. Cushing was a clerk in a store, when Mrs Weigart entered, &, mistaking her for a female of his acquaintance, he stepped up to her & patted her on the shoulder. Instantly discovering his mistake, he made a humble apology. Mrs Weigart, however, greatly offended, went home & told her husband, who armed himself in search of Cushing, found him, & shot him dead on the spot.

John B Dillon, one of the Irish exiles, a very eloquent man, has permission to return to Ireland. The announced was communicated to him by the British Ambassador at Wash. –N Y Mirror

Mrs Martha E Cubbedge, of Gillisonville, S C, aged 64, died recently under very painful circumstances. Previous to her death her residence had been repeatedly visited by thieves who stole various articles. Her son, determining to detect the intruder or intruders, kept watch in the yard all night with a loaded gun. The son, seeing a retreating figure at the door, fired, without taking aim, for it was too dark to do so. He heard his mother say, "You have shot me." Mrs Cubbedge died a few days afterwards from the injuries received.

Chicago, Aug 17. The dwlg of Mr Merchant, near Picatonica, was struck by lightning on Sat. Mrs Merchant & 4 of her children were killed.

A few days ago 3 men were hung at Smithville, Clay Co, Missouri. A fracas occurred, in which John W Douglass was killed, Wm Ross & John Ross, father & son, were dangerously & Ira Tritt severely stabbed, by Saml & Wm Shackelford & John W Callaway. The Shackelfords are said to have been connected with a gang of horse thieves. A gang of citizens hung the three of them. When the election took place on Monday these men were still hanging upon a tree in full view of the people. On Tuesday the bodies were cut down.

On Sep 6 next there is to be a grand gathering of the descendants, & those connected with them, of Edmund Rice, who was born in 1594, settled in that part of Sudbury which is now **Wayland** in 1639, & died at Marlboro in 1663. The place of meeting is to be on the old ancestral homestead, in the south part of Wayland, 1½ miles from Saxonville, at 10 o'clock. –Springfield [Mass] Republican

Died: on Aug 14, in her 79th year, Amelia, Consort of Bryant Johnson, deceased, of Farifax Co, Va, but for the last 43 years a resident of the Dist of Columbia. She died, as she lived, in great peace & an abiding hope of a blissful eternity.

Died: on Aug 13, at Norfolk, Va, in his 38th year, Mr Enoch L Reynolds, of Wash City, & late clerk in the ofc of the Sec of the Treasury. His funeral will take place from Odd Fellows' Hall, 7th st, on Monday, at 4 o'clock.

MON AUG 21, 1854
Trustee's sale of frame house & lot at auction: on Sep 19, by deed of trust from Saml Byington & wife to the subscribers, recorded in Liber J A S No 4, Folios 92 thru 98, of the land records for Wash Co, D C: sale of lot 1 in square 502, with a good frame house, situated at the corner of 4½ st & N st. –Walter Lenox, Henry Naylor, trustees -Green & Scott, aucts

Died: on Aug 18, after 2 days' illness, Wm Clarance, infant son of Jas & Deborah Mankin, aged 9 months.

Died: on Aug 19, in Gtwn, John Austin, only son of Chas & Sarah Abbot, aged one year. His funeral is this afternoon at 5 o'clock from the residence of his father on Gay st.

Died: on Aug 19, Joseph Gregory, aged 4 months & 19 days, only child of John F & Mary Ann Ellis.

Circuit Court of Wash Co, D C. In the matter of Polly Jennings, a lunatic. The cmte reported to this Court that he had sold the real estate directed to be sold, that is to say, lot 1 in square 513, Wash City, to John Walker, for $850, & lot 2 in square 513 for $378.36, & the *purchasers had complied with the terms of the sale.
[*Only one name given.] -Jno A Smith, clerk

In Chancery. Wm A Smallwood against John Addison, Wm Addison, Washington Van Hamm, Cornelia Van Hamm, Clarence Van Hamm, Henry Van Hamm, & Jonathan Prout. Trustees in the above cause have sold at auction, on Aug 19, to Jonathan Prout, part of lot 1 in square 796, fronting on 4th st, with brick dwlg house thereon, for $1,125; & also part of lots 4 & 5, in square 1,001, fronting on 11th st, for $107.45; & to Theodore Mosher the wharf & water privileges of lots 3 & 4 in square 826, with the warehouse thereon, for $1,260; & also lots 2 & 3 in square 824, for $367.93; & to Mary N Fulmer lot 10 in square 824, with the brick dwlg house thereon, for $1,320; & all the purchasers have fully complied with the terms of the sale. –Jno A Smith, clerk

Orphans Court of Wash Co, D C. Letters of administration on the personal estate of Jos Elgar, late of Wash Co, deceased. –Ann Elgar, admx

Miss Corbin, the daughter of Francis Corbin, of Va, long a resident of Paris, was married recently to Vicompte de Dampierre.

Whereas a paper purporting to be the last will & testament of Eliza Gamble, late of Queen Ann's Co, Md, deceased, in which Harrison Keene & Rebecca Keene are named as nephew & niece of said deceased, & to whom property is devised, & who are supposed to reside in the State of Ky; ordered by the Orphans' Court of Queen Ann's Co that said heirs & legatees of said Eliza Gamble, deceased, appear before this Court on the first Tue in Nov next. –Saml T Harrison, Reg/o Will for Queen Ann's Co.

Trustee's sale: by 2 deeds of trust from Wm Dowling to Edwin C Morgan & Wm E Howard, the same recorded in the land records for Wash Co, D C: sale on Sep 23 of lots 9, 10, & 11, in square 566, with improvements. –E C Morgan, W E Howard, trustees

Valuable Rappannock Estate for sale: pursuant to a decree of the Circuit Court of Caroline Co: public auction on Oct 4, of the tract of land called **Liberty Hill**, of which the late Dr John Taylor died seized. The tract borders on the Rappahannock river, in said county, & contains some 1,341 acres. The bldgs consist of a frame dwlg, 2 stories high, & all necessary out-houses.

TUE AUG 22, 1854
Trustee's sale of a 2 story frame house & lot: on Aug 8, by deed of trust from Henry B Robertson & Mahaley Jane Robertson his wife, dated May 11, 1854: sale of lots 51 & 52 in square 465, improved by house & back bldg. –Craven Ashford, trustee –Green & Scott, aucts

Saml R Kramer died at Harrisburg, Pa, on Thu. He was one of the oldest printers in the State of Pa.

Murders in Texas: 1-Victoria Advocate: on Jul 27 Edward Mitchell killed Conrad Hecheiser, on the Aranosa, in Victoria Co, by stabbing him with a dirk in the back of the neck. Hecheiser died instantly, & Mitchell made his escape. 2-Central Texas of Jul 29: Col Wade, who is just down from Madisonville, said that Nash, the man who killed young Wiseman, was shot againt on Wed, & instantly killed by someone in the dark.

Wanted, a Preceptor for 3 or 4 boys, from 13 to 16 years of age, competent to teach the Latin, Green, & French languages, as well as the usual English branches. Salary $300. Address Mrs Geo Carter, Bellefield, near Upperville, Fauquier Co, Va.

Fatal accident near Eagle River. The Lake Superior Journal of Aug 5: Dr Pratt, physician at the Minnesota Copper Mine, Mr Kershon, formerly a clerk in the same company, & a Canadian voyager, were drowned, & Mr Revere, of Boston, narrowly escaped with his life. Their frail canoe was submerged by a huge wave.

Central Academy, corner of E & 10th sts, will be resumed on Sep 4. –J W Winans, R B Dietrick, principals

WED AUG 23, 1854
Household & kitchen furniture at auction on Aug 30, at the residence of Mrs Wallingsford, on 4½ st, between C & Pa ave. -Green & Scott, aucts

Trustee's sale in square 536, 4½ & south D st. Under decree of the Circuit Court of Wash Co, D C, sitting in equity, in a cause wherein W W Corcoran is plntf & Chas Kiernan is dfndnt: sale on Aug 30, of lot 6 in square 536, with improvements. A Myde, trustee -Green & Scott, aucts

Household & kitchen furniture at auction: on Aug 30, at the residence Mrs Wallingsford, on 4½ st, between C & Pa ave. -Green & Scott, aucts

Trustee's sale in square 536, 4½ & south D st: under a decree of the Circuit Court of Wash Co, D C, sitting in equity, in a cause wherein W W Corcoran is plnts & Chas Kiernan is dfndnt: sale on Aug 30, of lot 6 in square 536, with improvements. -A Myde, trustee -Green & Scott, aucts

Mrd: on Aug 20, by Rev Mr Hodges, Luke Anderson to Miss Fanny Clarke, all of the District of Columbia.

Died: on Aug 21, at her residence in Wash City, Mrs Louisa Savary Preuss, aged 67 years. Her remains will be taken to the family burial ground, **Montazile**, PG Co, on Wed morning at 6 o'clock.

Wash Corp: 1-Nomination of John M Stevens for lumber measurer, vice John W Ferguson, deceased: confirmed. 2-Account of G E Slatford for cleaning & walling the sewer Pa ave: referred to the Cmte on Improvements. 2-Ptn of Jas Casparis, praying the remission of an unexpired license: referred to the Cmte on Improvements. 3-Ptn of John McKim, praying permission to rebuild & enlarge 2 sites of a frame back bldg in square 904: referred to the Cmte on Improvements. 4-Ptn from Jos Rappetti & others, asking the re-pavement of the west front of square 904: referred to the Cmte on Improvements. 5-Ptn of Lewis Hoping & others, property holders in 5th & 6th sts, in regard to the improvement of square 482: referred to the Cmte on Improvements.

Col M M Payne, U S 4th Regt of Artl, appointed Govn'r of the U S Military Asylum near Wash City. The appointment was made by the Board of Com'rs, of which Gen Winfield Scott is Pres.

Wash City appointments: The Mayor has appointed Amon Duvall, Ebenezer Cross, Wm Ready, Alonzo Brest, & John Hodgkins, members of the Auxiliary Guard, in place of the same number removed on Sat last.

U S appointments: Wm H Thomas appointed by Col Jas G Berret, Postmaster of Wash City, a clerk in that ofc, at $1,400 per annum, vice Jos W Davis, removed; & Capt E Branch Robinson appointed Collector of the Port of Washington, vice Mr Thomas, resigned.

Andrew K Starke, of Wash Co, Md, has been appointed general superintendent of the works of the Chesapeake & Ohio Canal Co, & Mr Lamby has been appointed superintendent of the division near Gtwn, vice Mr Atchison, who declined longer serving. -Union

The co-partnership under the firm of Shekell & Bailey is dissolved by mutual consent. The business of the late firm will be liquidated. –Jas H Shekell
Jas H Shekell having purchased the interest of Josiah R Bailey will conduct the business at the old stand, No 5, opposite Centre Market.

Large dwlg for sale: new double house on the corner of G & 18th st, recently occupied by Hon Edw Everett: possession immediately. Apply to me at the ofc of Riggs & Co, A Hyde.

Valuable real estate & wharf property for sale: belongs to the estate of John C Vowell, deceased, & John S Miller, on the east side of Union, between King & Prince sts, in the city of Alexandria, Va, adjoining the property formerly owned by Phineas Janney on the north & of Wm N McVeigh, on the south. Refer to Francis L Smith, or Saml Miller, Alexandria, Va.

Orphans Court of Wash Co, D C. Letters testamentary on the personal estate of Jeremiah Cissell, late of Wash Co, deceased. –Sidney Evans, exc

Large dwlg for sale: new double house on the corner of G & 18th st, recently occupied by Hon Edw Everett: possession immediately. Apply to me at the ofc of Riggs & Co, A Hyde.

Notice: the partnership existing under the name of Mitchell & Reynolds, as Auction & Commission Merchants & Real Estate Agents, is this day dissolved by mutual consent. –Geo W Mitchell, Jos Reynolds

THU AUG 24, 1854
North Carolina: S J Person has been appointed a Judge of the Superior Court vice Judge Settle, resigned. Romulus M Saunders, well known in Congress & as Minister to Spain, has also resigned the ofc of Judge of the Superior Court.

Cmder David G Farragut, accompanied by his family, sailed from N Y on Sat last in the steamship **Star of the West** for Calif. He goes to take charge of the Navy Yard, now being constructed, about 28 miles from San Francisco. He takes the sloop-of-war **Warren**, now lying at San Francisco, as his residence, until such time as a suitable bldg can be erected.

Peter Crowel, [alias Baltimore Pat,] & Jos Donley, are charged with having, during a riot in Phil, murdered a watchman named Mooney. These 2 seamen arrived at the Brooklyn Navy Yard last week in the store ship **Relief**, from a 3 years' cruise, & were arrested just as they had been paid off. Their conduct on board the **Relief** during her return voyage had been so bad that it was found necessary to keep them in irons nearly all the way.

Fatal accident at Chester Springs, Chester Co: Anna Deacon & Kate Buckbee, of Phil, with a young man, were going to the springs when the reins broke. Miss Deacon was killed when she leapt from the vehicle, & Miss Buckbee was injured when she was thrown out. -Phil Ledger

The Fincastle [Va] Democrat states that the infant daughter of Mr John Britt, residing about a mile from Fincastle, while playing in her father's spring-house on Thu, fell upon a piece of a saucer & cut her throat. She bled to death in a few moments.

Mobile Tribune: on the authority of a letter from Greenville, Butler Co, a few days before, in a general melee, Felix Gafford had his throat cut & died one day after, J Williams & John Caldwell were shockingly cut up & are probably dead; & Wm Williams, Franck Gafford, & Henry Caldwell were all seriously wounded.

Mr Peter Kilmore, of Capake, N Y, was out hunting, when his dog jumped against him & discharged the whole contents of his gun in his breast. The accident took place on Aug 7, & he died the next Friday.

John T Crandell, aged about 17 years, a step-son of Dr R Finley Hunt, of Wash City, accidentally shot himself yesterday & died in 2 or 3 minutes afterwards. In company with another youth, he went in the morning in a boat over to Mason's Island on a hunting excursion. His gun accidentally went off when he seized it after spotting some birds. He fell back, & delivered a fond farewell to his mother, & expired. He was of a good character, & his family is in sad bereavement.
+
Died: On Aug 23, from the accidental discharge of his gun, John Thos Crandell, in his 18th year. His funeral will take place this afternoon, from the residence of his father, Dr R Finley Hunt. [Aug 25th newspaper: The Scott Guards, a fine volunteer company of quite young men, paraded yesterday & accompanied to their last resting place the remains of their fellow-member, John T Crandell.]

Mrd: at the residence of Absalom B Woodruff, Paterson, N J, by Rev Wm B Hornblower, Miss Charlotte G, daughter of Gen Geo De Wolfe, deceased, of the Island of Cuba, to Edw P Goode, of Wash City. [No date given-current item.]

Died: on Aug 22, in Wash City, Kendall, youngest daughter of Wm & Jennie Stickney.

Died: on Aug 22, Katharine Theodosia, infant daughter of Robt W & Katharine T F Barnard, aged 2 months & 22 days.

First Ward: Chas A Davis is a candidate, & Luther R Smoot is a candidate, for a seat in the Board of Common Council to fill the vacancy occasioned by the death of O S Paine. [Aug 29th newspaper: Davis received 800 votes; Smoot 297 votes; & Mr Perkins 2 votes. So Chas A Davis was elected to fill the vacancy.]

The creditors of Saml Chew, & all persons having claims upon the proceeds of his real estate conveyed to Jas A S Lawrence by deed of trust dated Jul 7, 1838, are notified to exhibit their claims to me on or before Sep 15 next. –Walter S Cox, trustee of Saml Chew.

New Boot & Shoe Store: Saml W Taylor & Co, Pa ave, next to Messrs Geo & T Parker, opposite Brown's Hotel.

FRI AUG 25, 1854
Fire at Richmond, Va, on Mon, destroyed the tobacco factories of Gentry & Hatcher & of J W Atkinson. Several firemen ventured into one of the burning bldgs, when the division wall gave way & fell, killing Nicholas Walsh & Wm Ligon.

The Charleston papers announce the death of Hon Danl Elliott Huger, a distinguished citizen of S C, who formerly for a brief period, from 1843 to 1845, represented S C in the U S Senate. He has been identified with the public service of his State, as a Member of the Legislature, a Judge, a State Senator, & finally a member of the U S Senate. [No death date given-current item.]

Household & kitchen furniture at auction: on Aug 28, at Mrs Hall's, on 11th st, between G & H sts. -Green & Scott, aucts

Rare & elegant estate for sale: I offer my Farm called *Antrim*, in Carroll Co, Md, near the village of Taneytown, containing 500 acres of land. All the improvements are new, the mansion house is 50 feet front by 110 feet in depth, 2 stories & attic, finished at a very large cost in the best possible style. Many out-bldgs, & 2 Switzer barns. The title is indisputable. –A G Ege, Antrim, Carroll Co, Md.

SAT AUG 26, 1854

Household & kitchen furniture at auction: on Sep 2, by deed of trust from J V N Throope, dated Jul 6, 1854, in front of the Auction store. –A E L Keese, trustee -Green & Scott, aucts

The events that have recently occurred in Spain have brought Gen O'Donnell before the public more than at any previous period. O'Donnell, a Spaniard by birth, is, as his name implies, of Irish origin. His family have been long settled in Spain, & the names of his father & uncle, the Counts of Lubisbal, must be familiar to the readers of the history of the Peninsular war, or of the Duke of Wellington's despatches. They were ofcrs of distinction during the war of independence, at least in comparison with the military men that Spain produced at that period. Leopold O'Donnell, the present Minister of War, entered the army young, some years before the death of Ferdinand. After the death of the King in 1838, he remained faithful to the Christine cause, while his 3 brothers, Juan, Carlos, & Henrique, & his 2 brothers-in-law, passed over to the camp of Zumallacarregui, who raised the standard of Don Carlos in the Basque Provinces. Even Madame O'Donnell, the mother of the Minister, joined the Carlist cause, & while her son commanded in the name of Queen Isabella the province of Giupuscoa, his mother accepted & long filled the ofc of lady of honor to the wife of Don Carlos, at their sylvan court of Onate, in the same province.

Calif: W H Sheppard, convicted of the murder of Henry C Day, was executed at San Francisco on Jul 28. He protested his innocence to the last.

Died: on Aug 23, in Gtwn, after a week's illness, J Anderson Jones, 3rd son of Capt John C Jones, of *Clean Drinking*, Montg Co, Md. By his sudden death his family has been deprived of a most affectionate & devoted son & brother.

Died: on Aug 21, in Harrisburg, Pa, after a short illness, Sarah Emma, the beloved wife of Wm H Maruqis, of Wash City, in her 28th year.

Died: yesterday, Thos Jordan, in his 84th year. His funeral is this afternoon, at 4½ o'clock, from his late residence on L st, between 8th & 9th sts.

Harrisburg, Pa, Aug 25. Courtland C Johnson was hung here today for the murder of his wife & a man named Collier. There was a large crowd of spectators.

The London papers are full of the details of a trial of Mr John Carden, of Barrane, Ireland, on a charge of attempting a violent abduction of Miss Arbuthnot, who is the sister of Mrs Gough, wife of Hon Capt Gough, the son of Lord Gough, lately advanced to the peerage for his services in India. The lady had been to church with 3 other ladies, her sister, Miss Lyndon, & Mrs Gough. On their way home Mr Carden, with 2 or 3 retainers, stopped the carriage. The 3 ladies were dragged from the carriage, but Miss Arbuthnot fought bravely. Miss Eleanor L Arbuthnot proved herself too much, not only for Mr Carden, but even for another big fellow, who nearly tore the clothes from her back. The noise of the struggle drew several persons to the scene, & their interference prevented Mr Carden from carrying out his design, one of the persons giving him a flogging with a whip. The jury found the dfndnt guilty of an attempt to commit a felon, the punishment for which is 2 year's imprisonment.

Peter Fox, a man of good character, had on Wednesday morning for the first time gone to work at the Catholic Cathedral in Buffalo, his job being to point the plastering & finish the outside ornamental work. On his return to the job after having gone home for lunch, he ascended the scaffolding on the outside of the Church, when the scaffolding gave way, & he fell 72 feet. He lived but a short time. Mr Fox leaves a family of 6 or 7 little ones.

MON AUG 28, 1854
Franklin Pierce, Pres of the U S A, recognizes Ernest Carl Angelrodt, who has been appointed Consul of Baden at St Louis, in Missouri. –Aug 25, 1854

Died: on Aug 26, in Wash City, in her 59th year, Mrs Eliz Pulizzi, widow of the late Sgt Maj Venerand Pulizzi, U S M C. Her funeral will be this afternoon at 3 o'clock from her late residence on I st east, near the Navy Yard.

Died: on Sunday, John Somerfield Hughes, youngest child of Robt B & Eliza Frances Hughes, aged 5 years. His funeral will be this day at 4 o'clock, from his father's residence, on 12th st, Island.

Died: Thu, Robert Latimer, infant son of John & Cordelia Goldin, aged 13 months.

Died: on Aug 24, at Edinburgh, Saratoga Co, N Y, where he was on a visit with his mother & 2 little sisters, Charles Amos Hunt, aged 5 years & 10 months, an amiable & intelligent scholar of the E st Baptist Sabbath School, & youngest son of Amos Hunt, of Capitol Hill, Wash City.

Having procured the services in my family of Mr Wm Thurmond, who is a graduate of the Univ of Va in the Ancient & Modern Languages & Chemistry, & competent to teach all the common English branches, I am desirous of receiving into my family 3 or 4 boys, from 10 to 14, who will in all respects be treated as my own children. The rate is $160 for a term of 10 months. –Jas K Marshall, Leeds, near Markham Station, Fauquier Co, Va.

Stephen Simpson died in Phil a few days ago. He was at one period of his life an editor, & gained considerable celebrity as a political writer, especially by his essays against the U S Bank, over the signature of Brutus, published in Duane's Aurora.

In Store & for sale: wines, brandy, cider vinegar, sugar, & fresh spices of all kinds. -Wm Linton, corner & of 7th & D sts.

TUE AUG 29, 1854
Household & kitchen furniture at auction on Sep 11, at the two houses occupied by Prof D E Groux, on Pa ave, between 6th & 7th sts. -Jas C McGuire, auct

Household & kitchen furniture at auction on Sep 4, at the late residence of Mrs Preuss, deceased, on I st, between 18th & 19th sts. -Green & Scott, aucts

The house of Abraham Simpson, near Poughkeepsie, N Y, was burnt early on Thu. Mr Simpson was absent from home. His wife was badly burnt, & their 5 children perished in the flames.

I will sell at private sale my Farm, containing 101 acres, situated on the Columbia Turnpike, about 4 miles from Wash: improvements consist of a good frame house & barn, both new. –Harvey Bailey, Alexandria Co, Va

The venerable Rev Leonard Woods, of Andover, Mass, died there on Thu, at the age of 81 years. He was born in Princeton, Mass, Jun 19, 1774, & graduated at Harvard in 1796: ordained Pastor of the Fourth Congregation Church in Newbury, Dec 5, 1798, & left it on May 26, 1808. In 1810 he was installed Prof of Theology at Andover, at which place he had ever since resided. –N Y Com Advertiser

John Muller, a German, who confessed that he some time ago murdered a man in N J, & was sent home for trial by the U S Consulat Port-au-Prince, died in prison on Wed last. Some persons attribute his death to the gnawing of conscience, whilst others doubt whether he had really committed a murder.

Riot reported to have taken place at Adairsville, Cass Co, Ga, on Sat week. Jas Blackwell, marshal, was shot & killed; deputy marshal Hillburn was severely cut on his head; Saml Dobbs, freight engineer on the railroad, was shot but the ball glanced his head; Mr Ely, fireman, is thought to be fatally wounded.

Mrd: on Aug 21, in Wash City, by Rev Mr Hill, Auren Knapp, of N Y, to Miss Mary E Norflet, of Norfolk, Va.

Died: on Aug 28, at Wood Cot, PG Co, Md, Mrs Mary Louisa Dangerfield, wife of Col Wm Henry Dangerfield, & daughter of Mrs Rebecca Winn, of Wash City. Her funeral will be this day, at 4 o'clock, at the **Congregational burying ground**.

Died: on Aug 28, in Wash City, of dysentery, Joseph Borrows, 2nd son of Josiah R & Anne E Bailey, aged 2 years. His funeral will take place on Wed at 4 o'clock, from the residence of his father, on D st, near 7th.

Died: on Aug 28, Thomas Delvin Berry, only son of Thomas B & Fannie L Berry, aged 1 year & 2 months. His funeral is tomorrow at 10 o'clock, from Mrs E Ferguson's, East Capitol st, Capitol Hill.

Died: on Aug 26, John Massey Moore, youngest daughter of Danl D & Mgt Davidson, aged 1 year, 4 months 5 days.

John Townsend, Pres of the Commercial Bank at Albany, & formerly Mayor of that city, died there on Sat, in his 73rd year.

Orphans Court of Wash Co, D C. Letters of administration, with the will annexed, on the personal estate of Jas Nourse, late of Wash Co, deceased.
–Sarah H Nourse, admx w a

Portsmouth [N H] Journal of Aug 26. In the Washington Union of the present week we see the official announcement of the appointment of John McClintock as Naval Ofcr at the Custom-house, Portsmouth, N H. His term expires under his old appointment this day, & on Monday next he enters on his 94th year, & on the discharge of the duties of his new four years' commission. Capt John MClintock was born on Aug 28, 1761, the son of Rev Dr Saml McClintock, of Greenland, who was chaplain in the army of the Revolution at the battle of Bunker Hill. John McClintock, at about 16, entered the service in the private armed ship **Alexander**, of 20 guns. At 17 he was mater's mate, & was entrusted with conducting a prize into the West Indies. He remained in the service 4 years lacking one month, not being in any public ship, he receives no pension for Revolutionary services. The emolents of the ofc last year were less than $400. Let the guns be fired & the flags be displayed when he enters his ofc on Monday next.

Has the history of even Spanish revolutions ever offered more sudden vicissitudes of fortune than appear in the case of Col Garrigo, who was taken in an early skimish, tried by a court-martial, condemned to death, & saved by the Queen at the earnest intercession of his wife, & has now, within only a few days, been by the same Queen created a general ofcr & appointed to the command of the cavalry of the garrison at Madrid?!

The editor of the Wheeling Times received a watermelon weighing 63 pounds. It was a specimen of the crop of Mr Edwin Baldin, of Anne Arundel Co, Md.

Terrible visitation of cholera in the family of Mr Aaron Daniels, a respectable farmer, residing about 3 miles north of Ottowa, Ill. The first victim was Miss Minerva Daniels, aged 17, who died on Sat; on Mon, Jonathan Daniels, son, aged 20 years; Ruth Ann Daniels, aged 14 years; Judith Daniels, aged 11 years; Aaron Daniels, 4 years; & on Thu Mrs Aaron Daniels, aged about 40 years. The family was widely connected, & among the visiters the following fell victims: On Mon, Geo Head, son of Thos Head, aged 18 years; Louis Parker, child of Mrs Parker, daughter of Aaron Daniels; Mrs B Flemings, sister of Mrs A Daniels; Alvah Channel, living with A Daniels; Miss Kingsley, school teacher, who had been boarding in the family; & Mr Garret Galvin, who had assisted in burying the family of Mr Daniels. The disease spread in no other families. –St Louis Rep of 24th.

WED AUG 30, 1854
Premptory sale of new 2 story house & lot on 12th st, between M & N sts, late in the occupancy of Jno W Phillips. The above property will be sold to remove an incumbrance now resting on it. –R Phillips, trustee of Angelina D Phillips
-Jas C McGuire, auct

Horrid stage accident. As one of the stages of Messrs Flagg, Caldwell & Co, of Lynchburg, was proceeding from the canal to the South Side Railroad depot, on Sat last, & it turned over injuring Mr Robt Ritchie, who had his hand mashed & torn, & his wife had a severe flesh wound. Mrs Russell & Miss Martha M Russell were bruised. Dr Carrington had both legs badly broken, & died in a few hours. Dr D G Potts was bruised. Mr E W Burwell & Mr Wells were considerably injured. The accident is attributable to the recklessness of the driver of the stage, who was intoxicated at the time.

Wash Corp: 1-Ptn of LeRoy Edwards for the remission of a fine: referred to the Cmte of Claims. 2-Cmte of Claims: asked to be discharged from the further consideration of the ptn of H Hersberg: discharged accordingly. 3-Ptn of E G Handy, claiming a portion of a fine: referred to the Cmte of Claims.

The death of Gen Nicholas Haight, of N Y, an active ofcr of the war of 1812, is announced by a Corresponding State Cmte of the veterans. [No death date given-current item.]

Appointments by the Pres. 1-*Robt J Armstrong, of Iowa, 3rd Auditor of the Treasury, vice Francis Burt, appointed Govn'r of Nebraska Territory. 2-Thos C Porter, late Surveyor of the Port of New Orleans, Collector of Customs, vice Solomon W Downs, deceased. 3-Wm E Starke, Surveyor of the Port of New Orleans, to fill the vacancy occasioned by the promotion of Thos C Porter to the collector ship. The vacancy in the appraiser's ofc occasioned by the promotion of Wm E Starke has not yet been filled. -Globe [Aug 31st newspaper: *The new Third Auditor is Robt J Atkinson, & not Robt J Armstrong, as the appointee to this important ofc.]

Calamity at Louisville: by proclamation of Mayor Speed, all business was suspended throughout the city & the bells tolled, in observance as a day of mourning for the victims of the awful tornado of Sunday. The funeral services were preached by Dr Brackenridge's church, where an immense concourse were gathered to hear Dr Morrison, the pastor of the demolished church. List of some of the killed: Mrs Vildabee & 3 children; Mr Taylor & child; Mr Godfrey; Mrs Salisbury; wife of Mr Salisbury, city pump maker; Miss Headley; aged about 11 years; John McGowan, ; Mr Sweeney, carpenter; Mrs Martin, wife of John N Martin, saddler; Mrs Wicks, wife of Capt Wm Wicks; niece of Mrs Martin; Mr Barbour; Alex McLelland, of the Ky Locomotive Works; Mr R Davis, a resident of New Albany; & Mr McBride & child. One or two others not yet identified. [Sep 1st newspaper: names of those wounded: Mrs Taylor, wife of Mr Taylor who was killed, & child, both seriously; Miss Duff, 3 ribs broken; Mrs Pennebaker, slightly; Mrs Morsell, dangerously, no hopes of recovery; Miss Morsell, aged 18 years, severely, but will probably recover; Mrs Hewitt & child, badly, but will recover; Washington Ragan, seriously; Miss Cooper, severely; Mr Bradley, bricklayer, had an eye knocked out while efforts were being made to rescue him from the ruins. Mr Jos Lilley, on 10th st, was much injured & part of his back bldg was blown down. The large house owned by Col Saml Churchill, was unroofed. The residence of Mr J Callahan, 9th & Magazine, was considerably injured. The beautiful family residence of Col Wm Riddle, on Ky st, was unroofed. Two brick houses on 12th st were unroofed; one belonged to Mr Short & the other to Mrs Nugent. A row of 21 brick cottages, on Ky st, belonging to Messrs Cochran & Mussleman, were all completely unroofed.]

The U S sloop-of-war **Constellation** was launched at the Gosport Navy Yard on Sat. She is a new edition of the brave old frig of that name which, under the command of the gallant Truxton, won for our navy, while in its earliest infancy, imperishable laurels, & continued to be while she floated a "crack ship" in the navy. Some of her timber has been worked into the new ship.

Mrd: Aug 29, by Rev S C Clarkson, Lt Egbert Thompson, U S Navy, of N Y, to Miss Emily B, only daughter of the late Ignatius Mudd, of Wash.

Mrd: Aug 25, by Rev Mr Hodges, Jos Hodges to Miss Eliz I Jett, both of PG Co, Md.

Fatal affray on Fri: Mr John Turner, of Portsmouth, Va, was shot by Mr Thos H Cocke, while the two were engaged in a dispute in front of the residence of Mr Turner, killing him almost instantly. The deceased leaves a wife & 5 children. Cocke surrendered himself to the authorities.

THU AUG 31, 1854

Extensive sale of new & used household furniture on Sep 5, at the House-furnishing Ware-rooms of R B Reeves, on 7th st, immediately opposite the Patent Ofc. —Thos J Fisher, trustee -Jas C McGuire, auct

The State of Georgia some time ago authorized the erection of a monument in honor of the heroic services of Pulaski during the Revolutionary war, & particularly of his gallant conduct at Savannah, at the siege of which he fell, on Oct 9, 1779. This work had just been completed in N Y by Mr R E Launitz, the Russian sculptor. It is a square column, 60 feet in height, with a Corinthian cap, & surmounted by the statue of liberty. Within the panels of the pedestal are inserted appropriate designs, wrought in basso relive. It is to be erected in a few weeks in Monterey square, Savannah, & in ceremonies incident thereto the public authorities will participate.

Mrd: on Aug 12, by Rev Stephen Merrick, Mr Nicholas Beck to Miss Matilda Harrison, both of Wash.

Died: on Aug 30, at the residence of her father, Mrs Harriet Valinda Farquhar, widow of the late R C Farquhar, & daughter of Rev John Scrivener, leaving 3 orphan children. Her funeral is this afternoon at 4 o'clock, from the Methodist Episcopal Church South, on 8th st, between H & I sts.

Died: on Jul 19, on board the ship **Francis P Sage**, 12 degrees south of the equator, Atlantic, on his passage home, Fred'k W De Krafft, of Gtwn, D C.

Died: Aug 20, Ida, aged 17 months & 4 days, only daughter of Ambrose & Lucina H Carner. Her funeral is this morning at 10 o'clock, at their residence, B st, Capitol Hill.

Wash City Ordinances: 1-Act for the relief of Jos Cross: sum of $4 to be paid to Cross, late Com'r of the eastern section of the canal, for expenses incurred in repairs to said canal. 2-Act for the relief of Richd G Briscoe: the sum of $31.50 be paid to him being the amount erroneously assessed to Briscoe for improvements on his property.

In Chancery. Virginia: In the Circuit Court of Fred'k Co. Jun 17, 1854. P C L Burwell, adm with the will annexed of Zachariah Sanks, deceased, cmplnt, against Joshua Sanks, John Sanks, son of Geo Sanks, deceased, Eliz Fenton & others, legatees of said Zachariah Sanks, deceased, & others, dfndnts. It appearing to the Court that Joshua Sanks, a brother of the testator, John Sanks, son of Geo, & Eliz Fenton, a sister of the testator, have not come forward to claim their shares in said estate, & that their residences are unknown, it is ordered that the said administrator do pass the share of said last named parties, amounting to $723.10 to the Receiver of this Court, who is directed to loan out the same until the further order of the Court, taking bond with good personal security. And it is further ordered that the Master Com'r, Wm L Bent, do proceed to make diligent inquiry as to the residence of said last named absent dfndnts, by communicating with those likely to know the family & by publication in the Richmond Enquirer & the Nat'l Intell, & such other papers as may be the probable residence of said parties. –J Kean, C C. Com'rs Ofc, Winchester, Va, Aug 28, 1854. The above parties are notified that their shares are held in the above named Circuit Court, & will be paid to them upon proof of their identity. -Wm L Bent, Com'r

Bladensburg Academy will begin its next session on Sep 1. Apply to the Principal, H T Wheeler.

FRI SEP 1, 1854
Sale by order of the Orphans Court of Wash Co, D C, on Sep 6, on the farm belonging to the estate of the late Capt Wm Easby, a short distance beyond Rock Creek Church, the following articles, viz: 100 hewn House logs; lumber & shingles; 550 chestnut posts; lot of manure; 20 cords of word; wrought & cast iron; lot of wheat & rye, in the straw; lot of corn & potatoes in the fields growing. By order of the execs. -Jas C McGuire, auct

Sale by order of the Orphans Court of Wash Co, D C, on Sep 8, at Easby's Shipyard, I shall sell the following articles belonging to the estate of the late Capt Wm Easby, viz: large punching machine; 2 scows; wooden crane; fire engine; copper pump; lumber wagon; pair timber wheels; cart; 2 anvils; 2 pair bellows; lots of blacksmiths' tools; bolts; cast & wrought iron; iron screw press; iron windlass; portable forge; lot of doors & lumber. -Jas C McGuire, auct

Sale by order of the Orphans Court of Wash Co, D C, on Sep 7, in front of my Auction Rooms, the following personal property of the late Capt Wm Easby, viz: 6 work horses, 6 carts & harness; 3 wagons & harness; carryall; 3 cows & heifer; ploughs; cultivators; straw cutter; picks; hoes; shovels; axes; cutting box; jack screw; wheelbarrows; rakes; saws; augurs; cradle; & scythe. -Jas C McGuire, auct

Mrd: on Aug 24, by Rev Mr Boyle, Mr Jas M Woodward to Mrs Mary E Bates, both of Washington.

The Roman Catholic Bishop of Buffalo has directed that no more than 5 carriages shall accompany any corpse to the church or cemetery, & the Catholics have, with few exceptions, shown a disposition to obey the order cheerfully.

Rev Dr McJimsey, pastor of the Graham Church, [Associate Reformed,] about 4 miles from Walton, Delaware Co, N Y, died on the 26th ult, at the advanced age of 82 years. He had been pastor for the Graham Church 60 years. On the Sunday previous to his decease he traveled 10 miles to fulfil an appointment.

Knoxville [Tenn] papers contain the following mixture under their matrimonial head: Mrd: on Jul 10, in Knoxville, Tenn, by Zach Boothe, Mr Patrick Welch to Miss Sarah E Davis.
Died: in Knoxville, on Jul 24, Mr Patrick Welch.
Mrd: on Aug 12, at Knoxville, Tenn, by W R Seay, Thos Collins to Mrs Sarah E Welch, relict of the late Patrick Welch. This is the progressive age!

Died: on Aug 31, in Balt, Mrs Caroline Harrington, wife of Geo Harrington, of Wash City. Her funeral will be performed at the Cathedral in Balt, this morning, at 7 o'clock, & her remains will be desposited at 11 o'clock in the vaults of St Patrick's Church in Wash City.

Died: on Aug 30, Samuel, 3rd son of Chas A & Eliza Anderson, aged 2 years & 6 months.

A bethrothed young woman shot by her lover: on Sun Danl McArthur was sitting in the same room at Cincinnati, with Catharine Desmond, a young lady to whom he was engaged. She was reading a book, & her lover was teasing her trying to transfer her attention to himself. Finally he took a double barreled shot gun, pulled the trigger, intending to blow out the candle. Unfortunately the gun was loaded & he saw his bethrothed sink to the floor, bleeding & dying. The unhappy man surrendered himself to the police. The dead & the living were to have been married in about 2 months. –Cincinnati Gaz, 29th.

Jas B Dodson & Louis F Perry have this day formed a copartnership under the firm of Dodson & Perry, for the buying & selling of Furniture Dry Goods, Mr Louis F Perry having bought out the interest of Mr D Clagett, of the late firm, in that business. –Jas B Dodson, Louis F Perry. [D Clagett is retiring from the business.]

SAT SEP 2, 1854
Intelligence of the death of Mr Downs, Collector of New Orleans, [an Ex-Senator,] have rendered to be true. [No death date given-current item.]

Washington Seminary will resume on Sep 4. –H J De Neckere, S J, Principal

Died: on Aug 26, at the residence of Dr P B Bowen, in Culpeper Co, Va, Wm Fillison, son of Woodville & Sarah M Latham, of Wash City, aged 10 months & 7 days.

Alexandria Boarding School will commence on Oct 2. The number of students is limited to 60. –Benj Hallowell, Henry C Hallowell, Francis Miller, Alexandria, Va

Orphans Court of Wash Co, D C. In the case of Welhenmina Letmate, admx of Christian Letmate, deceased, the admx & Court have appointed Sep 23 next, for the settlement of the estate of said deceased, of the assets in hand. –Ed N Roach, Reg/o wills

Death of a veteran. Norfolk Herald: Wm Rogers, a native of Poole, England, who, at age 21, about the beginning of the present century, entered the U S naval service as a seaman, & served in the Mediterranean squadron, under Com Preble in our war with Tripoli. He was one of the gallant crew, headed by the late Cmdor [then Lt] Stephen Decatur, who in 1808 executed the brilliant achievement of boarding & burning the frig **Philadelphia** in the harbor of Tripoli & under the guns of its batteries. [No death date given-current item.]

MON SEP 4, 1854
Household & kitchen furniture at auction: on Sep 7, at the late residence of Venerando Pulizzi, deceased, on South I, between 6th & 7th sts. –F S Walsh, exc -Green & Scott, aucts

The steamer **Timour** No 2, left St Louis on Aug 23, for Weston & St Joseph. On Sat, about 3 miles below Jefferson city, her 3 boilers exploded. Many were blown into the river. Among the victims whose bodies were recovered is Mr Chas Dix, brother of the captain.

Died: on Sep 2, Mrs Ann Birth, widow of the late Jas Birth, in her 73rd year. Her funeral will be from her late residence this morning at 9½ o'clock.

TUE SEP 5, 1854
Household & kitchen furniture at auction: also carpenter shop & finished work: on Sep 12, by deed of assignment for the benefit of their creditors, made by Geo W Scroggan & Thos B Davis to the subscriber as trustee, at the residence of the above named gentlemen, at the corner of South C & 13½ sts west, on the Island, all the house-hold effects in the 2 houses. To be sold at auction the two houses in which they reside, nearly new, & the lot on which they stand, being lot 4 in square 264, with the Carpenter's shop, work benches, & finished work. The title is indisputable. –John L Smith, trustee -Green & Scott, aucts

Household & kitchen furniture at auction on Sep 11, at the residence of Wm Gadsby, Pa ave, next to the corner of 3rd st. -Green & Scott, aucts

The Princess Charlotee Julia Zenaide Bonaparte died on Aug 8 at Rome, where she has resided for many years. She was the oldest daughter of Jos Bonaparte, ex-King of Naples & of Spain. She was married in Jun, 1822, to her cousin, Chas Lucien Bonaparte, son of Lucien Bonaparte, [brother of Napoleon I,] & the actual Prince of Canino. She has left many children, who all reside in Rome. Prince Canino himself has for several years resided in France. He is a distinguished as a man of science, but is reported to have not very estimable personal qualities. His character has long prevented his living upon good terms with the Princess, his late wife, who was exceedingly amiable & intelligent. She was born in Paris on Jul 8, 1801

Saml Chilton, Atty & Counsellor at Law, Wash City, D C, has this day associated with him J D Latham, of said city. Ofcs: 7th st, over the Exchange Bank.
-Saml Chilton, J D Latham

District of Columbia, Wash Co, to wit: in virtue of a warrant from Wm R Woodward, a Justice of the Peace for said county, dated Aug 30, 1854, to me directed, commissioning me to summons 12 freeholders, inhabitants of the said county, to meet on the lands of Ann Robey, widow of Theophilus Robey, deceased, & Theophilus Robey, Danl Lightfoot & Sarah Eliz Lightfoot [late Robey] his wife, John Robey, Barbara James, Jarome Davis, Wm Lachlen & Sarah Lachlen his wife, & J C Harmer, assignee of Uriah Robey, legal reps & heirs at law of Theophilus Robey, deceased, on Oct 18, 1854, for the purpose of assessing what damage the owner or owners may sustain by reason of the new road about to be opened though the said land, leading from a point on the old Milkhouse Ford Road, near the house occupied by Thos Mattingly, to a point on the road leading from the mill of Price Shoemaker to the old Paper Mill above, at or near the mouth of Broad Branch.
-J D Hoover, Marshall for D C

Francis B Habersham, late associate editor of the N Y Courier & Enquirer, died at his residence in Brooklyn a few days since of typhoid fever, after an illness of 6 weeks. He was a native of Georgia, & descended from one of the oldest families of that State. He graduated at one of the Phil Medical Colleges, but, after several years of Southern practice as a physician, abandoned the profession & became an editor.

John Lynch, Collector of the Port of Richmond, Va, died at the Huguenot Springs on Fri last.

Mrd: on Jul 13, 1854, at **Fort Union**, New Mexico, by Rev Mr Smith, Miss Emily Virginia Macrae to Capt Geo Sykes, U S A.

Died: on Sep 4, in Wash City, Mrs Matilda M, consort of Wm Jos Smith, in her 39th year.

Died: on Sep 1, in Rockville, Md, very suddenly, Mr David Little, for more than 20 years a resident of Wash City.

Died: on Sep 3, Susan, youngest daughter of J R & Mary M Zimmerman. Her funeral is this morning at 10 o'clock, from the residence of the parents, 9th st, between D & E sts.

Wheeling, Va, Sep 2. An arch of the bridge now in course of construction for the Hempfield road, near this city, fell today, killing the contractor, Mr Jas McCartney, & one of the workmen.

Dr S J Cockerille, Dentist, Pa ave, between 11th & 12th sts.

Dissolution of the copartnership under the firm of Evans & Fant, which expires by limitation this day, by mutual consent. H G Fant is alone to use the name of the firm in the final settlement of their business. –F S Evans, Hamilton G Fant
+
Hamilton G Fant, Banker & Dealer in Exchange Stocks, etc, Pa ave, between 4½ & 6th st, Wash, D C. Claims against the Gov't collected.

For sale: a new & well finished 2 story brick house on Va ave, between 3rd & 4½ sts. Apply to the subscriber at the Wash City Savings Bank-Edw Simms.

WED SEP 6, 1854
Brvt Lt Col John McClelland, of the Corps of Topographical Engineers, died recently at Knoxville, Tenn, of cholera. Col McC was the brother of Sec McClelland, of the Interrior Dept. He leaves a widow, formerly Miss Walker, of Wash City, & has a family of children, all of whom are now at Piney Point. -Star [Sep 8th newspaper: obit of Col John McClellan: born in Franklin Co, Pa, he entered the Military Academy in 1822; graduated as brvt lt in the 3rd Artl on Jul 1, 1826; transferred to the 1st Artl in 1827; promoted to an adjutancy in 1831; in 1833 advanced to a 1st Lt, & appointed adj of the Artl School for Practice at **Fort Monroe** during the same year. On Nov 19, 1836, he resigned. He was recalled into the service as a captain of Topographical Engineers on Jul 7, 1838; & received a brvt of major in Aug, 1848, for meritorious conduct in the battles of Contreras & Churubusco in Aug, 1847; in the same month he received the brvt of lt col for his gallant services in the military operations before the city of Mexico on Sep 13, 1847. He was struck down in the meridian of life at age 49 years.]

Household & kitchen furniture at auction: on Sep 13, at the residence of L R Smoot, on K st, between 26th & 27th sts. -Green & Scott, aucts

Household & kitchen furniture at auction: Sep 8, at the residence of Mr Henry C Neale, on 12th st, 3rd door from Mass ave. –Geo F Dyer; Edw S Wright, auct

Household & kitchen furniture at auction on Sep 8, at the late residence of Hon Danl Mace, on B st, corner of 3rd st west. -Green & Scott, aucts

Wash Corp: 1-Ptn of Mrs Catharine White for the remission of a fine: referred to the Cmte of Claims. 2-Ptn of Jas Crook for the remission of a fine: referred to the Cmte of Claims. 3-Ptn of Geo Hercus, asking to be refunded certain moneys paid for a license, which license was not used by him: referred to the Cmte of Ways & Means.

Died: on Sep 1, Jesse F Plowman, aged 17 years & 3 months, youngest son of Jesse & Eliz Plowman.

Died: on Aug 18, Jesse Plowman, aged 10 months & 11 days, son of Wm R & Eliz Plowman.

Died: on Sep 3, at the Marine Barracks, Wash, Cpl John Gilchrist, formerly of N Y.

Died: on Sep 5, George, son of Prudence E & Wm H Frazier, aged 1 year, 2 months & 2 weeks. His funeral is this morning at 9 o'clock, from the residence of his father, on 8th st, between M & N sts.

THU SEP 7, 1854
Trustee's sale of frame house & lot at auction: on Sep 28, by deed of trust from Beedey Wise to the subscriber, dated Aug 29, 1850, recorded in Liber J A S No 56, folios 93 thru 95, of the land records for Wash Co, D C: sale of lot 34 in square 411, with frame house. –J Fitz Bartlett, trustee -Green & Scott, aucts

Dr Robt M Patterson, late Director of the U S Mint, died in Phil on Sep 5. He was Pres of the American Philosophical Society, & formerly Prof of the Universities of Pa & Va.

The celebrated **Warm Springs**, in Bath Co, Va, was sold at auction on Sep 1 for $50,000. Messrs Mays, Francisco, & a gentleman residing in the neighborhood were the purchasers. There are about 3,000 acres of grazing land attached to the **Springs**.

Liberty [Bedford Co] Sentinel of Fri: Jas H Wilson, Editor & Proprietor of the Roanoke Republican, died at the residence of Rev Nelson Sale, in this county, on Sunday last, after a protracted illness. He was a young man of talent & gave promise of much usefulness.

Mrd: on Sep 6, by Rev Dr Cole, Geo P Krafft to Mrs Sarah Ward, all of Wash City.

Mrd: on Sep 5, by Rev F Israel, Durbin Tucker to Sarah Ann Dove, all of Wash City.

Died: yesterday, after a long illness, Mr Jas Y Freeman, in his 66th year. Mr Freeman was a native of Guernsey, but has been a resident of Wash City for the last 30 years, & was highly esteemed by all who knew him. His funeral will take place from his late residence, on D st, between 9th & 10th sts, this afternoon, at 4 o'clock.

Obit-died: on Fri last, in Wash City, after a short illness, Mrs Sarah Eliz Ketchum, wife of Capt Wm H Ketchum, & daughter of Wm C & Mary Stoddart Easton, of Mobile. Mrs Ketchum was born in Wash City on Jul 22, 1829, & was a few days over 25 years old. She has left 3 children, all very young.

At the wedding celebration of Cyrus H Larkin on Friday, bells were struck, tin pans were clanged, & a gun was twice discharged, which took effect on Edmund Adams, age 18 years. He lingered until Sat night, when he died. Both men had resided for a long time in Elgin, & belonged to highly respectable families. –Chicago Journal of Monday week.

Albany, Sep 6. Mrs Gen Stewart, of Balt, died suddenly on board the steamer **Hendrick Hudson** at the wharf in this city.

The undersigned, by virtue of a commission issued from the Circuit Court of St Mary's Co, Md, to value & divide the real estate of John Mattingly, late of said county, deceased, hereby give notice that they will meet on the premises of said deceased, on Nov 9 next, for the purpose of executing the aforesaid commission.
John F Dent　　　　　　　Henry Hammette　　　　　John Blakistone
Morris Shanks　　　　　　Albert Burch

Orphans Court of Wash Co, D C. Letters of administration on the personal estate of Susan Devenport, late of Wash Co, deceased. –Wm M Mann, adm

Mrs Wm Q Force, intending to instruct her daughter at home, proposes to receive 6 pupils for companions in study. Residence 10th st, between D & E sts.

Large plantation & residence at auction, together with stock, near Memphis, Tenn. Contains 1,600 acres. The remains of a mill on Big Creek, lately burnt down, owned by John Ralston, will be offered for sale: 200 to 300 acres. –S S Bembert, Big Creek, Shelby Co, 12 miles from Memphis, Tenn

FRI SEP 8, 1854
Household & kitchen furniture at auction on Sep 14, at the residence of B N Hutchinson, on north K, between 6th & 7th sts. -Green & Scott, aucts

Trustee's sale of brick house & lot at auction: on Oct 10, by deed of trust from Jos Radcliff & wife to the subscribers, dated Apr 16, 1850, recorded in Liber J A S No 14, folios 240 to 246, of the land records for Wash Co, D C: sale of lots 1 & 22 in square 455, with a fine brick house: at the corner of 6th st west & F st north, in Wash City, D C. –Walter Lenox, Henry Naylor, trustees -Green & Scott, aucts

Trustees sale of house & lot at auction: on Oct 9, by deed of trust from Wm Talbert & wife to the subscribers, dated Jan 10, 1850, recorded in Liber J A S No 10, folios 274 to 280, of the land records for Wash Co, D C: sale of lot 22 in square 977, situated on 11th st east, between M & N sts south. –Walter Lenox, Henry Naylor, trustees -Green & Scott, aucts

On Thu last the farm of Danl Jacobs, deceased, in Wash Co, Md, containing 102 acres of land, near the Hagerstown & Waynesboro road, was sold to Jacob Hykes for $91.70 per acre. The mountain land belonging to the same estate sold for $35.05 per acre; also the farm of Christian Sheller for $47 per acre, & the farm of Nathan McDowell, to John Fox, of Pa, at $90 per acre.

Mrd: on Sep 5, in N Y, by Rev Spencer H Cone, D D, Robt B Morrell, of Phil, to Miss Sallie C McCorkle, daughter of the late Jos P McCorkle, of Wash City.

Died: on Sep 7, at the residence of her son-in-law, Thos Cookendorfer, Mrs Susan Burnes, in her 82nd year, after a protracted illness. Her funeral is this afternoon, at 4 o'clock, from Mr Cookendorfer's residence, on E st, near 6th.

Died; on Aug 22, in York, Ill, Stephen J Ober, in his 34th year, late of Wash City.

Phil, Sep 7. Edw C Lewis, formerly a Lt of the Pa volunteers in Mexico, was arrested on Fri last charged with numerous forgeries of land warrants. He was held in $2,500 bail. Failing to appear for a hearing yesterday & today, his bail has been forfeited.
[Sep 11th newspaper: Lt Lewis was arrested in Phil on Friday last charged with numerous forgeries of land warrants, & was held in $2,500 bail, but, failing to appear for a hearing, his bail has been forfeited.]

U S Patent Ofc, Wash, Sep 6, 1854. Ptn of Henry Burden, of Troy, N Y, praying for the extension of a patent granted to him on Dec 10, 1840, for the improvement in machines for rolling puddle balls or other masses of iron in the manufacture of iron, for 7 years from the expiration of said patent, which takes place on Dec 10, 1854. –Chas Mason, Com'r of Patents

SAT SEP 9, 1854
An interesting little daughter, aged about 12, of Mr Chas Stuart, paver, at 11th & Boundary sts, was on Thu accidentally killed by her brother, aged about 7, who hastily took down a gun to kill a bird on a tree near the window.

Died: on Sep 8, at the residence of her father, Mary E, wife of Wm H Falconer, & eldest daughter of Jos & Octavia Bryan, in her 30th year, after a long & protracted illness. Her funeral is on Sep 10, at 3 o'clock, from the residence of her father, on N Y ave.

Died: on Aug 8, Mary, consort of Jas Maxwell. Her funeral is this morning at 9 o'clock, from her late residence, on 4th st, between I & K sts.

Died: on Aug 7, Mrs Susan C Klinehanse, wife of Geo D Klinehanse, in her 41st year. Her funeral is this afternoon, at 4 o'clock, from the residence of her husband, on 7th st east, Navy Yard.

Died: on Sep 8, Mary Hammond, in her 6th year, youngest daughter of Wm B & Eliz G Todd. Her funeral is this afternoon at 5 o'clock, from the residence of her father, corner of C & 3rd sts.

Batesville, Ark, Aug 14, 1854. Batesville has received a heavy blow in the death of Rev Jas F Green, of the Presbyterian Church, who died from cholera at Memphis. We also learned of the death of Capt Geo Buckley, who was contractor for the river mail from Aberdeen to this place. He was very highly respected by all who knew him.

Most fiendish act ever recorded by the Rowan [N C] Whig. In Cabarrus Co, last week, a man by the name of Holbrooks hung his own son. He had sent the boy to a neighbor's to procure something to eat & the boy returned without it. He then sent him back & he again returned without it. His father took him out to a tree & hanged him. Holbrooks then fled, but has been apprehended.

On Monday, as a boy named Macey & a son of the late Judge Barculo were playing around the academy at Poughkeepsie, N Y, during recess, on turning a corner their heads came in collision with such violence as to rupture a blood-vessel & cause the death of young Barculo. The other boy was seriously injured & taken home insensible.

MON SEP 11, 1854
Among the passengers who arrived at N Y on Fri last from Calif are Hon John W Davis, late Govn'r of Oregon; Lt E G Beckwith; Capt Morris; Lt Baker, Dr Scheill; & Mr Snyder, of the Central Pacific Railroad surveying party; & Maj Heintzlemann, Lt McLean, & Lt O'Donnell, of the 2nd Infty U S Army.

Fine stock of Devon Cattle, Horses, Hogs, Farming Utensils, Carriage, Wagons, Carryall, Guns, & Furniture, at auction: on Sep 20, at the farm recently sold by B Forrest, in Montg Co, Md, lying between the Rockville & Brookville roads, near Tennallytown, adjoining the farms of Messrs Bradley & Watkins.
-Green & Scott, aucts

A highly esteemed young man, Franklin Knowles, residing not far from Cairo, was killed by a reaper: he & his brother were reaping with a patent reaper, drawn by 2 horses; the reaper disturbed a nest of bumblebees; the bees attacked Mr Knowles, who running forward, fell and the horses became frightened and dragged the reaper over Mr Knowles body. Although not killed outright, the pain was so intense that he was thrown into the lockjaw & died the next day. –Belleville [Ill] Advertiser

Mrs Fish, whose death we record today, [says the N Y Express] is the mother of Hamilton Fish, U S Senator, & widow of the late Col Fish, a gallant ofcr in the U S Army, & one of the old Knickerbockers. Mrs Fish was a lineal descendant of old Govn'r Stuyvesant, & has lived herself to the good old age of four score years. [No death date given-current item.]

A little son, age about 9 years, of Mr E A Smith, who resides in Richmond, was shockingly burnt on Tue last by the explosion of a powder flash. He was loading a child's brass cannon, & lit the powder with a candle.

The Balt Patriot says that Saml Williams, a colored man, has one of the finest farms in Wash Co, Md. At age 38 years he was a slave in Stafford Co, Va, but subsequently purchased his freedom from his own earnings. He then bound himself to years of servitude until he could purchase his wife & children, which he accomplished when he was 50 years of age. He now owns a farm worth $10,000 & personal property amounting to several thousand more, all earned by his own labor. He is now 73 years of age.

Mrd: on Aug 12, on board U S frig **Cumberland**, lying in the harbor of Spezzia, Sardinia, Lt Johnston B Creighton, U S Navy, to Edwina H, daughter of Cmdor S H Stringham, commanding U S squadron in the Mediterranean.

Mrd: on Sep 7, by Rev Mr Hodges, Wm A Scott to Miss Ann Rebecca Scott, all of Wash City.

Mrd: on Sep 7, in Germantown, Pa, by Rev Luther Albert, Harrison P Lewis, of Wash City, to Lizzie B, daughter of Chas Lewis, of Phil.

Died: on Sep 10, Robt A Carter, a clerk in the ofc of the Sixth Auditor of the Treasury. His funeral will be from his late residence, [Mrs Preston's,] on 12th st, between E & F sts, at half-past 3 o'clock this afternoon.

Died: on Sep 1, at **Longwood**, Montg Co, Md, Elisha W Williams, in his 76th year, afer a protracted illness of 12 months. In all the relations of life, as husband, father, neighbor, friend, & master he was unexampled. He had for 12 years been a member of the Episcopal Church. In character he was retiring, upright, & kind.

Died: on Sep 8, Anne Mandeville, infant daughter of J M Carlisle, in her 14th month.

$100 reward for runaway negro boy Allen West, about 19 or 20 years of age. He has a brother belonging to Richd B B Chew, a sister belonging to Thos Talburtt; & his father belongs to Col Wm D Bowie, & stays at his **Bellfield Farm**; & relations living in Wash City. –Chas Clagett, living near Upper Marlboro, PG Co, Md.

Rev Wm Chittenden, a clergyman of the Presbyterian denomination, committed suicide at Watertown, N Y, by hanging himself on Sat week. He had for some 20 years past at times exhibited symptoms of aberration of mind, during which he was much depressed. He was much beloved by those among whom he ministered.

TUE SEP 12, 1854
Trustee's sale of valuable property: on Sep 21, by deed of trust from Philip Boteler & wife to the subscriber, recorded in Liber J A S No 24, folios 346 thru 348, of the Land Records for Wash Co: sale of lot 16 in square 169, with a very large brick livery stable. –N Callan, trustee -Jas C McGuire, auct

Household & kitchen furniture at auction: on Sep 15, at the residence of Wm Lee, No 2, **Walker's Row** 9th st, opposite the Patent Ofc. -Jas C McGuire, auct

Edmund P Hunter, of Martinsburg, died suddenly at Berkeley Springs on Sat last. He was a gentleman of great worth & extensive popularity, known throughout Va as having been a valuable member of the legislature.

Hon John Black, for many years a member of the U S Senate fom the State of Mississippi, & late of Louisiana, died at Winchester, Va, on Aug 29.

I certify that Judson H Thorn, of Wash Co, D C, brought before me as a stray trespassing upon the enclosures, a small roan Horse. –Saml Grubb, J P
Owner of the above horse is to prove property, pay charges, & take him away.

The only surviving child of John T Lyle, of Fayette Co, Ky, aged about 13 or 14 years, was accidentally killed at his father's residence on Sat last. In passing between an ox-cart & the corn-crib the oxen started & crushed him in such a manner as to cause his death in a few minutes. He was the last of their children left them.
-Lexington Observer

Appointment by the Pres: Wm M Harrison, Collector of the Customs at Richmond, Va, vice John Lynch, deceased.

Mrd: on Sep 11, in Wash City, by Rev Dr Eliot, of St Louis, Mo, Frank A Eliot, of Phil, to Mary J Whipple, adopted daughter of the late Prof W R Johnson, of Wash.

Soldiers of the war of 1812 are to assemble in front of the City Hall, on Sep 12, at 10 o'clock, from whence they will repair to the Railroad depot, to unite with the soldiers of the Mexican war in escorting the Old Defenders to the avenue. –John S Williams, Pres late Convention

Mr D C Taylor, of Moriah, Essex Co, N Y, writes the Whitehall Chronicle that on Tue a house near the village, occupied by Mr Baldwin, was burnt down, & the whole family, consisting of Mr B, his wife, & 4 children, perished in the flames, being literally burnt to ashes. The house was in a clearing near the woods in which the fires had lately raged, & it is supposed caught from a fresh outbreak of these fires.

Chas Z Abrams, committed to jail in Richmond, Va, on a charge of killing his wife near Bacon's Quarter Branch, committed suicide on Tue by hanging himself at the door of the cell where he was confined.

Obit, died: on Sep 10, in Wash City, Mrs Eliz Benton, wife of Hon Thos H Benton, aged 60 years. Her protracted illness of several years was born with patience. Deprived of utterance, of all her energies, Mrs Benton still preserved the bearing of one whose mind would not allow the most prostrating affliction to overthrow the fine character it had formed. The religious faith, severe to herself, was nurtured in her father's house & among the Virginia Puritans of Rockbridge, stood the test of 30 years, spent amidst the fashionable life of Washington. The ruling feeling in Mrs Benton's heart was her devotion to her husband. She has made her home wherever his business called him. When she felt the approach of the crisis which terminated her life she led her daughter to the vacant chair in which her husband worked, &, by look & gestures, made it apparent that she required his recall from Missouri, where he was on business. It was too late. She walked to the bed in the next apartment, from which she was never able to rise again. Her funeral will take place this afternoon at 4 o'clock, from the residence of Col Benton, on C st. [Sep 14th newspaper: the funeral of Mrs Eliz Benton, took place Tue from her late residence on C st. Her illness was of several years' duration. Col Benton is at this time in the State of Missouri. Gen Henderson, Gen Jesup, Hon R H Stanton, of Ky, Hon Mr Ashe, Mr Seaton, Cmdor McCauley, Hon Mr Singleton, & F P Blair acted as pallbearers. Among others who followed the remains to the tomb was the Pres of the U S & all members of the Cabinet. –Sentinel] [Sep 30th newspaper: Hon Thos M Benton retuned to Wash some days ago, & is at his residence in Wash City. He has, we are glad to learn, the comfort of the presence & company of all his daughters & his grandchildren.]

Piano for sale: at Constable's Sale: by 5 writs of fieri facias, against the goods & chattels of J H Eberbach, I have levied upon 1 piano to satisfy the 5 executions, one in favor of Lawrence & Myers, one in favor of Wisenfeld & Co, & 2 in favor of J W Baden, & 1 in favor of Green & Scott: auction on Sep 16, at the auction store of Messrs Campbell & Co, on Pa ave, between 9th & 10th sts. –A E S Keese, Constable

WED SEP 13, 1854
Beautiful cottage property for sale: fronting on 9th st, running back to an alley, & to the lot of the Church of the Ascension, with all the bldgs thereon, known as *Mrs Humphey's Cottage*. On 9th st is a large public sewer; gas pipes pass by the property; & water, from never failing public wells, is in the immediate vicinity, & wells can be sunk on the premises. -Green & Scott, aucts

Capt Downing, No 55 on the list of Captains, & lately in command of the U S sloop-of-war **Jamestown**, has been deprived of his commission by the sentence of a court-martial, with the Pres' approval. It is a matter of regret that an ofcr who had been more than 40 years in service, & 17 years at sea, should now be deprived of his vocation.

Boston, Sep 11. The wife & daughter of Hon Nathl B Borden, of Fall River, Mass, died of cholera between Saturday morning & Sunday night.

Wash Corp: 1-Cmte on Improvements: asked to be discharged from the further consideration of the ptn of Geo W Talburtt, agent for Jane Woodruff: discharged accordingly. 2-Ptn of Wm B Kirby & others in reference to a sewer: referred to the Cmte on Improvements. 3-Ptn from Augustus Ladd, praying damages for injury sustained from alteration in grade: referred to the Cmte of Claims.

Mrd: in Balt City, by Rev John A Gere, John Reese, of Wash City, to Virginia Bowen, of Balt. [No date given-current item.]

Died: on Sep 10, at the residence of her son-in-law, Rev H W Dodge, Upperville, Va, Mrs Phebe Brown, aged 73 years, widow of the late Danl Brown, of Wash City.

Died: on Sep 2, at St Paul, Minnesota, William Fletcher, infant son of the late Danl H Dustin, & grandson of Judge Sargent, of Wash City.

Improved real estate at public auction: farm know as ***Bellemeade***, in Stafford Co, Va: on Oct 4: contains 288½ acres; comfortable dwlg, kitchen, smoke-house, ice-house, carriage house, over-seer's house, quarters for hands, barn, & stable. Address the subscriber at Fredericksburg, Va-John B Wiltberger.

THU SEP 14, 1854
$100 reward for runaway negro boy Israel, between 20 & 21 years of age. –Hugh Perrie, living near Nottingham, PG Co, Md.

The Hartford Times of Sep 7 announces the following deaths in a single family from cholera: Patrick Dillon, 2 weeks since, was attacked, but recovered. A few days after his wife died, then 2 daughters, then a nephew, & then his mother. One daughter & a son escaped.

Notice, that in 1842 a warrant was issued to my late wife, Jane Cosby, by the Register of the Land Ofc of Va, numbered 8,914, for 533¼ acres of land, being her share of land bounty as one of the heirs of Lt John Carson, of the Continental Line, & which was lost, & a duplicate of which has since been given: now, therefore, be it known to all whom it may concern that I shall apply to the Gen Land Ofc of the U S for scrip on said warrant, the same being now due to Jane F & others, the children of the aforesaid Jane Cosby, deceased, of whom I am guardian. –Lewis F Cosby, Guardian -Abingdon, Jul 15, 1854

Carriage for sale, good second-hand carriage for sale, which may be seen at the subscriber's house, on G st, between 6th & 7th sts, near Bates' Soap Factory. There are 2 months' license, which will be given with it. [Subscriber's name not given.]

Died: yesterday, in Wash City, Wm Kahoe. His funeral will take place today at 4 o'clock, from his late residence, Capitol Hill, 2nd st, between Mass & Md aves.

Valuable & highly improved property near Wash, D C, for sale. The Farm called **Edgewood**, in Montg Co, Md, containing about 188 acres, with a dwlg house 45 feet front, containing 11 rooms, exclusive of cellar & servants' rooms; & necessary outbldgs. Apply to Chas S Wallach, La ave, Wash, D C.

FRI SEP 15, 1854
Cholera at Martinsburg, Va: the Gaz of Wed give the following list of deaths up to 6 o'clock on Tue morning: Sep 8-Thos Turner; Mrs Poisal, consort of Jacob Poisal, sr; Mrs Wilson, widow; A Pentony's child; Mr Underdonk's child; Miss Catharine Homrich; Mrs McIntire, consort of Robt McIntire; Mrs M J Hess, consort of David Hess. Sep 9-Miss Ann Hutchinson. Sep 10-A Morrison; Mrs Caskie, consort of Jas Caskie; German girl at R Webster's; Mrs Locknow; Mrs Raenbal, consort of Geo Raenbal; Mr Longhammer's child; Mr Underdonk; Adam Pentomy. Sep 11-Mrs John Weller, consort of John Weller, died of bilious pleurisy; Mr Harboker, German; A Pentony's child; John Synder's child; Horace Woodward; Edwin Merchant; Staub's cooper, Rockhammer; T Seary's child.

Household & kitchen furniture at auction: on Sep 18, at the residence of Mr J Iardella, corner of B st south & N J ave. -Green & Scott, aucts

Trustee's sale of valuable bldg lots at auction: on Oct 4, by 2 deeds of trust from Wm Gadsby, one dated Nov 12, 1845, the other Jun 11, 1847, recorded in the land records for Wash Co, D C: lot 2 in square 534; & lot 11 in square 786, being in Wash City, D C. Also, on Oct 5, I shall sell at the auction room of Green & Scott, by the same deeds of trust, lot 213, in Beatty Hawkins' addition to Gtwn, D C. Also, pew No 49, in Trinity Church, Wash City. –Henry Naylor, trustee -Green & Scott, aucts

Savannah: the deaths there on Sat last were 33, mostly from yellow fever. Dr Wildman is dead; & both Dr Schleys' are dead. The two Mr Burroughs are also dead. S T Chapman, editor & proprietor of the Savannah Courier died on Sat, & R B Hilton, principal editor of the Savannah Georgian died on Sunday. Many physicians are sick, among them Drs West, Wells, Wayne, Ellis, & Arnold. All are worn out.

Mrd: on Sep 12, by Rev Mr Hodges, Francis Osborn to Miss Isabella Reed, of Wash City.

Mrd: on Sep 12, in Foundry Parsonage, by Rev E P Phelps, Mr Jas A Moore to Miss Rachel Ella Deputy, both of Balt City.

Mrd: on Sep 12, at Balt, in Grace Church, by Rev Dr Wyatt, Lucius Campbell Duncan, Counsellor-at-Law, of New Orleans, to Miss Mary Rebecca Smith, daughter of the late Dennis A Smith, of Balt.

Died: yesterday, Chas T Kirby, printer, aged 35 years. His funeral will take place this afternoon at 3½ o'clock, from his late residence No 334 Fifth st, above Mass ave. His friends & members of the Columbia Typographical Society are invited.

Died: on Sep 14, Richard Gromly, son of Jos F & Mary Isabel Hodgson, aged 7 months & 10 days. His funeral is this morning at 10 o'clock, from the residence of his parents, K st north, between 6th & 7th sts.

Wash City Ordinances: 1-Act making appropriation to pay Hanson Brown for extirpation of thistles in 5th Ward: the sum of $20. 2-Act granting permission to John McKim to rebuild & enlarge a frame back bldg in square 904: provided, the consent of the Pres of the U S be obtained, also, the consent of the property holders within 24 feet. Approved: Sep 8, 1854

SAT SEP 16, 1854
Fatal accident in Harrison township, Ohio, on Sep 3: Mr Asa Crockett was engaged in felling timber, the butt of a tree which he had chopped down clung to the stump, & in passing under the trunk for the purpose of getting to the other side it fell, striking him with tremendous force on the temple, crushing his skull. His 3 children were with him at the time, the eldest 9 or 10 years old. Death put an end to his suffering. -Ohio Northwest, Sep 6.

Going the rounds of the newspapers: all the family of the late Gen Taylor who occupied the White House are dead-the Gen, his wife, his daughter, Mrs Bliss, & Col Bliss. Mrs Fillmore & her daughter are also dead. There is at least one error in it. Mrs Bliss is not dead. She was but lately in fine health, &, with her sister, Mrs Wood, & was on a visit to Wash City.

Mrd: on Sep 6, at **Morven**, the residence of her father, by Rev Chas E Ambler, Jas K Marshall, jr, to Fannie L, daughter of Maj Thos M Ambler, of Fauquier Co, Va.

Mrd: on Sep 14, by Rev Mr Hodges, Sylvester Carroll to Miss Mary Diamond, of PG Co, Md.

Trustee's sale of Montg Co, Md, land: by decree of the Circuit Court for Montg Co, as a court of equity, in the case of Agnes Clarke & others vs Wm Glover & wife: the subscriber will offer at public sale, on Oct 10, at the court-house door in Rockville, the large real estate of which the late Hanson Clarke died seized, in said county, containing 940½ acres, divided into the following lots, viz:
No 1 Lot on Old Bladensburg road, adjoins a 60 acre lot bought by Mrs Emily Beall from the estate of the late Thos Gettings, containing 67½ acres.
No 2 Lot continguous to No 1 on the road from Colesville by **Bond's Mills** to Washington: with a small tenement: contains 180½ acres.
No 3 adjoins No 2, fronts on Washington road from Colesville, & contains 157½ acres.
No 4 lies on the eastern side of the Washington road: contains 124½ acres.
No 5 contains 205¾ acres & fronts on the Washington road.
Not 6 lies between No 5 & the lands of Mr Barnes & Mr Joy: contains 127¼ acres.
No 7 lies nearly south of & adjoins No 5: contains 51½ acres.
No 8 contains 25½ acres, & adjoins the lands of Mr Richardson & of Mr Davis.
-W *Veirs Bouic, trustee [*Veirs below is Viers.] [Oct 14th newspaper: all the lots have been sold except lots 2 & 3.]

Montg Co land for sale: public sale on Oct 10, at the Court-house door in Rockville, Montg Co, Md: two lots of land: one contains 72 acres, on the turnpike road; the other in the same vicinity contains 112¼ acres: both are well wooded, but unimproved, & are portions of the real estate of the late Jas B Higgins.
–W *Viers Bouic, John M Kilgour, trustees [*Viers above is Veirs.]

Hartford, Conn, Sep 15. Chief Justice Saml Church, of this State, died at Newton, on Wed, in his 70th year.

N Y, Sep 15. Warrants have been issued for the arrest of Gen Munson & J Lockwood, agents of the Sing Sing Prison, C C Childs, jr, clerk, & another ofcr of the prison, upon the charge of perjury & fraud, in their official relations, upon the complaint of the Legislative Cmtes Com'rs, now in session at Sing Sing.

Dr Nathan Smith Lincoln has removed to No 430, 15th st, Washington. Having been for several years past the assistant of Prof Nathan R Smith at Balt, Dr L will give particular attention to Surgery & Diseases of the Eye.

To the next of kin & the distributees of Edw Herndon, late of Campbell Co, Va: said Edw Herndon died in 1845 without issue, & by his will, after certain specific bequests, he directed that the balance of his estate should be equally divided between his sisters, Sarah Samuels, Eliz Baker, Catharine Durham, Mary Herndon, & his brother, Reuben Herndon. This will was duly probated in Campbell Co Court, & Y W Robertson qualified as exec. A suit has been instituted in the Circuit Court of Campbell Co, by John T Irving & wife against the exec & legatees of said Edw Herndon for a settlement & division of said estate. It appears from the Comr's report that all of the residuary legatees died in the life-time of the testator, it is contended that said residuary legacy has lapsed, & is to be divided equally among the distributees of said Edw Herndon. And the undersigned has been ordered by said court to advertise for said distributees to appear & make themselves parties to said suit. Said residuary estate is worth $4,000 to $5,000. The following were the brothers & sisters of said Edw Herndon: Lewis Herndon, Benj Herndon, Jas Herndon, John Herndon, Reuben Herndon, Mary Herndon, Sarah Samuels, Eliz Baker, & Catharine Durham. The parties interested will please state under which brother or sister of the testator they claim; the names & residence of all the children of said brother or sister, & in the case of the death of any child, the name of the widow or husband, as the case may be, & children of the same; & as far as practicable will furnish the evidence of their relationship to said decedent.
—Chas R Slaughter, Lynchburg, Va

MON SEP 18, 1854

Rt Rev Edw Barron, D C, Catholic Misionary Bishop of the Coast of Africa, died at Savannah on Sep 12. In consequence of impaired health, Bishop Barron was on leave of absence from his charge, & had been temporarily residing in Florida. On his way to the North, a few weeks since, he stopped at Savannah, & when the epidemic broke out he concluded to remain to render such service as might be required. He was far advanced in years, & fell in a noble cause. On the same day Rev Joshua S Payne, a young minister of 24 years, belonging to the Methodist Episcopal Church, was struck down in the discharge of his pastoral duties, of the same disease.

Died: on Sep 7, at Barrytown, Dutchess Co, N Y, Mrs Harriet Leavenworth, widow of the late Gen Henry Leavenworth, U S Army. When her gallant husband was ordered to the frontier, hundreds of miles in the wilderness, to protect the inhabitants from the invasions of the savages, she, like a faithful wife, was at his side, regardless of the many dangers, hardships, & privations she had to endure. After the death of Gen Leavenworth she returned to N Y, & has resided most of the time at Newburg.

Mrd: on Sep 12, by Rev Edw Eells, at Forest Home, Boone Co, Ky, Geo Wm Ranson, of Jefferson Co, Va, to Olivia M Todd, daughter of Dr B F Bedinger.

Mrd: on Sep 14, at Willard's Hotel, in Wash City, by Rev A F N Rolfe, of N C, Mr Bushrod W Vick to Miss Eudora Higgins, all of Balt, Md.

Died: yesterday, in Wash City, in his 28th year, Jos A Keenan, M D, late of Wash City, but formerly of Balt, where his funeral service will be performed, on Sep 19, in St Peter's Church, Poppleton st, at 8 o'clock A M.

Capt Johnson, cmder of the canal boat **Waterford**, lost his life on Sunday while attempting to save the life of his wife. She was on board the boat, & when near Oriskany she fell overboard. He jumped in to rescue her, having on a heavy overcoat. As he neared the shore, finding himself exhausted, he thrust her forward so that she was saved, but he sank & was drowned. –N Y Commercial Advertiser

TUE SEP 19, 1854
Close-out sale at the Furniture Store of E B Reeve, on 7th st. –Thos J Fisher, trustee -Jas C McGuire, auct

Household & kitchen furniture at auction: on Tue, at the residence of Rev Dr Butler, on C st, between 4½ & 6th sts. -Jas C McGuire, auct

Chancery sale: by decree of the Circuit Court of Wash Co, D C, in equity, made in the cause of Jas Lynch vs Hugh Lockery, Jane Lockery, Ambrose S Lynch, & al, No 817, dated May 31, 1854, I will offer at public auction on Oct 11: a lease for 99 years, renewable forever, of the eastern most part of lot 17 in square 729, fronting 27 feet on East Capitol st: improved by a 2 story brick house. The whole of lot 26 in square 728, fronting on A st north: with a 2 story brick house. –Walter S Cox, trustee -Jas C McGuire, auct [Oct 25th newspaper: auction postponed until Nov 15.]

Mrd: on Sep 18, by Rev Wentworth L Childs, of St Alban's Parish, D C, Ogden W Blackfan, of Trenton, N J, to Mary Agnes, daughter of Dr T Watkins, of Wash City.

Mrd: on Jul 31, by Rev Wm Norwood, Pastor of Christ Church, Gtwn, Jos T Coldwell, of Petersburg, Va, to Virginia Josephine, youngest daughter of the late Wm A Williams, of Wash City.

Mrd: on Sep 14, at St James Church, Richmond, Va, by Rev Dr Empie, Pollard Webb, of Wash City, to Miss Mildred C Christian, daughter of the late John H Christian, of Richmond.

Mrd: on Sep 13, in Gardiner, Maine, by Rt Rev Geo Burgess, Dr W McKendree Tucker, of Wash City, to Caroline A, daughter of the late Capt Jas Blish, of Hallowell.

Died: on Sep 18, after 12 hours' illness, Mary Adelaide, the beloved daughter of Wm A & Frances E Griffith.

Died: yesterday, suddenly, in Wash City, Mr Benj Hadley, aged 42, formerly of Boston.

Died: on Aug 9, 1854, at his residence near Boonville, Missouri, Col Thos Russell, late of Berkeley Co, Va, aged 56 years.

Died: on Sep 16, Frank, aged 2 years, son of J P & S A Keller, of Wash City.

The proprietors offer for sale the **National Hotel**, Wash City: embraces more than 40,000 feet of ground, on Pa ave: contains upwards of 350 rooms. Apply at the Hotel.

Circuit Court for Montg Co, as a Court of Equity. French Forrest & others vs Moreau Forrest & others. The ptn of John Dawson, of said county, respectfully represents to the honorable the Circuit Court for Montg Co, that Jos Forrest departed this life in 1845, possessed of a large real estate in said county, & leaving 8 heirs at law, of whom Zachariah Forrest is one. Your petitioner further represents that such proceeding have been had in the above cause in this Court that Richd J Bowie had been appointed as trustee to make sale of said real estate for partition amongst the heirs at law of said Jos Forrest, deceased, & several portions thereof sold, & the proceeds thereof now subject to the order of this Court. Your petitioner further shows that, on Mar 29, 1845, he recovered before Jesse T Higgins, a Justice of the Peace for said county, a judgment against said Zachariah Forrest for $20.46 debt, with interest from date, & cost 58½ cents, & that on Jul 7, 1846, he sued out of fieri facias on said judgment, & caused the same to be levied on the same day on the said lands; all which will more fully appear by reference to said writ of fieri facias & the inventory & constable's return herewith filed, marked D, 1, 2, & 3. Your petitioner alleges that he several times offered at public auction the said interest of Zachariah in said land in virtue of said writs, but failed to sell the same for want of buyers, & it was finally understood that said trustee should pay the said claim out of the proceeds of the sales of said land. Wherefore, your petitioner prays the Court to direct the said trustee pay the said claim of your petitioner, & all interest & costs thereon, out of the portion of the said Zachariah of the proceeds of the sales of said lands, & for such other & further relief as the case may require, & as in duty. –W Veirs Bouic, Solicitor for Petitioner

In the Circuit Court of Montg Co, as a Court of Equity. French Forrest & others vs Moreau Forrest & others. It is Aug 25, 1854, adjudged & ordered by the Court that the within named petitioner, by causing a copy of the foregoing petition & of this order to be inserted in the Nat'l Intell, once a week for 1 month before Nov 1 next, give notice to the said Zachariah Forrest of the object & substance of said petition, & warn him to appear in this Court, in person or by solicitor, on or before Feb 1 next, to answer the premises & show cause, if any he have, why an order ought not to pass as prayed. –Nicholas Brewer, Circuit Judge -Jas G Hening, Clerk

Savannah: the interments on Thu amounted to 34, of which 20 died of yellow fever. Dr Stephen N Harris died on Fri, Mr Jonathan Olmstead, cashier of the Maine Bank, died the same day.

Farm & Mill near the Manassas Gap railroad for sale: a small farm in Prince Wm Co, Va: containing 52 acres, improved by a 2 story frame dwlg. The property is well known at *Waterfall Mills*. –Wm Q Force, Real Estate Agent, 10th & D sts.

WED SEP 20, 1854
Household & kitchen furniture at auction: on Sep 23, in front of the Auction Store, 6th st & Pa ave, by order of the Orphans Court of Wash Co, D C: the personal effects of Harriet E Jardine, deceased. -Green & Scott, aucts

Household & kitchen furniture at auction: & pianoforte: on Sep 26, at the residence of Mrs Peyton, 4½ st & Pa ave. -Green & Scott, aucts

Official, Dept of State, Wash, Sep 18, 1854. Information had been received from the Acting Consul at Hong Kong, Henry Anthon, jr, of the death in the hospital at that place of the following named American seamen:

Frank Silvee, Jul 17	J Williams, Dec 7
L Bourrows, Oct 30	O Leginshaw, Nov 30
W Elliott, Oct 25	J Lewis, Nov 19

Respecting the small sums of money found on the persons of W Elliott & J Williams, further information can be obtained by application to this Dept.

Gtwn lot: by deed of trust from heirs-at-law of Mrs Sarah Peter, deceased, I will sell, at public auction, on Oct 24, parts of lots 24 & 25 in Gtwn, D C, adjoining the residence of Geo Poe, jr, fronting 67½ feet on Bridge st & the same on Prospect st, having a depth of 240 feet between said streets. On payment of purchase money the subscriber will convey to the purchaser all the estate of Mrs Sarah Peter at the time of her death & of her heirs-at-law in the said lot of ground. –Jno Marbury, trust

Mrd: on Sep 18, by Rev Jas H Brown, Mr John Rutherford to Miss Sarah Ann Richardson, all of Va.

Mrd: on Sep 19, by Rev Jas H Brown, Mr Jas H Posey to Miss Mary E Jefferson, both of Alexandria, Va.

Died: on Sep 19, in Wash City, after a lingering illness, of consumption, Mr John Kerby, in his 26th year. His funeral is this afternoon at 4 o'clock, from the Infirmary, on E st, between 4th & 5th sts.

Died: on Sep 8, after a long & painful illness, of dropsy, Mr Francis H Darnull, aged 37 years.

Mr John L Barnhill, one of the principal accountants of the Gen Land Ofc, died on Monday, at his residence on the Island, in Wash City. He died of well-defined cholera. Mr Barnhill was about 40 years of age, & had been for more than 20 years connected with the Gen Land Ofc, entering the bureau orginally as a messenger. He was unmarried. He had just returned from a visit to Saut Ste Marie, Mich, & other points in the Northwest, whither he was dispatched on official business.

THU SEP 21, 1854
Household & kitchen furniture at auction: on Sep 27, at the residence of Hon W S Ashe, on H st, east of 10th st. -Jas C McGuire, auct

A young man, Edwin R Keyes, late of Pinceton, Mass, was strangled to death in a car-shop at Cleveland, Ohio, on Sep 14. He was adjusting something near the planing machine when his neckerchief became entangled & he was choked.

Died: on Sep 20, near Davisonville, Anne Arundel Co, Md, Marcellus Gallaher, of Wash City, youngest son of John S Gallaher, aged 23 years & 3 months, leaving a wife & one child, & numerous relatives & friends to mourn his early death.

Hon Alexander W Stow, late Chief Justice of the State of Wisconsin, died in Milwaukee on Sep 14. Judge Stow was widely known throughout the West as well as in the State of N Y as an able lawyer & an upright judge.

FRI SEP 22, 1854
Mr Saml Nicholls, Editor of the N Y Sunday Mercury, was run over by one of the Third ave cars in N Y on Monday & so severely injured that he died on Tue. He was attempting to jump upon the front platform of the car, when his foot slipped & he fell underneath the wheels, the car passing over his limbs. He had been connected with the city press for about 15 years. He was a native of Hempstead, near London, & was educated to the profession of the law. -Times

Hon Asa Spencer has sent to the Govn'r of Md his resignation as Circuit Judge for the 8th judicial district, to take effect from Sep 30, 1854.

Geo Kremer died at his residence in Union Co, Pa, on Sep 11, in his 80th year. He represented the Union Co district in Congress during Mr John Quincy Adams' administration, & was the author of the absurd & calumnious & long since exploded charge of political bargain between Mr Clay & Mr Adams.

Lt Alonzo Davis, U S Navy late cmder of the U S brig **Porpoise**, attached to Cmdor Ringgold's North Pacific Exploring Expedition, & who had but a few days since returned, died at Wilmington, Del, on Tuesday.

The funeral of the late Marcellus Gallaher will take place from his father's residence, on 9th st, at 11 o'clock this morning.

Died: on Sep 5, Catharine Chauncey Hand, eldest daughter of the late Jos W Hand, of Wash City, aged 24 years. For 3 years her life was clouded by painful & protracted disease, yet her last hours were full of peace & sure hope & trust in the Redeemer.

Died: on Sep 20, at his late residence, **Hermitage**, Montg Co, Md, Mr Saml Fitzhugh, in his 68th year. His funeral will be from the Church of the Ascension, H st, on Fri, at 4 o'clock.

Died: on Sep 21, John Irvin Miller, of Missouri, in his 19th year. His funeral will take place tomorrow at 8 o'clock A M, from Mrs Mary Harrod's, 4th st, between N Y ave & K st.

Died: on Sep 19, at **Edgehill**, Prince Wm Co, Va, Helen, wife of John S Ewell, & eldest daughter of N M McGregor, of Wash City, aged 25 years.

Died: on Sep 21, John Sands, youngest child of Jas S & Eliz J Holland, in his 4th year. His funeral will be this afternoon at 3 o'clock, from his parents' residence, 412 9th st, between H & I sts.

Died: on Sep 14, at Leesburg, Va, in her 2nd year, Sally Moore Orr, daughter of John M & Orra L Orr.

N Y, Sep 21. Rt Rev Jonathan Mayhew Wainwright, Provisional Bishop for the Diocese of N Y of the Protestant Episcopal Church, who has been ill here for some days past, died this evening, in his 66th year. [Sep 25th newspaper: Bishop Wainwright was born in Liverpool, England, in 1792, of American parents. He was educated at Harvard Univerity.

Young Mr W Cookman Hutchens, a page in the Senate, has generously given $7 out of his limited pay to the Washington Monument fund, being a dollar a month for the whole time he was employed.

N C Nelson, postmaster at Keesville, Essex Co, was arrested on Monday by Mr North, special agent of the Post Ofc Dept, charged with robbing the mails. Nelson is editor of the Administration organ at Keesville, & was a delegate to the Soft Convention from Essex Co. The clerks in the ofc were also arrested. -Albany Argus of Tues. [Sep 25th newspaper: Mr Nelson was committed to jail in default of procuring bonds, in two sureties in the sum of $5,000, for his appearance at the U S District Court.]

Valuable Illinois land for sale: in Jefferson Co, Ill: 320 acres in the farm, & from 80 to 85 acres under good fencing; with dwlg house. –B L Bogan, 521 12th st north

Orphans Court of Wash Co, D C. Letters of administration on the personal estate of Nathan Towson, late of Wash Co, deceased. –Wm M Caldwell, adm

SAT SEP 23, 1854
The Richmond Enquirer announces that Mr Wm W Dunnavant has purchased the interest of the late Thos Ritchie, jr, in the Enquirer establishment, & the paper will henceforth be published in the name of Ritchie, Pryor & Dunnavant.

Household & kitchen furniture at auction: on Sep 28, at the residence of Mr Carner, on north B st, between Delaware ave & First st east. -Jas C McGuire, auct

Household & kitchen furniture & pianoforte at auction: on Sep 29, at the residence of G E Tingle, 11th & E sts. -Green & Scott, aucts

Runaways were committed to the jail of Wash Co, Md, on Sep 15, 4 negroes, viz: Sidney about 40 years old; John is 21 or 22 years old; Townsend is about 16 or 17 years old: the above negroes say they belong to Hamilton Rodgers, of Loudoun Co, Va. Also, Peter Lee, about 30, says he belongs to Wm Guelick, of Loudoun Co, Va. Owner of the above described negroes are required to prove property, pay charges, & take them away, else they will be discharged according to law. -Wm Logan, Sheriff

Cumberland Miners' Journal of yesterday: we announce the death of Archibald Cary, the Editor of this paper, who died last Wed, after a severe illness of 2½ weeks.

Mrd: on Sep 21, by Rev Jas H Brown, Mr Alfred W Andrews to Miss Ann Virginia Moore, both of Va.

Mrd: on Sep 19, by Rev T B Dooley, Mr John T Weaver, of Calif, to Miss Virginia Macdaniel, daughter of the late Ezekeil Macdaniel, of Mason Co, Va.

Died: on Sep 21, in Wash City, Timothy J Tuomy. Requiescat in pace!

Died: on Sep 21, Dorsey Brown, only child of Jas & Ann E Smith, aged 22 months & 11 days.

St Louis Republican contains the annexed list of removals & appointments of Postmasters in Illinois: 1-Fred'k M Mead, appointed at Union, vice C D Cannon, removed. 2-Jas W Marlow, appointed at Crystal Lake, vice Wm Jackman, removed. 3-Marcus B Burdick, at Belden, vice Danl Wayne. 4-Saml B Groat, at Huntley Grove, vice B Bunn, jr. 5-Jacob W Brewster, Mail Agent on the Chicago & Galena Railroad, vice Jonathan Kimball, removed.

Hon John W Taylor, for many years a prominent statesman of N Y, has died. He was born in Saratoga Co in 1784; his father was a zealous actor in the scenes of the Revolution, & the son partook of the spirit of patriotism. Mr T was a law student of the late Abraham Van Vechen, of Albany. In 1811 he was elected a member of the Legislature of N Y, & elected to Congress, & was continued a member of the House of Reps. In 1841 he was attacked by paralysis, from the effects of which he never recovered. In Sep, 1843, Mr Taylor removed to Cleveland, & has resided with his son-in-law, Mr W D Beattie, where the evening of his life had been made pleasant as possible. Although enfeebled in body, his mind was a storehouse of facts, until a few weeks of his death. –Cleveland Herald [No death date given-current item.]

Wm G Thomas was nominated by a Democratic Convention on Thu last, for the ofc of Mayor of the Balt City.

About 40 children, boys & girls, started from N Y on Wed to fine homes in the West. They are sent out by the Children's Aid Society in charge of Mr E P Smith. Most of them are orphans gathered out of the streets.

Mrs C F Greer has several large furnished rooms for rent, with or without board. The house is on East Capitol st, Capitol Hill.

MON SEP 25, 1854
For rent: two new & handsome well finished 4 story brick houses on K st, near the corner of 4th. Inquire of Jas Henry, at the Capitol, or J T Clements, I st near 4th st.

In Chicago, on Wed, Casper Lower, one of the day police, was killed by Patrick Cunningham while the former was conveying him to the watch-house. Cunningham had been disorderly throughout the day, for which he was arrested.

The Masonic Fraternity at Richmond have made arrangements to pay special funeral honors to the late Edmund P Hunter, who at the time of his death was Grand Master of the State of Va. The ceremonies will take place on Nov 4. A Judson Crane has been invited to deliver a eulogy of the deceased, & has consented to do so.

Cincinnati Gaz of Sep 21. Accident on the C H & D Railwway, on North Canal st, near Carr, yesterday. The train, Conductor Whitney, containing 120 persons was coming towards the depot. The switch lever broke & the cars were thrown with immense violence down an 18 foot stone embankment into the Whitewater Canal, in which there was about 4 feet of water. A son of Henry F Moore, carpenter, John St, near 8th aged 7 years, was fatally injured. He was in charge of his aunt, Mrs Ann W Davis, who had an arm broken & so badly lacerated that it is the opinion of her physician the arm must be amputated. Mrs Henrietta Rosenbush, a German woman, who lived in Greenville, Ohio, is in critical condition. She was in company with Mr S Brachman, who is much injured. Mrs Canfield & Mrs O'Brien, of Dayton, were badly bruised, but both will recover. ___ Grundy, who resides on 7th st, was bruised & is supposed to have internal injuries. Jas B Milliken, of Hamilton, bruised but not seriously hurt. Danl Mulford, an old man, who resides on Vine st, received several contusions on the body & head. Dr Smith, of Dayton, & Geo McCullough, of **Fort Wayne**, Ind, slightly injured. The wife of Patrick McCrail, of May st, Newport, Ky, bruised over one eye. Martin Mason, who keeps the Exchange at Hamilton, cut in the face. Andrew Wilson, of the firm of Andrew & Wilson, was bruised. Mr Russell, who was with Mr Wilson, was quite seriously injured. Capt Hilt, of Middletown, slightly injured. Chancey Couch was slightly injured. Washington Terry, who resides on Carr, between Cutter & Linn sts, was slightly injured.

The Car Place, at St Louis, was struck by lightning on Sep 18th, & the house was blown to pieces. Messrs Catoir & Edward were instantly killed. Messrs Beaugeau & Auguste, sleeping in the upper story of the bldg at the time were slightly injured.

The St John [N B] Courier chronicles the death at Mispeck, [N B,] on Sep 11, of Esther, relic of the late Thos O'Brien, aged 113 years. She was a native of South Carolina, & emigrated to New Brunswick in 1783.

Freeman's Journal: Archbishop Hughes has summoned a Council of the Bishops of the province of N Y of the Roman Catholic Church, with their theologians & heads of religious orders, to assemble at the Cathedral in N Y on the 1st Sun in Oct. The suffragan Bishops of this province are: Rt Rev Drs: McClosky, Bishop of Albany; Fitzpatrick, Bishop of Boston; Timon, Bishop of Buffalo; O'Reilly, Bishop of Hartford; Loughlin, Bishop of Brooklyn; Bayley, Bishop of Newark; & de Geesbriand, Bishop of Burlington, Vt.

A monument has been erected to the memory of the late Hon Levi Woodbury in the **Auburn Cemetery**, at Portsmouth, N H. With the exception of the Weare Monument at Hampton Falls, there is none more elevated in N H.

Mrd: on Sep 21, in St Alban's Parish, by Rev Mr Childs, Zachariah Collins to Nancy Barber, all of the District.

Died: on Sunday, after a lingering illness, Winifred S, youngest daughter of Leonard & W S Harbaugh, aged 2 years & 3 months. Her funeral will take place from the residence of her parents, on F st, this afternoon, at 3½ o'clock.

Died: on Sep 15, in Middleburg, Loudoun Co, Va, Richard Henry, youngest child of Lt Danl F & Mgt A Dulany, aged 13 months.

Died: on Sep 23, after a lingering illness, Mary Elizabeth, aged 5 years, 4 months & 28 days, daughter of Thos F & Mgt Stewart.

Obit-died: Hon Wm Plumer, a distinguished statesman of N H, died at his residence in Epping, on Sep 18, after an illness of about a week. His complaint was the dysentery, & his age was about 64 years. He received his education at Dartmouth College, & studied law with his father, the late ex-Govn'r Wm Plumer, but was never known as a practising lawyer. He was frequently elected a member of both branches of the Legislature of N H, serving as a member of the House from 1819 to 1825. The father of Mr Plumer died at Epping, Dec 23, 1850, at the advanced age of 91 years, having been Govn'r of N H in 1812, 1816, 1817, & 1818, U S Senator from 1802 to 1807, & a member of the State Legislature at various times.

Rt Rev Francis Xavier Gartland, Roman Catholic Bishop of the Diocese of Georgia, died at the residence of M Prendergast, in Savannah, on Sep 20, of yellow fever. He was born in Dublin, & his parents came with him to this country while he was yet an infant. He was educated at Mount St Mary's College, entered the priesthood at Phil, was consecrated Bishop of the Diocese of Georgia in 1850, arrived in this city in Nov of that year, & entered upon his duties. –Savannah Republican

TUE SEP 26, 1854
Wm C Worthington, a prominent lawyer & former member of the Legislature of Va, died at Charlestown, Jefferson Co, on Friday last.

Died: on Sep 22, in Wash City, after a protracted illness, Mary Ellen, consort of Geo Burns, in her 25th year, with a bright hope of a blissful immortality.

Died: on Sep 21, in Wash City, John Irving Miller, in his 19th year, late of Nebraska Territory. It may be consoling to the parents & friends of this young man to know that during his illness every attention was paid him which the best medical attendance & nursing could effect.
+
Died: on Sep 22, in Balt, Mr Joshua Cole, jr, printer, late of Wash City, in his 19th year. Three weeks ago both of the young men whose deaths are above recorded left Wash in fine health for a pleasure trip to Charleston, S C, where they contracted the fever of which they died after their return.

Died: on Sep 21, Mrs Johanna O'Regan, a native of Bentry, county of Cork, Ireland, aged 63 years.

Died: on Sep 23, in Wash City, of consumption, Virginia Josephine, wife of H A Hayden, & daughter of Hon Henry Dodge, aged 25 years & 5 months.

Died: on Sep 24, Kate K, aged 14 months, youngest child of Jas & Mgt Selden. Her funeral is this morning at 9 o'clock, from the residence of her parents, I st, between 19th & 20th.

Orphans Court of Wash Co, D C. Letters of administration on the personal estate of Pius W Williams, late of Wash Co, deceased. –Henrietta Williams, admx

WED SEP 27, 1854
Soon after the discovery of the late frauds by Robt L Schuyler, the Directors of the New Haven Railroad Co, by advice of counsel, determined to prefer criminal charges against him. Having ineffectually sought by the police in the States & in Canada, it is now supposed that he sailed for Europe immediately after the discovery of the frauds.

Wash Corp: 1-Ptn of Michl Muntz for the remission of a fine; same for Andrew Henson: both referred to the Cmte of Claims. 2-Ptn of Moses Lee, complaining of an illegal arrest by a police ofcr, & asking an investigation of it: referred to the Cmte of Claims. 3-Dr Saml A Storrow, to be physician for the poor of the 1st Ward, vice Dr Edwin C Moore, resigned, to take effect from Oct 1. 4-Theodore Wheeler to be Com'r of the Asylum.

Mrd: on Sep 26, by Rev Mr Dashiel, Mr Warren Lowe, of PG Co, Md, to Mrs Louisa C Allen, of Wash City.

Mrd: on Sep 18, by Rev Mr Alig, Jas R May to Miss Mary A Childress, both of Wash City.

Died: on Sep 26, in Gtwn, Mrs Christina Hobbs, in her 76th year. Her funeral is this afternoon, at 3:30 o'clock, from her late residence, 3rd & Warren sts.

Died: on Sep 25, in her 60th year, Mrs Ann, wife of Mr Jacob Kleiber. Her funeral is this morning, at 10 o'clock, from the City Hall.

Died: on Sep 26, Charlotte Young, daughter of Jas & Jane Lynch, aged 16 months & 2 days. Her funeral is this afternoon at 4 o'clock, from the residence of her parents, on East Capitol st, Capitol Hill.

Died: on Sep 19, at **Edge Hill**, Prince Wm Co, Va, Helen Woods, wife of John S Ewell, & daughter of N M McGregor, of Wash, D C, aged 25 years & 17 days. May God temper the wind to the shorn lamb, her infant son, the object of her tender care & devoted love; & may her disconsolate husband, her fond parents, her loving relatives & friends, find a solace in their bereavement from the hand of Him who only can bind up the broken heart. –J E

The Buffalo Courier: Lawrence Myers died in that city of hydrophobia, on Monday. He leaves wife & 5 small children in rather needy circumstances.

Rev Isaac Lewis, D D, a venerable clergyman of the Presbyterian church, died at N Y on Sat, in his 82nd year.

Public Schools: Wash, D C. Ofcrs: John T Towers, Mayor & ex officio Pres. Chas A Davis, Sec V Harbaugh, Treasurer. Trustees: Geo J Abbot, Robt Farnham, Flodoardo Howard, Thos Donoho, Peter F Bacon, V Harbaugh, F S Walsh, C P Russell, Thos Altemus, Wm B Randolph, P M Pearson, & S Yorke Atlee

Principals:
Mr S Kelly	Miss E Parsons	Miss Jane Moss
Miss M A S Davis	Miss L H Randolph	Miss Connell
Mrs M E Rodier	Miss F Henshaw	Mr J E Thompson
Miss M G Wells	Miss E V Billing	Miss M A Milburn
Miss A K Lowe	Mr John Fill	Mrs S J Thompson
Miss M E Middleton	Mrs C D Martin	Mrs M A Skidmore
Miss C Campbell	Mrs W M McCathran	Miss M A Lee
Mr Thos M Wilson	Miss F Elvans	Miss A A Adams
Mrs S P Randolph	Mrs M F Freeman	
Mrs R M Ogden	Mrs E Clark	

Assist Principals:
Mrs E M Kelly	Mr Hector Grant	Mr J F Goldsmith
Miss S E Coale	Miss C McCarthy	Miss J Acton
Miss Harriet Baker	Mrs E Myers	Miss H U Henshaw

THU SEP 28, 1854
Calvert College, near New Windsor, Carroll Co, Md: bldgs erected in 1850: scholastic year commences on the 3rd Monday of Oct, divided into 2 sessions, Winter & Summer Session. Tuition, Boarding, & Washing: $125. –A H Baker, Pres

The **Burgess estate**, so called, on Broad st, Boston, covering about 8,400 square feet of land, with old bldgs thereon standing, was sold at auction on Monday for $50,000, Mr W G Merrill being the purchaser.

Mrd: on Sep 26, at St Matthew's Church, by Rev Mr Donelan, W E Greenwell to Margret, youngest daughter of the late Nathl Manning, of Va.

Died: on Aug 30 last, in Berryville, Clarke Co, Va, Mr B H Sinnott, formerly of Washington, but for the last 8 years a resident of Clarke Co, Va.

The very desirable Hotel which has been occupied for the last 9 years by Mr Gadsby is now for rent. This property is located on Pa ave & 3rd st. Inquire of either of the subscribers: S P Franklin, John Purdy, D W Middleton, or Wm B Todd.

Hon Leonard Jarvis died at his residence in Surry, Maine, on Sep 18, aged 72 years.

Obit-died: Rt Rev Edw Barron, D D, Missionary Bishop [Roman Catholic] of the West Coast of Africa, on Sep 12, of the direful pestilence, yellow fever, that is now scourging the South, in Savannah. He was the brother & heir to the Rt Hon Sir Henry Winter Barron, Baronet, of Waterford, in the Kingdom of Ireland. He was soon followed to the grave by Rt Rev Dr Gartland, Bishop of Savannah.

FRI SEP 29, 1854
Louisville Journal: fortunate family. In the present Congress there are 2 members who are brothers, Israel *Washburn, jr, who represents the Penobscot district in Maine, & S B *Washburne, who represents the Galena district in Ill. Another brother, Mr C C *Washburne, has been nominated for Congress by his political friends in Wisconsin. If elected, we presume it will be the first instance in the history of our country that 3 brothers have held seats at the same time in Congress. [There are two other brothers in the House of Reps: the Messrs Stanton, one from Tenn, the other from Ky. They both went from the District of Columbia, of which they are natives-that is, Alexandria, which has since then been reconveyed to Va. They are both Democrats & men of ability & influence.] [*Washburn/Washburne: copied as written.] [Oct 17th newspaper: We copied a paragraph lately stating that the Messrs Washburn, in the next Congress, would make the first instance of 3 brothers being in Congress at the same time. A friend reminds us of a former case of 3 brothers being in Congress together, namely, in 1826-27, etc. They were Wm & John Findlay, Senator & Rep from Pa, & Jas Findlay, Rep from Ohio.]

Dates from Acapulco, Mexico, to Aug 24th, report the death of Gen Nicholas Bravo, after 34 years of military service. [No death date given.]

C R Weld, Sec of the Royal Society of London, a gentleman of scientific & literary attainments, & brother-in-law of the celebrated poet, Tennison, arrived in Wash City yesterday. H expressed himself in terms of high admiration of the the Library of Congress. He also visited the Pres of the U S, by whom he was handsomely received. -Union

Wm Livingston, of Canawana, N Y, was accidentally killed on Sep 17th, while gunning in the woods, when his gun accidentally discharged.

U S Patent Ofc, Wash, Sep 24, 1854. Ptns of Caroline S Williams, admx of Thos R Williams, deceased, of Moreau Station, N Y, praying the extension of a patent granted to said Thos R Williams on Sec 14, 1840, for improvements in machinery for hardening bats in felting, for 7 years from the expiration of said patent, which takes place on Dec 14, 1854. Also, by the same, on the same dates, the patent for an improvement in machinery for forming bats for felting. –Chas Mason, Com'r of Patents

A little daughter of Philo Robbins, formerly of Monson, was burnt to death st Shushan, Wash Co, N Y, on Sep 13th. She was at play with some matches & a candle & she set her clothes on fire.

Peleg S Blake, of Taunton, age 22 years, was killed by the accidental discharge of his gun one day last week, as was also Philander S Smith, of Jersey city.

Two intoxicated men, Patrick Muloy, of Castleton, & Jeffrey Pentegrass, of Sudbury, were run over by a railroad train between Rutland & Sutherland Falls, Vt, on Tue. Muloy was instantly killed. Pentegrass had his arm taken off, & died the next day.

A rowboat was swamped by the swell of the steamer in the North River, opposite N Y, on Sunday, & Bridget King, Eliza Brady, & Geo Mulder, were drowned.

John Morse, of Salem, was proceeding to bed, he missed his footing & fell down a flight of stairs, breaking his neck by the fall.

On Tue last a party of Cincinnatians went to the woods in the neighborhood of Hillsborough on a sporting expedition. On Wed, Jos Cridlan, shot & instantly killed another of the party, Jas Glancey, who had laid down to rest. Glancey leaves a wife & 4 children. Cridlan is almost insane in consequence of this occurrence.

Savannah: the death of Dr A B Brantley is announced. He died in Scriven Co on Sunday, in his 28th year. He was a son of the late Wm Brantley, D D, Pres of the Charleston College. There were 118 deaths from yellow fever last week at Charleston. The Savannah Georgian of Tue states that the number of interments have been lingering for some days. No doubt the sickness is subsiding.

An admirable portrait of Rev Mr Sunderland, painted by Mr Saml Walker, artist, is now on exhibition at Galt & Bro's, jewelers, Pa ave.

The Picture of **Mount Vernon**, painted by our old fellow-citizen, Mr Wm McLeod, is now on view at Taylor & Maury's, & will be raffled for, at the request of his numerous friends & admirers.

Mrd: on Sep 28, at the Wesley Chapel parsonage. By Rev Jas H Brown, Mr Robt Cole to Miss Martha Sherbertt, both of Md.

Mrd: on Tue, by Rev John C Smith, Mr John Smith to Mrs Phoebe Ann Vibber, of N Y.

Died: on Sep 12, at the *Bower*, Jefferson Co, Va, in her 78th year, Mrs Nancy Clayton Kennedy, widow of the late John Kennedy. For many years she resided at Balt, but for the last 35 years past has lived in Va. She leaves 4 sons: John P & Anthony Kennedy, of Balt, & Andrew & Pendleton Kennedy, of Va.

Dancing Academy will resume on Oct 7. He has leased the beautiful hall now in course of erection, 9th & D sts. Apply at Mr John F Ellis' Music Store, Pa ave, near 10th st. –Prof H W Munder

SAT SEP 30, 1854
Dr John T Miller, a popular physician of Flat Rock, was found dead in a pasture about 4 miles from that village on Fri last. He & his horse had been killed by lightning during the thunder storm on Thu, & had evidently fallen instantly dead. -Paris [Ky] Citizen, 22nd.

A stranger fell in the street at Dayton, Ohio, on Sep 16, & immediately expired. It was ascertained that it was Ezekiel Clark, a resident of Wash Co, Pa, who was on his way to Ill, where he was in the habit of purchasing cattle for the Eastern market. He had on his person 2 gold watches & $11,443, including $4,000 in drafts on N Y.

Emily Jane Skiller, a girl of 3 years, was scalded to death by falling into a kettle of boiling tomato sauce in N Y on Sunday.

Executor's sale of valuable real estate in PG Co, Md: by the last will & testament of the late Henry H Waring, the undersigned, exc of the said H H Waring, will offer at public sale, on Oct 19, *Waring's Lot*, supposed to contain 160 acres of land, more or less. Improvements are a good dwlg house & other necessary out-bldgs.
-Dyonisius Sheriff, Exc of H H Waring

At the request of the neighborhood **gas lights** have recently been introduced into our streets, for which each of us, in proportion to the extent of our property on the street, pays a monthly rate for the benefit of the gas company. I for one would have not joined in the petition had I known at the time that by the arrangement with the gas company the lights are to be extinguished at midnight, particularly as we pay a rate for which the company can well afford to let them burn all night when there is not sufficient moonlight, as is the usual mode. –A property holder & resident on H st. -Wash Item

Mr Gore, the English Charge d'Affaires at Montevideo, died of apoplexy on Jul 30.

In Circuit Court for PG Co, as Court of Equity. John B Webster & others vs Chas B Calvert & others. The object of this suit is to procure a decree for the sale of certain real estate, in said county, of which Jas G Webster, late of said county, died seized & possessed. John G Webster departed this life on Dec 3, 1852, intestate, having before that time purchased of a certain Chas B Calvert, of said county, a part of a tract of land known as a part of *Fordshops' Kindness*, in said county, containing 311 acres, leaving Sarah Webster, his widow, & the following children, your oratrix; John B Webster & Saml Webster, & your orators Mary A Meade, wife of Theodore Meade, Eliz A Jenkins, Wm Webster, Jas G Webster, Philip L Webster, Susan Vernon, wife of Walter Vernon, Mary Jane Tenley, wife of Geo Tenley, Louisa Moore, wife of Marsham Moore, & Geo Webster, his only children; Isaiah Drane, Mary Ellen Drane, Robt Drane, & Julia Ann Trunnel, wife of Wm Trunnel, children of a deceased daughter, Ann Drane; the said Geo Webster having died since his said father, leaving Mgt Webster, his widow, & the following children: Hiram Webster, Geo Webster, Catherine Strider, wife of John Strider, Rosetta Meade, wife of Robt Meade, Ann M Heath, wife of John Heath, & Mgt Linsley, wife of Saml Linsley, his only heirs. That the said Jas G Webster paid to the said Chas B Calvert the whole amount of the purchase money for said real estate, but died before having received a deed for the same; that, since the death of said Jas G, the said Sarah Webster, his widow, has procured a commission to issue from this court, to assign & lay off her dower in said real estate, which has been executed; that it would be greatly to the interest & advantage of all the parties interested to have said real estate sold, as well the residue thereof as also the remainder interest in that part assigned to said widow, as & for her dower; that the said Mgt Webster, Hiram Webster, Geo Webster, John Strider, & Catherine his wife, Robt Meade & Rosetta his wife, John Heath & Ann his wife, Saml Linsley & Mgt his wife, Isaiah Drane, Mary Ellen Drane, Wm Trunnel & Julia Ann his wife, reside out of the State of Md. Absent dfndnts are to appear in this Court on or before the first Monday of Nov next. –Owen Norfolk, Clerk County Court of PG Co.

Mrd: on Sep 28, by Rev Jas H Brown, Mr Jas H Granger to Miss Mgt Young, both of Wash, D C.

Mrd: on Sep 26, at Colebrook, N H, by Rev J B Hill, Cornelius B Adams, of Wash City, to Miss Martha B Loomis, daughter of Gen L Loomis, of Colebrook.

Mrd: on Sep 28, in the F st Presbyterian Church of Wash City, by Rev P D Gurley, D D, Rev Nathan C Chapin, of Wisconsin, to Miss Mary A Fountain.

Mrd: on Sep 28, in Wash City, by Rev G W Samson, Mr Wm Beagle to Miss Henrietta Byer, both of Wash.

Mrd: on Sep 13, 1854, in Boston, by Rev R W Cushman, D D, Mr Hiram Corson, jr, of Wash, to Mademoiselle Caroline Rollin, of Paris, France.

Died: on Jul 29 last, at Waco Village, McClellan Co, Texas, after a few days' illness of congestion of the brain, Dr Jonathan Edwards Jackson, formerly of Wash City, youngest son of Mrs Col Tuley, of Clarke Co, Va, & grandson of the late Rev O B Brown, of Wash City.

Died: on Sep 29, Mrs Mgt Duckworth, aged 83 years, a resident of Wash City for the last 50 years. Her friends & the friends of W H Gunnell are invited to attend her funeral on Oct 1, at 4 o'clock, from C st, between 3rd & 4th sts.

N Y, Sep 29. A police ofcr, Jas Cahill, was shot dead this morning whilst attempting to arrest some burglars. Three men have been arrested on suspicion.

Boston, Sep 29. Thos Casey was executed at Cambridge today for the murder of his wife. He was swung at the appointed time, & after hanging some 20 minutes it was discovered that his heart still throbbed & his neck was unbroken. He finally strangled after painful struggling.

Appointments by the Pres: 1-Jas Ramsey, Collector, Plymouth, N C, re-appointed. 2-Wm P Keyburn, Assist Appraiser, New Orleans, vice Francis Leech, appointed Appraiser.

Trustee's sale: by decree of the Circuit Court for Anne Arundel Co, passed in a cause in which Thos R Tongue & others are cmplnts & Thos O Tongue & others dfndnts, the subscriber, as trustee, will offer at public auction, on Oct 5, at the Exchange in the city of Balt, the valuable Farm on West River, in said county, devised by John Collinson to Mrs Harriet Waters, containing between 400 & 500 acres, situated within 1½ mile of navigable water, at Tracey's Landing, 5 miles of Fair Haven, & 6 miles of Galesville. This property is in the richest part of Anne Arundel Co, & adjoins the lands of Alex'r Franklin, Edw Hall, Thos J Hall, Wm Hall, St James' or **Herring Creek** Parsonage, Mrs Compton, John Netwell, & Wilson Stallings. The improvements consist of dwlg, overseer's house, all necessary barns & outhouses. –Wm H G Dorsey, trustee -Gibson & Son, aucts

MON OCT 2, 1854
Household & kitchen furniture at auction: on Oct 4, at the residence of John B Clagett, on C st, between 4½ & 6th sts. -Jas C McGuire, auct

Household & kitchen furniture at auction: on Oct 5, at the residence of Mrs Swartze, D st north & 3rd st west. -Green & Scott, aucts

The New Orleans papers announce the death of John Kane, who died from wounds received during the late mob doings in that city. Kane is the 7th victim of these disgraceful outrages.

Hon John Beverley Robinson, Chief Justice of Upper Canada, & Hon Louis Hypolite Lafontaine, Chief Justice of the Lower Province, have been created Baronets of the United Kingdon of Great Britain & Ireland.

The Murfreesboro [Tenn] Telegraph: the trial there last week of Col Robt Rucker for the murder of his brother-in-law, Dr W A Smith, resulted in a verdict of murder in the 2nd degree & 10 years' imprisonment. It is probable a new trial will be applied for, & if it be granted that an appeal will be taken to the Supreme Court.

Dr Stevens, coroner, on Thu held an inquest on the body of Malinda Harman, a young lady aged 20 years, at the Balt cemetery, said she came to her death by poison. The body was exhumed & examined. Mr Ringgold, wife of Justice Ringgold, was sworn, & said that Malinda lived in her house; she was taken ill, & sent to the drug store & got some magnesia; when it came to the house it was placed on the mantel, where lay some arsenic that had been procured to kill rats. Miss Harman went to the mantel & took what she supposed was magnesia, but it was arsenic. She died in 10 or 12 hours. Verdict: death from taking arsenic by mistake. –Balt Sun

The Odd-Fellows, Temperance Societies, Red Men, & Fireman appeared yesterday to attend the funerl of the late Edw McCubbin, a member of the several Orders. His remains were taken to Alexandria. The procession was quite imposing & solemn.

Two young Germans, Christian Glantz & Henry Glantz, brothers, were out gunning near Bladensburg on Fri, &, on being remonstrated with by Edw W Duvall, a resident on the premises, as to the danger of their pusuit, an altercation ensued when one of the young men deliberately shot Mr Duvall, who died later that day from the effects of the wound. The Germans were arrested in Wash City, & committed to jail for further examination. They stated they committed the act in self-defense. [Oct 7th newspaper: Mr Edw W Duvall, of PG Co, did not die & is likely to recover. The examination of the trespassers had been delayed to await the result of Mr Duvall's wound.]

At Worcester, Mass, on Tue, Mrs Martha Whitcomb was found dead in her bed at the house of her son-in-law, & by her side was the lifeless corpse of her grandchild, aged 7 months. Mrs Whitcomb had taken the child to her bed in order to assist its mother in weaning it, but it is supposed she expired suddenly in the night from heart disease, with which she had been some time afflicted. At the time of her death appearances indicated that her arm fell across the face of the infant, & as it stiffened in death the child was unable to extricate itself, & was smothered.

Hon Jos W Jackson, a Rep in the last Congress from the State of Ga, died at Savannah, of the epidemic prevailing there, on Thu last.

Mrs Eliz McCarty, of Mattapoisett, while stepping on the cars of the train for N Y on Thu, fell from the steps & was so badly crushed that she died soon after.

Dr John W Shields, a young physician of Fred'k Md, accidentally killed himself on Tue last by the discharge of his own gun whilst on a gunning excursion.

A fatal accident occurred on one of the islands of Lake Winnipisseogee on Sep 24. Aurin Brown, a young lad, while out gunning, was accidentally killed when his own gun discharged.

Died: on Oct 1, Mrs Ann Royall, at a very advanced age. Her funeral is this afternoon, at 3 o'clock, from her late residence on B st north, Capitol Hill.

Died: on Oct 1, in Wash City, Wm Cash, a native of the county of Wexford, Ireland, for many years a resident of Wash City. His funeral will take place from St Peter's Church, Capitol Hill, this evening, at 3 o'clock.

TUE OCT 3, 1854
Yellow fever appeared at Darien, Ga, & 12 deaths are reported, among the victims are Capt Wing, proprietor of the Mansion Housse, & his assistant Geo W Clensey. The interments at New Orleans for the week ending Sep 24 were 504, of which 341 were deaths from yellow fever.

The Baton Rouge papers announced the death of Col Stephen Henderson, an aged & highly respectable resident of that town. At one time he edited the Louisiana Register & at another the Baton Rouge Gaz. At the time of his death he was the financial partner of the firm of Hill & Henderson, of Baton Rouge.

Court martial is sitting on board the ship **North Carolina**, at N Y, trying the deserters from the raze **Independence**. Three more of the runaways, making 9 in all, have been caught. There are now only two of the gang at large. The ringleader, David Hazzard, was arrested a few days after the occurrence. He was yesterday placed on trial for threatening the life of Midshipman Miller. Hazzard was recognized as a seaman who passed by the name of Dimon in the Pacific squadron in 1849. On that cruise he & four others attempted to desert the service. The command was under Passed Midshipman Gibson. They threw him overboard & fled. Gibson was picked up by a boat. Two were caught & hung from the yard-arm of the flag ship **Savannah**, & the remaining three, of which Hazzard was one, whilst under arrest had their punishment commuted. –Corr of Balt American

The Cambridge Chronicle announces the death, on the 25th ult, of Henry C Rawlings, a member of the Senate of Md from Caroline Co.

A gentleman in Amherst Co, Va, Mr W Lavender, who had been annoyed for some time by a dog, poisoned some milk a few days ago & forgot to inform his family with the fact. Three of them died almost instantly, & others were dangerously ill.

Charlottesville [Va] Advocate of Fri: about 3 weeks ago at Sweet Springs, Mrs Harris, wife of Lt Harris, of the navy, & daughter of Gov Troupe, of Ga, had her clothes catch fire, & before she was rescued was burnt in a most shocking manner. Her constant prayer was for death. Her brother, a young Mr Troupe, & her brother-in-law, Mr Dent, of Ga, were also badly burnt in their efforts to save her. Her condition last week was somewhat improved, though still very painful & critical.

Wash City Ordinance: 1-Act for the relief of E G Handy: to pay him $6.77, being 1/3rd the amount of fine made by him out of Chas Keirnan for violation of a law of this Corp, & the costs on the same, the judgment obtained in 1849.

Hartford [Conn] Times of Sep 22. All our citizens venerate the **Charter Oak**, the grand old tree that shielded the written charter which continued to be our organic law until 1818. The tree stands upon the Wyllys' place, now owned & occupied by Hon I W Stuart, who has kindly cared for it. A few years since some boys kindled a fire within its trunk. Mr S put the fire out, & at considerable expense, had the hollow enclosed by a door with a lock & key. On Sep 22 the New Haven fire companies had their annual muster & visited the famous oak. Mr S invited them to enter the hollow trunk, when 24 men belonging to Capt McGregor's company entered together. Twenty-eight of Capt Thomas' company then entered. By placing 28 full grown men in an ordinary room of a dwlg one may judge of the great size of the famous old Charter Oak. [Some 4 or 5 years ago, at the request of a gentleman of Wash, Judge T S Williams, of Conn, sent him acorns from the tree; they were placed in the hands of a skillful gardener, & are now growing finely. They are designed to be transplanted in the parks & reservations of the metropolis. -Nat Intell]

Public sale of a most desirable lot, or lots, on the Heights of Gtwn, D C: sale on Nov 3, on the premises of the northern portion of the **Tudor Place** square, containing 1 acre, 2 roods, & 35 feet, as per plat, more or less, & bounded by Congress st on the east, Road st on the north, Valley st on the west, & the dividing line from the southern portion of said square on the south. This property may be sold as a whole or divided. –Geo W Peter, Agent for B W Kennon, exc

Orphans Court of Wash Co, D C. Letters of administration on the personal estate of Thos Hall, late of Wash Co, deceased. –L R Holmead, adm

Orphans Court of Wash Co, D C. In the case of Mary A M Jones, admx of Gen Roger Jones, deceased: the admx & Court have appointed Oct 21, for final settlement of the estate of said deceased, of the assets in hand. –Ed N Roach, Reg/o wills

WED OCT 4, 1854
Household & kitchen furniture at auction: Oct 6, at the residence of Rev Alex'r Duncanson, at Va ave & 2nd st, near the Navy Yard. -Green & Scott, aucts

Household & kitchen furniture at auction: on Oct 9, at the residence of Lt Bisselle, at the corner of Pa ave & 21st st, in **Gadsby's Row**. -Green & Scott, aucts

Hon Presley Ewing, a Rep in Congress from the 3rd district of Ky died of cholera last Wed, at the Mammoth Cave, in Ky.

Mr Geo Steers has entered upon his duties as Naval Constructor at the Brooklyn Navy Yard, & has commenced laying down his lines for the new war-steamer **Niagara**, which is to be the largest ship ever built in this country. The entreme length will be 345 feet; depth of hold, 31 feet; breadth of beam, 55 feet; draught when loaded, 22 feet 9 inches; displacement 5,500 tons. –N Y Times

A letter from Lima, Peru states that Jos F Haley, a printer from Portland, Me, has been convicted there of counterfeiting Gov't notes, having struck off $600,000 worth. He was at first sentenced to be shot, but through the efforts of Mr Clay, the American Minister, his punishment was reduced to 5 years in the chain gang.

A daughter of Hon Caleb B Smith, at a recent county fair at Connersville, Ind, received the highest prize, a side-saddle worth $100, as being the best lady-rider of all who presented themselves as competitors.

Wash Corp: 1-Act for the relief of Jos Smoot: referred. 2-Cmte of Claims: act for the relief of Andrew Henson: passed. Same cmte: asked to be discharged from the further consideration of the ptns of Moses Lee; of Solomon Heflebower; & of Michl Muntz: discharged accordingly.

Mrd: on Sep 6, by Rev S A H Marks, Mr Jas M Larcomb to Miss Jane Catharine Windsor, all of Wash City.

Mrd: on Sep 26, by Rev S A H Marks, Mr Wm Carrington to Sophia E Watson.

Mrd: on Oct 3, by Rev Andrew G Carothers, Mr Chas Schussler to Mrs Mary Hudal, all of Wash City.

Mrd: on Oct 3, by Rev S A H Marks, Mr Thos Pierce to Miss Charity Ann Allen, both of PG Co, Md.

Mrd: on Tue, in the Fourth Presbyterian Church, by Rev John C Smith, John T Moss to Ann Virginia, daughter of John G Schott, all of Wash City.

Wash Co, D C. Writ of fieri facias issued on Sep 26, 1854: I have levied on the property of Chas E Mundy, to satisfy said execution in favor of Wm I Webb, to wit: one mortising machine, 10 window frames; a lot of door stuff, dressed, a lot of sash stuff, dressed, 8 cleats; & a small lot of lumber: public sale on Oct 10, in front of the Bank of Wash. –Wm Cox, constable

Trustee's sale of a large stock of groceries: on Oct 9, at the store of C W Coleman, near the Market. –Edw S Wright, auct

Orphans Court of Wash Co, D C. In the case of Saml Stott, adm of Thos S Bingey, deceased: the adm & Court have appointed Oct 24 for the final settlement of the estate of the deceased, with the assets in hand. –Ed N Roach, Reg/o wills

THU OCT 5, 1854
Administrator's sale of the personal effects of Jos L C Handy, deceased: on Oct 7, by order of the Orphans Court of Wash Co, D C, in front of our auction store: household & kitchen furniture, gold watches, swords uniform, wearing apparel, & trunks. –Green & Scott, aucts

Mr Mahlon Loomis, of Cambridgeport, Mass, has perfected a new style of artificial teeth, the peculiarity of which is that both teeth & plate are of one piece & of the same material. No metal plate is used, nor are there any joints around the teeth.

Five gentlemen from Calif report to the Western Texan that in Durango, Mexico, they found in prison 3 Americans, named Wm Shirley, of Broome Co, N Y; Wm Rodgers, of Stark Co, Ohio; John Gaines, of Dayton, Montg Co, Ohio. These men have been in a dungeon 4 years & 3 months, during 2 years of this time they were chained down to the floor, in total darkness. They were imprisoned on the charge of murder & robbery, & had been unable to get a trial, & respectable Mexicans admitted that there was no proof to convict them. They say that they have repeatedly written to the American Minister in Mexico, but do not believe he received them.

Mrd: on Oct 3, in Balt, by Rev Mr Morrison, at Christ Church, Wm B Walworth, of Plattsburg, N Y, to Jennie Gray, daughter of the late Col Henry W Gray, of Balt.

Mrd: on Oct 3, at Wilmington, Delaware, by Rev A D Pollock, Mr Champion Bissell, of N Y C, to Miss Mary Josephine, youngest daughter of Hon John Wales.

Died: on Oct 4, Mrs Catharine Gibson, in her 85th year, a native of St Mary's Co, Md, but for the last 50 years a resident of this District. Her funeral will be from the residence of her son, R Gibson, D & 12th sts, this morning at 10 o'clock.

Died: on Oct 4, in Wash City, Jas Davis, in his 71st year. His funeral will take place from his late residence, on 7th st, between L & M sts.

Died: on Oct 3, Joseph Frederick, only son of Jos A & Eliz G Deeble, aged 21 months. His funeral will be from his father's residence, on I, between 9th & 10th sts, this afternoon, at 4 o'clock.

Wash police ofcrs who had judgments in Sep, 1854:

Washington Hurley	R R Burr	John A Willett
Jos B Peerce	Wm Martin	Isaac Stoddard
W H Barnaclo	A R Allen	U B Mitchel
Wm A Boss	John H Wise	J M Busher
R G Handy	J Simonds	
J F Wollard	Josias Adams	

-John Davis, Chief of Police

The following young gentlemen have just passed the preliminary examination for admission into the Naval Academy at Annapolis, & have received from the Sec of the Navy appointments as Acting Midshipman:

Geo Dewey, Vt, 1st Congressional Dist	Jas M Wadsworth, Pa, 23rd
Chas H Swasey, Mass, 2nd	Henry F Young, Pa, 1st
Thos Starr Spencer, Conn, 3rd	Wm C Whittle, jr, Va, 4th
West Van Santvoord, N Y, 11th	Hamilton A Brown, N C, 8th
Richardson Mallet, N Y, 5th	Wm Alex Kerr, N C, 5th
Beatty P Smith, N Y, 29th	Chas S Wheeler, N C, 8th
Allen V Reid, N Y, 31st	Richd Wheeler, N C, 1st
Alden W Belknap, N Y, 10th	John Grimball, S C, 3rd
John F Wright, N Y, 18th	Iverson A Hines, Ga, 2nd
John Adams Howell, N Y, 28th	Vernon H Vaughan, Ala, 2nd
C M Schoemaker, N Y, 11th	Geo Strong Storrs, Ala, 3rd
Chas O Judson, N Y, 27th	Nicholas J Lane, Ala, 5th
Robt H Yates, N Y, 18th	Clarius Phillips, Ala, 1st
Arthur McKinstry, N Y, 33rd	Alfred P DeShields, La, 2nd
Geo F Merriam, N Y, 23rd	Thos Reddington, La, 1st
Thos Ewing, N J, 1st	Curtis P Hinman, La, 3rd
H M Blue, N J, 3rd	J C R Mullary, Texas, 1st
Jas L Stanborough, N J, 4th	Johu Bradley, Texas, 2nd
Jas Ross, jr, N J, 5th	T W W Davies, Tenn, 1st
Geo B White, Pa, 7th	Luther C May, Tenn, 3rd
Augustus S Walls, Pa, 10th	Saml Mulliken, Ky, 1st
Norman H Farquhar, Pa, 11th	Edw G Furber, Ohio, 17th
Edmund Taylor, Pa, 12th	Albert Kantz, Ohio, 6th
Richmond L Jones, Pa, 8th	Lucius H Gibbs, Ohio, 6th
Henry Broderick, Pa, 13th	Roderick S McCook, Ohio, 17th

John A Purdee, Ohio, 15th
Henry L Howison, Ind, 2nd
Roderick Prentiss, Ind, 10th
Richd S Collum, Ind, 2nd
Edwin McCook, Ill, 4th
Henry F Condict, Ill, 1st
Horace Hulbard, Ill, 3rd
Joshua Bishop, Mo, 6th
Chas B Cleveland, Mo, 3rd

Wellington Triplet, Mo, 2nd
Myron H Beaumont, Mich, 2nd
C S Livingston, Fla
Saml Adams, Fla
Elias V Andrews, Minn
Philip Smith, New Mexico
Franklin Lee Ridgely, Oregon
-Star

Court of Chancery of the State of Delaware, in & for Newcastle Co. Wm R Work & M Meigs, as guardian of Eliz W & Mary Ann Work, vs Wm Henry McBeath, Rebecca C Ellett, Ellen H Davis, & Henry T Ellett. Aug 25, 1854-Petition for partition filed. And now, to wit, this Sep 16, 1854, it appearing in this Court that the said Rebecca C Ellett, Ellen H Davis, & Henry T Ellett, do not reside in the State of Delaware, on motion of Victor du Pont, solicitor for petitioners, it is ordered by the Court that they appear before the said court at the next term, to wit, on Feb 19, 1855, & show cause, if any they have, why partition of the premises may not be made agreeably to the prayer of the petitioners. –Peter B Vandever, Reg of Chancery

Peoria Republican: terrible effects of lightning in that city on Sunday week. it burst with all its fury upon the residence of Capt Morrison, on 3rd st, the bolt first struck the chimney, another passed down the dining room, & a third passed into the second story. At the foot of the stairs two sons of Capt Morrison were lying in the hall, & the oldest was struck & in half a hour life was extinct. The body to all appearances, was not injured in the least. The other brother was terribly lacerated, both thighs being furrowed vertically to the bone by a number of gashes. The physician in attendance has but little hopes of the sufferer's recovery. Capt Morrison was in the dining room at the time & he too was struck, but in a moment recovered from the shock. His daughter, a young girl, escaped injury. Two ladies in the house were unhurt. The bldg presented this morning a frightful appearance, having been riddled from the roof to the cellar.

Boston Journal: the schnr **Ontario**, Capt H G Penniman, went on a ledge of rocks about 3 miles below Long Island, on Fri, & in 3 hours became a total wreck. Four of the men were lost: David Beals, of Rockland, mate, aged about 20; Chas Reed, of New Orleans, about 23; Geo Kess, of St George, Maine, 19; & an Irishman, name unknown. The captain escaped after remaining on the wreck all night.

Fair Hill Boarding School for Girls, Sandy Springs, Montg Co, Md. The 8th term will commence on Nov 6. Refer to Benj Hallowell, C C Smoot, J M Johnson, Thos Waters. –R S Kirk, Mary W Kirk, W H Farquhar, Olney Post Ofc

To the creditors & next of kin of Susan Dillihunt, deceased. By order of the County Court of Fauquier, Va, made at its Sept term last, one of the Com'rs of the Court was directed to convene the creditors of Susan Dillihunt, deceased, to show cause, if any they can, why the fund of the intestate now in the hand of Richd H Carter, her administrator, should be be distributed, & also to ascertain who are the legal distributees of the estate. You are notified I shall attend at my ofc in Warrenton, Va, on Oct 30, 1854, to receive proof of the matters referred to. –John Q Marr, Com'r

FRI OCT 6, 1854
Telegraphic report: alleged defalcation by Saml Davidson, late Surveyor General of Calif to the amount of $12,400. –Boston Daily Advertiser

The **old Lutheran Church** in Winchester, Va, lately destroyed by fire, was built in 1764. It was occupied during the Revolution by British Hessian prisoners, & was one of the old relics which every body desired to see preserved. It was used in 1851 for a Democratic Convention, & not long after was struck by lightning. Its demolition was the work of an incendiary.

Miss Mary Reed, of Va, well known as a vocal & instrumental performer & competent teacher, will instruct a class in one or more of the schools of Wash City. References: Rev Dr Tustin, Rev Dr Dashiell, J J Miller, R W Latham, & Wm P Faherty.

Mrd: on Oct 4, at the Nat'l Hotel, by Rev Jas H Brown, Mr Henry A Ware to Miss Jane G Starling, both of Va.

Mrd: on Oct 3, by Rev E P Phelps, Mr Wm W Hollingsworth to Miss Lavinia D, daughter of John M Donn

Mrd: on Oct 5, by Rev E P Phelps, at Foundry parsonage, Mr John W Campbell to Miss Alcinda Moss, both of Alexandria, Va.

Mrd: on Oct 5, by Rev Dr Butler, of Trinity Church, Dr David Porter Heap to Lizzie, daughter of John C Bowyer, of Wash City.

Died: yesterday, in Wash City, Mrs Catherine Flinn, in her 89th year, a native of Ireland, county of Wexford. Her funeral will take place this afternoon at 4 o'clock, from her residence on F st, near 11th.

Died: on Oct 5, George Nelson, infant son of John A & Dolly Ann Ruff, aged 2 years. His funeral is this afternoon at 4 o'clock, from his parents; residence, on E st, between 5th & 6th sts.

SAT OCT 7, 1854
Reminiscences with the early history of the Gov't: 1-The first business Pres Washington submitted related to treaties with the Northern tribes of Indians & those Northwest of the Ohio. 2-Mr Jefferson desiring to return, Wm Short was nominated on Jun 16, & confirmed Minister to France on Jun 17, 1789. 3-Arthur St Clair was nominated & consented to on Aug 20, 1789, as Govn'r of the Western Territory. Pres Adams, on Jan 1, 1798, nominated him to be Govn'r of the Territory Northwest of the River Ohio for another period established by law, & was confirmed on Jan 12, 1798. He was dismissed from ofc by Pres Jefferson on Nov 22, 1802, for language considered disrespectful to the Congress of the U S in asserting the doctrine of Territorial sovereignty. 4-On Sep 11, 1789, the Pres nominated Alex'r Hamilton, of N Y, to be Sec of the Treasury of the U S, which, with other nominations, was confirmed. 5-On Sep 24 the Pres nominated for the Supreme Court of the U S the following: John Jay, of N Y, Chief Justice; John Rutledge, of S C; Jas Wilson, of Pa; Wm Cushing, of Mass; Robt H Harrison, of Md; & John Blair, of Va, Associate Judges. 6-On Sep 25, 1789, the Pres nominated & the Senate confirmed Thos Jefferson as Sec of State, Edmund Randolph as Atty Genr'l, & Saml Osgood as Postmaster Gen. 6-On Jun 7, 1790, the Pres nominated the following to fill ofcs established by law withing the Territory of the U S south of the River Ohio: Wm Blount to be Govn'r; David Campbell & John McNairy to be Judges; & Danl Smith to be Secretary. 7-On Oct 31, 1791, Thos Johnson, of Md, was nominated as one of the Associate Justices of the Supreme Court, in place of John Rutledge, resigned. On the same day Timothy Pickering was nominated to be Postmaster Gen, in place of Saml Osgood, resigned. 8-On Dec 22, 1791, Pres Washington nominated Governeur Morris, of N Y, as Minister for the U S at Paris, & Thos Pinckney, of S C, as Minister at London. 9-On Apr 11, 1792, the Senate confirmed the nomination of Anthony Wayne to be a Maj Gen in the Army, in place of Arthur St Clair, resigned. 10-On Apr 16, 1792, the nomination of Jas Wilkinson as Brig Gen was confirmed.

Columbus [Ga] Times: announce the death of Gen Hugh A Haralson, a favorite with the people of Ga. He was for many years a member of the Ga Legislature & Rep in Congress, & voluntarily retired into private life. [No death date given-current item.]

Mr Geo W Green, a banker, has been committed to jail at Chicago on a charge of having poisoned his wife with strychnine. The evidence thus far produced against him, taken before a coroner's jury, is circumstantial & ex-parte.

Mr Saml Head, of Hooksett, N H, was killed there on Fri by falling on a circular saw which cut off his arm & leg.

Mrs Christopher Bishop, of Rochester, N Y, was dreadfully burnt & died one night last week from trying to fill a fluid lamp while it was burning.

Mr Peterson, of Troy, N Y, died there of intemperance on Thu.

Wm Mears, of Provincetown, Mass, was killed on Monday by the giving way of the block of bldg he was trying to remove.

Mrd: on Oct 4, by Rev Mr Gurley, Mr John G Clarke to Bertha, youngest daughter of Wm Michlin, all of Wash City.

For rent: the farm of the late Cornelius Barber, containing 700 acres & upwards, on the Wycomico, St Mary's Co, Md: bldgs are commodious. Immediate possession. Apply to Wm Redin, Gtwn, D C.

MON OCT 9, 1854
Ellis Buffington & Wm England, Cherokee Indians, recently met each other on Grand River, in the Cherokee Nation, & in a fight with pistols & bowie-knives both were killed.

Mrd: on Sep 11 last, near McConnellsville, Ohio, Henry C Derrick, son of the late Wm S Derrick, of Wash City, to Emma, daughter of Gen B W Conklin, of that State.

Mrd: on Oct 4, by Rev Dr Gurley, John G Clarke to Bertha M, daughter of W Mechlin, all of Wash City.

Mrd: on Oct 4, at St John's Church, in Gtwn, by Rev Mr Tillinghast, Rev John D Powell, of Va, to Annie Leake, daughter of the late John M Hepburn.

Died: on Oct 6, Ann Elizabeth, infant daughter of Chas H Lane, aged 6 months. For of such is the Kingdom of Heaven.

Meeting of Nat'l Lodge No 12, at Masonic Hall, this evening, 7:30. Members are desired to be punctual in their attendance. -S Bulow Erwin, sec

Master Bakers of Wash meeting held this day at Odd Fellows' Hall, it was resolved, that the 1 lb loaf will be sold to shops at 4½ cents, & to families at 5 cents. -A Noer, Pres

Orphans Court of Wash Co, D C. Letters of administration on the personal estate of Robt A Carter, late of Wash Co, deceased. –Jas H Durham, adm

$50 reward for runaway negro boy Bill Nelson, 18 years old. –Andrew Martine, 590 12th st, Island.

Harman Blennerhassett, the 2nd son of Harman Blennerhassett, of the island in the Ohio river which bears that name, died in N Y on Sep 17, after a protracted illness. He was an artist of considerable eminence. The only surviving member of the family, Jos L Blennerhassett, now lives in Troy, Missouri.

Danville, Pa, Oct 6. Boiler explosion at the Montour Iron Works destroyed a frame dwlg. The family of John Farley lived upstairs, & one of his two children was instantly killed, & the other, a little girl, was dangerously if not fatally wounded. In the lower story 3 children of Barney McGuire were hurt. A boy, John Search, has died of his injuries, & John Priest, John Diesinger, John Adams, Alex'r Wands, Michl Levy, Isaac Hines, Wm Butler & Jos Shuggart are badly wounded & scalded, some seriously.

Incident at the last commencement of the Rochester Univ: one member of the graduating class, Mr R C Fenn, of Rochester, is totally blind. When his theme was announced Pres Anderson remarked to the audience that Mr Fenn, at the close of his junior year, in performing some chemical experiments in private, lost his eyesight entirely from the effects of an explosion, but that from unflagging energy & by aid of a devoted brother & attached class-mates he had been able to complete the studies of the course with honor. He was led forward by his brother, while there was scarcely a tearless eye in all that vast assemblage of near 2,000 souls. His subject was "The Lost Senses," the object of which to demonstate the proposition that blindness is preferable to deafness. Mr Fenn retired amid the prolonged applause of the audience.

TUE OCT 10, 1854

Sale on President's Square on Nov 1, of the dwlg on H st now occupied by Rev Dr Pyne. The house is large & well built. -Jas C McGuire, auct

The sudden death of young Mr Draper, son of the ex-Consul at Paris, is announced by M Gaillardet in his French Courier correspondence. Near Dieppe he was clumbing up a precipice & fell, & a young fisherman seeing him was so alarmed that he too fell, from a congestion of the brain.

Judge Nimrod E Benson, one of our oldest citizens, died. He was the model of a man & a Mason. He held the ofc of Receiver of the Land Ofc at this place for the last quarter of a century, & discharged his duties with fidelity. –Montgomery [Ala] Journal [No death date given-current item.]

Obit-died: yesterday, in Wash City, Wm Darby, in his 80th year. He was a native of Pa, but in his infancy removed with his parents to the Ohio, when the whole trans-Alleghany counry was a wilderness, inhabited only by fierce & savage tribes of Indians. He was a man of singular sincerity, probity, & benevolence. His funeral will take place today at 4 o'clock, from Mrs Clare's boarding-house.

Mrd: on Oct 3, in Trinity Church, N Y, by Rev Smith Pyne, of Wash, Capt Chas Wilkes, U S N, to Mary H Bolton, daughter of the late Henry Lynch, of N Y.

Mrd: on Oct 6, by Rev F Israel, Thos Brown to Mrs Nancy Wyman, all of Wash City.

The list of wrecks & casualties at sea, registered at Lloyd's during the present year sine Jan 1st last, discloses a frightful catalogue of ships missing, & which are now given up as lost, having, it is supposed, foundered with all hands on board. This list does not include the losses of the ship **Madagascar** & the ill-fated screw steamer **Glasgow**, with which upwards of 580 unhappy creatures were lost. Of the 48 lost, a large number were vessels bound across the Atlantic, carrying many passengers. Among them were the following: the ship **Waterloo**, from Liverpool to N Y; the ship **Ann**, Capt Atkinson, from Quebec for Bristol; the ship **Leviathan**, of & from N Y for Liverpool; the ship **Joanna**, from N Y for Dunkirk; the ship **American Lass**, Capt Cousins, from St John's, Newfoundland, for Oporto; the ship **Emma Field**, from Bath, [U S,] for Liverpool; the ship **Gipsey**, Capt Stephensen, from St John's for Greenock. Also, the ship **Arco**, of N Y; the ship **Agnes Hall**, from Montevideo; the ship **Wilberforce**, ship **Syria**, ship **Urgent**, ship **Antilles**, ship **John Wickliffe**, ship **Gov Briggs**, ship **Wm Thompson**, ship **Sarah**, [Peterson,] ship **Ann Tift**, ship **Spectator**, ship **Red Rover**, ship **Richard Watson**, & the ship **Abbe**, of Bridgport. -Balt American

Died: on Oct 9, Sarah Ann Whitney, aged 21 years. Her funeral will be Wed at 3 o'clock, from the residence of her father, Jos Whitney, C st, between 12th & 13th sts.

Died: on Oct 9, Mr Chas Stewart, in his 60th year, a native of Chas Co, Md, but for many years a resident of Gtwn, D C, & for the last 5 years a resident of Wash City. His funeral is this afternoon at 3 o'clock, from his late residence, 11th & R sts.

Died: on Oct 5, in Fauquier Co, Va, aged 3 years, Mary Selden, daughter of Richd M & Edmonia Heath.

Detroit, Oct 9. The steamer **E K Collins**, which left here last night with a large number of passengers for Cleveland, took fire about midnight, near Maiden, & was soon completely enveloped in flames. Among the missing are Mr Dibble, of N Y, Saml Whalon, & Thos Cook, the Pittsburgh railroad agent. [Oct 14th newspaper: List of passengers missing from the **E K Collins**: W H Stone, Berksville, Ohio; ___ Dibble, N Y; S Powell, Cleveland; L Whalen, Cleveland; T Cook, agent Pittsburgh Railroad, Cleveland; Mrs Nelly, waiter's wife; Mrs Watrous & child, Ashtabula, O; a colored man from Va.]

Valuable farm & tobacco plantation for sale: I wish to sell my Farm in Todd Co, Ky, 1 mile from Graysville, Ky, containing 1,328 acres. For terms apply to the undersigned near Turnersville, Robertson Co, Tenn. -G A Washington

WED OCT 11, 1854
Household & kitchen furniture at auction: on Oct 19, at the house on 6th st, between E & F sts, recently occupied by Hon C J Faulkner. -Jas C McGuire, auct

The Rondout [N Y] Courier states that Thos Smith, an Englishman, in the employ of Elihu Brown, of Rondout, engaged in grinding lime, was found dead on Wed of last week entangled in the machinery. He was a sober & industrious man.

Wm Jaqueline Taylor, local editor of the Richmond "Penny Post," died on Oct 9, after a brief illness.

Sister Monica, [Miss Riley of Phil,] of the Augusta Branch of the Institution of St Vincent of Paul in that city, died at Augusta on Tue last of yellow fever.

Mrd: in Groton, Mass, by Rev Edwin Bulkley, John Kendall, of Wash City, to Eliz Lawrence, daughter of Joshua Green, M D. [No date given-current item.]

Mrd: on Jul 30, by Rev Dr Scott, Mr Chas Wheatleigh, of London, England, to Miss Sally J Ansel, of Balt, Md.

Wash Co, D C. I certify that a stray Chickasaw Mare was trespassing upon the premises of Jeremiah T Baden. –Thos C Donn, J P [Owner is to come forward, prove property, pay charges, & take her away. –Jeremiah T Baden, near Benning's Bridge]

THU OCT 12, 1854
Loss of the steamer **Arctic**, with 226 passengers, exclusive of children, 175 employees, a valuable cargo, & heavy mail. It left Liverpool on the Sep 20, many returning from a European tour of pleasure, only 32 are known to have been saved. Account is furnished by Mr Geo H Adams, the express messenger of the Adams & Co, who was on board the steamer. On Sep 27 at 12 o'clock M, in a dense fog. We came in contact with a bark-rigged iron propeller, with black hull: speed of the **Arctic** about 13 knots an hour; shock was slight, damage to the other vessel was frightful. Capt Luce instantly ordered the quarter boats cleared away; the order was countermanded; water was pouring in the bows of the **Arctic**; the stern sunk; panic seized all on board. The barque **Huron**, of St Andrews, N B, Capt A Wall, bound for Quebec, took us on board from 6th boat. By the humane captain of the Huron & Mr Wellington Cameron, a son of the owner, we were received with great kindness, our wounds dressed, fires kindled, & food & clothing provided. On Sep 28 Capt Wall hung out extra lights, fired rockets, & kept a horn blowing, in hopes of falling in with the remainder of the boats. His endeavors were fruitless. On Sep 29 he spoke the ship **Lebanon**, Capt Story, bound for N Y, by whom 18 of our number were taken off, & well treated. Those saved in the 6th boat: taken to Quebec by the **Huron**: Jas Abry, ship's cook; Luke McCarthy, Jos Connolly, Richd Makan, Thos

Conroy, Jas Conner, John Drury, Christian Moran, Jas Ward, & Christopher Callaher, firemen; Thos Wilson, assist engineer; Robt Bryan, David Barry, & Erastus Miller, waiters. Arrived at N Y in the **Lebanon**: Edw Brian, Patrick Mahon, Thos Garland, Patrick Casey, Patrick Tobin, & Dobbin Carnagan, firemen; Thos Brennan, assist engineer; John Connolly, engineer's steward; Thos Stanson, ofcrs steward; Jas Carnagan, porter; Michl McLoughlin, boy; Peter McCabe, picked off the raft, waiter; Wm Nicolls, Trescoa; Henry Jenkins, Scilly Island; Jas Thompson, New Orleans; Capt Paul F Grann, N Y; Geo H Burns, Phil: passengers; Francis Dorian, N Y, 3rd ofcr. Names of persons known to be in the ship's boats: The five boats which may have reached land or been picked up are known to have contained Mr Gurley, 1st ofcr; Thos Wilde, boatswain; Mr Ballam, 2nd ofcr; Mr Graham, 4th ofcr; Mr Moore, N Y, passenger; Mr Rogers, chief engineer; Mr Drown, 1st assist; Mr Walker, 2nd assist; Mr Willet, 3rd assist; Danl Donnelly, John Moran, John Flanagan, & Patrick McCauley, firemen; Mr Dingnel, Mr Kelly, & Mr Timpson, engineers; & a young man named Robinson, under instructions in the engineers' dept, besides sailors & quartermasters. The last seen on the quarter-deck, fastening life-preservers, & who must have sank with the ship or perished on the raft, were Capt Luce & son, Mrs E K Collins, Master Coit Collins, Miss Collins, Mr Brown & family, [connexion of the senior of the firm of Brown, Shipley & Co, Liverpool;] Mr Thomas, importer of hosiery, N Y, Mr Adams, Brooklyn; Mr Bowen, Cincinnati; Mr Chas Springer, Cincinnati; Jas Muirhead, jr, Petersburg, Va; Mr Hewitt, Mrs Hewitt, & daughter, Fredericksburg, Va; Mr Wood, N Y, Mr Ysaki, Mr Schmidt, Miss Murton, Falmouth, England; a nephew of Mr Bloodgood, hotel keeper, Phil, residing in Albany; the Duke de Grammont, of the French Embassy; 2nd steward, wife & child; Annie, a colored girl, & Mary, stewardesses; Miss Jones, Mr Petrie & lady, Stewart Hollin, Wash, D C; J Cook, Opelousas, La, & many more. Mr Comstock, brother to the cmder of the ship **Baltic**, was drowned by the capsizing of a boat whilst being lowered. Another list of persons saved, forwarded by telegraph from Halifax. They are only those saved in the boat of Wm Ballam, the 2nd mate: B C Ward, W Gihon, jre, W P Rathbone, T Hennesey, E M Juss, Dr Maycer, ___ Dupasner, H Moore, J McMath, J Bogart, W Young, W W Gilbert, E Mitchell, Geo Dowdt, C Du Laenit. Crew: John L Crib, purser; Mark Graham, 4th mate; David Reed, Boatswain's mate; Wm Ballam, 2nd mate; John Lagner, 1st assist engineer. Seamen: Allen, Weeks, Lynn, Davis, Humphreys, Tupper, Page, Jones, McGee, McRath, Blake, Joskens, Smith, Thomas, Fleming, & Burley, carpenter. Firemen: Draper, Canon, Egan, Larkin, Mahin, Mercer, & Hardwick, a bed-room servant, & Waddington, Raal, & Baker, waiters. The subjoined is a list of the passengers who left Liverpool in the steamer **Arctic**:

Mr H Arbuckle	Mr Babcock & lady
Mr W Adams	Mr Babcock, jr
Mr G F Allen & family	Mr A Banche
Mr E Burch	Mr Burnes
Mr W B Brown & lady	Mr Brown & family
Miss Maria Brown	Mr A Benedict & lady

Miss Brun
Mr Brady
Mr J Barrill
Mr W Barer
Mrs Bryan
Mr Bedford & friend
Mr G Brown
Miss Benjamin
Mr P Bush & son
Mr W W Bowen
Miss Bronson
Mr Berry
Mr W W Comstock
Mr Christie
Mr D Cannon
Mrs Craige
Mr Culman
Mr Cooke
Mr H Christian & friend
Mr F Copp
Mr S Cuiner
Mrs E K Collins & dght
Mr C Collins
Mr J B Cooke
Mr T Catherwood
Mrs Child & dght
Mr Dupassem & friend
Mr W Day & family
Mr Deigrade, friend & servant
Mr Dawson & lady
Mrs Drew
Mr G Dodds
Mrs Edgecombe & child
Mr Eggers
Mr C Fabricotti
Miss Ford
Mr John Fryer
Mr Ferguson
Mr Frank
Mr Favenscroft
Mr Fass & friend
Mr Grant, lady & child
Mr F W Gale, lady & servant
Mr Gibon

Mr A Garcia
Mr Geiger & lady
Mr P T Grann
Mr A Garcia
Mr Guilliam
Duc deGrammont & servant
Mr E Guynett & family
Mr Guynets & family
Mr E Henry
Mr J B Hogg
Mr Hirsch & family
Mr Hewitt & lady
Mr Hinde & friend
Mr W J Henessey
Mr Hilger & friend
Mr Hollub
Mr J Holbrook
Mrs Mary Hodson & infant
Miss Hayse
Mr Howland & son
Miss Hasard
Mr F Hilbroner
Mr H Hatcher & friend
Mr Jeffords
Mr T C Jones
Mr P Johnson
Mr H Jenkins & lady
Miss Jones
Mr H K Koon
Mr Lenotre & family
Mrs J Lindsay
Miss A Lais
Mr Lochmfranet
Mr J Lynch & lady
Mr Musterd
Miss Jane Murton
Mr C T Mitchell
Miss Mansay
Mr Millville
Mr Morris
Mrs Major, friend, & child
Mr Major & friend
Mr H Moore
Mr G McCracken

Mr J McMath
Mr McGlyrin
Mr McDougal
Mr R Madison
Mr J Muirhead
Miss Mitchell
Mr Mayer
Mr W Nicolas
Mr T Newman & son
Mr Niven
Mr North
Mr S L Noakes
Mr Newbould
Mr C Petrie & lady
Mrs Perrin
Mr G P Pearson
Mr W Perkins
Capt D Pratt & lady
Mr Pratt
Mr Pasive & 4 friends
Mr Patterson
Mr F Rhine
Mr T Robson
Mrs Ridge & friend
Mr Ravenscroft
Mr Robinson
M H Reed
Miss Revell
Mrs Ropes & son
Mr W P Rathbone
Mr M A Stone
Mrs Scott
Miss Stewart
Miss A Stone
Mr T Shuster, lady, & 2 dghts
J G Smith
Miss Smith
Mrs & Miss Stone
Mr Scheibler
Mr E Sandford
Mr C Springer
Mr C St John
Lady J Smith
Mr Schmidt
Mr Sherbourn
Mr Jas Smith
Mr H Thomas
Mr J Thompson
Mr B C Wood
Mr R S Williams & lady
Mr Wallace
Mr Waterman
Mr S M Woodruff
Mr Woodruff & lady
Mr Waring
Mr Winterburne
Mr Wiborg & friend
Mr B C Wood
Mr J Young
Mr D Yoasi
Mr J Zollogi

Mrd: on Oct 10, in St John's Church, Gtwn, by Rev N P Tillinghast, Chas R Sherman, of Wash, to Sally, daughter of the late Peyton B Page, of Va.

Administrator sale of the personal effect of Capt Jos L C Hardy, deceased: by order of the Orphans Court of Wash Co, D C. Auction in front of our store, 6th & Pa ave, on Oct 14, of: wearing apparel, uniform, trunks, gold watch, books, bookcase, swords, 2 second-hand buggies, 1 family carriage, brandy, whiskey, & peach brandy. -Green & Scott, aucts

Mrd: on Oct 5, by Rev Jas H Brown, Mr John T Daniel to Miss Ophelia E Faulkner, both of Va.

Mrd: on Oct 8, by Rev Jas H Brown, Mr Geo J Lynch to Miss Eliz Ann Osborne, all of Wash City.

Dave Thomas, the negro who murdered Mr Wm H Butler in Caroline Co, Md, on Sep 27, has been tried at Denton & convicted of murder in the 2nd degree & the verdict had induced many citizens to threaten to resort to the lynch law on Thu last, the day on which he was found guilty. We received a letter that said a large crowd assembled on Sat night, broke the jail open, took the prisoner out & hung him from a plank which they nailed to a window on the outside, in the 2nd story of the jail bldg, suspending him until life was extinct. His body was cut down & conveyed back to the jail. The mob then released & set at liberty 2 other prisoners, one of whom had been sentenced to the penitentiary. The sheriff had been seized & tied by the mob. This is one of the most daring outrages ever perpetrated in Md. –Balt Sun

Thos Jefferson, Edmund Pendleton, Geo Wythe, Geo Mason, & Ludwell Lee composed the cmte in the Legislature of 1776 which reported the first scheme for colonizing the free negroes of Va. Africa was suggested as the site of the colony.

The Poughkeepsie Herald says that in the Sept Circuit Court of that district the jury returned a verdict against a teacher for $365, for flogging a girl, Frances Gershom, 17 years old, for disobedience. The Judge charged the jury that the teacher stood in the place of a parent, & had a right to correct a pupil, but in so doing must exhibit a parent's feelings. The means used to preserve order should be adapted to the sex, age, & habits of the pupil.

Lost Heiress. Catharine Byrne, alias McGuinness, has become heiress to upwards of L20,000 in Ireland, but she cannot be found. Patrick Byrne, the husband of Catharine McGuinness, was, it appears, sentenced to transportation some years ago at the Antrim assizes. Soon after the execution of the sentence he was left property mentioned by a distant relative. This property was transferred to his son, Thos Byrne, who was then in America, & who has since died, leaving it, with other sums, to his mother; & now the relatives are in a state of great anxiety as to the existence or fate of the interested party.

Died: on Oct 11, Jas Edmonston, in his 35th year. His funeral will take place this afternoon at 3 o'clock, from his late residence on Mass ave.

Died: on Oct 10, in Wash City, Dr Louis R Fechtig, in his 31st year, leaving an afflicted wife & 2 infant children to mourn their great bereavement. Dr Fechtig had but recently removed to this city & settled himself in the practice of medicine.

Died: on Oct 9, in Mobile, of yellow fever, Chas H Carmichael, son of Dr E H & Sarah Carmichael, aged 22 years.

Died: on Oct 3, at Lafayette, Ind, Albert Hebard, the only son of Roswell C & Annie Ellsworth Smith.

Died: on Oct 10, of typhoid fever, Mr Jno S Marll, in his 39th year. His funeral is tomorrow at 2 o'clock, from his late residence on K, between 3rd & 4th sts.

FRI OCT 13, 1854
Lynn, Mass, last week. Chas Johnson, 15 years of age, standing in the doorway of his father's house, was killed when his gun exploded, the whole charge of shot entering his body.

Loss of the steamer **Arctic**: Thos Brennan, oiler, Edw Brian, Patrick Mahon, Patrick Carey, & Patrick Tobin, fireman, survivors of the wreck, who were saved in the same boat with Mr Burns, corroborate his statements. They were saved in the Francis metallic life-boat No 727, with Mr Dorian, 3rd ofcr. Alex'r Grant, fireman, Michl Russell, coal passer, John Riley, coal passer, & several passengers, floated off from the **Arctic** on doors, planks, spars, & other frail rafts, which, it is feared, could not sustain them long amid the heavy sea. Among the families most afflicted are E K Collins & Jas Brown, of Brown Brothers & Co. Mr Collins lost his wife, his only daughter, & a son. Mr Brown has lost his son, W B Brown, with his wife & child; his daughter, Mrs Geo F Allen, with her husband & child; & his daughter, Miss Maria Brown, aged about 18.

Sir Geo Arthur, who distinguished himself in the Napoleon wars & was Govn'r of Jamaica & Lt Govn'r of Canada, died recently in England.

Mr S P Hoover has removed from his old stand to a new & elegant Shoe Store in Iron Hall. The carpenter's work was by Messrs Baldwin & Son; the painter's by Messrs Parker & Spaulding. It is a very handsome establishment. –Wash News

Wash City Ordinances: 1-Act for the relief of Jas Robertson: the sum of $4.21 be paid to him, being the amount of fines & costs imposed on him. 2-Act for the relief of Wm M Ellis & brother: the sum of $56.03 be paid to them for repairs done to the suction of the Union Fire Co.

Obit-died: on Jul 29 last, at Waco Village, McClellan Co, Texas, Dr Jonathan E Jackson, of Millwood, Va, after a few days' illness, of congestion of the brain. He graduated at Princeton College in 1849 & received his medical degree at the Univ of Pa in 1852. He has located himself in Texas for the practice of his profession. His near relatives may console themselves with the assurance that he has departed with the respect & admiration of all who knew him.

Mrd: on Oct 12, at Foundry parsonage, by Rev E P Phelps, Mr Francis W Ashley to Miss Mgt D Gregory, both of Alexandria, Va.

Died: on Oct 11, Wm Frush, of apoplexy, in his 77th year, a native of Balt Co, but for the last 50 odd years a resident of Gtwn, D C. His funeral will be from his late residence, Green st, this afternoon at 3½ o'clock.

Mrs G H Gates has taken the Store 368 east side of 7th st, near I st, for carrying on the Millinery & Fancy Business in all its branches.

Fall Millinery: Miss E E McDonald, successor to Mrs Ann H Clark, will open on Oct 14. Store 3 doors from the Post Ofc, south side of Bridge st, Gtwn.

Official, Dept of State, Wash, Oct 11, 1854. Information received from Thos Savage, in charge of the U S Consulate at Havana, of the death near that place of Peter Hogan, recently belonging to the late American brig **Mary**, of N Y.

SAT OCT 14, 1854

Hon Gideon Tomlinson died at his residence, in Fairfield, Conn, on Oct 8. He was a Rep in Congress from 1819 to 1827; filled the ofc of Govn'r of his State; was in 1830 chosen a Senator in Congress, which station he held until 1837.

Local: we are grieved to hear by the family of Mr Thos Hewitt, of Wash City, that he & his wife were on the steamer **Arctic**, & are believed to be among the lost. He was the son of Thos Hewitt, long Register of Wash City, & both himself & family have numerous relatives & friends here.

Mr Henry A Chouteau, of the banking house of Benoist & Chouteau, at St Louis, died there on Oct 7, after several days' suffering, from the effects of a wound received by the accidental discharge of his gun.

Boston, Oct 13. 1-We have today received from St John's [N F] papers by the **Europa**, which announces the arrival of the steamer **Vesta**, which was in collision with the **Arctic**, but makes no mention of her having rescued 31 of the steamer **Arctic**, as announced by our telegraph from Halifax yesterday. 2-The steamer **Europa** arrived here last night from Halifax and had on board some passengers from the **Arctic**, amongst whom are Mr Mitchell, of Charleston, & Mr DeSaussuer, of New Orleans. They assert that the wife & family of Mr Collins were lost, beyond all doubt, as they were seen on deck when the steamer sunk. So also the family of Mr Brown, who shared the same fate.

Mrd: on Oct 10, at the Church of the Epiphany, by Rev J W French, Dr T C McIntire to Sarah E, daughter of Col John S Williams.

Mrd: on Oct 11, at ***Oakwood***, by Rev Wm M Nelson, John R Mitchell, of Wash, to Fannie Perkins, daughter of Dr John W Gantt, of Albemarle Co, Va.

Mrd: on Oct 11, by Rev G W Samson, Mr Geo W Mitchell, of Annapolis, Md, to Miss Martha A Brayfield, niece of Mr Saml Devaughn, of Wash, D C.

Squatter sovereignty illustrated. The Lawrence Association of Kansas Territory has formed a gov't with a view to the settlement of Kansas by the free people of the North. Today we proceeded to the election of ofcrs under our new constitution, with the following results: for Pres, D C Robinson, of Rochester, N Y; for Vice Pres, F Fuller, Worcester, Mass; for Sec, C S Pratt, Boston, Mass; for Treasurer, L Gates, Worcester; for Reg of Deeds & Claims & Clerk of Court, E D Ladd, Milwaukie, Wisc; for Surveyor, Scarles, Brookfield, Mass; for Marshal, J Grover, Richmond, N Y; for Arbitrators, [any one of whom to hold court,] J Mailey, Lynn, Mass; Taylor, Boston; Brice, Worcester; for Council, Mallory, Lincoln, Willis, Emery, Tappan, Morgan, Haskall, Harrington, Johnson, & Cracklin.

Rev Thos Chilton, formerly of Ky, died recently at Montgomery, Texas. In 1819-20 he was a member of the Ky Legislature; in 1821 he was a clergyman; about 1824-5 he was elected clerk of the Ky Senate; in 1827 he was elected to Congress in the Hardin district of Ky, & re-elected in 1829; & at the end of his term, in 1835, he retired. He devoted the remainder of his life to preaching, lastly in Texas.
--Frankfort Commonwealth

For rent: the residence of the late Gen Towson, F & 17th st. Inquire on the premises.

MON OCT 16, 1854
Mrs Fishback, of Cincinnati, the wife of Judge Fishback, of that place, was injured last week by the explosion of camphene gas, from the effects of which she died. Is it not surprising that, in despite of the almost daily record of disasters from camphene, people will persist in its use?

Household & kitchen furniture at auction: on Oct 18, at the residence of C Wierman, on 15th st, between N Y ave & H st: superior parlor & chamber furniture.
-Green & Scott, aucts

Mr Parker, who lives on the Blue Ridge, south of Arnold's Vally, Va, accidentally shot his brother a few days ago, while fixing his rifle. Both were young men of families.

Household & kitchen furniture at auction: on Oct 17, at the late residence of Alex'r Forrest, deceased, on N Y ave, between 6th & 7th sts. -Green & Scott, aucts

The Louisville Journal announces the death of Rev John L Waller, LL D, who has long labored in the cause of virtue as the editor of a religious paper published in that city. He was 44 years old.

Among the passengers lost in the steamer **Arctic**: 1-Prof Henry Reed, a native of Phil, a grandson of Gen Reed, of Revolutionary memory, & brother of W B Reed, Atty Gen of Pa. He graduated at an early age at the Univ of Pa, & after legal study was admitted to the bar. Mr Reed was on his return to his native city. He was married to a grand-daughter of Bishop White, & was 55 years of age. 2-Edw Sandford: was a native of Seneca Co; brother of the late Lewis H Sandford, Assist Vice Chancellor & afterwards Judge of the N Y Superior Court. He became the law partner of John L Graham, of this city. Mr Sanford sailed in the packet ship **Mercury**, of the Havre line, on Jul 2 last, with his wife & 6 children, the eldest of whom is about 17 years of age. He left his wife & children in Paris, where he had leased a house for 3 years, for the purpose of giving his children a continental education. On the voyage to Europe the ship **Mercury** encountered an iceberg, which seriously injured that vessel, & endangered the lives of the passengers. The last suit in which Mr Sanford was engaged he was associated with the late N B Blunt, & took leave of him in Court on his departure for Europe. Mr Sandford was about 45 years of age. 3-F Catherwood: was extensively known as an artist of great merit: he was the painter of the panoramas of Jerusalem, Lima, & other cities. He was the companion of the celebrated traveler, the late John L Stephens, on his visit to Central America. 4-Abner Benedict: was a distinguished lawyer of this city: was a native of Conn, & was on his return from an excursion undertaken for recreation from the active business of life. 5-Mr Jacob Morris: a resident of Phil; member of the Board of Managers of the Pa Institution of the Blind. 6-The Duc de Grammont: a young French nobleman of distinguished family, who was dispatched to this country as an attaché to the French embassy at Wash. More than 6 months ago he was appointed to the post. He was but 21 years old. 7-Mr Mahlon Day: one of the oldest printers & publishers in N Y, & was highly respected. His wife & daughter were with him on board the **Arctic**. [The steamer **Arctic** was built in N Y by Wm H Brown: she measured 3,500 tons register & cost $700,000.]

+

Mr Beverly C Wood, who was one of the passengers on board the **Arctic**, was the 3rd son of the late Silas Wood, of N Y, who has found a grave in the waters, his 2 brothers having been previously drowned in the Mississippi river.

+

Intelligence received of the rescue of Capt Luce, the noble cmder of the unfortunate steamer **Arctic**, with several passengers & crew, by the ship **Cambria**, which arrived at Quebec on Fri. Saved were: J C Luce, late capt; Geo F Allen, of N Y, Jas Smith, of Miss; Fred'k May, all passengers; & J A Govet Francois, of the ship **Vesta**. The following firemen, belonging to the **Arctic**: Patrick Noran, Alex Grant, Michl Russell, John Riley, & John Patterson.

+

Forty-five persons who were saved from the wreck of the steamer **Arctic** in the 2 boats under the charge of Wm Baalham, the 2nd mate, 38 arrived at Boston from Halifax on Thu. The passengers agree that Mrs Collins & her son & daughter were drowned. Indeed, it does not appear that a single female escaped.

Explosion on Fri in the distillery of Messrs Furman & Co, at Wmbsburg, N Y: Wm Real, engineer, was killed; Patick Baglin, a fireman, was fatally hurt.

Murder in N Y: John Gilforgs, while going home through 9th ave, was shot by an unknown German, who mortally wounded him & escaped.

Mrd: on Oct 10, at St James Church, Richmond, Va, by Rev Geo Cummins, Lt Jas P Roy, U S Army, to Miss Kate S, eldest daughter of David Bridge.

Mrd: on Oct 4, at **Rosemont**, by Rev F N Whittle, Isaac Tyson, of Balt, to Miss Fannie H, eldest daughter of Howard F Thornton, of Clarke Co, Va.

Died: on Oct 13, in Wash City, Virginia, wife of Wm Collins, in her 27th year.

Died: on Oct 14, Estelle, youngest child of P Louis & Louisa M Rodier, aged 10 months.

Died: on Oct 7, in Bennington, Vt, Gen Henry Robinson, in his 67th year. Gen Robinson was extensively & favorably known, & leaves many sincere friends in Wash City to sympathize with his relatives in their loss.

Pestilence at Savannah: To the long list of faithful physicians who have fallen in the discharge of their duties to the sick since the epidemic we add another worthy name Dr Cullen. Wildman, Wells, Harris, Ellis, Hartridge, Schley, Gordon, Brantly, Saussy, 9 noble spirits, have been joined by a tenth, Dr P W Cullen. He was a native of Columbia, S C; practiced a short time in Charleston; from that place he came to Savannah 2 years since. His age could not have been more than 30.

TUE OCT 17, 1854
Mrd: on Oct 15, in Wash City, by Rev G W Samson, Mr Wm James to Miss Mgt Ballantine.

Mrd: on Oct 12, at Beverly, Va, Miss E B Frame to Mr A R H Ranson, both of Jefferson Co, Va.

Died: on Oct 16, Geo W Thompson, in his 43rd year. His funeral will be today at 3 P M, from his late residence, corner of L st south & 3rd st west.

The official term of Govn'r Brigham Young, of Utah Territory, expired on Sep 29. His successor has not been agreed upon. Young will not be re-appointed, but it is well known that no man not a Mormon could govern that lawless & impious community without the material aid of one of two well appointed regiments. The Sec of the Territory, A W Babbit, formerly delegate in Congress, will direct affairs until the further action of the Pres.

Hon Jared Perkins, a Rep from Mass in the last Congress, died at his residence in Nashua on Sat last.

Archbishop Kenrick, of Balt, was amongst the passengers who sailed from N Y for Liverpool, on Sat, in the steamer **Atlantic**. We learn that he was accompanied by Rev Mr Foley, Rev Dr O'Connor, & Rev Dr Timon, all of whom are going to Rome, by invitation of the Pope, to attend the meeting of Bishops to be held at the close of Nov next. The administration of the diocese during the absence of the Archbishop is vested in the Rev Fr L'Homme & the Rev H B Coskery.

Mr Guynet, a French importer, who lost his life in the steamer **Arctic**, is supposed to have had with him diamonds & other jewelry to the amount of $150,000.

WED OCT 18, 1854
Household & kitchen furniture at auction: on Oct 31, by deed of assignment for the benefit of his creditors, made by Thos B Davis, to the subscriber, as trustee: at the residence of said Davis, next to the corner of south C & 13½ sts west, on the Island. -John L Smith, trustee -Green & Scott, aucts

On Sat last Nathl Jellison was killed in Lewiston, Maine, by a stone thrown from a blast a quarter mile off.

On Tue the venerable Pres of Magdalen College, Oxford, Martin Jos Routh, D D, entered his 100th year. Dr Routh, on the death of Dr Geo Horne, in the year 1791, was elected Pres of Magdalen College.

Jas Moran, another one of the parties injured in the late riots at New Orleans, has died of his wounds. He makes the 8th victim.

Danl Chandler, of Concord, N H, has been sentenced to the State prison for life, on conviction of having altered a switch which caused a train of cars to be thrown from the track of the Concord railroad.

Mr Wm W Story, son of the late Justice Story, now in Italy, has finished a statue of his father, on which he has been for some time engaged. Ths statue has been shipped from Italy for America. It has been pronounced by judges who have seen it to be a perfect work of art.

Govn'r Seymour has appointed M Alex'r Vattemare a 3rd commissioner to represent N Y at the Paris Exhibition in 1855.

A judiciary cmte of San Francisco reported in favor of paying Mrs Greenhow $10,000, as compensation for the loss of her husband, who was killed by falling from one of the bad sidewalks of the city.

Wash City Ordinances: 1-Act for the relief of Saml Cook: the sum of $5 be paid to him for grading south G st, between 4th & 5th sts. 2-Act for the relief of C Baker: the sum of $42.50 be paid to him for overpaying for a license to keep a tavern.

Valuable farm for sale: the subscriber is desirous to sell his excellent Farm: contains 186 acres; has a 2 story house, built in 1852, barn & other out-bldgs, lies on the Gtwn & Rockville turnpike, 6 miles from Wash City. –S C Denton, Tennallytown

Mrd: on Oct 17, in Wash City, by Rev Stephen P Hill, at the 10th st Baptist Church, Mr Jos Knowles Lewis to Miss Virginia Clarke, all of Wash.

Died: on Oct 17, Mary, consort of Edw Cowling, in her 58th year, a native of Cornwall, England, but for the last 22 years a resident of this District. Her funeral will take place this afternoon at 3 o'clock, from her late residence, on G st, between 13 & 14th sts.

Died: on Oct 17, Mary Jane, wife of A H Brown, of Wash City, & eldest daughter of the late A B Murray, of Balt.

THU OCT 19, 1854
European Correspondence: Paris, Oct 2, 1854. 1-The Siecle announces the sudden death of M Auguste Jullien, one of its editors. The event took place yesterday just as he was about to begin his day's labor. He was the son of M Jullien de Paris, who was well known as the secretary of Robespierre, as a writer of merit. 2-M Pagnerre, the well-known publisher, died yesterday at St Ouen-l'Aumone, near Pontoise. He was Sec-Gen of the Provisional Gov't in 1848. 3-Fifty <u>Sisters of Charity</u> & three <u>Lazarist Missionaries</u> left Marseilles on the 26th in the steamer **Gange** for Constantinople. Gen Espinasse also left in the same vessel.

Orphans Court of Wash Co, D C. In the case of Jesse T Peck, adm of Amos Bateman, deceased: the adm & Court have appointed Nov 14 next for the final settlement of said estate, of the assets in hand. –Ed N Roach, Reg/o wills

Death of a Revolutionary patriot. One of the few remaining participants in the American Revolution closed his earthly career last week. Dr Wm Hale, of Hollis, N H, died on Tue, at the advanced age of 92 years. He joined the American army in 1777; was then a medical student, though but 15 years of age; continued in the army connected with the medical staff for 3 years; for two-thirds of a century he was an esteemed physician in his native place.

Moses Stebbins, of South Deerfield, Mass, has an apple tree which the Amherst Express says was planted one hundred years ago. It is 18 feet in circumference, & bears a sweet apple called the belly-bound.

Died: on Oct 18, Miss Virginia A Howell, in her 16th year. Her funeral will take place this afternoon at 3 o'clock, from the residence of her mother, on 9th, between G & H sts.

Died: on Oct 12, at Thomaston, Me, Mrs Lucy F K Thatcher, in her 87th year. She was the daughter of Maj Gen Henry Knox, of the Revolutionary army, & the mother of Lt H K Thatcher, of the U S Navy. She died where she would have chosen to die-in her own house; the noble old mansion erected by her venerable parent, Gen Knox, the friend & intimate associate of Washington. That elegant old house, with all its Revolutionary treasures, in which her parents breathed their last, was her home during the latter years of her widowhood; & to her, as the last surviving child, of Gen Knox, were all its treasures entrusted. –Boston Traveller

Died: on Oct 12, at Brooklyn, Henry Waller, civil engineer, of Baton Rouge, La, eldest son of the late Henry Waller, of Sing Sing, N Y.

Troy Budget of Oct 16. Arthur C Nelson, the late Keesville postmaster, who had been confined in jail her to await trial before the U S District Court, which opens this week in Albany, on charge of robbing the mails, made his escape last night with the aid of a small saw & rope. He left a note directing that the effects he left behind should be addressed by express to his friends in Plattsburgh, who, upon your presenting a bill for my expenses with you, they will no doubt pay.

Wm Richards, one of the Mormon saints, lately deceased in Utah, leaves 20 widows emancipated by his death.

Maj Lee, of the 8th Infty, U S Army, was not long since killed on the way from **Ringgold Barracks** to the Presidio, in Texas.

Anna Howard has recovered a verdict of $13,000 damages in a suit in the Hudson, [N Y] county court against Wm K Hall, Superintendent of the Harlem Railroad, for breach of promise of marriage. [Dec 19th newspaper: Wm K Hall, at that time superintendent of the Harlem railroad, has applied for the benefit of the insolvent act, submitted to imprisonment in the Hudson Co jail, N J, & recently obtained a discharge from his debts, by means of which he escapes the penalty & leaves the young lady without redress. –Cincinnati Advertiser]

Jas Pollick, aged about 50, who occasionally assisted the hostler at F McKeown's hotel, Phil met an awful death on Sat from the bite of a vicious horse. He had been warned not to go near the horse, but he went in the stall & the animal made a sudden attack upon him; seizing him by the throat & completely severed his windpipe.

FRI OCT 20, 1854
Hugh A Garland, a prominent member of ths St Louis Bar, died on Oct 14. He was a native of Nelson Co, Va, & represented Mecklenburg Co in the Legislature several years. He was elected Clerk of the House of Reps in Dec, 1838. In 1850 he published a Life of John Randolph, which passed through several editions. He leaves many relatives & friends in Va.

Wm S McKee, one of the editors of the St Louis Democrat, died on Oct 13.

Yellow fever has appeared in Washington, La, & many citizens have fled, although there have been only 3 deaths. Col Fitzpatrick, Register of the Land Ofc at Opelousas & a Lt in the Mexican war, was the first victim. It also appeared in the parish of Plaquemine, & Dr Hay & 9 others have died.

Notice: I hereby caution & forewarn all persons from crediting any person or persons whomsoever on my account, as I am determined to pay no such accounts unless my written order is produced with the account. Given under my hand Oct 19, 1854. -Levi Pumphrey

Buffalo Republic of Tue: Mr Pardon Teft, of Eden, called upon us this morning to tell us of the fatal accident which occurred in that town yesterday. About 40 citizens of Eden Valley were removing an old bridge over 18 mile creek, to substitute with a new one, when the bridge gave way. Deacon John Carter & Curtis Hubbell, two of the most prominent citizens of that town, were fatally injured and died soon after.

Washington Sentinel: we all regretted much that one fine young man belonging to the steamer **Arctic** was not saved. His name is Stewart Holland, & his post was at the gun, firing signals. He kept firing the gun till the vessel sunk. We saw him in the very act of firing as the vessel disappeared below the waves. He was the son of the Doorkeeper of one of the Houses of Congress. –P Tobin's Account

Died: on Oct 11, at Salem, the residence of his father, of typhoid fever, Abner Floweree, in his 27th year. Intelligent, enterprising, & public-spirited, he was widely known & largely esteemed in the county. He was the much-loved son & brother.

SAT OCT 21, 1854
Household & furniture at auction: at the house over Mr Muller's Drug store, on Pa ave, between 4½ & 6th sts. -Green & Scott, aucts

By order of the Orphans' Court of PG Co, the undersigned as guardian of Oliver H Perry, will sell at public sale, at the late residence of Mrs Esther Y Ferguson, near the **Long Old Fields**, in said county, on Nov 21, 8 likely negroes, men, women, & children. Terms of sale cash. –Wm F Berry, guardian of O H Perry

Is Friday an unlucky day? On Friday:
Aug 31, 1492, Christopher Columbus sailed on his great voyage of discovery.
Oct 12, 1492 he discovered land.
Jan 4, 1493, he sailed on his return to Spain, which if he had not reached in safety the happy result would never have been known.
Mar 15, 1498, he arrived at Palas in safety.
Nov 22, 1493, he, though unknown to himself, discovered the continent of America.
Mar 5, 1496, Henry VII, of England gave to John Cabot his commission which led to the discovery of North America. This is the first American State paper in England.
Sep 7, 1555, Melendez founded St Augustine, the oldest settlement in the U S by more than 40 years.
Nov 10, 1620, the ship **May Flower** with the Pilgrims made the harbor of Provincetown; & on the same day signed that august compact the forerunner of our glorious present Constitution.
Dec 22nd, the Pilgrims made their final landing at Plymouth Rock.
Feb 22, Geo Washington, the father of American freedom, was born.
Jun 17, Bunker Hill was seized & fortified.
Oct 7, 1777, the surrender of Saratoga was made, which had such power & influence in inducing France to declare for our cause.
Sep 22, 1780, the treason of Arnold was laid bare, which saved us from destruction.
Jul 5, 1776, the motion of Congress was made by John Adams, seconded by Richd Henry Lee, that the United Colonies were, & of right ought to be, free & independent. -Woonsocket Patriot.

Mrd: on Oct 19, by Rev Mr Stanley, Norval Wilson Burchel, of Alexandria, Va, to Miss Sarah F Landon, of Wash City.

Mrd: on Jul 9, by Rev Mr Doll, Mr J W Rowan to Mrs Agnes McGill, both of Wash City.

Mrd: on Oct 12, in N Y C, by Rev Edwin Harwood, Rector of the Church of the Incarnation, Lewis Johnson Davis, of Wash, D C, to Mgt Jane, daughter of Chas M Keller, of N Y.

Died: on Oct 18, at the residence of her son, Dr R W Wheat, near Dumbires, Va, Mrs Rachel Wheat, aged 84 years. She was for many years a resident of Wash City, & for more than half a century a worthy & devoted member of the Methodist Church.

Orphans Court of Wash Co, D C. In the case of Ruth A Peaco & John W Chew, excs of Wm H Peaco, deceased, the excs & Court have appointed Nov 7 next for the final settlement of the estate with the assets in hand. –Ed N Roach, Reg/o wills

C H Munck, Practical Gunsmith, Dealer in Guns & Pistols, has removed his establishment from D st to Pa ave, opposite the Nat'l Hotel.

In Equity: Alfred Shaw & Julia his wife & Mary Welsh, against Catharine & Mgt Welsh. The parties above named & David Welsh, guardian & also trustee, are to appear on Nov 28, in the City Hall, Wash, & I shall state the accounts of the said trustee & guardian, & ascertain the distributable shares in the trust fund; when & where they & all parties are hereby required to attend. –W Redin, trustee

A dispatch from Dr McRae, dated at York Factory on Aug 4, has been received by the Govn'r of the Hudson Bay Territory, narrating the discovery of the remains of Sir John Franklin & his unfortunate company. It is stated that they were starved to death in the spring of 1850, to the northwest of Fox River. [Dec 6th newspaper: The Journal of Commerce says: "Dr Kane was when last heard from at *Smith's Sound*, & it is improbable that any of his party should have since then found their way down to the Back river, where Sir John Franklin is supposed to have perished. We fear that the story will prove to be a distorted version of the account of Dr Rae, originating in the substitution for his name of that of Dr Kane."]

Circuit Court of Wash Co, D C-in Equity. Wm E Thursby, John Thos Thursby, Robt Alfred Thursby, Caroline Thursby, & David Uriah Thursby, vs. Martha Ann Thursby, Miriam L Thursby, Eliz Verlinda Thursby, & Sarah Thursby. The above cause is to report whether the western most feet front of lot 7 in square 75, in Wash, can be specifically divided between the above parties, heirs at law & widow of Wm Thursby, deceased, & whether it would be for the advantage of said parties to have the same sold. The said parties are to appear at the Auditor's room, City Hall, to be heard regarding the premises, on Nov 27. –Walter S Cox, special auditor
[Dec 8th newspaper: W Redin, trustee, reported having sold on Nov 24, 1854, the westernmost 23 feet front part of lot 7 in square 75 in Wash City, leaving that front on the public street, with the old frame bldg thereon, to Alfred Wetherill, for $650, & the purchaser has complied with the terms of the sale. –Jno A Smith, clerk]

Circuit Court of Wash Co, D C, as Court of Chancery, Oct Term, 1854. Jeremiah Williams & wife & others, vs Mary Rhodes & others. John Marbury, the trustee, reports that he has sold lot 14 in square 224, in Wash City, D C, part of the estate of Ann Stewart, deceased, containing 4,618 square feet, to A E Pacetti for $4,618.75; & lot 15 in same square, part of the same estate, to Robt Cruit, the same containing 5,370.10 square feet, for $5,102.30: the purchasers have severaly complied with the terms of sale. –Jno A Smith, clerk

Circuit Court of D C : Edw Chapman & others, cmplnts, against Henry H Dodge & others, dfndnts. In the matter of the estate of Mgt Davidson: Edw Chapman, trustee, reported the sale of part of the real estate of Mgt Davidson, deceased: sold, to wit: lot 1 in square 372, to R & L Els, for $2,815.65; lots 2, 3, & 4 in square 372, to J Bryan, for $4,332.79; lot 9 in square 372, to S L Harris, for $1,121.33; lot 17 in square 372, to Henry Johnson, for $1.612.69; lots 5, 6, & 10 in square 373, to J Bryan, for $2,931.63; lot 21 in square 316, to J W Simms, for $742.50; lots 22 & 23 in square

316, to Mitchell & Reynolds, for $1,428.75; lot 24 in square 316, to H E Woodbury, for $708.75; lot 2 in square 342, to C W Bennet, for $1,025; lot 10 in square 342, to Mitchell & Reynolds, for $757.64; lot 5 in square 340, to H G O'Neal, for $847.50; lot 17 in square 342, to G Hartwell, for $442.73; lots 36 & 37 in square 367, to Sampson Simms, for $321.10; lot 10 in square 315, to H C Neale, for $656.78; lots 12 thru 15 in square 281, to L V Dovilliers, for $2,210.50; lots 8 & 9 in square 283, to N Vedder, for $1,275; lots 41, 42, & 43, in square 248, to J C G Kennedy, for $2,752.82½; lots 44 & 45 in square 248, to Mitchell & Reynolds, for $1,764; lot 46 in square 248, to J C G Kennedy, for $886.32½; lots 14 thru 17 in square 385, to W B H Brown, for $7,846.14; lot 18 in square 385, to Alex'r McIntire, for $1,903.83; lots 19 & 20 in square 385, to Allen Pollock, for $3,714.33: the several purchasers have complied with the terms of sale. -Jno A Smith, clerk

Circuit Court of Wash Co, D C: Edw Chapman & others, cmplnts, vs Henry H Dodge & others, dfndnts. In the matter of the estate of Eliz A Chapman, Edw Chapman, the trustee, sold the part of the real estate of Eliz A Chapman, deceased: Lot 1 in square 213 to Edw Swann for $664.59; lot 5 in square 215 to N W Burchell for $606.53; lot 2 in square 248 to D Breed for $2,388.75; lot 23 in square 248 to N Callan for $673.90; lot 10 in square 281 to J A M Duncanson for $552.62; lot 12 in square 315 to John L Kidwell for $700.56; lots 4 & 5 in square 367 to Edw Swann for $735; lot 10 in square 372 to S L Harris for $1,168.57; & the several purchasers have complied with the terms of the sale. –Jno A Smith, clerk

MON OCT 23, 1854

Rev John Bapst, a Catholic clergyman of Bangor, Maine, who was tarred & feathered at Ellsworth, Maine, on Oct 14, has recovered from his injuries. He was stopping at the house of Mr Kent, which was surrounded & broken into about midnight by a crowd of rowdies. Mr Bapst fled to the cellar, but was dragged out, stripped, & rode on a rail, during which cruel treatment he was robbed of his watch & wallet. He was finally carried to a shipyard & there tarred & feathered & abused. His persecutors then left him alone to suffer or to find his way to Mr Kent's house. The immediate cause of the outrage was the fact that Mr Bapst had been connected with a controversy respecting the right of the authorities to enforce the reading of a book in school on the part of scholars whose parents objected to it. The citizens of Maine will doubtless condemn this Ellsworth outrage almost unanimously. [Oct 25th newspaper: Several Protestant citizens of Bangor, Maine, have presented Rev Mr Bapst with a valuable gold watch, as an evidence of their regret for the disgraceful outrage.]

Household & kitchen furniture at auction: by order of the Orphans Court of Wash Co, D C. Also, two first rate work horses, carts, & harness, & superior milch cows: on Oct 26, at the residence of the late Jabez Travers. -Jas C McGuire, auct

Groceries, liquors & hardware at auction on Oct 25, at the Grocery Store of Mrs Hall, at 3rd & H sts. -Green & Scott, aucts

Geo Thompson, of Grafton, Mass, was killed by the accidental discharge of his gun on Tue afternoon, while on a hunting excursion.

Rev Saml K Jenning, M D, died at Balt on Thu at the age of 84 years. Few men were more generally known in the Methodist Church. He was one of the founders of the Methodist Protestant Church, & for a number of years held a professorship in the Phil Medical College.

Saml Dunham, a soldier in the Revolutionary war, died at Mansfield, Ct, on Oct 12, at the age of 100 years & 20 days. He was the oldest Revolutionary pensioner in the State, & possibly in the U S. Mr Dunham leaves 2 brothers, one of whom is 95 & the other 97 years of age. Both of them were soldiers of the Revolution, & one of them, to the disgrace of the country, is now the inmate of an almshouse.

Among the passengers by the ship **Africa** were the wife & daughter of Rev Dr Jonas King, the well-known missionary of the American Board at Athens, Greece.

Mrd: on Oct 17, at Gtwn, D C, by Rev B F Brooke, Mr D W Edmonston, jr, to Miss Marion J Daw, of Gtwn, D C.

Died: on Oct 14, at the residence of Dr Bayne, in PG Co, T S Hoxton, M D, in his 25th year. Dr H graduated at the Univ of Md in the session of 1851; returned home & entered upon the duties of the practice. Society will long deplore his loss.

Jos Huggins, Jeweller, 214 Pa ave, 2 doors above Willard's Hotel, is now selling off his entire stock, very low for cash.

Orphans Court of Wash Co, D C. Letters of administration on the personal estate of Mary E Gates, late of Wash Co, deceased. –John N Gates, adm

TUE OCT 24, 1854
Household & kitchen furniture at auction: on Oct 31, at the residence of Mrs Offley, 285 B st, between N J ave & 1st st. -Jas C McGuire, auct

Saml Drake died on Oct 17, near Louisville, Ky, at age 87. He was the pioneer of the Western drama. He was the father of those well known performers, Alex'r & Julia Drake. He was himself an actor of no ordinary claims to distinction. He was born in England Nov 8, 1768 & emigrated to N Y in the middle of his life. Later he emigrated to Ky with his talented family, & became the successful manager of reputable theatrical companies in Louisville, Lexington, Frankfort, & Cincinnati.

Cornelius Moran, about 14, was instantly killed at Phil yesterday by being run over by a train of cars, when he attempted to leap on the cars while they were in motion.

Died: on Oct 23, in Wash City, Spencer, the only child of Archibald & Ruth Roane, aged 23 months. His funeral is this day at 3 o'clock, from Mrs Gassaway's, D st.

Methodist Metropolitan Church: the corner-stone of this edifice, on the corner of 4½ & C sts, was performed yesterday: prayer by Rev L F Morgan; Scripture lessons by Rev C C Phelps; address by Rev Bishop Simpson; collection under the superintendence of Rev H Slicer; corner-stone laid by Dr W B Magruder, Grand Master of Masons for D C; & doxology & benediction by Rev Jas H Brown.

Died: on Oct 22, Wm Hunter, of Wash City, in his 87th year. He was born at Brunswick, N J, & spent his youth mainly in England, after having been captured by a French man-of-war, & with his parents, carried into France. Being left an orphan at an early age in a foreign land, he was placed in a printing ofc, where he served the usual period & acquired a knowledge of the printing art. In 1793 he returned to the U S & established a French & American paper in Phil, & became associated in business with Matthew Carey, with whom his friendship continued uninterrupted to the dying hour of that useful man. In 1795 Mr Hunter removed to Washington, Pa, & established the Telegraph. In 1797 he married Anne Morrison, of Bedford, Pa, who lived to mourn his loss. He removed to Washington, Ky, where he established the Mirror, removing subsequently to Frankfort, Ky, he published the Palladium. Early in Gen Jackson's administration Col Hunter removed to Wash City, & in 1829 received an appointment in the 4th Auditor's ofc, which he retained til his death. His funeral will take place this afternoon, from his late residence on 12th st, between H & I sts. [No time given.]

Upon a requisition of the Govn'r of Md, Christian & Chas Henry Glantz, charged with the crime of assaulting with intent to kill Mr E W Duvall, near Bladensburg, will be removed from Washington to PG Co for trial

Orphans Court of Wash Co, D C. The estate of Azariah Fuller. On the application of Geo Lowry, administrator of said Azariah Fuller, it is ordered by the Court that Nov 11 next be appointed for making distribution of the assets in the hands of the administrator among the creditors of the deceased. –Ed N Roach, Reg/o wills

Orphans Court of Wash Co, D C. Letters testamentary on the personal estate of Geo W Thompson, late of Wash Co, deceased. –Joanna M Thompson, excx

WED OCT 25, 1854
St Louis, Oct 22. The Santa Fe mail has arrived at Independence. Mr R H Weightman, who recently killed Mr F X Aubrey in a personal re-encounter, has been acquitted of the charge of murder.

Mr Edwin Williams, the well-known statist & geographer, died at his lodgings in N Y on Sat, aged 57 years. He was the editor of Wms' Annual Register & the Statesman's Manual. He was a native of Norwich, Conn, to which place his remains were conveyed for interment. His disease was cholera, which is said to have been superinduced by eating an unwholesome oyster on Fri night. -N Y Com Adv

A little boy, between 3 & 4 years old, son of Mr McDermott, on D st, was run over yesterday by a baggage wagon, at 7th & D sts, & severely hurt.

Died: on Oct 23, Dr Richd O Cochrane, only surviving brother of Jno T Cochrane, of Wash City, in his 31st year. His funeral will be from the residence of his brother-in-law, Mr Jas A Magruder, West st, Gtwn, this day at 3½ o'clock.

Died: on Oct 23, after a lingering illness of 4 months, Agricol Favier, in his 57th year. His funeral will be from his late residence today, at 10 A M.

Wm Linkins has taken the store adjoining Saml Duvall's grocery store, Pa ave, in which he designs keeping a stock of fresh meats, vegetables, & fruit. He will continue the butchering business as heretofore.

Wash Corp: elected Trustees of the Public Schools:
J F Polk
C W Bennett
J P Dickinson
Peter F Bacon
Wm Lord
T J Magruder
Grafton D Hanson
Wm Dixon
Chas W Davis
S York Atlee
John Knight
Peter M Pearson

Boots & Shoes. I have this day associated with me my son, Wm T Griffin. The business will hereafter be conducted under the name of Griffin & Son.
–Thos B Griffin

Orphans Court of Wash Co, D C. Letters of administration, will the will annexed, on the personal estate of Eliza C Lyles, late of Wash Co, deceased. –Thos Marshall, adm, will annexed

THU OCT 26, 1854

Household effects & furniture at auction: on Oct 28, at the auction rooms, removed from residence of Hon Gerret Smith for convenience of sale. -Jas C McGuire, auct

Household & kitchen furniture at auction: on Nov 1, at the residence of Dr Arthur, on Pa ave, between 12th & 13th sts. -Jas C McGuire, auct

Household & kitchen furniture at auction: on Nov 1, at the residence of Wm Flye, on K, between 8th & 9th sts. -Green & Scott, aucts

Household & kitchen furniture at auction: on Nov 2, at the residence of Mrs Gibbons, on Indiana ave, between 1st & 2nd sts. -Jas C McGuire, auct

Naval Intelligence: Private letter from Hong Kong: Cmder Ringgold, of the U S Surveying Expedition, has been deemed incapacitated for duty on account of mental aberration, & is now bound home on board one of the storeships of the squadron. He is a brother of the gallant Major Ringgold who fell in Mexico. Capt Rodgers, of the ship **Vincennes**, succeeds to the command of the Surveying Squadron. [Oct 28th newspaper: On Jul 22 Cmder Ringgold was sitting up & talking with Dr Parker. He was then just convalescent; had been delirious in his sickness, & then showed occasional symptoms of a wandering mind, though his conversation was for the most part rational.]

The whole number of the company in Sir John Franklin's two ships **Erebus** & **Terror**, when they left England, May 24, 1845, nearly 10 years since, was 138. These, it is probable, have all perished. The names of the ofcrs are thus stated:

The ship **Erebus**:	The ship **Terror**:
Sir John Franklin, capt	Richd Crozier, capt
Jas Fitzjames, cmder	Lts: Edw Little
Lts: Graham Gore	Geo H Hodgson
Hon T D LeVesconie	John Irving
Jas Wm Fairholme	Total: 68 ofcrs & crew

Francis Burt, Govn'r of the Territory of Nebraska, died on Oct 18, at Bellevue City, which place he had only reached on Oct 6. He had but lately resigned the post of Third Auditor of the Treasury to accept the new honor in the new Territory.

Sing Sing Chronicle: Miss Eliz Valentine, a maiden lady, residing near Hunt's Bridge, Westchester Co, & much respected, died on Tue last, suddenly. Heart disease is supposed to have been the cause of her death.

Mrs Mgt Lenox, widow of the late Peter Lenox, has given $1,000 to the Catholic Orphan Asylum of Wash City.

Orphans Court of Wash Co, D C. Letters of administration on the personal estate of Jas Edmonston, late of Wash Co, deceased. –Chas Edmonston, adm

Died: on Oct 6, in Gtwn, after a brief but painful illness, in his 63rd year, Francis Lowe Darnall, of PG Co, formerly of Anne Arundel Co, Md, leaving a wife & large family to deplore his death.

Died: Oct 25, after a lingering illness, Jas Quinn, in his 15th year. His funeral will be from the house of Mr Thos Gallagher, on 4th, between G & H sts, today at 3:30 P M.

Wash City Ordinance: 1-Act to pay G W Slatford for repairing the sewer on 6th st west: sum of $87. 2-Act for the relief of Capt Jos Smoot: to pay him $425, to refund to him the cost of replacing the stone wall, coping, railing, & steps, which were removed by the authority of the Corp in regarding K st, between 12th & 13th sts.

Sudden deaths at N Y, Oct 25: by cholera, superinduced by eating oysters: John H Carnell, cashier of the Mechanics' Bank; Jas Foster, jr, agent of a Line of Packets; & Morris Davidson, counselors-at-law. They all died after a few hours' illness.

FRI OCT 27, 1854
Relics of the Franklin expedition: the crest & motto of Lt Fairholme, of the vessel **Terror**. Among the silver forks recovered from the vessel **Esquimaux** is one bearing the initials H D S G, which is doubtless those of H D S Goodsie, Assist Surgeon of the expedition; & that bearing the initials of A McD, doubtless belonged to Surgeon A McDonald, who was also one of the companions of Franklin.
–Balt American

Miss Martha Parker, in an action for slander against a man named Spencer, tried last week in the Oneida [N Y] Circuit Court, obtained a verdict for $2,500 damages.

Cholera in Martinsburg, Va: deaths there since the re-appearance of cholera.
Oct 17: Andrew Hagerman' child; Jane, colored woman of P C Pendleton, at S Alburtis'.
Oct 18: Washington Kroesen; Mrs Anna C Hoe, consort of John B Hoge; Mrs Eliza Baker, consort of Mr Saml Baker, & Mr Chas Bowman.
Oct 19: Wm Floyd
Oct 20: Chas D Stewart, aged about 76 years; Mr Stetson's child; Isaac Waters' child, not cholera; Miss Rebecca Hutchinson; Maria Lyle, colored.
Oct 21: John Snowdeal's child
Oct 22: Mrs Maria Cooper
Oct 23: Mr R H Fletcher's child, not cholera; Mr Henry Crim's child, not cholera.
Oct 24: Miss Sallie Turner

Mrd: on Oct 19, at Chantilly, Fairfax Co, Va, by Rev R Post, D D, of Charleston, S C, Wm M Post, M D, of S C, to Mary C Stuart.
+
Mrd: on Oct 19, at Chantilly, Fairfax Co, Va, by Rev R T Brown, Rev Addison B Atkins, of Phil, to Ellen C Stuart, both daughters of the late Chas Calvert Stuart.

Died: on Oct 2, after a long & painful illness, Mrs Sarah Jane Hammond, in her 38th year. Her funeral is this afternoon at 3 o'clock, from the residence of her mother, Mrs Tate, on D, between 6th & 7th sts.

Died: on Oct 25, in Gtwn, Mrs Isabella H Bemis, wife of Mr N P Bemis; & on Oct 26, Mrs Frances Annette Tyler, wife of Mr Wm W Tyler, both daughters of the late Carter L Stevenson, of Fredericksburg, Va. Their funeral will take place from the residence of Mr Tyler, on Fred'k st, near 1st st, Gtwn, at 11 o'clock.

Died: on Oct 25, at Balt, Wm Schroeder, well known as among the oldest & most estimable citizens of that city. He was for many years engaged in mercantile pursuits, but was recently, & until a short time since, Sec of the Nat'l Fire Ins Co.

Died: on Oct 24, at **Oak Hill**, Montgomery Co, Md, Mary Louisa, daughter of Edmund H & Emily Brooke, aged 7 years & 7 months.

SAT OCT 28, 1854
At Galveston, Texas, on Oct 16, Mrs Seawell was accidentally shot by one of her sons, who were quarrelling, & one of them holding a pistol threatened to shoot his brother. She was endeavoring to separate them when she received the mortal wound. [Nov 1st newspaper: Mrs Sewell, who was shot a few days ago in a scuffle between her 2 sons, has died of the wound.]

Mrd: on Oct 26, by Rev Mr Hodges, Saml Cross to Miss Victoria J Miller, all of Wash City.

Died: on Oct 27, in Wash City, Mrs Mary Mgt Jullien, aged 77 years, a native of France, but for the last 52 years a resident of Wash City. Her funeral will be from her late residence on 13th st, on Oct 29, at 2 o'clock.

Died: on Oct 26, Nellie L, eldest daughter of Dr J L Fox, U S N, aged 6 years & 7 months. Her funeral will be on Sat, at 3:30 o'clock, from the residence of her grandfather, Cmdor Morris.

Died: on Oct 27, Amelia R, daughter of Dwight R & Marceila Waters, aged 22 months. Her funeral will be this afternoon at 3 o'clock, on 8th, between M & N sts.

Wm West, an aged & esteemed citizen of Jefferson Co, Va, shot his son-in-law, Jefferson Smith, dead on Friday last. Smith was intemperate & treated his wife cruelly. Smith followed her to her father's house with a gun & attempted to break into his kitchen. West fired & Smith fell dead. Mr West surrendered himself, & was held for trial.

Household & kitchen furniture at auction: on Nov _, at the residence of Mrs Davis, in *Gadsby's Row*, Pa ave, near 21st st. -Green & Scott, aucts

In Equity. John S Blackford & others, against Martha Blagrove, admx, & Josephine Blagrove, heir of H B Blagrove. The above parties are to appear on Nov 4 in my ofc in City Hall, Wash, & the account of the personal estate of Henry B Blagrove will be stated, with the view to see if it is necessary to sell any part of his real estate for the payment of his debts. –W Redin, auditor

Wash City Ordinance: 1-Act for the relief of Maurice Holoran: the sum of $26.67 be paid him, balance due for grading & graveling D st, between 14th & 15th sts.

Late San Francisco papers: Indian massacre in Oregon. On Aug 22 a party of 18 men left *Fort Boise* to recuse 3 ladies & a number of children who were supposed to be in the hands of a party of Winnass Indians, who attacked Mr Alex'r Ward's train from Missouri, on Aug 20th. On arriving, they found the bodies of Alex Ward & his eldest son Robt, young Amon, about 17; Saml Mulligan, Chas Adams, Wm Babcock, Miss Ward, Mrs White, Mrs Ward & 3 children. Newton Ward, a surviving boy, said that Dr Adams & Mulligan fought bravely. In a statement from Mr Masterson, a brother of Mrs Ward & Mrs White, he said it appears that the booty the Indians carried off consisted of 41 head of cattle, 5 horses, & about $2,000 or $3,000 in money, besides guns & pistols. Maj Raynes, cmder at *Fort Dallas*, sent out 30 regulars & 30 volunteers, all mounted, & under the command of Maj Haller.

MON OCT 30, 1854
Appointments by the Pres: 1-Geo L Curry, of Oregon, to be Govn'r of the Territory of Oregon. 2-Wm H Farrar, of Oregon, to be Atty for the Territory of Oregon. 3-Benj F Harding, of Oregon, to be Sec of the Territory of Oregon.

The remains of Gov Burt, late Govn'r of the Territory of Nebraska, arrived at St Joseph, Mo, on Oct 24 in charge of a cmte appointed by Acting Govn'r Cuming to accompany them to S C.

Mrd: on Oct 24, at Honeywood, Va, by Rev D Francis Sprigg, Wm Leigh to Mary White Colston, daughter of the late Edw Colston.

Mrd: on Oct 26, at Fred'k, Md, by Rev Mr Atkins, Jos C Isaac, of Wash, D C, to Miss Maria L B Macgill, of Fred'k, Md.

Died: on Oct 28, Mr Michl P Mohun, aged 30 years & 7 months. His funeral is this afternoon at 2 o'clock, from his late residence on 11th st, near the Navy Yard Bridge.

Died: yesterday, after a long & painful illness, Lawrence O'Brien, a native of Ireland, county Wexford, aged 33 years. His funeral is today at 3 o'clock, from his late residence on Md ave, near 7th st.

Died: on Oct 23, at his residence in Woodsfield, Ohio, after a lingering illness, Hon Jos Morris, aged 59 years. He was a native of Green Co, Pa, but emigrated to Ohio at an early period of her history. He represented his district in the 28th & 29th Congresses.

Orphans Court of Wash Co, D C. Letters of administration on the personal estate of Wm Kough, late of Wash Co, deceased. –Geogiana Kough, admx

Orphans Court of Wash Co, D C. In the case of Henry C Mathews, exc of Rosanna Brown, deceased, the exc & Court have appointed Nov 18 next, for the settlement of the estate of said deceased, of the assets in hand. –Ed N Roach, Reg/o wills

TUE OCT 31, 1854
Mrd: on Oct 26, by Rev J A Russell, John Tayloe, of Chatterton, to Mary Willis Lewis, daughter of Daingerfield Lewis, of Marmion, all of King George Co, Va.

Mrd: on Oct 24, at Norwich, N Y, Dr S A H McKim, of Wash, to Miss Caroline L Gibbs, of the former place.

Died: on Oct 30, Mrs M D V King, wife of Jas A King, of a brief illness, in her 18th year. Her funeral is today at 3 o'clock, from the residence of her father Jos Peck, 527 H st, between 6th & 7th sts.

Died: on Oct 30, Frank Stakely, aged 8 months, son of P F & Cornelia M Wilson. His funeral is this afternoon at 3:30 o'clock, from the residence of his parents, 426 11th st, between H & I sts.

Died: on Oct 23, at St Augustine, Fla, after a short illness, Mrs Rachel Parker Miller, aged 25 years, wife of Andrew J Miller, of that city, & only daughter of Dr John Westcott, Surveyor Genr'l of Florida. Mrs Miller spent the past fall with her friends in Wash City, & left here some 4 weeks since in good health. Her sudden decease will be severely felt by her numerous friends & relatives in Wash City & in the States of Pa, N Y, & N J, her native State. -D

Orphans Court of Wash Co, D C. Letters testamentary on the personal estate of Jeannett B Phillips, late of Wash Co, deceased. –Jos Follansbee, exc

Dancing Academy at Carusi's Saloon: Mr John Cochen announces that his school is now open. Lewis Carusi, in retiring from the profession, tenders his thanks to the public who have so liberally patronized him. Mr Cochen, for many years a teacher in N Y, Norfolk, & other cities, & last year in this city & Gtwn, has taken his saloon. -Chas Tucker, agent at the saloon.

WED NOV 1, 1854
Administrator's sale: by order of the Orphans Court of Wash Co, D C: furniture, bricklayers' tools, at auction, on Nov 7, the personal effects of Jas Edmonston, deceased, at his late residence on Mass ave, between 5th & 6th sts. -Green & Scott, aucts

Intelligence received of the formation of a new State in Liberia, called the State of Maryland. A constitution was adopted on May 29, & on Jun 6 the following State ofcrs were elected: Govn'r, Wm A Prout; Lt Govn'r, B J Drayton; Senators, I T Gibson, A Wood, Thos Fuller, & John B Bowen; Delegates, Danl F Wilson, Chas Harmon, John Cooper, Henry Pinkett, & John E Molten; High Sheriff, Saml S Reynolds; Coroner, Peter Siscoe. Thos Mason was appointed Sec of State. The Govn'rs inauguration took place on Jun 8.

Hart Stevens, aged about 17, belonging in Guilford, Ct, was accidentally killed on Fri by the accidental discharge of a gun.

Wash Corp: 1-Ptn of Euredice F Simms, admx of E Simms, deceased, asking to be refunded a portion of the amount paid for a license: referred to the Cmte on Finance. 2-Act for the relief of W W Demaine: referred to the Cmte on Finance. 3-Ptn of Richd A Boardman, asking indemnity for injury done his property by the revision of the grade of L st: referred to the delegation from the 6th Ward. 4-Ptn of Benson Collam & others, praying for the erection of lamp-posts on North Captiol st & Delaware ave: referred to the Cmte on Improvements.

N Y oyster excitement. Dr Jas R Chilton has analyzed a number of the oysters now on sale in N Y, & has certified that they are entirely wholesome. Mr Cornell, the cashier of a bank, had been ill for 7 months, &, though improving, was in feeble health at the time he partook of the oysters. It is not believed he died from eating oysters.

Miss Eliz Green, of Oldtown, Me, recently instituted a suit against Mr DeWolf for breach of promise of marriage. Mr DeWolf argued his own case upon the trial, but the jury gave a verdict for the fair plntf of damages in the sum of $1,625.

Mrd: yesterday, in Wash City, by Elder R C Leachman, Mr Wyatt S Berry, of Vandalia, Ill, to Miss Mary Eliz Moore, of Wash.

THU NOV 2, 1854
From 27 trees Luther Hatch, of Marshfield, Mass, gathered last week 100 barrels of Baldwin apples.

Trustee's sale: by decree of the Circuit Court of Wash Co, D C, passed in the cause wherein Wm E Thursby & others are cmplnts, & Martha Ann Thursby & others are dfndnts: auction on Nov 24, of the westernmost 23 feet front part of lot 7 in square 75, in said city, with the old frame house thereon. –W Redin, trustee
-Jas C McGuire, auct

The Alabama papers state that Hon Jas Abercrombie, a Rep in Congress from that State, recently killed a man in the State of Florida. The particulars are not given, but it appears that Mr Abercrombie was discharged after a judicial investigation, thus implying that the homicide was justifiable.

Nicholas Beehan, who has been on trial for several days at Riverhead, N Y, for the murder of the Wickham family, has been found guilty & sentenced to be hung.

The Calif Christian Advocate reports the case of a man arrested there for bigamy, on whose examination the following facts were elicited: a certificate was produced that Jas Mulqueen & Sarah J Summers were married in the parish church of Streatham, Surrey, Apr 10, 1848. Much corroborative testimony show a legal marriage, according to the common & civil laws of England & the U S; that a Catholic priest, Francis Llebaria, Vicar-Gen, had assumed to annul this marriage, & to marry Mr Mulqueen to Miss Mgt Bride, on Jun 25 last. Certificate of this priest: Having attended to all the reasons present by Mr Jas Mulquuen, & finding out that Mrs Sarah Summers, his pretended wife, was not baptized, neither dispensation has been given in order to contract legally before the Church; &, further, not being married by any magistrate lawfully authorized, we declare such a marriage had never existed, & is null & void. Therefore both parties remain as free as before. –Francis Llebaria, Vicar-Gen, San Francisco, Jun 24, 1854. Mulqueen was committed for trial, the Vicar General's certificate, of course, being no justification in the eye of the law.

Jos Peterson was an actor long attached to Norwich Theatre. In Oct, 1758, he was performing the Duke, in Measure for Measure, which he played in masterly style. Mr Moody was the Claudio. In the 3rd act, where, as the Friar, Peterson was preparing Claudio for his execution, he dropped into Moody's arms & never spoke again. Mr Moody was a second time destined to receive the last breath of a fellow perfomer. Mrs Jefferson, an actress, expired in his arms, when she had a sudden pain while in the midst of a hearty laugh during a rehearsal. The death of John Palmer, of Drury Lane Theatre, on Aug 2, 1798, while performing in the play of the Stranger, at the Liverpool Theatre, fell on his back & instantly expired. –Biographia Dramatica

Died: in Wash City, of typhoid fever, Thos Booth Roberts, in his 44th year. His remains were taken to Phil & interred on Oct 28, in **Laurel Hill Cemetery**. [No death date given.]

Died: on Oct 30, at the residence of Mr John Mellor, Md ave & 10th sts, in her 19th year, Emily Mary Dunne, of disease of the heart.

Died: on Oct 6, of cholera, at St Paul, Minn, Washington Terrett, in his 83rd year, after an illness of 4 days. At the time of his death Mr Terrett was engaged on duty in the Pay Dept of the U S Army. Mr Terrett was one of 4 brothers who, within the last 9 years, have been in the military service of the U S, the sons of the late Capt Geo Hunter Terrett, of Fairfax Co, Va. Three of this gallant band met death in early manhood. Capt Burdett A Terrett, of the 1st Dragoons, accidentally shot himself with a pistol at **Fort Scott**, Mo, while dismounting from his horse, in the spring of 1845; Lt John Chapman Terrett, Adj 1st Infty, was killed on Sep 21, 1846, while gallantly fighting at the battle of Monterey; the sole survivor is Brvt Maj Geo Terrett, of the Marines, now stationed at the Wash Navy Yard. Upon the increase of the army during the war in Mexico Washington Terrett was appointed 2nd Lt of the Voltigeur Regt; served some months as quartermaster till appointed adj, in which capacity he served till the disbandment of his regt at the close of the war. He was engaged in 4 of the decisive battles in the valley of Mexico; wounded at Milino del Rey; highly distinguished in the report of his Col for courage & good conduct in the storming of Chepultapec. His brother, Maj Terrett, won his laurels at the same battle on the opposite side of the Fort. -W

Orphans Court of Wash Co, D C. Letters testamentary on the personal estate of John Fred'k Speiser, late of Wash Co, deceased. —Maria Speiser, excx

Orphans Court of Wash Co, D C. Letters of administration on the personal estate of David Rowland, late of Wash Co, deceased. —Dan Rowland, adm

Dissolution of the copartnership under the firm of Thompson & Carner, merchant tailors. —J R Thompson, Ambrose S Carner [The business will be continued by A S Carner at the late stand, Morfit's bldg, 4½ st.]

FRI NOV 3, 1854
Household & kitchen furniture at auction on Nov 8, at the residence of Mrs Willis, corner of F & 13th sts. -Green & Scott, aucts

Household & kitchen furniture at auction on Nov 9, at the residence of John A Brennen, on Pa ave, between 3rd & 4½ sts. -Green & Scott, aucts

John E Norris, [Dem] formerly of Wash City, has been elected Commonwealth's Atty for Berkeley Co, Va, by a majority of 93 votes over Norman Miller, [Whig,] to supply the vacancy occasioned by the death of Edmund P Hunter.

The Monroe [Michigan] Sentinel: Mr Powell, an old Revolutionary soldier, 95 years of age, with his wife, 75, left here on the 18th ult for Nebraska, in company with several citizens. Mr Powell is remarkably vigorous, capable of chasing a deer with a rifle a-shoulder 26 miles a day.

Nathan Childs, jr, of St Louis, formerly of Balt, has recovered $2,550 damages from the Dirs of the Bank of Missouri, to indemnify him for the expense he was put to a few years ago in defending himself in a suit brought against him by the bank on a charge of embezzling $120,000, & of which he was acquitted. This is the second case determined in favor of Mr Childs, & the aggregate damages amount to $4,910.

John McCarron, who was convicted of murder at Boonville, Oneida Co, in Mar last, but was granted a new trial, was tried on Tue last, at Rome, & the jury again found him guilty. The prisoner was sentenced to be executed on Dec 15 next.

From the Little Rock [Ark] Democrat, we learn that Dr Solon Borland, late Minister to Central America, has opened an apothecary store in company with Dr J J McAlmont, & has resumd his professional vocation.

Sir John Franklin was born at Spilsby, in Lincolnshire, in 1786; at age 14 he entered the British navy as a midshipman on board the ship **Polyphemus**, in which capacity he served at the battle of Copenhagen. In 1803 he accompanied his relative, Capt Flinders, on a voyage of discovery to the South Seas, & was shipwrecked on the coast of New Holland. He was afterwards signal ofcr on board the ship **Bellerophon** [the ship on board which Napoleon took refuge in 1815] at the battle of Trafalgar, & in 1814 served as Lt upon the ship **Bedford**, which carried the allied sovereigns to England. In 1815 he was at the attack upon New Orleans, which ended so disastrously for the British. In 1818 he was appointed to the command of the brig **Trent**, which formed part of the polar expedition, under Capt Buchan.

Mrd: on Nov 1, at the Church of the Advent, in the city of Boston, by Rt Rev Bishop Southgate, Ezra Williams, of Wash City, to Miss Sarah Townsend, of Medfield, Norfolk Co, Mass.

Mrd: on Oct 31, in F st church, by Rev J M Henry, Miss Esther A Nugent, formerly of Harrisburg, Pa, to Mr Chas Stott, of Wash City.

Mrd: on Nov 2, by Rev Mr Reese, Mr Chas Temple Wood to Miss Sarah Amanda Ratcliffe, daughter of Mr Jos Ratcliffe, all of Wash City.

Mrd: on Oct 31, at Trinity Church, by Rev Mr Clarke, Mr John S Guyther to Miss Sarah M Holton, both of St Mary's Co, Md.

Died: on Oct 30, in Wash City, Mrs Louisa M, wife of Mr John M McFarland, of Wash City, in her 26th year. Her end was peace.

Died: on Oct 5, at the residence of his son-in-law, Dr John H Thomas, in the Parish of St Martin, La, Mr Edw J Heard, at the age of 72 years. He was born in Chas Co, Md. In 1837 he removed to Atakapas, & in 1838 established his plantation on Lake Catahoula. He had the gratification of seeing a large family of children grow up around him, respectable & in the enjoyment of wordly comfort, as a result of his efforts. He was an honest & faithful member of the Roman Catholic Church. –S

Charleston, Sep 1. Lt Govn'r Farger died at New Orleans on Oct 29 of yellow fever.

In Equity. A F Offutt & Co against John Davis, Jos P Davis, Geo W Beall, Richd P Jackson, & others. The parties above named are to meet at my ofc on Nov 10, City Hall, Wash, where an account of the personal estate of Richd Davis, deceased, will be stated. –W Redin, auditor

SAT NOV 4, 1854
The body of the late Govn'r Burt, Govn'r of Nebraska, arrived in this city last evening, attended by Messrs Ward B Howard, of N Y, B Green, of Ohio, & J Doyle, & W R Jones, of S C, the cmte appointed by Acting Govn'r Cumming to convey the remains of the late Govn'r to their last resting place in South Carolina.

Mrd: on Nov 2, by Rev W F Speaks, Wm C Harper to Ann Eliza Speaks, all of Wash.

Died: on Nov 3, Sarah J Keith, youngest daughter of the late John & Mgt Keith, in her 17th year. Her funeral is this afternoon at 3 o'clock, from the residence of her uncle, John Tretler, on 9th st, between G & H sts.

Died: on Oct 21, at Byron, Ogle Co, Ill, after a brief illness, Mr David Rowland, of Wash City, in his 86th year.

The firm of Donn & Bros was dissolved on Oct 31 by mutual consent. John M Donn, the senior partner, withdraws from the business. –John M Donn, G W Donn, O P Donn The House-furnishing business will be continued by the subscribers at the old stand on 9th st, corner of D. –Donn, Bro & Co

For sale: <u>Antietam Iron Works</u> in Wash Co, Md, containing about 1,290 acres.
-W B Clarke, Balt City

MON NOV 6, 1854
Household & kitchen furniture at auction on Nov 8, at the residence of Miss Catherine Boone, at the corner of East Capitol st & 3rd sts. -Green & Scott, aucts

Benj Johnson Barbour, son of the late Govn'r Jas Barbour, delivered the Valedictory Address at the Va Agricultural Fair. It is spoken of as a very happy effort.

Troops for Texas. The ship **Metropolis** sailed from N Y on Sat for Brasos San Jago, with a detachment of 270 recruits. Ofcrs who accompanied the detachment: Lt Col Wm Chapman, 5th Infty, commanding; Lt H R Selden; Lt J C Booth, 4th Artl, Quartermaster & Commissary; Lt J H McArthur, 5th Infty; Lt H C Bankhead, 5th Infty, Adj; Lt W Jenkins, 1st Artl; Lt A Smead, 4th Artl; Lt D H Brotherton, 5th Infty; Assist Surgeon, J R Smith, U S A.

Chicago, Ill, Nov 3. Accident on Wed night, from the breaking of an axletree of the engine, near Minoka station, the result, it is said, of running over a horse upon the track. The engine & a portion of all of the cars were thrown from the track: Mr W G Brown, engineer, was fearfully scalded; his brother, acting as fireman, had both legs broken; a gentleman named Carpenter, from Poughkeepsie, N Y, was terribly burnt; J W Albion, of Monroe Co, Ohio, burnt & badly scalded; Sarah Albion, of Monroe Co, Ohio, burnt & scalded; Mrs Cox, of Wash Co, Iowa, severely injured. Catherine Laughlin, of Wash Co, Iowa, was seriously injured. Mgt Laughlin, of Gettysburg, Pa, was seriously if not fatally injured. J M Carpenter, of Canandaigua, one of the injured, died this afternoon.

Death caused by joy. Howard [Md] Advocate: Mr Jacob Timanus, father of Mr Wm J Timanus, who had just returned from Calif, & the joy occasioned by his safe return contributed in a degree to the father's death.

Died: on Fri, after a few hours' illness, at his late residence on Capitol Hill, in Wash City, Wm Parker Elliot, Architect, leaving a wife & 6 children & a large circle of relations & friends to lament his sudden & premature death in the meridian of life & of usefulness. Mr Elliot was in his 46th year, & although a native of N J, had been a resident of Wash City nearly all his life. In the relation of husband, father, friend, & citizen his character was most exemplary. He was during several years surveyor of Wash City. His funeral will take place, from his late residence on Capitol Hill to St Peter's Church, this morning at 9 o'clock. [Nov 7th newspaper: the funeral of the late Wm P Elliot, which was yesterday postponed at the suggestion of some of his numerous friends, will, after a full consultation with his attending physicians & several medical & other friends take place from the late residence of the deceased, this day, at 9 o'clock, on which melancholy occasion the friends of the family are invited to attend.]

Died: on Nov 5, Louis Vivans Drury, aged 18 months. His funeral will take place from St Matthew's Church this day at 2½ o'clock P M.

Died: on Sat, in Wash City, after brief but excessive suffering, Kate Douglas, aged 3 years & 6 months, daughter of Jos L & Melinda Williams. This is the second victim of scarlet fever in this household within 9 days. Rebecca Jane is scarcely cold in her grave when the sister, Katy, follows to the gloom of earth & glory of Heaven; Katy darling, [as the bright & joyous little creature sportively called herself.] Her funeral is this day at 12 o'clock, from Mr Williams' residence, 367 C st.

Died: on Nov 4, Alice, only daughter of Geo & Mary E Emmerich, aged 5 years, 1 month & 19 days.

The Annapolis Republican says there is now living in the *Swamp*, in the lower section of Anne Arundel Co, a man by the name of Richd Crandell, who is 106 years old, & is very active & sprightly, & speaks of the improvements he intends to make on his farm like a man of 40 or 50.

Mrd: in Norfolk, by Rev Mr O'Keefe, Mr Richd G Broughton, jr, to Miss Emily R daughter of Wm Ward. [No date given-current item.

Short way of getting a divorce. Albany [N Y] Argus: As my husband, Jos Rentz, has left me without any provocation, & I have seen or heard nothing of him this last year past, I hereby declare that unless he returns in 3 days from this date I shall take it as a divorce, & shall marry again immediately. –Johanna Rentz

Louisville [Ky] Democrat of Oct 26. Last week, while the play The Robbers, was being performed at the theatre in 3rd st, Mr Meyer, one of the actors, was shot at by Mr Aldersbers, an actor, the gun containing a hard ball of paper. It struck Mr Meyer in the arm, causing a severe wound. Mortification ensued & on Sat night the sufferings of the unfortunate man were relieved by death.

Orphans Court of Wash Co, D C. Letters testamentary on the personal estate of Lawrence O'Brien, late of Wash Co, deceased. –Jas O'Brien, exc

Orphans Court of Wash Co, D C. Letters of administration on the personal estate of Agricol Favier, late of Wash Co, deceased. -Jas C McGuire, auct

TUE NOV 7, 1854
Bldg lots of the Heights of Gtwn for sale: well known property known as *Lee's Hill*: front 398 feet on Road st. –Barnard & Buckley, aucts

Household & kitchen furniture at auction: on Nov 13, at the residence of Geo Burns, on F st, between 6th & 7th sts. -Green & Scott, aucts

One hundred years ago: We have 2 volumes of the Md Gaz published at Annapolis in 1745-6; the only newspaper published in Md at the time. From the Gaz: in the number of May 20, 1746, we are informed that "on Friday last Hector Grant, Jas Horney, & Esther Anderson, white servants, were executed at Chester, in Kent Co, pursuant to their sentence, for the murder of their late master. The men were hanged & the woman burned."

Edw D Ingraham, an eminent lawyer, & U S Com'r at Phil, died there yesterday.

Household & kitchen furniture at auction: on Nov 13, at the residence of Judge Platt, on north G st, between 10th & 11th sts. -Jas C McGuire, auct

In consequence of the death of the late Agricol Favier, his celebrated Mineral Water Establishment, for the last 12 years in successful operation, is for rent or lease for any number of years, together with the dwlg, & out-houses. Also, horses & wagons. It is within a few minutes walk of the Pres' House & public Depts. For particulars inquire on the premises.

Mrd: on Oct 31, by Rev Chas A Davis, Mr Southey S Parker to Miss Isabella Waters, all of Wash City.

Died: on Friday last, at Alexandria, Va, Caroline Huntington, aged 1 year, only daughter of J H & Mariana B Lathrop.

For sale, the finest riding horse in the District. Apply at the Stable of Jas T Essex, Water st, Gtwn.

WED NOV 8, 1854
People around the country are grieved to hear of the illness of the venerable Mrs Hamilton, widow of Gen Alex'r Hamilton. She has been a resident of Wash City for many years & is now in the 97th year of her age. It is 50 years since the death of her distinguished husband. She is the daughter of the patriot Gen Schuyler, of the Revolutionary army.

Hon Wm W Farmer, Lt Govn'r of the State of Louisiana, died on Oct 29 at New Orleans, whither he has been called by business & was stricken down by yellow fever. He was elected Lt Govn'r in 1852, having previously served in the Legislature & been Pres of the State Senate.

Rev W A Macy sailed from N Y on Monday for Hong Kong to engage in the service of the American Board as a missionary to the Chinese. Numbers are already converted.

The Macon Messenger says that Sam D Scovil, Book-keeper in the Agency of the Marine Bank at that place, has absconded with $10,000 of the funds of the institution. He had previously borne a very good character for industry & sobriety.

Mrd: on Tue, by Rev J C Smith, Dr Thos R Chew, of New Orleans, to Miss Mary Caroline, daughter of E B Grayson, of Wash City.

Mrd: on Nov 7, in the Fourth Presbyterian Church, by Rev John C Smith, W Blair Lord, of Balt, to Louisa L Willis, of Wash.

Died: on Nov 6, at his late residence, near Bladensburg, Mr John Brereton, in his 42nd year. His funeral is this afternoon, at 2 o'clock. His friends & those of the family are invited to meet at J F Harvey's [Undertaker,] No 410 7th st, at 1 o'clock, where hacks will be in readiness to convey them to his late residence.

Died: on Nov 3, in Alexandria, Va, Horace Holmes Moss, youngest son of John M Johnson, Postmaster of the House of Reps U S, aged 2 years & 6 months.

Wash Corp: 1-Ptn of Gaffin Nalley, asked the remission of a fine: referred to the Cmte of Claims. 2-Ptn of John E Bates & others, for a gravel footwalk along 3rd st east: referred to the Cmte on Improvements.

The Columbus [Ohio] Fact of Oct 27 says: Nicholas Satto, convicted in the U S Court of robbing the mail, was yesterday sentenced to 10 years' imprisonment in the penitentiary. Satto was mail-carrier between Washington [Guernsey Co] & Sarahsville.

THU NOV 9, 1854
Household & kitchen furniture at auction: Nov 15, at Cmder's Quarters, Wash Navy Yard, a portion of the private effects of Capt L M Powell. -Jas C McGuire, auct

Mrd: on Nov 7, at Trinity Church, by Rev Mr Clark, Henry D Hatton, of PG Co, Md, to Miss Sarah C Wilson, of Wash City.

Mrd: on Oct 19, at Keokuk, Iowa, by Rev J T Umstead, Arthur Wolcott to Clara daughter of the late Brig Gen Belknap, U S Army.

Died: on Oct 22, at St Augustine, Fla, Mr Burwell Stark Randolph, in his 54th year.

The new Mayor of Balt, Saml Hincks, has taken the oath of ofc, & will enter upon the discharge of his duties on Monday next.

Wanted: a Teacher competent to teach the usual academical branches in a select school of lads, 3 miles north of Wash. Address Geo McCeney, through this ofc.

Notice: the original Land Warrant No 1,579, issued Aug 18, 1783, for 2,666 2/3 acres of land, to Given Summerson for his services as a Midshipman in the State Navy of Va; Land Warrant No 576, issued May 14, 1783, for 200 acres of land, to Burnell Bacon for his services as a Capt in the Va State Artl or Continental Establishment; Land Warrant No 2,563, issued Feb 21, 17__, for 2,666 2/3 acres of land to John Vaughan for his services as a Lt in the Va State Line; Land Warrant No 84, issued Dec 31, 1782, for 4,000 acres of land, to Jas Quarles for his services as a Capt in the State Line of Va, have been lost, mislaid, or destroyed. Application will be made to the Gen Land Ofc for the issue of scrip upon duplicates of said warrants. -John F Webb, for the heirs

Providence Journal: John Howland, age 97 years, died in Providence on Sunday. He entered the Revolutionary army & was with Washington at Trenton & Princeton, & with Gen Spencer in Rhode Island. He was the leading man in establishing a common school system & held many municipal ofcs. He was several years Pres of the Mechanics' Assoc & 21 years Treasurer of the Savings Institution, which he was mainly instrumental in bringing into existence. He was an honest & useful citizen.

Chancery sale: by decree of the Circuit Court of Wash Co, D C, in equity, in the cause of Wm J Gray & Susan R Stinger vs Nathan Gray, Benj Gray, et al, No 898, dated Dec 13, 1853: public auction on Nov 30, on the premises: 1-Lot 105 in Beatty & Hawkins' addition to Gtwn, having a front of 70 feet on the north side of 1st st & a dept of about 150 feet. 2-Lots 115, in the same addition, fronting 70 feet on the south side of 2nd st, running back about 150 feet. These lots are fine bldg sites. This property is resold by order of the Court, in consequence of an accidental omission in the advertisement of the previous sale. –Walter S Cox, trustee -Edw S Wright, auct

FRI NOV 10, 1854
Mrs Eliz Hamilton, the venerable relict of Alex'r Hamilton, closed her earthly career at her residence in Wash City, on Nov 9. She was the 2nd daughter of Philip S Schuyler, of Albany, & was born on Aug 9, 1757. She was married to Alex'r Hamilton, then one of the Aids of Gen Washington with the rank of Lt Col, on Dec 9, 1780, their being not quite a year's difference in their ages. They lived together in the enjoyment of every blessing that could render wedded life happy for 24 years, & she survived her husband more than half a century. Hamilton was placed at the head of the Treasury Dept & carried on the Govn't finances. Mrs Hamilton lived to the very advanced age of 97 years & 3 months, & died without a struggle, in full communion with the Episcopal Church & surrounded by her surviving children.

Household & kitchen furniture at auction: On Nov 16, at the residence of A B Little, 264 8th st, between M & N sts. -Green & Scott, aucts

Died: on Nov 6, of consumption, Addison Conway, in his 46th year.

An American by the name of Ansley was arrested in Paris last month, under the international treaty to that effect, for forgeries committed upon a bank in New Orleans. On Oct 16 the unsuspecting gentleman called at the Legation to get his passports [which gave his name as Dupont] vised for Italy, when he was arrested, & taken to the conciergerie to await orders from New Orleans.

The heirs & reps of Rudolphus Brill, deceased, on whose estate letters testamentary were granted by the Orphans' Court for Wash Co, Md, in 1801, are notified to appear in this court on or before May 1, 1855, & establish their right to the funds now in the hands of the undersigned, as administrator de bonis non, with the will annexed, of said deceased. –John R Sneary, adm d b n, w a

In Equity: Jos H Hilton against John Rodier & Pauline Rodier, heirs of Martha P J Smart. The personal estate of Mrs Smart will be stated, & an inquiry instituted whether the same is sufficient to pay her debts; &, if not, what portion of her real estate it is necessary to sell for the purpose. Meeting at my ofc, City Hall, on Nov 18, 1854. –W Redin, auditor

Miss Lamphier & Mrs Ditty will open Winter Millinery on Nov 4.

SAT NOV 11, 1854
The steamer **Yankee Blade** left San Francisco on Sep 30 for Panama, & was wrecked the following day. She had on board 800 passengers, besides her crew & firemen, when she struck the reef rocks off Point Arguello, 15 miles above **Point Conception**. A heavy fog hung upon the coast, which was the cause of the disaster. Names of those known lost are: four children of Mrs Longstown, Mrs Breman & child, Mrs Sumner & child, Mrs Smith & child, Mr Moore & child, & Frank Mitchell. There were terrible scenes of pillage on board after the vessel struck, & before the passengers were rescued by the steamer **Goliah**. All the specie on board, amounting to $153,000, was lost. The ship is a total wreck, having washed to pieces.

Trial at N Y of Capt Jas Smith, master of the ship **Julia Moulton**, on a charge of piracy, for being concerned in the slave trade, has resulted in a verdict of guilty. Jas Wills, the chief mate of the brig, swore positively to the carrying of 646 slaves from Africa to Cuba, & burning the brig afterwards. He also named the owners of the brig, in N Y, who fitted her out for the slave trade in Feb last.

Fred'k Gedge, the acting Pres of the Covington & Lexington Railroad Co, committed suicide on Tue by throwing himself across the track of that road at the time of the passing of a train. His head was severed from his body.

Mrd: on Oct 30, in Boston, by Rt Rev Bishop Fitzpatrick, Edw Gassett to Maria W Percival, adopted daughter of Capt John Percival, of the U S Navy.

Boston, Nov 10. Capt McDonald, of Gloucester, England, arrived here today charged with killing a man at Cape Breton. It is expected that the prisoner will be claimed under the Ashburton extradition treaty.

Public sale of an elegant estate: *Ingleside*, in Wash Co, D C, contains about 140 acres of land; divided by the Old Mill Road into 2 parts. The farm side contains about 100 acres, the house side about 41 acres. The farm side is between the old Wash Race Course, lying west of 14th st, & Piney Branch bridge, bounded by Rock Creek on the south & by the county road to *Pierce's Mill* on the north, less than 2 miles from Pa ave & 14th st. The farm has been divided into sites containing from 5 to 20 acres each. The Mansion house is bounded on the east by the estate of Col Wm Selden, north & west of Piney Branch; it is an irregular Italian Villa residence about 150 feet front by varied depths of from 30 to 60 feet. Numerous out-bldgs. Title indisputable. Lithographed plans of the property may be seen at my counting-room. -Jas C McGuire, auct

Died: on Oct 7, at Galveston, Texas, of yellow fever, Jas Percival, aged 21, nephew & adopted son of Capt John Percival, of U S Navy, a young man of much promise.

Died: on Nov 9, in Wash City, Geo Johnson, aged 71 years. His funeral will take place from his late residence on K st, this day, at 10 o'clock.

Died: on Nov 10, in Gtwn, Capt Chas Cruikshank, in his 61st year. His funeral will be from his late dwlg near St John's Church, Gtwn, at 3 o'clock this day.

Died: on Nov 2, at his residence in Wash City, of dropsy of the chest, Wm Lee Boak, formerly of Berkeley Co, Va, aged 49 years. Mr Boak has been for 3 years a highly respectable delegate in the Legislature of Va, & at the time of his death was a clerk in the Gen Land Ofc. He was deservedly popular, gentle & kind of demeanor.

MON NOV 13, 1854
The Tunnel Bridge, on the Balt & Susquehanna Railroad burned a few days since, & the frame work of the bridge fell through. Among the spectators was Eli Rheem, age 12 years, who had the forethought to stop the express passenger train due from York, unaware of the impending danger. He stood on the tracks, running towards the approaching train with his hands raised, caught the attention of the engineer, who reversed his engine, & stopped with 400 yards of impeding destruction. The passengers, when they viewed the precipice over which they were near being dashed, liberally rewarded the boy for his presence of mind & daring, & the Board of Dirs appropriated $100 as an additional recompense. Of the 20 persons present, most of them men, he only had forethought sufficient for the occasion. –Balt American

The funeral ceremonies of Mrs Alex'r Hamilton, who died in Wash City on Thu last, took place yesterday at Trinity Church, in N Y C.

Superior groceries & wine at auction on Nov 16, at the family grocery of Messrs R W Robertson & Co, Pa ave, between 17th & 18th sts. Sale of all their stock. -Jas C McGuire, auct

Trustee's sale of brick house & lot at auction: on Dec 5, in front of the premises, by deed of trust from Beedy Wise to the subscriber, dated Aug 29, 1850, recorded in Liber J A S No 56, folios 93 thru 95, of the land records for Wash Co, D C: all of lot 34 in square 411, with improvements, brick house, in Wash Co. –J Fitz Bartlett, trustee -Green & Scott, aucts

Executor's sale of household & kitchen furniture at auction: on Nov 15, by order of the exec: the personal effects of Jeannett B Phillips, deceased, at her late residence, East Capitol st, between 1st & 2nd sts. –J Follensby, execs -Green & Scott, aucts

Since the election riot at Wmsburg, on Tue, Mr Wm Henry Harrison, a very estimable citizen, has died of injuries he received, & Mr John H Smith is believed, cannot recover. The riot would have been much more serious if Mayor Wall had not called out a company of artillery & 2 companies of infantry. [Nov 16th newspaper: Mr John H Smith, who attempted to rescue Harrison from the mob, has died of the injuries he then received.]

The Marine Bank of Savannah, Geo, has offered $1,000 for the apprehension & delivery to them of Saml D *Scovill, age 26 years, who absconded from Macon on Oct 29 with $10,000 of the funds of that institution. [Nov 25th newspaper: *Scoville was arrested at the Planters' House under the assumed name of Lewis. –No date given-current item as of Nov 25, 1854.] [*2 spellings of Scovill/Scoville.]

Wm H Arrison, the man charged with sending the infernal machine by which Mr Allison & his wife were killed last summer at Cincinnati, has been arrested at Muscatine, Iowa, & is to be sent to Cincinnati for examination.

The Wheeling Intelligencer has been furnished with the account of a quilt made by Miss Magdalene Miller, of Fish Creek, Va, containing 7,913 pieces in the middle, 1,756 in the border, & 2,500 yards of boss.

2nd Lt Jas P Llewellen, of the 1st Artl, & 2nd Lt Melancthon Smith, of the 8th Infty, have resigned.

A gentleman in South Brooklyn has been presented by Mrs Cowden Clarke with the veritable jug that Shakespeare aforetime owned.

Robt F Poe, Pres of the Augusta [Geo] Bank, died a few days ago.

The Jefferson [Ind[[Railroad Co have been mulcted in $2,100 damages for killing a child of Alva Dullet.

Sarah Canby, aged 107 years, recently died at New Liberia, La. She was born in N Y C on Dec 25, 1746.

At the burial of Marshal de St Arnaud the flags of France & of England, for the first time in history covered the same coffin, & Musselman cannon resounded in sign of grief at the funeral of a Christian general.

Official: Dept of State: Wash, Nov 10, 1854. Information received from Thos Wm Ward, U S Consul at Panama, at New Granada, that Thos Kenlan, a citizen of the U S, who fell overboard & was drowned in the harbor of Iaboga on the night of Jun 29 last. Mr Ward has forwarded to this Dept an inventory of the effects left by the deceased.

Rev John C Smith, D D, Pastor of the Fourth Presbyterian Church in Wash City, was among the passengers in a car which was thrown down an embankment on the South Side Railroad, between Petersburg & Lynchburg, Va, on Thu last. He was brought home on Sat last, where he lies in much pain from the bruises & contusions, but has no permanent injury. One of the firemen was killed. Among those severely bruised were Mr Alfred King, coachmaker, of Richmond, Mr & Mrs Ely, Mr Venable, the mail agent, Mr Davis, the conductor, Mr Jones, the engineer, Mr J B Hillard, Mr Wood, & Mr Wilson, of Cumberland Co; Mrs Smith, of Prince Edward; Mr Anderson, & Mr Bruce, of Lynchburg.

Mrd: on Oct 31, at **Woodlawn**, Montg Co, Md, by Rev Mr Hutton, John T Towers, Mayor of Wash, D C, to Miss Eliza, daughter of Dr Wm P Palmer, of the former place.

Mrd: on Nov 9, by Rev F Israel, Thos Herbert to Miss Mgt Lucas, all of Wash City.

Mrd: on Nov 9, by Rev G W Samson, Mr Jas A Hall to Miss Emma Roby, both of Wash City.

Mrd: on Oct 14, in San Francisco, Calif, at the residence of Judge Thompson, by Rt Rev Bishop Kip, Capt E O C Ord, U S Army, to Miss Mary Mercer Thompson.

Died: on Nov 12, after a very brief illness, Catharine Virginia, daughter of Wm C & Mary Viginia Morrison, aged 14 months. Her funeral will take place this afternoon, at 3½ o'clock, from the residence of her grandfather, Chas E Mix, on High st, opposite 4th st, Gtwn.

Orphans Court of Wash Co, D C. In the case of Robt M English & Richd Henderson, adms of David English, deceased: the adms & Court have appointed Dec 2 next for the settlement of the estate of said deceased, of the assets in hand.
–Ed N Roach, Reg/o wills

Liverpool, Nov 1. The Queen-Mother of Bavaria is dead.

In Chancery: Shaw et al vs Welsh et al. Order of Ratification Nisl. John F Ennis, the trustee in the above cause, having reported on May 18, 1854, after due notice, he sold lot 20 in square 199, in Wash City, to Wm Flaherty, for the sum of $1,025.28; & that afterwards on May 20, 1854, said Flaherty transferred & assigned all his right, title, & interest to the said lot, & premises unto one Jas O'Brien; & that the said O'Brien has since complied with the terms of the sale. –Jno A Smith, clerk

TUE NOV 14, 1854
Trustee's sale of brick house & lot at auction: on Dec 14, by deed of trust from Wm D Acken to the subscriber, dated Aug 11, 1853: recorded in Liber J A S No 66, folios 147 to 150, of the land records of Wash Co, D C: public auction of part of lot 17 in square 374, fronting on I st, between 9th & 10th sts 33 feet 4 inches, running back the same width 105 feet, with dwlg erected thereon. –Henry Naylor, trustee -Green & Scott, aucts

The American Organ, the first of a new daily & weekly paper under this title appeared yesterday in this city. It is published by an Association of Native Americans, & is under the editorial control of Vespasian Ellis, as principal, R M Heath, as assistant; & printed by Josiah Melvin.

Funeral ceremonies appropriate to the event were performed on Nov 8, at Frankfort, Ky, on the occasion of the re-interment of the remains of the late Govn'r Chas Scott, Hon Wm T Barry, & Maj Bland Ballard & wife, in the cemetery of that place. The remains of Mr Barry were lately brought from Liverpool. Orations were delivered by Thos L Crittenden, Theodore O'Hara, & Humphrey Marshall.

On Sat at Bel-Air Market, Balt, Chas Richter was shockingly burnt when an ethereal oil lamp exploded. Two others were badly burnt. –American

Warren Terry, of Enfield, Ct, died on Nov 7, having received a charge of shot in one of his thighs while drawing a loaded gun with the muzzle towards him from a wagon 10 days before.

Mr Larkin Thompson, of Chesterfield, N H, was accidentally killed on Fri last while in the woods felling trees. He was much esteemed.

Accident near Tigerville, parish of Terrebonne, La, on Oct 21. W H Morning & W L Armstrong, two intimate friends, were in the woods hunting, when the gun of Morning accidentally went off, striking Armstrong, severing the jugular vein, & causing almost instant death.

Mr Chas W Stewart, of Wash City, long a faithful & obliging Assist Door-keeper of the House of Reps, has created both pain & surprise to all who knew him. He was found lying dead on the sofa in the Speaker's room on Sunday, having evidently taken strychnine of some other poison. His estimable family have the sincere sympathy of the community.
+
Died: on Nov 12, suddenly, Chas W Stewart, for many years an ofcr of the House of Reps of the U S. His funeral will be on this morning at 11 o'clock, from his late residence on Missouri ave, between 3rd & 4½ sts.

Mrd: in the Church of the Epiphany, by Rev Mr French, Mr Elasah Moran to Miss C Angeline Moran, both of Wash City. [No date given-current item.]

$100,000 worth of real estate in the city of Knoxville, Tenn, including business houses & residences, mills & mill site, & vacant lots, at public auction, in Knoxville, Jan 9, 1855. –J W J Niles -C H McGhee

By order of distrain & to me directed, for house rent due & in arrears by Wm L Boak to B J Simmes, agent for Virginia Simmes, I shall sell for cash, on Nov 17, at the Columbia House, a very large assortment of household & kitchen furniture at public auction: . –A E S Keese, bailiff

For rent, the comfortable 2 story brick dwlg, 441 I st, between 9th & 10th sts. Apply to Mrs Caroline Cox, Mass ave, near 10th st, or to the undersigned, at the ofc of Chubb Brothers. -A H Barrow

WED NOV 15, 1854
Household & kitchen furniture at auction: Nov 21, at the residence of Philip Griffith, Sec to the British Legation, West & Congress sts. –Barnard & Buckey, aucts

The English papers say that the amount of repeating pistols, or revolvers, manufactured by Mr Colt, during the last 2 years, amounts to 200,000. The Viceroy of Egypt has lately ordered 5,000 of them for the equipment of his cavalry; & the British Board of Ordnance dispatched, some time ago, 10,000 to the Baltic fleet.
Household & kitchen furniture at auction: on Nov 21, at the residence of A H Barrow, on I st, between 9th & 10th sts. -Jas C McGuire, auct

Household & kitchen furniture at auction: on Nov 21, at the residence of A H Barrow, on I st, between 9th & 10th sts. -Jas C McGuire, auct

Affray on Sat last at Gordonsville, Orange Co, Va, between Mr Thos S Baker, formerly a mail agent on the line of the Railroad, & Mr Brannam, of Orange, & another citizen of that county named Gibson, in the course of which Baker was severely beaten. Baker shot & killed Brannam. Gibson was standing close & was severely wounded, & died. The difficulty was caused by a game of cards. Mr Brannam had a wife & children. Baker is in jail at Orange Court-house.
-Alexandria Gaz

The papers announce the death at N Y, Fri last, of Mr Chas S T Burke, one of the best comedians of the day, trained by the Jefferson family, & a favorite of the public.

Tue week was the day set in the criminal court in St Louis for the trial of Wilson C Baker, charged with an assault with intent to kill Hoffman, who was subsequently killed by the wife of the accused. The dfndnt failing to appear, his recognizance of $3,000 was declared forfeited.

Meeting of the <u>soldiers of the war of 1812</u> was held at the City Hall yesterday, when Col John S Williams was called to the chair, & Richd Burgess appointed sec. A cmte of 3 was appointed by the chair: Maj Gen Geo McNeir, Jas A Kennedy, & J W McCulloh. Delegates appointed by the chair:

Col John S Williams	Col Peter Force	Wm Dant
Richd Burgess	Gen Jas Thompson	Reuben Berry
*Geo W P Custis	Philip Hines	Jas Laurenson
John S Gallaher	Geo Petrie	*Capt De La Roche
Jas W McCulloh	C R Johnson	*Wm Thomas
Wm P Young	Isaac Holland	G C Grammer
Benj C Ridgate	Wm Clarke	Edw Simms
Maj Geo McNeir	Gen W Briscoe	Francis Lord
Dr Tobias Watkins	Col Wm Doughty	Jesse Plowman
Col W B Randolph	Saml McKenney	John Allen
Jas A Dennedy	Walter Stewart	
Dr Wm Jones	Col Jas L Edwards	

[*Added per the list in the Nov 17th newspaper.]

Teacher wanted: from Jan 1 next, to assist in a Classical & Mathematical Academy, in Charlestown, Jefferson Co, Va. Address P H Powers, Charlestown, Va.

Wanted, a gentleman well qualified to teach the Latin & Greek languages in the Alexandria Academy. --B L Brockett, Alexandria, Va

Died: on Tue, in Wash City, Richd Hanson Weightman, son of R H & Susan B Weightman, aged 6 years & 2 months. His funeral will take place from the residence of his grandfather, R S Coxe, 4½ st, between C & La ave.

For sale: 40 to 50 acres of good land, 4 miles from Wash. The land can be seen by calling on the subscriber, near Tennally Town, D C: Chas R Belt.

THU NOV 16, 1854
The Calif swindler, Meiggs, should not be confounded, in name or connexion, with the respectable family of Meigs in N Y, Phil, & Washington.

Chancery Sale: by decree of the Circuit Court of Wash Co, D C, in a cause wherein John B Kibbey & others are cmplnts & Eliz F Marceron, Jos B Marceron, & others are dfndnts: the trustee will, on Dec 8, at auction, in front of the premises, sell the property on N J ave, Wash: part of square 690, with dwlg house & other improvements thereon. –W Redin -Green & Scott, aucts

On Sat, while the family of Mr John Hoye, a trunk maker in Syracuse, NY, were sitting about the breakfast table, a pot of varnish which was drying upon the stove ran over & exploded. Mr Hoye & his wife were terribly burnt, but not believed dangerously. An infant son was burnt so badly that there was no chance of his recovery. Two daughters were severely but not dangerously burnt. –Albany Reg

Anderson B Graham, of Wayne Co, N Y, a respectably connected young man, has been arrested upon a charge of forging bounty land papers, on some of which he has obtained land warrants under the name of E C Ludlow.

David Hoffman, formerly a distinguished lawyer of Balt, died in N Y on Sat of apoplexy, aged 70 years. He left Balt some 6 or 7 years since, & took up his residence in London. –Balt Sun

Arrival of U S Troops: Col E J Steptoe arrived at Salt Lake City with his command, en route for Calif, on Aug 31. The ofcrs under Col Steptoe are Maj Reynolds, Capt T Ingalls, Quartermaster & Commissary; Lts Tyler, Mowry, Livingston, Chandler, & Allston; & H R Wirtz, Surgeon. There are about 175 soldiers.

Mrd: on Nov 15, by Rev John C Smith, Mr Bernard M Campbell, of Balt, to Miss Emily Jane Moore, daughter of Mr Wm W Moore, of Wash City.

Wash Ordinances: 1-Act for the relief of Wm Brown, agent for the heirs of Mary Young, deceased: the Register is to refund the amount paid by him for taxes on improvements erroneously assessed on lot 4 in square 1,075, for the year 1854. 2-Act for the relief of John S Gallaher: to pay him $9.45 for taxes on personal property illegally paid, the same having been paid twice.

Orphans Court of Wash Co, D C. Letters testamentary on the personal estate of Addison Connoway, late of Wash Co, deceased. –Wesley Hyatt, exc

For sale, a good garden farm, of 105½ acres, on the Eastern Branch, 1½ miles above the Anacostia Bridge: with two comfortable dwlg houses & out-bldgs. Inquire of David Cole, on the premises, or of David A Hall, C st, corner of 3rd, Wash, D C.

Wood-land for sale: a tract of 228 acres in Prince Wm Co, Va, 2½ miles from navigation. –H N Gilbert, Land Agent, Pa ave, near the Capitol.

FRI NOV 17, 1854
Desirable market garden at auction: on Nov 22, at the rooms of J H Hartwell, [formerly E N Stratton:] lots 1 thru 3, & 13 thru 18, in square 1,072, fronting south A & B sts & 16th st east, containing 43, 365 square feet. –Geo F Dyer, auct

Household & kitchen furniture at auction: on Nov 28, at the residence of Jno T Reed, on 12th st, 2nd door north of the Kirkwood House. -Jas C McGuire, auct

San Francisco Herald of Oct 23. The last rumor relating to the purchase of the Sandwich Islands was that the American Gov't had agreed to give King Kamehameha $800,000 per annum during his life, & the same to the heirs apparent while he exists, in consideration for their surrendering their claims to the sovereignty of the U S Gov't. Intrinsically the value of the Islands amounts to but little.

Hon Wm Starr Miller died at his residence in N Y C on Nov 9.

The N Y papers publish the particulars of the distressing shipwreck on Monday of the vessel **New Era** on the Jersey coast. There were about 400 souls on board when she struck, of which only 155, including the ofcrs & crew, were saved. A large amount of money & valuable trinkets were found upon the corpses, which remain in the hands of the coroner. The surviving passengers reached N Y on Tue & Wed.

The funeral of Mrs S W Karns, for many years a member of the Methodist Episcopal Church, took place yesterday from the Jane Street Methodist Episcopal Church. The deceased was 117 years, 3 months & 16 days old; born in this country in 1737, when Geo Washington was only 5 years old; was taken to Ireland when an infant & resided in Cork, but after marriage returned with her husband to the U S. Her father was a Scotchman; her mother an Irish lady. She was the mother of 22 children, 2 of whom survive her. She was active & vivacious during life, & showed no signs of imbecility up to the time of her departure. –N Y Day Book

Mr Wm North died suddenly on Tue at N Y, impelled to the melancholy rashness of self-murder. He was found in his chamber a corpse, prussic acid being undoubtedly the cause of his death. -Times

Mrd: on Nov 14, by Rev Jas R Eckard, Mr H W Blunt, of Gtwn, to Miss Marion A Coolidge, daughter of the late Edmond Coolidge, of Wash.

At Rutland, Vt, week before last, Jim Morton, alias M Matthews, & John Gil, alias Saml Becroft, arrested in Canada, & Chas Sexton & Wm Mintzer, arrested in Phil some time since, were all tried for forging a check to the amount of $3,000 on the Rutland Bank, Vt. $1,000 was found on Mintzer, but he was placed upon the stand as a witness, & on his evidence the other 3 were convicted on 2 charges, forgery & false pretences. –Troy Whig

The brothers Glantz were arrested several weeks ago in Wash, charged with being concerned in the shooting of Mr Duvall, near Bladensburg, by which that gentleman's life was endangered. They were taken to Md. On Monday last the grand Jury of PG Co, presented the elder brother simply for an assault, & the younger, a boy, for an assault & battery. The trial is set for next April. The first was released in the sum of $100, the second for $500, for appearance at court. On Tue night they both returned to Wash City. -Sentinel.

Died: on Nov 15, Jas E Wall, in his 26th year. He was beloved by a large circle of friends & acquaintances. His funeral will take place today at 2½ o'clock, from his late residence on 11th st west, near Md ave.

Died: on Oct 30, in Scotland, Concordia Parish, La, William, only son of Field & Mary W Dunbar, aged 1 year.

Dissolution of the co-partnership under the firm of J G Smith & J O Fowler, in the lumber business, Wash City, by mutual consent. The business will hereafter be conducted by said J G Smith. –J G Smith, Jos O Fowler, Wash.

I wish to sell part of my farm nearest to & binding on the west side of the Balt & Wash Railroad, opposite the village of Bladensburg: about 50 acres of good quality. Apply to the undersigned, at Gtwn, D C, or Mr Scott, at the Bladensburg Depot. -H C Matthews

SAT NOV 18, 1854
Chancery sale: by decree of the Circuit Court of Wash Co, D C, in equity, in the cause of Jno S Blackford & others vs Martha Blagrove & Josephine Blagrove, No 1,109, dated Nov 14, 1854, I will offer at public auction, on Dec 8 next, on the premises, all that piece & lot of ground on Montg st, in Gtwn, D C, being a part of lot 13 of Holmead's addition to Gtwn, beginning at the s w intersection of Montgomery & Olive sts; to the northern boundary line of a lot formerly conveyed by the late H B Blagrove to Geo W Godey. –D W Edmonston, jr, trustee -Edw S Wright, auct

Yesterday the Perseverance Fire Co attended to the grave the remains of their companion, John Watson; & the Odd Fellows followed to his last resting-place the body of their brother, Jas E Wall. After life's fitful fever, they sleep well.

Boarding: Mrs E T Duvall, 331 Pa ave, opposite Brown's' Hotel, Wash.

Teacher wanted: to instruct 3 small boys. Address J Waring, Chaptico, St Mary's Co, Md.

Two valuable tracts of land in King Geo Co, Va, for sale. As atty for the heirs of Francis T Fitzhugh, deceased, I shall offer on Dec 21: 1-**Belle Isle**, on Machodock Creek, containing about 700 acres. 2-**Millford**, opposite to **Belle Isle**, contains 500 acres. Call upon Mr Johnson Fitzhugh, who resides at **Millford**, or the undersigned W R Mason, King Geo, Va

Indian murders on Oct 21 about 200 miles above **Fort Kearny**, as we were seated at the evening repast-a shot from a rifle killed one of our number. The names of this unfortunate part are given as follows: Udolphe Wolfe, N Y, shot in the ankle; Harvey Wickoff, N Y; Benj Woods, St Louis; Saul Mantel, St Louis; Silas Nodway, killed; Wm Nodway, killed; Hiram Woodruff, killed; Henry Law, N Y, killed. The St Louis Democrat discredits this story because the banks of the Platte have no timber on them between Kearny & Laramie, while the spot indicated would be upon the north fork of the Platte.

Teacher wanted for my sons, a young man who is a good English & Latin scholar. Address W A Cocke, Cartersville, Cumberland Co, Va.

I have this day disposed of my interest in the Steam Factory to my sons, Messrs W H & H C Baldwin. The business will hereafter be conducted under the firm of Baldwin Brothers. –A Baldwin

Chas H Peverelly, on trial in N Y for arson, the indictment alleging that he set fire to his own store in N Y on Jul 6, was found guilty on Monday. Theodore Peverelly, brother of Chas, has been held to bail in the sum of $5,000 to appear for trail on a charge of being an accomplice in the crime.

The house of Madame Baury, No 2 Waverly Pl, has been undergoing repairs, the family being absent. Bridget Welsh, an Irish woman, some 40 years of age, a faithful domestic in the family, was sent on Sat last to prepare the house for their reception. She engaged Ellen Hollan, about 16, to assist her. Both were found dead in the attic yesterday, having evidently been suffocated by gas which escaped from a pipe in the 1st story, from which a chandelier had been removed.
–Boston Transcript of Tue

MON NOV 20, 1854
Rev John Brady, pastor of the Roman Catholic Church in Hartford, Conn, died suddenly on Thu night of cholera. He had resided in Hartford many years & had the very general respect of its citizens.

Cincinnati despatch of Nov 17: at New London, Butler Co, Ohio, on Thu, the tower of the new Congregational Church in course of construction fell on the workmen & others, & killed Robt Jones, Nathl Jones, John C Jones, & wounded 10 others. John C Jones is a wealthy Welchman, generally known among his countrymen. [Nov 22 newspaper: names of the wounded: Abner Francis, John Davis, John W Jones, Evan Evans, Elias Williamson, Edw Jones, Thos Jones, Jas Scott, Wm Atherton, & Jacob Phillis. Two or three, it is thought, will have to undergo amputations.]

On Thu, at the U S Naval Asylum in Phil, Wm C Riggs, an aged pensioner of the institution, was killed by being pushed down by Anthony Prussock, another pensioner, during a quarrel between them. Riggs struck his head, causing concussion of the brain. He was nearly 70 years of age, & was a participator in the gallant deed carried into effect in the harbor of Tripoli on Feb 16, 1804, when the frig **Philadelphia** was burnt. He was one of the crew on board the ship **Intrepid**, under command of Decatur.

Fort Snelling Court Martial. A trial was held, a short time since, of Capt Napoleon J T Dana, Assist Quartermaster U S Army, upon grave charges of illegal conduct, disobedience of orders, neglect of duty, & fraudulent conduct. He was acquitted. The honorable acquittal from a court of such exalted character is the highest compliment which could be paid Capt Dana. The Court sitting in judgment comprised the following ofcrs: Brig Gen Hitchcock, Cols May, C F Smith, Baker, Brown, Majs Sibley, Garnet, Hays, Raines & Merchant. –St Paul [Minn] Pioneer

Mrd: on Nov 16, in Lynchburg, Va, by Rev J D Mitchell, Leonard H Lyne, of the U S Navy, to Miss Mary Boothroyed, daughter of Mr Thos Ferguson, of Lynchburg.

Died: yesterday, in great peace, John N Lovejoy, sr, at the advanced age of 85 years. He was perhaps one of the oldest residents of Wash City, & none enjoyed more fully the love & respect of all who were favored with his acquaintance. His funeral will take place from the Foundry Church, corner of G & 14th ts, tomorrow at 2 P M.

U S Patent Ofc, Wash, Nov 18, 1854. Ptn of Squire Whipple, of Albany, N Y, praying for the extension of a patent granted to him on Apr 24, 1841, for an improvement in the construction of iron truss brudges, for 7 years from the expiration of said patent, on Apr 24, 1854. –Chas Mason, Com'r of Patents

No 1,046. Equity. Thos Baker & Bernard Givenny, excs of Terrence Looby, against John McGarvey & Josh McGarvey. The above parties & creditors of Chas McGarvey are to appear on Nov 26 next, at my ofc, in the City Hall, Wash, for an account of the personal estate of said Chas McGarvey, to inquire whether the same is sufficient to pay his debts, & if not, what portion of his real estate it is necessary to sell for the purpose. –W Redin, auditor

Died: on Nov 13, at Williamstown, Mass, Mr Jesse Sabin, the father-in-law of Hon Robt McClelland.

Orphans Court of Wash Co, D C. Letters of administration on the personal estate of Chas W Stewart, late of Wash Co, deceased. –Chas S Wallach, adm

TUE NOV 21, 1854
Extensive wholesale stock of groceries at auction: on Nov 27, at the warehouses of Messrs Waters & Shoemaker, Water st, Gtwn. –Waters & Shoemaker –Barnard & Buckey, aucts

At Phil, on Fri, Mrs Brewey was burnt by the accidental upsetting of a fluid lamp. She lingered in great agony until the next morning, when death came to her relief.

The Bishop of Hartford [Conn] & his flock are at enmity. The Bishop refused to allow the remains of Fr Brady, the former pastor of the church, & who at the time of his death was under suspension, to be buried in the churchyard. The people persisted & ultimately carried their point.

Two brothers, who are described as fast young men, named Joel H Wicker & L D Wicker, aged 22 & 18 respectively, have been arrested at Chicago, Ill, for robbing the post-ofc of that city.

Circuit Court of Wash Co, D C. West et al vs Bowie et al. The trustee in this cause having reported that he has sold parts of lots 74 & 75 of Old Gtwn to Jas F Essex for $582.81; part of lot 75 to Richd Ellis for $725; parts of lots 74 & 75 to Waters & Shoemaker for $885.75; part of lot 75 to John Ellis for $687.50; part of lot 75 to Jos Waters for $527.50; lot 33, in Beatty & Hawkins' Addition to Gtwn, to Thos Brown for $305; & lot 148, in the same addition, to Eben Brown for $600; & the purchasers have complied with the terms of sale. –Jno A Smith, clerk

U S Patent Ofc, Wash, Nov 20, 1854. Ptn of Franklin Ransom & Uzziah Wenman, of N Y C, praying for the extension of a patent granted to them on Feb 13, 1841, for an improvement in the mode of applying water to fire engine, so as to render their operation more effective, for 7 years from the expiration date of Feb 13, 1855. -Chas Mason, Com'r of Patents

Dr Wm Turk, the oldest surgeon in the American navy, died yesterday at Newark, N J. He entered the service on May 15, 1800.

Maj Arthur T Lee, of the U S Army, who was reported to be killed in New Mexico by Indians, is alive & well. A letter dated Oct 9th was received from him by a friend of his in Sunbury, Pa.

Mrs Lucy Brashear, who was the first woman ever married in Louisville, died recently in Madison Co. She was present at the siege of Boonsborough in 1776, & was born in Va Jul, 1761. —Louisville Courier

Intelligence received of the death, in Texas, of Brvt Maj Geo W F Wood, of the U S Army. He was a native of Phil, & entered the army as 2nd Lt of Infty in 1838.

The carpenter shop of Mr Wm H Thomas, at the foot of Capitol Hill, was destroyed by fire on Sunday night. Two sets of tools were burnt, & the loss is at $500. There were several false alarms during the day.

Two Sheffield silver-plated baskets, with gold & silver medals attached, are at the store of Messrs Wabriner & Semkin, made to the order of the Washington encampment of Masons, is to be presented to their brother, V V French. The inscription: "Presented to Sir Knight B B French by Washington Encampment No 1." -Star

Knights Templar meeting on Nov 22, a 6:30. —Wm J Rhees, Recorder

Balt, Nov 20. The drying house of Jacob Johnson, in Marlboro township, Montg Co, Pa, containing 2 tons of gunpowder, exploded this morning, killing Henry Whistler & Josiah, his son. The bldg was entirely destroyed.

WED NOV 22, 1854
Trustee's sale of valuable property: by deed of trsut from Philip Boteler & wife to the subscriber, recorded in Liber J A S No 24, folios 346 thru 348, of the Land Records for Wash Co: I shall sell lot 16 in square 169, with a very large brick livery stable. -Jas C McGuire, auct

In Lowell, Mass, on Sat night, Mr Richd Seaton was robbed of his watch by a fellow who put over his mouth a cloth wet with some liquid which nearly strangled him, & left him to be discovered by the police in a senseless condition. The scamp was subsequently arrested.

Wash Corp: 1-Act for the relief of Matilda Ann Beall: referred to the Cmte of Claims. 2-Ptn from Evan Hughes for the remission of a fine: referred to the Cmte of Claims. 3-Cmte of Claims: act for the relief of Corbin Baker: passed. Same cmte: act for the relief of Evan Hughes: passed. 4-Cmte on Improvements: bill for the relief of Wm R Woodward: passed.

Groceries & liquors at auction on Nov 24, at the grocery store of Mr H C Purdy, in the old Railroad Depot, on Pa ave, between 2nd & 3rd sts. -Green & Scott, aucts

Wash City Ordinances: 1-Act for the relief of Chas H Tillett: fine imposed on Chas H Tillett, an orphan boy, for peeling the bark off a tree in front of Lafayette Square, is remitted; provided said Tillett or his friends pay the cost of prosecution. 2-Act for the relief of Jas Barry: fine imposed on him is remitted: provided he pay the costs thereof. 3-Act to pay Geo Neitzes for work done on G st: sum of $57.27. 4-Act for the relief of Chas Edmonston: the Register is to omit from the tax books the assessment made for 1854 on 2 brick houses lately erected by Chas Edmonston on I st, between 10th & 11th sts, in square 344, they not having been liable to assessment for said year.

On Nov 12 Mr Cyril Bienvenu, a hightly respectable citizen of New Orleans, went hunting in the Parish of St Bernard, accompanied by a favorite negro. In crossing Lake Leri they were exposed to a severe norther. The following day Mr Sckismanski found him dead in his canoe. His remains were consigned to the grave at Terre aux Boeufs yesterday. In a strange coincidence, about 10 days ago, Mr Bienvenu lost a younger brother, who, while hunting, fell upon a pointed stake receiving an injury which proved mortal. A third brother was some years ago severely wounded, while engaged in the same dangerous sport, that he had to suffer amputation of a limb.
-New Orleans Bee

Drowned, yesterday, at the Four Mile Run, near Swash Channel, on the road to Alexandria, Jas Moir, in his 22nd year. His body was not found. When it is discovered leave information with Stewart Downs, at the Navy Yard. The deceased had friends at Balt.

A negro boy belonging to Mr Sasser, of PG Co, was accidentally killed yesterday on Pa ave. The wagon of Mr Sasser, laden with his produce, was proceeding to Gtwn, when the deceased fell from the wagon, which the man driving stopped with the wheel resting upon the boys' neck. Life was found to be extinct.

Mr Thos C Connolly was last evening elected Superintendent of the Exhibition of the Metropolitan Mechanics' Institute, to be commenced on Feb 8 next.

Mrd: on Nov 16, by Rev Mr Hodges, Zadock Williams, of Wash City, to Miss Mary Morton, of Balt.

Mrd: on Nov 21, by Rev R L Dashiel, Mr Josephus Perry to Miss Catharine Miles, all of Wash City.

THU NOV 23, 1854
Cemeteries. The new *Georgetown Cemetery* is one of the prominent attractions to visiters, & the *Glenwood Cemetery*, lately laid out in the vicinity of Wash, will soon be also an object of interest.

Mr De Cueto, the esteemed Minister from Spain, was driving a pair of fine & spirited horses, attached to a light vehicle, when they became unmanageable & dashed with headlong speed down the avenue, from 13th st. They encountered a furniture car, which they upset. Mr Cueto was injured in the head & neck but was able to walk to a carriage, in which he was conveyed to his residence. The horses were not hurt. [Nov 30th newspaper: Mr De Cueto is in his 8th day of illness. He is still low. He has today been informed, for the first time, of the cause of his injury, but he has heard it with great incredulity. He remembers most of the incidents of the last 2 weeks, but has no knowledge of being thrown from his carriage & injured. –Globe]

Circuit Court of Wash Co, D C-in Chancery. Anthony Holmead vs John F Ennis, adm, & Thos C Wells, Susan Sears, Gilbert D Kean, & Harriet Kean, heirs-at-law of Catherine E Dent, deceased. Auction, on the premises, Dec 18, of all that lot of ground in Wash City: lot 7 in square 580. –R H Laskey, trustee -Green & Scott, aucts

The Methodist Episcopal Church at Hyattstown, Montg Co, Md, was burnt to the ground on Sat night last, it having caught fire from the stove-pipe during the services in the evening, but not discovered until it was enveloped in flames & totally destroyed.

Circuit Court of Wash Co, D C-in Equity. Jas Adams, Jos Ingle, et al, vs John P Ingle, Hardage Lane, et al. As special auditor to inquire into the property, known as the **Old Capitol**, being lots 14 thru 19 in square 728, are susceptible of specific partition among the parties to the above cause. Said parties to appear before me at City Hall on Nov 28. –Walter S Coxe, Special Auditor

F W Risque, of Gtwn, a gentleman of means, of enterprise, & a lover of the arts, recently purchased in N Y C a marble statue representing the "Dying Gladiator," copied from the celebrated antique statue in the museum of the capitol in the Eternal City. The copy is by Gott, a sculptor of eminence, & is pronounced perfect by John Gibson, Emelius Wolf, Crawford, & by other artists of celebrity. Mr Risque paid $3,000 for it, & its arrival is expected hourly, for exhibition in the bldg of Mr Morrison, on 4½ st, near Pa ave, Wash City.

At Yarmouthport, Mass, on Sat, while a lad, Joshua H Bassett, was hunting with a playmate, he accidentally shot himself in the leg, & death ensued in a few hours.

Mrd: on Nov 16, at St Louis, Missouri, by Rt Rev Bishop Hawks, John R Triplett to Sallie A, daughter of Maj Benj Walker, U S Army.

Mrd: on Nov 22, at Alexandria, Va, by Rev Mr Johnstone, Rev Chas H Hall, of Fayetteville, N C, to Miss Annie S, youngest daughter of the late Geo H Duffey, of Alexandria.

N Y, Nov 22. Rev Horatio Potter was today consecrated provisional Bishop of the diocese of N Y. The sermon was preached by Bishop Talford, of Montreal.

Phil, Nov 22. Thos P Cope, an aged & highly esteemed merchant of this city, died here today in his 88th year.

Balt Sun: on Sat the jury in the case of Fred'k Loebig, charged with the murder of Mathias Smith, came into the court & rendered a verdict of not guilty. The wife of the prisoner stood weeping by the side of her husband.

In Chancery. A P West & others against Mary Bowie [late Oden,] Wm D Bowie, & others. Auditor to state the account of the trustee, & ascertain the shares of the cmplnts & dfndnts in the trust fund; & also to audit the claims made by Mrs Eliza Lucas & Mrs McDaniel & others, who have paid taxes for parts of lots 74 & 75, in Old Gtwn, & for lot 33, in Beatty & Hawkins' addition to said town. Audit on Nov 19 at my ofc in Gtwn, where all persons interested are to attend. –W Redin, auditor

SAT NOV 25, 1854

First ascent of **Mount Hood**, Oregon, estimated to be 18,861 feet high, even more lofty than Mount Shasta, & heretofore unexplored. The narrative is given by the editor of the Oregonian, who started on Aug 4, with a party of gentlemen, under the guidance of Capt Barlow, an old mountaineer, to ascend the peak. We were to meet Judge Olney & Maj Hallar, of the army, on the south side of the snow peak. At a high altitude Judge Olney, Maj Hallar, & Capt Travaillot exhibited dizziness in the head & were unable to go further. We got to the ridge & could distinctly see Mounts Jefferson, Three Sisters, McLaughlin, St Helen's, Rainier & Adams; also, Fremont's Peak & Shasta Butte Mountain, in Calif. On the 11th the party reached Portland, having been just a week engaged in the exploration.

Coroner Woodward held an inquest in the County Jail on Thanksgiving Day on the body of Bill, alias John Thomas, who was found dead in his bed on the same morning. He had been committed for theft while laboring under a malady which caused his death. Thomas was an old offender, having been 4 times in the Penitentiary. Thus sadly ends a wicked career.

The Phil papers of Thu announce the death of the venerable Thos P Cope, in his 87th year. His father, Caleb Cope, was a native of Chester Co, & son of Oliver Cope, an original proprietor of land under Penn. The old homestead-a farm about 30 miles west from this city-still remains in the possession of the family. The log cabin which was erected on the premises by the grandfather of the deceased, & beneath whose humble roof were born his 8 children, consisting of 6 boys & 2 girls, is yet standing, though nearly a century & a half old.

An old mine has recently been discovered on the farm of John L Neely, in Solebuy township, about 2½ miles below New Hope, on the Delaware river, in Bucks Co, Pa.

Judge Alex'r Wells died at San Jose on Oct 31.

Circuit Court of Wash Co, D C-in Equity. Wm A Smallwood, vs John Addison, Wm Addison, Washington Van Hamm, Cornelia Van Hamm, Clarence Van Hamm, Henry Van Hamm, Henry Van Hamm, & Jonathan Prout. Auditor to state the account of the trustee on Nov 29 at the auditor's room, City Hall. -Walter S Cox, special auditor [Note-Henry Van Hamm was listed twice.]

Valuable estate for sale: by decree of the Circuit Court for PG Co: public sale, on the premises, on Dec 14, the fine Farm which the late Robt Ghiselin occupied, near the village of Nottingham, PG Co, Md, containing about 360 acres: with 2 large tobacco houses, servants quarters, overseer's house, stable, corn-house, all in good repair. -C C Magruder, trustee
+
Orphans' Court of PG Co, Md: public sale of valuable negroes, on Dec 13 next, on the farm occupied by the late Robt Ghiselin, 10 valuable servants, most of them prime young men & field hands; among the lot is an excellent cook woman. At the same time will be sold a stock of work horses, oxen, cows, sheep, & hogs, & farming implements. –C C Magruder, adm d b n c t a, of Marg A Ghiselin.

MON NOV 27, 1854
Household & kitchen furniture at auction: on Nov 29, at the store of Mr T S J Johnson, 310 Pa ave, between 9th & 10th sts. –Geo F Dyer, auct

Beautiful residence in Lafayette Square at public auction: on Dec 11, on the premises, the residence lately occupied by Thos Ritchie, deceased, adjoining the residence of W W Corcoran, fronting south on Lafayette square: fronts 54 feet & 9 inches on north H st. -Jas C McGuire, auct

From Europe: Chas Kemble, the distinguished actor, is dead, at age 79 years.

Administrator's sale of valuable horses, carriages, buggies, cart, sets of harness, saddles & bridles: by order of the Orphans Court of Wash Co, D C. The adm will sell the above at public sale, on Nov 30, at the Auction Store of Rothwell & Brown, on La ave. -Chas S Wallach, adm -Rothwell & Brown, aucts

During the recent session of the Vt Legislature Miss Lucy Stone received 7 votes for the ofc of Brig Gen of Militia.

New Family Grocery: at the old stand under Odd Fellows' Hall, 502 7th st. —Geo W E Kennedy

In Conn last week Geo A Peters, an ex-councilman, & Madison Peters, his son, were convicted of rescuing from the custody of a police ofcr a prisoner, the son of the ex-councilman, who, with a gang of lads, was stoning a man, & taken into custody, when he was rescued by his father & brother. The evidence was clear, & the Court sentenced the dfndnts to a fine of $10 & costs each, & confinement in the county jail for 24 hours. The fine was paid & the parties committed.

From Calif: 1-Dr Robt Semple died near Colusa, on Oct 25, from injuries received by a fall from his horse. He was one of the earliest settlers of Calif, & was president of the convention which formed the constitution of the State in 1849. 2-Hon Alex'r Wells, Assoc Justice of the Supreme Court of Calif, died at San Jose on Oct 31. His death appears to have been sudden & unexpected, but no particulars are given. 3-John Dougherty was recently drowned in the Alta Lagoon, near San Francisco, while wading out for some ducks that he had shot.

Chas Willey, of Cherryfield, Me, while on a hunting excursion on Fri last with a young man, Gilbert M S Hill, was shot by the latter, who, being separated from him, supposed him to be a deer or some other animal.

Home Hill Boarding School for Boys: was opened the first Monday in Jan, 1854, in the neighborhood of Falls Church, Fairfax Co, Va. Address R F Judson, Falls Church, Fairfax Co, Va, for particulars.

For sale: valuable Farm adjoining Mr Lansdale's, containing 53 acres of good land: about 5 miles from Gtwn, near the Rockville Turnpike Road. Also, a tract of 40 acres near Alexandria. The above Farms wil be sold on liberal terms or exchanged for city property. Apply to Edw Swann, 26 La ave, near the City Hall.

TUE NOV 28, 1854
Fine 3 story carpenter's shop at auction: on Dec 8, in front of the premises, the bldg formerly occupied by Davis & Garrett, & now by Thos Davis & W Norris, in Jackson Alley, in Reservation No 10. -Green & Scott, aucts

St Louis Republican; the case of Mrs Mary C W Baker, for the murder of Wm O Hoffman, in that city, in May last, went to the jury on Nov 21st. They were out near 2 hours, & then returned a verdict of not guilty.

At Pittsburg, Pa, on Sat week, Danl Husk ordered his little son to hold a lighted candle while he filled a camphene lamp. An explosion took place, & the lad & 2 children who were at play were enveloped in flames. One of the children died, & the recovery of the other two was deemed next to impossible. Mr Husk & wife were likewise badly burnt.

Died: yesterday, in Wash City, Mrs Catharine F Alexander, relict of the late Walter Stoddard Alexander, of Alexandria Co, Va, in her 70th year. This most excellent lady was the 2nd child of the late Col Baldwin Dade, of Va, & was born at Lochobar, near the city of Alexandria. Her illness, though short, was severe. She leaves a large circle of relatives & friends left to deplore her loss. Her funeral will take place today at 2 o'clock, from the residence of her son, Oscar Alexander, on I st, between 6th & 7th sts, where the friends of her family & of her sister, Mrs Julia Terrett, are invited to attend.

Albany, Nov 27. Phelps, convicted of the murder of his wife at West Troy, has been sentenced to be hung on Jan 13.

John Andrews, of Topsfield, Mass, aged 16 years, accidentally shot & killed himself while hunting squirrels with his father on Thu. The lock of his gun got caught by a twig & the gun discharged.

WED NOV 29, 1854
Household & kitchen furniture at auction: by order of the Orphans Court of Wash Co, D C: auction on Dec 2, in front of the auction rooms, the furniture & effects of C R Byrne, deceased. -Jas C McGuire, auct

The power of atty given by me to Jas Towle has been fully revoked, & is hereby revoked. The deed of trust under which he has advertised my property for sale has been fully satisfied, & I forewarn all persons from purchasing under it.
–Wm D Acken

Funeral of a Roman Catholic Priest. The remains of Rev Mr Lilly, late Vice Pres of Loyola College, Balt, were brought to this city by the cars this morning. They were accompanied by the Rev Messrs Early, McManus, McColgan, Dolan, & others, from Balt, including a cmte of the Young Catholics' Friend Society. The cortege was met at the depot by friends & clergymen of Wash City & Gtwn, & by Rev Mr Blox, of Alexandria, Va. The corpse was removed in funeral procession to Gtwn, where, after services, it was deposited in the burial ground of **Gtwn College**. The deceased had been for some time a professor in the Washington Catholic Seminary on F st.
-Globe

Wash City Ordinance: 1-Act for the relief of Jas M Wright: to pay him $2.91, reimbursement for taxes overcharged & paid by him in 1854. 2-Act for the relief of P W Dorsey: to pay him $40.95, the amount of taxes twice paid on a lot of ground at 7th & H sts, in square 428. 3-Act for the relief of Corbin Baker: Register to refund him $38.33, the amount overpaid on a license to keep a tavern, he having paid for a whole year, while the license took effect from Jul 14, 1854.

Orphans Court of Wash Co, D C. Letters of administration on the personal estate of Wm P Elliot, late of Wash Co, deceased. –Mary A Elliot, admx

Phil, Nov 28. In the Criminal Court today, Dr Stephen T Beal was sentenced to 4 years & 6 months' imprisonment in the county jail. Previous to the sentence he made a speech in which he asserted his entire innocence.

THU NOV 30, 1854
Orphans Court of Wash Co, D C. Letters of administration on the personal estate of Jas Cuthbert, late of Wash Co, deceased. –J B Wilson, adm

Dissolution of the copartnership in the Dry-goods business, under the firm of Maxwell, Sears, & Colley, by mutual consent, on Nov 1, John S Maxwell withdrawing from the firm. –Jno S Maxwell, Jas W Sears, J W Colley.
Sears & Colley will continue the Dry-goods trade at the old stand, 523 7th st.

Valuable real estate for sale: Farm in Montg Co, Md, 3 miles from Rockville, containing by estimation 800 acres of land. The house is commodious with numerous out-bldgs. –Alex Kilgour, Atty & Agent

Abolitionist held to bail. Boston, Nov 29. In the U S Circuit Court today, Judge Sprague presiding, Rev Theodore Parker was arraigned on the charge of inciting a riot last summer & aiding in the attempt made to rescue Anthony Burns, the fugitive slave. Mr Parker waived the reading of the indictment, & gave bail in the sum of $1,500 to appear for trial at the March term of the court.

<u>Ladies Furs,</u> Furs! Great bargains in Stone Marten, Fitch Marten, Siberian Squirrel, Mink & Rock Martens. Children's furs in abundance, cheap. –W F Seymour, 132 Bridge st, Gtwn.

Mrs B Gregg will open a handsome assortment of winter Millinery on Dec 2, at Mrs Hill's, between 10th & 11th sts, Pa ave, south side, No 277.

FRI DEC 1, 1854
Arrest of counterfeiters: Chas O'Donnel, master, & Saml James, a hand, belonging to the canal boat **J H Stone**, were committed by Capt Burch for trial before the Criminal Court. The notes they attempted to pass, purport to be issued of the Merchants' Bank, at Lynchburg, Va. -Globe

At the Centre Market yesterday, a son of Mr Stanley, 9 or 10 years of age, who resides on the Island, was seized in the crowded market place by an angry bulldog, from which he could not be rescued until the animal was killed by blows from a number of cleavers. The child was not dangerously hurt, protected by the thickness of his clothing. The owner of the dog was fined $3. –Globe

Mexican boundary commission: from the San Antonio Ledger. Maj Emory & party leave our city in a few days. Sixteen of the most experienced frontiersmen have selected to accompany the expedition: Col Emory, commanding; C Radzeminski, sec; L W Emory, clerk; John H Clark, assist astronomer; Hugh Campbell, W R Likins, assists; Col M T W Chandler, in charge of magnetic & meterorological observations; David Hinckle, assist; C R R Kennedy, surgeon; Lt Turnbull, quartermaster.

Mrd: on Nov 14, at the Wesley Chapel parsonage, by Rev Jas H Brown, Mr Caleb B Ricard to Miss Mgt Ann Reed, both of Montg Co, Md.

Mrd: on Nov 28, by Rev Jas H Brown, Michl Shay to Mrs Rebecca Fage.

Mrd: on Nov 29, in Wash City, by Rev P D Gurley, Warner P Jones, of Lynchburg, Va, to Miss Rebecca L Paxton, of New Orleans.

Mrd: on Nov 16, in Balt, by Rev Myer Levin, John A Hunnicutt, of Wash, to Mary C B, eldest daughter of Saml C Moran, of Chas Co, Md.

Mrd: on Wed, by Rev John C Smith, Rev J Eames Rankin, Pastor First Presbyterian Church, Pottsdam, N Y, to Miss Mary H, daughter of Cyrus Birge, of Wash City.

Died: on Nov 28, in Wash City, at the residence of her Uncle, Jas Nokes, after a severe illness of 24 days, of typhoid fever, Susan B Curtis, of Phil, aged 20 years, daughter of Asa Curtis, U S Navy.

Died: at Port Tobacco, Chas Co, Md, Jas A Berry, in his 30th year. [No death date given-current item.]

Died: on Nov 23, in Balt, in his 46th year, Lt Saml E Munn, of the U S Navy. He was one of the oldest ofcrs of his grade, but had not been in active service for a number of years.

Died: on Nov 22, at Malvern, near Theological Seminary, Fairfax Co, Va, Margaretta Jane Johns, wife of Bishop Johns, & eldest daughter of Dr J T Shaaff, deceased.

Departure of missionaries: Rev H R Hitchcock & wife, Rev Geo Pierson & wife, & Rev Wm O Baldwin & wife sailed from Boston on Tue for Honolulu. Mr & Mrs Hitchcock have been connected with the Sandwich Islands mission more than 20 years, & they now return to Molokai, their island home, with 2 sons. Mr & Mrs Baldwin are to occupy a vacant station at the islands. Mr & Mrs Pierson are bound to Strong's Island, where they expect to be associated with Rev Mr Snow.

The War Dept received information of the death of C A Hinckley, at **Fort Arbuckle**, Cherokee Nation. The deceased arrived at the post on Sep 25, complained of being unwell & exhibited symptoms of derangement of mind. On Oct 10, he inflicted wounds in the region of the heart which almost instantly caused his death. His remains were interred with every mark of respect by the ofcrs of the post. Nothing is known of his relatives, & it is hoped this notice may reach then, as he left a small amount of property at the post. -Star

On Monday Capt Robt McCerren & Capt Beatty, of N Y, started in a sailboat on a duck-shooting excursion. The boat capsized in a squall. Capt McCerren was carried into deep water by the waves & perished. Capt Beatty succeeded in making land.

SAT DEC 2, 1854
Fenton Peters & his wife Jane were arrested at New Orleans last week by the sheriff of the parish of Jefferson on the charge of having abducted a boy named Denis Langton from the plantation of his guardian, Mr Pierre Sauve, above Carrollton. It appears that the boy is the heir of an estate of $30,000, & that Mrs Peters is the only surviving sister of his deceased mother. In case of the boys' death she would be sole heir to the estate. They are to be examined in Carrollton, where the alleged offence was committed.

On Sat last Mr Mordecai Thompson & Mr Adolphe Henry started in a small sail boat for Bay Monte for hunting. Yesterday their lifeless bodies were found frozen to death in the boat. –Mobile Tribune, 22nd ult

Several members of the family of Maj Israel Pierson, of West Bloomfield, N J, were shockingly injured on Tue by the bursting of a lamp containing burning fluid. A 9 year old girl died the next morning; an older daughter is much injured; the mother & a little boy are considerably burnt.

Mrd: on Thu, by Rev John C Smith, Mr Geo H Walker to Miss Mary O Anderson, all of Wash City.

Died: on Dec 1, in Wash City, Helen, infant daughter of Hamilton G & Josephine Fant. Her funeral will take place on Sunday at 4 o'clock, from the residence of Mrs Smith, 233 F st.

Obit-died: [from the Madison [Indiana] Banner: In our paper on Monday we announced the death of Hon Williamson Dunn, in his 73rd year, at his late residence in this county. In 1809 or 1810 he removed from Danville, Ky, to this county. A good man has fallen in our midst, & we all feel the loss. [No death date given.]

Loudoun, Fauquier, & Fairfax lands & real estate in Alexandria for sale. By decree of the Circuit Court of Alexandria Co, rendered at Nov term, 1854: public auction of the real estate of which the late Dr Wm L Powell died seized, viz: 1-*Coon-skin tract*, about 600 acres, in Loudoun Co. 2-*Oakendale tract*, in Fauquier Co, on the Little River, containing about 700 acres: with small dwlg & usual out-houses. 3-*Fairfax Farm*, containing 505 acres, lying on the waters of Accotink. 4-The Three story Brick Dwlg & lot of ground on King st, between Wash & Columbus sts, in the city of Alexandria, the residence of the late Dr Wm L Powell, & now occupied as a Boarding-house by the Misses Thurston. 5-An undivided lot of ground in the s w corner of Wolfe & Union sts, in the city of Alexandria, known a the *Old Distillery Lot*. The farms in Loudoun & Fauquier will be sold in front of Rufus Smith's Hotel, in Middleburg, on Dec 30. The other property will be sold in front of the Mayor's ofc, in Alexandria, on Jan 6, 1855. –Burr P Noland, Lawrence B Taylor, Com'rs

Circuit Court of Wash Co, D C-Oct Term, 1854. Abram Barnes & others vs John Mason & others. John Marbury, trustee, reported that he has sold the following lots of land lying in Wash City, viz: to Wm Marshall, lot 73 in square 17, for $193.48; lot 14 in same square for $163.48; lot 2 in square 31, for $322.87; lot 10 in square 31, for $256.80; lot 8 in square 44, for $191.55; to Jas M Mason, lots 5 & 6 in square 28, for $682.78; to G C Grammer, lot 2 in square 55, for $564.30; lot 15 in same square, for $671.30; to A F & G B Hines, lot 1 in square 55, for $534.62; to Geo W Mitchell, lots 14 & 15 in square 31, for $573; to Jos N Fearson, lot 28 in square 28, for $415; lot 1 in square 42, for $229: & that the parties have complied with the terms of sale. –John A Smith, clerk

Buffalo, Dec 1. Wm Darry was hung in this city this morning for the murder of his wife. [Dec 9th newspaper: Wm Darry, a ship carpenter, who murdered his wife Mary on Aug 14, 1852, at Buffalo, was executed in that city on Fri week. He had been married but 3 months. His dying words were that the assault, which resulted in his wife's death, was committed while he was under the influence of liquor, & that she loved him, & never gave him cause to injure her.]

MON DEC 4, 1854
Household & kitchen furniture at auction: Dec 7, in front of the Auction Rooms, the effects of Hon E Everett. -Jas C McGuire, auct

Stock of family groceries at auction: on Dec 6, at the store of Mr David Hines, [who is about to change his business,] corner of Pa ave & 20th st. -Jas C McGuire, auct

Trustee's sale of groceries, horse, carryall, & spring wagon: on Dec 8, by deed of trust dated Dec 2, 1854, recorded among the land records of Wash Co, D C, at the Grocery Store of Henry G Murray, corner of 8th st east & K st south, near the Navy Yard. –John C E Hamilton, trustee -Green & Scott, aucts

On Nov 22 a very aged & then unknown man was knocked down on the corner of 42nd st & 3rd ave, N Y, by one of the cars, which caused injuries which resulted in death soon afterwards at Bellevue Hospital. He was buried in Potter's Field at the expense of the city. It now appears the deceased was Mr John L Norton, nearly 85 years of age, who lived in Pearl st, & was worth more than $500,000. On Friday the blind son of the deceased, upwards of 60 years, & Brock Carroll, his grandson, called upon the clerk to the coroner, who examined the record of inquests for their benefit, which resulted in the dress & articles found in the pockets of the deceased being recognized as those belonging to their venerable relative. They at once took steps to recover the remains of the deceased & give then a respectable interment in **Greenwood Cemetery**. -Express

Columbia Typographical Society: last Sat the following ofcrs were elected for the ensuing year:
Wm Woodward, Pres
Wm M Belt, Vice Pres
Thos Rich, Rec Sec
Wm M McLane, Corr Sec
Michl Caton, Treas

Mrd: on Nov 29, by Rev Mr Leavel, at **Ellerslie**, Dr Bushrod Taylor, of Clarke Co, Va, to Miss Elvira Lane, daughter of Jas Jett, of Rappahannock Co, Va.

Died: on Dec 3, Eliz C, the beloved wife of Ferdinand Butler, & daughter of Jos Abbott. Her funeral will take place on Tue at 2 o'clock, from the residence of her husband, corner of 14th st & Pa ave.

Died: on Oct 9, in Thibodaux, La, of yellow fever, Dr Walter B Young.

Died: on Oct 17, in Houma, La, John Y Young, for many years a resident of Gtwn, D C.

Died: on Nov 9, near Thibodaux, La, of yellow fever, Dr Thos F Young.

Mrs Ann H Scott, opposite Jackson Hall, is prepared to accommodate a mess of boarders. She has several very fine rooms.

TUE DEC 5, 1854
Trustee's sale: 2 deeds of trust from Geo W Garrett & wife to the subscriber, dated May 26, 1853, & Jun 27, 1854, [& by direction of Chas Calvert, trustee & exec of Solomon Drew, the party secured thereby,] public auction, on the premise, of part of lot 6 in square 459, Wash City, containing 673 square feet of ground, known as lot C on the plan of the heirs of Solomon Drew, with the 4 story new brick dwlg house thereon. –W Redin, trustee -Green & Scott, aucts

Sale of valuable collection of Books & Congressional Documents: by order of the Orphans Court of Wash Co, D C: by order of the administrator of the estate of the late Chas W Stewart. –Rothwell & Brown, aucts, La ave

Trustee's sale, by deed of trust from Geo W Garrett & wife to the subscriber, dated Jul 6, 1854, [& by direction of Messrs Simonton & Rittenhouse, the parties secured thereby,] the following property at auction, on Jan 8, 1855: part of lot 6 in square 459, Wash City, known as lot C on the plan of the heirs of Solomon Drew, with 4 story new brick dwlg house thereon. –W Redin, trustee -Green & Scott, aucts

Chancery sale: by decree of the Circuit Court of Wash Co, D C, in equity, passed in a cause between Terrence Looby's excs & Chas McGarvey's heirs: auction on Dec 28, of part of lot 1 in square west of square 4, in Wash City, situated on the n w corner of K st & 27th st, with 2 story brick dwlg & store thereon; also, one undivided half part of lot 11 in the same square, fronting on 27th st. This property is the corner immediately west of the Brewery near the K st bridge, over Rock Creek, in the 1st Ward. –John F Ennis, Wm R Woodward, trustees -Green & Scott, aucts

New members of the 33rd Congress, second session, Dec 4, 1854. Chas S Lewis, Rep elect from the 11th district of Va, vice John F Snodgrass, deceased; F M Bristow, 3rd district of Ky, vice Presley Ewing, deceased; Isaac Teller, 12th district, & Henry C Goodwin, 22nd district of N Y, vice Gilbert Dean & Gerrit Smith, resigned.

Died: on Dec 4, Mrs Anna M Mohun, consort of Mr Francis Mohun, in her 43rd year. Grief for the unexpected death of this lady extends beyond the family circle, for to neighbors & friends she presented the example of a good & useful life. Her funeral will be from her late residence on 6th st, between E & F sts, on Wed, at 9:30 o'clock. The funeral service will be held at St Patrick's Church at 10 o'clock the same day.

Rooms to let: 1-C W Boteler, Iron Hall, Pa ave, between 9th & 10th sts. 2-Mrs D E Groux, 349 Pa ave, opposite Brown's Hotel. 3-Jas L Smith, City Post Ofc: if the rooms are not engaged soon the whole house, furnished as it is, would be rented to a small family for 4, 6, or 12 months. 4-Furnished dwlg at 13th & H st: apply on the premises, or to Nicholas Callan, or to W C Reddall, Dept of State. 5-Mrs Spaulding: F & 9th sts. 6-Mrs E E Alexander: 502 I st, between 6th & 7th sts. 7-Elegant parlors & bed chambers, on north 15th st: C Weirman. 8-Mrs R E Wheeler, F & 13th sts, in the Boarding-house formerly kept by Mrs Willis. 9-Jas A Wise, 7th st, between G & H sts.

Mrd: on Nov 23, by Rev J McKin Duncan, C K Green, of Detroit, to Sarah, daughter of Jotham Lawrence, of Exeter, N H.

Mrd: on Nov 28, at Zanesville, Ohio, by Rev J M Platt, Maj J Van Horne, U S Army, to Miss Mary S Gilbert, daughter of the late Chas C Gilbert, of that place.

Valuable farm in the State of Va & Town lots in Alexandria & Wash City for sale. In Berkeley Co: about 530 acres, opposite old *Fort Frederick*, Md. In Morgan Co: farm called *Dunmore*, on the Warm Spring Run & the Potomac River, opposite the town of Hancock, Md, for many years tenanted by Cromwell Orrick, containing upwards of 1,100 acres. In Hampshire Co: tract on Buck Island Run, called *Lockheart's*, or the *Cat-tail Run Tract*, containing about 500 acres. **Coal land**, known as one of the *Martin Surveys*, lying on the top of the Alleghany mountains, containing between 700 & 800 acres: 7 miles from Reese's Tavern. Price $16 per acre. Hardy Co: tract known as *Kittle Lick Survey*, at the head of New Creek, containing 501 acres: price $10 per acre. In Alexandria-15 acre lot, in Alexandria & partly in Fairfax Co. Lot on Wolfe & Pitt sts. 2 acre square & lot on Pitt, Royal, & Oronoka sts, for many years occupied by Mr Robt Brockett as a brickyard, & lot on Pitt & Oronoka sts, 63 feet 5 inches on Pitt st & opposite the square, also occupied by said Brockett for the same purpose. In Washington: lot 8 in square 536 on Va ave. Apply to Ch Lee Jones, Atty at Law, Wash.

For sale or rent: one of those new dwlg houses on C st, between 1st & 2nd sts: contains 6 large chambers, a fine large parlor, fashionably finished, a commodious dining room, & well arranged kitchen. Hot & cold water & gas pipes throughout the house. Bathing room, arranged for hot, cold, & shower baths; & pump in kitchen; bells from every room; cooking range in the kitchen & furnace in the cellar. –John B Ward, in the adjoining house, or at the corner of 12th st & Canal.

The widow of Wm Bradford, Atty Gen of Washington's Administration in 1794-95, died at her residence in Burlington, N J, on Thu last, in her 90th year, having survived her husband 60 years. She was the last surviving widow of the accomplished men who composed Gen Washington's Cabinet. Mrs Bradford was the only daughter of Hon Elias Boudinot, Pres [for some time] of the old Continental Congress, Commissary Gen of Prisoners during the Revolution, & the first Director of the Mint of the U S, an ofc to which he was appointed by Washington & retained by Jefferson.

In Chancery: in the Circuit Court for Worcester Co, Md. Saml S McMaster vs The Board of Foreign Missions of the Presbyterian Church of the U S A, & the Board of Missions, John Williams, & others. The bill states that Ann P White, late of Worcester Co, deceased, by her last will & testament, dated May 20, 1839, duly proved, among other things bequeathed the remainder of her money to remain in the hands of Lewis West & David H White, with directions to them to pay over the interest thereof to her mother every year while she was a married woman, & in the event of her said mother becoming a widow then the whole sum to be hers, & to be at her disposal; & if her said mother should die a married woman, then she leaves the whole of said fund in the hands of her executor to be applied to the support of missionaries in India, under the direction of the Gen Assembly's Board of Mission of the Presbyterian Church in the U S, & all the rest & residue of her property to her mother. By said will Geo Hudson was appointed exec thereof, & letters testamentary were granted him, by virtue whereof he presented himself of the personal estate of said Ann P White, but died before he had completed the administration thereof, & letters de bonis non, with a copy of the will annexed, were granted unto the cmplnt, Saml McMaster, who proceeded to complete said administration, & paid off the debts & legacies enjoined by said will to be paid off before the death of the mother of said testatrix; after the payment of which there remains in his hands $4,521,88l; of which sum $500 are to be paid, as the said cmplnt supposes, to John White, son of Ambrose J White, a legatee under said will; leaving still undisposed of in his hands $4,021.88; all which money was invested by order of the Orphans' Court of Worcester Co, & still is invested, as the cmplnt received it, as follows: $850 in the stock of the Farmers' Bank of the State of Delaware, & $2,671,88 in the promissory note of David H White, of Phil. The cmplnt further states that he has annually paid the interest on the said money to Sarah R Williams, mother of said testatrix, & wife of John Williams, during her life; that, by order of the Orphans' Court of Worcester Co, he retained $300 to meet anticipated expenses, of which he still had $125 undisposed of to be added to the amount above mentioned; that the said Sarah Williams, mother of said testatrix, died during the present year, & her husband, John Williams, still survives her; & since her death several persons claim said fund, to wit: John Williams, who was husband of said testatrix's mother, who has instituted suit at law therefore; Wm Townsend, Mary Odell, Justus M Bratten, Arra Clayvell, wife of Wm Clayvell, Joshua Atkinson, Geo Atkinson, whose residence is unknown, Mary Chapman, wife of Jas Chapman, of Accomac Co, Va, Esther Dix, wife of John Dix, & Thos Atkinson, who are the next of kin of said testatrix, & threaten to institute legal proceedings against cmplnt therefore; also the Board of Foreign Missions of the Presbyterian Church of the U S A, & the Board of Missions, said to be incorporated under the laws of the State of N Y, who also threaten legal proceedings against cmplnt for said fund, & who claim under the said last will & testament, by reason of which opposing claims, being unable to ascertain to whom said fund belongs, & being ready & willing to pay the same over to whichever of said parties may be justly entitled, the cmplnt asked that the said parties claiming may interplead & be restrained from proceeding at law against him, & he offers to bring the money into Court for the benefit of whoever may be found entitled, to which end the cmplnt asks a subpoena against said John William, Wm Townsend, Mary Odell, Justus M Bratten, Wm Clayvell & Arra his wife, Joshua Atkinson, John Dix & Esther his wife, & Thos Atkinson, residents of the State of Md, commanding them to appear in said Court; & also an order of publication against the said Geo Atkinson, Jas Chapman & Mary his wife, non-residents as aforesaid, & against the Board of Foreign Missions of the Presbyterian Church of the U S A, & the Board of Missions, corporations not created by the laws of this State, warning them to appear in said Court by the 3rd Tue in May next. –Edw D Martin, clerk of the Circuit Court of Worcester Co, Md.

WED DEC 6, 1854
Administrator's sale of real estate: lot 7 in square 126, fronting on north H st, between 17th & 18th sts, opposite the residence of Hon H Fish. –Geo McNeill, R S French, adms -Green & Scott, aucts

Wash Corp: 1-Act for the relief of Gaffin Nally: referred to the Cmte of Claims. 2-Act for the relief of Mrs Louisa J Wadsworth; act for the relief of John H O'Neill: both referred to the Cmte on Finance.

Hon Jesse D Bright, of Indiana, was yesterday elected Pres of the Senate of the U S by a very large vote-indeed without any serious apparent opposition.

Mrd: on Dec 3, in Wash City, by Rev Mr Hodges, Mr Wm Lawson to Miss Rebecca Hulse, all of Wash.

Alta Calif of Nov 9. Fatal duel over politics between Achilles Kewen & Col Woodlief, on Nov 8, at Oakland. Present were friends of Kewen, Messrs Wake, Briarly, & Robt Wood; friends of Woodlief were Capt Skerrett & Maj McDonald. The arms chosen were Mississippi yagers; at 40 paces. The ball from Mr Kewen's rifle passing completely through the body of Col Woodlief & out of his back, killing him instantly. His body was brought over to the city last evening. When the wife of the dead man looked upon all that remained of the former partner of joys & sorrows, who, but a few short hours before, had gone forth in the prime of manhood, is said to have been effected in the extreme. Mrs Woodlief accompanied her husband on the occasion, & stopped in San Antonio while the party went out. She returned with the body to the Tehama House. Devereux J Woodlief was born in Greenville Co, Va, & moved to Texas more than 20 years ago; was elected a colonel in the Texan army, & was in active service during the revolution there; was one of the Texas Rangers; in the Mexican war he accompanied the American forces as an amateur warrior; was an accurate marksman; had been engaged in a number of duels, had been wounded a number of times in battle, & carries to his grave 3 bullets in his body. He came to Calif in 1849, & was collector of the foreign miners' tax in Calaveras Co.

On Sunday last Mrs Kirk, an elderly lady residing on F st, attempted to fill an ethereal oil lamp while the wick was still burning, when the liquid took fire. Her son-in-law was fortunately at hand, & saved the life of Mrs Kirk, who was so badly burnt that much of the skin from her left side came off with her clothing. Is there no law to prevent the use of explosive materials?

Mrd: on Nov 30, at the Foundry Parsonage, by Rev E P Phelps, Mr Thos J Adams to Miss Annie Wright, both of Wash City.

Mrd: on Dec 5, by Rev E P Phelps. Mr Jas W St Clair to Miss Mary E Burche, both of Wash City.

Mrd: on Nov 30, at the residence of Capt John Edrington, Stafford Co, Va, by Rev J M Henry, of Wash, Col Saml Simpson, late U S Consul at Bombay, [British India,] to Miss Ella A Edrington.

Died: on Dec 2, at Rockville, Md, Sarah S Prout, eldest daughter of the late Wm Prout, of Wash City. The adorning trait of her character was a tender & faithful devotion to her remaining parent. She bore with cheerfulness & patience a lingering & painful illness, & departed in full faith of a happy immortality.

THU DEC 7, 1854

House of Reps: 1-Ptn of Jas S McGinnis, register, & Theodore Sherer, receiver of the land ofc at Chillicothe, Ohio, praying additional compensation for their labors.

Wash City Ordinances: 1-Act to refund to Jos Howard the amount paid by him for lots 9 & 10 in square 1,089, sold at tax sale on Mar 26, 1851; the said lots having been improperly sold, not being taxable property. 2-Act for the relief of W W Demaine [Assist Surveyor:] the sum of $177 be paid to him, to reimburse him that amount laid out & expended by him on Corp surveys during the last 16 weeks.

Died: on Dec 3, suddenly, but in great peace, at Lewisburg, Va, Mrs Lizzie S, wife of Rev Wm Harden, of the Balt Annual Conference, & eldest daughter of Rev Henry Slicer, aged 24 years & 6 months. Not lost; only gone before.

Died: on Dec 2, Mrs Eliz Ellen, consort of C G Wildman, in her 38th year.

Masonic meeting this evening at 7 o'clock, at Masonic Hall, E & 19th sts. Brothers of other lodges are fraternally invited. –S Bulow Erwin, sec

New piano for $200: rosewood case, perfect in every respect. We have also in store Pianos from the renowned manufactories of Hallet, Davis & Co, Bacon & Raven, & Knabe, Gaehle & Co. Old Pianos taken in exchange. At the Music, Stationery, Perfumery, & Fancy Good Store of John F Ellis, 306 Pa ave, near 10th st.

Independence, Mo, Dec 5. The Salt Lake mail has arrived. On Nov 13 a party under charge of John Jamieson, while coming to the States, were attacked by a party of Indians, [supposed to be Sioux,] 6 miles this side of **Fort Laramie**, & all of them killed. They were: John Jamieson, Jas Wheeler, Thos Hackett, & a passenger named Chas A Rincard, who was robbed of $10,500 in gold. The soldiers found & took care of the bodies of the murdered men. No escort could be granted at the post, & the mail of Nov could not go further than Laramie; that of Dec has returned to Independence.

Mrs A M Maddox'r Boarding House, 437 E st, between 6th & 7th sts. Board with or without rooms.

FRI DEC 8, 1854
Medical word & surgical instruments at public sale: on Dec 14, at my Auction Rooms, the collection belonging to Dr Warfield, who has declined his profession. -Jas C McGuire, auct

Trustee's sale: by deed of trust from Mrs Eliz Ann Laub, dated Jun 1, 1852, to the subscriber, & by the direction of Geo Poe, jr, the holder of one of the notes secured by the said deed, the following property, or such part as may be necessary to raise the debts secured thereon, will be sold at auction, on the premises, on Jan 9 next, namely: part of lot 29 in square 250, Wash City. Also, parts of lot 1, 29, & 30, in square 250. Also those other parts of lots 1, 29, & 30 in square 250 with the dwlg house & other bldgs thereon. –W Redin, trustee -Jas C McGuire, auct

Household & kitchen furniture at auction: & Chickerin Piano, on Dec 12, at the residence of G W C Whiting, Franklin Row. -Jas C McGuire, auct

New Boot & Shoe Store: Saml W Taylor & Co, have opened the spacious new store 339 Pa ave, next to Messrs Geo & T Parker's.

Senate: 1-Ptn from Isaac S Smith, asking remuneration for losses sustained due to the annulment of his contract for the construction of a light-house on Horse-shoe Reef, in the Niagara river. 2-Ptn from John Thomas, asking an examination of his improvement for the better preservation of the lives of those who travel in ocean, lake, & other steamers carrying passegers. 3-Ptn from Sam Crapin, asking that the pension allowed him may be made to commence from the time of his disability.

Last evening, as a carriage containing two daughters & servant of Alex'r Lee were returning from the Navy Yard, the carriage was upset. None were seriously injured, except the oldest daughter was cut by her falling on the glass of the carriage. The accident is ascribed to the inebriety of the driver.

Died: on Oct 19, Robt R Gatton, Consul of the U S at Mazatlan.

Died: on Dec 6, in Wash City, Thos Hodson, aged 73, a native of Lincolnshire, England, but for several years past a resident of PG Co, Md.

Died: on Wed, Mr Geo W Mounts. His funeral will take place from his father's residence, Bridge st, Gtwn, this afternoon at 3 o'clock.

SAT DEC 9, 1854
The regular term of the Hardin [Ky] Circuit Court is in progress in Elizabethtown. Thos M Yates, one of the jurors who granted the verdict of not guilty in the Ward case, is upon trial for perjury. He was indicted by the grand jury, along with several others of the same jury.

Chancery sale: by decree of the Circuit Court of Wash Co, D C, in the cause of Jos F & Mary F Ritter vs Wm H & Horatio G Ritter, dated Nov 22, 1854: public auction on Jan 2, 1855, on the premises, the following property in Gtwn: 1-Part of lot 40, of old Gtwn, fronting on the east side of Duck lane or Market st. 2-Parts of lots 40 & 80, of old Gtwn, fronting on the east side of Duck land or Market st; with the dwlg house of the late Peter Ritter & several small tenements. 3-Part of lot 80, with a 2 story brick dwlg. –Wm R Woodward, Walter S Cox, trustees -Ed S Wright, auct

Capt Robt Burnett died at his house in Orange Co, N Y, on Nov 29. He was born on Feb 22, 1762, & was at his death 92 years, 8 months & 8 days old. Capt Burnett was appointed a lt in the Regt of Artl in the service of the U S, commanded by Col John Lamb, on Jun 29, 1781, being then only 19 years of age, & continued in the service during the war. He was esteemed as a brave & efficient ofcr, & when the American army marched into N Y, at the evacuation of the city by the British troops, had the honor of commanding the American Guard, which relieved the British rear guard stationed in the Bowery.

Accounts from the Crimea announce the death of Col the Hon Francis G Hood, commanding the 3rd Btln of the Grenadier Guards. His father, Lt Col Francis Hood, was killed on the heights of Aire, in the South of France, in 1814, & he himself has met death in an equally noble manner, at the head of his btln before Sebastopol. He is the great grandson of the first Lord Hood, of naval renown, who was elevated to the peerage in 1782 for his celebrated victory over the French fleets under the Count de Grasse, in the West Indies. Col Hood was brother to the 3rd Viscount who succeeded his grandfather. He has been 27 years in the Grenadier Guards.

Wm J Brown, special mail agent of the Post Ofc Dept, on Fri last arrested John M Watson, postmaster at Rainsborough, Highland Co, Ohio, on a charge of robbing the mail. Counterfeit notes, placed in a decoy letter, are said to have been paid out by Watson.

The N Y Chamber of Commerce have adopted resolutions recommending to Congress that an expedition be sent in search of Dr Kane, the Arctic navigator.

Rev Geo D Cummins, of Richmond, Va, has accepted the Rectorship of Trinity Church, in Wash City, pursuant to a unanimous invitation extended him by the Vestry of said church.

Mrd: on Oct 26, at Marmion, King Geo Co, Va, by Rev Mr Russell, John Tayloe to Mary Willis Lewis, daughter of Daingerfield Lewis, all of the same county & State.

Died: on Dec 7, in Montg Co, in her 76th year, Mrs Mgt Culver, consort of the late Burgess Culver, & sister to the late Michl Connelly. May she rest in peace!

Died: on Dec 8, Wm Dowling, a native of Wash. His funeral is this morning at 10 o'clock, from the Infirmary.

Died: yesterday, after a long & painful illness, in her 50th year, Mary Eliz Maguire, wife of Jas Maguire, formerly of the U S Marine Corps. Her funeral will take place tomorrow, from the residence of the family, on H st, near 14th st.

The Life of Horace Greeley, Editor of the N Y Tribune, by Jas Parton. 12 mo, cloth, 450 pp, illustrated. Price $1.25. Will be published Dec 18.

Opened this day a beautiful assortment of Embroidered & Lace Goods, at the Ladies' Fancy & Trimming Depot, 12 Market Space. –Ruth A Peaco

Official: Dept of State, Wash, Dec 7, 1854. Information has been received at this Dept, through the U S Consul at Vera Cruz, of the death of Robt R Gatton, late U S Consul at Mazatlan, Mexico. Also, of Wm Foster, a citizen of the U S, lately residing in the State of New Leon, Mexico. Information has been received from the U S Consul at Callao, Peru, of the death of the following American seamen at Bella Vista Hospital, in that city, via: John Haro, late of ship **Baltimore**. Hiram Dawson, late of ship **Inez**. Abraham Wilson, late of ship **Joans**. Arthur Watty, late of ship **Pelican State**. G W Games, colored, late of ship **Lancashire**. Francis Hall, colored, late of ship **Hugh Birkhead**; Wm L Hogue, of Indiana, late of ship **Queen of the Clippers**. Geo Hood, of Indiana, late of ship **Kate Hays**.

Teacher wanted, the services of a young lady qualified to teach the English branches, & also French & music. Address B Shumate, Weaversville, Fauquier Co, Va.

All persons troubled with smoking chimneys can have them effectually remedied by calling in person or address through the post ofc, Philip Macky, 4th & I st.

The Rhyme & Reason of Country Life, exquisitely illustrated, by Miss Cooper, daughter of Fennimore Cooper. For sale at Taylor & Maury's Bookstore, near 9th st.

MON DEC 11, 1854
From Calif: Dennis O'Brien was executed at Mokelumne Hill Fri last for the murder of Michl Ryan. His true name, he said on the gallows, was Wm O'Brien, & he was from Ballina Co, Tipperary, Ireland. Thompson, who was to have been hung at the same time, has had his sentence commuted by Gov Bigler to 7 years' imprisonment.

Abraham Quady, the last of the Nantucket Indians, died at Nantucket on Nov 25.

The dwlg house of the late venerable Thos Ritchie, on H st, is to be sold at auction today. It is in a beautiful position, & described as a commodious & very desirable residence.

Rev Chas A Davis, for several years an efficient clerk in the Gen Land Ofc, & member of the Common Council of Wash City, has resigned both situations to resume his duties as a minister of the Gospel. He has joined the Virginia Conference of the Methodist Episcopal Church South, & has been assigned to the charge of Trinity Church, Richmond, Va.

Mrd: on Dec 7, in Wash City, at St John's Church, by Rev Smith Pyne, Stephen B Luck, U S Navy, to Eliza, youngest daughter of the late Com J D Henley.

Fire at Richmond, Va, on Thu at the Richmond Penitentiary. The superintendent, Mr Morgan, lost much of his furniture by having it thrown from a 2nd story window. During the excitement a convict, Elias Helms, made his escape.

Rev Thos March Clark, D D, was consecrated Bishop of the Protestant Episcopal Church, Rhode Island, on Dec 6.

U S Patent Ofc, Wash, Dec 9, 1854. Ptn of Moses & Saml Pennock, of Kennett Square, Pa, praying for an extension of a patent granted to them on Mar 12, 1841, for an improvement in seed drills, for 7 years from the expiration of said patent, on Mar 12, 1854. –Chas Mason, Com'r of Patents

TUE DEC 12, 1854
Trustee's sale of horses, wagon, carry-all & gear, vinegar, counter & scales: on Dec 14, by deed of trust from Henry G Murray, dated Dec 2, 1854, in front of the Auction Store. -Green & Scott, aucts

Trustee's sale of valuable & improved property: by deed of trust from Ira A Hopkins & wife, dated May 10, 1854, recorded in Liber J A S No 77, folios 441 thru 444, of the land records of Wash Co, D C: sale of lots 17 & 18 in square 725, in Wash City, with a two story cottage frame house & other out-bldgs: corner of 1st & C sts, 2 squares north of the Capitol grounds. –Jas Adams, trustee -J C McGuire, auct

Double homicide: an affray occurred at Jackson, Miss, on Nov 30th between Mr R D Shackelford & Mr Flanders, in front of the house of Mr Taylor, with whom they boarded, when the latter interfered as a peace-maker. Shackelford shot Taylor. Shackelford was shot in the breast by some person unknown, & died in a few minutes. Taylor died on Dec 2.

Senate: 1-Ptn from A M Winn, asking that he may be indemnified for advances he made in aid of the indigent sick & suffering population at Sacramento city prior to Oct 13, 1849, under the direction of Gen Riley, then Military Govn'r of Calif. 2-Ptn from Geo M Torrence, asking that the pension granted him may be made to commence from the time of his disability. 3-Ptn from G R Drake, asking a patent for a chain pump. 4-Ptn from Harvey Lindsley, asking an appropriation to compensate him for extra salary as acting charge d'affaires at Canton from Jan 17 to Apr 14, 1854. 5-Ptn from Joshua Shaw, for compensation for the use by the Govn't of the percussion cap & lock for small arms & wafer primers, to be employed in the firing of cannon. 6-Ptn from Dr J Winthrop Tayloe, surgeon, U S Navy, asking to be allowed the difference of salary between acting & passed assist surgeon. 7-Ptn from the widow of Lt Col J McClellan, late U S Army, asking to be allowed a pension. 8-Ptn from the heirs of Capt Underwood, of the Revolution, asking an increase of pension; & from widow of John Vincent, asking a pension. 9-Ptn from Henry Ruggles, of Brooklyn, N Y, asking for an exchange of waste land belonging to the Govn't for land belonging to him adjoining the navy yard at that place. 10-Ptn from Mary Okill, asking remuneration for losses sustained by her father due to advances made by him in 1779 for the use of the Gov't. 11-Documents in relation to the rank of A S Taylor, an ofcr in the marine corps: submitted. 12-Ptn from Roswell H Haskins, asking to be discharged from a judgment in favor of the U S against him as bail of P A Barker, late collector of the customs at Buffalo Creek.

House of Reps: 1-Joint resolution for the relief of the children of Capt Thos Porter, deceased: passed.

The Hannah More Academy, Wilmington, Delaware: will commence its 26th session on Feb 1st & end on Jul 1, 1855. Principals: Misses C & I Grimshaw & A H Grimshaw, A M, M d. French teacher: Mademoiselle Durand. Music teacher: Miss Susie Pavitt. References: Rt Rev A Lee, D D, Alfred du Pont, C I du Pont, Henry Latimer, E C Stotsenburg, Hon Jno M Clayton, Delaware; Hon Wm J Duane, T C Percival, Wm Welsh, Wm B Page, M D, Prof Carson, Phil; Rev R B Duane, Honesdale, Pa; Rev G T Bedell, Beverly W Mason, N Y; Rev H V D Johns, D D, Balt; Rev W W Spear, Charleston, S C; Hon Langdon Cheves, Columbia, S C; Capt Josiah Tattnall, Capt L F du Pont, S Sharp, M D, U S Navy.

Dissolution of the copartnership exising under the firm of Darden & Young, in the Drug & Apothecary business, 9th & I sts, by mutual consent. –D D Darden, Wm H Young The undersigned is retiring from the firm. –D D Darden

Mrd: on Dec 11, by Rev F Israel, John H Hurst to Miss Ann V Bicksler, both of Fairfax Co, Va.

Va Conference of the Methodist Episcopal Church South, assembled at Norfolk, adjourned on Thu last. The following are appointments for the Wash district: W W Bennett, Presiding Elder; J A Duncan, Wash; J D Coulling, Alexandria; A G Brown, Rock Creek; Jos Amiss, Howard; W D Judkins, Fairfax; Fairfax Mission to be supplied; W L Murphy, Potomac; J S R Clarke, Leesburg; P F August, W P Twyman, Loudoun; W F Bain, Manassah; J D Blackwell, J F Poulton, Warrenton; Thos A Pierce, Springfield; Jos E Potts, South Branch.

The death of Hon John R Grymes, of New Orleans, is announced in the papers of that city as having taken place on Dec 3. He was a native of Orange Co, Va, & in the 68th year of his age.

Another of the few survivors of our Revolutionary struggle has gone to rest. Maj Robt Burnett, of Newburgh, N Y, was buried on Sat week. Among the mourners was a compatriot, Usual Knapp, now 95 years old, who belonged to Washington's Life Guards. Maj Burnett was 92 years old. [No death date given.]

Dr Sion Madison Wm Danl Lancaster Miller has been convicted at Montg, Ala, of the murder of A G Jones, & sentenced to the penitentiary for life. Jas Patton, a respectable citizen of New Orleans, who was some time since convicted of killing Mr W Turnbull, has also been sentenced to the penitentiary for life. He is believed to be insane.

WED DEC 13, 1854
Household & kitchen furniture at auction: on Dec 19: the personal effects of the late A Favier, in front of the Auction Rooms. -Jas C McGuire, auct

House of Reps: 1-Ptn of Hugh E Vincent & Danl B Vincent, of Charleston, S C, to change the name of the barque **Como**. 2-Ptn of Horace Brown, of Milo, Me, for bounty land. 3-Ptn & papers in behalf of the widow & children of Caleb Wood, deceased, were withdrawn from the files, & referred to the Cmte on Invalid Pensions.

Wash Corp: 1-Ptn of J S Hollingshead in reference to the exhibition of a work of art: referred to the Cmte on Police: passed. 2-Ptn of Philip Kraft, praying for the correction of an error in the grade of square 481: referred to the Cmte of Claims.

Dress & Cloak Making: Brown's Bldg. –Mrs R Cady

Bedford, the residence of Dr Fitzhugh, in King Geo Co, Va, accidentally took fire last week from a spark from the chimney, & was burnt down. **Bedford** was one of the old seats of Va hospitality.

Levi Blossom has fled from Milwaukie with funds belonging to the Lake Shore Railroad: amount could be about $150,000. –Chicago Democrat

Abraham A Ackerman, age 20 years, & lately a clerk in the Ohio Life & Trust Co at N Y, was arrested on Sat charged with abstracting a draft for $5,000, & causing it to be twice drawn.

Mrd: on Dec 7, in Wash City, at Trinity Church, by Rev Wm J Clarke, J Bartram North to Addie W, daughter of the late Wm Lippincott, of Phil.

Senate: 1-Ptn from Miguel Montiel, an ofcr in Col Domingo's company of spies in the Mexican war, asking that bounty land be granted to all the members of said company. 2-Ptn from Susan Palmer, widow of an ofcr of the last war with Great Britain, asking bounty land. 3-Ptn from Denison E Seymour, representing that he was induced to enlist in the corps of engineers by certain misrepresentations, & asking some remuneration for losses sustained & sufferings in consequence thereof. 4-Ptn from Wm A Cameron, asking passage of an act for the settlement of the claims of John Denman & Geo Towley, of N J, for cattle furnished for the use of the army during the Revolution. 5-Additional documents in the case of Jas Bell's heirs: submitted. 6-Ptn from Justin Spaulding, asking pay for his services as chaplain on board the U S ship **Independence** when in the harbor of Rio Janeiro: he states he was a missionary of the Methodist Church resident at Rio, that the ship was without a chaplain, & that he performed all the duties, such as preaching, visiting the sick, & burying the dead, during all the time she remained at the station. 7-Documents relating to the claim of Judge Schley & Judge Wetherell for compensation for extra services while U S judges for the Territory of Michigan: submitted. 8-Ptn from the heirs of Jas Heard, deceased, of the continental army, asking the half-pay for life to which said Heard was entitled. 9-Ptn from Ebenezer Hitchcock, asking a pension for services in the war of 1812. 10-Cmte on Military Affairs: recommended passage of: bills for the relief of Simeon Stedman; of Chas W Carroll; of Eleanor Hoople, of the province of Canada; & bill granting bounty land to Cornelius Coffey. 11-Bill for the relief of Thos T Russell, of Fla: introduced. 12-Rev Henry Slicer was declared duly elected chaplain of the Senate for the present session.

Death of a miserly woman. Jeanne De Lux died in N Y a few days ago from injuries received by being run over by an omnibus. She was 65 years of age, & the Journal of Commerce thus speaks of her: she was a most reluctant tax-payer; living in a secluded apartment; she was last year assessed for only $10,000, though the house she occupied & owned was well worth $25,000. The Public Administrator now show that she owed bonds to the value of $80,000, making her entire property at least $100,000. She is only known to have a nephew residing in Cincinnati. She died without leaving a will.

Died: on Sep 5, 1854, at sea, aboard the U S frig **Susquehanna**, & buried at Simoda, Japan, Dr Jas Hamilton, U S Navy. His family has met an irreparable loss & the navy deprived of an efficient ofcr, as his scientific attainments were of the first order.

Wash City Ordinances: 1-Act for the relief of E Owen: fine is remitted provided Owen pay the costs. 2-Act for the relief of John Hall, for keeping a male dog without a license: remitted: provided Hall pay the costs. 3-Act for the relief of Evan Hughes: $5 to be refunded to him, that being the amount of the fine imposed on & paid by him for violating the law relating to tying horses to tree boxes.

Orphans Court of Wash Co, D C. Letters of administration on the personal estate of Michl P Mohun, late of Wash Co, deceased. –Rosella A Mohun, admx

Household & kitchen furniture at auction: Letters of administration on the personal estate of Chas Pruess, late of Wash Co, deceased. –Gertrude Pruess, admx

The Trustees of St Vincent's Orphan Asylum have re-established their house for destitute orphan boys, under the care of the **Christian Brothers**, Wash, D C.

Trustees:
Rev Edw A Knight, Pres	Thos Carbery, Treas
Rev Jas B Donelan	Wm Hickey, Sec
Rev Timothy J O'Toole	

Lady Managers:
Mrs Henrietta H Boone, 1st Directress	Mrs Jane Noyes
Miss Catharine M Johnson, 2nd Directress	Mrs Mary Elliot
	Mrs Jospehine Young
Mrs Henrietta Kennedy, Treas	Mrs Catharine Roche
Mrs Catharine A Masi, Sec	
Mrs Catharine Simms	

Gentlemen Managers & Visiters of Boys' Asylum & of Parish Day Schools connected therewith:
Dr W J C Duhamel	Geo Harvey
Chas Keenan	Jos Redfern
Edw Simms	Peter Conlan
Seraphim Masi	Rudolph Eichorn
John C Fitzpatrick	Dr Alex'r Semmes
Wm J Wheatley	Geo Mattingly
Thos Bayne	Robt Mahoney
Peter Brady	John T Cassell

THU DEC 14, 1854
Under our obituary head, says the Balt American of Dec 11, we have the notice of the demise of our respected townsman, Edmund Didier, Pres of the Mutual Fire & Marine Ins Co of Balt. [No other information.]

Died: Maj Lowd, gallant ofcr at St Augustine, Fla. Maj [then Capt] Lowd was stationed in this city between 1837 & 1840, in command of a company of the 2nd Artl, who were fresh from the Indian wars in Florida. Capt Lowd was here with his family for a long time, & formed the friendship of many of our citizens. He & his command served in the Mexican war. He was brevetted for gallantry in one of the first battles, under Gen Taylor, on the Rio Grande. He remained in the line during the war. –Rochester Amer [No death date given-current item.]

Hon John Scott Harrison, of Ohio, has been called home because of the serious illness of his mother, the relict of Gen Harrison.

Senate: 1-Letter from Brig Gen Thos Machin, of the volunteers of the war of 1812, asking that an appropriation be made to pay the expenses of a convention of soldiers of that war to be held in Wash City Jan 8, 1855, & that said convention be allowed the use of one of the Halls of Congress: referred to the Cmte on Military Affairs. 2-Ptn from Reuben H Grant, asking payment of a claim against the Choctaw Indians. 3-Bills for the relief of Isaac Swain; & relief of Israel Ketcham: both passed. 4-Bill for the relief of J S Graham & Walker H Finnal: passed.

For sale, the Estate of the late H R W Hill: extensive & valuable sugar plantation only 15 miles above the city of New Orleans; also, 260 acclimated negroes. By J A Beard & May. Auction on Jan 16, 1855, on the plantation, called *Live Oak Point Plantation*: containing about 2,000 arpents of sugar land, with all improvements thereon. –J A Beard, auct   Acts of sale before Wm Christy, N P, at the expense of the purchaser.

FRI DEC 15, 1854
Anniversary Ball & Supper of the Columbia Typographical Society will be held at Jackson Hall on Jan 10, 1855: arrangements by Mr Tho Eckhardt: tickets $2, admitting a gentleman & ladies.

Managers:

Hon J T Towers	J F Haliday	S Lamborne
Hon W W Seaton	Wm Towers, sr	E C Dyer
Hon Peter Force	J Dowling	E Ward
Hon R C Weightman	W W Moore	H Walker
A G Seaman	T W Howard	E S Cropley
G S Gideon	E B Robinson	J H Thorn
W Woodward	M Caton	G W Cochran
Jas English	W Fitzgerald	J Bowen
C Alexander	J W Davis	Robt Waters
C W Dunnington	C Wendall	J S Cunningham
L Towers	J F Tenholm	F Jefferson
A B Claxton	H Polkinhorn	Wm G Moore
J S Gallaher	Geo Cochran	J L Smith
F Edmondson	J Chedal	

Cmte of Invitation & Reception: [white rosette]

C F Lowrey	G Whittington	J Cunningham
Thos Rich	Wm H Dennesson	Geo Rock
Chas McPherson	J McIntyre	J T Waters
Jesse Judge	S Culverwell	J B Tate
P Rodier	J Melson	Jos Mattingly
F W Gould	J Larcombe	J Hurley

Wm Towers, jr	F M Detweiler	J Robinson

Cmte on Refreshments: [tri-colored rosette]

Wm E Morcoe	Jno Sessford, jr	Geo Duvall
Saml Robinson	T D Sultzer	Chas Schell

Floor Managers: [red rosette]

Wm L Jones	John Judge	F R Dorsett

Executive Cmte: [blue rosette]

Wm M Belt	J T Halleck	Harrison Bowen
Wm L Jones	Wm McLean	
Chas Canfield	Geo Caton	

Family Groceries at auction: on Dec 18, at the store of Mr W H Tenney, corner of Bridge & High sts, his entire stock. –Barnard & Buckey, aucts

Household & kitchen furniture at auction: on Dec 20, at the residence of J B Sellick, K st, between 6th & 7th sts. -Jas C McGuire, auct

Household & kitchen furniture at auction: on Dec 21, at the residence of Jas Morss, 12th between E & F sts. -Jas C McGuire, auct

Senate: 1-Ptn from Susannah H Burnham, in behalf of the heirs of Jos Hill, an ofcr of the Revolution, asking to be allowed commutation. 2-Ptn from Jane Rudolph, of S C, a widow of a Revolutionary ofcr, asking a pension. 3-Ptn from the children of the late Jabez B Rooker, asking compensation for the services of their father as clerk to the Cmte on Public Bldgs. 4-Ptn from the administrator de bonis non of Col Wm Brent, an ofcr of the war of the Revolution, asking to be allowed the commutation pay to which that ofcr was entitled. 5-Ptn from Michl Hanly, for an increase of pension. 6-Ptn from Fred'k Zarracher, asking compensation for expenses incurred & losses sustained in entertaining, by order of the U S Marshal, a posse of men [a large body of U S marines & others] called out to aid in the suppression of the riot at Christiana, Pa, & sustain the supremacy of the law. 7-Ptn from Edw Harte, asking compensation for services performed under direction of the Com'r of Patents.

Died: on Dec 14, after a few days' illness, Mrs Mary Quinn, in her 74th year. She was a native of Wexford, Ireland, but for a number of years a resident of Norfolk, Va, & late of Wash City. Her funeral is this evening at 3 o'clock, from the residence of her son-in-law, John J Joyce, 13th & F sts.

House of Reps: 1-Act for the relief of Amos Knapp: re-referred to the Cmte on Invalid Pensions. 2-Bill for the relief of Thos Hurst, a sgt in the Marine Corps: referred to the Cmte on Naval Affairs. 3-Memorial of Mrs Mary Benseil, of Phil, asking for a pension on account of the Revolutionary services of her husband. 4-Ptn of Jane M Rudolph, of Charleston, S C, widow of Capt Thos C Rudolph, praying for a pension.

SAT DEC 16. 1854

Household & kitchen furniture at auction: on Dec 19, at the residence of J W Hauptman, 509 11th st, 3 doors south of Pa ave. –Green & Scott, aucts

Large dwlg-house for rent: finding it necessary to occupy a smaller tenement, I will, [though somewhat reluctantly,] rent the large 3 story house now occupied by me on 9th st, between E & F sts. –John S Gallaher, 461, 9th st, Wash City

For sale, a small Farm of about 24 acres, about 6 miles from Wash, with a small frame house, stable, & corn-crib. –Henry J Adams, Atty-at Law, 489 7th st.

New Book: History of the Origin, Formation, and Adoption of the Constitution of the United States, with Notices of its Principal Framers. By Geo Ticknor Curtis, in 2 vols, N Y: Harper & Brothers, 1854.

Senate: 1-Bill for the relief of John A Bowes, agent in charge of the property of the U S at Michigan City, in the State of Indiana: referred. 2-Bill for the relief of Stephen Bunnel, of the State of Indiana: referred. 3-Bill for the relief of Gad Humphreys; of Isaac Swain; of Israel Ketchan: each referred. 4-Bill for the relief of Saml Colt was passed informally. 5-Bill for the relief of Hiram Moore & John Hascall: passed over informally. 6-Bill for the relief of Ferdinand Clark; of Adolphus Meier & Co, of St Louis; & of Wilson & Brothers, of St Louis, Mo: recommended they pass: passed. 7-Bill for the relief of Chas A Kellett: recommended that it do not pass: rejected. 8-Bill for the relief of the children & heirs of Maj Gen Baron De Kalb was considered. Mr Peckham moved to reduce the sum proposed in the bill from $90,500 to $66,000, being satisfied that the latter sum was the amount really due. Mr Letcher moved to reduce the appropriation in the bill to $27,400, the amount of the claim without interest: which was disagreed to. Bill was laid aside.

Prince Napoleon, the heir to the throne, has returned to Constantinople, owing, it is said, to ill health.

Official, Dept of State, Wash, Dec 14, 1854. Information communicated to this Dept, by the Minister Resident of Bremen, that Mr John Wolff, of St Louis, Mo, has, on his own application, been discharged from his duties as Bremen Consul in that city; & that there will not be, for the present, another consul appointed in his place.

Mrd: on Nov 27, at Memphis, Tenn, by Rev Dr Page, Hon Wm C Dawson, of Ga, to Mrs Eliza M Williams, of Memphis.

Mrd: on Dec 14, in Christ Church, by Rev W Hodges, Rev Edmund Roberts, Rector of St Peter's Parish, Peekskill, N Y, to Helen L, daughter of Maj A A Nicholson, of the U S Marine Corps, Wash.

Mrd: on Dec 14, in Wash City, by Rev Mr Cheneworth, Mr Thos P White to Miss Esther Ann Marshe, eldest daughter of Thos Marshe, all of Wash City.

Mrd: on Dec 13, by Rev Mr Cheneworth, Enoch M Norris, of St Mary's Co, Md, to Miss Sarah, daughter of Zadock Williams, of Wash.

Mrd: on Dec 7, by Rev S A H Marks, Mr Basil W Ducket to Miss Caroline Eckton, both of PG Co, Md.

Mrd: on Dec 7, by Rev S A H Marks, Mr Washington Berry to Miss Columbia Skidmore, of the District of Columbia.

Died: on Nov 22, at St Augustine, Fla, where he was temporarily residing, John Bliss, late a Lt Col in the U S Army. Most of his life was spent in the camp; he was a 1st Lt of the 11th Infty in 1812; in May, 1813, he was promoted to a captaincy & was distinguished for his gallantry & wounded in the battle of Niagara Falls in 1814. In 1818 & 1819 he was instructor in infty tactics & commandant of cadets at West Point, where he married a daughter of Andre Ellicott, who, with an only son, survives him. In 1823 he was made Major by brevet for 10 years' faithful service. As Major of the 1st Infty, in 1830, he commanded his regt in the battle of Badaxe, & was made Lt Col in 1836. He resigned his commission in 1837, & has since resided at Meadville, Pa, & Buffalo, N Y.

The Rockville [Md] Journal states that the dwlg-house & all the furniture, except the piano, of Dr Franklin Waters, of Medley's district, in Montg Co, were entirely destroyed by fire on Dec 3.

U S Patent Ofc, Wash, Dec 15. 1854. Ptn of Wm Perrin, of Lowell, Mass, praying for the extension of a patent granted to him on Mar 24, 1841, for an improvement in machines for cutting square joint dove-tails, for 7 years from the expiration which takes place on Mar 24, 1855. –Chas Mason, Com'r of Patents

Circuit Court of Wash Co, D C-in Chancery. Wm S Laurie & others against Jas C Hall & Lizzie Delle Laurie. The trustee has reported that on Nov 22, 1854, he sold to Jas C Hall that piece of ground in Wash City, being contained in square 226, fronting on Pa ave, together with improvements, for $5,500, & the purchaser has complied with the terms of sale. –Jno A Smith, clerk

The Purchase of **Mount Vernon**. Mr John A Washington declares himself entirely unwilling that **Mount Vernon** should pass from his possession, unless to the State of Va or to the U S. The reasons assigned have much force: one of which is that, as a private possession, in the dispersion of families & changes of fortune, it might be converted to uses inconsistent with the veneration due to the memory & character of him with whose life it is so intimately connected.

Boston, Dec 15. Wendell Phillips was arraigned this morning on an indictment for participation in the Burns riot, by inciting the rioters in a speech which he delivered in Faneuil Hall. He gave bonds to answer.

Winchester Virginian: two men, N J Copenhaver & Wm Spur, on Sat made an unprovoked attack, at the Fountain Hotel, upon W J Smith, killing him on the spot. The villains were arrested near Strasburg, the Mayor of Winchester having offered a reward of $500.

A few evenings ago, as Mr J M Berrien, of Rome, Ga, was riding in the cars to Augusta, with his family, a stranger took a seat beside him & succeeded in administering to him chloroform until he became insensible. He then cut his overcoat & extracted from his side pocket $5,160; & his wallet from his pantaloons, containing about $1,000, & made good his escape.

MON DEC 18, 1854
The *Jefferson Wigwam*, an ancient Revolutionary relict, the house in which Jefferson wrote the Declaration of Independence, was among the bldgs in Phil lately destroyed by fire.

Jas *Fitzgibbon, formerly a night porter & clerk in the N Y post ofc, was on Sat last convicted before Judge Betts of abstracting packages containing money from the U S mail. The lowest penalty for the offence is 10 years' imprisonment. [Dec 30th newspaper: *Fitzgibbons was sentenced to 10 years in the State prison for mail robbery.] [*Fitzgibbon/Fitzgibbons]

The English Generals slain at Inkermann. Sir Geo Cathcart, G C B, was a member of what has been most appropriately styled a family of fighters. He was the son of the celebrated Earl Cathcart, many years English Ambassador at St Petersburgh, & brother to the present Earl Cathcart, who so distinguished himself at Waterloo. His age was 62. Sir George was the ofcr who gave Wellington's famous order to the guards to "charge." He was a soldier of great renown & experience, & died on the battle-field-the field of his fame. Brig Gen Strangways served in the campaign in Germany in 1813-14. In 1815 he was with the royal artillery at Quatre Bras & Waterloo, in which last battle he was wounded. Brig Gen Thos Leigh Goldie had been nearly 30 years in the service, having entered it as ensign Jun 13, 1825.

Nicholas Beehan, alias Beheehan, the murderer of the Wickham family, was hanged at Riverhead, L I, on Fri. –N Y Commercial Advertiser

Mrd: on Dec 17, by Rev H B Closkery, in the Cathedral, Balt, Wm Graham Scott, of Wash, to Miss Anna Virginia Devlin, of the same place, daughter of Lt Devlin, late of the Marine Corps.

Died: on Oct 2 last, at his residence in Bryantown, Dr Walter F Boarman, in his 57th year.

From Texas. 1-David Dean, a member of Capt Travis' company, killed Mr Kirk, a messmate of his, in Fredericksburg. The murder was dastardly & cold-blooded. He managed to disarm Kirk, & then blew his brains out. Dean was in custody, strictly guarded by 15 men. 2-Capt Walker encountered a party of Indians, killed several, & recaptured 19 American horses.

The U S steam frig **Cumberland**, Capt Harwood, bearing the broad pennant of Cmdor S H Stringham, with the U S steam frig **Saranac**, Capt Long, arrived at Villa Franca on Nov 18 from Toulon. The ofcrs & crew are all well, but anxious to return to the U S, having been absent nearly 3 years. Ofcrs of the U S ship **Falmouth**, which sailed from Norfolk, Dec 14, on a cruise:

Cmder, Thos Danah Shaw
1st Lt, Saml R Knox
2nd Lt, Francis Winslow
3rd Lt, John Wilkinson
4th Lt, Abner Read
Purser, Francis B Stockton
Surgeon, J J Brownlee
Assist Surgeon, Michl O'Hara
Acting Master, Thos W Brodhead
Passed Midshipman, Geo E Belknap
Midshipman: John Cain, jr
& Wm G Dozier
Clerk to Cmder, J R Woolson
Boatswain, Francis A Oliver
Gunner, Jas A Litteston
Carpenter, Geo Wisner
Sailmaker, John J Sanford

Fancy Goods & Toys: Mrs H Clitch, at the old stand.

Dissolution of copartnership existing under the firm of Geo W Garrett & Co, by mutual consent, Geo W Garrett retiring. –G J Thomas, John F Dyer, Geo W Garrett

Dr Saml Parkman, an eminent surgeon of Boston, died in that city on Sat.

I certify that Dr John Fairfax, of Wash Co, D C, brought before me, as strays, trespassing on his enclosures, a large Cow; also, a yearling Bull. –C H Wiltberger Owner is to come & prove their property, pay charges, & take them away from the farm of Mrs Sanders, on Rock Creek Church road. –John C Fairfax

TUE DEC 19, 1854
Senate: 1-Ptn from Jno T Sprague, of the army, asking that the widow of Maj Gen Worth may be allowed the pension her husband was entitled to for disability incurred in the late war with Great Britain: referred. 2-Ptn from Robt Mills, architect in Wash, D C, asking an examination of his plan for supplying Wash City with water: referred. 3-Documents relating to the claim of Mary Felch for bounty land for the services of her husband as chaplain during the war of 1812: referred. 4-Ptn from John H Horne, asking that money required from him by the Gov't for land may be

refunded with interest: referred. 5-Ptn from B F H Wetherall, legal rep of Jas Wetherall, late a Judge of the Territory of Michigan, asking compensation for the adjustment of land title in said Territory: referred. 6-Ptn from Josiah S Little, asking to be remunerated for land of which he was deprived by the treaty of Washington: referred. 7-Ptn from Emily L Slaughter, widow of the late Cmder Slaughter, for a pension: referred. 8-Additional documents in support of the claim of the legal reps of Isaac Shelby: referred. 9-Cmte on Pensions: bill for the relief of May Rutherford, widow of Saml Rutherford; & for the relief of Sydney P Pod, of the State of Maine: recommended their passage. Same cmte: bill for the relief of Catharine B Arnold. Same Cmte: asked to be discharged from the further consideration of the ptn of Mary Felch, & that it be referred to the Cmte on Public Lands: agreed to. 10-Resolved, that the Cmte on Naval Affairs be instructed to inquire into the expediency of sending a steamer & tender to the Arctic seas for the purpose of rescuing or affording relief to passed assist surgeon E K Kane, of the U S Navy, & the ofcrs & men under his command. 11-Bill for the relief of Col Wm Grayson: introduced. 12-Bill from the House of Reps for the relief of the heirs of Baron De Kalb, the brave soldier who lost his life in the service of our country, at the disastrous battle of Camden: referred to the Cmte on Revolutionary Claims. 13-Bill for the relief of J H F Thornton, Lawrence Taliaferro, & Hay Taliaferro, sureties of D M Thornton, late a Purser in the U S Navy: passed.

House of Reps: 1-Mr Bennett moved to reconsider the vote by which the House, on Fri last, referred to the Cmte of the Whole the bill for the relief of Betsey Nash, returned from the Senate with an amendment granting $3,000 to the widow of Jas C Bachelder, who was killed at Boston, during the Bruns fugitive slave riot, on May 26, 1854, while assisting the U S marshal for the district of Mass in executing a law of Congress. Mr Bennett referred to the case of Betsey Nash as one which commended itself to the consideration of the House. Her claim had been before the Pension Cmte since 1822, & the proof in its justice was perfected in 1831, & at nearly every succeeding Congress a bill had been reported for her relief. It was as honest a case as had ever been presented, & its settlement should no longer be delayed. Betsey Nash is very infirm, & probably could not live very long. The bill & amendment were then made the special order of the day for the next Friday three weeks.

Mrd: on Dec 14, by Rev S A H Marks, Malacki Farr to Miss Amelia E Owens, of the District of Columbia.

Mrd: on Dec 18, by Rev S A H Marks, Mr Levi G King to Miss Rebecca Jones, of the District of Columbia.

Leeches, 5,000, in excellent order, today received & for sale in lots to suit.
-J F Callan, Druggist, E & 7th sts.

Circuit Court of Worcester Co, in Chancery. Littleton P Franklin vs Edgar H Purnell & others. The object of this suit is to procure a decree for the sale of the real estate of Jas R S Purnell, late of said county, deceased, for the payment of his debts. James died intestate in 1848 indebted to Henry Franklin in the sum of $883, on his bill obligatory dated Aug 3, 1847, with interest from the date thereof; that after the execution of said bill Henry died intestate, & administration of his personal estate was committed to John R Franklin, who, as administrator, assigned the said bill to Littleton P Franklin for value received; that the said Jas R S Purnell left as his heirs at law his children, Edgar H Purnell, who resides in parts unknown, of the full age of 21 years, Geo W Purnell, a minor, residing in the State of Louisiana, Wm Purnell & Wilmer Purnell, both minors, residing in Worcester Co; that administration of all the personal estate of said James hath been granted to Wm T J Purnell, of Worcester Co; & that the same is insufficient to pay the debts due & owing by said James at the time of his death. Absent dfndnts to appear in this Court on or before the 3rd Tue in May next. –Edw D Martin, clerk

Circuit Court of Worcester Co, in Chancery. Chas G Dale vs Jos Godfrey & others. Object of this bill is to procure a decree for the sale of the real estate of Geo Godfrey, late of said county, deceased, for the payment of his debts. George died intestate in 1854 indebted to said Chas G Dale & to divers other persons; that administration of his personal estate was committed to Jos Godfrey, & that it is insufficient for the payment of his debts; that the following persons are heirs at law of said George, upon whom has devolved his interest in all his real estate, to wit: Jos Godfrey, Belitha Godfrey, Wm J Godfrey, Ann Taylor wife of Josiah Taylor, Jos W Holloway, Eliz Godfrey, Mrs Ann Godfrey, John W Godfrey, & Emmeline Godfrey; that the said Jos Godfrey, Belitha Godfrey, Ann Taylor wife of Josiah Taylor are all of full age & reside in Worcester Co; that Jos W Holloway, Wm J Godfrey, Eliz Godfrey, Mary Ann Godfrey, John W Godfrey, & Emmeline Godfrey are residents of some of the Western States, of whom Jos W Holloway, Wm J Godfrey, Eliz & Mary Ann Godfrey are of full age, & others are infants under the age of 21 years. Absent dfndnts are to appear in this Court, on or before the 3rd Tue in May next. –Edw D Martin, clerk

Canton Tea Co: 510 7th st: partnership formed under firm of Hall & Henning, opens Dec 18th, a large assortment of Teas, Coffees, & Spices. -P W Hall, G C Henning

WED DEC 20, 1854
Mme Boye Danstrom died a few weeks ago in Stockholm. The Washington public, just some months ago, delighted to the singing of this lady, & will receive the news of her death with deep regret. Even last year before her journey to the U S, she had contracted a severe disease of the chest, which ultimately caused her death.

Gen J P Duval, long a citizen of Florida, died at Tallahassee, Fla, on Dec 7. He was the brother of the distinguished & lamented Gen W P Duval, &, like him, was intimately connected with the early American settlement of the Territory. -Floridian

Wash Corp: 1-Ptn from Henry W Ferguson & John W Young, for the remission of a fine: referred to the Cmte of Claims. Ptn from Isaac A Montross for the same. 2-Act for the relief of Elias E Barnes: passed. 3-Act for the relief of John McGarvey: passed. 4-Bill for the relief of John Considine: passed.

Senate: 1-Ptn from Wm B Wood, asking that a pension may be allowed the widow of Geo M F Wood, an ofcr of the army, who died of yellow fever while in the discharge of his duty in Texas. 2-Cmte on Military Affairs: adverse reports on the ptns of Jas P Heath, & of Saml Clendenin. Same cmte: asked to be discharged from the further consideration of the bill for the relief of Thos T Russell, of Fla, & that it be referred to the Cmte on Public Lands: agreed to. 3-Cmte of Claims: recommended the passage of the bill allowing rations to Brig Gen John C Wool. Same cmte: recommended the passage of the bill for the relief of Lincoln Bates. Same for the bill for the relief of Polly Carver. 4-Cmte on Pensions: bill for the relief of Zabina Rawson, & recommended its passage. Same cmte: bill for the relief of Parmelia Allen, late the wife of John Blue: submitted a report.

House of Reps: 1-Bill to incorporate the Mutual Fire Ins Co of D C: granted them the necessary powers to insure property, etc: it declares Ulysses Ward, Thos Blagden, F Howard, J C McKelden, John Van Reswick, P W Browning, & Mathew G Emery, their present & future associates, a body politic & corporate.

Lot of valuable negroes at public sale: by order of the Orphans Court, sale on Jan 11 next, at the residence of the late Dr Richd Duckett, near Queen Ann, PG Co, 17 servants. –C C Magruder, adm de bonis non of Thos Duckett.

On Tue last the scaffolding of the new Roman Catholic Church, now bldg in Chicago, Ill, gave way & 6 workmen were precipated to the ground. Andrew Foster was instantly killed.

Mrd: on Dec 9, at **Elm Grove**, near Jacksonville, Ill, the residence of Mrs E C Duncan, by Rev L M Glover, Chas E Putnam, of Davenport, Iowa, to Miss Mary L, daughter of the late Gov Jos Duncan, of Ill.

New Orleans, Dec 18. W H Wilder, a lawyer, & one of the most prominent of the Cuba fillibusters & Lopez sympathizers, was convicted today of forging land warrants.

Circuit Court of Wash Co, D C, in Equity. John S Blackford et al vs Martha Blagrove & Josephine Blagrove. D W Edmonston, jr, trustee, reported that he had sold all that piece & lot of ground on the s e corner of Montg & Olive sts, Gtwn, D C, being a part of lot 13, of Holmead's addition to Gtwn, fronting 20 feet, more or less, on Montg st, & running back the same width 54 feet, with the frame bldgs thereon, to Robt McPherson for $1,005, & that he has complied with the terms of sale. –Jno A Smith, clerk

THU DEC 21, 1854
Obit-died: on Dec 10, in Phil, Mrs Ann Bayard, widow of Jas A Bayard, of Delaware; in her 77th year. Her father, Richd Bassett, was the first U S Senator elected by the State of Delaware: held his seat from 1789 to 1793. Her husband, Jas A Bayard, was elected to represent the State of Delaware in the lower House of Congress from 1797 to 1803; in 1801 was appointed Minister Pleni of the U S at the Court of France; in 1804 was elected U S Senator from Dela; re-elected in 1810; in 1813 Pres Madison appointed him, in connexion with John Quincy Adams & Albert Gallatin, Envoy Extra & Minister Pleni to negotiate a treaty of peace with Great Britain, under the mediation of the Emperor of Russia. He died in 1815, in his 48th year, leaving Mrs Bayard a widow for nearly 30 years. Richd Bayard, one of her sons, has been twice elected to rep the State of Dela in the U S Senate, between the years 1836 & 1845; Jas A Bayard, another son, represents the same seat in the U S Senate heretofore occupied & so long by his grandfather, his father, & his brother.

Household & kitchen furniture at auction: on Dec 27, at the residence of Rev Chas A Davis, on H st, near 20th st. -Jas C McGuire, auct

John R Cooke, an eminent lawyer & a member of the Va State Convention of 1829, died at Richmond on Fri last.

Senate: 1-Ptn from the heirs of John Gales, asking to be allowed the bounty land to which their father was entitled: referred. 2-Ptn from Eliza J Rogers & Sarah Ann De Wolf, only children & heirs of Rev Wm Rogers, a brigade chaplain in the Revolution, asking to be allowed bounty land.

Trustee's sale of Montg Co Land: at public auction, on Jan 9, at the Court-house door in Rockville, that part of the real estate of the late Thos Gittings which was assigned to the widow for her dower. It lies on the road from Colesville to Wash, about 8 miles from the latter place: 191 acres: with a pretty good dwlg house, frame stable, & out-bldgs. The property will be sold free of the incumbrance of the widow's dower. –W Veirs Bouic, trustee, Rockville, Md

Mrd: on Dec 19, in the First Presbyterian Church, in Wash City, by Rev Wm McLain, Edw B Wheelock, of New Orleans, to Mary Louisa Clack, daughter of the late Capt John H Clack.

For sale, improved Farm in D C: called **Glenellen**, contains 102½ acres of choice land; with a large sub-stantially built dwlg, 56 feet in length by 40 feet in depth. The society in the neighborhood is of the very best kind. Apply to the subscriber, in person or by letter, on board the U S steamer **Michigan**, at Erie, Pa. –Wm A T Maddox, Capt U S Marines. Or to Mr Thos Marshall, & Mr John H King, living near the farm; ofc of the latter No 35 south High st, Gtwn. And to Chubb Brothers, Bankers, & Mr Jas Towles, Property Agent, Wash.

Died: on Dec 19, Jos W Beck, in his 61st year. His funeral will be from his late residence, Capitol Hill, on Fri, at 2 o'clock.

Wash City Ordinances: 1-Act for the relief of Wm R Woodward: to pay him $366.90, a balance due for walling **Tiber Creek** though a portion of square 630. 2-Act for the relief of Gaffin Nally: fine imposed on the son of Gaffin Nally, for a misdemeanor at the Eastern Market-house is remitted: provided Nally pay the costs of prosecution. 3-Act for the relief of Mrs Louisa J Wadsworth: the sum of $800 be paid to her for expenses for the stone-wall, coping, railing, & steps, which were removed by the authority of the Corp in regarding K st.

FRI DEC 22, 1854
Senate: 1-Ptn from Wm G Ridgely, chief clerk in the bureau of yards & docks, asking to be allowed arrears of salary: referred. 2-Cmte on Public Lands asked to be discharged from the further consideration of the ptn of Jacob Dodson, & that it be referred to the Cmte on Military Affairs: agreed to.

House of Reps: 1-Bill for the relief of C E Greneaux. 2-Mr Bridges asked Mr Eliot if the gentleman was acquainted with Judge Cranch? Mr Eliot said, "I am." Judge Cranch's wife & my grandmother were sisters. Mr Bridges: does not the gentleman know that Judge Cranch has been entirely incapable of discharging the duties of his ofc for the last 5 years, & that he had during that time regularly drawn his salary of $2,900 a year? Mr Eliot: Under our Constitution, we have no pensions.

Jas Lowry, N Y fireman, was killed at a fire in N Y on Wed.

The store of Mr Wm P Pouder, at Balt, was robbed Wed night of silks, velvets, & other fancy goods to the amount of about $3,000.

The English papers brought the intelligence that John Gibson Lockhart, the eminent Scottish author, died of paralysis, at Abbottsford, on Nov 25. He was the son of a Scottish clergyman, & was born at Glasgow in 1792. His writings brought him into an intimacy with Walter Scott, which resulted in his marriage to the novelist's daughter, Charlotte Sophia Scott, in Apr, 1820. Mrs Lockhart died in 1837, & we believe his children are all deceased. –Phil Bulletin

Died: on Dec 10, in his native place, Norfolk, Va, Dr Joel Martin, of the army.

Died: on Sat last, in Nottingham District, Mr Jas N Baden, an old & highly respected citizen.

Died: on Dec 21, Mrs Ann Eliza Wood, wife of Edw Wood, sr, aged 68 years. Her funeral will be this afternoon at 2 o'clock, from her late residence on 13th st, near B st, Island.

$500 reward for runaway negroes Jason Williams & Andrew Snowden, late the property of John Coal, of PG Co, Md, deceased. Jason is about 40 years old & Andrew is about 27 years old. –N C Stephen, Admr C T A of John Coal, deceased.

Appointments by the Pres by & with the advice & consent of the Senate:
Mark W Izard, to be Govn'r of Nebraska, vice Francis Burt, deceased.
Jacob Sorber, to be Postmaster at Wilkesbarre, Pa, vice John Richard, resigned.
Thos M Pegues, to be Postmaster at Camden, S C, vice John M Gamewell, resigned.
Fairman F Taber, to be Postmaster at Natchitoches, La, vice Timothy Lacoste, resigned.
Jacob C Martin, of Ark, to be Receiver at Little Rock, Ark, vice B F Danley, resigned.
Albert Greenleaf, of D C, to be Navy Agent at Wash, for 4 years, vice A G Allen, resigned.

Orphans Court of Wash Co, D C. Letters of administration on the personal estate of Henry Ismann, late of Wash Co, deceased. –A Gross, adm

SAT DEC 23, 1854
Trustee's sale: by deed of trust from Martha E Dixon, dated Feb 15, 1854, the following property at auction, in front of the premises, on Jan 16: part of the eastern half of lot 6 in square 518, Wash City, with the brick dwlg house thereon.
-W Redin, trustee -Green & Scott, aucts

Hon Levi Foulerod, a Senator in the Legislature of Pa, from Phil Co, died on Thu. He was a member of the Democratic party, & had 2 years of his term yet to serve.

Wm H Martin, a clerk in the post ofc in Balt was yesterday convicted of purloining letters from the mails. The penalty is 10 years imprisonment in the penitentiary.

Mrd: on Thu, by Rev John C Smith, Mr John H Gardner to Miss Anna E J Harvey, all of Wash City.

Died: on Dec 19, after a protracted illness, Miss Martha A Baden, in her 20th year, formerly of PG Co, Md.

House of Reps: 1-Bill for the relief of the legal reps of John H Stone: recommended it pass. 2-Bill for the relief of the legal reps of Col Francis Vigo: recommended that it be rejected. 3-Bill for the relief of John Shaw: referred.

Orphans Court of Wash Co, D C. Letters of administration on the personal estate of Jas M Smith, late of Wash Co, deceased. –Wm Bell, exc

Trustee's sale: by decree of the Circuit Court of PG Co, Md, in equity: public sale on Jan 18 next: at the late residence of Oliver B Magruder, deceased: the real estate of which he died seized & possessed, supposed to contain about 700 acres of land, about 4 miles from Bladensburg, with a comfortable frame dwlg nearly new & every necessary bldg for farming operations. –N C Stephen, trustee

Circuit Court of Wash Co, D C-in equity. Stinger et al vs Gray et al. The trustee reported that he has sold lot 105, in Beatty & Hawkins' addition to Gtwn, to Chas Slemmer for $997.50, & lot 11, in same addition, to Richd Pettit for $840, & the purchasers have complied with the terms of sale. –Jno A Smith, clerk

MON DEC 25, 1854
Three men in the employ of Mr Fillion, stone-cutter, were precipitated last week from the roof of a 5 story bldg in course of erection at Louisville. Geo Schweigert was instantly killed, & Jos Schall & Wm Absalon, were very seriously hurt.

By the caving of a bank near the Bergen station, on the N Y & Erie Railroad, on Tue, Wm Connell was instantly killed; Patrick Carran was crushed so that his life is despaired of.

At the burning of a hotel in Birchville, C W, a few nights ago, John Jacobs, agent, perished in the flames.

Dr Proctor, of Brighton, Canada, was accidentally shot dead, as he was sitting in his parlor, by a lad who was firing at a mark.

On Dec 4 Stephen T Noble & Jos O'Neil, 2 Kansas pioneers who went out with one of the N Y companies, were drowned in the Missouri, near Weston, by the snagging of a boat.

Died: on Dec 24, Lizzie Livingston, daughter of Dr Wm Gunton, & wife of Rev Wm Ives Budington, recently of Charlestown, Mass, but now of Phil. Her protracted & painful illness she bore with sweet submission. Her funeral will be tomorrow at 11 o'clock, from the residence of her father.

In Chancery. John S Blagrove & others against Martha & Josephine Blagrove: the creditors of Henry B Blagrove, deceased, are to file their claims on Dec 30 at my ofc, in the City Hall, Wash. —W Redin, auditor

WED DEC 27, 1854
Senate: 1-Ptn from the heirs of David Tomlinson, asking to be allowed commutation pay. 2-Ptn from Geo Fitzsimons, a soldier wounded in the war of 1812, asking that his pension may be made to commence from the time of his disability. 3-Bill to increase the pension of Patrick C Miles: passed.

Catalogue sale of books, periodicals & stationery: on Dec 27, all the stock in trade of Jno Elder & Co, 7th st, near La ave. -Jas C McGuire, auct

Criminal Court-Wash. Stephen F Lucas, who was convicted last week of obtaining money under false pretences from Chubb Brothers, & had a new trial, was again convicted on Saturday last.

Mrd: on Dec 24, by Rev Andrew G Carothers, Mr Chas Edmonds, of Albany, to Miss Sarah Ann Dougherty, of Wash City.

Mrd: on Dec 23, by Rev Jas H Brown, Mr Saml Johnston to Miss Eliz E Yost, both of PG Co, Md.

Mrd: on Dec 14, by Rev J Stratton, at **Hollywood**, Adams Co, Miss, Mr Dudley M Haydon, of Ky, to Miss Anna, daughter of Jas A Gillespie.

Balt, Dec 26. Saml Wilkinson, a contractor for carrying the mail between Milford, Dela, & Cambridge, Md, has been arrested as an accomplice in a series of mail robberies in connexion with Wm Williams, a clerk in the post ofc at Milford, who has been heretofore arrested. Both are now in jail in Dover, Dela, awaiting a trial.

N Y, Dec 26. The land belonging to the Parker Vein Co on George' creek, Md, was sold here this afternoon at auction for $250,000. It was bought in for the benefit of the stockholders.

For sale or rent, with or without furniture, the well built & commodious house, occupied by the subscriber, in **Franklin Row**. Immediate possession given if desired. -B H Chean

Bailiff's sale: by order of distrain for house rent due & in arrears & several writs of fieri facias: against the goods & chattels of Anton Lehmann: I have seized furniture & cooking utensils & stove, at 7th & La ave, Wash City, know as the Columbia Place, in the basement of said house, formerly kept as a restaurant by said Lehmann. -A E S Keese, bailiff

THU DEC 28, 1854

Senate: 1-Ptn from Jas Walling, an American citizen who had been impressed on board a British man of war, & who surrendered himself as a prisoner during the war of 1812, & was sent to Dartmoor prison. He asks to be compensated for the loss of time & suffering endured while in his captivity: referred. 2-Ptn from Jno Holden, asking to be allowed the half pay to which his father was entitled for his Revolutionary services.

Warren Moore, aged 16 years, died in Orange Co, N Y, on Dec 12, of hydrophobia. He was bitten by a dog in Athol about 6 weeks previous to his death, but felt no bad effects from the bite until Sat.

House of Reps: 1-Bill granting a pension to Dolly Empson.

Wash Corp: 1-Bill for the relief of Mrs Mary Nevitt: referred to the Cmte of Ways & Means. 2-Bill for the relief of Jos D Lafontaine: passed. 3-Ptn of John O'Dwyer for the remission of a fine: referred to the Cmte of Claims. 4-Ptn from Henry B Robinson for an increase in his salary as assist clerk of the Centre Market: referred to the Cmte on Finance. 5-Act for the relief of Matilda Ann Beall: passed. 6-Nomination from the Mayor for Wm Dixon to be Intendant of the Asylum, in the place of Benj E Gittings, resigned, to take effect from Jan 1 next; John P White to be Com'r of the Asylum, in place of Wm Dixon, appointed intendent of the Asylum: nominations confirmed.

Mrd: on Wed, by Rev John C Smith, Jasper S Lloyd, of Cincinnati, Ohio, to Miss Jane Randall, of Wash City.

Mrd: on Dec 26, in Wash City, by Rev W Hodges, John Rowland to Miss Anna Lockor, of PG Co, Md.

Circuit Court of Wash Co, D C-in equity. Wm J Gray vs Nathan Gray, Benj Gray, Jas M Gray, Edw Gray, Mgt Gray, Eliza Gray, Louisa Gray, Griffith Gray, Eliza Jane Gray, Robt & John Gray, et al. The ptn states that the petitioner appointed administrator of Nathan Gray, deceased, Jefferson Co, Ky; that he received no personal assets, & made payments from his private means for the funeral expenses, amounting to $230.05, & there is not personal estate to reimburse him; that by decree of this court the real estate of said Nathan Gray, in Gtwn, was sold by W S Cox, trustee, who has the proceeds in hand. It asks that he may be paid the sum of $230.05 out of the proceeds of sale, & states that the above dfndnts are non-residents. Absent dfndnts are to appear in person or by solicitor, on or before the first Monday of May next. –Jas S Morsell, Assist Judge Circuit Court of Wash Co, D C -Jno A Smith, clerk

Died: on Dec 27, Mrs Sarah Pilling, in her 77th year. Her funeral will take place on Dec 29, at 2 o'clock, from her late residence on 15th st.

Orphans Court of Wash Co, D C. Letters of administration on the personal estate of Jos W Beck, late of Wash Co, deceased. –Jas A Tait, E G Handy, admx

Notice to Creditors. By deed of assignment from Wm B Hart, dated Nov 14, 1854, the undersigned has been appointed trustee for the benefit of the creditors of the said W B Hart. –E R Sprague

FRI DEC 29, 1854
Circuit Court of Wash Co, D C–in equity. Kitty E A Gassaway vs Jno H Gassaway, Jane A Gassaway, Nicholas Gassaway, Wm A Gassaway, Laura Gassaway, Mary A Darne wife of A C H Darne, & Lavinia Peter wife of Geo Peter. Bill of reviver: in Jan 1847, she filed her original bill against Hanson Gassaway, her late husband, setting forth her marriage with said Gassaway, his subsequent insanity & refusal to support her, & his ownership of certain property in Wash, & praying allowance of alimony; that the Court passed an order requiring said Gassaway to pay to said cmplnt $2 weekly for her support, pendent elite; that in Mar, 1847, said Hanson Gassaway filed his answer to said bill, that the general replication was filed & interrogatories to accompany a commission to take proofs; since which said Gassaway died, leaving as his heirs at law John H Gassaway, Jane A Gassaway, Nicholas Gassaway, Wm A Gassaway, Laura Gassaway, Mary A Darne wife of A C H Darne, & Lavinia Peter wife of Geo Peter, all of whom are non-residents, & said Wm A & Laura Gassaway are minors. It further states that said Hanson Gassaway had purchased some lots in Wash, which he caused to be conveyed to E M Linthicum by an absolute deed, intended as a security for a debt; that they exceed in value the amount of the debt, & the cmplnt is entitled to & prays for alimony out of the surplus. The property consists of lot 9, in Davidson's subdivision of square 267; lot 1, in Wilson & Callan's subdivision of said square; lot 7, in Davidson's subdivision of the same square; lot K, in Wilson & Callan's subdivision of same; the east part of lot 2, in square 72, & lot 6 in the same square. Dfndnts to appear in this Court, in person or by solicitor, on or before, the first Monday of May next.
–Jas S Morsell –Jno A Smith, clerk

Col A R Woolley, a veteran ofcr, formerly of the army, has a petition before Congress for relief against an alleged unjust dismissal from service by the sentence of a Court-Martial. He has requested us to place the annexed brief extracts from a report on his case by Gen Shields, of the Senate, from the Military Cmte: In 1829 he was subjected to trial upon certain charges, & found guilty of having punished a private soldier with a few lashes; the court sentenced him to be dismissed from the service; the sentence was approved by the Pres. In the opinion of this cmte, the court-martial that tried & condemned Lt Col Woolley was irregularly constituted, both as to number & rank.

Household & kitchen furniture at auction: Jan 4, at the residence of Mrs Gildmeister, 21 4½ st, near C st. -Green & Scott, aucts

The Detroit papers mention that a young man, Wm H Gregg, went into the woods in pursuit of a deer for his sick father. On his return he was shot by a lad of 16, Simon Shirts, who, instead of going to help him, ran a mile to tell that he had mistaken a man for a deer. Gregg did not survive long.

Mrd: on Dec 26, in Wash City, at the E street Baptist Church, by Rev G W Samson, assisted by Rev Prof Huntington, Prof R P Latham, of Richmond, Va, to Miss Ida Bacon, daughter of J S Bacon, D D, Pres of Columbia College.

Died: on Dec 16, suddenly, at his residence in Chas Co, Md, Mr E Rudhall Pye. The deceased was greatly endeared to an extensive circle of friends & relatives by his many amiable qualities. May he rest in peace!

Thos W Dorr, of Rhode Island, died on Wed at Providence. He was the leader & hero of a party which, 12 or 13 years ago, attempted to overthrow the Gov't of Rhode Island by revolutionary means, in which purpose he was defeated by the People of the State. He fled to N Y, & then to N H. Upon returning to R I, he was arrested, tried & convicted of treason, & sentenced to the State prison for life. Several years ago he was liberated by act of the Legislature, & in 1853 the Legislature relieved him from all the civil disabilities which he had incurred in Consequence of his revolutionary enterprise. Mr Dorr had been in bad health for some time previous to his death.

Obit-died: on Oct 31 last, in his 74th year, at *Clifton*, his residence in Clarke Co, Va, David H Allen. For several years past his health had been declining, & for the last 6 months he was unable to leave his chamber. He was one of the few survivors of a class of men once numerous in Va, who had fine talents & liberal education, added to that the advantage of hereditary wealth. He graduated at Princeton College in 1802, during the Presidency of Dr Smith. As a husband & father, he was affectionate & thoughtful. A Virginia gentleman of the old school.

SAT DEC 30, 1854
Senate: 1-Ptn from Oscar W Turk, asking payment for serices rendered as a clerk in the Fourth Auditor's ofc.

Cholera in Messina: 22,000 fell victims to cholera from Aug 22 to Sep 10. On Aug 27 it became impossible that the bodies could be buried. The English Consul, Mr Barker, his brother & to 2 sisters died; so did the Sardinian Consul & his numerous family; also the Tuscan consul.

Homicides at Augusta, Ga, during Christmas. On Sat Saml Wilson, a painter, was shot & killed in the street by Wm A Archer, who is now in jail for his crime. On Monday a man named Attoway was killed by a blow on the head with a brick. The offences are ascribed to "rum doings."

On Thu, at Phil, Andrew Dunbar was killed by Jos Kenny. They had been at a tavern together, but got into an altercation, when Kenny fired a pistol, killing Dunbar.

On Sep 20 the English troop ship **Charlotte**, from Calcutta to Queenstown, was wrecked on a reef in Algoa bay. There was on board a detachment of the 27th Regt, consisting of the following ofcrs: Capt Stapylton, Capt Warner, Lt Maguire, Ensign White, Dr Kidd, 168 rank & file, 14 women, & 26 children. Of the survivors it was ascertained that out of 168 rank & file about 18 were saved. Of the crew, which consisted of 24, only Capt Affleck, his son, the 1st mate, ship's butcher, cook, steward, & 2 others were saved. The total drowned is 117.

Yesterday the house of Mr Jos Sears, at Naugatuck, Ct, was robbed. Mrs Sears received frightful wounds & a young child was murdered to prevent it from giving an alarm. Mr Sears, who slept in another part of the house, was not awakened. The murderers escaped.

Mrd: on Dec 28, in Wash City, by Rev W Hodges, Robt V Henry to Miss Mgt K Stanfield, all of Wash.

Mrd: on Dec 13, by Rev W Hodges, Enoch M Norris, of Chas Co, Md, to Miss Sarah Williams, of Wash.

Mrd; on Dec 23, at Foundry Parsonage, by Rev E P Phelps, Mr Armstead T Mills, of Fairfax Co, Va, to Miss Eliz E Germon, of Wash City.

Mrd: on Dec 28, at the Navy Yard, Wash, by Rev Mr Hodges, John W Lynn to Miss Emily Bell, both of PG Co, Md.

Mrd: on Dec 21, at Gtwn, D C, by Rev Mr Sutherland, Morris Adler to Catharine, daughter of the late Danl Kurtz, of that place.

Died: on Dec 28, Mr John D Brown, of Wash City, in his 39th year. His remains will be taken to Norfolk, Va, for interment, leaving this morning by the train of cars at half past 8 o'clock. He came to this city a few years since with nothing to rely upon but his own unaided exertions. He established himself in a prosperous business. He was a devoted & affectionate husband, & in his death his bereaved & afflicted wife & children have sustained an irreparable loss.

A

Abbot, 39, 285, 297, 337
Abbott, 5, 39, 414
Abercrombie, 381
Abert, 39, 75
Aborn, 249
Abrams, 321
Abry, 355
Absalon, 440
Acken, 270, 394, 409
Acker, 39
Ackerman, 237, 425
Ackley, 39
Acton, 39, 58, 288, 337
Adae, 22
Adam, 76
Adams, 14, 33, 39, 52, 63, 82, 91, 108, 114, 118, 157, 162, 178, 186, 210, 282, 288, 292, 316, 331, 337, 341, 348, 349, 351, 353, 355, 356, 369, 378, 405, 418, 423, 430, 437
Addison, 18, 28, 39, 106, 107, 109, 123, 140, 234, 239, 264, 298, 407
Adkinson, 282
Adler, 445
Adrain, 195
Adrian, 39
Adrien, 170
Affleck, 445
Ager, 1
Agg, 237
Ahrents, 119
Aiken, 251, 264, 280
Aitkin, 86
Albert, 91, 95, 319
Albion, 385
Alcott, 23
Alday, 107
Aldersbers, 386
Aldis, 137
Alexander, 20, 24, 39, 54, 146, 177, 196, 241, 255, 283, 409, 415, 428

Alig, 336
Alison, 193
Allemander, 186
Allen, 25, 33, 49, 67, 73, 75, 86, 96, 113, 119, 193, 199, 205, 234, 246, 294, 336, 346, 348, 356, 360, 363, 396, 436, 439, 444
Allerton, 153
Allison, 34, 66, 217, 222, 392
Allston, 397
Allyn, 19, 124
Almy, 39, 56
Altemus, 337
Alton, 8
Alvord, 215, 284, 285, 286
Ambler, 325
American Flag, 224
American Organ, 394
Ames, 240
Amey, 5, 199
Amiss, 424
Anderson, 39, 60, 103, 114, 157, 164, 198, 232, 242, 254, 299, 311, 353, 387, 393, 412
Andrae, 39
Andrews, 66, 102, 151, 225, 231, 239, 254, 264, 280, 296, 332, 349, 409
Angelrodt, 304
Angley, 66
Angus, 97, 195, 231, 239, 255
Ansel, 355
Ansley, 390
Ansman, 195, 270
Anspach, 278
Anthon, 329
Anthony, 249
Antietam Iron Works, 384
Antisel, 261
Anton, 91
Antrim, 303
Apaches, 151
Apperson, 73, 156, 292
Appich, 261

Appleton, 39, 185
<u>Appointments by the Pres</u>, 33, 56, 68, 70, 72, 90, 100, 124, 128, 130, 136, 152, 176, 214, 223, 241, 273, 275, 277, 308, 342, 378, 439
Arbuckle, 356
Arbuthnot, 304
Archbishop of Vienna, 171
Archbold, 2
Archduchess Sophia, 171
Archer, 33, 76, 103, 445
Arctic, 355
Arena, 65
Arfwedson, 37, 49, 237, 274
Arlington House, 79, 175
Armigo, 57
Armijo, 202, 229
Armstead, 219
Armstrong, 18, 55, 75, 82, 83, 308, 395
Arnold, 3, 9, 29, 51, 92, 95, 99, 106, 111, 147, 167, 168, 240, 254, 281, 285, 324, 369, 434
Arnot, 116
Arnott, 192
Arrison, 222, 392
Arth, 39
Arthur, 360, 375
Arwedson, 167
Aschwanden, 38
Ash, 67
Ashburton, 391
Ashe, 133, 321, 330
Ashford, 92, 219, 246, 298
Ashley, 360
Ashman, 290
Ashton, 143
Aspinwall, 20, 21
Atchison, 77, 300
Atherton, 401
Atkins, 248, 377, 378
Atkinson, 39, 64, 76, 167, 171, 302, 308, 354, 417
Atlee, 337, 374

Atocha, 112, 170
Attoway, 445
Atwood, 238
Aubrey, 373
Auburn Cemetery, 334
Aubury, 235
Auchinlick, 20
Audubon, 55
August, 424
Auguste, 334
Aurand, 232
Ausman, 254
Austin, 8, 189, 261
Auvergne plantation, 279
Aveihle, 39
Averill, 52, 86, 190
Avery, 106, 211, 212
Ayers, 252
Aylmer, 109, 156
Ayot, 131
Ayres, 27
Ayton, 65

B

Baalham, 363
Baasen, 241
Babb, 72
Babbit, 19, 88, 364
Babcock, 18, 220, 356, 378
Bach, 248
Bachelder, 183, 434
Backus, 144
Bacon, 63, 87, 91, 93, 121, 178, 218, 277, 291, 337, 374, 389, 419, 444
Baden, 40, 77, 322, 355, 439
Badger, 116, 240
Baggerby, 270
Baggerly, 212, 255, 281
Baglin, 364
Bailey, 80, 91, 118, 220, 226, 300, 305, 306
Bain, 192, 424
Baird, 18, 165, 278
Baja, 155

Baker, 14, 26, 52, 53, 58, 60, 69, 134, 139, 167, 187, 203, 210, 222, 258, 260, 264, 270, 275, 280, 281, 287, 318, 326, 337, 356, 366, 376, 396, 401, 403, 408, 409
Balard, 24
Balch, 119, 283
Baldin, 307
Baldwin, 31, 39, 89, 121, 137, 207, 212, 245, 255, 272, 280, 321, 360, 400, 411
Balestier, 100, 274
Balkeman, 53
Ball, 39, 73, 191
Ballam, 356
Ballantine, 364
Ballantyne, 278
Ballard, 5, 17, 25, 394
Ballast, 13
Ballenger, 91
Balster, 25, 245
Balt, 39
Baltimore, 39
Baltzell, 40
Bamberger, 191
Banche, 356
Bankhead, 17, 385
Banks, 265
Bannister, 262
Bapst, 371
Baptiste, 220
Barbarin, 241
Barber, 135, 146, 172, 334, 352
Barbour, 154, 308, 385
Barclay, 106
Barculo, 318
Barelli, 241
Barer, 357
Bargy, 234
Barker, 219, 263, 424, 444
Barlow, 7, 180, 289, 406
Barnaclo, 81, 348
Barnacloe, 92
Barnard, 30, 125, 166, 245, 302

Barnes, 25, 27, 39, 63, 80, 119, 129, 137, 140, 168, 190, 204, 218, 219, 325, 413, 436
Barnhill, 330
Barnitz, 141
Barnwell, 56
barque **Abeona**, 123
barque **Como**, 425
barque **Concordia**, 291
barque **Huron**, 355
barque **Kilby**, 19, 20, 21, 33, 197
barque **Mount Vernon**, 123, 281
barque **Oleona**, 281
barque **Zenobia**, 180
Barr, 137, 191, 244
Barratts, 33
Barrell, 132
Barrett, 8, 40, 138
Barrill, 357
Barron, 39, 287, 326, 338
Barrow, 395
Barrundia, 271, 276
Barry, 2, 8, 9, 39, 40, 90, 102, 103, 356, 394, 404
Barstow, 17
Bartalis, 186
Bartlett, 315, 392
Bartoll, 33
Barton, 21, 245, 275
Bartonsville, 245
Bartruff, 214
Bassett, 36, 153, 405, 437
Bassuett, 81
Bastianelli, 184
Bastow, 294
Batchelder, 182, 237, 262
Bateman, 39, 366
Batemen, 86
Bates, 28, 40, 102, 239, 264, 310, 323, 388, 436
Battle, 40, 231
Batts, 236
Bauer, 173
Baughman, 278

Baum, 219, 247
Baury, 88, 97, 400
Bawtree, 234
Baxter, 10
Bayard, 18, 124, 437
Bayley, 334
Bayliss, 83
Baylor, 39, 72, 263
Bayly, 38, 40, 191
Bayne, 40, 138, 372, 427
Beagle, 341
Beal, 410
Beale, 90
Beall, 16, 28, 39, 51, 75, 91, 107, 149, 174, 234, 325, 384, 403, 442
Bealle, 39
Beals, 349
Bean, 97, 98, 123
Beard, 168, 428
Beardsley, 39, 119
Beattie, 333
Beatty, 6, 78, 141, 412
Beaubien, 26, 114, 123, 264, 280
Beaugeau, 334
Beaulieu, 155
Beaumont, 131, 200, 349
Beaver Dam Meadows, 141
Bechtel, 25
Beck, 31, 106, 219, 309, 438, 443
Beckett, 30
Beckham, 240
Beckwith, 318
Becroft, 399
Bedell, 70, 78, 190, 424
Bedford, 357, 425
Bedinger, 68, 73, 191, 223, 254, 327
Bee, 264
Beebe, 9, 199
Beebee, 281
Beecher, 13
Beehan, 381, 432
Beelen, 277
Beers, 229
Beggs, 119

Begnan, 170
Beheehan, 432
Beider, 59
Beirne, 50
Belden, 136, 199, 274
Belding, 220
Belin, 133
Belknap, 117, 348, 388, 433
Bell, 21, 30, 161, 202, 205, 215, 221, 256, 426, 440, 445
Belle Isle, 400
Bellemeade, 322
Bellfield Farm, 320
Bellows, 78
Belmont, 68, 223
Belt, 40, 92, 106, 164, 397, 414, 429
Belton, 21, 24
Bembert, 316
Bemis, 377
Bemus, 73
Benbridge, 53
Bender, 199
Bendon, 131
Benedict, 356, 363
Benjamin, 177, 357
Bennet, 176, 371
Bennett, 24, 48, 100, 116, 123, 160, 189, 199, 252, 254, 280, 290, 374, 424, 434
Benning, 39, 355
Benoist, 361
Benseil, 429
Benson, 10, 240, 353
Bent, 310
Bent's Fort, 162
Benter, 256
Bentley, 121, 213, 214, 217
Bently, 281
Benton, 38, 321
Bentz, 25
Benzinska, 240
Bequette, 277
Bergershausen, 39
Bergman, 39

Berkler, 26
Berne, 158
Berret, 300
Berrien, 432
Berry, 28, 36, 40, 65, 87, 144, 150, 203, 204, 207, 289, 306, 357, 368, 380, 396, 411, 431
Berryhill, 66, 67
Berryman, 73, 231, 239
Bertram, 295
Bestor, 14, 40
Bett, 39
Bettencourt, 241
Bettinger, 2
Betts, 432
Bevens, 241
Beverly, 293
Bibb, 10, 11
Bickley, 40, 143
Bicksler, 424
Bienvenu, 404
Biewend, 218
Bigelow, 261
Bigler, 422
Biglow, 39
Billing, 288, 337
Bindon, 49
Bingey, 347
Bingham, 285
Birch, 39, 92, 111, 164, 181, 186, 238
Bird, 36, 40, 83, 86, 106, 123, 157, 160
Birdsall, 203
Birdwell, 66
Birge, 411
Birns, 155
Birth, 40, 312
Biscoe, 170
Bishop, 9, 29, 51, 95, 182, 240, 254, 281, 349, 351
Bishop of Buffalo, 311
Bishop of Hartford, 402
Bispham, 27, 58, 60, 80, 123
Biss, 40

Bissell, 176, 347
Bisselle, 346
Bixby, 205
Black, 1, 101, 220, 271, 320
Blackbun, 141
Blackburn, 31, 141, 148, 269
Blackfan, 327
Blackford, 237, 378, 399, 437
Blackwell, 306, 424
Blagden, 40, 436
Blagrove, 378, 399, 437, 441
Blair, 17, 169, 204, 226, 321, 351
Blake, 9, 57, 151, 213, 280, 289, 339, 356
Blakeney, 195
Blakistone, 4, 316
Blanchard, 248
Blanchet, 181
Blandford, 234
Blaney, 50, 254
Blatchford, 68
Blaurak, 25
Blays, 76
Bledrod, 66
Blennerhassett, 352
Blish, 328
Bliss, 286, 325, 431
Bloecher, 39
Blokin, 236
Bloodgood, 356
Bloomer, 181
Blossom, 425
Blount, 351
Blox, 409
Blue, 48, 50, 58, 157, 348, 436
Blunt, 146, 147, 246, 363, 398
Boak, 391, 395
Boals, 58
Boardman, 8, 380
Boarman, 38, 170, 433
boat **Flying Cloud**, 200
boat **G W Sparhawk**, 224
boat **J H Stone**, 410
boat **Waterford**, 327

Bocock, 104, 226
Bodeman, 17
Bodisco, 30, 35, 38, 294
Bogan, 247, 332
Bogard, 145
Bogardus, 14
Bogart, 356
Boggs, 106, 119, 286
Bogusch, 168
Bogy, 212
Bohrer, 39, 92, 241
Boileau, 54
Bolling, 245, 270
Bolton, 353
Bomford, 39, 99
Bomino, 291
Bonaparte, 235, 294, 313
Bond, 39, 260
Bond's Mills, 325
Bonner, 17
Bonton, 255
Booker, 7, 131
Boone, 385, 427
Booth, 39, 250, 385
Boothe, 311
Boothroyed, 401
Booton, 145
Borcherdt, 169
Borden, 322
Borders, 184
Borland, 22, 68, 207, 383
Borliace, 131
Borrows, 168
Boss, 348
Bosten, 86
Boswell, 20
Bosworth, 74
Boteler, 40, 81, 320, 403, 415
Boudinot, 416
Boughton, 276
Bouic, 158, 325, 328, 437
Bouldin, 163
Boullgay, 93
Bourne, 31

Bourrows, 329
Bouton, 50, 54, 194, 282
Bowan, 56
Bowditch, 203
Bowen, 40, 141, 199, 231, 239, 284, 312, 322, 356, 357, 380, 428, 429
Bower, 209, 340
Bowers, 165
Bowes, 430
Bowie, 9, 38, 103, 147, 169, 174, 218, 232, 262, 320, 328, 402, 406
Bowling, 289
Bowman, 40, 69, 73, 137, 196, 220, 242, 376
Bowne, 48, 75, 220
Bowyer, 350
Boyce, 112
Boyd, 5, 53, 92, 97, 100, 174, 177, 212, 228, 233, 244
Boyer, 94
Boykin, 97, 156
Boyle, 26, 39, 56, 104, 198, 262, 265, 310
Boynton, 135, 174, 231, 239
Brachman, 334
Brackenridge, 308
Bracket, 163
Bradbury, 235
Bradford, 33, 39, 209, 416
Bradley, 20, 22, 39, 40, 56, 65, 93, 118, 178, 207, 219, 221, 223, 242, 247, 248, 265, 308, 319, 348
Brady, 18, 50, 58, 231, 260, 280, 339, 357, 400, 402, 427
Braiden, 98
Brandt, 231
Brangbridge, 14
Brannam, 396
Brantley, 339
Brantly, 364
Brashear, 403
Bratten, 417
Bravo, 170, 338
Braxton, 153

Bray, 39, 128, 157
Brayfield, 362
Breaker, 228
Breckenridge, 39, 40, 108, 288
Breed, 371
Breeding, 49
Brehon, 241
Brelsford, 287
Breman, 390
Bremen, 206
Brennan, 356, 360
Brennen, 382
Brenner, 39
Brent, 39, 40, 95, 118, 120, 234, 245, 429
Brereton, 39, 100, 127, 388
Bresneham, 187
Brest, 300
Brethrem, 122
Brevard, 100
Brewer, 76, 104, 329
Brewey, 402
Brewster, 333
Brian, 356, 360
Briarly, 418
Brice, 362
Bride, 381
Bridge, 364
Bridges, 39, 438
Bridgman, 130
Brien, 8
Briethaupt, 40
brig **Abby Frances**, 282
brig **Advance**, 122
brig **Amelia**, 282
brig **Amella**, 199
brig **Caledonia**, 247
brig **Enterprize**, 275
brig **Gen Armstrong**, 29, 204
brig **Glamorgan**, 225, 281
brig **Hallowell**, 232, 234, 281
brig **Heda**, 233
brig **James Rose**, 232, 234, 281
brig **Jane**, 48, 51, 244, 254

brig **Jasper**, 122
brig **John Dutton**, 4
brig **Kate Boyd**, 195, 239
brig **Mary**, 361
brig **Perry**, 225
brig **Porpoise**, 331
brig **Rescue**, 122
brig **Trent**, 383
brig **Union**, 214
brig **Wizard**, 281
Briggs, 50, 106
Brigham, 93, 264, 268
Brighardt, 261
Bright, 126, 418
Brill, 390
Brindle, 25
Bringham, 172
Brintnall, 165
Briscoe, 28, 40, 76, 87, 177, 240, 294, 309, 396
Bristow, 415
Britt, 301
Brockenbrough, 31
Brocker, 31
Brockett, 396, 416
Brockwell, 119
Broderick, 348
Brodhead, 9, 16, 433
Brodie, 80, 284
Bromberg, 10
Bronaugh, 195, 254, 270, 274, 282
Bronson, 54, 157, 357
Brook, 12, 232
Brooke, 12, 37, 40, 60, 77, 83, 102, 257, 293, 372, 377
Brookes, 5
Brooks, 20, 24, 35, 48, 86, 107, 162, 241, 258
Broom, 40
Brotherton, 151, 286, 385
Broughton, 386
Brown, 8, 12, 18, 19, 23, 24, 27, 30, 32, 37, 39, 40, 50, 51, 52, 71, 76, 83, 102, 105, 109, 118, 124, 140,

144, 146, 156, 161, 175, 182, 184,
191, 193, 195, 200, 202, 208, 216,
218, 219, 220, 223, 232, 240, 244,
248, 252, 254, 255, 258, 260, 261,
264, 270, 279, 280, 281, 282, 293,
296, 322, 324, 329, 330, 332, 333,
340, 341, 342, 344, 348, 350, 354,
355, 356, 357, 358, 359, 360, 361,
363, 366, 371, 373, 377, 379, 385,
397, 401, 402, 407, 411, 415, 421,
424, 425, 441, 445
Browne, 162
Brownell, 238
Browning, 115, 119, 247, 436
Brownlee, 433
Bruce, 393
Bruckley, 8
Brun, 357
Brutus, 305
Bryan, 26, 98, 150, 215, 218, 244,
264, 266, 318, 356, 357, 370
Buchan, 383
Buchanan, 5, 56, 225, 238
Buchly, 184
Buckbee, 301
Buckey, 30, 39, 166
Buckland, 250
Buckland Farm, 145
Buckles, 121, 254, 263, 281
Buckley, 318
Buckner, 7, 131, 239, 266, 282
Budd, 36
Buddy, 75
Budington, 440
Buel, 20
Buell, 82, 94
Buffington, 352
Buffum, 277
Bulger, 198, 292
Bulkley, 94, 355
Bull, 102, 110, 210
Bullock, 240
Bunn, 333
Bunnel, 430

Bunting, 102
Burch, 4, 40, 135, 248, 289, 316, 356,
410
Burche, 6, 10, 39, 40, 274, 418
Burchel, 369
Burchell, 371
Burchill, 28
Burden, 317
Burdett, 96
Burdick, 333
Burdsall, 210
Burford, 14
Burgess, 57, 220, 260, 328, 396
Burgess estate, 337
Burgevin, 174
Burke, 8, 19, 20, 21, 26, 39, 289, 396
Burkholder, 245
Burkhols, 25
Burley, 356
Burnes, 317, 356
Burnett, 421, 425
Burnham, 81, 244, 429
Burnley, 2
Burns, 53, 57, 269, 335, 356, 360,
386, 410
Burnt Mills, 204
Burr, 39, 95, 160, 167, 195, 348
Burroughs, 131, 324
Burrows, 180
Burt, 4, 277, 308, 375, 378, 384, 439
Burton, 14, 24, 89, 149, 196
Burwell, 191, 307, 310
Busby, 63
Busche, 40
Busey, 191
Bush, 40, 357
Busher, 348
Bushrod, 153
Bussell, 240
Bust, 103, 127
Buthmann, 65
Butler, 6, 8, 14, 29, 37, 39, 40, 56, 87,
104, 123, 146, 156, 160, 178, 195,
216, 223, 233, 254, 256, 265, 270,

278, 279, 292, 293, 327, 350, 353, 359, 414
Butt, 92
Butterfield, 239
Buttle, 39
Button, 25
Byer, 341
Byington, 39, 157, 297
Byrle, 256
Byrne, 10, 11, 40, 58, 61, 127, 159, 163, 359, 409
Byrnes, 236
Byron, 240

C

Cabell, 124, 249
Cabot, 40, 162, 369
Caden, 11, 40
Cady, 425
Caffee, 65, 289
Cahill, 342
Cahoon, 18, 124
Cain, 73, 433
Caine, 6
Calan, 40
Calbe, 25
Caldwell, 28, 38, 260, 301, 307, 332
Calhoun, 273
Call, 78, 213, 255, 270, 275, 281
Callaghan, 170, 204
Callahan, 40, 308
Callaher, 356
Callan, 11, 40, 64, 65, 320, 371, 415, 434, 443
Callaway, 297
Callin, 41
Callis, 138
Calvert, 160, 173, 186, 194, 197, 200, 229, 265, 341, 414
Calvert College, 337
Camanches, 151
Cameron, 24, 48, 163, 190, 355, 426
Cammack, 75
Camp, 26, 57, 149, 220

Campan, 52, 75, 83
Campau, 212, 255, 280
Campbell, 24, 37, 40, 76, 108, 117, 118, 124, 195, 201, 223, 275, 287, 322, 337, 350, 351, 397, 411
Camper, 186
Campt, 62
Canaan Lands, 242
Canaway, 67
Canby, 185, 248, 393
Canfield, 132, 144, 283, 287, 334, 429
Canino, 313
Cannon, 14, 40, 241, 268, 333, 357
Canon, 356
Cantin, 192
Cantrill, 67
Cantwell, 194
Capen, 212, 255, 280
Carbaugh, 85
Carbery, 91, 159, 164, 274, 427
Carden, 20, 304
Carey, 26, 360, 373
Cargill, 237
Carland, 25
Carlisle, 23, 146, 320
Carlos, 303
Carlton, 61, 78, 123, 212, 255, 279, 280
Carma, 192
Carmichael, 22, 140, 359
Carmick, 242
Carmines, 136
Carnagan, 356
Carnahan, 257
Carne, 31
Carnell, 376
Carner, 69, 309, 332, 382
Carothers, 104, 165, 219, 274, 346, 441
Carpenter, 27, 258, 385
Carr, 40, 112, 199, 285
Carran, 440
Carrico, 41
Carrier, 93

Carrington, 307, 346
Carroll, 8, 40, 77, 118, 174, 198, 220, 243, 288, 325, 414, 426
Carrolls, 179
Carson, 57, 69, 267, 323, 424
Carter, 41, 113, 153, 176, 200, 258, 299, 319, 350, 352, 368
Cartwright, 103
Carusi, 117, 246, 380
Carvalle, 11
Carver, 31, 244, 264, 436
Cary, 332
Casados, 271
Casey, 195, 283, 342, 356
Cash, 27, 51, 240, 252, 268, 275, 281, 344
Caskie, 226, 323
Casparis, 120, 300
Cass, 37, 38, 132, 144, 206, 223, 263
Cassa Blanca, 250
Cassaday, 152
Cassat, 277
Cassell, 16, 83, 427
Cassen, 270
Catalano, 166
Cathcart, 432
Catherwood, 357, 363
Catoir, 334
Caton, 40, 414, 428, 429
Catons, 179
Catron, 117
Cat-tail Run Tract, 416
Cattlett, 54, 139
Cavalier, 146
Caxillo, 254, 263, 275, 280
Cayle, 8
Cazillo, 212
Cemeteries, 404
Cemetery of Gtwn, 38
Cent__, 68
Chah-yah-yep-kah, 67
Chamberlain, 174, 202, 204, 220, 271
Chamberlayne, 52
Chamberlin, 58

Chambers, 40, 114, 182, 185, 190, 213
Champion, 48, 50, 58, 78, 123, 280, 282
Chanault, 152
Chancellor, 133
Chandler, 14, 19, 21, 33, 41, 67, 133, 149, 177, 197, 290, 365, 397, 411
Chandonet, 34
Channel, 307
Channing, 203
Chapin, 113, 251, 341
Chapman, 19, 27, 57, 102, 128, 149, 175, 196, 255, 282, 286, 324, 370, 371, 385, 417
Chappell, 243
Charlton, 29, 80
Charter Oak, 345
Chase, 18, 21, 68, 72, 88, 149, 257, 260, 276
Chatard, 221
Chatfield, 220
Chaudonet, 131
Chauncey, 275
Chean, 441
Chedal, 428
Cheerer, 157
Cheetham, 161
Cheever, 40, 51, 241
Chellar, 205
Chenery, 67
Cheneworth, 431
Cheney, 262
Chenoweth, 102, 277
Cherbonnier, 120
Chesapeake & Ohio Canal, 158
Chesebro, 33
Chesly, 195
Cheves, 424
Chew, 5, 40, 79, 218, 259, 302, 320, 369, 388
Chick, 209
Chickering, 138
Child, 357
Children's Aid Society, 333

455

Childress, 165, 336
Childs, 3, 14, 135, 327, 334, 383
Chilton, 283, 285, 313, 362, 380
Chiltonk, 286
Chipley, 245
Chism, 148
Chittenden, 240, 264, 270, 320
Chitty, 115
Choate, 162
<u>Cholera in Messina</u>, 444
Chouteau, 361
Christian, 31, 67, 148, 233, 327, 357
Christian Brothers, 427
Christie, 357
Christy, 236, 428
Chronchey, 113
Chub, 30
Chubb, 17, 199, 287, 395, 438, 441
Chubbuck, 187
Church, 325
<u>Church of the Ascension</u>, 161
Churchill, 99, 145, 178, 308
Cilley, 92
Cissel, 256
Cissell, 221, 247, 301
Cissil, 248
<u>citizens of Gtwn</u>, 60
Clabaugh, 75
Clack, 437
Claffin, 100
Claflin, 18, 50, 58, 60
Clagett, 28, 48, 204, 311, 320, 342
Claiborne, 136
Clancey, 152
Clancy, 25
Clare, 353
Clarendon, 3
Clark, 4, 9, 24, 25, 31, 37, 40, 51, 56, 66, 67, 70, 72, 82, 101, 136, 148, 158, 163, 183, 186, 217, 242, 245, 337, 340, 361, 388, 411, 423, 430
Clarke, 40, 41, 83, 85, 92, 106, 120, 121, 124, 139, 147, 166, 180, 207, 219, 241, 253, 288, 299, 325, 352, 366, 384, 392, 396, 424, 425
Clarkson, 309
Claude, 122
Claxon, 24
Claxton, 9, 428
Clay, 13, 197, 331, 346
Clayton, 275, 424
Clayvell, 417
Clean Drinking, 303
Cleary, 11
Clemens, 40, 124, 181, 236
Clements, 40, 101, 112, 241, 333
Clendenen, 281
Clendenin, 212, 255, 436
Clendennin, 259
Clensey, 344
Clerke, 187
Clermont, 69
Cleveland, 202, 213, 234, 349
Cliff, 131
Clifford, 6, 25
Clift, 131
Clifton, 444
Clinton, 131, 176
Clitch, 433
Close, 265
Closkery, 432
Closson, 285
Cloud, 36
Clough, 7, 146
Cloverdale, 141
Cluskey, 28
Clusky, 241
Clyne, 114
Coal, 439
Coal land, 416
Coale, 244, 287, 337
Cobb, 24
Coburn, 40
Cochen, 380
Cochran, 23, 41, 60, 219, 228, 247, 308, 428
Cochrane, 12, 123, 212, 255, 282, 374

Cock, 40, 50
Cockburn, 168
Cocke, 95, 116, 171, 309, 400
Cockerell, 40
Cockerille, 314
Cockran, 56
Coddington, 40
Coffee, 71, 279
Coffey, 220, 264, 426
Coffin, 279
Coghlan, 24
Cohen, 76
Coke, 12
Colclazer, 219
Coldwell, 327
Cole, 24, 40, 41, 88, 170, 204, 220, 240, 264, 270, 315, 335, 340, 398
Colegate, 147
Coleman, 15, 41, 114, 194, 251, 347
Colemar, 8
Colgate, 21
Collam, 380
Colley, 410
Collier, 304
Colligan, 88
Collins, 25, 40, 41, 142, 177, 202, 221, 229, 233, 256, 311, 334, 356, 357, 360, 361, 363, 364
Collinson, 342
Collum, 349
Colmesuil, 195
Colmus, 121
Colston, 378
Colt, 9, 64, 200, 204, 395, 430
Columbus, 369
Comb, 98
Combe, 118
Combs, 93, 107, 262
Compton, 342
Comstock, 356, 357
Conally, 24
Condict, 146, 349
Cone, 317
Conegham, 25

Conelly, 40
Congregational burying ground, 306
Congressional Burial Ground, 115, 198
Congressional Burying Ground, 216
Conklin, 352
Conlan, 289, 427
Conly, 185
Connell, 258, 337, 440
Connelly, 41, 67, 68, 421
Conner, 41, 69, 132, 356
Connis, 148
Connolly, 212, 355, 356, 404
Connor, 40, 156, 213
Connors, 267
Connoway, 397
Conoley, 41
Conrad, 140
Conroy, 40, 356
Considine, 170, 436
Conway, 25, 41, 389
Coody, 83, 239
Cook, 7, 27, 58, 60, 67, 69, 121, 123, 157, 172, 195, 218, 254, 262, 280, 354, 356, 366
Cooke, 215, 357, 437
Cookendorfer, 317
Cookingham, 163
Cookson, 191
Coolidge, 87, 130, 398
Coombe, 118
Coombs, 40, 41
Coon-skin tract, 413
Cooper, 2, 5, 14, 21, 25, 27, 30, 53, 61, 68, 80, 82, 92, 127, 131, 167, 170, 197, 240, 244, 251, 252, 287, 308, 376, 380, 422
Cope, 40, 406
Copeland, 27
Copely, 8
Copenhaver, 432
Copley, 105, 174
Copp, 101, 357
Coppinger, 87

Corbet, 107
Corbett, 25, 259, 271
Corbin, 159, 298
Corbins, 134, 153
Corbion, 134
Corbit, 13
Corcoran, 41, 74, 101, 115, 193, 226, 299, 407
Cord, 26
Cornell, 380
Corson, 60, 342
Corwin, 190
Cory, 60
Cosby, 182, 215, 323
Coskery, 365
Costello, 41
Costin, 18
Cotter, 240
Couch, 334
Coulling, 424
Coulter, 167, 220
Councilman, 129
Counsellor, 228
Courtright, 236
Cousin, 100, 133, 259
Cousins, 354
Cowling, 366
Cox, 40, 87, 96, 111, 115, 123, 144, 262, 302, 327, 347, 370, 385, 389, 395, 407, 421, 442
Coxe, 2, 62, 219, 221, 248, 263, 396, 405
Coxen, 41
Coyle, 1, 40, 79, 242, 258
Cozzens, 27
Cracklin, 362
Cragin, 65
Craig, 32, 68, 138, 212
Craige, 357
Crain, 4
Cramphin, 41, 110, 200
Crampton, 3
Cranch, 160, 438
Crandall, 133, 157, 212, 255, 280
Crandell, 138, 219, 302, 386
Crane, 172, 246, 333
Crapin, 203, 420
Crary, 164
Crawford, 41, 213, 273, 405
Creamer, 103
Creighton, 20, 101, 184, 319
Cressey, 213
Cresson, 82, 87
Creutzfeldt, 78
Crib, 356
Cribben, 255, 263, 282
Cridlan, 339
Crim, 376
Cripps, 68
Crispin, 283
Crittenden, 394
Crobin, 83
Crockett, 66, 324
Croggon, 40
Croix, 194, 281
Crommelin, 240, 241
Crook, 315
Crooker, 261
Cropley, 87, 428
Crosby, 20, 239, 266, 282
Cross, 40, 51, 94, 113, 149, 174, 191, 300, 309, 377
Crossan, 241
Crouch, 235
Crouchey, 142
Crowel, 301
Crowell, 49, 80
Crown, 41, 128, 231
Crozier, 203, 375
Crues, 225
Cruikshank, 221, 391
Cruit, 41, 106, 370
Crump, 40
Crutchet, 40
Crutchett, 217
Cruttenden, 40
Cryer, 40
Cubbedge, 296

Cuiner, 357
Culbertson, 66, 67, 68, 152, 246
Culienane, 41
Cullen, 115, 364
Cullings, 241
Culman, 357
Culver, 28, 71, 113, 123, 187, 212, 280, 421
Culverwell, 428
Cuming, 378
Cumming, 70, 223, 384
Cummings, 76
Cummins, 364, 421
Cunningham, 29, 32, 186, 204, 213, 246, 333, 428
Curran, 152, 212, 254, 263, 280
Currie, 25
Curry, 25, 67, 72, 378
Curtin, 216
Curtis, 13, 117, 411, 430
Curwen, 161
Cushing, 9, 176, 220, 255, 280, 296, 351
Cushman, 31, 277, 342
Custis, 80, 175, 396
Cuthbert, 170, 410
Cutler, 192
Cutter, 8, 172, 190, 218
cutter **Hamilton**, 54
cutter **Marcy**, 236
Cuvillier, 40
Cyr, 96

D

D'Estaing, 57
Dabney, 83
Dade, 409
Daggett, 13
Dale, 41, 63, 435
Dalley, 32
Dalnese, 237
Daly, 130, 140, 181
Dana, 68, 159, 223, 401
Dane, 190

Danforth, 131
Dangerfield, 306
Daniel, 68, 117, 140, 223, 358
Daniels, 253, 307
Danley, 439
Danstrom, 435
Dant, 41, 256, 396
Darby, 4, 134, 157, 231, 239, 254, 264, 280, 353
Darcy, 66
Darden, 424
Dardenne, 97, 123
Dardennus, 60
Darien, 106
Darling, 213
Darnall, 187, 206, 376
Darne, 265, 443
Darnell, 41
Darnold, 136
Darnull, 330
Darry, 413
Dashiel, 336, 404
Dashiell, 98, 102, 155, 258, 265, 278, 350
Davant, 285
David, 41, 176, 287
Davidge, 137, 233
Davidson, 41, 56, 59, 67, 151, 215, 306, 350, 370, 376
Davies, 348
Davis, 15, 16, 22, 24, 41, 42, 45, 68, 70, 77, 79, 87, 95, 98, 105, 115, 119, 127, 129, 138, 149, 154, 157, 168, 189, 191, 195, 200, 203, 205, 220, 231, 244, 255, 263, 277, 282, 286, 288, 300, 302, 308, 311, 312, 313, 318, 325, 331, 334, 337, 348, 349, 356, 365, 369, 374, 378, 384, 387, 393, 401, 408, 419, 423, 428, 437
Davison, 238
Daw, 372
Dawes, 71, 132

Dawson, 38, 157, 187, 206, 242, 328, 357, 422, 430
Day, 25, 41, 69, 213, 214, 260, 281, 303, 357, 363
Day's Neck, 156
Dayton, 242
De Angules, 181
De Bevoice, 183
de Bodisco, 30, 35, 38, 108
De Bow, 278
de Chaumont, 32
De Cueto, 405
de Dampierre, 298
de Geesbriand, 334
de Grammont, 363
de Grasse, 421
De Haven, 122
de Kalb, 59
De Kalb, 430, 434
De Krafft, 309
de Lambelle, 168
De Lano, 284
De Lux, 426
De Neckere, 311
De Selding, 41
de St Arnaud, 393
De Taroni, 143
De Treville, 124
De Wolf, 141, 437
De Wolfe, 302
Deacon, 25, 301
Deale, 119, 179, 184
Deaman, 139
Dean, 415, 433
Deany, 53, 58, 78, 281
Deas, 157
Deasy, 265
Deavor, 245
Decatur, 39, 312, 401
Decker, 59
Deckerhoff, 254, 280
Deckson, 41
Decomb, 228
Dedieman, 224

Deeble, 348
Deering, 164
Degges, 41
Deggle, 23
deGrammont, 357
DeHaven, 157
Dehl, 236
Deigrade, 357
Deitz, 41
DeKraff, 41
DeKrafft, 163
Delagrave, 109
Delany, 8
Delery, 93
Delius, 206
Delmas, 258
Demaine, 380, 419
Dement, 227, 284, 286
Demera, 34
Dempsey, 149
Denany, 235
Denecker, 112
Denison, 56, 117
Denman, 62, 72, 241, 426
Dennedy, 396
Dennesson, 428
Dennett, 142, 231, 239
Denny, 24, 28, 276
Dent, 216, 253, 316, 345, 405
Denton, 218, 366
Depriest, 116, 139
Deputy, 324
Derby, 131
Dermott, 41, 149, 196
Derr, 208
Derrick, 352
Desaules, 156
DeSausseur, 361
Deschell, 25
DeShields, 348
Deshler, 285
Desmond, 311
Desouga, 135
Desouza, 135

Deter, 41
Detweiler, 429
DeVaughan, 227
Devaughn, 41, 362
Develin, 69
Devenport, 316
Devereux, 241
Devlin, 8, 41, 75, 83, 244, 432
Dewey, 348
DeWolf, 380
Dexter, 32
DeZeyk, 157
Diamond, 43, 325
Dibble, 354
Dickens, 114
Dickenson, 41
Dickerhoff, 23, 97, 123, 195
Dickerman, 41
Dickerson, 124, 211
Dickins, 95, 244
Dickinson, 18, 374
Dickson, 127
Didier, 427
Diehl, 25
Diemateri, 237
Diesinger, 353
Dietrick, 299
Diffenderffer, 76
Digges, 41, 193, 201, 289
Diggle, 41
Diggs, 76
Dileway, 247
Dillihunt, 350
Dillingham, 25, 49, 61
Dillon, 296, 323
Dimon, 344
Dingley, 31
Dingnel, 356
Dinsmore, 243, 250
Dinwidde, 84
Ditty, 390
Divins, 207
<u>divorce</u>, 4, 386
Dix, 192, 312, 417

Dixon, 41, 123, 163, 184, 210, 247, 254, 374, 439, 442
Dobbin, 226
Dobbs, 306
Dodds, 357
Dodge, 28, 87, 91, 98, 144, 163, 198, 230, 242, 262, 322, 336, 370, 371
Dodson, 311, 438
Doherty, 8
Dolan, 8, 409
Doll, 369
Doly, 73
Domereq, 27, 57
Domingo, 426
Donaghan, 20
Donahoe, 242
Donaldson, 71, 220, 223
Donaval, 279
Donelan, 16, 85, 146, 148, 176, 192, 203, 337, 427
Donley, 301
Donn, 41, 191, 207, 228, 350, 355, 384
Donnelly, 11, 24, 356
Donoho, 106, 337
Donohoe, 41
Doolan, 226
Dooley, 11, 332
Dooling, 26
Dorian, 356, 360
Dority, 56
Dorn, 70
Dorr, 244, 444
Dorrell, 61
Dorsett, 429
Dorsey, 8, 10, 21, 41, 114, 152, 171, 228, 232, 244, 264, 270, 276, 281, 342, 409
Doty, 93
Doubleday, 111
Dougherty, 41, 143, 222, 408, 441
Doughty, 396
Douglas, 41, 80, 185

Douglass, 21, 41, 119, 145, 177, 259, 297
Doulin, 41
Dousman, 48, 58, 60, 281
Dove, 41, 96, 115, 191, 207, 316
Dove Spring Tract, 141
Dovilliers, 371
Dow, 124
Dowahy, 8
Dowd, 277
Dowdt, 356
Dowling, 8, 41, 256, 298, 422, 428
Downer, 41, 268
Downes, 203, 289, 292
Downey, 67
Downing, 24, 41, 157, 322
Downs, 293, 308, 311, 404
Downy, 53
Doyle, 174, 384
Dozier, 433
Drake, 372, 423
Drane, 341
Draper, 135, 208, 353, 356
Drayton, 380
Drew, 41, 173, 357, 414, 415
Droat, 1
Drown, 356
Drummond, 41, 261
Drurio, 210
Drury, 34, 155, 164, 170, 356, 386
Du Laenit, 356
du Pont, 349, 424
Duane, 424
Dubois, 165
Duchess Louisa, 171
Duchet, 21
Ducket, 431
Duckett, 20, 24, 27, 436
Duckworth, 342
Dudley, 258
Duel, 95
Duer, 192, 196, 203, 255
Duff, 3, 9, 212, 255, 308
Duffey, 41, 56, 405

Duffield, 144
Duffy, 120, 161, 276
Dugan, 276
Dugg, 282
Duhamel, 427
Duke de Berry, 136
Duke de Grammont, 356
Duke of Parma, 136
Dulaney, 41
Dulany, 41, 110, 335
Duley, 162
Dulie, 41
Dulin, 265, 274
Dullet, 393
Dulong, 25
Dunbar, 399, 445
Duncan, 14, 129, 209, 210, 324, 415, 424, 436
Duncanson, 41, 191, 346, 371
Dungan, 58
Dunham, 20, 372
Dunkin, 58
Dunlan, 41
Dunlap, 41, 66, 265
Dunlop, 249
Dunmore, 416
Dunn, 260, 412
Dunnavant, 332
Dunne, 382
Dunning, 5, 27, 30, 53, 244, 252, 280
Dunnington, 428
Dunscomb, 144, 204
Dupasner, 356
Dupassem, 357
Duplaigne, 141
Dupont, 185, 390
Durand, 424
Durfee, 240
Durham, 326, 352
Durity, 30
Durque, 25
Durr, 41, 289
Dustin, 250, 277, 322
Dutton, 25, 76

Duval, 108, 436
Duvall, 41, 287, 300, 343, 373, 374, 399, 400, 429
Dwyer, 72
Dyer, 14, 18, 41, 83, 93, 143, 207, 315, 398, 407, 428, 433
Dykeman, 25

E

Eagan, 207
Eagle, 254
Ealott, 236
Eames, 68, 127, 223
Eareckson, 228
Earl of Aberdeen, 256
Earl of Selkirk, 192
Earl of Uxbridge, 167
Earle, 169, 271
Early, 409
Easby, 42, 68, 203, 207, 266, 268, 295, 296, 310
Easley, 66, 67
Eastburn, 50, 292
Easterbrook, 261
Eastham, 121
Eastland, 62, 162
Easton, 24, 49, 60, 157, 220, 241, 316
Eaton, 21, 140, 204, 236, 251
Ebbetts, 163
Eberbach, 322
Eccleston, 2
Eckard, 53, 63, 130, 398
Eckhardt, 428
Eckloff, 41, 82
Eckton, 431
Edelin, 41, 118, 207
Edes, 135, 207, 267
Edge, 99, 145, 178
Edge Hill, 276, 337
Edgecombe, 357
Edgehill, 331
Edgewood, 323
Edini, 60
Edmonds, 441
Edmondson, 428
Edmondston, 42
Edmonston, 359, 372, 376, 380, 399, 404, 437
Edrington, 419
Edward, 334
Edwards, 27, 42, 51, 58, 62, 64, 66, 69, 78, 108, 123, 154, 157, 174, 213, 220, 255, 280, 307, 396
Eells, 327
Egan, 356
Ege, 303
Eggers, 357
Eggleston, 102
Ehrhard, 25
Eichhorn, 101
Eichorn, 427
Eirhstedt, 272
Elder, 441
Eldridge, 214
Elgar, 208, 298
Eliot, 210, 321, 438
Eliott, 212
Elkins, 217
Ellerslie, 179, 414
Ellett, 349
Ellicott, 41, 42, 61, 219, 292, 431
Elliot, 42, 107, 284, 385, 410, 427
Elliott, 13, 36, 95, 114, 259, 264, 270, 275, 329
Ellis, 1, 27, 41, 42, 51, 91, 100, 209, 212, 240, 252, 254, 268, 270, 275, 281, 297, 324, 340, 360, 364, 394, 402, 419
Ellmore, 223
Ellsworth, 90
Elm Grove, 436
Els, 370
Elvans, 61, 223, 288, 337
Ely, 164, 306, 393
Emack, 118
Emerson, 173
Emery, 84, 362, 436
Emmart, 241

Emmerich, 386
Emmons, 120, 231, 239
Emory, 230, 277, 411
Emperor of Japan, 225
Empie, 327
Empson, 442
Engel, 25
Engelbuch, 25
England, 352
English, 8, 137, 144, 149, 394, 428
English Hill, 216
Ennis, 25, 198, 394, 405, 415
Enroughty, 37
Ensign, 296
Ervin, 172
Erving, 42, 68
Erwin, 116, 123, 194, 352, 419
Eskridge, 102, 213
Esnard, 122
Espey, 42, 140
Espinasse, 366
Espy, 248
Essex, 387, 402
Estabrook, 223
Estep, 42, 103
Estes, 195
Etchison, 79
Etheridge, 205
Ettienne, 204
Etting, 245
Eubanks, 103
Evans, 37, 42, 50, 58, 63, 92, 133, 157, 191, 205, 207, 220, 221, 235, 265, 273, 301, 314, 401
Eve, 274
Everett, 38, 173, 300, 301, 413
Everick, 42
Everist, 86
Everly, 11, 50
Eversfield, 2
Every, 123
Ewell, 238, 331, 337
Ewing, 69, 266, 346, 348, 415

F

Fabricotti, 357
Factor, 57, 194, 255, 280
Fagan, 30, 281
Fage, 411
Faherty, 350
Fahey, 87
Fahs, 2
Fairfax, 233, 433
Fairfax Farm, 413
Fairholme, 375, 376
Fairman, 132
Faith, 176
Falconer, 318
Fales, 42
Falleegger, 26
Fallon, 8, 96
Fanning, 95, 114, 212, 255, 259, 282
Fant, 19, 314, 412
Farens, 290
Farger, 384
Farish, 23
Farley, 83, 353
Farmer, 387
Farmington, 292
Farnesworth, 20
Farnham, 83, 278, 337
Farnsberth, 252
Farnsworth, 21, 248
Farquhar, 38, 130, 290, 309, 348, 349
Farr, 56, 434
Farragut, 301
Farrar, 253, 378
Farrell, 26, 42
Farren, 186
Farrenberg, 249
Fasnaught, 292
Fass, 357
Fatio, 274
Fauerbach, 25
Faulkner, 37, 73, 126, 193, 206, 220, 247, 263, 274, 281, 355, 358
Favenscroft, 357
Favier, 240, 241, 374, 386, 387, 425

Fawcett, 141
Fearson, 164, 207, 413
Fechtig, 359
Felch, 433, 434
Felker, 52, 93
Fellow, 14, 58
Fendall, 293
Fenn, 353
Fennal, 131
Fenton, 310
Fenwick, 28, 42, 146, 271, 289
Ferdinand, 303
Ferguson, 92, 223, 270, 300, 306, 357, 368, 401, 436
Ferne, 25
Ferrill, 163
Ferris, 221
Ferry, 209
Fertig, 67
Fessenden, 192
Field, 19, 20, 24, 27, 29, 154, 220, 282
Fields, 37, 80, 174
Fierney, 8
Fiester, 184
Fifield, 67
File, 204
Fill, 288, 337
Fillion, 440
Fillison, 312
Fillmore, 261, 267, 268, 325
Finch, 105
Finck, 131
Finckel, 216
Findlay, 338
Finkel, 197
Finlay, 241
Finley, 239, 240, 250
Finn, 145
Finnal, 428
Finnall, 121, 255, 263
Finnigan, 10
First, 260
First ascent, 406
Fischer, 42

Fish, 13, 319, 418
Fishback, 362
Fisher, 9, 24, 36, 42, 50, 54, 92, 141, 161, 168, 178, 194, 220, 250, 255, 282, 309, 327
Fisk, 42
Fitch, 48
Fitnam, 274
Fitts, 13
Fitzgerald, 11, 42, 43, 216, 428
Fitzgibbon, 432
Fitzgibbons, 432
Fitzhugh, 118, 242, 331, 400, 425
Fitzjames, 375
Fitzpatrick, 11, 27, 57, 61, 124, 176, 180, 289, 334, 368, 390, 427
Fitzsimmons, 78, 180
Fitzsimons, 441
Flagg, 86, 205, 307
Flaherty, 394
Flanagan, 356
Flanders, 114, 423
Fleck, 24
Fleming, 356
Flemings, 307
Fletcher, 42, 56, 97, 204, 376
Flinders, 383
Flinn, 222, 294, 350
Flora, 18
Flournoy, 124
Floweree, 368
Floyd, 12, 37, 144, 229, 244, 376
Flye, 375
Fogg, 18, 142
Foley, 53, 260, 365
Follansbee, 379
Follensby, 392
Folsom, 42
Foltz, 157, 218
Forbes, 34, 135, 141, 172
Force, 91, 316, 329, 396, 428
Ford, 31, 42, 77, 90, 103, 136, 146, 150, 357
Forde, 12

Fordshops' Kindness, 341
Forman, 103
Forrest, 42, 131, 207, 247, 319, 328, 329, 362
Forrester, 151, 187, 241
Forsythe, 284
Fort Arbuckle, 412
Fort Belknap, 111
Fort Boise, 378
Fort Dallas, 378
Fort Des Moines, 152
Fort Du Quesne, 84
Fort Erie, 250
Fort Ewell, 175
Fort Frederick, 416
Fort Griswold, 268
Fort Hamilton, 165
Fort Hill, 246
Fort Independence, 37, 287
Fort Kearny, 400
Fort Laramie, 419
Fort Leavenworth, 34
Fort Madison, 180, 287
Fort McHenry, 181
Fort Monroe, 29, 314
Fort Myers, 215
Fort Necessity, 84
Fort Niagara, 51
Fort Scott, 382
Fort Simpson, 263
Fort Snelling, 19, 401
Fort Steilacoom, 180
Fort Taylor, 235
Fort Union, 313
Fort Wayne, 266, 334
Fosset, 76
Foster, 42, 113, 163, 195, 205, 257, 376, 422, 436
Foulerod, 439
Foulkes, 42
Fountain, 341
Fowke, 42
Fowler, 42, 81, 119, 149, 232, 260, 278, 399

Fowler Tract, 141
Fox, 25, 304, 317, 377
Foy, 42, 89, 217
Frailey, 124
Frame, 364
Francis, 401
Francisco, 315
Francois, 363
Frank, 357
Franklin, 88, 122, 156, 240, 247, 338, 342, 370, 375, 376, 383, 435
Franklin Row, 441
Franks, 26, 42
Frantman, 162
Fraser, 157
Frasier, 76, 160, 258, 259, 274
Frasy_er, 173
Frazee, 252
Frazer, 50, 58, 60, 97, 255, 280, 281
Frazier, 42, 114, 141, 160, 212, 315
Frederic, 22
Free, 42
Freeman, 12, 27, 30, 206, 212, 215, 255, 280, 288, 316, 337
Freer, 42
Frelinburger, 274
Frelinghuysen, 131
Fremont, 19, 20, 21, 33, 35, 37, 116, 211, 239, 264, 284, 286
French, 4, 9, 54, 64, 68, 75, 113, 121, 149, 164, 170, 246, 273, 293, 361, 395, 403, 418
Frestel, 79
Frick, 76, 145
Fridley, 170, 204, 219, 231
Friel, 25
frig **Cumberland**, 319, 433
frig **Massachusetts**, 157
frig **Philadelphia**, 17, 50, 312, 401
frig **Phoebe**, 289
frig **Saranac**, 139, 433
frig **Susquehanna**, 2, 426
Frink, 258, 264, 280
Frizzle, 139

Frohlick, 119
Frost, 73, 175
Frush, 361
Fry, 84, 189
Frye, 42, 55, 105, 121, 244
Fryer, 357
Fudge, 181
Fuller, 181, 362, 373, 380
Fulmer, 298
Fuqua, 55
Furber, 348
Furman, 364
Furnass, 13

G

Gadsby, 42, 313, 324, 338
Gadsby's Row, 346, 378
Gaehle, 419
Gaenslen, 80
Gafford, 301
Gaien, 103
Gaillardet, 353
Gaines, 62, 92, 129, 144, 347
Gaither, 225
Gale, 5, 233, 357
Gales, 80, 88, 437
Gallagher, 18, 151, 241, 376
Gallaher, 330, 331, 396, 397, 428, 430
Gallant, 10, 26, 42
Gallatin, 437
Gallaudet, 36
Gallion, 170
Galt, 137, 231, 339
Galvin, 307
Gamble, 50, 298
Gambrill, 146, 150
Games, 422
Gamewell, 439
Gammander, 236
Gannon, 172
Gansvort, 131
Gantt, 118, 232, 361
Garber, 284
Garcia, 122, 357

Garden, 138
Gardere, 13
Gardiner, 33, 89, 100, 111, 112, 152, 197, 227
Gardner, 18, 20, 21, 25, 42, 56, 145, 165, 178, 212, 439
Garfield, 110
Garland, 106, 152, 215, 356, 368
Garlick, 218
Garner, 104, 117, 216
Garnet, 401
Garratt, 96
Garresche, 268
Garret, 41, 68, 115
Garrett, 15, 42, 408, 414, 415, 433
Garrigo, 307
Garrison, 68
Garrizan, 8
Garth, 124, 292
Gartland, 335, 338
<u>Gas Light Co</u>, 60
gas lights, 340
Gaskins, 21
Gass, 212, 254, 275, 280
Gassaway, 42, 82, 227, 265, 373, 443
Gassett, 390
Gaston, 42, 218
Gates, 19, 20, 21, 24, 33, 42, 110, 154, 197, 205, 233, 290, 361, 362, 372
Gatewood, 176, 244
Gathright, 279
Gatlin, 94
Gatling, 66, 68
Gatton, 420, 422
Gault, 42
Gavazzi, 267
Gedge, 390
Gee, 174
Geffers, 168
Geiger, 357
Gelacking, 42
Gender, 9
Gentry, 96, 302
George, 279

Georgetown Cemetery, 404
Gerard, 51, 240, 252
Gere, 322
Gerk, 24
Germon, 445
Gershom, 359
Gettener, 136
Gettings, 325
Ghiselin, 80, 135, 407
Gibble, 277
Gibbons, 17, 211, 375
Gibbs, 19, 72, 79, 131, 348, 379
Gibon, 357
Gibson, 42, 48, 50, 52, 58, 62, 65, 102, 131, 134, 149, 160, 172, 221, 231, 232, 273, 280, 342, 344, 347, 380, 396, 405
Gideon, 5, 30, 48, 50, 54, 207, 244, 428
Gihon, 356
Gil, 399
Gilbert, 27, 38, 70, 356, 398, 415
Gilchrist, 315
Gildermeister, 197
Gildmeister, 444
Gilforgs, 364
Gilgon, 26
Gilhooley, 272
Giliad, 65
Gilkeson, 245
Gill, 191, 246, 254
Gillan, 42
Gillen, 8
Gillespie, 441
Gilliam, 268
Gilliss, 161
Gilman, 137
Gilmer, 249
Gilmore, 26
Girard, 19
Gitt, 271
Gittings, 437, 442
Givenny, 401
Giveny, 69

Gladmon, 39
Gladstone, 256
Glancey, 339
Glanding, 88
Glantz, 343, 373, 399
Glass, 129
Glen, 243
Glenellen, 438
Glenn, 237, 247, 280
Glenwood Cemetery, 257, 265, 404
Glover, 87, 209, 325, 436
Goddard, 42, 115, 195
Goddart, 234
Goddin, 156, 292
Godey, 207, 399
Godfrey, 42, 237, 240, 308, 435
Goggin, 52, 116, 134, 255, 280
Goheens, 42
Goings, 125
Goins, 96, 115
Gold, 8
Golden, 4, 106, 125
Goldie, 432
Goldin, 304
Golding, 54
Goldsborough, 82, 179
Goldschmidt, 134
Goldsmith, 98, 288, 337
Goldthwaite, 240
Gonder, 212, 255, 282
Gonzales, 106
Good, 295
Goodal, 220
Goode, 302
Goodger, 268
Goodman, 272
Goodrich, 50, 92, 261, 273
Goodsie, 376
Goodwin, 42, 415
Gordon, 2, 3, 9, 17, 24, 50, 61, 103, 139, 223, 261, 268, 286, 364
Gore, 275, 341, 375
Gorman, 12
Gormley, 241

Gormly, 53
Gosline, 15, 131
Gossett, 23
Gott, 405
Gough, 304
Gould, 428
Goulston, 234
Goundie, 72
Gove, 240, 264, 270
Gowen, 218
Gower, 66, 67
Grace, 155
Gracie, 286
Graef, 128
Graeff, 25
Graff, 42
Grafton, 186
Graham, 20, 21, 24, 25, 59, 121, 123, 128, 177, 185, 201, 237, 255, 256, 257, 263, 272, 273, 295, 311, 356, 363, 397, 428
Grahame's Farm, 232
Grammar, 207
Grammer, 229, 396, 413
Granger, 240, 341
Granghan, 8
Grann, 356, 357
Grant, 284, 286, 287, 337, 357, 360, 363, 387, 428
Graves, 70, 181
Gray, 62, 111, 132, 147, 173, 187, 225, 276, 278, 347, 389, 440, 442
Gray's Tract, 65
Grayson, 113, 388, 434
Great, 25
Greble, 286
Greeley, 113
Green, 8, 9, 18, 27, 42, 50, 51, 56, 58, 68, 85, 99, 100, 123, 149, 215, 223, 248, 252, 263, 275, 280, 294, 318, 322, 351, 355, 380, 384, 415
Green Hill, 201
Green Valley, 141

Greene, 48, 66, 104, 161, 180, 211, 221, 232, 239, 244, 254, 264, 286
Greenhow, 142, 179, 365
Greenleaf, 10, 106, 439
Greenock, 85
Greenway, 24
Greenwell, 337
Greenwood Cemetery, 414
Greer, 42, 141, 196, 220, 333
Gregg, 68, 252, 410, 444
Gregory, 67, 80, 289, 360
Greneaux, 438
Gretton, 20
Grey, 42, 256
Grial, 119
Griffin, 42, 58, 122, 374
Griffith, 25, 102, 266, 294, 328, 395
Griggs, 42
Grignon, 9, 51, 199, 240, 252, 280
Grimball, 348
Grimes, 87, 125, 144, 247
Grimshaw, 424
Grinder, 57
Grinnell, 122
Grist Mill, 141
Groat, 333
Groff, 236
Gromly, 324
Gross, 25, 135, 252, 439
Grosvenor, 134, 198
Groux, 305, 415
Grove, 287
Grover, 202, 362
Groves, 202
Grubb, 219, 320
Grundy, 334
Grymes, 425
Gtwn Cemetery, 251
Gtwn College, 409
Gtwn Gas Light Co, 282
Guelick, 332
Guest, 102, 107, 183
Guild, 100
Guile, 18

Guilliam, 357
Guinard, 213
Guion, 258
Gulager, 104, 254
Gulich, 259
Gulick, 157
Gull, 246
Gunnell, 59, 211, 342
Gunner, 269
Gunnison, 34, 35, 36, 72, 78, 282
Gunter, 52, 271
Gunton, 116, 138, 210, 440
Gurley, 53, 147, 251, 341, 352, 356, 411
Gurman, 127
Gusman, 114, 281
Guster, 73
Guthrie, 273
Guthrin, 82
Guy, 288
Guynet, 365
Guynets, 357
Guynett, 357
Guyther, 384
Gwin, 266
Gwyn, 220
Gwynn, 289, 293

H

Haag, 26
Haage, 25
Habersham, 313
Hacker, 277
Hackett, 136, 419
Hackner, 143
Hadley, 328
Hagan, 224, 252
Hager, 18
Hagerman, 376
Hagerty, 42, 170
Hagner, 137, 183
Hague, 17, 53
Haight, 135, 308
Haile, 243

Haines, 43
Halden, 27
Hale, 366
Haley, 24, 101, 346
Halfield, 14
Haliday, 159, 173, 279, 428
Hall, 1, 18, 32, 43, 58, 71, 137, 147, 149, 157, 158, 180, 196, 207, 213, 214, 217, 218, 229, 238, 243, 288, 294, 303, 342, 345, 367, 372, 393, 398, 405, 422, 426, 431, 435
Hallar, 406
Halleck, 283, 286, 429
Haller, 378
Hallet, 419
Halliday, 43, 54
Halligan, 43
Halloran, 42, 43
Hallowell, 130, 312, 349
Halstead, 18, 50, 58
Halsted, 216, 274, 280
Halstend Tract, 156
Halter, 122
Ham, 48, 107, 182
Hamersley, 289
Hamilton, 3, 11, 14, 27, 50, 58, 65, 72, 114, 142, 157, 160, 176, 180, 221, 246, 280, 289, 351, 387, 389, 391, 413, 426
Hamilton & Rossville, 126
Hammette, 316
Hammond, 18, 50, 58, 71, 80, 102, 216, 274, 281, 318, 377
Hancock, 33, 164, 286
Hand, 53, 167, 175, 331
Handy, 26, 307, 345, 347, 348, 443
Hanes, 201
Hank, 102
Hankins, 48, 51, 244, 254, 268
Hanley, 93, 179
Hanlon, 173, 279
Hanly, 155, 429
Hannah, 25
Hanscom, 27

Hanson, 7, 14, 18, 42, 46, 47, 51, 102, 142, 216, 374
Hanway, 167
Haralson, 351
Haran, 122
Harbaugh, 207, 247, 335, 337
Harboker, 323
Hardaway, 37
Harden, 419
Hardesty, 43
Hardin, 64, 92, 223
Harding, 3, 18, 378
Hardisty, 161
Hardwick, 356
Hardy, 14, 43, 66, 177, 358
Hare, 186
Harjo, 67
Harkness, 43
Harley, 86
Harlon, 163
Harman, 210, 343
Harmer, 313
Harmon, 43, 124, 243, 380
Harness, 242
Harney, 99
Haro, 422
Harper, 22, 42, 84, 122, 384, 430
Harrington, 113, 116, 135, 172, 311, 362
Harris, 43, 88, 93, 99, 128, 145, 150, 157, 166, 220, 221, 238, 255, 277, 329, 345, 364, 370, 371
Harrison, 43, 106, 187, 259, 261, 309, 321, 351, 392, 428
Harrod, 331
Harrover, 149, 219
Harshman, 43
Harslaw, 101
Hart, 24, 25, 57, 72, 121, 222, 277, 443
Harte, 100, 429
Hartley, 213, 218
Hartridge, 364
Hartwell, 371, 398

Harvey, 18, 86, 106, 109, 117, 147, 207, 388, 427, 439
Harvy, 144
Harwood, 181, 369, 433
Hasard, 357
Hascal, 172
Hascall, 36, 53, 88, 430
Haseltine, 123
Haskall, 362
Haskell, 224
Haskett, 42
Haskins, 94, 101, 192, 424
Haslam, 208
Hastings, 121
Haswell, 171
Hatch, 31, 110, 181, 381
Hatcher, 57, 302, 357
Hathaway, 165
Hatton, 135, 388
Hauptman, 430
Havenner, 37, 85
Haw, 164, 207
Hawes, 123
Hawke, 43
Hawkins, 284
Hawks, 405
Haxall, 245
Hay, 140, 368
Hayden, 336
Haydon, 441
Hayes, 32, 162, 236, 241
Hays, 84, 227, 401
Hayse, 357
Hayward, 142
Hazel, 123
Hazle, 43, 91
Hazlitt, 296
Hazzard, 344
Head, 80, 307, 351
Headley, 308
Headly, 83
Heald, 109
Healey, 8, 26
Healy, 8, 25

Heap, 350
Heard, 196, 220, 384, 426
Heart, 51, 72
Heath, 5, 20, 91, 125, 198, 341, 354, 394, 436
Hebard, 360
Hecheiser, 299
Heflebower, 346
Heine, 24
Heinrich, 25
Heinricke, 24
Heintzlemann, 318
Heister, 16
Heitmiller, 42, 193
Hellen, 11, 93, 218
Heller, 24
Helm, 37, 136
Helms, 423
Hempstead, 57, 230, 254, 280
Hempstone, 240
Hemstead, 26
Henderson, 43, 98, 135, 177, 212, 221, 232, 282, 293, 321, 344, 394
Hendley, 89, 94, 184, 294
Hendrickson, 125, 158
Henessey, 357
Hening, 329
Henke, 43
Henley, 235, 423
Hennesey, 356
Hennessy, 69, 238
Henning, 43, 435
Henry, 20, 24, 136, 163, 168, 169, 220, 248, 333, 357, 383, 412, 419, 445
Henry VII, 369
Henshaw, 106, 109, 191, 288, 337
Henshone, 236
Hensley, 5
Henson, 336, 346
Henwood, 106
Hepburn, 43, 92, 352
Hepner, 176
Herb, 52
Herbemont, 214
Herbert, 94, 199, 254, 256, 393
Hercus, 315
Herett, 208
Herkimer, 25
Hermitage, 295, 331
Hernandez, 81, 113, 123, 212, 255, 280
Herndon, 80, 326
Herr, 236
Herrick, 111, 128
Herriman, 70, 222
Herring, 220
Herring Creek, 342
Herron, 162, 241
Hersberg, 307
Hess, 323
Hesse, 22, 37, 128
<u>Hessian prisoners</u>, 350
Hevner, 126
Hewitt, 308, 356, 357, 361
Hewlett, 290
Hews, 251
Heyer, 163
Hibbs, 42
Hickey, 43, 176, 251, 427
Hicks, 151, 195, 241, 248, 254, 270
Hicky, 267
Higdon, 42
Higgins, 43, 56, 158, 277, 325, 327, 328
Higginson, 203
Highams, 290
Hight, 284
Higney, 25
Higway, 24
Hilbert, 76
Hilbroner, 357
Hildebrand, 72
Hildreth, 35, 128, 161
Hilger, 357
Hill, 1, 7, 19, 28, 42, 74, 89, 98, 129, 137, 149, 158, 169, 181, 188, 224,

242, 292, 306, 341, 344, 366, 408, 410, 428, 429
Hillard, 393
Hillburn, 306
Hiller, 123
Hillery, 259
Hilles, 124
Hillman, 163
Hillmans, 163
Hillock, 25
Hilt, 334
Hilton, 10, 24, 37, 207, 324, 390
Hinckle, 411
Hinckley, 412
Hincks, 388
Hinde, 357
Hindman, 43, 261
Hine, 54
Hines, 3, 42, 126, 234, 348, 353, 396, 413
Hinman, 348
Hinrichsen, 102
Hinshaw, 101
Hinton, 59
Hirsch, 357
Hirst, 151
Hitch, 233
Hitchcock, 195, 401, 411, 426
Hite, 238
Hitz, 55
Hoag, 225
Hoban, 11, 24, 43
Hobart, 33
Hobbie, 29, 108, 109
Hobbs, 336
Hodge, 9, 97, 123, 254, 264, 281
Hodges, 56, 61, 75, 114, 135, 162, 174, 183, 203, 209, 216, 233, 299, 309, 319, 324, 325, 377, 404, 418, 430, 442, 445
Hodgkins, 300
Hodgson, 324, 375
Hodson, 357, 420
Hoe, 376

Hoff, 10
Hoffman, 20, 55, 63, 134, 143, 196, 213, 214, 217, 396, 397, 408
Hofman, 236
Hogan, 184, 194, 244, 361
Hogarth, 267
Hogg, 357
Hogue, 422
Holan, 43
Holbrook, 155, 211, 357
Holbrooks, 318
Holcomb, 106
Holden, 80, 442
Holeman, 70
Holgate, 195
Holker, 236
Holladay, 7
Hollan, 400
Holland, 40, 331, 368, 396
Hollenback, 292
Hollidge, 135
Hollin, 263, 356
Hollingshead, 425
Hollingsworth, 350
Hollins, 43, 76, 106, 194, 263
Holloway, 256, 435
Hollub, 357
Hollywood, 441
Holman, 237, 263
Holmead, 8, 59, 100, 184, 207, 345, 399, 405
Holmer, 137
Holmes, 106, 121, 157, 163, 212, 284, 287
Holoran, 378
Holstead, 154
Holsteen, 66
Holt, 18, 207
Holton, 384
Holtzbecker, 124
Holtzman, 39, 43, 125, 290
Homans, 42
Home Place, 141
Homer, 8, 16

Homrich, 323
Hone, 75
Honey, 240
Hong, 14
Hood, 421, 422
Hooe, 27, 50, 58, 69, 92, 123, 149, 281
Hook, 194, 195
Hooper, 66, 261
Hoople, 220, 264, 426
Hootee, 207
Hoover, 42, 66, 102, 127, 313, 360
Hoping, 300
Hopkin, 155
Hopkins, 423
Hopley, 24
Hord, 140
Horn, 291
Horn's Point, 179
Hornblower, 302
Horne, 365, 433
Horner, 157, 217, 239
Horney, 387
Horton, 42, 101
Hosach, 17
Hoss, 76
Hotchkiss, 5, 93, 123, 240
Hough, 102, 113, 189, 242
Houghton, 205
Hourine, 229
House, 92, 107
House Tract, 156
Houser, 188
Houslet, 165
Houston, 2, 148, 176, 191, 206, 210
Houzam, 43
Hovey, 205
Howard, 43, 63, 66, 76, 84, 149, 205, 254, 264, 285, 288, 337, 367, 384, 419, 428, 436
Howe, 3, 48, 67, 182, 209
Howell, 2, 214, 348, 367
Howes, 210, 244, 249, 257

Howison, 195, 213, 214, 217, 263, 276, 349
Howland, 357, 389
Howle, 213, 293
Howse, 207
Hoxton, 372
Hoy, 7
Hoye, 43, 397
Hoyle, 139, 238
Hoyt, 48, 78
Hubbard, 59, 93, 156
Hubbell, 368
Hubbs, 236
Hubotter, 277
Hudal, 278, 346
Huddy, 94
Hudson, 14, 18, 50, 58, 60, 100, 123, 280, 417
Huebschmaun, 70
Huger, 52, 303
Huggins, 372
Hugh Birkhead, 422
Hughes, 7, 25, 43, 72, 131, 169, 180, 185, 267, 304, 334, 403, 426
Huglebergor, 48
Huidekoper, 182
Hulbard, 349
Hull, 261
Hulse, 169, 418
Humbert, 151
Humboldt, 143
Hume, 50
Hummel, 67
Hummer, 110
Humphrey, 104, 195, 263
Humphreys, 30, 43, 188, 263, 265, 275, 356, 430
Humpster, 236
Hunn, 13
Hunnicutt, 411
Hunsberger, 107, 292
Hunt, 12, 60, 83, 117, 181, 192, 248, 277, 302, 305

Hunter, 2, 36, 111, 125, 226, 242, 258, 261, 277, 320, 333, 373, 383
Huntington, 1, 78, 131, 258, 387, 444
Hunton, 145, 260
Huntt, 42
Hurd, 62, 151
Hurley, 8, 104, 156, 221, 348, 428
Huron, 355
Hurst, 424, 429
Husk, 408
Hussey, 231, 239
Huston, 94, 123, 134
Hutchens, 331
Hutchins, 67
Hutchinson, 99, 316, 323, 376
Hutton, 393
Hutty, 172
Hyatt, 11, 72, 100, 267, 397
Hyde, 93, 106, 179, 189, 193, 227, 300, 301
Hykes, 317
Hyland, 224

I

Iardella, 198, 276, 323
Iddins, 43, 207
Independent, 161
Ingalls, 100, 397
Ingersoll, 3, 90
Inghram, 121, 213, 214
Ingle, 43, 118, 147, 229, 233, 405
Ingleside, 391
Ingraham, 161, 280, 387
Ingram, 88, 94, 135, 272
Irby, 19
Irley, 19
Irving, 269, 290, 326, 375
Irwin, 48, 80
Isaac, 378
Isaacs, 223
Iseman, 43
Ismann, 439
Israel, 102, 149, 174, 194, 197, 227, 242, 316, 323, 354, 393, 424

Izard, 223, 439

J

Jack, 79, 196, 213, 214, 217, 281
Jackman, 333
Jackson, 16, 43, 59, 68, 73, 96, 108, 147, 165, 182, 219, 223, 230, 279, 291, 294, 342, 344, 360, 373, 384
Jacobs, 27, 91, 317, 440
James, 128, 152, 163, 194, 197, 256, 313, 364, 410
Jamieson, 142, 419
Janney, 65, 300
Janvier, 288
Jaqua, 67
Jarboe, 43, 87
Jardine, 219, 329
Jarero, 244
Jarrero, 112, 151, 239, 264
Jarrerro, 231
Jarvis, 146, 338
Javis, 215
Jay, 22, 27, 91, 292, 351
Jayne, 262
Jeffers, 83, 228, 232
Jefferson, 81, 88, 90, 133, 228, 288, 330, 351, 359, 381, 396, 416, 428
Jefferson Wigwam, 432
Jeffords, 357
Jeffrey, 168
Jeffries, 135, 210, 213
Jellison, 365
Jemison, 94, 123
Jenifer, 43
Jenkins, 43, 66, 137, 215, 341, 356, 357, 385
Jenks, 48, 51, 244, 254
Jenning, 372
Jennings, 2, 11, 65, 68, 132, 134, 138, 152, 153, 157, 159, 188, 212, 235, 255, 280, 297
Jerauld, 212, 255, 281
Jerault, 168
Jervey, 70

Jessup, 291
Jesuit, 28
Jesup, 17, 87, 92, 261, 321
Jett, 70, 309, 414
Jewell, 110
Joelinski, 25
Johanneson, 236
Johannet, 60
Johns, 120, 191, 238, 411, 424
Johnson, 20, 24, 43, 49, 50, 53, 57, 58, 70, 72, 75, 76, 78, 93, 106, 114, 118, 123, 163, 179, 186, 187, 204, 207, 221, 223, 258, 266, 280, 281, 297, 304, 321, 327, 349, 351, 357, 360, 362, 370, 388, 391, 396, 403, 407, 427
Johnston, 65, 194, 269, 441
Johnstone, 217, 405
Jolly, 59
Jomans, 295
Jones, 2, 7, 9, 15, 26, 31, 43, 51, 58, 59, 60, 63, 64, 68, 87, 88, 101, 110, 113, 120, 136, 140, 144, 149, 159, 161, 176, 182, 188, 193, 194, 199, 204, 210, 212, 215, 216, 230, 240, 241, 243, 244, 245, 251, 253, 254, 255, 262, 263, 275, 277, 280, 281, 282, 284, 294, 303, 346, 348, 356, 357, 384, 393, 396, 401, 411, 416, 425, 429, 434
Jordan, 43, 239, 264, 268, 275, 304
Jorgan, 282
Jose, 66
Joskens, 356
Joy, 325
Joyce, 85, 138, 166, 429
Joyner, 114, 123
Judd, 19, 20, 21, 33
Judge, 292, 428, 429
Judkins, 424
Judson, 187, 233, 348, 408
Jullien, 366, 377
Junemann, 247
Junkin, 18

Juss, 356

K

Kahlert, 104
Kahoe, 323
Kale, 25
Kamehameha, 398
Kane, 122, 343, 370, 421, 434
Kanncaster, 58
Kanoshe, 35
Kantz, 348
Karg, 24
Karns, 398
Katzenberger, 43
Kavanaugh, 43
Kealey, 44
Kean, 310, 405
Kearney, 131
Keating, 289
Keech, 211
Keefe, 49, 386
Keenan, 43, 277, 327, 427
Keene, 229, 298
Keeron, 8
Keese, 83, 303, 322, 395, 441
Kehle, 43
Kehrman, 225
Keirnan, 345
Keith, 384
Kele, 55
Keleher, 289
Kellar, 43
Keller, 83, 87, 191, 213, 328, 369
Kellet, 27
Kellett, 30, 53, 430
Kelley, 43, 44, 91, 121, 224, 238
Kellogg, 116
Kellup, 220
Kelly, 11, 17, 24, 43, 57, 60, 101, 102, 106, 128, 142, 191, 210, 224, 252, 254, 260, 273, 280, 287, 337, 356
Kelsey, 239
Kelson, 25
Kemble, 170, 407

Kemp, 58, 236
Kendall, 8, 11, 27, 97, 236, 355
Kendrick, 14
Kenlan, 393
Kenly, 76
Kennard, 223
Kennedy, 3, 9, 24, 38, 53, 76, 88, 106, 164, 207, 225, 244, 245, 252, 267, 276, 281, 340, 371, 396, 407, 411, 427
Kenney, 3, 80
Kennon, 261, 345
Kenny, 234, 445
Kenrick, 365
Kent, 124, 232, 371
Keppler, 43, 102
Kerby, 330
Kern, 35, 43, 78
Kerner, 25
Kernion, 93
Kerr, 11, 17, 39, 43, 100, 186, 259, 348
Kersey, 98
Kershon, 299
Kess, 349
Kessler, 63
Ketcham, 428
Ketchan, 430
Ketcher, 25
Ketchum, 220, 316
Kettlewell, 106
Kewen, 418
Key, 43, 44, 130
Keyburn, 342
Keyes, 158, 330
Keys, 102, 185
Kibbey, 107, 149, 270, 397
Kidd, 445
Kidwell, 43, 207, 241, 371
Kieckhoefer, 115
Kierman, 43
Kiernan, 193, 209, 299
Kilgour, 158, 325, 410
Killy, 8

Kilmon, 191
Kilmore, 302
Kimball, 333
King, 13, 20, 34, 43, 44, 51, 53, 56, 57, 65, 78, 98, 113, 155, 160, 194, 198, 202, 220, 226, 227, 231, 239, 244, 254, 255, 268, 271, 275, 280, 289, 295, 339, 372, 379, 393, 434, 438
King of the Heruli, 293
Kingsbury, 283
Kingsley, 307
Kinner, 210
Kinney, 43, 261
Kinnier, 216
Kinsey, 124
Kinsie, 113
Kinsvy, 286
Kintring, 62
Kintsing, 80
Kip, 393
Kirby, 14, 65, 133, 241, 322, 324
Kirk, 43, 130, 349, 418, 433
Kirkland, 246
Kirkwood, 62
Kitcham, 248
Kite, 134
Kittle Lick Survey, 416
Kleiber, 336
Klein, 178
Kleindeist, 43
Klinehanse, 318
Klock, 52
Klokey, 260
Klunk, 253
Kmarthla, 67
Knabe, 419
Knapp, 24, 61, 109, 123, 195, 306, 425, 429
Knight, 28, 43, 83, 99, 132, 201, 374, 427
<u>Knights Templar</u>, 403
Knock, 139
Knott, 43, 136

Knotts, 102
Knowles, 44, 129, 319
Knowlton, 25, 100
Knox, 258, 367, 433
Koon, 357
Kossuth, 186
Kough, 379
Krafft, 315
Kraft, 425
Kramer, 298
Kranworth, 256
Kremer, 331
Kribben, 212
Kroesen, 376
Krouse, 256
Krugar, 141
Kuept, 25
Kummer, 43
Kurtz, 43, 91, 445
Kyle, 88, 250

L

L'Engle, 80
L'Homme, 365
la Croix, 252
La Croix, 234
La Reintree, 97, 123, 254, 264, 280
Labadie, 241
Lablache, 119
Laboutte, 62
Lacey, 44
Lachlen, 313
Lacoste, 439
Lacrade, 21
Ladd, 121, 206, 322, 362
Ladies Furs, 410
Lafayette, 79
Lafont, 93
Lafontaine, 343, 442
Lagner, 356
Lahey, 8
Laidlaw, 165
Laidler, 44
Lais, 357

Lake, 185, 220
Lakeman, 238
Lamb, 104, 421
Lambart, 106
Lambelin, 71
Lamberson, 32
Lamberton, 163
Lamborne, 428
Lamby, 300
Lammond, 179
Lamotte, 99
Lamphier, 390
Lamy, 255
Lanagan, 184
Lancaster, 44, 178, 240, 256, 289
Lander, 26, 263, 271
Landing, 63
Landing Tract, 156
Landon, 143, 369
Landreaux, 57
Landrum, 268
Landsdale, 114
Landstreet, 102, 179
Lane, 112, 118, 119, 134, 145, 178, 207, 278, 348, 352, 405, 414
Laney, 281
Langdon, 103, 286
Langhorne, 212
Langley, 44, 52, 174, 274
Langlots, 209
Langton, 15, 412
Lanny, 275
Lansdale, 75, 117, 277, 408
Lapaugh, 187
Larcomb, 346
Larcombe, 428
Lare, 44
Larker, 219
Larkin, 142, 255, 316, 356, 394
Larnard, 284, 287
Larned, 180, 262, 283
Larner, 139
Larny, 194, 263
Larrabee, 122, 141, 231

Larrimore, 150
Laskey, 127, 405
Latham, 18, 50, 58, 154, 221, 231, 254, 270, 280, 312, 313, 350, 444
Lathrop, 387
Latimer, 142, 220, 287, 304, 424
Laty, 76
Laub, 241, 420
Lauderback, 66
Laughery, 254, 263, 280
Laughlin, 385
Launitz, 309
Laurel Hill Cemetery, 382
Laurenson, 396
Laurie, 44, 147, 207, 431
Lavalette, 72, 142, 206, 281
Lavender, 240, 345
Law, 33, 44, 400
Lawrence, 25, 29, 102, 239, 244, 252, 302, 322, 415
Lawrenson, 50
Lawson, 51, 123, 177, 418
Lawton, 86
<u>Lazarist Missionaries</u>, 366
Lazenby, 96, 101
Le Case, 221
Le Caze, 149, 254
Le Roy, 117
Lea, 71, 88, 123, 124
Leach, 44, 249, 264, 270, 280
Leachman, 380
Leadbettar, 44
Leake, 352
Leakin, 76
Learin, 145
Leary, 12, 100
Leavel, 414
Leaven, 145
Leavenworth, 18, 51, 58, 64, 69, 78, 121, 259, 261, 281, 326
Leavil, 178
Leavin, 178
Leber, 102
Ledyard, 144

Lee, 19, 26, 53, 61, 128, 140, 153, 159, 185, 197, 199, 225, 239, 244, 254, 259, 285, 288, 320, 332, 336, 337, 346, 359, 367, 369, 402, 420, 424
Lee's Hill, 386
Leech, 342
<u>Leeches</u>, 434
Lees, 180
Lefevre, 44
Leffiers, 76
Leftwich, 190
Leginshaw, 329
Lehmann, 158, 441
Leigh, 378
Lemmon, 187
Lempark, 236
Lendrum, 194, 255
Lenman, 65
Lenotre, 357
Lenox, 23, 28, 44, 64, 247, 297, 317, 375
Lenthall, 34
Leonard, 31
Leslie, 150, 283
Letcher, 430
Letmate, 312
Letter, 13
Leutze, 216
Leveley, 13
Levelly, 18
Levely, 24, 55
Levering, 184
Levermore, 67
LeVesconie, 375
Levin, 411
Levy, 112, 151, 231, 239, 244, 264, 353
Lewis, 1, 9, 18, 21, 32, 44, 49, 51, 58, 73, 99, 104, 128, 131, 133, 145, 163, 170, 178, 204, 205, 209, 216, 231, 236, 250, 255, 274, 280, 317, 319, 329, 337, 366, 379, 392, 415, 421

Lezron, 178
Libbey, 87, 144
Liberty Hill, 298
Lightbourn, 107
Lighted, 44
Lightfoot, 237, 313
Lightford, 290
Lightner, 210
Ligon, 15, 302
Likins, 411
Lilley, 90, 308
Lillington, 294
Lilly, 409
Lincoln, 326, 362
Lind, 134
Lindsay, 44, 57, 357
Lindsley, 44, 118, 205, 223, 423
Linkins, 374
Lins, 99
Linsley, 341
Linthicum, 147, 242, 443
Linton, 132, 250, 305
Lippard, 63
Lippincott, 425
Lippitt, 134, 263
Lipscomb, 243
Liscomb, 53
list of wrecks, 354
Liston, 44
Littele, 192
Litteston, 433
Little, 26, 44, 54, 148, 251, 314, 375, 389, 434
Littlefield, 180
Littlejohn, 118
Live Oak Point Plantation, 428
Livingston, 41, 338, 349, 397, 440
Llebaria, 381
Llewellen, 44, 392
Lloyd, 16, 40, 44, 171, 179, 240, 289, 354, 442
Lloyds, 171
Lochmfranet, 357
Locke, 44

Lockery, 44, 327
Lockhart, 438
Lockheart's, 416
Locknow, 323
Lockor, 442
Locksey, 194
Lockwood, 325
Locust Hill, 125, 144
Loebig, 406
Loeser, 19, 20, 21, 33, 140
Loftin, 59
Logan, 332
Loker, 44
Lomax, 248
Lombard, 137
Lombardi, 44
Long, 44, 107, 145, 245, 284, 285, 286, 433
Long Green, 16
Long Old Fields, 368
Longberry, 275
Longey, 236
Longhammer, 323
Longman, 203
Longstown, 390
Longstreet, 253
Longuemare, 234
Longwood, 320
Looby, 69, 401, 415
Lookingbill, 220
Loomis, 12, 50, 105, 254, 341, 347
Lorch, 237
Lord, 44, 128, 193, 217, 374, 388, 396
Lore, 188
Loring, 273, 277, 295
Lot, 18
Loud, 192
Louey, 64
Loughborough, 227
Lougheny, 212
Loughlin, 334
Love, 183
Lovejoy, 401
Lovell, 66

Low, 27, 195, 255, 282
Lowd, 427
Lowder, 205
Lowe, 181, 287, 336, 337, 376
Lower, 236, 333
Lowrey, 428
Lowrie, 272
Lowring, 32
Lowry, 44, 69, 373, 438
Loyd, 105
Lucas, 44, 97, 393, 406, 441
Luce, 355, 356, 363
Lucey, 155
Luck, 423
Luckett, 155
Luckie, 124
Luco, 132, 157, 212, 281
Ludlam, 25, 206
Ludlow, 28, 397
Lumpkin, 13, 44
Lumsden, 102
Lundy, 163
Lunky, 163
Lunt, 44
Lusby, 44, 88
Lusky, 288
Lutener, 17, 84
Lyle, 320, 376
Lyles, 374
Lynch, 33, 40, 44, 57, 92, 220, 264, 268, 270, 313, 321, 327, 336, 353, 357, 359
Lyndon, 304
Lyne, 401
Lynn, 25, 356, 445
Lyon, 254, 264
Lyons, 87, 90, 91, 99, 144, 207
Lytle, 33

M

MacAnliffe, 26
Macay, 3
Macdaniel, 332
Mace, 315
Macey, 318
Macfarlan, 50
Macfarland, 245
MacFarland, 92
Macgill, 378
Machin, 428
Mackall, 50, 120, 157, 244
Mackay, 45, 52, 95, 114, 212, 282
Mackey, 212
Mackleet, 67
Macklet, 66
Macky, 422
Macnamara, 156
MacNamara, 139
Macomb, 11, 86, 144
Macrae, 29, 260, 313
Macy, 387
Madan, 241
Maddin, 186
Maddon, 210
Maddox, 45, 49, 69, 289, 419, 438
Madi, 45
Madison, 34, 51, 80, 92, 251, 261, 358, 437
Maes, 271
Maffit, 80
Magar, 44, 45
Mageham, 267
Magill, 245
Magnolia, 79
Magraw, 228
Magruder, 22, 49, 64, 75, 135, 151, 166, 207, 232, 292, 373, 374, 407, 436, 440
Maguire, 47, 202, 240, 422, 445
Mahin, 356
Mahon, 62, 356, 360
Mahoney, 8, 427
Maiden Bower, 103
Mailey, 362
Main, 121
Major, 44, 357
Makan, 355
Makin, 139, 162

Malahy, 24, 25
Malcomb, 53
male attire, 34
Maller, 124
Mallet, 149, 221, 254, 348
Mallory, 362
Malone, 248, 274
Malus, 93
Manchester, 7
Mangate, 44
Mankin, 207, 297
Mann, 203, 241, 256, 277, 316
Manning, 337
Mansay, 357
Mansfield, 195, 260
Mansion Square, 85
Mantel, 400
Manypenny, 202
Manzy, 157
Marbury, 188, 190, 203, 217, 329, 370, 413
Marcellus, 87
Marceron, 112, 397
March, 66
Marcy, 3, 67
Markle, 66
Marks, 20, 22, 23, 30, 44, 162, 191, 288, 346, 431, 434
Markwood, 45
Marlett, 63
Marling, 277
Marll, 360
Marlow, 333
Marnay, 131
Marquis of Lansdowne, 256
Marr, 156, 350
Marriott, 68, 76
Marsh, 226, 235
Marshal, 69
Marshall, 20, 23, 29, 45, 84, 92, 124, 167, 177, 191, 245, 289, 305, 325, 374, 394, 438
Marshe, 431
Marten, 131

Martin, 8, 18, 28, 34, 54, 63, 66, 76, 77, 92, 101, 138, 184, 195, 256, 266, 279, 288, 308, 337, 348, 417, 435, 439
Martin Surveys, 416
Martine, 130, 352
Martini, 45
Maruqis, 304
Marvin, 195
Marx, 245
Maryman, 123, 274
Masi, 44, 77, 427
Mason, 2, 21, 38, 44, 49, 61, 69, 71, 74, 94, 100, 123, 130, 156, 166, 179, 190, 200, 208, 212, 226, 231, 245, 249, 253, 257, 274, 277, 302, 317, 334, 339, 359, 380, 400, 401, 402, 413, 423, 424, 431
Massi, 11
Master Bakers, 352
Masters, 189
Masterson, 378
Matchler, 25
Mateson, 173
Mather, 209
Mathew, 25
Mathews, 241, 255, 263, 379
Matlock, 66
Matthew, 274
Matthews, 2, 70, 82, 101, 128, 145, 151, 159, 172, 181, 212, 246, 282, 289, 399
Matthews Farm, 141
Mattingly, 44, 62, 83, 212, 254, 259, 280, 289, 313, 316, 427, 428
Maud, 45
Maury, 44, 58, 60, 106, 191, 198, 202, 339, 422
Mauzy, 50, 281
Maxey, 45
Maxwell, 18, 139, 192, 284, 287, 318, 410
May, 99, 111, 164, 193, 199, 293, 336, 348, 363, 401, 428

Maycer, 356
Mayer, 25, 75, 358
Mayo, 73, 106, 121, 281
Mays, 315
McAlister, 25
McAlmont, 383
McAnany, 51
McAnaspie, 53
McArthur, 311, 385
McAtee, 121
McAvoy, 244
McBeath, 184, 349
McBlair, 27, 57, 199, 230, 245, 254, 280
McBride, 44, 308
McCabe, 117, 356
McCalla, 203, 247
McCandless, 44
McCann, 16
McCarron, 383
McCarru, 8
McCarter, 59
McCarthy, 44, 45, 130, 170, 232, 276, 288, 337, 355
McCartney, 66, 314
McCarty, 21, 177, 207, 245, 344
McCathran, 183, 219, 288, 337
McCaulay, 50
McCauley, 72, 88, 191, 221, 321, 356
McCeney, 388
McCerren, 412
McCleary, 25, 286
McCleland, 220
McClellan, 7, 195, 314, 424
McClelland, 105, 241, 314, 402
McClennan, 271
McClintock, 306
McClokey, 170
McClosky, 334
McClure, 67
McColgan, 409
McColligan, 152
McConchi, 44
McConnell, 157, 197

McCook, 284, 348, 349
McCorkle, 44, 317
McCormich, 45, 136
McCormick, 7, 9, 45, 54, 78, 100, 143, 210, 226, 228
McCoubray, 45
McCowley, 240
McCoy, 44, 115, 210, 216
McCracken, 5, 45, 357
McCrail, 334
McCubbin, 45, 53, 343
McCulloh, 100, 396
McCullough, 334
McCutchen, 106, 160
McCutcheon, 26
McDaniel, 3, 406
McDermott, 45, 374
McDonald, 45, 53, 120, 126, 158, 361, 376, 391, 418
McDonnell, 53
McDougal, 358
McDowell, 72, 317
McElderry, 54, 254
McEldery, 75, 83, 171
McElfresh, 45
McElheney, 282
McElhenny, 212
McElhiney, 263
McElhiny, 255
McElray, 171
McElwrath, 81
McFail, 232
McFarland, 249, 261, 384
McFeely, 51
McFenan, 268
McGarvey, 238, 401, 415, 436
McGee, 45, 98, 181, 356
McGhan, 77
McGhee, 395
McGill, 25, 185, 206, 369
McGinnall, 256
McGinnis, 67, 106, 419
McGinniss, 173
McGirk, 52, 259, 264, 270, 281

McGlyrin, 358
McGowan, 308
McGrath, 170
McGregor, 16, 45, 122, 149, 202, 331, 337, 345
McGuffey, 208
McGuinness, 359
McGuire, 3, 26, 28, 45, 66, 91, 96, 163, 173, 177, 194, 225, 255, 263, 265, 275, 281, 353, 420
McHanney, 128
McHenry, 152
McIntire, 126, 180, 234, 290, 323, 361, 371
McIntosh, 24, 157, 175
McIntyre, 26, 55, 428
McJimsey, 311
McKay, 27, 51, 240, 252
McKee, 162, 368
McKelden, 84, 119, 207, 436
McKenna, 5, 8
McKenney, 44, 207, 396
McKenny, 176
McKenstry, 224
McKenzie, 103, 162
Mckeon, 180
McKeon, 235
McKeown, 367
McKim, 120, 300, 324, 379
McKinsie, 144
McKinstry, 196, 348
McKneely, 212, 263, 281
McKnew, 89
McKnight, 44, 45, 121, 152, 207, 213, 214, 217, 237
McKoy, 175
McKuen, 44
McLain, 23, 437
McLanathan, 59
McLand, 99
McLane, 24, 26, 30, 64, 88, 123, 414
McLaughlin, 25, 90, 96, 185
McLean, 1, 18, 44, 49, 56, 71, 140, 162, 181, 220, 262, 318, 429
McLellan, 254, 271
McLelland, 308
McLeod, 109, 339
McLoughlin, 356
McLure, 67
McManus, 24, 132, 139, 167, 174, 177, 233, 409
McMaster, 416, 417
McMath, 356, 358
McMillan, 33, 174
McMinn, 249, 264, 270, 280
McMoreland, 45
McMullen, 101
McNail, 129
McNairy, 351
McNally, 215
McNamara, 24
McNamee, 6, 44
McNeal, 261
McNeelly, 274
McNeely, 255
McNeil, 25, 212
McNeill, 102, 418
McNeir, 106, 396
McNerhany, 198
McNew, 247
McNutt, 283
McPeck, 45
McPherson, 45, 207, 428, 437
McQudlan, 45
McRae, 72, 189, 213, 370
McRath, 356
McVea, 212, 255, 263, 281
McVeigh, 300
McVey, 149, 231, 239, 252, 274
McWilliams, 241, 289
Mead, 169, 333
Meade, 9, 51, 73, 80, 157, 194, 212, 341
Meaders, 68
Mears, 27, 50, 58, 60, 73, 111, 112, 280, 352
Mechlin, 37, 352
Medary, 223

Meddart, 44
Meem, 245
Meier, 51, 430
Meiggs, 397
Meigs, 349, 397
Meinzesheimer, 181
Meir, 9
Meise, 4
Melcher, 106
Melendez, 369
Mellen, 265
Melleville, 270
Mellor, 382
Mellus, 20
Melson, 428
Melville, 217
Melvin, 394
Menard, 212
Menhall, 66
Menou, 160
Mentzer, 246
Mercer, 58, 160, 286, 356, 393
Merchant, 19, 20, 21, 162, 231, 239, 258, 264, 280, 296, 323, 401
Meredith, 141
Merida, 44
Meriwether, 70
Merkel, 44
Merman, 44
Merriam, 348
Merrick, 208, 213, 309
Merrifield, 205
Merrilist, 44
Merrill, 1, 37, 92, 99, 115, 337
Merriman, 292
Merritt, 246, 277
Merryman, 44, 228
Messersmith, 195
Messervy, 176
Metcalf, 76, 81, 157, 253
Methodist Episcopal Church, 405
Methodist Metropolitan Church, 373
Metoyer, 220, 255, 270, 275
Meyer, 25, 386

Meyers, 25, 100, 138
Meyn, 25
Michaels, 168
Michel, 93
Michler, 283
Michlin, 352
Mickum, 194
Middleswarth, 233
Middleton, 10, 28, 44, 149, 203, 207, 287, 337, 338
Mier, 24
Milbern, 207
Milburn, 44, 59, 106, 117, 227, 260, 288, 337
Mile, 44
Miles, 24, 203, 210, 237, 289, 404, 441
Miles farm, 183
Milholland, 76
Miller, 10, 18, 22, 24, 25, 44, 45, 47, 52, 61, 87, 89, 97, 100, 106, 123, 163, 181, 193, 194, 195, 207, 213, 229, 233, 241, 254, 255, 261, 279, 280, 288, 300, 312, 331, 335, 340, 344, 350, 356, 377, 379, 383, 392, 398, 425
Millford, 400
Milligan, 42, 259
Milliken, 32, 334
Mills, 44, 100, 202, 210, 215, 433, 445
Millson, 174, 227
Millville, 357
Miltenberger, 76
Milvers, 25
Mines, 25
Minnehein, 170
Minor, 66
Mintzer, 399
Mitchel, 348
Mitchell, 18, 20, 24, 45, 48, 50, 53, 66, 69, 70, 89, 90, 91, 108, 151, 183, 190, 195, 244, 247, 250, 252,

255, 270, 280, 299, 301, 356, 357, 358, 361, 362, 371, 390, 401, 413
Mix, 202, 393
Mixel, 25
Mobley, 152
Mocabee, 292
Moellor, 107
Moffitt, 69
Mohun, 117, 379, 415, 427
Moir, 404
Molesworth, 256
Molony, 68
Molten, 380
Mondy, 253
Monke, 25
Monnaghan, 8
Monroe, 52, 79, 108, 125, 217
Montague, 193, 240
Montaner, 96
Montazile, 299
Montgomery, 167, 214, 231, 275, 284, 289
Montiel, 426
Montour, 353
Montpelier, 92
Montross, 436
Moody, 277, 381
Mooers, 86, 131
Mooney, 301
Moore, 21, 25, 36, 44, 45, 53, 56, 65, 69, 71, 77, 93, 95, 99, 101, 117, 118, 133, 144, 151, 156, 167, 183, 209, 220, 229, 234, 241, 242, 263, 270, 306, 324, 332, 334, 341, 356, 357, 380, 390, 397, 428, 430, 442
Moran, 24, 60, 154, 356, 365, 373, 395, 411
Morass, 3, 48, 51, 244, 252, 281
Morcira, 241
Morcoe, 84, 229, 429
Mordecai, 3
More, 172, 212, 254
Morehead, 66, 141
Moreland, 45, 245

Morell, 254, 264, 281
Moreno, 96
Morey, 211
Morfit, 133, 382
Morfitt, 172
Morgan, 2, 25, 45, 60, 91, 105, 114, 146, 149, 166, 181, 194, 201, 214, 220, 229, 232, 264, 278, 281, 285, 289, 298, 362, 373, 423
Morganthall, 67
Moriarty, 8
Morison, 176
Mormon, 213, 364, 367
Morning, 395
Morrell, 209, 317
Morris, 25, 45, 67, 78, 87, 99, 115, 130, 168, 200, 289, 318, 351, 357, 363, 377, 379
Morrison, 44, 72, 124, 195, 236, 308, 323, 347, 349, 373, 393, 405
Morrow, 45, 70
Morrrison, 10
Morse, 25, 74, 107, 200, 201, 213, 255, 270, 339
Morsell, 33, 119, 146, 164, 205, 219, 308, 442, 443
Morss, 44, 129, 209, 429
Mortimer, 256
Morton, 219, 227, 231, 399, 404
Morven, 325
Mosche, 51
Moscrip, 44
Moseley, 273
Mosely, 71
Moses, 6, 24, 44, 80, 142
Mosher, 298
Moss, 288, 337, 347, 350, 388
Motler, 98
Mott, 296
Motzer, 259
Moulder, 44
Moulon, 199, 216
Moulton, 158
Mount Auburn, 292

Mount Hood, 406
Mount Vernon, 79, 169, 249, 339, 431
Mount Vernon Association, 249
Mount Vesuvius, 206
Mounts, 131, 420
Mountz, 44
Mower, 88
Mowry, 397
Moyer, 258, 271
Moylan, 168, 231, 239
Mrs Humphey's Cottage, 322
Much, 247
Mudd, 44, 252, 289, 309
Muhlenberg, 16
Muhlenburg, 59
Muirhead, 356, 358
Mulder, 339
Mulford, 334
Mullary, 348
Muller, 305, 368
Mulligan, 378
Mulliken, 348
Mullin, 21
Mullins, 286
Muloy, 339
Mulqueen, 381
Mumford, 146
Munck, 369
Munder, 340
Mundy, 347
Munk, 70
Munn, 411
Munnymon, 228
Munroe, 277
Munson, 325
Muntz, 336, 346
Murphey, 245
Murphy, 8, 56, 63, 71, 117, 424
Murray, 8, 20, 21, 24, 33, 45, 48, 70, 80, 91, 96, 228, 240, 246, 276, 366, 413, 423
Murrays, 179
Murrell, 207

Murry, 18
Murton, 356, 357
Musterd, 357
Mustin, 120
Myde, 299
Myer, 44, 80, 164, 219, 288
Myerle, 34, 161, 232, 240
Myers, 13, 30, 44, 45, 52, 76, 108, 166, 215, 245, 284, 290, 322, 337

N

Nahant House, 198
Nailor, 45, 129
Nalley, 98, 288, 388
Nally, 216, 418, 438
Napoleon, 187, 228, 383, 430
Narden, 45
Nash, 1, 148, 195, 238, 254, 268, 280, 299, 434
National Hotel, 328
Naton, 294
Naylor, 23, 45, 64, 77, 164, 291, 297, 317, 324, 394
Neale, 45, 46, 240, 315, 371
Needles, 153
Neely, 407
Neil, 45
Neilson, 45, 139
Neitzes, 404
Nelly, 354
Nelson, 8, 10, 48, 51, 56, 58, 81, 117, 123, 137, 184, 209, 214, 239, 269, 276, 280, 332, 352, 361, 367
Netwell, 342
Neville, 296
Nevins, 52, 95, 114
Nevitt, 294, 442
Newbold, 187, 206
Newbould, 358
Newcome, 34
Newman, 172, 191, 241, 358
Newton, 34, 45, 96, 175, 248
Nicholls, 45, 110, 330
Nichols, 161, 227

Nicholson, 45, 75, 88, 118, 174, 199, 430
Nickerson, 7
Nicolas, 358
Nicolls, 356
Nightingale, 211, 221, 232, 239, 264
Niles, 395
Niven, 358
Nixdorff, 45
Noakes, 358
Noble, 49, 294, 440
Nodway, 400
Noer, 352
Nokes, 411
Nolan, 261
Noland, 413
Noran, 363
Norflet, 306
Norfolk, 77, 341
Noriega, 277
Norris, 45, 278, 383, 408, 431, 445
North, 215, 238, 332, 358, 398, 425
Norton, 191, 414
Norwood, 34, 38, 171, 327
Nottingham, 25
Nourse, 36, 45, 120, 123, 129, 147, 190, 244, 251, 257, 293, 306
Nowland, 84
Noyes, 45, 147, 198, 427
Noyman, 124
Nugent, 308, 383
number the houses, 231
Nye, 88, 116, 231, 239, 254, 264

O

O'Branham, 48
O'Brien, 8, 53, 77, 267, 334, 379, 386, 394, 422
O'Bryon, 112
O'Conner, 8
O'Connor, 25, 241, 286, 365
O'Conor, 235
O'Couter, 45
O'Donnel, 410

O'Donnell, 303, 318
O'Donnghue, 84
O'Donoghue, 45, 233
O'Donohoe, 38
O'Dwyer, 442
O'Ferral, 45
O'Hara, 140, 394, 433
O'Harra, 45
O'Larey, 100
O'Neal, 371
O'Neale, 10, 45, 243, 274
O'Neil, 52, 440
O'Neile, 241
O'Neill, 90, 117, 418
O'Niel, 116
O'Reilly, 334
O'Sullivan, 165, 223
O'Toole, 11, 144, 174, 202, 427
Oak Hill, 257, 377
Oak Hill Cemetery, 188
Oakendale tract, 413
Oakleigh, 133
Oakley, 49
Oakwood, 361
Oates, 113
Oats, 164
Ober, 317
Odam, 207
Odell, 417
Oden, 9, 146, 406
Odoacer, 293
Oertly, 204
Offley, 372
Offutt, 55, 97, 149, 384
Ogden, 11, 277, 288, 337
Ohio & Mississippi railroad, 191
Okill, 424
Old Capitol, 405
Old Distillery Lot, 413
old Lutheran Church, 350
Olds, 176, 241
Oliver, 6, 25, 433
Olmstead, 17, 30, 72, 213, 214, 329
Olmsted, 280

Olney, 406
One hundred years ago, 387
Oneonta, 168
Oothoudt, 220
Opey, 199
Ord, 393
Orem, 288
Orman, 67
Orme, 11, 87, 144
Ornfield, 30
Orr, 331
Orrick, 416
Osborn, 87, 185, 324
Osborne, 359
Osbourn, 169
Osgood, 351
Osler, 67
Osman, 67
Osterloh, 38
Otis, 34
Ould, 270
Over the Creek, 232
Overton, 155
Owen, 45, 68, 92, 121, 223, 266, 273, 426
Owens, 434
Oyster, 164, 207

P

Pace, 220
Pacetti, 370
packet **Kate Kearny**, 75
Packwood, 92
Page, 10, 49, 137, 143, 178, 228, 287, 356, 358, 424, 430
Page, 45
Paget, 167
Pagnad, 66
Pagnerre, 366
Paige, 194, 255, 268
Paine, 46, 187, 191, 260, 265, 284, 287, 290, 302
Pairo, 135
Palfrey, 241

Pallhuben, 84
Pallhuber, 36
Palmer, 121, 130, 150, 218, 248, 279, 286, 381, 393, 426
Palmerston, 256
Pancoast, 45
Pandally, 75
Pardon, 294
Parish, 68, 195
Park, 196
Parke, 105, 283
Parker, 2, 6, 22, 33, 45, 46, 54, 64, 67, 98, 106, 117, 137, 149, 163, 183, 209, 221, 240, 248, 263, 264, 265, 270, 278, 302, 307, 360, 362, 375, 376, 387, 410, 420
Parkman, 433
Parks, 24, 67
Parrel, 101
Parren, 232
Parrot, 221
Parry, 54
Parsons, 17, 45, 61, 123, 147, 199, 217, 259, 288, 337
Parton, 50, 105, 123, 280, 422
Partridge, 2, 28, 111
Paschall, 190
Pasive, 358
Paskiewitch, 276
Pat, 301
Patten, 125
Patterson, 1, 55, 66, 129, 185, 207, 215, 224, 244, 275, 315, 358, 363
Patton, 33, 86, 128, 425
Paulding, 50, 75
Paulent, 131
Pauleut, 15
Pauls, 124
Pavie, 264, 270, 275
Pavitt, 424
Pavle, 239
Paxton, 60, 411
Payne, 89, 115, 211, 220, 240, 300, 326

Payson, 128, 221
Payster, 27
Payton, 25
Peabody, 240
Peace, 162
Peaco, 79, 369, 422
Peake, 45, 118, 252
Peale, 254
Pearce, 240, 264, 274, 275
Pearson, 45, 131, 147, 191, 337, 358, 374
Peck, 10, 63, 69, 85, 102, 173, 202, 366, 379
Peckham, 430
Peddicord, 166
Peden, 176, 223
Pedrick, 274
Peerce, 348
Pegram, 249, 285
Pegues, 439
Pelham, 273
Pellet, 249
Pember, 194
Pembroke, 181
Penby, 69
Pender, 286
Pendergrast, 78, 123
Pendleton, 191, 209, 237, 340, 359, 376
Penington, 8
Penly, 81
Penn, 143, 234, 240, 242, 259, 264, 280, 406
<u>Penn Female College</u>, 272
Pennebaker, 308
Penniman, 349
Pennock, 423
Penny, 13
Penrice, 241
Pentegrass, 339
Pentomy, 323
Pentony, 323
Pepper, 91, 151, 191
Percival, 238, 390, 391, 424

Perea, 229
Peres, 202
Perin, 80
Perkins, 16, 34, 53, 92, 240, 266, 284, 285, 291, 302, 358, 361, 365
Perrie, 323
Perrin, 358, 431
Perrine, 234
Perry, 109, 120, 185, 189, 207, 225, 248, 263, 275, 311, 368, 404
Person, 301
Peter, 45, 261, 265, 329, 345, 443
Peterkin, 214
Peters, 38, 48, 59, 69, 80, 154, 209, 229, 233, 252, 274, 408, 412
Peterson, 351, 354, 381
Petrie, 356, 358, 396
Pettengill, 18
Pettibone, 45, 46, 157, 254, 281
Pettigrew, 136
Pettit, 147, 216, 241, 440
Peugh, 46, 193
Peverelly, 235, 400
Peyton, 81, 292, 329
Phagan, 5, 24, 53, 244
Phelps, 7, 25, 102, 171, 180, 192, 193, 210, 227, 265, 268, 273, 292, 324, 350, 360, 373, 409, 418, 445
Phifer, 58
Philip, 46, 47
Philips, 24, 150, 240, 241
Phillips, 31, 45, 46, 145, 209, 256, 265, 307, 348, 379, 392, 432
Phillis, 401
Phoenix, 182
Phyfe, 119
Piatt, 130
Pickering, 351
Picket, 210
Pickett, 72, 186
Pickrell, 87, 91, 144, 207
Piedmont estate, 260
Piemont, 7

Pierce, 16, 22, 73, 76, 86, 96, 97, 102, 108, 123, 125, 139, 142, 158, 164, 169, 217, 218, 254, 264, 280, 281, 304, 346, 424
Pierce's Mill, 391
Pierre, 45
Pierson, 411, 412
Pigott, 23
Pilgrim Burial Place, 31
Pilgrims, 369
Pilling, 443
Pinckney, 100, 270, 351
Pinkett, 380
Pinkney, 125, 234
Pitler, 67
Pittman, 52, 95, 114
Pittsley, 6
Pizzini, 241
Plant, 21, 191, 219, 278
Plater, 104
Platt, 18, 387, 415
Pleasants, 166, 187, 206
Plowden, 241
Plowman, 315, 396
Plumer, 173, 335
Plummer, 213
Plumsill, 46
Plympton, 67, 99
Pod, 434
Poe, 28, 240, 261, 278, 329, 392, 420
Pogue, 2
Point Conception, 390
Pointer, 48
Poisal, 323
Polanes, 106
Polk, 70, 127, 374
Polkinhorn, 428
Pollard, 45
Pollick, 367
Pollock, 101, 347, 371
Poman, 26
Pomeroy, 33, 88
Pomroy, 18, 23, 53
Poncin, 194

Pool, 52, 55, 101, 132, 216, 244, 264
Poole, 220
Pope, 225
Porcher, 74
Porter, 2, 53, 64, 72, 99, 213, 214, 217, 220, 230, 233, 253, 254, 261, 274, 275, 281, 282, 288, 289, 308, 350, 424
Posey, 101, 177, 241, 330
Post, 113, 377
Potomac Pavilion, 192
Potter, 78, 99, 133, 240, 241, 266, 293, 406
Potts, 307, 424
Poucin, 256, 282
Pouder, 438
Poulton, 424
Pourman, 124
Powell, 26, 63, 89, 226, 245, 352, 354, 383, 388, 413
Power, 25
Powers, 3, 126, 396
Praco, 122
Prain, 14
Prata, 93
Prather, 45, 195
Pratt, 103, 110, 232, 299, 358, 362
Preble, 312
Prendergast, 335
Prentiss, 349
<u>Presbyterian Church</u>, 49
Prescott, 223
Presher, 199
Preston, 38, 45, 46, 122, 152, 228, 319
Prettyman, 278
Preuss, 299, 305
Prewitt, 194
Price, 66, 101, 109, 145, 185
Priest, 353
Princess of Spain, 53
Pringol, 228
Printz, 81
Priolean, 60
Prioleau, 220, 255

Prior, 175
privateer **General Armstrong**, 224
privateer **Nonsuch**, 55
Proctor, 10, 21, 60, 78, 169, 440
Prospect Hill, 214
Prott, 45
Prout, 45, 298, 380, 407, 419
Provest, 45
Provis, 156
Pruderoski, 162
Prudhomme, 241
Pruess, 427
Pruit, 89
Pruitt, 87
Prussock, 401
Pryor, 332
Pulaski, 57, 309
Pulizzi, 304, 312
Pullen, 220
Pullin, 20
Pumphrey, 37, 92, 157, 160, 165, 260, 368
Purcell, 76
Purdee, 349
Purdy, 91, 204, 338, 403
Purl, 45
Purnell, 435
Purris, 71
Putnam, 152, 184, 270, 436
Pye, 444
Pyne, 28, 38, 75, 87, 137, 145, 226, 353, 423

Q

Quackenbosh, 295
Quady, 422
Quaries, 121
Quarles, 258, 389
Queen, 21, 46, 247
Queen Isabella, 180
Queen Victoria, 180
Queen-Mother, 394
Quigley, 152
Quin, 46, 150

Quinan, 80
Quinn, 179, 376, 429
Quirk, 25
Quitman, 165

R

Raal, 356
Raborg, 213
Radcliff, 120, 206, 208, 317
Radzeminski, 411
Rae, 122, 370
Raenbal, 323
Rafferty, 8
Raftrice, 265
Ragan, 29, 186, 308
Ragland, 207
Raiford, 68
Raines, 401
Raley, 46
Rallston, 249, 264
Ralston, 97, 316
Ramsay, 60, 242
Ramsey, 12, 86, 342
Rand, 233
Randal, 286
Randall, 46, 128, 183, 229, 234, 442
Randolph, 2, 80, 118, 133, 229, 251, 287, 288, 292, 337, 351, 368, 388, 396
Random, 247
Rankin, 21, 177, 411
Ransom, 402
Ranson, 93, 191, 327, 364
Raoul, 218, 242, 259, 264, 280
Rappetti, 300
Ratcliff, 85
Ratcliffe, 94, 115, 383
Rathbone, 356, 358
Ratrie, 46
rattlesnake, 196
Raven, 419
Ravenscroft, 358
Rawlings, 218, 345
Rawlins, 79

Rawson, 240, 264, 436
Ray, 7, 12, 46, 106, 122, 161, 234
Rayburn, 105
Raymond, 220, 264, 270
Raynes, 378
raze **Independence**, 344
Rea, 195, 228
Read, 38, 198, 433
Readel, 243
Reading, 46
Ready, 300
Real, 364
Reardon, 68
Rechter, 170
Records, 188
Reddall, 415
Reddick, 212, 255
Reddin, 24, 206
Redding, 226
Reddington, 348
Redfern, 427
Redin, 33, 93, 118, 147, 209, 352, 370, 378, 381, 384, 439
Redstreak, 46
Reed, 14, 89, 131, 135, 156, 238, 324, 349, 350, 356, 358, 363, 398, 411
Reeder, 223
Reedy, 26
Rees, 36
Reese, 59, 89, 102, 216, 322, 383, 416
Reeside, 174
Reeve, 29, 184, 327
Reeves, 52, 202, 309
Regan, 135, 170, 336
Reginald, 230
Reid, 29, 105, 224, 248, 348
Remington, 166
Reminiscences, 351
Renner, 293
Renshaw, 11, 240
Rentz, 386
Rettberg, 86
Rettlebusch, 26
Revell, 358

Revere, 299
Reybold, 91, 112, 183
Reyburn, 280
Reymert, 73
Reynold, 185
Reynolds, 33, 108, 144, 190, 228, 297, 301, 371, 380, 397
Reynoldson, 46
Rhea, 111, 277
Rheem, 391
Rhees, 403
Rhine, 358
Rhodes, 85, 123, 135, 203, 204, 219, 249, 370
Riall, 261
Ricard, 411
Rice, 220, 240, 245, 297
Rich, 205, 237, 414, 428
Richard, 69, 212, 255, 439
Richard III, 253
Richards, 13, 31, 46, 213, 279, 367
Richardson, 3, 4, 8, 46, 66, 67, 71, 81, 88, 127, 208, 270, 325, 329
Richaud, 281
Richmond, 53
Richter, 394
Ricker, 214
Ricketson, 61
Riddick, 1
Riddle, 164, 308
Ridely, 120
Ridenour, 279
Rider, 46, 86, 170, 173
Rider's Grove, 228, 235
Ridgate, 396
Ridge, 358
Ridgely, 5, 50, 107, 172, 233, 242, 349, 438
Ridgway, 46
Ridick, 73
Ridout, 171
Riggs, 46, 115, 300, 301, 401
Rignald, 259

Riley, 25, 46, 53, 105, 131, 139, 229, 355, 360, 363, 423
Rincard, 419
Ringgold, 56, 87, 164, 283, 287, 331, 343, 375
Ringgold Barracks, 367
Riordan, 234
Ripley, 123, 177, 213, 261
Risque, 160, 405
Riston, 148, 170, 176, 192
Ritchie, 175, 226, 249, 261, 307, 332, 407, 422
Riter, 46
Rittenhouse, 19, 53, 147, 415
Ritter, 10, 77, 421
Rives, 46, 78, 165, 278
Roach, 46, 54, 163, 312, 346
Roane, 295, 373
Robbins, 339
Roberts, 18, 26, 59, 78, 99, 143, 182, 196, 259, 274, 280, 382, 430
Robertson, 18, 55, 73, 87, 94, 163, 230, 242, 246, 277, 293, 298, 326, 360, 392
Robespierre, 366
Robey, 45, 46, 313
Robins, 218
Robinson, 7, 27, 63, 71, 183, 184, 196, 228, 234, 241, 245, 249, 254, 255, 276, 300, 343, 356, 358, 362, 364, 428, 429, 442
Robson, 358
Robt, 99
Roby, 393
Roca, 123
Roche, 121, 189, 242, 396, 427
Rocices, 122
Rock, 428
Rockhammer, 323
Rodgers, 137, 275, 332, 347
Rodier, 46, 287, 337, 364, 390, 428
Roemmelle, 169, 171
Roemmle, 169

Rogers, 26, 80, 97, 102, 116, 163, 207, 274, 285, 312, 356, 437
Rogon, 25
Roland, 83
Rolfe, 327
Rollin, 342
Rollins, 46, 247, 248, 256
Rollston, 270
Roman, 93, 220, 280
Rood, 176
Rooker, 112, 293, 429
Root, 13, 108
Roper, 230
Ropes, 358
Rose, 219, 228, 256
Rosemont, 364
Rosenbaum, 240
Rosenbush, 334
Rosi, 106
Ross, 46, 92, 107, 128, 212, 227, 297, 348
Roszel, 102
Rothwell, 45, 46, 91, 106, 407, 415
Rotler, 46
Roundtree, 269
Rousseau, 198
Roussin, 13
Routh, 365
Row, 280
Rowan, 369
Rowe, 2, 27, 50, 58, 60, 81, 149, 294
Rowland, 24, 46, 67, 382, 384, 442
Roy, 7, 131, 364
Royal, 97, 199
<u>Royal Family</u>, 180
Royall, 133, 344
Rozsell, 105
Rubini, 119
Rucker, 343
Rudd, 61, 240
Ruddock, 277
Rudolph, 34, 37, 199, 429
Ruff, 191, 350
Ruffin, 95

Rufflin, 222
Ruger, 285
Ruggles, 46, 99, 424
Ruppel, 26, 227
Ruppell, 26, 278
Rusewurn, 60
Rush, 112, 179, 186, 251, 284, 286
Russell, 27, 46, 51, 81, 99, 100, 123, 195, 199, 244, 254, 256, 280, 282, 284, 307, 328, 334, 337, 360, 363, 379, 421, 426, 436
Rutherford, 220, 264, 329, 434
Rutland, 127
Rutledge, 351
Ryan, 53, 137, 422
Ryer, 49, 80

S

S tphen, 117
Sabin, 402
Safford, 136, 165
Sailor, 18
Sale, 315
Salisbury, 308
Salivero, 122
Sallhausen, 21
Salmon, 24
Saloman, 54
Salomon, 52, 73, 143, 195
Salony, 148
Sample, 140
Sampson, 113, 202, 235, 238
Samson, 8, 61, 251, 341, 362, 364, 393, 444
Samuels, 326
Sanders, 98, 168, 272, 275, 289, 433
Sandford, 20, 358, 363
Sands, 72, 133, 175, 331
Sanford, 24, 161, 221, 253, 363, 433
Sanger, 95, 114, 239, 259
Sangster, 103
Sanks, 310
Sansbury, 162
Santvoord, 348
Sanxay, 66, 67
Sargeant, 46
Sargent, 31, 50, 66, 67, 68, 131, 138, 179, 191, 322
Sartiges, 51
Sasser, 404
Satterlee, 20, 21, 33
Satto, 388
Sauer, 146
Sauger, 52
Saul, 86
Saunders, 54, 92, 199, 205, 301
Saussy, 364
Sauve, 240, 412
Savage, 125, 132, 237, 238, 248, 263, 289, 361
Sawtelle, 286
Sawyer, 23, 24, 26, 33, 131, 144, 291
Saxton, 25, 246
Sayton, 5
Scaggs, 207
Scarles, 362
Scarritt, 235, 257, 283, 287
Schall, 440
Schaub, 46
Scheerer, 25
Scheibler, 358
Scheill, 318
Schell, 21, 429
Schenck, 24, 97, 161, 237
Scherf, 46
Schlegel, 46
Schlessinger, 206
Schley, 162, 364, 426
Schleys, 324
Schlobecker, 189
Schlosser, 102
Schmidt, 159, 356, 358
Schmidts, 25
Schnebley, 46
Schneider, 238
schnr **Ann**, 27, 195, 255, 282
schnr **Brothers**, 236
schnr **Drumscale**, 199

schnr **Enterprise**, 172
schnr **Eufalia**, 157
schnr **Eufaula**, 105, 282
schnr **Grampus**, 17, 195, 254
schnr **Hannah Ann**, 105
schnr **Harriet**, 214
schnr **Lamartine**, 122
schnr **Manchester**, 122
schnr **Moselle**, 4
schnr **Ontario**, 349
schnr **Oregon**, 149
schnr **Tempest**, 7
Schoemaker, 348
Schonair, 253
Schooler, 276
Schott, 197, 347
Schouler, 173
Schroeder, 223, 377
Schultz, 26, 46, 218
Schultze, 170
Schussler, 107, 346
Schutte, 278
Schutter, 104, 197
Schuyler, 131, 336, 387, 389
Schwarr, 274
Schwartze, 6, 23, 229
Schweigert, 440
Schweitzer, 25
Sckismanski, 404
Scory, 102
Scott, 9, 46, 47, 72, 89, 92, 110, 142, 152, 154, 171, 179, 187, 193, 197, 198, 204, 212, 216, 228, 235, 261, 289, 300, 319, 322, 355, 358, 394, 399, 401, 414, 432, 438
Scounnell, 8
Scovil, 388
Scovill, 392
Scribner, 177, 207
Scrivener, 46, 47, 121, 156, 309
Scroggan, 312
Scroggins, 52
Scroode, 31
Scudder, 184

Seabrook, 231, 242
Seaman, 428
Search, 353
Searles, 67
Sears, 139, 203, 240, 405, 410, 445
Seary, 323
Seaton, 80, 88, 122, 321, 403, 428
Seaver, 99
Seawell, 99, 377
Seay, 311
Seely, 1
Seibels, 68, 223
Seibert, 47, 289
Seitz, 94
Selden, 156, 267, 336, 354, 385, 391
Seldon, 46
Selkirk, 206
Sellhausen, 49, 170, 202
Sellick, 429
Semkin, 403
Semmes, 8, 46, 177, 229, 241, 249, 427
Semple, 408
Sems, 46
Seneca Mills, 163, 242
Sengstack, 46, 55
Sergeant, 62, 71, 225
Sessford, 174, 429
Settle, 301
settlement of Calif, 169
Seufferle, 93
Severance, 140
Sewal, 162
Sewall, 47, 102, 123
Seward, 130, 157
Sewell, 71, 105, 144, 377
Sexton, 399
Seymore, 135, 231, 239
Seymour, 195, 365, 410, 426
Shaaff, 411
Shackelford, 85, 205, 240, 297, 423
Shad, 46
Shakespeare, 392
Shamly, 25

496

Shand, 137
Shang, 236
Shanklin, 58
Shanks, 316
Shannon, 29
Sharp, 66, 73, 424
Sharretts, 127
Shaw, 46, 104, 174, 195, 212, 217, 277, 370, 394, 424, 433, 440
Shay, 411
Sheahan, 10, 26
Sheckett, 46
Shecklels, 6
Shedd, 121
Sheehan, 24, 26
Sheer, 272
Sheffield, 273
Sheirburn, 136
Shekell, 300
Shelby, 434
Shelden, 1
Sheldon, 147
Shell, 8
Sheller, 317
Shelter, 47
Shelton, 220
Shepard, 230
Shephard, 260
Shepherd, 93, 179
Sheppard, 46, 303
Shepperd, 286
Sherbertt, 340
Sherbourn, 358
Sherburne, 15, 213
Sherer, 419
Sheriff, 88, 292, 340
Sherman, 208, 358
Sherrad, 33
Sherrard, 245
Sherwood, 193
Shiel, 236
Shields, 75, 105, 199, 267, 344, 443
Shillington, 172
ship **Abbe**, 354

ship **Aberdeen**, 258
ship **Africa**, 372
ship **Agnes Hall**, 354
ship **Alexander**, 306
ship **American Lass**, 354
ship **Ann**, 354
ship **Ann Tift**, 354
ship **Antarctic**, 19, 20, 21
ship **Antelope**, 8
ship **Antilles**, 354
ship **Arco**, 354
ship **Baltic**, 356
ship **Baltimore**, 422
ship **Bedford**, 383
ship **Bellerophon**, 383
ship **Boxer**, 275
ship **Cadmus**, 19
ship **Cambria**, 363
ship **Charles Wharton**, 248
ship **Charlotte**, 445
ship **Constitution**, 109
ship **Cyane**, 106, 137
ship **Dale**, 81
ship **Emblem**, 89
ship **Emma Field**, 354
ship **Erebus**, 375
ship **Essex**, 5, 289
ship **Falmouth**, 433
ship **Francis P Sage**, 309
ship **George**, 96
ship **Gipsey**, 354
ship **Gov Briggs**, 354
ship **Independence**, 426
ship **Inez**, 422
ship **Intrepid**, 401
ship **James Drake**, 109
ship **Joanna**, 354
ship **Joans**, 422
ship **John Wickliffe**, 354
ship **Julia Moulton**, 390
ship **Kate Hays**, 422
ship **Lancashire**, 422
ship **Lebanon**, 355
ship **Leviathan**, 109, 354

ship **Madagascar**, 354
ship **May Flower**, 369
ship **Mercury**, 363
ship **Metropolis**, 385
ship **North Carolina**, 344
ship **Orosimbo**, 11
ship **Pelican State**, 422
ship **Plymouth**, 82
ship **Polyphemus**, 383
ship **Portsmouth**, 236
ship **Powhatan**, 138
ship **Queen of the Clippers**, 422
ship **Red Rover**, 354
ship **Relief**, 301
ship **Richard Watson**, 354
ship **Russia**, 295
ship **Sarah**, 354
ship **Savannah**, 344
ship **Spectator**, 354
ship **Staffordshire**, 4, 8
ship **Syria**, 354
ship **Terror**, 375
ship **Three Bells**, 19, 20, 21, 184
ship **Townsend**, 294
ship **Urgent**, 354
ship **Vincennes**, 375
ship **Virago**, 177
ship **Waterloo**, 109, 354
ship **Wilberforce**, 354
ship **Wm Thompson**, 354
Shipley, 356
ships of war **Phoebe & Cherub**, 5
ships **Raritan** & **Vandalia**, 7
Shirley, 347
Shirman, 259
Shirts, 444
Shiver's Tract, 156
Shoemaker, 2, 313, 402
Shoenberger, 229
Shorey, 18
Short, 308, 351
Shorter, 46
Shreve, 71
Shryock, 46

Shubrick, 100
Shucking, 58, 60
Shugert, 130, 132, 133
Shuggart, 353
Shuking, 37
Shullsburgh, 230
Shumate, 422
Shunk, 283, 286
Shurman, 24
Shuster, 183, 358
Shuster farm, 183
Shyne, 266
Sibley, 99, 401
Sibrey, 47
Sickler, 68
Siebels, 251
Siebert, 289
Sigler, 213, 255, 270
Sigourney, 165
Sill, 283
Silova, 294
Silvee, 329
Silvers, 166
Silverton, 17
Simmes, 395
Simmonds, 282
Simmons, 20, 22, 46, 53, 128, 157, 282
Simms, 16, 46, 64, 94, 121, 126, 158, 248, 314, 370, 371, 380, 396, 427
Simonds, 4, 213, 214, 255, 263, 280, 348
Simons, 17, 69
Simonton, 9, 24, 105, 126, 167, 188, 281, 415
Simpson, 46, 140, 226, 236, 305, 373, 419
Simpsonville, 226
Simpton, 9, 51, 204, 240, 252, 253, 281
Sinchcomb, 46
Sinclair, 145
Singles, 67
Singleton, 216, 321

Sinnott, 338
Sinon, 104, 265
Siscoe, 380
Sister, 46
Sister Monica, 355
Sisters of Charity, 366
Sisters of Mercy, 267
Sitgreaves, 87
Skerrett, 418
Skidmore, 288, 337, 431
Skiller, 340
Skinner, 71, 86
Slack, 2, 228
Slacum, 88, 157
Slade, 47
Slater, 46
Slatford, 300, 376
Slaughter, 284, 326, 434
Slavin, 48, 50, 58, 81, 157
Slemmer, 147, 284, 285, 440
Sleven, 73
Slicer, 102, 373, 419, 426
Sloan, 80
Sloat, 180
sloop-of-war **Cherub**, 289
sloop-of-war **Constellation**, 308
sloop-of-war **Cyane**, 194, 263, 290
sloop-of-war **Jamestown**, 157, 322
sloop-of-war **Plymoth**, 146
sloop-of-war **Warren**, 301
Sludt, 26
Slye, 155
Smack, 36
Small, 202, 294
Smalley, 286
Smallwood, 22, 119, 298, 407
Smart, 33, 390
Smead, 285, 286, 385
Smedberg, 146
Smidt, 24
Smiley, 50
Smith, 4, 6, 8, 9, 14, 15, 18, 19, 20, 23, 24, 25, 26, 28, 29, 34, 46, 47, 49, 51, 53, 54, 55, 58, 60, 69, 72, 76, 78, 80, 83, 87, 89, 90, 92, 94, 95, 101, 102, 107, 111, 113, 118, 120, 121, 122, 123, 126, 129, 135, 136, 147, 149, 157, 158, 161, 163, 168, 169, 173, 178, 179, 181, 183, 185, 188, 189, 191, 195, 199, 200, 201, 202, 203, 204, 205, 207, 210, 212, 213, 215, 216, 221, 224, 225, 231, 234, 239, 241, 242, 248, 251, 252, 253, 254, 255, 259, 264, 265, 266, 272, 273, 280, 281, 282, 285, 286, 291, 293, 295, 297, 298, 300, 312, 313, 314, 319, 324, 326, 333, 334, 339, 340, 343, 346, 347, 348, 349, 351, 355, 356, 358, 360, 363, 365, 370, 371, 375, 378, 385, 388, 390, 392, 393, 394, 397, 399, 401, 402, 406, 411, 412, 413, 415, 420, 428, 431, 432, 437, 439, 440, 442, 444
Smith's Sound, 370
Smithson, 114
Smoot, 99, 219, 229, 232, 233, 302, 314, 346, 349, 376
Smull, 152
Smyth, 156
Sneary, 390
Snell, 215
Snelling, 236
Snodgrass, 128, 193, 198, 220, 255, 280, 415
Snow, 18, 50, 58, 152, 217, 274, 281, 411
Snowdeal, 376
Snowden, 181, 439
Snyder, 10, 13, 318
Socor, 258
Sohler, 241
Solden, 60
Solomon, 256
Somerell, 182
Somerfield, 304
Somers, 8, 60, 69
Somerville, 9, 73

Sontag, 217
Soper, 86, 160, 170
Sorber, 439
Sotheron, 186
Sothoron, 47, 103
Southall, 171
Southgate, 80, 383
Southmayd, 157
Southmead, 105
Southwark, 20, 21
Southworth, 21, 48, 106, 109
Spafford, 133
Spalding, 240, 294
Sparrow, 258
Spaulding, 360, 415, 426
Speake, 46, 102
Speaks, 384
Spear, 424
Spearing, 47
Speed, 111, 308
Speer, 219
Speiden, 93, 218
Speir, 253
Speiscer, 282
Speiser, 382
Spence, 68, 188
Spencer, 58, 90, 162, 261, 330, 348, 376, 389
Spilane, 24
Spohn, 260
Spooner, 291
Spotswood, 79
Sprague, 18, 70, 410, 433, 443
Sprigg, 174, 175, 378
Spriggs, 290
Spring, 178
Spring Garden farm, 183
Springdale, 245
Springer, 18, 152, 356, 358
Springman, 46
Sprung, 58
Spur, 432
Squibb, 226
St Clair, 351, 418

St John, 358
St Vincent of Paul, 355
Stabs, 236
Stacy, 63
Stafford, 14, 49, 50, 58, 60, 62, 78, 123, 204, 281
Stakely, 379
Stallcup, 191
Stallings, 10, 46, 54, 342
Stallions, 71
Stamp, 23
Stanborough, 348
Stanfield, 445
Stanford, 218
Stanhope, 288
Staniford, 146
Stanley, 17, 98, 149, 161, 369, 410
Stansburg, 76
Stansbury, 69, 124, 129, 209, 229, 293
Stanson, 356
Stanton, 154, 241, 283, 321, 338
Staples, 18, 51, 58, 60, 227, 242, 280
Stapylton, 445
Stark, 246
Starke, 300, 308
Starkweather, 223
Starling, 71, 350
Starry, 240
Statham, 114
Staub, 323
Stealey, 83, 210
steamboat **Georgia**, 59
steamboat **Thomas Collier**, 125
steamboat **Velante**, 100
steamer, 15, 363
steamer **Arctic**, 355, 356, 360, 361, 363, 365, 368
steamer **Atlantic**, 365
steamer **Caroline**, 101
steamer **E K Collins**, 354
steamer **Europa**, 361
steamer **Falcon**, 122, 140, 154, 281
steamer **Fanny**, 15, 195
steamer **Gange**, 366

steamer **Gazelle**, 181
steamer **George Law**, 106
steamer **Glasgow**, 354
steamer **Goliah**, 390
steamer **Hendrick Hudson**, 316
steamer **Hermann**, 141
steamer **Kate Kearney**, 94
steamer **Kate Kearny**, 82
steamer **Michigan**, 438
steamer **Nelly Baker**, 198
steamer **Nevada**, 163
steamer **Niagara**, 346
steamer **Ohio**, 122
steamer **Omstepe**, 99
steamer **Queen City**, 281
steamer **Royal Arch**, 103
steamer **San Francisco**, 14, 19, 20, 21, 24, 29, 33, 37, 109, 140, 154, 197, 233, 275
steamer **Secretary**, 163
steamer **Timour**, 312
steamer **Union**, 14
steamer **Vesta**, 361
steamer **Virago**, 126
steamer **Yankee Blade**, 390
steamers **Pearl & Natchez**, 17
steamship **Brother Jonathan**, 99
steamship **Massachusetts**, 194
steamship **Star of the West**, 301
steamship **Winfield Scott**, 4
steam-tug **Titan**, 21
Stearns, 135
Stebbins, 366
Steck, 70
Stedman, 48, 426
Steel, 102, 221, 290
Steele, 46, 93
Steen, 220
Steene, 264, 270
Steenrod, 27, 51, 244, 254, 263, 270, 280
Steers, 346
Steevens, 199
Steimart, 25

Steiner, 99, 162
Steinman, 25, 218
Steles, 273
Stelle, 92
Stem, 111
Stembel, 157
Step, 25
Stephen, 22, 439, 440
Stephens, 121, 363
Stephensen, 354
Stephenson, 131
Stepper, 152
Steptoe, 132, 397
Sterling, 225, 255
Sterun, 217
Stetson, 376
Stettheines, 56
Stettinius, 179
Steuart, 24, 57, 76, 203, 283, 285
Stevens, 65, 106, 125, 170, 198, 263, 300, 343, 380
Stevenson, 18, 377
Steward, 149
Stewart, 22, 46, 47, 88, 92, 149, 160, 189, 191, 192, 199, 200, 207, 208, 247, 272, 289, 316, 335, 354, 358, 370, 376, 395, 396, 402, 415
Stickney, 47, 302
Stidder, 294
Stillman, 186
Stinchcomb, 180
Stinger, 111, 147, 389, 440
Stirling, 196
Stobo, 84
Stockbridge, 176
Stockely, 196
Stockton, 50, 195, 214, 433
Stockwell, 21, 24
Stoddard, 348
Stoddart, 316
Stoke, 46
Stoll, 258, 264, 280
Stone, 26, 73, 93, 136, 169, 354, 358, 407, 440

Stoneman, 283
Stoner, 66
storeship **Fredonia**, 221
storeship **Relief**, 233
Storm, 91
Storms, 230
Storrow, 336
Story, 188, 355, 365
Stotsenburg, 424
Stott, 47, 185, 347, 383
Stotts, 277
Stow, 330
Stowell, 182
Strader, 268
Strain, 106, 126, 137, 177, 258, 267
Straley, 257
Strange, 76
Strangways, 432
Stratton, 3, 46, 59, 398, 441
Straw, 66
Streeter, 208
Stribling, 161, 193, 194
Strickland, 128
Strider, 341
Stringham, 319, 433
Strode, 117
Strong, 23, 47, 81, 221, 348
Strother, 235
Struthers, 256
Stuart, 27, 61, 153, 199, 220, 238, 245, 285, 318, 345, 377
Stubbs, 46, 217, 241
Studley, 100
Sturgess, 46
Sturgiss, 268
Stuyvesant, 319
Sullivan, 8, 17, 24, 34, 76, 91
Sultzer, 429
Summerfield, 198
Summers, 62, 100, 131, 149, 239, 381
Summerson, 121, 389
Sumner, 95, 114, 264, 390
Sunderland, 49, 169, 215, 265, 272, 274, 339

Surrell, 68
Suter, 237
S-uter, 46, 47
Sutherland, 102, 114, 233, 445
Sutlenberger, 25
Sutton, 46
Swain, 112, 175, 221, 428, 430
Swamp, 386
Swan, 9, 59, 233
Swan Tavern, 295
Swann, 3, 140, 157, 163, 264, 281, 371, 408
Swansman, 237
Swartze, 342
Swasey, 348
Sweeney, 8, 274, 308
Sweeny, 65, 131, 146, 267
Sweet, 27
Sweeting, 37
Sweitzer, 284
Swift, 258
Switzer, 66
Sydenham, 179
Sykes, 313
Sylvester, 32, 47, 99
Sympton, 1
Synder, 323

T

Tabbs, 118
Taber, 205, 439
Tabler, 47
Tabor, 260
Tainter, 205
Tait, 443
Talbert, 174, 317
Talbot, 103
Talburtt, 320, 322
Talcott, 206, 283, 287
Talford, 406
Talfourd, 115
Taliafero, 93
Taliaferro, 5, 47, 128, 153, 193, 194, 259, 434

Talty, 289
Tamburtal, 119
Taney, 22, 117
Tanner, 207
Tape, 182
Tappan, 362
Tapscott, 129
Tarleton, 72, 128, 170
Tarlton, 135
Tarner, 102
Taroni, 143
Tarver, 135
Tasker, 73
Tastet, 120
Tate, 141, 377, 428
Tatnall, 81
Tattnall, 198, 424
Tauburan, 66
Tayloe, 43, 47, 134, 153, 159, 379, 421, 424
Taylor, 1, 7, 19, 20, 21, 24, 29, 38, 47, 50, 57, 73, 76, 80, 84, 95, 106, 108, 122, 127, 134, 159, 169, 176, 181, 195, 197, 212, 213, 223, 242, 254, 255, 257, 281, 298, 302, 308, 321, 325, 333, 339, 348, 355, 362, 413, 414, 420, 422, 423, 424, 427, 435
Tearney, 228
Teel, 66
Teeling, 234
Teft, 368
Teller, 415
Temple, 258
Ten Eyck, 157
Tench, 4
Tenholm, 428
Tenley, 341
Tenney, 21, 24, 87, 92, 122, 429
Tennison, 338
Terrett, 15, 47, 91, 382, 409
Terrill, 81
Terry, 66, 334, 394
Testader, 20
Tewksbury, 294

Thatcher, 367
Thaw, 192
Thayer, 205
Theilick, 47
Theodoric, 293
Theudley, 6
Thody, 27
Thoma, 91
Thomas, 12, 23, 26, 31, 47, 48, 51, 73, 84, 92, 99, 127, 145, 148, 178, 194, 222, 223, 235, 244, 248, 254, 300, 333, 345, 356, 358, 359, 384, 396, 403, 406, 420, 433
Thompson, 14, 24, 26, 27, 49, 50, 52, 61, 62, 66, 67, 69, 71, 75, 110, 118, 133, 141, 149, 151, 152, 162, 175, 182, 193, 195, 203, 218, 220, 221, 223, 229, 233, 236, 237, 244, 248, 253, 262, 271, 288, 309, 337, 356, 358, 364, 372, 373, 382, 393, 394, 396, 412, 422
Thorn, 140, 320, 428
Thornley, 100, 186
Thornton, 176, 199, 207, 259, 364, 434
Thracher, 122
Throckmorton, 47
Throope, 303
Thruston, 47
Thurber, 205
Thurman, 265
Thurmond, 305
Thursby, 370, 381
Thurston, 93, 413
Thwing, 291
Thyson, 119
Tiber Creek, 170, 217, 438
Ticer, 125
Tidball, 193, 245
Tidrick, 152
Tighe, 186
Tilghman, 47
Tillett, 404
Tilley, 167

Tillinghast, 28, 238, 352, 358
Tillis, 215
Tilton, 273
Timanus, 385
Timon, 334, 365
Timpson, 356
Tingle, 332
Tiniece, 131
Tobin, 8, 356, 360, 368
Todd, 47, 204, 265, 318, 327, 338
Todhunter, 231
Todshinder, 292
Toledano, 93
Tomlin, 86
Tomlinson, 361, 441
Tongue, 342
Tool, 27
Topp, 158
Topping, 53, 210
Torrants, 195
Torrence, 165, 231, 280, 423
Torrents, 220
Touro, 34
To-wah we ke, 67
Towers, 56, 130, 198, 337, 393, 428, 429
Towle, 72, 213, 214, 217, 234, 282, 409
Towles, 58, 69, 438
Towley, 426
Town, 124
Townes, 103, 247
Townsend, 71, 139, 220, 247, 286, 306, 332, 383, 417
Towson, 47, 247, 250, 251, 261, 283, 287, 332, 362
Tracey, 342
Tracy, 27
Traherne, 31
Travaillot, 406
Travers, 47, 371
Traverse, 266
Travis, 86, 433
Trayer, 15

Treadwell, 131, 285
Tree, 130, 139
Trego, 64, 88
Tretler, 384
Treville, 131
Triplet, 349
Triplett, 405
Tripp, 163, 216, 280
Tritt, 297
Trock, 47
Trook, 260
Troop, 103
Troupe, 345
Trousdale, 68
Trowbridge, 86, 137, 144
True, 10
Trumbull, 220
Trumpet, 24
Trundell, 228
Trunnel, 341
Truston, 106
Truxton, 53, 308
Tubbs, 144, 209
Tucker, 18, 67, 92, 153, 179, 227, 316, 328, 380
Tuckerman, 176
Tudor Place, 242, 345
Tuely, 266
Tuley, 342
Tully, 26
<u>Tunnel Bridge</u>, 391
Tuomy, 332
Tupper, 356
Turberville, 153
Turk, 402, 444
Turley, 52, 233
Turnbull, 58, 128, 145, 246, 285, 411, 425
Turner, 7, 33, 47, 81, 88, 124, 241, 261, 309, 323, 376
Turpin, 30
Turtin, 75
Turvin, 183, 233
Tustin, 249, 350

Tweed, 235
Tweeny, 13
Twyman, 424
Tyler, 6, 31, 114, 161, 241, 242, 260, 377, 397
Tyson, 364

U

Umstead, 388
Uncle Sam, 283
Underdonk, 323
Underhill, 212
Underwood, 118, 149, 172, 273, 424
Upman, 273
Upson, 141
Urriza, 221
Utermehle, 292

V

Valentine, 375
Van Bibber, 103
Van Braam, 84
Van Brunt, 105, 157, 254
Van Buren, 215, 262, 284, 285, 286, 287
Van Derge, 126
Van Derveer, 52
Van Derze, 149
Van Dieman, 38
Van Dusen, 158
Van Hamm, 298, 407
Van Horn, 254
Van Horne, 415
Van Lear, 239
Van Ness, 47, 61, 85, 236, 252
Van Patten, 47
Van Ranst, 240
Van Rensselaer, 18
Van Reswick, 237, 436
Van Riswick, 117, 239
Van Sanford, 25
Van Vassel, 98
Van Vechen, 333
Van Voast, 197

Van Vorst, 20, 21, 33, 140
Van Wart, 135, 231, 239
Van Wyck, 75
Vanderslice, 71
Vandever, 349
Vandruff, 199
Vanhorn, 105
Vanmeter, 79
Vanscriver, 290
Vanvort, 19
Vanwick, 131
Varady, 186
Varick, 67
Varker, 175
Varn, 57
Varnon, 279
Varnum, 224
Vasques, 88
Vattemare, 365
Vaughan, 71, 121, 348, 389
Vedder, 371
Vein, 441
Veitch, 47
Vell, 115
Venable, 47, 247, 393
Vension, 216
Vermilie, 137
Vermillion, 21, 106
Vernon, 47, 341
vessel **Charles Wood**, 82
vessel **Esquimaux**, 376
vessel **James Maull**, 82
vessel **John Dutton** to **Emma Eager**, 3
vessel **New Era**, 398
vessel **Perservancia**, 180
vessel **Terror**, 376
vessels **Erebus & Terror**, 375
Vesta, 363
Vethake, 141
Vibber, 340
Vick, 327
Vickers, 76
Victor, 236

Vigil, 210, 256
Vigo, 73, 440
Vildabee, 308
Villard, 47
Villepigue, 285
Vincent, 149, 221, 232, 254, 267, 424, 425
Vincinanza, 136
Vineyard Farm, 227
Vinson, 13, 126
Vinter, 131
Virgil, 268
Vise, 100
Vocable, 47
Vocke, 65
Vodder, 179
von Blonay, 37
Von Moschysker, 84
Vondersmith, 90
Voorhees, 73
Vosburgh, 131
Voshell, 188
Voss, 61, 84, 265
Vowell, 47, 300
Vroom, 68
Vrooman, 71

W

Wabriner, 403
Waddel, 177
Waddington, 356
Wade, 299
Wadsworth, 77, 94, 181, 348, 418, 438
Waggaman, 6, 95
Wagner, 47
Wailes, 239
Wainwright, 81, 144, 331
Waite, 99
Wake, 418
Walbach, 7, 237
Walderan, 271
Walen, 140
Wales, 347

Walker, 36, 47, 48, 94, 152, 157, 160, 161, 163, 171, 172, 173, 191, 193, 196, 215, 228, 236, 248, 273, 295, 297, 314, 339, 356, 405, 412, 428, 433
Walker's Row, 320
Wall, 47, 48, 151, 227, 232, 355, 392, 399
Wallace, 24, 25, 26, 116, 152, 213, 214, 217, 218, 237, 358
Wallach, 3, 157, 173, 265, 279, 323, 402, 407
Waller, 362, 367
Walles, 198
Walley, 5
Walling, 442
Wallingsford, 47, 167, 299
Walls, 348
Walrad, 67
Walsh, 23, 25, 47, 73, 109, 202, 229, 263, 274, 280, 302, 312, 337
Walter, 48, 95, 155, 256, 293
Walters, 185, 272
Walthall, 234
Walton, 122
Walworth, 86, 347
Wands, 353
War of the Revolution, 28
Ward, 6, 13, 15, 17, 19, 24, 47, 48, 50, 58, 60, 72, 146, 157, 159, 195, 232, 260, 281, 315, 356, 378, 386, 393, 416, 420, 428, 436
Ware, 212, 255, 350
Warfield, 420
Waring, 81, 85, 232, 273, 340, 358, 400
Waring's Lot, 340
Warm Springs, 315
Warner, 58, 76, 445
Warren, 32, 110, 195, 236, 277
Warring, 47
Warrington, 17, 30, 172, 199
Warrior, 122
Wartelle, 152

Warwick, 191
Wash City-1853, 1
Washburn, 118, 205, 220, 338
Washburne, 118, 338
Washington, 12, 19, 20, 22, 24, 29, 52, 79, 84, 92, 123, 134, 145, 160, 169, 175, 214, 216, 242, 246, 247, 275, 278, 280, 292, 294, 351, 354, 367, 369, 389, 398, 416, 425, 431
Washington Cemetery, 147
Waterfall Mills, 329
Waterman, 31, 219, 358
Waterous, 192
Waters, 47, 48, 52, 87, 144, 234, 342, 349, 376, 377, 387, 402, 428, 431
Watkins, 19, 20, 21, 226, 319, 327, 396
Watrous, 70, 354
Watson, 63, 66, 84, 96, 104, 174, 199, 255, 259, 281, 346, 399, 421
Watterston, 47, 59, 166
Wattles, 204
Watts, 261
Watty, 422
Waugh, 17, 207
Wayland, 297
Waylen, 103
Wayne, 117, 324, 333, 351
Weagley, 67
Weare, 334
Weatherford, 210
Weathers, 11
Weaver, 17, 48, 64, 93, 113, 332
Webb, 93, 111, 121, 135, 220, 224, 262, 264, 270, 278, 327, 347, 389
Webber, 169
Webster, 13, 31, 48, 76, 149, 162, 226, 258, 283, 286, 323, 341
Weed, 73, 157, 286
Weeden, 124
Weeks, 11, 50, 356
Weems, 66
Wehling, 10
Weigart, 9, 296

Weightman, 173, 373, 396
Weirick, 220, 255, 271
Weirman, 415
Weizick, 280
Welch, 24, 48, 72, 77, 195, 216, 240, 274, 311
Weld, 7, 338
Weller, 235, 323
Welles, 50, 281
Wellesley, 14
Wellesleys, 179
Wellford, 83, 239
Wellington, 86, 167, 303, 432
Wells, 51, 55, 73, 83, 194, 214, 230, 281, 307, 324, 337, 364, 405, 407
Welsh, 47, 55, 73, 83, 194, 281, 370, 394, 400, 424
Wendall, 428
Wendover, 224
Wendt, 25
Wenman, 402
Werner, 47, 168
Wesley, 121
West, 9, 61, 143, 147, 227, 262, 320, 324, 378, 402, 406, 416
West Market, 227
Westberry, 67
Westcott, 52, 107, 142, 152, 175, 254, 280, 379
Westerfield, 247
Westerly, 182
Western, 208
Western Military Institute, 266
Weston, 32
Westphalia estate, 16
Wetherall, 434
Wetherbee, 235
Wethered, 198
Wetherell, 426
Wetherill, 370
Weverton, 162
Whalen, 25, 354
whaler **George**, 32
Whalin, 68

Whalon, 354
Wharton, 34, 36
Wheat, 83, 103, 194, 212, 255, 257, 282, 369
Wheately, 94
Wheatleigh, 355
Wheatley, 427
Wheaton, 53
Wheelan, 47
Wheeler, 61, 91, 98, 117, 171, 277, 310, 336, 348, 415, 419
Wheelock, 437
Wheeney, 225
Whelan, 11, 34
Whipple, 12, 124, 136, 199, 321, 401
Whistler, 113, 403
Whitaker, 53, 183
Whitcomb, 205, 343
White, 14, 23, 25, 31, 33, 47, 53, 67, 68, 70, 122, 141, 160, 164, 181, 196, 223, 231, 239, 241, 252, 264, 315, 348, 363, 378, 416, 417, 431, 442, 445
Whitfield, 71, 124
Whiting, 420
Whitmore, 48
Whitney, 47, 72, 240, 275, 334, 354
Whittemore, 180, 189
Whittington, 428
Whittle, 348, 364
Whittlsey, 35
Whitworth, 241
Whyte, 240
Wiborg, 358
Wicker, 402
Wickham, 20, 190, 192, 381, 432
Wickliffe, 64, 83
Wickoff, 400
Wicks, 308
Wierman, 278, 362
Wilber, 81
Wilcox, 49, 94, 134, 273
Wilde, 356
Wilder, 250, 436

Wilderness, 141
Wilderness Farms, 141
Wildman, 324, 364, 419
Wilgus, 199, 254
Wilkerson, 47
Wilkes, 146, 353
Wilkins, 67, 148, 205
Wilkinson, 233, 351, 433, 441
Willard, 115
Willcott, 220
Willet, 10, 356
Willett, 54, 195, 348
Willetts, 222
Willey, 408
William, 417
Williams, 4, 30, 31, 32, 35, 47, 48, 50, 53, 54, 56, 66, 67, 70, 73, 76, 86, 96, 98, 104, 110, 144, 146, 162, 166, 179, 189, 198, 202, 203, 205, 215, 225, 242, 244, 252, 278, 280, 284, 294, 295, 301, 319, 320, 321, 327, 329, 336, 339, 345, 358, 361, 370, 374, 383, 386, 396, 404, 416, 417, 430, 431, 439, 441, 445
Williamson, 52, 67, 94, 95, 113, 114, 123, 254, 401
Willingham, 67
Willis, 9, 27, 51, 58, 64, 69, 128, 157, 281, 362, 382, 388, 415
Williss, 107
Willner, 47
Wills, 390
Wilson, 4, 13, 15, 18, 20, 40, 47, 48, 51, 58, 66, 68, 78, 91, 92, 100, 102, 106, 112, 134, 149, 157, 165, 169, 187, 188, 195, 212, 213, 220, 233, 251, 254, 266, 269, 280, 283, 287, 292, 315, 323, 334, 337, 351, 356, 379, 380, 388, 393, 410, 422, 430, 443, 445
Wiltberger, 6, 19, 20, 47, 70, 92, 322, 433
Wilts, 75
Wimbish, 66

Wimsatt, 47, 48
Winans, 128, 249, 299
Winchell, 152
Winchester, 58
Winder, 5, 19, 21, 22, 33, 47, 48, 51, 140, 144, 197, 284, 285
Windsor, 346
Wines, 130
Wing, 344
Wingate, 48, 67, 160
Wingenroth, 55
Wingfield, 81, 126, 171, 175
Winkley, 13
Winn, 276, 306, 423
Winship, 25
Winslow, 31, 50, 244, 433
Winslow Burying Ground, 31
Winston, 169
Winter, 21
Winterburne, 358
Winters, 244
Winthrop, 106
Wirtz, 20, 21, 397
Wise, 30, 51, 95, 130, 148, 149, 170, 223, 228, 315, 348, 392, 415
Wiseman, 299
Wisenfeld, 322
Wishart, 239, 264
Wisner, 66, 433
Wisong, 81
Withers, 60, 265, 284
Wittenauer, 23
Wizard, 268
Wolcott, 252, 388
Wolf, 405
Wolfe, 400
Wolff, 430
Wollard, 348
Wolverton, 162
Wood, 18, 32, 47, 54, 70, 86, 92, 111, 131, 211, 241, 268, 269, 325, 356, 358, 363, 380, 383, 393, 403, 418, 425, 436, 439
Woodbridge, 144

Woodbury, 53, 244, 254, 268, 334, 371
Wooderson, 294
Woodhull, 48, 181
Woodis, 217
Woodlawn, 393
Woodlief, 418
Woodruff, 109, 302, 322, 358, 400
Woods, 67, 269, 305, 337, 400
Woodson, 223
Woodward, 47, 151, 157, 173, 310, 313, 323, 403, 406, 414, 415, 421, 428, 438
Woodworth, 5
Wool, 1, 17, 73, 196, 254, 282, 289, 436
Woolard, 241
Wooley, 216, 236
Woolford, 188
Woolley, 443
Woolson, 433
Wooster, 221
Worcester, 47
Work, 349
Workman, 24
Wormley, 36, 47
Wormsley, 86, 123, 212, 255, 280
Worrell, 72, 146
Worth, 72, 261, 433
Wortham, 101
Worthen, 24, 30
Worthington, 49, 161, 213, 243, 335
Wosencraft, 174
Wotherspoon, 156, 284, 287
Wotton, 234
Wreford, 213
Wright, 19, 29, 30, 50, 54, 65, 86, 95, 111, 135, 163, 172, 173, 180, 194, 197, 199, 213, 253, 255, 262, 270, 282, 285, 315, 347, 348, 409, 418, 421
Wringfield, 124
Wroe, 48, 207
W-se, 47

Wurick, 62
Wyand, 56
Wyatt, 295, 324
Wyche, 223
Wykoff, 272
Wylie, 235
Wyllys, 345
Wyman, 112, 354
Wyrick, 47
Wyse, 19, 20, 21, 33, 154, 171
Wysong, 102
Wythe, 295, 359

Y

Yahrling, 93
Yates, 23, 55, 348, 420
Yeatman, 38, 48, 83
Yerby, 149

Yoasi, 358
Yost, 441
Young, 12, 24, 48, 59, 78, 86, 158, 166, 213, 220, 229, 239, 267, 336, 341, 348, 356, 358, 364, 396, 397, 414, 424, 427, 436
Young Mansion, 129
Ysaki, 356
Yulee, 273, 291

Z

Zachey, 7
Zantzinger, 60, 163, 208, 246
Zappone, 85, 138
Zarracher, 429
Zimmerman, 314
Zollogi, 358

Other Heritage Books by Joan M. Dixon:

National Intelligencer *Newspaper Abstracts
Special Edition: The Civil War Years
Volume 1: January 1, 1861-June 30, 1863*

National Intelligencer *Newspaper Abstracts
Special Edition: The Civil War Years
Volume 2: July 1, 1863-December 31, 1865*

National Intelligencer *Newspaper Abstracts 1854*

National Intelligencer *Newspaper Abstracts 1853*

National Intelligencer *Newspaper Abstracts 1852*

National Intelligencer *Newspaper Abstracts 1851*

National Intelligencer *Newspaper Abstracts 1850*

National Intelligencer *Newspaper Abstracts 1849*

National Intelligencer *Newspaper Abstracts 1848*

National Intelligencer *Newspaper Abstracts 1847*

National Intelligencer *Newspaper Abstracts 1846*

National Intelligencer *Newspaper Abstracts 1845*

National Intelligencer *Newspaper Abstracts 1844*

National Intelligencer *Newspaper Abstracts 1843*

National Intelligencer *Newspaper Abstracts 1842*

National Intelligencer *Newspaper Abstracts 1841*

National Intelligencer *Newspaper Abstracts 1840*

National Intelligencer *Newspaper Abstracts, 1838-1839*

National Intelligencer *Newspaper Abstracts, 1836-1837*

National Intelligencer *Newspaper Abstracts, 1834-1835*

National Intelligencer *Newspaper Abstracts, 1832-1833*

National Intelligencer *Newspaper Abstracts, 1830-1831*

National Intelligencer *Newspaper Abstracts, 1827-1829*

National Intelligencer *Newspaper Abstracts, 1824-1826*

National Intelligencer *Newspaper Abstracts, 1821-1823*

National Intelligencer *Newspaper Abstracts, 1818-1820*

National Intelligencer *Newspaper Abstracts, 1814-1817*

National Intelligencer *Newspaper Abstracts, 1811-1813*

National Intelligencer *Newspaper Abstracts, 1806-1810*

National Intelligencer *Newspaper Abstracts, 1800-1805*

www.ingramcontent.com/pod-product-compliance
Lightning Source LLC
Chambersburg PA
CBHW071431300426
44114CB00013B/1393